Inside Network Perimeter Security:

The Definitive Guide to Firewalls, VPNs, Routers, and Intrusion Detection Systems

Contents At a Glance

D0470397

Inside Network Perimeter Security:
The Definitive Guide to Firewalls, VPNs, Routers, and Intrusion Detection Systems

Primary Authors:
Stephen Northcutt
Lenny Zeltser
Scott Winters
Karen Kent Frederick
Ronald W. Ritchey

Contributing Authors:
Mark Edmead
Neil F. Johnson
Brian O'Berry
Daniel Martin

New Riders

www.newriders.com

800 East 96th Street, Indianapolis, Indiana 46240
An Imprint of Pearson Education
Boston • Indianapolis • London • Munich • New York • San Francisco

Inside Network Perimeter Security:

The Definitive Guide to Firewalls, VPNs, Routers, and Intrusion Detection Systems

Copyright © 2003 by New Riders Publishing

FIRST EDITION: July

International Standard Book Number: 0-7357-1232-8

Library of Congress Catalog Card Number: *2001096722*

06 05 04   8 7 6

Interpretation of the printing code: The rightmost double-digit number is the year of the book's printing; the rightmost single-digit number is the number of the book's printing. For example, the printing code 03-1 shows that the first printing of the book occurred in 2003.

Printed in the United States of America

Trademarks

Warning and Disclaimer

Publisher
David Dwyer

Associate Publisher
Stephanie Wall

Production Manager
Gina Kanouse

Managing Editor
Kristy Knoop

Acquisitions Editor
Elise Walter

Producer
Lenny Zeltser

Development Editor
Sydney Jones

Product Marketing Manager
Kathy Malmloff

Publicity Manager
Susan Nixon

Copy Editor
Karen A. Gill

Indexer
Christine Karpeles

Manufacturing Coordinator
Jim Conway

Book Designer
Louisa Klucznik

Cover Designer
Aren Howell

Composition
Amy Parker

Table of Contents

About the Authors

Primary Authors

Karen Kent Frederick is a senior security engineer for the Rapid Response Team at NFR Security. She holds a bachelor's degree in computer science from the University of Wisconsin-Parkside and a master's in computer science from the University of Idaho. Karen has more than 10 years of experience in various areas of IT, particularly system administration and information security. She holds four SANS GIAC certifications and also has the CCSA and MCSE + Internet certifications. Karen is one of the authors of *Intrusion Signatures and Analysis* (New Riders) and is a contributing author to the *Handbook of Computer Crime Investigation* (Academic Press). She also frequently writes on intrusion detection-related topics for `SecurityFocus.com`.

Stephen Northcutt created the Shadow Intrusion Detection System, the DoD Shadow team, the GIAC Security Certification Series, and the SANS Immersion Security Training education system—currently consisting of 11 tracks ranging from Security Essentials to Forensics. He authored or teamed to write *Incident Handling Step-by-Step* (New Riders), *Network Intrusion Detection—An Analyst's Handbook* (New Riders), and *Intrusion Signatures and Analysis* (New Riders). Before joining SANS, Stephen served as chief for information warfare at the Ballistic Missile Defense Organization. Currently, he is an instructor for the SANS Institute.

Ronald W. Ritchey is an authority in the areas of secure network design and network intrusion and regularly leads penetration testing efforts for Booz Allen Hamilton, where he has had the opportunity to learn first-hand the real-world impact of network vulnerabilities. He is also an active researcher in the field with peer-reviewed publications in the area of automated network security analysis. Ron holds a master's degree in computer science from George Mason University and is currently pursuing his Ph.D. in information technology at their School of Information Technology and Engineering. His doctoral research is attempting to automate network security analysis.

Scott Winters has been working in all aspects of networking and computer security for 12 years. He has been an instructor, author, network engineer, consultant, and systems administrator and has worked with various perimeter security solutions, firewalls, and infrastructure designs. He has SANS GIAC GSEC, and GCFW certifications, as well as MCSE, CNE, and Cisco CCNA and other technology certifications. Scott's other accomplishments include the authoring and editing of a SANS GIAC training and certification course and exam content. He has also been involved in the SANS GIAC mentoring program, and has served on the SANS GCFW advisory board.

Lenny Zeltser's work in information security draws upon experience in system administration, software architecture, and independent research. Lenny worked as a consultant to a major financial institution, co-founded a software company, and is presently a director of information security at Kiodex, Inc. He has also written and presented coursework for SANS, reverse-engineered malicious software, and is an active member of several GIAC advisory boards. Lenny holds a number of professional certifications, such as MCSE, CCSE, GSEC, GCFW, GCIA, GCUX, and GCIH, and has earned a bachelor's degree in computer science engineering from the University of Pennsylvania.

Contributing Authors

Brent Deterding works for TechGuard Security is St. Louis, Missouri. He chairs the SANS GIAC GCFW advisory board and is an Authorized Grader for the GCFW certification. He holds SANS GIAC GSEC, GCFW, GCIA, GCIH, and GSNA certifications, as well as the RHCE, and he has mentored nearly 50 students through GSEC training. Brent was recently married and enjoys domestication.

Mark Edmead, CISSP, SSCP, TICSA, is president of MTE Software, Inc., and has more than 22 years' experience in software development, product development, and network systems security. Fortune 500 companies have turned to Mark often to help them with projects related to Internet and computer security. He was managing editor of SANS Digest (Systems Administration & Network Security) and contributing editor to the SANS Step-by-Step Windows NT Security Guide. Mark previously worked for KPMG's Information Risk Management Group and IBM's Privacy and Security Group, where he performed network security assessments, security system reviews, development of security recommendations, and ethical hacking. His other projects included assisting companies to develop secure and reliable network system architectures for their web-enabled businesses. Mark is co-author of the book *Windows NT: Performance, Monitoring, and Tuning* (New Riders Publishing), and he developed the SANS *Business Continuity/Disaster Recovery Plan Step-by-Step Guide*.

Dr. Neil F. Johnson is the associate director and a senior research scientist for the Center for Secure Information Systems (CSIS) at George Mason University (GMU). He is also the president of Johnson & Johnson Technology Consultants, LLC (JJTC). He has extensive experience with many aspects of information security/assurance. Neil has more than 12 years of experience in application development, both in commercial companies including IBM and Sprint and within the U.S. government. In 1997, he began working at GMU's CSIS sponsored by the National Security Agency (NSA). He holds a bachelor's in business administration in information systems from

James Madison University, a master's of science in information systems, and a Ph.D. in information technology from George Mason University, focusing on information assurance. Through CSIS and his company, Dr. Johnson briefs various companies and government agencies on the subjects of information assurance and covert communications. He is a contributing author of the book *Information Hiding: Techniques for Steganography and Digital Watermarking* (Artech House) and the primary author of the book *Information Hiding: Steganography and Watermarking—Attacks and Countermeasures* (Kluwer) based on his research at CSIS/GMU.

Brian O'Berry has worked in IT for more than 20 years, beginning as an MVS systems programmer in the early 1980s, and then moving into a managerial role for IBM mainframe-based IT in the financial and insurance industries. There, he stayed until the Internet exploded on the scene. In the early 1990s, Brian switched career tracks and returned to his hands-on, technical roots by jumping into TCP/IP network design, implementation, and maintenance. He has focused on the network security arena for the past six years, first with a large consulting firm, and then moving into research. Brian currently works on the research faculty at George Mason University in Fairfax, Virginia.

Daniel Martin is a senior security specialist for Sprint E|Solutions Consulting Services, working on a plethora of projects ranging from network and firewall attack and penetration testing, operating system hardening, and network design and architecture. Over the past 10 years, his technical expertise has been quantified by many technical industry certifications, such as CISSP, SSCP, MCSE+I, MCT, SCSA, CCNA, CCSE, and GCFW. Daniel taught computer-related classes for Chattahoochee Technical Institute and serves as a member of SANS GCFW advisory board. Security has always been an exciting passion for Daniel, and with his understanding of the many facets of the network components, he is able to take security to a higher level. Daniel also loves being around his family and friends and spending time outdoors riding motorcycles. He wants to thank his lovely wife, Wendy, who sustained him with love, understanding, and a constant supply of Cokes during the long nights and weekends while he was working on this book and achieving various certifications.

About the Technical Reviewers

These reviewers contributed their considerable hands-on expertise to the entire development process for *Inside Network Perimeter Security: The Definitive Guide to Firewalls, VPNs, Routers, and Intrusion Detection Systems.* As the book was being written, these dedicated professionals reviewed all the material for technical content, organization, and flow. Their feedback was critical to ensuring that this book fit our reader's need for the highest-quality technical information.

Bill Bauer has been troubleshooting network operations and security for various ISPs and software companies since 1995. His background includes being a medic in the 101st Airborne and teaching swordfighting to medieval recreationists. He currently lives in Northern Virginia.

Sam Campbell spent some time in the medical imaging field with CT Scanners and Nuclear Medicine, and then returned to the UNIX world by joining the support services group of HP. After a number of years' experience with UNIX troubleshooting, Sam extended these skills by moving into the role of Internet services architect and security consultant. Sam has worked with a number of Australian government agencies and other companies on projects such as business-to-business private communications and PKI-enabled systems combining web, email, and data sharing. Sam has a BE(Elec), SANS GCFW, and an RHCE, among others, and would like to go rogaining again when the kids grow up.

Todd Chapman is a senior security consultant for gedas, USA, Inc., in Auburn Hills, Michigan where he is currently responsible for Volkswagen/Audi of America IT security. Prior to joining gedas USA, Inc., Todd spent three years working for an IT consulting company as a senior consultant, where he delivered a variety of services including system administration, security and networking, clustering, Perl programming, and corporate development and training. A board member of the SANS GCFW advisory board and a member of the Metro Detroit Linux Users Group and the System Administrators Guild (SAGE), Todd is certified as a Red Hat Certified Engineer (RHCE), Microsoft Certified Systems Engineer (MCSE), HP Certified IT Professional in System Administration, Check Point Certified Security Administrator (CCSA), GIAC Certified Intrusion Analyst (GCIA), and as a GIAC Certified Firewall Analyst (GCFW). Todd earned a master's degree in computer science from Oakland University, (Auburn Hills, Michigan) and a bachelor's degree in mechanical engineering from Michigan State University (East Lansing, Michigan). He currently lives in Ferndale, Michigan where he spends his free time playing Ultimate Frisbee.

Clément Dupuis is an avid contributor to the security community and strongly believes in knowledge sharing to improve the overall state of security. He is a retired member of the Canadian DoD, where he was employed as a communications and IT specialist for more than 20 years. Clément is currently employed as the subject matter expert and senior security consultant for the fifth largest IT services provider in North America, with more than 13,000 employees. He is a Global Incident Analysis Centre, Certified Firewall Analyst (with honors) as well as a Certified Intrusion Analyst. Being a member of the SANS advisory board, he is directly contributing to the development of the GCFW certification and is one of the two authorized graders (AG) of the practical exams required to pass the certification. Clément contributed to the SANS Securing Linux Step-by-Step book and the SANS Security Awareness initiative. He is a member of the Commonly Accepted Security Practices and Recommendation for UNIX (www.caspr.org) and an active supporter of the Open Source Security Testing Methodology Manual (www.osstmm.org). Clément is a technical reviewer of security books published by New Riders Publishing and regularly writes security articles for the Télé-Université Online Journal. He is also one of the security experts from the Security Clinic at www.itsecurity.com. Clément is the maintainer of the CISSP Open Study Guides web site at www.cccure.org, a web site that is dedicated to helping those studying to become CISSPs (Certified Information System Security Professionals). As such, he has written several of the study guides for the 10 CISSP domains.

Dan Goldberg, an active member of the GCFW advisory board and a grader for GCFW practicals, is currently a security consultant at Xerox Corporation and is working on projects involving intrusion detection systems, reverse proxy services, VPNs, and firewall deployment. Prior to working at Xerox, Dan designed extranet systems that enabled the successful launch of a manufacturing company's e-commerce and b2b initiatives. Dan also worked for Eastman Kodak Company and Bausch & Lomb in security and network engineering positions. He got his start in infosec during the 1990s as a U.S. Army information security officer for an infantry division staff element. He holds the GCFW and CCNA certifications.

Jeff Stevenson is a principal engineer with C-Cubed Corporation, where he provides support to the Space and Naval Warfare Systems Center (SPAWAR) in Charleston, South Carolina. Jeff currently holds several certifications, which include the GCFW, MCSE, and CCNA. Before computers entered his life, Jeff earned a degree in mathematics from The Citadel. After that, he managed to spend several years traipsing around the world as a nuclear submarine officer. Now, when he's not fixing a network or securing some Microsoft product, he enjoys being active with the Cub Scouts, playing with his Linux/OpenBSD toys, and catching "script kiddies" going after his home computers.

Sergei Ledovskij started experimenting with computers at the age of 12, and has been in the UNIX and network security field since he was 17. Presently, he works as a security consultant for a Finnish company and holds MCP and GCFW certifications. His main areas of expertise are operating systems and network security.

Tell Us What You Think

As the reader of this book, you are the most important critic and commentator. We value your opinion and want to know what we're doing right, what we could do better, what areas you'd like to see us publish in, and any other words of wisdom you're willing to pass our way.

As the associate publisher for New Riders Publishing, I welcome your comments. You can email or write me directly to let me know what you did or didn't like about this book—as well as what we can do to make our books stronger.

Please note that I cannot help you with technical problems related to the topic of this book, and that due to the high volume of mail I receive, I might not be able to reply to every message.

When you write, please be sure to include this book's title and author as well as your name and phone or fax number. I will carefully review your comments and share them with the author and editors who worked on the book.

Email: feedback@pearsontechgroup.com

Mail: Mark Taber
            Associate Publisher
            800 East 96th Street
            Indianapolis, IN 46240 USA

Preface

The flight from Lihue to San Francisco is about five hours and allows me some of my most productive work time. The phone doesn't ring, the dog doesn't ask to go outside, and my personal firewall doesn't start blinking because someone is trying to scan my computer.

I was enjoying working on this book when a scene on the airplane entertainment televisions caught my eye. It was a video history of United Airlines, which started by delivering airmail in rickety old airplanes with exposed cockpits. Today, modern, fast, sophisticated aircraft have an incredible safety record. The airline industry has gone from an oddity—a great tool to entertain the crowds at a county fair—to an industry that is crucial to our way of life and economy. The airlines in the United States were essentially grounded for about three days following the terrorist attack of September 11, 2001, and the U.S. Congress scrambled to give them money.

By exploring what has changed in the airline world, you will see both the past and the future of our industry, information technology (IT). Like the airline industry, IT history has rickety platforms. We have benefited from rapid advances in technology. We have seen a decline in personal service. We are headed for continuous inspections, a defense-in-depth approach, and we are every bit as vulnerable and at the same time crucial to the economy.

Rickety Planes

What if we flew in computers? That gives crash a whole new meaning, doesn't it? Well, if we did, I am sure you would agree that we would all be dead. I would love to say operating systems are really improving, but it isn't so. I waited a month after Windows XP was officially shipping to get my version, and it was factory installed on a new Dell laptop. I opened the box and installed my Linsky's wireless networking card. The XP even had a driver for it. I downloaded the Microsoft critical updates. Yes, that's right—one month and already five critical updates. I rebooted the machine; it came back up and hardcrashed. It reminded me of the heady days of NT 3.51, with the genuine bluescreen of death with about a page of writing that displayed for maybe three seconds. It took me about an hour to get the stupid thing back to life, and I supposedly know something about computers. I was ready to heave the gorgeous new state-of-the-art laptop across the room. And I just kept thinking to myself: How could Microsoft ship something this bad?

Please don't get me wrong. I am not a Microsoft basher at heart. I think Windows 2000 is a pretty cool operating system. Microsoft will come out with updates and better drivers, and it won't stay this horrible. My point though, is really simple. A lot of people died in the early days of the airline industry and as I say, if we flew in those early planes today, most of us would be dead.

Now here is the kicker: Firewalls and VPNs are nothing but software applications that are built on these rickety operating systems. One of the primary themes of this book is never to trust the operating system, to expect perimeter components to fail. This book will show you techniques for failover, layering defense components instrumentation to detect anomalies, and troubleshooting. In the early days of perimeter defense, the only choice that information security practitioners had was to layer their perimeter software on these rickety operating systems.

Perl Leigh Gates

In 1984, if you said CIA to me, I would have thought about the spy shop, not confidentiality, integrity, and availability, the three primary dimensions of security. I was a network builder for the Department of Defense, which uses large, high-end, fast networks. Security was something that was implemented with a physical airgap, which remains a worthy notion. The Morris worm, an early UNIX worm that essentially shut down the Internet for a couple of days, was the first time I even started thinking about security.

A couple of years later, I attended a firewall class given by Tina Darmohray at a tiny conference called SANS. She explained a firewall architecture with two firewall systems: one of them was called Perl, and the other was Leigh, and they were her Perl Leigh Gates (Pearly Gates). The joke was more worth a tired smile. My head ached from all the new material I was learning. As I made my way home, I kept wondering: Why two firewalls? Why not just one?

Whenever people made a physical analogy to a firewall, they always compared it to a castle. The main point was that there was one way in and one way out, with a number of chokepoints as you entered the structure. Why was Darmohray talking about two firewalls? Well, for one thing, those early firewalls were not efficient, and performance was a significant issue.

Just then as I was driving, a Navy F14 Tomcat flew over the highway and it hit me. Two engines. Navy planes always have at least two engines. After all, pilots who are flying over the ocean don't want an engine failure to force them into the drink. They don't have advanced failover or anything, but with two firewalls, if one of those rickety operating systems flames out, your network still has some connectivity.

This book discusses a number of perimeter designs. Some are more focused on security, whereas others are focused on performance. Some focus on uptime and help you to understand how to choose these designs based on your organization's requirements.

> **Note**
>
> One of the reasons that early airplanes were so dangerous is that a large number of them were hand built. Even if the planes were built in a factory, after a couple of years, they might as well be hand built because of the number of times they were repaired and modified.
>
> Today, you can get appliance firewalls, factory built, plug and go. It's not guaranteed that their OS is hardened, but you do know that the OS on the appliance is factory built, consistent, and probably stripped of unneeded programs. These appliances are one of the most interesting technological advances in computing.

Rapid Advances in Technology

Modern aircrafts have wings, fly through the air, and land on the ground—that is about all they have in common with the first airplanes. The advances in airframe design, materials, avionics, navigation and route selection, and airport operations make it difficult to believe that people ever considered getting into the early airplanes.

I would love to say that modern perimeter systems are so advanced that it is inconceivable that we ever tried to protect our systems with those early firewalls, but we haven't made that much progress yet. However, hope prevails, and we certainly see evidence of improvement. Perimeter defense systems have come way down in prices; many can be upgraded by just downloading a new image. Some exciting architectural advances are on the way.

A free firewall, such as IPtables, is a nice software package and can save a lot of money. The decreased cost for perimeter security is incredible, especially for home users and small offices. Have you noticed how low the prices of the combination 802.11 wireless cable modem/DSL routers have dropped? It is speculated that prices are likely to drop even further. It is not impossible that we will see a $99.00 price point. Who would have ever thought we would see the day that a router would sell for less than $100.00? And these appliance routers are simple to configure—as simple as clicking a GUI. Even better, the perimeter defense appliance updates to the latest OS version with a single click right over the web. Subscription models that update daily or weekly are just around the corner. You might wonder why such a subscription model would be needed. The fundamental architecture of perimeter components is changing from a perimeter defense-only system to hybrid systems that combine perimeter defense, reporting sensors and possibly even vulnerability assessments that allow performing internal correlation. Intrusion signatures and vulnerability plugins change rapidly, some people download Snort signatures daily, hence the need for a subscription model.

This book discusses the importance of using the information that is collected by perimeter devices to help defend the network. The Ramen, Lion, and Leaves worms were detected first using technology that collects reports from perimeter sensors. Some of the services that use such techniques to provide security analysis are DShield at `www.dshield.org` or `www.incidents.org`, and ARIS at `www.securityfocus.com`. One of the upcoming models for security is continuous reporting, or operational readiness, and this requires sensors all over the network to constantly report in. The technology of network security is dynamic. It's important to have constant updates to maintain security in the face of the ever-changing threat.

It is worth mentioning that ease of use and good security might be orthogonal. If it were as easy to get into an airplane and fly as it is to get into a car and drive, the skies would be a dangerous place. Appliance wireless access points often aggregate all wireless and built-in wired ports into the same broadcast domains. Possibilities for attacks exist based on MAC address spoofing. Network designers, like pilots, need a combination of training and checklists and can't just insert Plug and Play appliances willy-nilly into the network.

Decline in Personal Service

More has changed on the human side of the airline equation than just the name change from stewardesses to flight attendants. The airlines seem to be testing the limits to see just how much abuse people will take—and they wonder why they occasionally deal with passenger rage. Sadly, the IT industry has never been big on personal service. There were exceptions, back in the glory days of big blue. We had a bit of trouble with an IBM mainframe, and they tossed a squad of technicians into an airplane and dropped them by parachute into our parking lot, while vice presidents would call every 15 minutes to apprise us of the location of the plane. Okay, I am kidding, but not by much.

Nowadays, the IT industry has two primary features: bad software and worse service. The same is true for information technology. Please allow me to illustrate this with an example. I just uninstalled my Symantec personal firewall this morning. The subscription for the personal firewall was six weeks away from needing to be renewed. The Symantec LiveUpdate launched every 30 minutes or so, cluttering my screen, demanding that I click OK twice to get rid of it. After three days of trying to find a way to make it chill out, I just uninstalled the Norton Personal Firewall.

One of the advantages of this book is that the entire author team has pragmatic experience with most of the commercial and freeware perimeter products on the market, including the rapidly changing personal firewall market. Again, we do not intend to bash any vendor—they each have their foibles. We devote an entire chapter of the book to implementing defense components such as personal firewalls at a host level, to help you avoid some of the common pitfalls, and to know what technology is available. I am not sure I believe any of the personal firewalls by any of the vendors provide anything approaching bulletproof protection, although they are an important and valuable layer of defense.

Continuous Inspections

One of the primary reasons that the aircraft industry has been able to make gigantic leaps in improving safety are the rigorous, complete, and continuous inspections for every component and process that is related to flying. This is the most important change that we need to make. When I teach at SANS, I often say, "Who reads the event logs every day?" Some hands go up. I try to memorize their faces and catch them alone at the break. Then I ask them, "What is in the logs? What recurring problems are there?" They usually cannot answer. This book can help you deploy sensors and scanners. An entire chapter is devoted to intrusion detection. Even your organization's software architecture is a security perimeter component, as you will learn in the software architecture chapter.

If you were to ask me what the growth industry in IT was, I would answer that consoles, sensors, and agents to collect and display information would be a strong candidate. Computer systems change rapidly. They are analogous to the barn stormer bi-plane that flew around county fairs. When something broke, a blacksmith, automobile mechanic, or seamstress fabricated a new part. We can add and uninstall software in a heartbeat, but when we do, we cannot get back to the place where we were before the change. We need to monitor for change continuously, and until we learn how to do this and rigorously enforce change control, flying in computers will be nearly certain death.

Defense in Depth

It is a tragedy when a single passenger plane crashes, worse when a plane full of people goes down, and an unspeakable horror when a plane is used as a weapon of terrorism. Today, airports are transforming into examples of defense in depth. Defense in depth is a primary focus of this book, and the concept is quite simple. Make it harder to attack at chokepoint after chokepoint. How many security systems or defensive layers would you have to defeat to rush through an airport race to a waiting, fueled, long-range jet, commandeer the plane, drive it out on the tarmac to take off, and use it as a missile? Many are obvious, such as security checkpoints, armed National Guard troops, locked doors, and tarmac controls. If you did manage to get it in the air, you would also have to defeat fighter aircraft. It isn't impossible, but it is unlikely that you could defeat the defense in depth that is now employed at airports.

Defense in depth is present in every chapter of this book, and is becoming easier to implement in information technology. High-speed programmable hardware boxes, such as Attack Mitigator from Top Layer can help protect our network borders from denial-of-service flooding attacks. Technologies we have already discussed in this Preface, such as appliance devices and personal firewalls, allow us to implement multiple layers for our perimeter with little cost or effort. New advances, such as wrappers for individual programs, are now appearing in groundbreaking products. As you read this book, you will learn how to architect your network so that it is resistant to attack. As we evolve as an information-based society, the importance of protecting intellectual property assets continues to rise.

Core Business Sector

In less than a century, airplanes have gone from being an oddity to being vitally important to the economy. Information technology has done the same in less time and continues to grow in importance. One of the primary keys to survival in business over the next few years will be managing the flow of information so that resources are available when they are needed with full integrity, while the confidentiality of proprietary and sensitive information is maintained. It is a big task, so we had better get started.

—*Stephen Northcutt and the authoring team*

Introduction

Welcome, and thank you for considering *Inside Network Perimeter Security: The Definitive Guide to Firewalls, VPNs, Routers, and Intrusion Detection Systems*. This book is a unique work because it has a consistent phrasing and style, yet it consolidates the experience of 17 information security professionals working together as a team of writers and reviewers. Our goal was to create a practical guide for designing, deploying, and maintaining a reliable network security perimeter. Protecting the network is not an easy task; it requires that you get to know different types of technologies and understand how they relate to each other. This is why we discuss key perimeter components, such as firewalls, VPNs, routers, and intrusion detection systems. We also explain how to integrate these devices with each other to form a unified whole. There is no single gadget that can protect our networks against all threats, which is why we focus on layered security architectures. This concept of defense in depth is present throughout the book, and we believe it holds a key to practical use of perimeter security techniques discussed here.

Who Should Read This Book

This is an intermediate- to advanced-level book for security professionals and system and network administrators who already have a good understanding of TCP/IP and related technologies. This is a valuable reference for individuals who are interested in examining best practices of perimeter defense and in expanding their knowledge of network security tools and techniques. Because the book was developed in close coordination with the SANS Institute, it is also an excellent supplementary resource for those who are pursuing the GIAC Certified Firewall Analyst (GCFW) certification.

Overview

We would like to introduce this book from a 50,000-foot view. Part I, "Perimeter Fundamentals" covers the first five chapters and serves as a foundation for later chapters. The first chapter presents an overview of everything we will talk about throughout the book. Other chapters in Part I discuss core perimeter security concepts, such as packet filtering, stateful firewalls, proxies, and security policy.

Part II, "Extending the Perimeter," comprises Chapters 6 through 10 and concentrates on additional components that make up a network security perimeter. Here, we examine the role of routers, network intrusion detection systems (IDSs), virtual private networks (VPNs), and host-centric defense mechanisms.

Good design is covered in Part III, "Perimeter Design," where we focus on integrating perimeter components into a unified defense architecture. Chapters 11–16 describe ways of achieving defense in depth that are appropriate for your needs and budgets, letting you apply what you have learned about security devices and approaches. In addition to discussing design fundamentals, we focus on topics such as resource separation, software architecture, and VPN integration. We also explain how to tune a security design to achieve optimal performance, and look at several sample architectures.

Part IV, "Perimeter Assessment," concludes the book by answering the famous question, "How do you know?," in Chapters 17–22. It presents a discussion of understanding what the perimeter systems are telling us, and of ensuring that the perimeter operates according to its design. We examine perimeter maintenance procedures, log analysis, and troubleshooting approaches. We also describe techniques for assessing the strength of your defenses and explain how to conduct an adversarial review of the network architecture. The last chapter summarizes defense-in-depth concepts that have been described throughout the book. It is a mirror in some sense of the first chapter, but it is used to wrap up prime concepts of the book.

We have also outfitted the book with several appendixes. Here, we provide sample Cisco access list configurations, discuss fundamentals of cryptography, and offer a general overview of network air gap devices. Designing, deploying, and maintaining a network security perimeter is a challenging journey, and we hope that our approach to network defense makes your path more comfortable.

Conventions

This book follows a few typographical conventions:

- New terms are set in *italic* the first time they are introduced.
- Whenever possible, we reference the Common Vulnerabilities and Exposures (CVE) database to allow you to obtain additional information about the vulnerabilities—for example, `http://cve.mitre.org/cgi-bin/cvename.cgi?name=CVE-2000-1027`.

- Program text, functions, variables, and other "computer language" are set in a monospace font—for example, `GET`, `ping`, and `access-lists`.
- We also use *italic* to indicate the use of a placeholder in the text. For example, in the following IOS command, you should substitute "gateway IP" with an actual IP address: `ip route 0.0.0.0 0.0.0.0 gateway IP`.

I

Perimeter Fundamentals

1

Perimeter Security Fundamentals

THE SECURITY OF YOUR NETWORK IS evaluated daily. A rich question to ask is, "Are you the one doing it?" The answer, hopefully, is that someone on your side is involved in assessment, but overwhelming evidence reports that you are not alone. Internet facing systems (computers with IP addresses that can be reached from the Internet) receive between seven and hundreds or even thousands of attack attempts every day. Many of these are simple scans and probes that we know how to defend against, but others catch us by surprise and the next thing we know we are in cleanup mode.

Does your organization have access to expertise in all aspects of network security, including networking, firewalls, Intrusion Detection Systems (IDSs), Virtual Private Networks (VPNs), anti-virus, UNIX security, and Windows security? In the pages ahead, we will show you how all of these work together. Can you definitively say how secure or insecure your network is? One of the most interesting developments in 2001 and 2002 has been the "rulers" developed by the Center for Internet Security. For the first time, we have widely accepted tools that give us a score, but we have a long way to go. Does everyone in your organization understand the policies related to information security and their implications? One hint that they do not is the famous expression, "But we have a firewall!"

Does that sound familiar? If you work in information security, you probably hear this more often than you would like to because it seems to express the opinion of many people, both technical and non-technical. We must understand that no single component can properly defend a network.

However, many components working together can. *Defense in depth*, a major theme of this chapter, is the process of layering these components to capitalize on their respective strengths. It is flexible, in that it allows us to select components based on technical, budgetary, and political constraints and combine them in a way that doesn't compromise the overall security or usability of the network.

In the next few sections of this chapter, we're going to define some common terms of the trade to ensure that we're all on the same page. Then we'll discuss the different pieces of defense in depth. We will close with a discussion of the Nimda worm and show how defense in depth would have helped protect your network.

Terms of the Trade

We need a common frame of reference when it comes to terms used throughout the book because one person's definitions might not be the same as someone else's. To that end, we'll define the perimeter, the border router, a firewall, an IDS, a VPN, software architecture, and those pesky De-Militarized Zones (DMZs), and screened subnets.

The Perimeter

What exactly is the perimeter? When a co-worker heard the term *perimeter*, he conjured up an image of a small squad of soldiers spread out on the ground in a circle. Another co-worker came up with the circling-the-wagons image. Before we move on, ask yourself "What is a perimeter?"

A *perimeter* is the fortified boundary of our network that might include the following:

- Routers
- Firewalls
- IDSs
- VPN devices
- Software
- DMZs and screened subnets

Border Router

Routers are the traffic cops (or villains) of networks. They direct traffic into, out of, and within our networks. The *border router* is the last router you control before the Internet. Because all of an organization's Internet traffic goes through this router, it often functions as a network's first *and* last line of defense through initial and final filtering.

Firewall

A *firewall* is a device that has a set of rules specifying what traffic it will allow or deny. A firewall picks up where the border router leaves off and makes a much more thorough pass at filtering traffic. Firewalls come in several different types, including static packet filters, stateful firewalls, and proxy firewalls. You might use a static packet filter such as a Nortel Accellar router to block a subnet, a stateful firewall such as a Cisco PIX to control allowed services, or a proxy firewall such as Secure Computing's Sidewinder to control content. Although firewalls aren't perfect, they do block what we tell them to block and allow what we tell them to allow.

IDS

An *IDS* is like a burglar alarm system for your network that is used to detect and alert on malicious events. The system might comprise many different IDS sensors placed at strategic points in your network. Two basic types of IDS exist: network-based (NIDS) and host-based (HIDS). NIDS sensors are devices that monitor network traffic for suspicious activity. NIDS sensors often reside on subnets that are directly connected to the firewall, as well as at critical points on the internal network. HIDS sensors reside on and monitor an individual host. In general, IDS sensors watch for predefined signatures of bad events, and might perform statistical and anomaly analysis. When IDS sensors detect bad events, they can alert in several different ways including email, paging, or logging the occurrence. IDS sensors can report to a central database that correlates their information to view the network from multiple points.

VPN

A VPN is a protected network session formed across unprotected channels, such as the Internet. Frequently, we reference a VPN in terms of the device on the perimeter that enables the encrypted session, such as a Nortel Contivity. The intended use might be for business partners, road warriors, or telecommuters. A VPN allows an outside user to participate on the internal network as if connected directly to it. Many organizations have a false sense of security regarding their remote access because they have a VPN. If an attacker compromises the machine of a legitimate user, a VPN can give that attacker an encrypted channel into your network. You might trust the security of your perimeter, but do you trust the security of one of your telecommuters on a cable modem at home or dialing up in a hotel room? Even if you do trust them and their security, can you trust the security of your VPN-connected business partner's remote access users?

Software Architecture

Software architecture refers to applications that are hosted on the organization's network, and defines how they are structured. For example, we might structure an e-commerce application by splitting it into three distinct tiers:

- The web front end that is responsible for how the application is presented to the user

- The application code that implements the business logic of the application

- The back end databases that store underlying data for the application

Software architecture plays a significant role in the discussion of a security infrastructure because the primary purpose of the network's perimeter is to protect the application's data and services. When securing the application, ensure that the architecture of the software and the network are harmonious.

DMZs and Screened Subnets

We typically use the terms DMZ and screened subnet in reference to a small network containing public services that are connected directly to and offered protection by the firewall or other filtering device. A DMZ and a screened subnet are different even though many people use the terms interchangeably. The term DMZ originated during the Korean War when a strip of land at the 38th parallel was off-limits militarily. A DMZ is an insecure area between secure areas. Just as the DMZ in Korea was in front of any defenses, the DMZ, when applied to networks, is located outside the firewall. A firewall or a comparable traffic-screening device protects a screened subnet that is directly connected to it. Remember this: A DMZ is in front of a firewall, whereas a screened subnet is behind a firewall. In the context of this book, we will adhere to these definitions. Note the difference in Figure 1.1.

A *screened subnet* is an isolated network that is connected to a dedicated interface of a firewall or another filtering device. The screened subnet is frequently used to segregate servers that need to be accessible from the Internet from systems that are used solely by the organization's internal users. The screened subnet typically hosts "public" services, including DNS, mail, and web. We would like to think these servers are bastion hosts. A *bastion* is a well-fortified position. When applied to hosts on a network, fortifying involves hardening the operating system and applications according to best practices. As attacks over time have shown, these servers are not always well fortified; in fact, they are sometimes vulnerable despite being protected by a firewall. As security professionals, we must fortify these hosts because they are the target of the majority of attacks and can be the method by which the world sees our organizations.

Now that we have defined the important security components, let's look at how defense in depth can use them to form a complete security picture.

Figure 1.1   The DMZ is located in front of the firewall; the screened subnet is isolated from the internal network, but it still enjoys the protections that the firewall offers.

Defense in Depth

Think of the security of your network like an onion. When you peel away the outermost layer, many remain underneath it. No concept carries more importance when discussing network security than this defense in depth, and you will see it used as the guiding principle behind designs and implementations throughout this book. Defense in depth helps you protect network resources even if one of the security layers is compromised. After all, no security layer can be guaranteed to withstand every attack it might need to face.

We operate in a real world of system misconfigurations, software bugs, disgruntled employees, and overloaded system administrators. Moreover, any practical security design needs to accommodate business needs that might require us to open certain firewall ports, leave additional services running on the server, or prevent us from applying the latest security patch because it breaks a business-critical application. Treating perimeter security components as parts of a coherent defense in depth infrastructure allows us to deploy them in a way that accounts for weaknesses and strengths of each individual component. Of course, given the requirements of your organization, you might choose not to have every component that is discussed in this chapter. The extent to which you need to apply network security layers depends on the needs and capabilities of your business.

Crown Jewels

Think of the information that would have significant adverse affects if compromised as your organization's crown jewels. What are your company's crown jewels? How well protected are they?

Take the case of CD-Universe. Maxim, a Russian cracker, compromised 300,000 credit card numbers late in 1999. CD-Universe refused to pay his $100,000 ransom demand. In response, Maxim posted 25,000 numbers on a web site on Christmas Day 1999.

CD-Universe had their crown jewels compromised and undoubtedly felt the effects in lost sales and consumer confidence. According to the 2001 Computer Crime and Security Survey, the average loss of an incident is more than $2 million (http://www.gocsi.com/prelea_000321.htm).

Given this, we as security professionals *must* consider what our organization's crown jewels are and what protecting them is worth when we implement defense in depth if we want to avoid similar problems for our organizations.

Defense in Depth: Components

What exactly does defense in depth entail? The simple answer is the perimeter, the internal network, and a human factor. Each of these comprises many components, which are independently not enough to secure a network. The key lies in each component complementing the others to form a complete security picture.

The Perimeter

When we think of network security, we most often think of the perimeter. The perimeter might contain any or all of the following:

- Static Packet filter
- Stateful firewall
- Proxy firewall
- IDS
- VPN device

In addition to these components, we must consider the design of the network. Typically, a static packet filter, such as a border router, is the first perimeter device that traffic entering a network encounters and the last perimeter device that traffic exiting a network encounters.

Static packet filters inspect basic information within every packet. Static packet filters can be either routers (Cisco router) or firewalls (Linux IPchains). The border device, which is often a router, is the first incoming and the last outgoing layer of your network security. It contributes to defense in depth by filtering traffic before it enters or exits your network. All too often, we only consider filtering incoming traffic, but then we don't get the full usability of our border router.

Improperly destined traffic might be internal addresses that hit your external interface or vice-versa, and they can be addressed with ingress and egress filtering. Border routers can also block traffic that is considered high risk from entering your network, such as traffic on the SANS Top 20 list (http://www.sans.org/top20.htm). ICMP is a favorite of attackers both for DoS attacks and reconnaissance, so blocking it in whole or in part is a common function of a border router. Block source-routed packets at the border router because they can circumvent defenses. The border router can also block out-of-band packets, such as SYN-FIN packets.

On February 9, 2000, web sites such as Yahoo! and CNN were DDoSed off the Internet, mostly by spoofed smurf attacks. A smurf attack involves sending an ICMP Echo Request (ping) to the broadcast address, resulting in a response from every host. In this case, spoofing allowed attackers to direct the large number of responses to a victim network. Ingress and egress filtering would have blocked the spoofed traffic and allowed them to weather the DDoS storm. Every network should have ingress and egress filtering at the border router to permit only traffic that is destined for the internal network to enter and traffic that is destined for the external network to exit. We will cover filtering—including ingress and egress filters—in Chapter 2, "Packet Filtering."

Static packet filters, such as routers, are faster at screening traffic than stateful or proxy firewalls. This speed comes in handy when you are under attack or when the firewall is already under a heavy load. What if you don't have a border router under your exclusive control? Given your situation this may be appropriate. If your Internet connection is relatively small (T1 or less), then a firewall might be sufficient. Firewalls take a much more thorough look at packets, but they cover the same functionality as a border router.

In addition to static packet filtering, stateful firewalls keep track of connections in a state table and are the most common type of firewall. This connection tracking is useful to defense in depth because a stateful firewall blocks traffic that is not in its table of established connections. The firewall rulebase determines the source and destination IP and port numbers that are permitted to establish connections. You should consider any reconnaissance you detect to be a strong indication of a pending attack. By blocking non-established, non-permitted connections, a stateful firewall helps to block reconnaissance.

Recon Is the Name of the Game

My cable modem at home receives several scans per day. Previously with the IPchains firewall I had in place, Nmap ACK scans would pass through and successfully scan me. They were successful because non-stateful, static packet filtering firewalls, such as IPchains, evaluated each packet independently and did not track state. The presence of the ACK bit made it appear that I had initiated the connection and the ACK was the response. Without a stateful firewall in place, reconnaissance of my machine was relatively easy.

Stateful firewalls are able to recognize and block traffic that is part of an unestablished, non-permitted connection, such as attempts at reconnaissance. The ability to block reconnaissance such as the Nmap ACK scan that hit your firewall make stateful firewalls a valuable part of defense in depth by adding another layer of security to your network. An alternative, and sometimes a complement to a stateful firewall, is a proxy firewall.

Proxy firewalls are the most advanced and least common type of firewall. Proxy firewalls are also stateful, in that they block any non-established, non-permitted connections. As with stateful firewalls, the firewall rulebase determines the source and destination IP and port numbers that are permitted to establish connections. Proxy firewalls offer a high level of security because internal and external hosts never communicate directly. Rather, the firewall acts as an intermediary between hosts. Proxy firewalls examine the entire packet to ensure compliance with the protocol that is indicated by the destination port number. Ensuring that only protocol-compliant traffic passes through the firewall helps defense in depth by diminishing the possibility of malicious traffic entering or exiting your network.

The process for a user behind a proxy firewall to connect to an external web site is as follows:

1. An internal client sends the proxy a request for a URL.
2. The proxy requests the URL from the external site.
3. The external site responds to the proxy.
4. The proxy sends the response to the internal client.

One Lucky Soul

When I was network security manager for a large company, I was the lucky soul who received the angry phone calls and emails when people received pornography in their email. I don't know if you have ever attempted to explain the concept of browser information harvesting to an angry group of managers, but they don't tend to make the connection. Attempting to make the connection for them can be quite hazardous to your career! I told them that I could use a set of internal proxy firewalls with a URL filter to solve part of the problem by not allowing users to browse pornographic sites or material.

Using proxy firewalls diminishes the possibility of malicious traffic that is entering or exiting your network by ensuring that only protocol-compliant traffic passes through. What happens if malicious traffic appears to be appropriate material and adheres to the protocol?

An IDS represents the eyes and ears of a network by monitoring the network and hosts from critical points for malicious activity. Typical network IDS sensor placement includes each network segment directly connected to the firewall, as well as critical points within the network. If malicious traffic enters your network, your network IDS should be able to detect it, as well as communicate what it sees. This is precisely how an IDS helps defense in depth.

For example, a network IDS could identify and alert on the following:

- DNS Zone Transfer requests from unauthorized hosts
- Unicode attacks directed at a web server
- Buffer overflow attacks
- Worm propagation

We have seen several successive worms bring down large international networks. If these companies had been able to identify and isolate the infected machines quickly each time a new worm hit, they could have kept their networks functioning. An IDS with the correct signature would facilitate that identification. An IDS can help identify malicious traffic that might otherwise appear normal to an untrained eye. For example, a DNS Zone Transfer is a legitimate and common operation for peered DNS servers to engage in. However, we should consider zone transfers outside of those hosts dangerous.

An IDS is extremely valuable to defense in depth by detecting and reporting malicious traffic. We cannot afford to underestimate the value of information that an IDS provides. Although an IDS represents the eyes and ears of a network, we are not completely blind without one. Correlation of router, firewall, VPN, and system logs can yield some information about suspicious activity on the network. These logs are not meant to replace the granularity and extensiveness of IDS logs, but to augment them. Logs from non-IDS perimeter components can help significantly when the network IDS logs are of no use, such as when the traffic is encrypted in route to a VPN device.

VPNs protect communications over unprotected networks, such as the Internet. They protect by offering confidentiality, integrity, and non-repudiation. Plainly, they can make sure that if a colleague sends you an email, no one else can read it, the information hasn't changed, and it's really from him. VPNs are appropriate for a wide range of applications, and are often useful when dedicated private lines are too expensive or impractical for connecting network nodes. Protecting communications over unprotected networks helps us defend our networks with depth.

VPNs are wonderful tools or wonderful weapons, depending on who is using them. By providing protected communications over unprotected channels, a VPN is a tool to legitimate users. If, however, the endpoints of a VPN connection are not secure, an attacker might be able to gain a protected channel into your internal network, giving him an awesome weapon.

Remember the large international network we just discussed that was crippled by worms? Each time a worm hit, the culprit was the same: a VPN user who was working from home. Users would surf the web using their personal broadband connections at night before logging onto the internal network the following day via the VPN. A worm infected their machines when they were connected to the Internet at night. When they connected to the internal network the following day, the worm propagated to the internal network and ran rampant.

VPNs offer significant cost savings over the previous alternative of frame relay. We can use a VPN to protect all traffic from one network to another (network to network), between two hosts (host to host), or from a single host to a network (host to network). Knowing this, the way in which we configure our networks becomes increasingly important.

All too often, security is not a primary concern to a business when putting a network in place. A secure architecture is vital to defense in depth because it segregates resources and provides for performance and redundancy.

We need to do the following when evaluating an architecture:

- Determine what resources need to be protected.
- Determine the risk.
- Determine business requirements.

With this information, we can make educated decisions regarding our network defenses.

A solid network architecture created with security in mind will segregate resources and provide for performance and redundancy. Segregating resources is vital to defense in depth, and we will look at it closely in Chapter 12, "Separating Resources." We must keep in mind that no matter how segregated a host is from a network viewpoint, its configuration must also be hardened.

At Least Lock the (Screen) Door

I recently encountered a network without a screened subnet or a DMZ. The DNS server resided on the internal network, which was an entire hub environment. When an attacker compromised the DNS server, he installed a sniffer and was able to glean internal passwords. If the DNS server had been on a switched screened subnet, the attacker's ability to sniff passwords would have been greatly inhibited.

The Perfect Onion

Recently I was on site with a client who was telling me all about his company's layered security. The company had proxy firewalls, a big border router, IDSs, VPNs, a good design—you name it. When I asked about the security of the public DNS server, he told me that "it was fine" and that with so much security in front, the company wasn't too worried about it. Talk about locking the door but leaving the window open!

The client had segregated and protected this DNS server quite well. However, in neglecting to harden the host, the company had wasted a lot of work on securing the rest of the perimeter. Further investigation revealed that an attacker could have easily compromised the server, obtained a shell, and exploited a trust relationship with the internal DNS server, leaving him inside the network with a critical server. I asked what else "was just fine."

This particular client just needed a little reminder that security is a process, not a product. Unfortunately, not everyone believes this. Many people tend to have tunnel vision when it comes to security; it is part of our job as information security professionals to open their field of view.

We've discussed how various pieces of the perimeter contribute to the overall security of our network through defense in depth. While vital, the perimeter is only one piece of defense in depth. Next, we examine a piece that many organizations neglect to properly address: the internal network.

The Internal Network

The internal network is the network that is protected by the perimeter that contains all the servers, workstations, and infrastructure with which a company conducts business.

So often, administrators of various types say "We can trust our own people." Organizations often neglect the security of the internal network because they don't consider an internal attack a risk. An internal attack doesn't have to be a malicious employee; it can be a careless employee as well. As organizations are learning each time a new worm comes out, they cannot afford to overlook the security of the internal network!

Let's shift gears for a minute. Conjure up an image of what you consider a highly skilled cracker. Imagine him attacking your network...while sitting at your desk. What would stop him?

On the internal network, we could have the following "perimeter" devices:

- Ingress and egress filtering on every router
- Internal firewalls to segregate resources
- Proxies to enhance performance and security
- IDS sensors to function as "canaries in a coal mine" and monitor the internal network

Internally, we can use the following:

- Personal firewalls
- Anti-virus software
- Operating system hardening
- Configuration management
- Audits

Personal firewalls are generally implemented as software modules that run individual machines, screening network traffic as it enters and leaves the system. Many are configurable on a per-application basis, meaning that the user determines which applications have rights to access the Internet or function as servers (accept incoming connections). Personal firewalls are cost effective, ranging from free to cheap. They help defense in depth by augmenting the perimeter on every host.

You might ask, "Why do I need a personal firewall if I'm behind a firewall at work?" A personal firewall at work can protect you from malicious programs, such as trojans, and other internal hosts, as is the case with malicious internal users. If you do not have a personal firewall and connect to the Internet outside of work (hotel room while traveling or work-from-home), you cannot assume that you are being protected.

You Did What!?

Recently, a non-technical co-worker asked me why her personal firewall kept popping up alerts. My curiosity immediately piqued, as I seriously doubted there was a hole in the company firewall. I discovered that she used a dial-up connection to check her personal email and it had created a tunnel to her machine. She was being probed from her dial-up network for a vulnerability her machine had. If she had not had a personal firewall in place, an attacker could have run rampant on the internal company network.

Personal firewalls are wonderful pieces of software that augment the perimeter. If a traditional firewall cannot be deployed at the network's entry point, personal firewalls are cost-effective alternatives, especially if the network hosts a small number of systems. Personal firewalls are also useful for mobile users who connect to a network outside of work. Almost every network needs firewall technology of some sort, be it with static packet filters, stateful firewalls, or proxy firewalls on the perimeter or the individual machines. Most networks with user-level workstations also need an anti-virus capability.

In many respects, anti-virus software and network IDSs are similar in that they frequently operate by examining data for signatures of known malicious intent. Anti-virus software typically looks at the data on the file system, whereas a network IDS examines data on the network. As vendors package anti-virus, personal firewall, and IDS technology into a single product, the line distinguishing the three becomes increasingly vague. The role of anti-virus in defense in depth is clear—it protects against malicious code.

Remember my non-technical co-worker who was checking her personal email through dial-up? Her personal firewall saved her. What if she had not installed a personal firewall? Depending on the attack, updated anti-virus signatures could have prevented her machine from becoming infected.

We can augment our anti-virus capability on the desktop through products that couple with perimeter components, such as firewalls and email servers. The effectiveness of anti-virus software drastically decreases if it is not regularly updated, or if it does not yet provide a signature to identify the latest virus or worm. This is often the case with worms, which surface and propagate quickly. Host armoring becomes quite important in the case of ineffective anti-virus software.

Host hardening is the process of tightening the configuration of the host's OS and applications with the purpose of securing any unnecessary openings on the system. This typically involves applying any OS and application patches, setting file system permissions, disabling unnecessary services, and enforcing password restrictions. If everything else fails, host hardening is the last layer protecting an individual system. That makes it vital to defense in depth.

What if my non-technical co-worker who was checking her personal email through dial-up had not installed a personal firewall *or* anti-virus software? If basic hardening had been performed, she would have had a much-reduced risk by not presenting a vulnerability that an attacker could exploit.

It is all too easy to forget about host hardening when multiple layers of defense are surrounding the system. The fact remains that those defenses are not perfect, and we need that last layer. The question of how to keep on top of host hardening naturally arises.

Configuration management is the process of establishing and maintaining a known configuration for systems and devices that are on the network. Large companies might have an automated means of manipulating the configuration of all hosts, whereas small companies might perform the process manually. Defense in depth benefits from the ability to enforce a standard configuration.

Configuration management can enforce the following:

- That all Windows machines have Service Pack x installed
- That all Linux machines have kernel $x.x.x$ running
- That all users with remote-access accounts have a personal firewall
- That every machine has anti-virus signatures updated daily
- That all users accept the acceptable use policy when they log on

Some of these naturally lend themselves to large-scale automation, whereas others we can accomplish manually.

Who Is Responsible for Configuration Management?

A client recently called me in to handle a worm outbreak. My first question of the systems administrator was if all hosts were up to the latest service pack and patch level. He had not updated them because every host had anti-virus software that each user was to update weekly. This did neither him nor I any good. I ended up cleaning the main server and giving the administrator a good week's worth of work updating configurations.

Configuration management is the best way to establish a standard, secure configuration so that damage from incidents, such as this one, is limited. It can also enable your organization to control unauthorized software installation. Configuration management is an important piece of defense in depth because it enforces a standard configuration. How can we verify that a configuration is a secure one that remains unchanged?

Audit is the process of resolving perception to reality and improving upon that. Internal staff or external consultants can perform audits. The information that is presented here applies to either situation. Verifying the current state of security and improving upon it is vital to defense in depth.

An audit typically progresses like this:

1. An informational meeting is held to plan the audit. At the first informational meeting, we find out what the client wants and expects and establish risks, costs, cooperation, deliverables, timeframes, and authorization.

2. Fieldwork begins (implement the audit). When the client is ready, we perform the audit in line with what we established in the planning session.

3. The initial audit report (technical report) takes place. You might prefer to give an initial audit report to the technical representatives of a client before their management sees the final report. You can give them one or two days to fix anything they can before the final report goes to management. This also ensures that the technical representatives know what their management will see and can offer clarification on any issues.

4. The final audit report (non-technical report with final technical report) takes place. The final audit report contains an executive summary, the general approach used, the specific methodology used, and the final technical report.

5. Follow-up occurs (verify recommendations are performed).

When the client is ready, we go back in to verify that the issues have been resolved.

Just like you go to your doctor on a regular basis for a physical to make sure you're as healthy as you think you are, you should check your network on a regular basis to ensure that your perception of and the reality of security coincide. Consider an audit preventative maintenance. An audit is the only tool in defense in depth to verify that everything is as it should be.

Securing the internal network with personal firewalls, anti-virus software, and host armoring is not a trivial task. Configuration management and audits can help you accomplish this. Addressing security on the perimeter and the internal network is not enough. Next, we will complete the network security picture by discussing the human factor.

The Human Factor

Frequently, we get caught up in the technical aspect of network security without considering the non-technical aspect. Things like rulebase optimizations, reading a packet in hex, and generating ACLs are certainly important to network security. What we typically forget is the human end of things, like the policies and awareness that goes along with the technical solution.

Policy determines what security measures your organization should implement. As a result, the security policy guides your decisions when implementing security of the network. An effective defense in depth infrastructure requires a comprehensive and realistic security policy.

Hallmarks of good policy include the following:

- Authority (who is responsible)
- Scope (who it affects)
- Expiration (when it ends)
- Specificity (what is required)
- Clarity (can everyone understand it)

Note

In the initial planning meeting with clients, the first thing I always ask for is the security policy. Many times, they give me a quizzical look and ask why I would need it. I try to explain to them that policy and security are not separate entities, but determine one another.

If only a lawyer could read your security policy, it needs to be re-evaluated. We'll take a good, long look at policy later in the book. A caveat about policy: It only works if someone reads it.

User awareness is like driver's education. You can do without it, but things go much easier with it. Users can reduce risk and help defense in depth if they are aware of policy and follow it.

To increase user awareness, you can require the following:

- Have every user sign an acceptable use policy annually.
- Set up a security web page with policies, best-practices, and news.
- Send a "Security Tip of the Week" to every user.

A direct benefit of aware users comes when considering social engineering attacks. For example, if users know not to give their password to other people, a potential attack might be thwarted. When users are aware of policy, there tend to be fewer policy violations and users feel more involved in security. Additionally, in the case of policy violation, if they are educated, they cannot claim they don't know.

Note

I'm reminded of a time in my intemperate youth when I used the phrase "I didn't know that; it was never communicated to me." regarding an acceptable use policy. I've heard this same phrase repeated in a number of different circumstances. There is not much to be said when you have a signature affirming that a user agrees to and understands a policy. I have found a signed policy statement to be more valuable than gold in terms of time and effort saved.

Remember: Defense in depth hinges on the human factor of policy and user awareness. Policy determines what security measures your organization should implement. Those security measures should reflect policy. Defense in depth is the means to policy implementation; it depends on it.

We've examined the components of defense in depth and how they contribute to security of the network. Defense in depth is a flexible concept that allows you to create an effective security infrastructure that reflects the requirements of your organization. For example, smaller organizations might not be able to afford some of the components we discussed, but alternatives usually exist. Regardless of the size of your organization, policy and user awareness are necessary. We'll finish off this chapter looking at a real-world case where defense in depth could have saved an organization a lot of time, effort, and money.

Case Study: Defense in Depth in Action

The Nimda worm hit the Internet on September 18, 2001, causing a DoS for many organizations. Nimda was unique in that it spread via four methods:

- IIS exploits
- Email
- HTTP browsing
- Network Neighborhood

These four propagation methods made Nimda particularly vicious, as it could infect server-server, server-client, or client-client. Nimda was able to infect the entire range of Windows operating systems.

A large international network of 10,000 servers was brought to its knees in a matter of hours because of Nimda. Every system, network, and security administrator in the organization could not stop it after it began. This organization discovered first-hand the cost of not heeding the defense in depth concept. Defense in depth could have mitigated Nimda.

How could they have used the perimeter to mitigate Nimda? Using their routers to preemptively block or restrict ports 80 and 135–139 inbound could have prevented infection via the first and fourth methods. A rate limiting switch would have been able to dampen the effects of a DoS in the case of mass infections. Stateful firewalls being utilized as simple packet filters to block or restrict ports 80 and 135–139 also would have helped. Proxy firewalls that were configured to block known strings within Nimda also could have helped. If the company had properly segregated public services on a screened subnet, few machines would have been facing the Internet. Given that Nimda achieved saturation in approximately 2.5 hours, it is safe to say that most organizations did not know of Nimda until it had penetrated their internal network. What could have mitigated Nimda on the internal network?

The internal network could have used many of the same components that the perimeter had available, such as routers, stateful or proxy firewalls, and IDSs. Additionally, the internal network could have contained personal firewalls that were capable of blocking methods one and four easily. They could have attempted to use anti-virus software to mitigate Nimda, but reliable cleaning methods were not available for some time. (The preferred cleanup method is still a complete rebuild.) Host hardening had the highest potential of success in blocking Nimda by preventing infection entirely. Nimda used an old exploit that administrators should have patched well before September 18. Had they applied the patch, they would have stopped all four propagation methods. Additionally, this vulnerability was widely known, and regular audits would have found this vulnerability. Had none of these mitigation methods worked, hope remained for containment.

Policy could have helped prevent the spread of Nimda. Given an incident-handling procedure, sections of the network could have been isolated to patch the vulnerabilities or contain the spread of the worm. If they had a user awareness program before the attacks, user behavior might have prevented infection (especially via email).

Why did Nimda run rampant when so many methods were available to mitigate it? Perhaps organizations had one or more important components of defense in depth missing. Perhaps organizations had the wrong pieces of defense in depth in place by focusing entirely on the perimeter while neglecting the internal network. Perhaps organizations didn't follow policy. Perhaps this particular organization and countless others like it will learn to address security before an incident rather than during or after.

Summary

This first chapter set the stage for the book; as you can see, you must understand defense in depth to improve the security of a networked organization. No silver bullets exist, and no single component can properly defend a network. You can deploy many components working together in such a way as to make attack difficult. Defense in depth is the term that describes the process of layering these components to capitalize on their respective strengths. It is flexible, and some hold strong opinions, but no single roadmap can select and deploy the various perimeter components. Our role is to design, build, and maintain the perimeter so that the overall security of the network is at an acceptable level, while providing an environment that is not so restrictive that it impairs the business operations of the organization. A defense in depth approach can be used to secure an individual machine or the largest network in the world. It is a powerful tool for defenders.

2

Packet Filtering

Packet filtering is one of the oldest and most widely available means to control access to networks. The concept is simple: Determine whether a packet is allowed to enter or exit the network by comparing some basic identifying pieces of information that are located in the packet's header. Packet filtering technology can be found in operating systems, software and hardware firewalls, and as a security feature of most routers.

The goal of this chapter is to explore the highlights and weaknesses of packet filtering technology and how to implement this technology successfully. We discuss the basics of TCP/IP and how it applies to packet filtering, along with the rules of how to implement packet filters using Cisco router access lists. We explore uses for rules that filter on source address, such as the allowance and prohibition of traffic from given hosts and ingress and egress filters. We also cover filters that examine destination addresses and make decisions based on port numbers and their uses for improved control of traffic flow. We examine the problems of the packet filter, including weaknesses to spoofing, fragmentation, control of return traffic, and the problems with poking an always-open hole in your defense. Finally, we explore the power of dynamic packet filters and ways that they can help correct many of the downfalls of static packet filtering.

TCP/IP Primer: How Packet Filtering Works

Before this chapter goes into the details of packet filtering, it is necessary to understand the construct and technologies behind the TCP/IP protocol and its associated packets.

Note

The next several sections provide a basic overview of the TCP/IP protocol. Advanced readers might find this review unnecessary and might prefer to skip ahead to the "The Cisco Router as a Packet Filter" section.

When systems on a network communicate, they need to speak the same language, or protocol. One such protocol is TCP/IP, the primary communications language of the Internet. To facilitate such communications, the information you send needs to be broken down into manageable pieces called *packets*. *Packet headers* are small segments of information that are stuck at the beginning of a packet to identify it.

Packets are directed, or routed, by the values that are located in their packet headers. These identifiers hold information about where the packets came from (source address), where they are going (destination address), the port number of the protocol with which they are communicating, as well as other information describing the type of service that the packet might support, among other things. When a TCP/IP packet arrives at a router, the router checks its destination to see whether it knows how to get to the place where the packet wants to go. If it does, it passes the packet to the appropriate network segment. The fact that a router passes *any* packet whose destination it is aware of is called *implicit permit*. As you can imagine, this would not be an effective way to protect your network because all traffic is allowed in as well as out! You need a method to control the information that is entering and exiting the interfaces of the router.

TCP and UDP Ports

The TCP part of TCP/IP stands for *Transmission Control Protocol*, and it is a reliable transport-oriented way for information to be communicated. *User Datagram Protocol* (UDP) is an unreliable transport protocol that works well with programs that don't rely on the protocol to make sure that their payload gets where it's going. Both TCP and UDP use ports to keep track of communication sessions. Certain ports are set aside as the particular port to contact a server through running a given service such as HTTP (port 80), FTP (port 21), Telnet (port 23), DNS (port 53), and SMTP (port 25). (These services and how to secure them are discussed in more detail later.) For an up-to-date informative list of all of TCP's and UDP's server-side ports and the services to which they are assigned, check out RFC 1700.

When a client contacts a server, it randomly picks a source port numbered above 1023 to go out through. Then the client contacts the server on a set port, such as port 23 for Telnet. When the server replies, the information leaves on port 23 and returns to the client on the random >1023 port on which it left. This is the only way that a packet filter can determine the service that it is filtering.

For example, you might want to filter out all Telnet traffic; you do so by blocking all traffic that is directed at TCP port 23. You might also want to allow all HTTP traffic that is coming to port 80. However, if someone is running a Telnet server on port 80 somewhere on your network, and all you have for protection is the aforementioned packet filter, the traffic passes. Packet filtering systems don't have the intelligence to look beyond the port number to determine what service is running at the application layer. For this reason, if you want to block access to a particular service that you are running on alternative ports, you need to keep this in mind when constructing filtering rules. Sometimes, web servers run on alternative ports, such as 8000, 8080, or the like; if you wanted to allow access to said web servers, then creating a packet filtering rule that allows in port 80 traffic wouldn't be enough.

TCP's Three-Way Handshake

To begin communicating, the connection-oriented TCP uses what's known as *the three-way handshake*. When Host A wants to connect to Host B to transfer data, it has to let Host B know that it wants to connect. Host A does this by sending a packet to Host B with the SYN or synchronization flag set, meaning "I want to start a new conversation." If Host B can and wants to converse back to Host A, it returns a packet with the SYN and ACK or Acknowledgement flags set, meaning, "Okay, let's talk." Finally, Host A returns the third part of the handshake, a packet with just the ACK flag set, meaning, "I'm glad you want to talk, so let's start talking!" With that, data begins transferring. The aforementioned flags represent whether it is an initial attempt at communication, a response, or a response to a response.

Packet filtering systems can use these flags to determine in what stage the three-way handshake traffic is currently. For example, if you didn't want to allow new connections from the outside, you could choose to only permit traffic that is flagged with ACK; the packets starting a new connection contain the SYN flag only.

The Cisco Router as a Packet Filter

The Cisco ACL is one of the most available packet filters found today. The means by which a Cisco router filters packets is known as an *access control list* (ACL). An ACL serves as a laundry list of things for the router to look at in the packet header, to decide whether the packet should be permitted or denied access to a network segment. This is the basis of the traffic control features of a Cisco router.

Routers are a convenient choice for network filtering because they are already a part of your network's infrastructure and are located at its furthermost edge. If you want to keep something out of your network, this is the best place to screen it. This section covers the basic syntax and usage of the Cisco ACL and its environment, the Cisco IOS. All examples in this chapter are illustrated through the use of Cisco ACLs (IOS version 12.1 or greater), although the theories that are demonstrated can be applied to any packet-filtering system.

An Alternative Packet Filter: IPchains

Although examples in this chapter are given as Cisco access lists, other software programs and devices use similar technology. Following is a sample of IPChains, one such program. IPChains is a popular packet-filtering system that comes bundled with many versions of Linux (perhaps adding to its popularity).

If you wanted to block HTTP traffic from anywhere to your host 200.200.200.2 and log the matches, you would use the Cisco ACL:

`access-list 111 deny tcp any host 200.200.200.2 eq 80 log`

With IPChains, you would use the following:

`ipchains -A input -i eth1 -p tcp -s 0.0.0.0/0 -d 200.200.200.2/32 80 -l -j DENY`

where -A input means to place this rule on the end of the existing input chain.

The -i eth1 tells IPChains to apply this rule to the interface eth1.

-p tells the protocol to watch for TCP.

-S parameter sets the source address. 0.0.0.0/0 tells to watch for any source address. The /0 is the wildcard, and it means to match the specified bits exactly. Because the wildcard is 0 in this case, don't match anything exactly or allow anything. This is equivalent to the Cisco "any" keyword.

-d is the destination address. In our example, it is equal to the host address 200.200.200.2 because the /32 wildcard mask is used. It tells IPChains to match the first 32 bits (or everything) exactly. This is equivalent to using the 0.0.0.0 wildcard or the "host" keyword in Cisco ACLs.

The destination address in this case is followed by the port number of the blocked protocol: 80 (for HTTP traffic). If the source port would have been filtered as well, it would have followed the source address.

-l means "log this information."

Finally, -j DENY stipulates that any matching packets should be dropped and not to send any information of this back to the sender. It is the counterpart to the Cisco "deny" keyword.

As you can see, although similar in function, static packet filters come in different forms. Despite the differences in appearance and syntax, after you have a grasp of packet filtering concepts, your knowledge can be applied to any of these filtration systems.

The Cisco ACL

The Cisco ACL is simply a means to filter traffic that crosses your router. It has two major syntax types: numbered and named lists, and it comes in several filtering types, including standard, extended, and reflexive, which will be discussed in this chapter. Numbered access lists are entered in the following format:

```
access-list <number> <criteria>
```

where the number is a given range that represents the type of access list it is. 1–99 represents standard IP lists, and 100–199 represents extended IP lists. Over time, these basic ranges were expanded to include 1300–1999 for standard and 2000–2699 for extended. Other access list number ranges are reserved for alternative protocols, and so on. The named access list uses the following format:

```
ip access-list <type> <name>
```

where the <type> code stands for standard, extended, and so on. The <name> code represents a unique name for the list. This can help make the list more identifiable. For example, "dnsinbound" might mean more to someone than the number "113" does.

Upon entering the preceding command to start list creation, you are dropped into a configuration mode just for that access list. Here, you can enter filtering commands in the following format:

```
permit|deny  <criteria>
```

Either type of ACL works well and can be used separately or together. Although standard and extended lists can be written in either format, reflexive access lists can use only the named format. To remove either type of ACL, re-enter it preceded by the word no.

Rule Order

Many of the access lists that are demonstrated throughout this text are deny access lists that show how to block a particular address or port. However, because of a concept called implicit deny, dropping such a list into an otherwise empty router configuration could cause the blocking of *all* traffic! *Implicit deny* takes place when as little as one access list is added to an interface on a Cisco router. The router stops its standard behavior of forwarding all routable traffic and instead begins comparing all packets that are received to the newly added access list. If the traffic doesn't match the applied access list(s), it is dropped. Adding one simple access list changes the behavior of the router entirely. Only packets that match the added access list are allowed.

When multiple rules are added, even more concerns arise. Because rules are processed from the top down and a packet only has to pass or fail one rule to be dropped or allowed into the network, it is imperative to put specific filters before general filters. Otherwise, a more general rule might allow a packet that you specifically have a rule written to deny later in the list. When a packet "matches" a rule, the packet is immediately dropped (if it is a deny rule), or forwarded (if it is a permit rule) without being tested by the rest of the access list.

Care must be taken when planning the order of access list rules. That is why a complete access list rule-base needs to be laid out in advance and built from the ground up. Adding rules carelessly is a sure recipe for disaster.

Note

Whenever possible, assemble your access lists following the precept of "allow what you need" rather then "deny what you don't."

Cisco IOS Basics

Before going into detail on the syntax of Cisco access lists, it is necessary to discuss the interface by which Cisco routers are configured. Cisco routers can be configured in one of several ways. They can be accessed through a serial connection to the console port on the back of the router, through a Telnet session, or by a web browser with newer models. After you have access to the router, actually getting it into configuration mode is a relatively easy process.

1. First, you receive the standard prompt (designated by the > symbol) `routername>` .

2. You must go into enable mode before configuration mode. Typing `enable` and pressing the Enter key accomplishes this. You are prompted for a secret password. After entering it, you are in enable mode, which is identified by the `routername#` prompt (designated by the number sign (#)).

3. To configure the router, enter terminal configuration mode by typing `config t` (which is short for configure terminal) and pressing Enter. You then see the global configuration prompt: `routername(config)#`. This is where you enter global configuration commands, including access lists.

4. You can enter interface configuration mode from the global configuration mode by typing `int s1`, where `int` stands for interface and `s1` is the interface name (in this case, serial1). This format is also carried into Ethernet interfaces (e0, e1, and so on) as well as other interface types. Typing the

interface command changes the prompt to the interface configuration prompt: `routername(config-if)#`. From here, you can type interface-specific commands, and this is where you can apply access lists to individual interfaces with the `access-group` command.

5. Exit any configuration level by typing the `exit` command. Completely exit out of configuration mode from any sublevel by pressing Ctrl+Z. Leave enable mode by typing `disable`.

Effective Uses of Packet-Filtering Devices

Because packet filtering is older technology and lacks the capability to differentiate between types of network traffic, you might be wondering why we are discussing it. What could be the possible use for this technology in a world that is filled with hi-tech firewalls that can track the services using knowledge of the way the protocols work to intelligently differentiate between incoming and outgoing traffic streams? Good question! Why use a PC when we have supercomputers? Sometimes a lighter weight, less expensive means to get things done is a major advantage. Because packet filters don't go to great depth in their analysis of traffic streams, they are faster than other firewall technologies. This is partially due to the speed at which the header information can be checked and partially due to the fact that packets don't have to be "decoded" to the application level for a decision to be made on them.

Filtering Based on Source Address: The Cisco Standard ACL

One of the things that packet filtering technology is great for is the blocking or allowing of traffic based on the IP address of the source system. Some ways that this technology can be usefully applied are filters blocking specific hosts (black-listing), filters allowing specific hosts (such as business partners), and in the implementation of ingress and egress filters. Any of these examples can be implemented on a Cisco router by using a "standard" access list.

The standard access list is used to specifically allow or disallow traffic from a given source IP address only. It cannot filter based on destination or port number. Because of these limitations, the standard access list is fast and should be preferred when the source address is the only criteria on which you need to filter.

The syntax for a standard access list is as follows:

```
access-list <list number 1-99> <permit |deny> <source address> <mask> <log>
```

Notice that the list number must be between 1 and 99. This is the only way that the Cisco IOS can identify the list as a standard ACL. The `mask` option is a required wildcard mask, which tells the router whether this is a single host we are filtering or an entire network range. (For more information on wildcard masks, check out the sidebar "The Cisco Wildcard Mask Explained," later in this chapter). The `log` option can be appended to tell the router to specifically log any matches of this filter. These log entries can be saved in local memory or more appropriately sent to a remote Syslog server. For more information on router logging, see Chapter 6, "Role of a Router" and Chapter 18, "Network Log Analysis."

The previously listed access list notation is entered in global configuration mode, and can be applied to the interface in the interface configuration mode with the `access-group` statement.

```
ip access-group <list number> <in|out>
```

The `access-group` command is used to specifically apply an ACL to an interface (by its list number) either inbound or outbound. Only one access list can be applied in one direction (in or out) per interface. This means a maximum of two applied ACLs per interface: one inbound and one outbound.

One of the confusing concepts of router ACLs is the way that applying filters "in" or "out" works. This is confusing because people normally visualize "in" as traffic moving toward their internal network, and "out" as traffic moving away from their network toward outside entities. However, this premise does not necessarily hold true when talking about the `in` and `out` keywords in Cisco router access lists. Specifically, the keywords tell the router to check the traffic moving toward (in) or away from (out) the interface listed.

In a simple dual interface router, this concept is more easily illustrated. Let's assume that you have an interface called e1 (hooked to your internal network) and an external interface called s1 (hooked up to the Internet, for example). Traffic that comes into the s1 interface moves toward your internal network, whereas traffic that goes out of the s1 interface moves toward the Internet.

So far this seems to be pretty logical, but now let's consider the internal e1 interface. Traffic that comes into e1 moves away from your internal network (toward the Internet), and traffic that goes out of e1 goes toward your internal network. Keep in mind when you apply `access-group` commands to your interfaces that you apply the access list in the direction that the traffic is traveling, in regards to the router's interface. You might be thinking, "What is the difference then, between inbound on the s1 interface and outbound on the e1 interface? Both refer to traffic that is moving in the same direction. Which is more appropriate to use?"

Tip

To maximize performance, filter traffic as it enters the router.

The less work that the router has to do, the better. Always try to filter traffic at the first interface it enters, or apply your filters "inbound" as much as possible.

Returning to our example, if something should be blocked (or permitted, for that matter) coming in from the Internet, it would make the most sense to block it coming in to the s1 (outside) interface. In addition, if something should be filtered leaving your network, it would be best to filter it inbound on the e1 (inside) interface. Basically, you should show preference to the `in` keyword in your access lists. Some specific exceptions to this rule exist, which involve certain access list types (such as reflexive ACLs) that require being placed outbound.

These examples often list the actual prompt for a router named *router*, to remind you of the command modes that the router will be in when entering the various commands.

The following is an example of an actual filter that uses the previous syntax and 190.190.190.x as the source network's IP address that you want to deny:

```
router(config)#access-list 11 deny 190.190.190.0 0.0.0.255
```

This filter's list number is 11. It denies any packet with a source network address of 190.190.190 with any source host address. It is applied to the interface inbound, so it filters the traffic on the way into the router's interface. Because this is a standard access list, it would probably be best to put this rule near the top of the pecking order. It is faster than more complicated access list types.

The command to apply the access list to your serial 1 interface would be this:

```
router(config-if)#ip access-group 11 in
```

where we are in interface configuration mode for the interface to which we are applying the access list, inbound.

The Cisco Wildcard Mask Explained

The wildcard mask is one of the least understood portions of the Cisco ACL syntax. Take a look at the following example:

```
access-list 12 permit 192.168.1.0 0.0.0.255
```

In this case, `0.0.0.255` represents the wildcard mask. It looks like a reverse subnet mask and represents the portion of the listed IP address range to filter against the traffic in question. Zeros mean "Test this portion of the address," and ones mean "Ignore this portion of the address when testing."

In our example, let's say a packet comes in with a source address of 192.168.2.27. Because the first octet of the wildcard mask is a zero, the router compares the first octet of the incoming packet to the value 192 that is listed in the access list. In this case, they are the same, so the router continues to the second octet of the wildcard mask, which is also a zero. Again, the second octet of the value of the source address of the incoming packet is compared to the value 168. Because they are also the same, the router continues to the third octet. Because the wildcard mask specifies a zero in the third octet as well, it continues to test the address, but the value of the third octet does not match, so the packet is dropped.

For the sake of example, let's continue to look at the fourth octet, even though in actuality the packet would have been dropped at this point. The wildcard's fourth octet is valued at 255. In binary, this equates to 11111111. In this example, the value 0 in the access list does not match the value 27 of the compared packet; however, because the wildcard wants us to ignore this octet, the access list allows the packet to pass (assuming that it hadn't failed on the previous octet). The concept might seem pretty easy with a wildcard value that deals with entire octets, but it gets tricky when you need to deal with an address range that is smaller than 255. The reality is that the router doesn't test octet by octet, but bit by bit through each of the octets.

What if you want to allow traffic from systems in the address range 192.168.1.16–192.168.1.31 only. The first three octets of the wildcard are easy: 0.0.0. It's the last octet that is difficult. It's time to grab your handy-dandy binary calculator. Consider what 16 looks like in binary: 0001 0000. Now look at 31: 0001 1111. The difference between these two binary values occurs in the last four bits. Therefore, the values between 16 and 31 are covered in the range 10000–11111. To allow those values, you need to place zeros in your wildcard mask for the portions that need to match exactly, and ones for the binary values that change. Because the last four bits are the only bits that change in the desired range, the wildcard mask reflects those four bits with ones. In binary, our wildcard mask is as follows:

```
00000000.00000000.00000000.00001111
```

Translated with our binary calculator, that is 0.0.0.15.

This wildcard mask works for any range of 15 addresses that you are comparing, so to make it work for 16–31, you must properly reflect the range in the IP address portion of the access list. Your final access list looks like this:

```
access-list 10 permit 192.168.1.16 0.0.0.15
```

A wildcard mask is always contiguous zeros and ones, without interruption, as in the example listed previously. In some cases, you need more than one ACL statement and wildcard mask to cover a range of network addresses. For example, if you want to block addresses in the range 232–255, you need the following two commands:

```
access-list 110 deny ip 192.168.1.232 0.0.0.7 any
```

to block the range 232–239.

You also need to specify this:

```
access-list 110 deny ip 192.168.1.240 0.0.0.15 any
```

to block the range 240–255.

Black-Listing: The Blocking of Specific Addresses

One popular use of the standard access list is the "black-listing" of particular host networks. This means that you can block a single host or an entire network from accessing your network. The most popular reason for blocking a given address is mischief. If your IDS shows that you are being scanned constantly by a given address, or you have found that a certain IP address seems to be constantly trying to log in to your systems, you might simply want to block it as a preventative measure.

For example, if your intranet web server should only be offering its information to your business locations in the continental United States, and you are getting a lot of hits from a range of IPs in China, you might want to consider blocking those addresses.

> **Warning**
>
> The blocking of "spoofed" addresses can lead to a denial of service condition. Always research IP addresses before uniformly blocking them.

The blocking of address ranges is also a popular way to band-aid your system against an immediate threat. For example, if a denial of service exists against one of your servers from a certain IP address, you could simply block all traffic from that host or network number. As another example, if you just found out that you had a widespread infection of a Trojan that contacted a remote IRC server, you could block all traffic coming from that IRC server. It would be more appropriate to block the traffic leaving your network to that destination, however, but that would require an extended access list because standard ACLs only filter on source address.

A sample access list to block access from an outside address range would be this:

```
router(config)#access-list 11 deny 192.168.1.0 0.0.0.255
router(config-if)# ip access-group 11 in
```

where the network number of the outside parties to be blocked would be 192.168.1.0–255. (Of course, this address range is part of the ranges that are reserved for private addressing, and is simply used as an example in this instance.) This access list would be applied to the external router interface, inbound.

Spyware

Once I was perusing my logs to check for Internet connections from my network during off-hours, to see if anything peculiar was going on. I noticed some connections that were initiated in the middle of the night from various stations, repeatedly contacting a similar network address. I did some research on the address and determined that the maker of a popular freeware program owned it.

After a brief inspection of one of the "beaconing" stations, I found that the freeware program in question was loaded on the system. Being completely paranoid (as all good security professionals are), I immediately set up a rule on my perimeter router to block all access to the network address in question. Many software packages search for updates regularly, and do not use these automatic "phoning home" sessions for malicious activity. However, as a firewall administrator, I have to be in control of my network's traffic flow. Besides, I do question why these packages need to "call out" several times a night.

Of course, my block was just a quick fix until I could unload the software at all of the "infected" stations, but if it somehow appeared again, I had no fear of the software gaining outside access. The moral of the story: It can be a lot easier to block a single network address at your perimeter router than to run from station to station to audit software.

"Friendly Net": Allowing Specific Addresses

Another way you can use a standard access list is to permit traffic from a given IP address. However, this is not recommended. Allowing access to an address in this matter, without any kind of authentication, can make you a candidate for attacks and scans that use spoofed addresses. Because we can only filter on source address with a standard ACL, any inside device with an IP address can be accessed. Also, it's impossible to protect individual services on those devices. If you need to set up access like this and can't do it through a solution that requires authentication or some type of VPN, it is probably best to at least use an access list that considers more than the source address. We'll discuss this more in the section on extended access lists.

Ingress Filtering

RFC 1918 pertains to reserved addresses. Private/reserved addresses are ranges of IP addresses that will never be distributed for public use. This way, these addresses can be used in internal networks without worry of accidentally picking network addresses that might correspond with a public address that you might want to access some day.

For example, imagine that you are in a world in which reserved private addresses don't exist. You are installing a new private network for your business that will have access to the Internet and will be running TCP/IP, so you will have to come up with a range of IP addresses for your stations. You don't want these stations to have public addressing because they won't be serving information to the Internet, and you will be accessing the Internet through a proxy server. You pick a range of IP addresses at random—let's say 190.190.190.0–255. You configure your stations and set up Internet access.

Everything is working great until the first time you attempt to access your bank's web site and receive an error. You call the bank, and the bank says that everything is fine on the bank's end. You eventually come to discover that the bank was right—nothing was wrong at their end. The bank's system that you were trying to contact has a public IP address of 190.190.190.10, the same address that you have configured for one of your own stations. Every time your web browser goes to send information to the bank, it never even leaves your internal network. You've been asking your CAD station for a web page, and because your CAD station doesn't run web server software, you've just been getting an error. This example should have painted a clearer picture of why reserved addresses are so important for the interrelationship of public and private TCP/IP networks.

The reserved ranges are as follows:

- Class A: 10.0.0.0–10.255.255.255
- Class B: 172.16.0.0–172.31.255.255
- Class C: 192.168.0.0–192.168.255.255

Because these ranges are often used as internal network numbers, they are good candidates for someone who is crafting packets or doing other malicious packet-transmitting behavior, including denial of service. Therefore, these ranges should be blocked at the outside of your network. In addition, the loopback address 127.0.0.1, the default address that all IP stations use to "address" themselves, is another candidate for being blocked, for the same reason. While you are blocking invalid addresses, you should also block the multicast address range 224.0.0.0–239.255.255.255 and the invalid address 0.0.0.0. Following is an example access list to accomplish this:

```
router(config)#access-list 11 deny 10.0.0.0 0.255.255.255
router(config)#access-list 11 deny 127.0.0.0 0.255.255.255
router(config)#access-list 11 deny 172.16.0.0 0.15.255.255
router(config)#access-list 11 deny 192.168.0.0 0.0.255.255
router(config)#access-list 11 deny 224.0.0.0 15.255.255.255
router(config)#access-list 11 deny host 0.0.0.0
router(config-if)# ip access-group 11 in
```

These access lists are similar to the last one, denying access to the IP address ranges that are listed in an inbound direction on the applied interface. Notice the host keyword when blocking 0.0.0.0 in the previous example. When blocking a single host, instead of following the IP address with the wildcard

0.0.0.0, you can precede the address with the keyword host. These lists have the same "implicit deny" that any access list does. This means that somewhere in access list number 11, a permit statement would have to exist, or all inbound traffic would be denied! An example of an appropriate permit statement might be one that allows the return of established traffic, like the following:

```
router(config)# access-list 111 permit tcp any any established
```

This is, however, an extended access list, which we'll talk more about later in the section "Filtering by Port and Destination Address: The Cisco Extended ACL."

It is also advisable to create a rule to block traffic coming into your network that claims to have a source address matching that of your internal network, to complete your ingress access list. Valid traffic from the outside world doesn't have to have the same addressing as your stations. However, if this traffic is allowed to pass, it could bypass security mechanisms that think the traffic is local. If you are using one of the standard private address ranges, this is already done. If you're not, it would look like this:

```
router(config)#access-list 11 deny 201.201.201.0 0.0.0.255
```

where your network address range is 201.201.201.0–255. This rule would be added to the previous list before the line that allows return traffic.

Ingress filters are an excellent example of a means to use packet-filtering technology to its fullest, on any network. Even if you have a stateful or proxy firewall, why not let your perimeter router use packet filtering to strip off this unwanted traffic? Let perimeter routers be the "storm-troopers" of your network, stripping off the undesirables before they even reach other internal protection devices.

Egress Filtering

Another use of standard access lists is for egress filters. The concept behind an egress filter is that only packets with your network's source address should be leaving your network. This seems like a forgone conclusion, but as stated in the section on ingress filters, Trojans and other nefarious programs might use a station on your network to send spoofed traffic to the rest of the world. By creating an ACL that only allows your subnet's address in from your network, you prevent this type of traffic from touching the outside world. Of course, this won't help if the program doesn't spoof the source address, but many such programs do to help slow the rate at which they can be traced. Such an access list would look like this, assuming an internal network address of 192.168.100.0:

```
router(config)#access-list 11 permit 192.168.1.0 0.0.0.255
```

Implicit deny takes care of denying all other source addresses. You could use an extended access list to tighten this down even more and limit things like the types of traffic and destinations that your stations are allowed to access. This ACL would be applied to the inside interface inbound, effectively on the outside edge of your router's network interface.

You might be wondering what the advantage is in implementing a rule such as this. "What will this do for me?" you might be asking yourself. Well, it is no different from dumping your tray at the local fast food restaurant; it's the good neighbor policy. It doesn't do anything for you directly (other than possibly prevent you from facing outside litigation), but if everyone did it, oh what a world we would live in. Imagine the effect on distributed denial of service attacks that use zombies stationed on innocent people's networks. These filters (assuming that the DoS zombies take advantage of some type of packet spoofing) could help cripple such zombies.

It is also possible to set up filters that prevent traffic from leaving your network from specified systems. For example, imagine that you have a top secret file server that has no Internet access. This system should only be contacted from inside stations, and should never contact the outside world, or be contacted from the outside world. You can place an ACL on the inside router interface inbound. It could be a part of the same access list that you used for your egress filter, but it would have to be placed above the egress filter because of the importance of rule order. If the top secret file server's IP address was 192.168.100.7, this is how the entire egress list would look:

```
router(config)#access-list 11 deny 192.168.100.7 0.0.0.0
router(config)#access-list 11 permit 192.168.100.0 0.0.0.255
```

The given host's packets would be filtered before the rule that allows all other systems on the 192.168.100 network to enter the router.

Tracking Rejected Traffic

When creating Cisco router access lists, one of the greatest downfalls of the `log` keyword is that it only records matches to the rule in question. Therefore, if the rule is a permit rule, then you lose the profoundly important information about which packets are being denied. To track the traffic that is being filtered by an implicit deny, add a "deny any" ACL with the `log` keyword (as seen in the example at the end of this note) to the bottom of the list in question. Functionally, the `deny  any  log` command does the same thing as the assumed implicit deny, but it facilitates the logging of denied traffic. One good application of this concept is to track abnormal traffic that is being filtered by the implicit deny at the end of an egress filter access list. Using this method allows a means to track all outbound traffic that has a source address other than that of your network. This is a great way to keep a handle on any strange things that might be trying to sneak out of your network! Here is a simple example of how you would tell the router to log blocked traffic:

```
access-list 11 deny any log
```

Filtering by Port and Destination Address: The Cisco Extended ACL

Another powerful use of packet filtering technology involves filtering on packet header information and port numbers. These examples can be applied in the form of specific "conduits" that allow one system to access another (*extranets*), allowing access to a specific public access system (web or DNS server), or allowing a specific type of traffic into the network (ICMP packet too big—unreachables). This functionality is enabled on a Cisco router using the extended access list.

The Cisco Extended ACL

The Cisco extended ACL offers additional features that allow more control of network traffic flow. Instead of only being able to filter on source address, we have the additional flexibility of destination address filtering, filtering based on protocol type, filtering on specific layer 4 port number information, flags, and more. With this additional granularity, the effectiveness of the Cisco router as a packet filter is greatly increased, making it viable for many security concerns.

The extended access list syntax is as follows:

```
access-list <number 100-199> <permit|deny> <protocol>  <source>
↪<source-mask> <source-port> <destination>  <destination-mask>
↪<destination port> <log|log-input> <options>
```

You should recognize the first entries in the syntax from the standard access list, up to the `protocol` keyword. This is where you would specify the protocol that you are interested in filtering. Possible selections are IP, TCP, UDP, and ICMP. Because TCP, UDP, and ICMP are all forms of IP-based traffic, when you use IP as the protocol on an access list, it permits or denies any of the other three traffic types. If we had used an extended access list to substitute for one of the standard access lists from the previous section, IP would have been the appropriate choice because it would have blocked all IP traffic types (UDP, TCP, and ICMP).

Remember the importance of rule order. Each incoming packet is checked by each access list in order from top to bottom. When a packet matches the criteria in any one of the access lists, an action is performed. If it is a permit filter, the packet is forwarded; if it is a deny filter, the packet is dropped. No rules test the packet beyond the rule that the packet matched. Use the following code to allow a particular packet in (let's say that its IP address is 205.205.205.1) if it is TCP, but deny entry if it uses any other IP protocol:

```
access-list 111 deny ip host 205.205.205.1 any
access-list 111 permit tcp host 205.205.205.1 any
```

The first rule would test true for a TCP packet of address 205.205.205.1. Because it is a "deny" rule, the packet would be dropped. The packet would never get to be tested by the second rule. If the two rules were reversed in order, with the TCP rule first, the filter would work correctly.

In the extended access list's syntax, the source address and mask should look familiar; the destination address and mask follow the same format, and simply mean "where it is going" instead of "where it is from." The keyword any can be used to represent the numerical range 0.0.0.0–255.255.255.255, or all addresses.

This is the first time that you see ports listed as part of an access list. As mentioned previously, ports are an important part of TCP/IP and the access lists. The <source-port> or <destination port> entry can specify the type of traffic you want to allow or disallow. When specifying a port number or name, you must also include an operator, such as eq (meaning equal to this port number), gt (for any port above this number), lt (for any port less than this number), and my favorite range (to list an entire contiguous range of port numbers. Use the syntax range <port1> <port2>, where <port1> is the first port in the range and <port2> is the last).

Extended access lists are configured and applied just like standard access lists, including the association of an access-group to an interface. Many options can be added to the end of the access list, such as log (as mentioned in the standard access list or log-input, which also displays the input interface and source MAC address), flags to check for, or the established keyword.

"Friendly Net" Revisited

As mentioned previously, allowing access to a given IP address is not a favored practice. The main reason for this is lack of control and the dangers of spoofing. Using a standard ACL to allow access is a problem because the only thing that we have control over is which IP address (or range) can access the entire inside network. This means that not only can the host or range of hosts specified access any station on the inside, but they also can do so on any port number. This is not good. Extended access lists can at least help tighten up that control. We can specify the destination host (or range) to which the host can connect, as well as the port on which they can communicate. This way, we can allow an outside trusted host to access our web server (only) on port 80 (only). Take a look at this example:

```
access-list 111 permit tcp host 100.100.100.1 gt 1023 host
➥200.200.200.2 eq 80 log
```

This example assumes that the trusted host is at address 100.100.100.1 and our target web server is at address 200.200.200.2. We only allow traffic from the trusted host on ephemeral ports, and only to port 80 on our web server. We add the log keyword to track traffic that is passing this rule.

This is not secure. All this guarantees is that you have control over those specified items, helping to lessen the ability of outsiders to exploit your defense. This ACL can be subverted in other ways.

Only allowing port 80 traffic doesn't ensure that only web traffic will transpire from the outside host to your web server. As a matter of fact, if a flaw exists to be exploited in your web server, and an attacker can get a Telnet program or other backdoor running on your web server on port 80, the server might as well be wide open. If this system is on your private network and not on a separate screened subnet, you are just a few leaps away to being fully compromised, especially if the web server has a trust relationship with any other mission-critical servers on your network.

Be sure to tightly harden the system if you elect to control access to its resources solely through the use of packet filters, without further authentication. If possible, run a multiple interface router (or packet filtering device) or multiple levels of packet filtering devices where you can structure a separate subnet for public access systems.

Filtering TCP and UDP Ports and ICMP Types

Another handy function of the extended access list is the filtering of certain types of traffic. You can control the types of traffic that leave your network, in effect enforcing your security policy. You can allow or disallow certain types of traffic that enter your network. Denying traffic to a list of popular Trojan program ports or to ports that programs use that conflict with your Internet usage or security policies (IRC, Napster, instant messenger programs, and so on) can also be an extra layer of defense. As stated previously, it makes more sense to only allow what you need. A more common use of port filtering is allowing traffic types that can enter or leave your network, like the example in the previous section. For a list of mission-critical ports that any environment should consider defending, see Appendix A of the SANS/FBI's "The Twenty Most Critical Internet Security Vulnerabilities," available at http://www.sans.org/top20.htm.

Another use for this type of filtering is to allow or disallow certain informative ICMP messages entrance to our network. ICMP is one of the most exploited of the protocols. It is being used for reconnaissance, denial of service attacks (such as Smurf), and more. It is recommended that you block incoming echo requests (`ping` and Windows `traceroute`), block any outgoing echo replies, and block time exceeded, for maximum security. All of the ICMP traffic types can be blocked with extended ACLs. The use of any ICMP blocking filters could affect network traffic control.

ICMP doesn't work like the other protocols. Instead of having port numbers, it uses type and code identifiers. It is basically set up to send error messages for protocols that can't (such as UDP and IP) and to send informational messages (such as router error messages telling that a host is unreachable). ICMP is used by popular end-to-end troubleshooting utilities such as `ping` and `traceroute`. ICMP can be controlled by using Cisco access lists with special ICMP keywords or ICMP type numbers, instead of port numbers such as TCP and UDP access lists.

To block ICMP echo requests (ICMP type 8), we could use a line in an extended access list such as this:

```
router(config)#access-list 111 deny icmp any any echo-request
```

The main difference between this access list and others we have done is the keyword at the end of the line. This keyword represents the ICMP type and code for echo-requests. It means, "Deny any ICMP traffic from anywhere to anywhere with the type and code set to echo-request." This filter would be applied on the external router interface to the Internet. Other ICMP traffic types can be filtered in the same way using their type-of-service keywords.

A better way to handle the ICMP blocking would be to allow only the types of traffic that you want and then deny the rest. For example, one important ICMP packet type to allow in is the `packet-too-big` ICMP unreachable messages (type 3, code 4). This is because without this message, you could have major communications issues. What if a host can't receive a packet because it is too large for it to handle and the router isn't allowed to return information to the host telling it that the packet is too large? How will the sender ever find out what is wrong and successfully communicate with the host? Luckily, in this example, Cisco has an ICMP keyword for the `packet-too-big` message. This keyword could be applied as follows, permitting the `packet-too-big` messages, but denying all other ICMP messages:

```
router(config)#access-list 111 permit icmp any any packet-too-big
router(config)#access-list 111 deny icmp any any
```

The filter would be applied as usual with an `ip access-group 111 in` command.

Problems with Packet Filters

Despite the many positive uses of packet filters, problems exist due to
inherent limitations in the way the packet filter works. Spoofed and fragmented traffic can bypass the packet filter if protections aren't properly
implemented. In addition, because of the always-open nature of a "permit"
static packet filter, issues exist with opening such a "hole." Finally, allowing
return traffic can be difficult using a technology that lacks the ability to track
the state of the current traffic flow. To successfully defend a network with
packet filtering, these weaknesses must be understood.

Spoofing and Source Routing

Spoofing means sending a packet that is addressed with false information, so it
appears to come from somewhere other than where it did. A packet can be
addressed as if it came from an internal host on the target network, one of
the private address ranges, or even another network entirely. Of course, a
packet doesn't do this on its own; the packet has to be crafted or created
with special packet-crafting software.

   If your defense isn't set up correctly and the packet gets through, it's possible that an internal host could believe that the packet came from a "trusted"
host that has rights to private information, and could in turn reply to the
spoofed address! You might be asking yourself, "If the packet appeared to
come from a station other than the one who sent it, where will the response
go?" Well, the answer in typical TCP/IP communication is to the *real* host,
who wouldn't know what to do with the packet, and would drop it and send
a reset to the originator. However, if source routing is enabled, the imposter
packet could carry source-routing information that would allow it to tell the
station where it needs to be sent to go home.

   Source routing allows a packet to carry information that tells a router the
"correct" or a better way for it to get back to where it came from, allowing
it to override the router's prescribed routing rules for the packet. This could
allow a devious user to guide return traffic wherever they want. For this reason, it is imperative to have source routing disabled. It is easily disabled in a
Cisco router with the following command typed at the global configuration
prompt:

```
router(config)#no ip source-route
```

However, by blocking any packet that claims to have an unusable address
before it can enter, we can help remove the problem. This is where ingress
filters come into play. The best place to cut off packets like these is where
they enter: on the perimeter router's interface that connects your network to
the Internet.

Fragments

Many of the great fragmenting attacks were originally designed to defeat packet filtering technology. Originally, some packet filtering technologies allowed all fragments to pass, which wasn't good. After this was recognized as a security concern, many systems began checking the first fragment to verify that the header information passed the tests set forth by the ACLs. If this initial fragment failed the test and didn't pass through the router, the rest of the fragments could never be reformed at the other side, in theory solving the problem.[1]

Because of the way packet filtering examines the header information, it could be defeated by splitting up the packet into such small pieces that the header containing TCP or UDP port information was divided. Because the first fragment was often the only fragment that many popular packet-filtering systems checked and that the IP address information would pass, the entire reassembled packet would be passed. In addition, packet filtering was discovered to be vulnerable to other fragmenting attacks, including attacks that allowed a second fragment to overlap a seemingly harmless TCP or UDP port in the initial fragment with deviously chosen port information.[2] Many clever ways were determined that could bypass the packet filter's inspection capabilities.

As time went by, packet filtering product manufacturers advanced their technology, and solutions were proposed to many of the common fragment attack methods. RFC 1858 defined methods to deter fragment flow—including dropping initial fragments that were smaller than a defined size or dropping second fragment based on information found in it.[3]

The most important point on using a packet-filtering defense to protect your network from fragment attacks is to verify that you have the latest firmware and security patches, or in the case of Cisco routers, IOS software. These updates reflect the changes made to defend against fragment attacks like those mentioned. For more complete fragment protection, some firewall technologies include methods such as fragment reassembly before packets are ruled on, the forming of tables that track decisions regarding initial fragments, and the basing of outcome of non-initial fragments on their predecessors. These technologies are not inherent in packet-filtering systems, and must be checked for when purchasing an individual product.

Cisco access lists can disallow fragmented traffic using the following access list as the first in an ACL series:

```
router(config)# access-list 111 deny ip any any fragments
```

This access list disallows any non-initial fragments that have matching IP address information, but allows non-fragments or initial fragments to continue to the next access list entry because of the `fragments` keyword at the end of the ACL. The initial fragments or non-fragments are denied or allowed based on the access lists that follow the preceding example. However, fragmented traffic is a normal part of some environments, and a statement like the previous example would deny this normal traffic, as well as maliciously fragmented traffic. This example would only be used in an environment that warranted the highest security to fragmentation attacks, without fear of the loss of potential usability.

Opening a "Hole" in a Static Packet Filter

One of the great flaws of static packet filtering is that to allow a protocol into a network, you need to open a "hole." It is referred to as a hole because no additional checking takes place of the type of traffic allowed in or out based on more intelligent methods of detection. All you can do is open an individual port on your protective wall; as with a bullet hole through a three-foot wall, you can't shoot anywhere else on the other side, but you can fire straight through the existing hole repeatedly. The importance of this analogy is that something must be on the other side at the port in question, or you won't be able to hit it.

It is recommended when opening a port using an access list of this type that you limit the target hosts as much as possible with the access list. Then if you have a secured server with all patches and no vulnerabilities (found as often as elves and four leaf clovers) that you are allowing to service this port, this isn't such a bad thing. However, if your host system is exploitable through whatever port number you have open, it is possible that any traffic can be sent through that "hole," not just the protocol that was running on the host inside.

Two-Way Traffic and the *established* Keyword

When we communicate with another host, it's not just us connecting to them, but also them connecting to us—a two-way connection. This presents a problem when it comes to preventing unwanted access with a packet filter. If we try to block *all* incoming traffic, we prevent the return connection from hosts we are trying to contact.

How can we allow only return traffic? The original answer that Cisco came up with was the `established` keyword for extended access lists. By adding the word `established` to an access list, any traffic, other than return traffic, is blocked, *theoretically*. The `established` keyword checks to see which flags are set on incoming packets. Packets with the ACK flag set (or `RST` flag) would pass, and only response traffic of the type specified could ever get through, right? Wrong! The combination of certain pieces of software and sneaky, nefarious users results in what's known as a *crafted packet*, which is a packet that the communicating host does not create in the normal way, but builds Frankenstein-style from software residing on a host. Users can set any flag they want.

What happens if a packet that was crafted with malicious intent appears with the ACK flag set in an attempt to sneak by the router's filters? The established keyword access list lets it go through, which isn't good. The good news is that an internal system that is listening for a new connection (initiated by a SYN packet) would not accept the ACK packet that is passed. It would be so offended by the packet that it would send a reset back to the originator, telling it to try again.

This sounds like a good thing, but it has two flaws. First, it proves that a station exists at the address to which the packet was sent. If a station didn't exist there, a rest package wouldn't be returned. This scanning technique works and is pretty stealthy as well. Second, because you are eliciting a response from a private system, you might be able to use this technique successfully for a denial of service. You could repeatedly hit internal systems with scores of ACK packets, which they would feverishly attempt to reply to with `RST` after `RST`. You further accentuate this by spoofing the source address on the ACK packets, so the targeted network would be feverishly firing resets back to another innocent network. Fortunately, the innocent network does *not* respond to the resets, preventing a second volley from being thrown at the target network.

Despite the drawbacks of the `established` keyword, it is one of the only static means by which a Cisco router can allow only return traffic back in to your network. The following is an example of an established access list:

```
router(config)#access-list 101 permit tcp any any est log
```

This basic extended access list allows any TCP traffic that has the ACK bit set, meaning that it allows only return traffic to pass. It is applied inbound on the outside router interface, and can log matches with the appended `log` keyword. It also allows `RST` packets to enter (by definition) to help facilitate proper TCP communication. A more secure version of this same list would be this:

```
router(config)#access-list 101 permit tcp any eq 80
➥192.168.1.0 0.0.0.255 gt 1023 log
```

```
router(config)#access-list 101 permit tcp any eq 23
➥192.168.1.0 0.0.0.255 gt 1023 log
router(config)#access-list 101 permit tcp any eq 25
➥192.168.1.0 0.0.0.255 gt 1023 log
router(config)#access-list 101 permit tcp any eq 110
➥192.168.1.0 0.0.0.255 gt 1023 log
```

In this case, the inside network address is 192.168.1.0–255. These access lists are applied inbound on the external router interface. By writing your access list this way, you allow traffic only from approved protocol port numbers (Web traffic, Telnet, email, and so on) to our internal network addresses, and only to ephemeral ports on our systems. However, an access list like this one still has problems. It does not support FTP for reasons we will go over in an upcoming section, and it only handles TCP traffic.

The *established* Keyword and the Problem of DNS

Remember that the previous ACL did *not* allow UDP traffic or ICMP traffic. The `established` (or `est`) keyword is only valid for TCP access lists. Access lists allow needed ICMP and UDP traffic, which would have to be included along side of this established access list, to form a comprehensive filter set. Without UDP, outside DNS is a real problem, disabling Internet functionality. This shows one of the biggest flaws of the `est` keyword as an effective defense mechanism. To facilitate Internet access with the `est` keyword, a UDP access list must be included, allowing *any* DNS return traffic. Remember that return traffic is coming to a randomly chosen port above 1023. That means that to effectively allow any DNS responses, we need an access list like this:

```
access-list 101 permit udp host 192.168.1.1 eq 53
➥172.16.100.0 0.0.0.255 gt 1023 log
```

This ACL assumes that the external DNS server's address is 192.168.1.1, and that your internal network is 172.16.100.0–255. By adding this line to your existing access list 101, you allow DNS responses to your network. However, you also leave yourself open to outside access on ports greater than 1023 from that external DNS server. Your security red alert should be going off about now! This would be a great argument for bringing DNS inside your perimeter; however, that DNS server would then need to be able to access outside DNS servers for queries and zone transfers. To allow the DNS server to make outbound DNS queries, a similar access list would need to be added to the router:

```
access-list 101 permit tcp any host 172.16.100.3 eq 53
access-list 101 permit udp any host 172.16.100.3 eq 53
```

This allows all traffic through port 53 to your inside (and hopefully well-hardened) DNS server. Ideally, such a public access server would be on a separate screened subnet for maximum security.

Remember that neither solution provides for additional UDP or ICMP support. If access to either is needed in your specific environment, more "holes" have to be opened.

Protocol Problems: Extended Access Lists and FTP

File Transfer Protocol (FTP) is a popular means to move files back and forth between remote systems. You need to be careful of outside FTP access because it could allow a malicious user to pull company information or server information (including password files) from inside servers. A user could upload files in an attempt to fill a hard drive and crash a server, upload a Trojan, or overwrite important server configuration files with ones that allow compromise of the server.

FTP is also one of the more complicated services to secure because of the way it works. Securing (or blocking) an incoming connection is relatively easy, but securing outgoing FTP connections is considerably more difficult. Let's take a look at a trace that shows standard FTP communication between a client and a server.

First is the outgoing connection with TCP/IP's 3-way handshake:

```
client.com.4567 > server.com.21: S 1234567890:1234567890(0)
server.com.21 > client.com.4567: S 3242456789:3242456789(0) ack 1234567890
client.com.4567 > server.com.21: . ack 1
Next is the incoming connection when establishing data channel:
server.com.20 > client.com.4568: S 3612244896:3612244896(0)
client.com.4568 > server.com.20: S 1810169911:1810169911(0) ack 3612244896
server.com.20 > client.com.4568: . ack 1
```

The first part of the communication is a normal three-way handshake, but when the data channel is established, things become complicated. The server starts a connection session from a different port (TCP 20) than the one the client originally contacted (TCP 21), to a >1023 port on the client that differs from the one that the client originally used. Because the server starts the connection, it is not considered return traffic and won't pass through extended access lists with the established keyword or dynamic reflexive access lists. In turn, to open the router for standard FTP, you must allow any traffic with a destination port of >1023 TCP ports and a source port of 20, which is a significant security hole.

One way to get around this problem is to use passive (PASV) FTP clients. PASV FTP works like active FTP until the data connection. Instead of connecting to the client from port 20 to a random port greater than 1023, the FTP server tells the client (through the port that the client last used to connect to it) what >1023 port it wants to use to transfer data. With this port number, the client establishes a connection back to the FTP server. Now let's look at a trace of our previous example's data connection, this time using PASV FTP:

```
client.com.4568 > server.com.3456: S 1810169911: 1810169911(0)
server.com.3456 > client.com.4568: S 3612244896:3612244896(0) ack 1810169911
client.com.4568 > server.com.3456: . ack 1
```

All traffic that comes from the server is established traffic, permitting extended lists with the `established` keyword to function correctly. Changing to passive FTP clients isn't a problem for most sites because most popular FTP clients support PASV mode. Most of the major web browsers support PASV mode FTP as well; however, it might require some minor setup, such as going to a preferences section and selecting PASV or passive FTP mode support. Using an ACL like the following example would be one way to handle PASV FTP:

```
router(config)#access-list 101 permit tcp any gt 1023 192.168.1.0
►0.0.0.255 gt 1023 est log
```

The Case of the Covert Channel

As a young security practitioner, I had the scare of my life. I randomly grabbed some log files and started looking through them, just giving a random spot check for anything that seemed out of the ordinary. About halfway through, I ran into a conversation between one of my network stations with an outside, unrecognized IP address.

The ports in question were disconcerting. The inside station was using TCP port 1741, and the outside port was much higher, in the 3000s. The higher number was an undefined port, but with a quick check of some port listings, I found that port 1741 happened to be defined as "Cisco net management." I wasn't familiar with this, but we were in a Cisco environment. The terror! The 3000 range port must have been a generated port, and the outside entity was contacting me on port 1741.

This log file caught the middle of the conversation, so I couldn't look at the beginning to verify that my theory was sound. I needed more information, so I went to my proxy log to check specifics on the connection. The outside entity appeared to be uploading some kind of FTP program to the station in question. This was getting worse instead of better.

I did more research to find out whose station had the DHCP assigned address in question during the transfer. The "malicious" IP address belonged to an FTP server. A tiny lightbulb went off in my head. I went to the user and asked if he had been doing any FTP downloads at the time in question. He concurred. He had been downloading a new version of an FTP client. Because we used PASV FTP, the data channel port number was not the default port 20, but a high numbered port determined as previously stated.

If you choose PASV FTP, be aware of false alarms regarding covert channels!

This ACL assumes that 192.168.1.0–255 are our internal network addresses and that they are part of a more complete access list allowing other, more standard traffic types. The problem with this access list is that despite the fact that only return traffic is allowed (in theory), you must leave open all > 1023 TCP ports for return access because you don't know what data channel port the FTP server that you are contacting will choose. Although this ACL is more secure than some of the previous options, it still isn't a strong security stance. Wouldn't it be nice if it were possible to find out what port number you were using to contact the PASV FTP server every time, and use that information to allow the traffic back in?

Dynamic Packet Filtering and the Reflexive Access List

Many of the problems that face static packet filtering, the Cisco standard, and extended access lists can be alleviated by dynamic packet filtering technology. The concept is that filters are built on-the-fly as needed and torn down after connections are broken.

Reflexive access lists are examples of dynamic packet filtering technology. A criterion is set up on the outbound interface that watches defined connection types to the outside world. When the traffic returns, it is compared to an access list that was dynamically created as the outgoing traffic left the network.

For example, perhaps you have a client that has an IP address of 192.168.100.2 and have set up a reflexive access list to check for TCP traffic using the Telnet port. The reflexive access list would see the client sending the Telnet packet out the greater than 1023 port (let's say 1072 was randomly picked) to port 23 on some IP address (let's say 100.100.100.1) of a Telnet server. The reflexive access list would then generate an incoming access list based on this outgoing connection. It would take the outgoing connection:

```
Client 192.168.100.2.1072 > telnet server 100.100.100.1.23
```

and reverse it into an incoming access list that permits traffic from 100.100.100.1 on port 23, to client 192.168.100.2 on port 1072, like this:

```
access-list 111 permit tcp host 100.100.100.1 eq 23 192.168.100.2 eq 1072
```

This dynamically generated list would be deleted after the connection was ended (a graceful FIN exchange or RST packet was sent). Because this access list type doesn't rely on the TCP flag bits set, it works with UDP and ICMP traffic as well. For non–TCP traffic, the connection is torn down after a time-out value expires. The time–out can be set per access list, or it can default to the global timeout of 300 seconds. This feature allows maximum security for return traffic because lists are created and removed for individual communication sessions. This capability to keep track of connections makes the reflexive access list the safest of the three access list types, but also the slowest.

Syntactically, reflexive access lists are basically a subset of extended access lists—specifically, "named" extended access lists. Named lists were created in Cisco IOS version 11.2 for two main reasons. First, large enterprises could run out of numbers for access lists using the old method. Second, its name could explain for what purpose the list was being used. We start by defining the list with `ip access-list extended` *name*, where *name* is the descriptive name used to define the access list. We follow this line with `permit` and `deny` lines, as shown next. They follow similar logic to numbered extended access lists. To move to a reflexive access list, all we have to do is add the `reflect` keyword to the end, followed by a name for the reflexive access list:

```
router(config)#ip access-list extended outfilter
router(config-ext-nacl)#permit tcp any any eq 80 reflect mypackets
router(config-if)#ip access-group outfilter out
```

Reflective access lists are different from ACLS in three primary ways: the `ip` before the `access-list` command (as with any named access list), the filter's name (`outfilter`), and the way that the prompt changes, which shows that we are now entering specific information into the previously named access list. In the permit line, we have the `reflect` keyword and the name of the reflexive access list with which we will be keeping track of our packet's connection information. Of course, the last line applies the list to the network interface, just like all previous examples, but now we do it by name. You might remember from the explanation of reflexive access lists that every connection has a dynamically created access list. These dynamic lists are created based on an access list like the one in the previous example. However, we need a component in the reverse direction to examine the packets when they come back in. Take a look at an example inbound filter:

```
router(config)#ip access-list extended infilter
router(config-ext-nacl)#evaluate mypackets
router(config-if)#ip access-group infilter in
```

This access list should look familiar, except for the second line. The `evaluate` line checks the incoming packet flow versus the reflexive access list information (in this case, `mypackets`) to see if it will pass the test of one of its dynamically created lists. We now have a complete reflexive access list with all of its components!

FTP Problems Revisited with the Reflexive Access List

Following is an example of a reflexive mode FTP filter that blocks incoming FTP traffic but allows outgoing passive FTP, along with any valid TCP traffic. This is a popular use of the reflexive access list: to allow anything outbound, and allow return (or response) traffic inbound.

```
router(config)#ip access-list extended filterout
router(config-ext-nacl)#permit tcp any any reflect packets
router(config-ext-nacl)#permit udp any any reflect packets
router(config-ext-nacl)#permit icmp any any reflect packets

router(config)#ip access-list extended filterin
router(config-ext-nacl)#evaluate packets

router(config-if)#ip access-group filterin in
router(config-if)#ip access-group filterout out
```

The `filterout` on this list permits all types of traffic out. Only TCP is necessary for FTP, but the others are added to demonstrate a popular configuration selection used with reflexive access lists, as mentioned previously. The `filterin` evaluates the return traffic of the previous outbound filter, and by the implied "deny all," it drops non-return FTP (and any other non-return) traffic. The last group shows the application of the `filterin` inbound and `filterout` outbound on the appropriate internal and external ports. Filter order isn't an issue, as the example appears here. It is possible to add other permit and deny access lists into this filter, being careful to ensure that nothing permitting TCP port 21 traffic comes before the rule in `filterin`, and that the `evaluate` line terminates the list. The `evaluate` line must *always* terminate the list.

You can test the effectiveness of a properly implemented PASV FTP client by making contact with a known PASV FTP server through the preceding filter. The only way to effectively allow Active FTP on a Cisco router is by using a part of the Cisco Secure Integrated Software (formerly the Firewall Feature Set) called context-based access control (CBAC), which inspects traffic and watches for inbound connections based on common behaviors of known protocols. Therefore, if you have to do secured outbound standard FTP on a Cisco router, consider the Cisco Secure Integrated Software.

Reflexive ACLs with UDP and ICMP Traffic: Clearing Up DNS Issues

One of the greatest advantages of reflexive ACLs over extended ACLs with the `established` keyword is that reflexive access lists can handle UDP and ICMP traffic. One place that this is helpful is with DNS traffic.

As previously mentioned, incoming UDP DNS return traffic is an issue because it can't be tracked by the established command; therefore, a specific access list must be made to allow DNS return traffic. With the reflexive access list, this is no longer necessary. Using the same access list used in the "FTP Problems Revisited with the Reflexive Access List" section, DNS return traffic is handled dynamically. Because the outgoing connection is aware of the ephemeral port that the DNS request is using, the dynamically created ACL can reflect (pardon the pun) that information, making a much more secure access control list.

Trouble in Paradise: Problems with Reflexive Access Lists

Yes, just when you thought you had found the panacea of packet filtering, the disclaimer comes about. Even reflexive access lists aren't perfect. However, due to the dynamic nature by which they are created and deleted, they are much more difficult to pass than other packet filters. One reset packet is all that is required to entirely remove a reflexively generated ACL.

Another issue with reflexive access lists is that they keep no record of TCP flags, so initial traffic could flow in without an alarm being sounded. How feasible is this? Look at the following example:

```
permit tcp host 100.100.100.1 eq 23 192.168.100.2 eq 1072
```

This is a dynamically generated reflexive access list example from a previous section. For someone to be able to use this access list as a conduit through to your internal network, the following would have to transpire:

1. Someone would have to know that this access list exists.

2. This access list would have to be created by an internal host contacting an outside entity.

3. Only a host at 100.100.100.1 using port 23 could start a viable communications channel through this access list.

4. The only host that could be contacted would be at address 192.168.100.2.

5. The contacted host would have to be listening to the ephemeral port 1072.

6. The sending host would have to know exactly what stage of communication the contacted host would be expecting to keep it from tearing down the dynamic access list.

7. This would all have to transpire before the generated access list was torn down.

If someone is this in-tune with your network and security structure and you don't have the reconnaissance capabilities to recognize that this person is watching you, you might be vulnerable on more levels than this one.

One thing can walk right through reflexive access lists: outbound traffic. If a virus or Trojan is on the internal network and wants to contact a malicious outside entity, the reflexive access list would let the traffic out and the return traffic from the conversation back in. The only way to defend against this with packet filtering is by limiting outbound access with an access list like this. (For an even stronger security stance, replace the second any with your internal network number.)

```
router(config)#ip access-list extended filterout
router(config-ext-nacl)#permit tcp any any eq 21 reflect packets
router(config-ext-nacl)#permit tcp any any eq 22 reflect packets
router(config-ext-nacl)#permit tcp any any eq 23 reflect packets
router(config-ext-nacl)#permit tcp any any eq 25 reflect packets
router(config-ext-nacl)#permit tcp any any eq 53 reflect packets
router(config-ext-nacl)#permit tcp any any eq 80 reflect packets
router(config-ext-nacl)#permit tcp any any eq 110 reflect packets
router(config-ext-nacl)#permit tcp any any eq 119 reflect packets
router(config-ext-nacl)#permit tcp any any eq 143 reflect packets
router(config-ext-nacl)#permit tcp any any eq 443 reflect packets
router(config-ext-nacl)#permit udp any any eq 53 reflect packets
router(config-ext-nacl)#permit icmp any any packet-too-big
router(config-ext-nacl)#deny ip any any log-input


router(config)#ip access-list extended filterin
router(config-ext-nacl)#evaluate packets

router(config-if)#ip access-group filterin in
router(config-if)#ip access-group filterout out
```

This way, controls exist for the types of traffic that are leaving the network. However, if the virus or Trojan happens to use one of these popular traffic types, you are just as vulnerable. This is why it is important to deploy extra layers of defense, such as virus checkers and host firewall defenses. Despite the fact that reflexive ACLs can be a more effective means to defend your network using dynamically generated host and port access lists, they still have the inherent limitations of packet-filtering technology that need to be considered before choosing them as your protection method of choice. They also put more of a burden on your router than static ACLs, so implement them with caution.

For two complete examples of reflexive access lists, refer to Appendix A, "Cisco Access List Sample Configurations."

Summary

Throughout this chapter, we discussed the many ways that packet filtering can be used as a means to secure the perimeter. We discussed the positive and negative points of using a packet filter as the means to control traffic flow based on address and port, and the weaknesses of the packet-filtering technology. We also discussed the improvement of packet filtering technology through the use of dynamic packet filters.

Despite weaknesses in the packet filter's capability to track information and understand what it is tracking, it still has many uses that can make it a valuable part of your perimeter defense. Filters can be utilized to screen out unwanted traffic at the perimeter, to prevent possibly dangerous traffic from leaving your network, and even to tailor incoming traffic that is allowed.

Packet filters can be used in conjunction with other firewalls as a layer of an intricate defense-in-depth posture, or as a stand-alone solution in lower risk areas or where budgets are tight. After all, protection of information is a balancing act between the value of the data and the cost to protect it.

Packet-filtering technology can be a useful means to protect your network as long as you implement it with due consideration to its strengths and weaknesses.

References

1 "Access Control Lists and IP Fragments." Cisco Systems, Inc. `http://www.cisco.com/warp/public/105/acl_wp.html`. December 2001.

2 "Access Control Lists and IP Fragments." Cisco Systems, Inc. `http://www.cisco.com/warp/public/105/acl_wp.html`. December 2001.

3 RFC 1858 "Security Considerations for IP Fragment Filtering." `http://www.ietf.org/rfc/rfc1858.txt`. October 1995.

3

Stateful Firewalls

T HE FOCUS OF THIS CHAPTER IS ON *STATEFUL FIREWALLS*, a type of firewall that attempts to track the state of network connections when filtering packets. The stateful firewall's capabilities are somewhat of a cross between the functions of a packet filter and the additional application-level protocol intelligence of a proxy. Because of this additional protocol knowledge, many of the problems that are encountered when trying to configure a packet-filtering firewall for protocols that behave in non-standard ways (as mentioned in Chapter 2, "Packet Filtering") are bypassed.

This chapter discusses stateful filtering and stateful inspection as well as various transport and application-level protocols. We also demonstrate some practical examples of how several vendors implement state and go over frequently used configuration examples of such firewalls.

How a Stateful Firewall Works

The stateful firewall predominately examines Layer 4 (Transport) and lower packet information, most often dealing with only Layer 7 (application) inspection for the packet that initializes a connection. If the inspected packet matches an existing firewall rule that permits it, an entry is added to the state table. From that point forward, the packets in that particular communication session are allowed access without call for further inspection because they match an existing state table entry. This method increases overall firewall performance (versus proxy-type systems that examine all packets) because only initial packets need to be unencapsulated the whole way to the application layer.

Conversely, because these firewalls use such filtering techniques, they don't consider the application-layer commands for the entire communications session, as a proxy firewall would. This equates to an inability to really control sessions based on application-level traffic, making it a less secure alternative to a proxy. However, because of stateful firewalls' speed advantage and their ability to handle just about any traffic flow (as opposed to the limited number of protocols supported by application-level proxies), they can be an excellent choice as the only perimeter protection device for a site or as a role player in a more complex network environment.

Note

Using a single perimeter protection device is often a financial necessity for smaller sites. However, despite the fact that only a single firewall is being implemented, other defense-in-depth options such as intrusion detection systems (IDSs), logging and monitoring servers, and host-level protection should also be used for a more secure network implementation.

Now that we have discussed the stateful firewall, for a better understanding of its function, let's discuss the meaning of *state* and how it is tracked in network communications.

Using a Firewall as a Means of Control

An important point that should be considered when discussing perimeter security is the concept of a firewall as a network chokepoint. A *chokepoint* is a place where something is funneled into a controllable single entry point for greater security. However, as the name implies, this area of limited entry also can be a place where bandwidth is compromised. A good example of a chokepoint in the real world is a metal detector at an airport. Imagine if a metal detector was the size of an entire hallway in the airport, and 20 or more people could walk through a single gate at one time. If the detector went off, it would be difficult for the inspectors to determine which party had triggered it and to be able to stop them to examine them further. More fine-grained traffic control is needed in such a situation. That is why the concept of a chokepoint is necessary in such a case; it allows one inspector to watch one party go through one metal detector at a time. The chokepoint offers additional control of the parties that are entering the airport. Like other chokepoints, this channeling of people for additional control can also lead to slowdowns in the process; in turn, lines often form at airport metal detectors.

Similar to an airport metal detector, a firewall offers a chokepoint for your network segment. All traffic that enters or leaves your network needs to pass through it for inspection. This additional control not only helps protect inbound and outward traffic flows but also allows a single point for examining and logging such traffic, verifying that if a breach exists, it is recorded.

The Concept of State

One confusing concept to understand when discussing the firewall and TCP/IP communications is the meaning of state. The main reason this term is so elusive is that it can mean different things in different situations. Basically, *state* is the condition of being of a given communication session. The definition of this condition of being for a given host or session can differ greatly depending on the application with which the parties are communicating and the protocols that the parties are using for the exchange. In turn, many vendors have varying definitions of what *stateful* technology is.

Devices that track state most often do so in a table. This state table holds entries that represent an individual communication session of which the device is aware. Every entry holds a laundry list of information that uniquely identifies the communication session that it represents. Such information might include source and destination IP address information, flags, sequence and acknowledgment numbers, and more. A state table entry is created when a connection is started out through the stateful device. Then, when traffic returns, the device compares the packet's information to the state table information to determine whether it is part of a current communication session. If the packet is related to a current table entry, it is allowed to pass. This is why the information that is held in the state table must be as specific and detailed as possible to guarantee that attackers will not be able to construct traffic that will be able to pass the state table test.

Listing 3.1 is a basic example of what state information looks like, as held by a Cisco router running reflexive access lists.

Listing 3.1   Excerpt from the State Table of a Cisco Router Using Reflexive Access Lists

```
Reflexive IP access list packets
  permit tcp host xx.yy.zz.45 eq 36204 host 192.168.1.1 eq smtp (10 matches) (time
  ↩left 295)
  permit tcp host xx.yy.zz.99 eq www host 192.168.1.1 eq 2151 (8 matches) ( time left
  ↩294)
  permit tcp host xx.yy.zz.247 eq www host 192.168.1.1 eq 2149 (10 matches) (time left
  ↩294)
  permit udp host xx.yy.zz.34 eq domain host 192.168.1.1 eq 2150 log (3 matches) (time
  ↩left 293)
  permit tcp host xx.yy.zz.247 eq www host 192.168.1.1 eq 2148 (16 matches) (time left
  ↩296)
  permit udp host xx.yy.zz.34 eq domain host 192.168.1.1 eq 2146 log (3 matches) (time
  ↩left 292)
```

In Listing 3.1, we see all the dynamically generated access lists that are formed by outgoing connections. (For more information on reflexive ACLs, refer to Chapter 2.) These access lists provide similar functionality to a state table in that they are keeping track of information for current communication sessions so that return traffic will be allowed back through the router successfully. Each entry starts with `permit` and then is followed directly by the protocol of the session in question. As you can see from the examples, both UDP and TCP are supported (as well as semi-stateful treatment of ICMP, although no ICMP examples are listed). The protocol is followed by the source destination address and source port, followed by the destination address and destination port. These addresses are formatted like an ACL, using the host prefix to designate that a single address is being specified, and the `eq` specifier to introduce the value of the destination or source port. (For more information on these labels, see Chapter 2.) Finally, the number of times that the particular rule has been matched is listed, followed by the time left before the dynamically allocated list is automatically removed.

Firewall Clustering and Tracking State

It is possible to cluster firewalls together to allow more bandwidth than a single firewall can handle on its own. This way, fast links can be accommodated. In this clustered state, any of the firewalls could possibly receive any part of a traffic flow. Therefore, although the initial SYN packet for a connection might be received on firewall 1, the final ACK response might come back to firewall 2. To be able to handle traffic statefully when stateful firewalls are clustered, a single shared state table must be available to all of the cluster members. This facilitates the complete knowledge of all traffic that other cluster members have seen. It is often accomplished using a dedicated communications cable between the members as a sort of direct link, solely for the sharing of vital state information. Such a mechanism affords an efficient means for the propagation of said state table information, allowing even the fastest communication links to operate without the problem of an incompletely updated state table.

Transport and Network Protocols and State

Transport protocols can have their connection's state tracked in various ways. Many of the attributes that make up a communication session, including IP address and port pairings, sequence numbers, and flags, can all be used to fingerprint an individual connection. The combination of these pieces of information is often held as a hash in a state table for easy comparison. The particulars depend on the vendor's individual implementation. However, because these protocols are different, so are the ways that their state can be effectively tracked.

TCP and State

Because TCP is a connection-oriented protocol, the state of its communication sessions can be solidly defined. Because the beginning and end of a communication session is well defined in TCP and because it tracks the state of its connections with flags, it is considered a stateful protocol. (For more technical details of how TCP/IP works, see Appendix A, "Cisco Access List Sample Configurations.") TCP's connection is tracked as being in one of eleven states, as defined in RFC 793. To truly understand the stateful tracking of TCP, it is important to realize the many stages that a TCP connection goes through. These states are as follows:

- CLOSED. A "non-state" that exists before a connection actually begins.
- LISTEN. The state that a host is in when waiting for a request to start a connection. This is the true starting state of a TCP connection.
- SYN-SENT. The time after a host has sent out a SYN packet and is waiting for the proper SYN-ACK reply.
- SYN-RCVD. The state that a host is in after receiving a SYN packet and replying with its SYN ACK reply.
- ESTABLISHED. The state that a connection is in after its necessary ACK packet has been received. The initiating host goes into this state after receiving a SYN-ACK, as the responding host does after receiving the lone ACK.

The process of establishing a TCP connection normally goes through these states as part of the three-way handshake, as shown in Figure 3.1.

TCP STATES
for the 3-Way Handshake

Figure 3.1   The TCP three-way handshake connection establishment consists of five well-defined states.

The remaining six of the eleven TCP connection states describe the tearing down of a TCP connection. The first state is used during an active close by the initiator and a passive close by the receiver, as shown in Figure 3.2.

TCP STATES
for a standard connection close

Figure 3.2   The active/passive closing of a normal TCP connection consists of six states.

- FIN-WAIT-1. The state a connection is in after it has sent an initial FIN packet asking for a graceful close of the TCP connection.
- CLOSE-WAIT. The state a host's connection is in after it receives an initial FIN and sends back an ACK to acknowledge the FIN.
- FIN-WAIT-2. The connection state of the host that has received the ACK response to its initial FIN, as it waits for a final FIN from its connection partner.
- LAST-ACK. The state of the host who just sent the second FIN needed to gracefully close the TCP connection back to the initiating host while it waits for an acknowledgment.
- TIME-WAIT. The state of the initiating host who received the final FIN and has sent an ACK to close the connection. Because it will not receive an acknowledgment of its sent ACK from the connection partner, it has to wait a given time period before closing (thus, time-wait); the other party has sufficient time to receive the ACK packet before it leaves this state.

Note

The time that the TIME-WAIT state is defined to pause is equal to the Maximum Segment Lifetime (MSL) as defined for the TCP implementation, multiplied by two. This is why this state is also called 2MSL.

- CLOSING. A state that is employed when a connection uses the non-standard simultaneous close. It is in this state after receiving an initial FIN and sending an ACK. After receiving an ACK back for its FIN, the connection will go into the TIME-WAIT state (see Figure 3.3).

TCP STATES
for a simultaneous connection close

Figure 3.3 The simultaneous close of a TCP connection, where both parties close actively, consists of six states.

You can determine the state of the TCP connection by checking the flags that are being carried by packets, as alluded to by the various descriptions of the states. The tracking of this flag information in combination with the IP address/port address information for each of the communicating parties can paint a pretty good picture of what is going on for the given connection. The only other pieces of the puzzle that might be needed for clarity are the sequence and acknowledgment numbers of the packets. This way, if packets arrive out of order, the dialog flow of the communication can be more easily discerned, and the use of replay attacks against a device-tracking state will be less likely to succeed.

Entries for TCP communication sessions in a state table are removed when the connection is closed. To prevent connections that are improperly closed from remaining in the state table indefinitely, timers are also used. Although the three-way handshake is transpiring, the initial time-out value used is typically short (under a minute), which is lengthened considerably (usually to an hour or more) after the connection is established. The time-out is lengthened because it is more likely that an established connection will gracefully close itself.

It would seem from what we have just covered that the state of any TCP connection is easily definable, concrete, and objective. However, when tracking the overall communication session, these rules might not always apply. What if an application that employs non-standard communication techniques was being used? For example, as discussed in Chapter 2, classic FTP uses a non-standard communication form when initializing its data channel. When considering the state of the two individual TCP connections that make up this connection, each of their states can be maintained in a normal fashion. However, the state of the FTP connection obeys different rules. You must understand the way that standard FTP uses one inbound and one outbound connection to be able to track the state of the FTP session. We will cover this issue in greater detail in the "Application-Level Traffic and State" section, later in this chapter.

UDP and State

Unlike TCP, UDP is a connectionless transport protocol. This makes the tracking of its state a much more complicated process. In actuality, a connectionless protocol has no state; therefore, a stateful device must track a UDP connection in a pseudo-stateful manner, keeping track of items that are specific to its connection only. Because UDP has no sequence numbers or flags, the only items on which we can base a session's state are the IP addressing and port numbers that are used by the source and destination hosts. Because the ephemeral ports are at least somewhat random, and they differ for any connection coming from a given IP address, this adds a little bit of credence to this pseudo-stateful method of session tracking. However, because the UDP session is connectionless, it has no set method of connection teardown that announces the session's end. Because of this lack of a defined ending, a state-tracking device will typically be set up to clear a UDP session's state table entries after a preconfigured time-out value (usually a minute or less) is reached. This prevents the entries from remaining in the table indefinitely.

Another point of concern with UDP traffic is that because it cannot correct communication issues on its own, it relies entirely on ICMP as its error handler, making ICMP an important part of a UDP session to be considered when tracking its overall state.

For example, what if during a UDP communication session a host can no longer keep up with the speed at which it is receiving packets? UDP offers no method of letting the other party know to slow down transmission. However, the receiving host can send an ICMP source quench message to let the sending host know to slow down transmission of packets. However, if the firewall blocks this message because it is not part of the normal UDP session, the host that is sending packets too quickly does not know that an issue has come up, and it continues to send at the same speed, resulting in lost packets at the receiving host. Stateful firewalls must consider such "related" traffic when deciding what return traffic should be returned to protected hosts.

ICMP and State

ICMP, like UDP, really isn't a stateful protocol. However, like UDP, it also has attributes that allow its connections to be pseudo-statefully tracked. The more complicated part of tracking ICMP involves its one-way communications. The ICMP protocol is often used to return error messages when a host or protocol can't do so on its own, in what can be described as a "response" message. ICMP response-type messages are precipitated by requests by other protocols (TCP, UDP). Because of this multiprotocol issue, figuring ICMP messages into the state of an existing socket-pair can be confusing to say the least. The other, easier-to-track way that ICMP is used is in a request/reply type usage. The most popular example of an application that uses this request/reply form is ping. It sends echo requests and receives echo reply messages. Obviously, because the given stimulus in these cases produces an expected response, the session's state becomes less complicated to track. However, instead of tracking based on source and destination addresses, the ICMP message can be tracked on request message type and reply message type. This tracking method is about the only way that ICMP can enter into a state table.

Another issue with ICMP is that, like UDP, it is connectionless; therefore, it must base the retention of a state table entry on a predetermined time-out because ICMP also does not have a specific mechanism to end its communication sessions.

Application-Level Traffic and State

We have covered in some detail the ways that state can be tracked at the Transport and Network protocol levels; however, things change when you are concerned about the state of the entire session. When a stateful device is deciding which traffic to allow into the network, application behaviors must be taken into account to verify that all session-related traffic is properly handled. Because the application might follow different rules for communication exchanges, it might change the way that state has to be considered for that particular communication session. Let's look at an application that uses a standard communication style (HTTP) and one that handles things in a non-standard way (FTP).

HTTP and State

HTTP is the protocol used for web access, and is the most commonly used protocol on the Internet today. It uses TCP as its transport protocol, and its session initialization follows the standard way that TCP connections are formed. Look at the following tcpdump trace:

```
21:55:46.1 Host.1096 > maverick.giac.org.80: S 489703169:489703169(0) win 16384 <mss
↪1460,nop,nop,sackOK> (DF)
21:55:46.2 maverick.giac.org.80 > Host.1096: S 3148360676:3148360676(0) ack 489703170
↪win 5840 <mss 1460,nop,nop,sackOK> (DF)
21:55:46.5 Host.1096 > maverick.giac.org.80: . ack 1 win 17520 (DF)
```

This Tcpdump trace shows the three-way handshake between a contacting client named Host and the SANS GIAC web server, Maverick. It is a standard TCP connection establishment in all aspects.

The following packet lists the first transaction after the TCP connection was established. Notice that in the payload of the packet, the `GET / HTTP/1.1` statement can be clearly made out (we truncated the output for display purposes):

```
21:55:46.6 Host.1096 > maverick.giac.org.80: P 1:326(325) ack 1 win 17520 (DF)
E..m."@....6.....!...H.P.0G...+.P.Dpe$..GET./.HTTP/1.1..Accept:.image/gif,.image
```

This is the first HTTP command that a station issues to receive a web page from a remote source.

Let's look at the next packet, which is truncated for display purposes:

```
21:55:46.8 maverick.giac.org.80 > Host.1096: P 1:587(586) ack 326 win 6432 (DF)
E..r..@.2..6.!.......P.H..+..0HGP.......HTTP/1.1.301.Moved.Permanently..Date:.Wed,.06.
↪Feb.2002.02:56:03.GMT..Server:.Apache..Location:.http://www.sans.org/newlook/home.php
↪..Kee
```

Notice that this reply packet begins to return the home page for the SANS GIAC web site at www.sans.org. As shown in the preceding example, protocols such as HTTP that follow a standard TCP flow allow an easier definition of the overall session's state. Because it uses a single established connection from the client to the server and because all requests are outbound and responses inbound, the state of the connection doesn't differ much from what would be commonly tracked with TCP. If tracking only the state of the TCP connection in this example, a firewall would allow the HTTP traffic to transpire as expected. However, there is merit in also tracking the application-level commands that are being communicated. We cover this topic more in the section "Problems with Application-Level Inspection" later in this chapter. Next, we look at how this scenario changes when dealing with applications that use a nonstandard communication flow, such as standard FTP traffic.

File Transfer Protocol and State

File Transfer Protocol (FTP) is a popular means to move files between systems, especially across the Internet. FTP in its standard form, however, behaves quite differently from most other TCP protocols. This strange two-way connection establishment also brings up some issues with the tracking of state of the entire connection. Would a firewall that only tracks the state of the TCP connections on a system be able to pass standard FTP traffic? As seen in Chapter 2, the answer is no. A firewall cannot know to allow in the SYN packet that establishes an FTP data channel if it doesn't take into account the behavior of FTP. For a stateful firewall to be able to truly facilitate all types of TCP connections, it must have some knowledge of the application protocols that are being run, especially those that behave in non-standard ways.

When using the application-level examination capabilities of a stateful inspection system, a complicated transaction like that used by a standard FTP connection can be dissected and handled in an effective and secure manner.

The stateful firewall begins by examining all outbound traffic and paying special attention to certain types of sessions. As we know from Chapter 2, an FTP control session can be established without difficulty; it is the inbound data-channel initialization that is problematic. Therefore, when a stateful firewall sees that a client is initializing an outbound FTP control session (using TCP port 21), it knows to expect the server being contacted to initiate an inbound data channel on TCP port 20 back to the client. The firewall can dynamically allow an inbound connection from the IP address of the server on port 20 to the address of the client. However, for utmost security, the firewall should also specify the port on which the client will be contacted for this exchange.

The firewall discovers on which port the client is contacted through the use of application inspection. Despite the fact that every other piece of information that we have needed thus far in this exchange has been Layer 4 or lower, the port number that is used by the server that is initializing the data channel is actually sent to it in an FTP port command from the client. Therefore, by inspecting the traffic flow between client and server, the firewall also picks up the port information needed for inbound data channel connection. This process is illustrated in Figure 3.4.

Figure 3.4 The stateful firewall examines the `FTP PORT` command to determine the destination port for the establishment of the FTP data channel.

Multimedia Protocols and the Stateful Firewall

Multimedia protocols work similarly to FTP through a stateful firewall—just with more connections and complexity. The widespread use of multimedia communication types, such as H.323, Real Time Streaming Protocol (RTSP), CUSeeME, Microsoft's NetShow, and more have demanded a secure means to allow such traffic to pass into the networks of the world.

All these protocols rely on at least one TCP control channel to communicate commands and one or more channels for multimedia data streams that are running on TCP or UDP. The control channels are monitored by the stateful firewall to receive the IP addresses and port numbers that are used for the multimedia streams. This address information is then used to open secure conduits to facilitate the media streams' entrance into the network, as shown in Figure 3.5.

The stateful firewall recognizes the control commands for the multimedia session to securely facilitate inbound access for incoming multimedia streams to follow.

Figure 3.5   The stateful firewall tracks the Multimedia Protocol's communication channel to facilitate the passing of incoming media streams.

Note

Some stateful firewalls are just now allowing the use of multistream multimedia applications, such as H.323 in conjunction with port address translation (PAT). This has been a long-time problem with multistream protocols because the multiple ports used per connection could easily conflict with the PAT translation's port dispersal.

Problems with Application-Level Inspection

Despite the fact that many stateful firewalls by definition can examine application-layer traffic, holes in their implementation prevent stateful firewalls from being a replacement for proxy firewalls in environments that need the utmost in application-level control. The main problems with the stateful examination of application-level traffic involve the abbreviated examination of application-level traffic and the lack of thoroughness of this examination, including the firewall's inability to track the content of said application flow.

In a means to provide better performance, many stateful firewalls abbreviate examinations by performing only an application-level examination of the packet that initiates a communication session, which means that all subsequent packets are tracked through the state table using Layer 4 information and lower. This is an efficient way to track communications, but it lacks the ability to consider the full application dialogue of a session. In turn, any deviant application-level behavior after the initial packet might be missed, and there are no checks to verify that proper application commands are being used throughout the communication session.

However, because the state table entry will record at least the source and destination IP address and port information, whatever exploit was applied would have to involve those two communicating parties and transpire over the same port numbers. Also, the connection that established the state table entry would not be properly terminated, or the entry would be instantly cleared. Finally, whatever activity transpired would have to take place in the time left on the time-out of the state table entry in question. Making such an exploit work would take a determined attacker or involve an accomplice on the inside.

Another issue with the way stateful inspection type firewalls handle application-level traffic is that they typically watch such traffic more so for triggers than for a full understanding of the communication dialogue; therefore, they lack full application support. As an example, a stateful device might be monitoring an FTP session for the PORT command, but it might let other non-FTP traffic pass through the FTP port as normal. Such is the nature of a stateful firewall; it is most often reactive and not proactive. A stateful firewall simply filters on one particular command type on which it must act rather than considering each command that might pass in a communication flow. Such behavior, although efficient, can leave openings for unwanted communications types, such as those used by covert channels or those used by outbound devious application traffic.

In the previous example, we considered that the stateful firewall watches diligently for the FTP port command, while letting non-FTP traverse without issue. For this reason, it would be possible in most standard stateful firewall implementations to pass traffic of one protocol through a port that was being monitored at the application level for a different protocol. For example, if you are only allowing HTTP traffic on TCP port 80 out of your stateful firewall, an inside user could run a communication channel of some sort (that uses a protocol other than the HTTP protocol) to an outside server listening for such communications on port 80 or through a web site service such as http://www.go2mypc.com. This is because the application inspection portion of most stateful firewalls really isn't meant to consider incorrect traffic. It is looking for certain trigger-application behaviors, but most often (with some exceptions), not the lack thereof. In the case of http://www.go2mypc.com, application-level inspection has no means to decipher what content is inappropriate.

> **Note**
>
> Despite the fact that standard stateful examination capabilities of most such firewalls could not catch deviant traffic flows like the covert channels based on commonly open ports, many vendors also offer content filtering or proxy-like features on their stateful firewall products to prevent such issues. FireWall-1 and the PIX both offer varying levels of content filtering, for example. However, such features are often not enabled by default and must be configured properly to be effective.

Another popular example of traffic that sneaks out of many otherwise secure networks are programs like AOL Instant Messenger, Gnutella, and other messaging and peer-to-peer file-sharing programs. These programs have the potential to transmit through any port, and because most stateful firewalls have at least one outbound port open, they will find their way out. Like the aforementioned "covert channel" example, the standard stateful firewall does not differentiate this type of traffic; it allows it to pass as long as it is using one of its available ports. Content-level filtering or a true proxy firewall that considers all application-level commands could be used to prevent such traffic.

Stateful Filtering and Stateful Inspection

Now that we have covered what state is and what it takes to track the state of a protocol's connection or an application session, we can move on to cover how firewalls filter on state. The definition of stateful filtering seems to vary greatly among various product vendors and has developed somewhat, as time has gone on. Stateful filtering can mean anything from the ability to track and filter traffic based on the most minute of connection details to the ability to track and inspect session information at the application level. With this loose interpretation in mind, let's define these terms for the purpose of this chapter.

Stateful filtering lately has been used to define the stateful tracking of protocol information at Layer 4 and lower. Under this definition, stateful filtering products exhibit no knowledge of application-layer protocols. At the most basic level, such products use the tracking of the IP addresses and port numbers of the connecting parties to track state. As mentioned previously, this is the only way that connectionless protocols can be tracked, but at best, this is only "pseudo-stateful." What about using this same method of stateful filtering for the tracking of the connection-oriented TCP? As mentioned previously, this method does not in any way track the TCP flags. TCP's flags define its connection states; therefore, although this method might be tracking some information from the various communication sessions, it is not truly tracking the TCP connection state.

More advanced forms of stateful filtering can also track sequence and acknowledgment numbers and the TCP packet flags. With the addition of these criteria, we can get truly stateful connection tracking for TCP, although we still lack the ability to differentiate traffic flows at the application level.

Stateful inspection, in contrast, has come to be used as a description of the devices that track state using all of the Layer 4 type information listed previously, as well as the tracking of application-level commands. All of this information can be combined to offer a relatively strong definition of the individual connection's state. Also, because Layer 7 information is being examined, extra insight into non-standard protocol behaviors is available. This allows normally troublesome protocols such as FTP and H.323 to be securely passed by the device without complication.

Note

Stateful inspection is a term originally coined by the security product manufacturer Check Point, the makers of FireWall-1, for the way FireWall-1 handles the tracking of state information. It comprises both the tracking of state using Layer 4 protocol information and the tracking of application-level traffic commands.[1]

In both stateful filtering and stateful inspection, the tracked state information is most often recorded into a state table that tracks the information until a connection is torn down (as with TCP) or until a preconfigured time-out is reached (TCP, UDP, and ICMP). Every vendor has its own implementation of these methods, and in the next several sections, we will look at some vendors' definitions of stateful filtering/stateful inspection as used in their products.

Stateful Firewall Product Examples

As stated previously, various firewall products handle the tracking of state in many different ways. This section lists some popular firewall products and explanations of how they handle state. We also show examples of each product's state table and examine a sample configuration of a stateful firewall.

Cisco Reflexive ACLs

As mentioned in Chapter 2, reflexive ACLs are a means to track UDP, TCP, and even ICMP communications moving in one direction (usually outbound) and a way to create a dynamic ACL for its return traffic. Under the definitions that we have named previously for state tracking, reflexive ACLs handle UDP and ICMP traffic about as pseudo-statefully as many of the more advanced firewalls that promise stateful protection. Even reflexive ACLs' ability to track TCP can be classified as stateful filtering by our previous definition, although Cisco reserves its definition of stateful product for its CBAC feature for routers and the Fixup commands that PIX firewalls use.

Netfilter/IPTables

Netfilter/IPTables are the two main pieces of the most recent incarnation of a firewall product that is freely available for Linux distributions. IPTables is the construct that is used to build the firewall rule sets. Netfilter is the bridge between the Linux kernel and the IPTables rule structure. It is the successor of the ipfwadm and IPChains products, with an ever-increasing list of features and functionality. It now offers stateful filtering with its connection-tracking capability.[2]

Connection tracking records the state of a connection based mostly on protocol-specific information. Administrators create rules specifying what protocols or specific traffic types should be tracked. When a connection is begun using a tracked protocol, IPTables adds a state table entry for the connection in question. This state table entry includes such information as the following:

- The protocol being used for the connection
- The source and destination IP addresses
- The source and destination ports
- A listing with source and destination IP addresses and ports reversed (to represent response traffic)
- The time remaining before the rule is removed
- The TCP state of the connection (for TCP only)
- The connection-tracking state of the connection

Following is an example of a state table entry for IPTables:

```
tcp 6 93 SYN_SENT src=192.168.1.34 dst=172.16.2.23 sport=1054 dport=21 [UNREPLIED]
➥src=172.16.2.23 dst=192.168.1.34 sport=21 dport=1054 use=1
```

The first line starts out listing the protocol in question followed by the protocol's numerical designation (6 for TCP). The next value, 93, represents the time remaining before the entry is automatically cleared from the state table. It then shows the state that the TCP connection is in. The source and destination IP addresses follow, and then the source and destination ports are listed. Because this is an initial connection (as demonstrated by the connection's TCP state), it lists that IPTables sees this connection as [UNREPLIED] and hasn't increased its time-out value yet. Next in the listing, we see a reversal of the original source and destination address and port information to allow return traffic. After the connection is established, the state table entry is altered, as we can see in the next example:

```
tcp 6 41294 ESTABLISHED src=192.168.1.34 dst=172.16.2.23 sport=1054 dport=21
➥src=172.16.2.23 dst=192.168.1.34 sport=21 dport=1054 [ASSURED] use=1
```

The [UNREPLIED] marker is removed after the first return packet. Upon establishment of the connection, the [ASSURED] marker is placed on the entry, and the time-out value (41294) is greatly increased.

Now let's consider the rules of IPTables.

> **Note**
>
> The following rule examples are basic for demonstration purposes only. They do not take into account egress filtering or the lockdown or allowance of specific services. For optimum security, rules that specifically designate only those individual applications that are allowed would be more appropriate.

Let's look at the syntax and how it works:

This first example rule is considered an OUTPUT rule. It defines which traffic can leave through the firewall (-A specifies that this rule will be appended to already existing rules).

```
iptables -A OUTPUT -p tcp -m state --state NEW,ESTABLISHED -j ACCEPT
```

This output rule determines which outbound communication will be ACCEPTed (as specified by the -j option). This particular rule deals only with the TCP protocol, as specified by the -p tcp option. It specifies in the --state section that NEW and ESTABLISHED traffic are allowed out of our network. This rule, as listed, allows no egress protection. All new outbound TCP traffic will be allowed because the NEW option is specified. NEW tells the firewall to watch for packets with a lone SYN flag that are initiating a connection and to create entries in the state table for every such occurrence. The ESTABLISHED option allows traffic that is part of an existing session that has previously been recorded in the state table to pass as well, which means that any standard TCP communications will be able to leave the network.

Another part of the command worth mentioning is the -m state. -m denotes what module should be used for the rule in question—in this case, the standard state module that comes with IPTables. Now let's examine the rule that will allow the return traffic for our connection back into our network:

```
iptables -A INPUT -p tcp -m state --state ESTABLISHED -j ACCEPT
```

This command appears identical to the preceding one, except that it is an INPUT rule, and only ESTABLISHED is listed under the -state section of the command. This means that *only* return traffic will be allowed inbound to our network as defined by the state table. IPTables determines whether incoming traffic is return traffic for the connection that was entered into the state table by checking it against the reversed connection information that is located in the state table entry. No new connections will be able to enter our network from the outside.

Even though most of the requirements of TCP stateful tracking are available in IPTables, one exception to this is the tracking of sequence and acknowledgment numbers, which can be added with the tcp-window-tracking patch.[3]

From our previous definition of the items held in the state table, you can see that the items needed to do a psuedo-stateful job of tracking ICMP and UDP are present. An example of a basic UDP output and input rule would be as follows:

```
iptables -A OUTPUT -p udp -m state --state NEW,ESTABLISHED -j ACCEPT
iptables -A INPUT -p udp -m state --state ESTABLISHED -j ACCEPT
```

These rules appear identical to those specified for TCP, except for the -p udp option listing.

ICMP rules look about the same:

```
iptables -A OUTPUT -p icmp -m state --state NEW,ESTABLISHED,RELATED -j ACCEPT
iptables -A INPUT -p icmp -m state --state ESTABLISHED,RELATED -j ACCEPT
```

The main differences are the -p icmp specification for protocol and a new entry in the --state section: RELATED.

The RELATED option is the means by which IPTables allows traffic that is already in some way associated with an established traffic flow to initiate a new connection in the state table and be passed through the firewall. This related traffic might be an ICMP error message that is returned for a UDP or TCP connection that is already held in the state table. It could also be the initialization of an inbound FTP data channel on TCP port 20, after state table information had already been logged for an inside station starting a control channel connection on TCP port 21.

As listed, our rule allows ICMP traffic inbound and outbound that is RELATED to existing ESTABLISHED traffic flows. Therefore, errors that are returned in response to existing TCP and UDP connections will pass. Because the NEW option is listed for outbound traffic, requests from ICMP programs such as Ping will be able to leave our network, and the ESTABLISHED option that is specified for inbound traffic will allow the replies to said traffic to return back through. However, inbound Ping requests will not be allowed in because the NEW option is not specified inbound.

The rules of conduct for defining RELATED traffic are included in connection-tracking modules. They facilitate the examination of application-specific commands, such as the way the ip_conntrack_ftp module facilitates the inspection of FTP's PORT command to allow the secure handling of standard FTP traffic. (For more information on how stateful firewalls handle FTP traffic, see the "File TransferProtocol and State" section earlier in this chapter.) These modules can be added on as new protocols are used in your environment.

To implement a module such as ip_conntrack_ftp to allow standard outbound FTP communications to be properly initialized through our IPTables firewall, it first has to be loaded with a command such as the following:

```
modprobe ip_conntrack_ftp
```

Next, a specific rule has to be created to inspect the related traffic. This can be accomplished in the case of FTP by making an INPUT rule that allows inbound TCP port 20 traffic with the state option of RELATED. This will allow the inbound port 20 traffic to connect if the inspection process deems it related to an existing connection in the state table. Here is a listing of such a rule:

```
iptables -A INPUT -p tcp --sport 20 -m state --state ESTABLISHED,RELATED -j ACCEPT
```

An OUTPUT rule will be needed as well to allow response traffic to return:

```
iptables -A OUTPUT -p tcp --dport 20 -m state --state ESTABLISHED -j ACCEPT
```

Notice that the -sport 20 option representing source port in the INPUT rule has changed to a -dport 20 or destination port option in the OUTPUT rule. This change is due to the reversal of communication roles for outbound versus inbound traffic.

Check Point FireWall-1

The Check Point FireWall-1 is one of the most popular stateful firewalls in use today. It is software based and can be loaded onto hardware server solutions of various platform types, including Windows NT and 2000, Solaris, and Red Hat Linux. It was also offered as a hardware appliance solution by Nokia. FireWall-1 uses a state table for the basic tracking of connections at the protocol level and an INSPECT engine for more complicated rules involving application-layer traffic and non-standard protocol behavior.

When deciding whether to allow a packet to pass, FireWall-1 tests it against the following data structures, in the order specified:

1. State table. First, FireWall-1 checks to see whether a connection is already logged in the state table for this particular incoming packet. If so, it is forwarded without further scrutiny.

2. Security policy. Next, if the state table did not contain an entry for the packet, the packet is compared against the security policy. If a rule allows the packet to pass, it will be forwarded on, and an entry for its communication session will be added to the state table.

TCP traffic is handled at a protocol level, much like previously shown examples. However, as of this writing, FireWall-1 does not track the sequence numbers of TCP connections.[4] When a communication ensues, because the first packet of a connection will not be reflected in the state table, it is tested against the security policy. If it is accepted based on one of the rules, it is added into the state table.

Tip

For the most complete stateful protection of TCP communication flows, be sure to use the latest version of FireWall-1. Specifically, FireWall-1 version 4 Service Pack 2 corrected a significant issue with accepting communication sessions that were initiated by an ACK packet.[5]

The rules that might allow traffic to pass are either one of the implied rules that are set up in the Security Policy tab or part of the rulebase that is created and maintained in FireWall-1's GUI interface. For an example of a rules listing and what the FireWall-1 GUI interface looks like, look at Figure 3.6.

As seen in Figure 3.6, designing a rule set for firewall products such as the FireWall-1 can be less demanding than some of the less user-friendly choices, such as IPTables. FireWall-1 allows you to use a GUI interface to represent your networks and systems as objects. You can elect to allow or disallow traffic for specific services by selecting appropriate options and referencing relevant objects. Rule order is one of the most critical things to keep in mind when designing such a rule set. It is vital to list specific rules at the top of the rule list before more general rules that might inadvertently apply to unwanted traffic types.

Figure 3.6   Check Point FireWall-1 offers a user-friendly GUI interface for editing its rule set.

> **Note**
>
> For more information on building a FireWall-1 rule base, see Lance Spitzner's paper titled "Building Your Firewall Rulebase" at www.enteract.com/~lspitz/rules.html.

FireWall-1 enforces time-outs for TCP connections to ensure that improperly terminated sessions that lack the common FIN packet exchange do not remain in the state table indefinitely. The initial timeout on a half-open connection (before the three-way handshake has been completed) is logged at 60 seconds by default. Upon completion of the three-way handshake, this timeout is increased to 60 minutes to allow for latency in communications. After the closing of the connection is initiated with a FIN packet, the timeout is dropped to 50 seconds to ensure that the state table entry is more quickly cleared if the graceful FIN exchange is not completed successfully.[6]

Note

The 60-minute time-out setting for TCP connections, as well as the default UDP timeout, can be adjusted in the Security Policy tab of the Properties Setup dialog box, as seen in Figure 3.7. Individual protocol timeouts can be modified in the init.def file. For more information about time-out handling for specific services, look at `www.phoneboy.com/faq/0203.html`.

FireWall-1 handles UDP traffic in much the same way that other stateful firewalls do. They use a pseudo-stateful method of tracking outbound UDP connections, and they allow inbound UDP packets that match one of the currently recorded communication flows. This process is accomplished through the recording of the IP addressing and port numbers that the communication partners use. A timer is used to remove the session from a state table after a predetermined amount of inactivity (see Figure 3.7).

Figure 3.7   The Security Policy tab of the Properties Setup dialog box for FireWall-1 contains many settings that define how FireWall-1 handles state.

FireWall-1 has special provisions for handling traffic based on remote procedure calls (RPCs), such as Network File System (NFS), whose ports are randomly generated by the portmapper service. The portmapper service runs on TCP and UDP ports 111 and handles the automatic generation of RPC programs' access ports. Because these ports are generated randomly, it would be nearly impossible to write a secure rule that could effectively permit such traffic. FireWall-1 solves this problem by tracking all specified portmapper traffic and actually caching the port numbers that portmapper maps to the RPC programs in use. This way, such traffic can be effectively tracked. This behavior can be enabled (as can other useful behaviors) under the Services tab of the Properties Setup dialog box (see Figure 3.8), although when possible, any RPC traffic that originates from the Internet should be blocked outright.

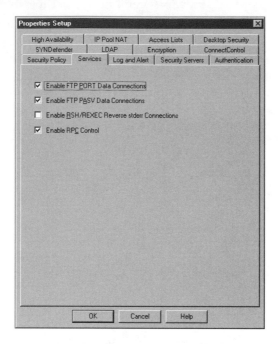

Figure 3.8   Many application-based behaviors can be allowed by the settings under the Services tab.

For a better understanding of the FireWall-1's tracking of state, look at its state table. Listing 3.3 is the Check Point FireWall-1 state table as decoded (it normally appears as rows of difficult-to-decipher numbers) by a Perl script (fwtable.pl) available format from Lance Spitzner's web site at http://www.enteract.com/~lspitz/fwtable.txt.

Listing 3.3   **A Check Point FireWall-1's State Table As Translated by Fwtable.Pl**

```
Src_IP               Src_Prt Dst_IP   Dst_Prt IP_prot Kbuf Type  Flags    Timeout
192.168.1.202 1783   192.168.1.207 137    17      0     16386 ffffff00 18/40
192.168.1.202 1885   192.168.1.207 80      6      0     28673 ffffff00 43/50
192.168.1.202 1884   192.168.1.207 80      6      0     28673 ffffff00 43/50
192.168.1.202 1797   192.168.1.207 23      6      0     16385 ffffff00 35/50
192.168.1.202 1796   192.168.1.207 22      6      0     16385 ffffff00 35/50
192.168.1.202 1795   192.168.1.207 21      6      0     16385 ffffff10 35/50
192.168.1.202 1798   192.168.1.207 25      6      0     16385 ffffff00 35/50
192.168.1.202 1907   192.168.1.207 80      6      0     28673 ffffff00 43/50
```

IP addresses, port numbers, and even time-out values can be clearly seen in the FireWall-1 state table represented by fwtable.pl.

The Cisco PIX Firewall

The PIX firewall statefully inspects traffic using Cisco's Adaptive Security Algorithm (ASA). The ASA is used to make a representative hash of each outgoing TCP and UDP packet, and then store it in a state table. When the TCP and UDP traffic return, because a representative entry is recorded in the state table, the traffic will be allowed to pass. ICMP traffic is a different matter. ICMP traffic is denied completely from the outside of the PIX, and a specific access list must be created to allow traffic as basic as the reply from a ping command. An example of such an access list, as commonly used for troubleshooting new PIX installations, would be this:

```
access-list ICMP-ACL permit icmp test address inside address range
access-group ICMP-ACL in interface outside
```

The first command creates an access list called ICMP-ACL that permits ICMP traffic from a specified test address to our inside address range. The second line applies that ACL inbound on the outside interface.

The fixup protocol command is used to start an advanced application-specific examination of outbound traffic of the type listed to the designated port. The Cisco PIX firewall supports this application-level examination of traffic for the following protocols through the standard fixup command: FTP, HTTP, H.323, RSH, SMTP, SQLNET, SIP, and SKINNY.

The fixups for these protocols can be added or removed from a PIX configuration and reconfigured for various port specifications. They are considered extraneous to the operations of the PIX. The PIX also offers built-in fixup support for these protocols: RTSP, CUSEEME, DNS, SUNRPC, XDMCP, H.323 RAS, TCP, and UDP.

These integrated fixups are not seen in the PIX's configuration. They work in the background in conjunction with the normal fixups for the advanced inspection of these particular types of traffic. Even if a fixup is not installed for a particular TCP or UDP traffic type, the PIX will still track the session in its state table and allow its return traffic re-admittance to the network.

Not all fixups are created equal. Each fixup tracks application-level information at different levels. This level of inspection might vary from making sure the traffic passes through NAT successfully to the monitoring for specific application-level commands. For example, the SMTP fixup is the most stringent of them all. Since PIX software version 4.2, the SMTP fixup has supplied a protection feature called "mailguard." This fixup allows only SMTP commands to pass through it successfully. Non-SMTP traffic commands are dropped, but the PIX still returns an OK to the sender as if the information were passed. This helps protect poorly defended mail servers from outside attacks. Other fixups, such as FTP and H.323, allow the return of non-standard communication traffic by monitoring the application-level commands that control the formation of their data channels.

Because the standard `fixup` command allows the specifying of the port number to be examined for the protocol, alternative configurations are supported. (This is not true for the built-in fixups.) For example, if you need to access a web server that is running on port 8080, use the following command:

```
Pixprompt(config)#fixup protocol http 8080
```

Such a `fixup` command will allow the creation of state table information for the listed outbound traffic type. Multiple fixups can be listed if more than one port number is used per protocol. The PIX's state tables contain ASA hashes based on the source and destination addresses, port numbers, sequence numbers, and TCP flags. Because PIX firewalls use truly random TCP sequence number generation, the connection is kept more secure.[8]

When the reply returns, the PIX checks the response against the state table and information that it knows about the behavior of the protocol in question. If the information checks out, it is allowed to pass. All other information is dropped unless it is specifically allowed using an access list.

The table listing connection state for a Cisco PIX can be viewed using the `show conn` command. Such a table can be seen in Listing 3.4.

Listing 3.4 **The Output From a Cisco PIX Firewall's** *show conn*
Command

```
TCP out xx.yy.zz.129:5190 in 172.16.1.33:1960 idle 629:25:50 Bytes 6737 flags UIO
TCP out xx.yy.zz.254:23 in 172.16.1.88:1053 idle 0:11:33 Bytes 226696 flags UIO
TCP out xx.yy.zz.254:23 in 172.16.1.76:1146 idle 256:09:15 Bytes 78482 flags UIO
TCP out xx.yy.zz.254:23 in 172.16.1.100:1660 idle 145:21:19 Bytes 9657 flags UIO
TCP out xx.yy.zz.254:23 in 172.16.1.100:1564 idle 641:51:05 Bytes 132891 flags UIO
UDP out xx.yy.zz.12:137 in 172.16.1.12:137 idle 0:00:03 flags
```

Notice that standard IP address and port information are tracked, along with
the time that entries will remain in the table. Also notice on the last entry for
a UDP connection that no flags are listed. Despite the fact that this output
shows current connections and can give you a good idea of what information is in your PIX's state table, this is not a true dump of the state table
because it lacks the information provided by the stored ASA hash. You will
notice, for example, that sequence numbers are not listed in this output.

To learn more about the way the PIX firewall operates and to better understand the configuration of a stateful firewall, we will look at a PIX firewall configuration using software version 5.3(1). The configuration will only include
those items that have to do with passing standard protocol information.

First, in the PIX configuration listing are commands that define the
interfaces:

```
nameif ethernet0 outside security0
nameif ethernet1 inside security100
```

This is a simple configuration with only two interfaces: an inside interface
and an outside interface. Notice the security levels (shown as `security0` and
`security100`). By default, all traffic can flow from a higher security numbered
interface to a lower one on a PIX, but none can flow from a lower interface
to a higher one. By default, this PIX cannot receive inbound traffic connections, but it can send anything out. These default behaviors can be adjusted
by using NAT and access lists.

To allow an inbound connection, two criteria must be met:

- A static NAT mapping must be configured to allow the inbound traffic
  flow to bypass NAT translation, assuming that NAT is used in your environment. If it is not, this criterion can be ignored.

- An access list must be made to allow the type of traffic in question. For
  highest security, inbound traffic should only be allowed when using a firewall with a DMZ port; public servers can be placed on their own
  screened subnet.

Because NAT will not be an issue, you only need to add an access list to disallow outbound connections. This prevents the traffic types that you want to disallow. You can also create an egress filter to verify that only authentic local traffic is leaving your network.

> **Note**
>
> This configuration as listed does not include support for egress protection. For optimum security, egress protection of some sort is suggested. For more information on egress filters, see Chapter 2.

The `nameif` interface commands are followed by the backbone of the PIX configuration: the `fixup` commands (as mentioned earlier in the section). These commands list the protocols and their associated port numbers that the PIX will inspect. Listed next are some popular choices:

```
fixup protocol ftp 21
fixup protocol http 80
fixup protocol h323 1720
fixup protocol rsh 514
fixup protocol smtp 25
fixup protocol sqlnet 1521
fixup protocol sip 5060
```

The next lines of this listing show the IP addresses and subnet masks that are assigned to both the inside and outside ports. These are displayed here as a point of reference for the NAT-related commands to follow:

```
ip address outside 192.168.2.178 255.255.255.240
ip address inside 172.16.1.10 255.255.0.0
```

In the next portion of the listing, we create two address pools of outside addresses for our NAT pool (reflected by the first line (`outside`) 2, and for PAT (`outside`) 1). If we were only using PAT, the first line would not be necessary.

```
global (outside) 2 192.168.2.180-192.168.2.190 netmask 255.255.255.240
global (outside) 1 192.168.2.179
```

Next, we define the inside addresses for pool 2 and 1. The first statement lists the pool of inside addresses that will be NAT address translated. All other IP addresses will be forced to use PAT.

```
nat (inside) 2 172.16.1.96 255.255.255.248 0 0
nat (inside) 1 0.0.0.0 0.0.0.0 0 0
```

The second line demonstrates a wildcard so that any IP address (other than those listed on the previous line) will be PAT translated. We know that this is a PAT translation command because it maps to the previous `global (outside) 1` command, which only has one public address.

PIX firewalls allow return traffic in conjunction with the NAT statement. The NAT and state tables combine to let it know which traffic is returning as part of an already started conversation.

The next statements are the defaults of a PIX configuration and were not added in this example. However, they are displayed to show the default time-outs for the NAT translation table (xlate), the connection listings (state table) (conn), and user authentication traffic listings (uauth):

```
timeout xlate 3:00:00
timeout conn 1:00:00 half-closed 0:10:00 udp 0:02:00 rpc 0:10:00 h323 0:05:00 sip
➥0:30:00 sip_media 0:02:00
timeout uauth 0:05:00 absolute
```

These time-outs can be adjusted at any time by simply retyping the preceding commands with new timeout values.

Summary

The firewall provides a secured method of controlling what information moves in and out of a defined ingress/egress point for your network. This concept of a network "chokepoint" allows increased control and a single target for the monitoring and logging of network traffic. This extra control does come at a price: an overall cost in performance.

The stateful firewall adds intelligence to the packet-filtering method of network communication control and can be classified in one of two ways. Stateful filtering has been popularly used to define the filtering of the state of packet flows based on information from Layers 4 and below. This definition is ambiguous because the amount of protocol information that is considered in the filtering can deviate between vendor implementations. Items such as source and destination IP address and port numbers, sequence and acknowledgment numbers, as well as flags and other Layer 4 information can all be considered.

Stateful inspection also monitors Layer 4 information (just like stateful filtering) and adds application-level examination to provide insight into the communication session. This offers a secure means to handle non-standard TCP/IP traffic flows. Stateful inspection offers a much more secure environment than a "dumb" packet-filter and performance advantages over a proxy firewall, making it an excellent compromise between the two technologies. However, the same features that give stateful application inspection a performance advantage over a proxy firewall also make it less secure in environments where all aspects of application-level communication must be considered.

In any case, the stateful firewall is an excellent fit as a single perimeter security solution for smaller environments. It performs well as a role-player in larger or more complex environments where multiple firewall technologies are implemented. Clearly, the stateful firewall is a solid choice and a strong performer in the current network landscape. In the next chapter, we examine a way to filter network traffic by taking advantage of application-level restraints that can be implemented using proxy firewalls.

References

1 Check Point. "Stateful Inspection Technology Tech Note." `http://www.checkpoint.com/ products/security/whitepapers/firewall-1_statefulinspection.pdf`. March 2002.

2 Netfilter/IPTables Documentation. "What Is Netfilter?" `http://www.iptables.org/ documentation`. March 2002.

3 Fabrice Marie. "Netfilter Extensions HOWTO." `http://netfilter.samba.org/ documentation/HOWTO//netfilter-extensions-HOWTO.html`. March 2002.

4 G. van Rooij. "Real Stateful TCP Packet Filtering in IP Filter." 2nd International SANE Conference. March 2000.

5 Lance Spitzner. "Understanding the FW-1 State Table." November 29, 2000. `http://www.enteract.com/~lspitz/fwtable.html`. March 2002.

6 Lance Spitzner. "Understanding the FW-1 State Table." November 29, 2000. `http://www.enteract.com/~lspitz/fwtable.html`. March 2002.

7 Dameon D. Welch. "TCP Timeout for a Specific Service." `http://www.phoneboy.com/faq/ 0203.html`. March 2002.

8 Cisco Systems, Inc. "Cisco's PIX Firewall Series and Stateful Firewall Security." `http://www.cisco.com/warp/public/cc/pd/fw/sqfw500/tech/nat_wp.pdf`. March 2002.

4

Proxy Firewalls

A PROXY SERVER, SOMETIMES CALLED AN *application gateway*, is a specialized application that provides communication via Internet protocols between the internal protected network and the outside world (Internet). In general, proxies work for programs based on the TCP/IP protocol. Proxy servers typically run a few programs (proxies) that can be secured and trusted. These programs are application specific, and each protocol that is being supported must have its own proxy service or be handled by a generic proxy. A proxy can also be a transparent program that is designed to move packets at any given port across a network boundary.

This chapter describes the basics of proxy firewalls and identifies some products to assist in building more secure firewalls through the use of proxied services.

Fundamentals

A proxy acts on behalf of the client or user for access to a network service and shields each side from a direct peer-to-peer connection. Clients establish connections, completing the three-way handshake to the proxy server. The proxy then establishes a connection to the destination server. The proxy server sends data that it receives from the client to the destination server and forwards data that it receives from the destination server to the client.

Strictly speaking, the proxy server is both a server and a client. It is a server to its client and a client to its destination server. One way to keep this straight is to call the listening end of the proxy the *listener* and the initiating side of the proxy the *initiator*. This leaves the client and server terms for the endpoints. The steps in making a connection through a proxy require various levels of authentication or trust of the software being executed to establish the connections.

The following is an example of the types of connections that are established through a proxy from an internal network to the Internet:

1. The user requests Internet services, such as HTTP, FTP, or Telnet.

2. Software on the client forwards the requests according to the security policy to the actual Internet services to be utilized.

3. The proxies provide connections by acting as gateways to the remote services.

4. The proxies perform all communication that is necessary to establish a connection with the external system while shielding the systems that are behind the firewall from being viewed by the external systems.

5. All traffic that is being routed between the internal user and the external systems is processed through the proxy gateways.

A proxy server typically runs on a dual-homed bastion host or gateway and supports one or more Internet protocols (see Figure 4.1). *Bastion hosts* are hardened systems that are configured for Internet-accessible functions. A dual-homed gateway consists of a host system with two network interfaces: one for the internal protected network, and one for the external network. These hosts permit no direct traffic between networks, and can be used to perform logging and auditing functions on the traffic that passes through them. The host's IP forwarding capability is disabled so that the host no longer routes packets between the two connected networks. The dual-homed gateway completely blocks IP traffic between the external and internal networks. Proxy servers on the gateway provide Internet connectivity and services. It might be advantageous to disable the IP forwarding capability explicitly to avoid having inadvertent IP traffic forwarding.

An example of a simple configuration for a dual-homed gateway is providing proxy services for email. The service on the firewall accepts all mail that is being addressed to internal users and then forwards it to internal systems or a centralized internal mail server. This type of connection appears transparent to the end user. It seems as if the connection is directly between the user's internal system and the external system.

Figure 4.1   A dual–homed (bastion) host with proxy services
is typically a gateway system with two network interfaces.

Because the data is communicated between the internal client and the bastion host, the client's internal IP address and certain protocol information are prevented from being broadcast across the Internet. By studying certain features of the packets—including the default settings for the Time to Live (TTL) field, window size, and TCP options—the operating system (OS) of the client can be determined. This technique of OS identification, known as *passive fingerprinting,* can be used by an attacker to determine what kinds of exploits to use against the client system.

These types of services/servers provide functionality for internal and external users while being outside of the internal network perimeter. Figure 4.2 provides an illustration of multiple servers outside of a protected network.

Figure 4.2   Multiple bastion hosts can reside outside of the protected
perimeter, each potentially serving a different purpose.

Ideally, one bastion host would be used to address one proxy service, the separation principle of security. No user accounts, compilers, or unneeded programs should be on the bastion hosts. Additionally, any unused services should be disabled; only those services that the proxy server offers should be enabled so that if a bastion or service were compromised, only one service would be affected. However, this might not always be feasible. Unfortunately, pooling all of the proxies on a single bastion host provides a potential single point of failure if successfully attacked.

In addition to the classically proxied protocols, such as Telnet, FTP, email, and news, organizations might need to provide access to the web (HTTP), multicast, and distributed protocols for music, video/audio, conferencing, database access, file sharing, and more. This results in a significant challenge for network security administrators as they battle to keep systems up-to-date and keep clients/users satisfied with service availability.

Application layer firewalls are beneficial because they have the capability to decode the application layer header information; therefore, they can provide more detailed audit log reporting. Next, we will discuss some of the various types of proxies and their typical applications.

Application Gateway Log Saves the Day

Long before CodeRed and Nimda, the defensive community noticed a large number of probes on ports 80, 8080, and 3128 TCP, all proxy servers ports. Analysts poured over Cisco router ACL logs, but they could not figure out what was going on. Bill Royds in Canada detected the activity on his Raptor firewall. The log is shown next:

```
Oct 1 06:47:02 gate gwcontrol: 201 http[3785494487]: access denied for
➡smak.mplik.ru to www.rusftpsearch.net [default rule] [no rules found]
➡Oct 1 06:47:02 gate httpd[7188]: 121 Statistics: duration=0.15
➡id=w7Ii3 sent=357
rcvd=402
    srcif=hme1 src=195.58.0.243/61332 srcname=smak.mplik.ru
    dstif=hme1 dst=206.253.222.89/80 dstname=www.rusftpsearch.net
    op=GET
arg=http://www.rusftpsearch.net/cgibin/pst.pl?pstmode=writeip&psthost=
➡167.33.61.23&pstport=80
    result="403 Forbidden" proto=http (request denied by gwcontrol)
```

You can see that the source computer smak is trying to go through the proxy to reach www.rusftpsearch.net. You can also see that it wants to reach the cgi-bin application pst.pl on the server. If successful, the Trojan software known as RingZero logs the presence of the proxy for use later. Because the application gateway firewall logged this additional information, the community was able to develop a response to the trojan.

Types of Proxies

Now that we have introduced the fundamentals of what a proxy is, we will examine some of the common variations on the theme. This section discusses forward and reverse proxies, application-level proxies, and circuit-level proxies, and most importantly, when you might want to implement each technology.

Reverse Proxy

At some point, the Internet became more hostile and organizations felt the need to deploy more secure perimeters than were possible with static packet filters. As the first firewalls were developed, internal users needed a way to get through the perimeter to Internet servers, and one solution was the proxy. As you already learned, a proxy is both a client and a server, so the forward/reverse notation is pretty ambiguous. Most people consider the internal user going through the proxy to reach the Internet service to be a *forward proxy*.

Reverse proxy describes a different use of proxy technology. A *reverse proxy* can be used outside the firewall to represent a secure content server to outside clients, preventing direct, unmonitored access to your server's data from outside your company. You can also use a reverse proxy for performance; multiple proxies can be attached in front of a heavily used server for load balancing. Forward or reverse applications could be the same proxy server; the difference is simply one of configuration.

As you can guess, a complex perimeter with proxies, tunnels, and packet filters in both directions can get ugly quickly. A simple labeling convention can really help when tracing network wiring diagrams. This is why we suggest using different terms for the four roles:

- C Client—The system requesting service
- S Server—The system with the desired Internet service
- L Listener—The side of the proxy awaiting connections from the client
- I Initiator—The side of the proxy that is making a connection to the server

Next, we move on to discuss two fundamentally different types of proxies: application and circuit.

Application-Level Proxy

Application proxies are custom client/server software programs that are implemented for each service to be under scrutiny by the firewall. A classic example is allowing outgoing HTTP traffic for external web access from all internal users.

A stricter policy might permit a particular user to telnet from an internal machine through the firewall; the controls ensure that all other users are denied access to the telnet proxy service. If the initiating activity is inbound, then authentication to establish this is the authorized user. A well-written application proxy can also protect against protocol attacks by only passing properly formed packets. This type of filtering guarantees a certain level of trust in the traffic that is being permitted through the firewall.

Circuit-Level Proxy

Another form of proxy firewall is the circuit-level proxy, also called a *circuit level relay* or *gateway*. This form of proxy takes packet filtering a bit further. Instead of just filtering based on IP addresses, port numbers, or other packet header information, *circuit-level proxies* validate and monitor each session that is established in the communication. Traffic is blocked unless a session is opened. A session is opened on behalf of the user through the client. The circuit-level gateway determines whether the connection is valid based on rules that might be related to destination IP address/port, source IP address/port, protocol that is used or requested, user ID, password, or even the time of day. Being able to handle rules associated with time and users is an advantage over packet-filter firewalls. Because these rules go beyond checking IP addresses, circuit-level proxies can handle UDP traffic by validating other information, making attempts to bypass firewalls via IP spoofing more difficult. Now let's investigate applying these technologies to firewalls.

Proxy or Application Gateway Firewalls

Firewalls fall into two broad categories: Network layer and Application layer. Network layer firewalls are limited to packet filters, whereas Application layer firewalls include the proxies.

Proxy firewalls provide greater ability for audit logging; however, they might require more configuration and reduce the number of services that are available to end users. This tradeoff is the classic ease-of-use versus security. Proxy firewalls require either modified client software (customized code) or modified user procedures (the users have to learn something new).

The earliest proxy firewalls required modified user procedures, including specifying a port number after a URL to access a web page (`http://www.mydomain.net:8080`). In such a case, port 80—the typical port used for HTTP—is blocked and the web server accepts only HTTP traffic on port 8080. Another modified procedure might be to FTP to one location before being allowed to FTP to the final FTP server. Early versions of proxies, such as the TIS Firewall Toolkit, required significant configuration that seemed complex. Proxy firewalls have made huge advances since then, but due to their roots, they have some significant advantages and disadvantages. We will investigate the problem of a proxy firewall when no proxy is available for an application that you need to run.

Advantages of Proxy Firewalls

Proxy firewalls have several advantages over other types of firewalls:

- Internal IP addresses are shielded from the external world because proxy services do not allow direct communications between external servers and internal computers.

- Administrators are able to monitor violations of the firewall's security policies using the audit records that proxy services can generate.

- User-based security is possible with proxy firewalls. Proxy services are effective at preventing unauthorized use at a per-user basis and can even support strong authentication.

- Proxy firewalls are not vulnerable to IP spoofing because connectivity is based on services instead of physical connections. IP addresses of machines within the internal protected network are not communicated through the proxy firewall.

- Proxy firewalls have better logging capabilities than filtering and routing firewalls and provide a single point for audit and control.

- Users do not log into the proxy servers. No user accounts are required on the bastion host. The proxy services function on behalf of the users.

- A proxy server provides a centralized point for the network, and traffic can be monitored closely. This might also create a bottleneck for network traffic, however.

- The topology of the internal protected network is hidden in proxy firewalls.

- Some proxies provide enhanced auditing facilities with tools to monitor the traffic.

- Robust authentication and logging are possible in proxy firewalls. The application traffic can be preauthenticated before it reaches internal hosts and can be logged more effectively than with standard host logging.

- Proxy firewalls have less complex filtering rules than packet filtering firewalls. The rules at the packet-filtering router are less complex than if the router needed to filter application traffic and direct the traffic to a number of specific systems. The router only needs to allow application traffic that is destined for the application gateway and can reject the rest.

Disadvantages of Proxy Firewalls

Although proxy firewalls provide increased security over packet-filtering firewalls, some disadvantages to using proxies include the following:

- Reduction of performance due to the additional processing requests required for application services. Application proxies are slower than packet filters.

- A new proxy must be developed for each new application or protocol to pass through the firewall.

- A limited number of services is available. Custom software or user procedures are required for each service. Access to other non-proxiable services remains unavailable.

- Inherent problems in operating systems and their components can affect the security of the firewall server. Proxy services are vulnerable to operating-system and Application-level bugs.

- The OS on the host that contains the proxy is exposed to external threats and might come under attack.

- Setting up a proxy service might be complex for each application that uses a gateway.

- Because a proxy server might be a bottleneck for the network, it might also become a single point of failure.

So far, we've looked into the basics of proxy servers and their role in developing a firewall solution. How can unsupported protocols be proxied? What happens if a service cannot be proxied?

When No Proxy Exists

Many factors can influence an inability to proxy a service. New services require that new proxies be developed, and proxy servers might not be available for the service desired. You might not be able to produce a modified client or have custom procedures to address the service.

Note

Many firewall administrators simply create a static packet filter type rule when they do not have a proxy. Be on the alert for this if you are auditing a firewall.

Most firewalls have a "generic proxy" capability that is similar to TCPproxy, designed to move packets across a network boundary. (TCPproxy is available at http://www.quietsche-entchen.de/manpages/tcpproxy-1.html). However, this type of proxy does not protect against inherent vulnerabilities in operating systems and protocols.

Sometimes alternatives are available to assist in proxying without a proxy server. One example is the use of a mail server to store and forward email. If you are serious about security, consider using a different tool to store and forward email than the tool you use on your internal hosts. This way, a single vulnerability is less likely to lay waste to your entire domain. For instance, if you use Microsoft Exchange as your mail server, you might choose a store and forward agent, such as Qmail or Sendmail. Additionally, tools such as application wrappers, can help to securely handle servers for which no proxies are available.

Unsupported protocols and services can still be partially secured through generic proxies and wrappers. If a proxy client/server is unavailable for a particular service, or if the source code of a protocol is not available for modification, another means of securing protocols is in the form of wrappers and generic proxies. The basic idea behind wrappers and generic proxies is to encapsulate the service to be used by software that adds security logic to the processing.

Protocol Issues for Proxies

In this section, we take a look at some basic protocol issues that are related to proxies. We also highlight some protocols that add security in communication, such as IPSec and SSL, which are commonly used to secure connections across the Internet.

IPSec is covered in detail in Chapter 8, "Virtual Private Networks," but for the moment, we want to show how the protocol does not adapt well to Network Address Translation (NAT) and proxy environments. In addition, the proxy sometimes hinders legitimate traffic from being able to pass through a perimeter; one emerging solution for this is Blocks Extensible Exchange Protocol (BEEP).

IPSec

One way to think of a proxy is a tube—that is, many times, the IP address, source, or destination ports change as the packet passes from one interface of the proxy to the other. This is a major problem for IPSec because the security associations are based on endpoint IP addresses.

This is one reason that IPSec appliances that sit outside the firewall and usually connect directly to the internal net are so popular. As we learned in our unenforceable policy discussion in Chapter 5, "Security Policy," if users can't go through the perimeter device, they find a way to go around the device.

SSL

Netscape Communications Corporation developed the SSL protocol, which allows secure connections across the Internet through an encrypted channel. Typically, SSL is used to protect HTTP traffic. However, other protocols, such as Telnet, can run on top of SSL.

Enabling SSL through your firewall can be done in the same way that you allow HTTP traffic—that is, if it's HTTP that you're using SSL to secure, which is usually the case. The only difference is that instead of simply relaying HTTP, communication must be established to permit SSL tunneling.

SSL provides privacy and integrity of a communication channel. The protocol is composed of two layers. The lowest level is the SSL Record Protocol that resides on top of the Transport Protocol Layer (TCP). The SSL Record Protocol acts as a wrapper to cryptographically encapsulate higher network layer protocols. One higher-level encapsulated protocol is the SSL Handshake Protocol. The SSL Handshake Protocol enables the client and server to authenticate one another and negotiates encryption algorithm and cryptographic keys to use before the application protocol transmits information. SSL is independent of application service and can be used to secure a variety of protocols without having a specialized proxy.

The details of SSL are beyond the scope of this chapter. The steps for establishing an SSL connection can become complex. The following steps outline the basics of an SSL Handshake to establish a secure channel (for more information about SSL, see `http://home.netscape.com/security/techbriefs/ssl.html`):

1. The client sends the SSL version number, cipher settings, randomly generated data, and other client-specific information that the server needs to communicate with the client.

2. The server replies by sending the SSL version number, cipher settings, random seed, and other server-specific information that the client needs to communicate with the server.

3. As part of this reply, the server sends its certificate and requests the client's certificate if authentication of the client is required.

4. The client authenticates the server based on information that is sent to the client from the server and the server's certificate.

5. If the server cannot be authenticated, an error is reported and the communication is terminated.

6. If the server can be authenticated, the client and server can exchange session keys to begin an encrypted session.

7. At this point, encryption algorithms have been agreed upon and public keys for the client and server have been exchanged (through their certificates).

8. The client creates and encrypts a secret with the server's public key and sends the encrypted secret to the server. (If client authentication is required, the client also digitally signs data that can be verified by the server, which holds the clients public key from the certificate exchange.)

9. The client decrypts the encrypted secret sent from the server. This decrypted secret and the encrypted secret that the client sent to the server are used together to form a session key (or master key).

10. The server authenticates the client's signature if client authentication is required. If the client cannot be authenticated, the communication is terminated.

11. If the client is authenticated, the server decrypts the encrypted secret that the client sent. This decrypted secret and encrypted secret sent to the client from the server are used together to form a session key (or master key).

12. At this point, both the client and the server have the same master key. This key will be used to encrypt further packets for a secure communication channel.

13. The client notifies the server that future packets will be encrypted.

14. The client sends an encrypted packet notifying the server that the client-side of the SSL Handshake has completed.

15. The server notifies the client that future packets will be encrypted.

16. The client sends an encrypted packet notifying the client that the server-side of the SSL Handshake has completed.

The SSL handshake is complete and the encrypted SSL session has begun. It takes longer to explain the process than it does to establish an SSL connection. From this point until the session is terminated, all traffic between the client and server for that session is encrypted. The basic idea behind this protocol is to add security logic to communication channels.

Tools for Proxying

Many available applications provide application or generic proxying capabilities.

SOCKS

SOCKS is a proxy toolkit that enables applications to be proxied without having specific proxy client/server software for each application. It enables hosts on one side of a SOCKS server to gain access to hosts on the other side of the SOCKS server without requiring direct IP connectivity. The SOCKS server redirects connection and service requests between hosts on either side of it. The SOCKS server performs authentication and authorization functions on requests, establishes a proxy connection, and relays data between hosts. The SOCKS proxy server is available from http://www.socks.nec.com/.

The SOCKS program needs two separate configuration files: one file to identify the allowable access, and another file to route the service requests to the appropriate proxy server. IP addresses and users can be identified for filtering. We will not go into the specifics of IP filtering with SOCKS or filter syntax here. See the SOCKS documentation for more information regarding installation and configuration.

To have applications work with the SOCKS proxy server, they must be "SOCKS-ified." Two applications are required for supported services. For example, two different Telnet programs are needed: one for direct communication, and one for communication via the SOCKS proxy server. SOCKS has instructions on how to "SOCKS-ify" a program, which includes steps for modification to work with the SOCKS server. Each application to be SOCKS-ified needs some modification. The client software communicates through the SOCKS server.

SOCKS includes two components: the SOCKS server and the SOCKS client. The SOCKS server is implemented at the Application layer, whereas the SOCKS client is implemented between the Application and Transport layers.

When an application client needs to connect to an application server, the client connects to a SOCKS proxy server. The proxy server then connects to the application server on behalf of the client, and relays data between the client and the application server. For the application server, the proxy server is the client.

For each TCP or UDP communication channel that the SOCKS protocol establishes, it transfers user information from the SOCKS client to the SOCKS server for user authentication and verifies the integrity of TCP and UDP channels.

As a generic proxy, the SOCKS protocol establishes communication channels, and manages and protects the channel for any application. As new applications come to market, SOCKS can protect them without requiring additional development.

Available SOCKS versions are SOCKSv4 and SOCKSv5. Traditional SOCKS through version 4 do not support UDP proxies. However, SOCKSv5 supports UDP proxying as well as a variety of authentication methods. SOCKSv5 is a much-improved version of SOCKS. The Internet Engineering Task Force (IETF) approved the standard (RFC 1928) generic, proxy protocol for TCP/IP-based networking applications. The basic functions of SOCKS are to make connection requests, set up circuit-level proxies, and relay application data. Version 5 provides additional authentication and UDP support.

SOCKS Version 4

The SOCKSv4 protocol defines the message format and conventions to allow TCP-based application users transparent access across a firewall. During proxy connection setup, the SOCKS server grants access based on TCP header information, including IP addresses and source and destination host port numbers. The SOCKS server also authorizes users using Ident (RFC 1413) information.

The SOCKS user community proposed and implemented a protocol extension to SOCKSv4 to eliminate the requirement for SOCKSv4 clients to resolve internal and external domain names. By appending the unresolved domain names to the SOCKSv4 client requests, SOCKSv4 servers can attempt to resolve domain names.

Because of its simplicity, SOCKSv4 is widely used as a network firewall. The SOCKSv4 protocol has two weaknesses: lack of strong authentication, and the requirement to recompile applications with SOCKSv4 client library. An IETF working group drafted and approved a new version of SOCKS, SOCKSv5. The working group completed three SOCKSv5-related standards: RFC 1928, RFC 1929, and RFC 1961.

SOCKS Version 5

The SOCKS version 5 protocol, also known as authenticated firewall traversal (AFT), is an open Internet standard (RFC 1928) for performing network proxies at the transport layer. It resolves several issues that SOCKS version 4 protocol did not fully address or omitted:

- Strong authentication. The SOCKSv5 authentication method negotiation is handled by the SOCKSv5 client/server communication. The application client identifies the authentication methods it can support to the SOCKSv5 server. The SOCKSv5 server, in turn, sends a message to the client identifying the authentication method the client should use. The authentication method is also determined based on the security policy defined in the SOCKSv5 server configuration. If the client's requited authentication methods fail to meet the security requirement, the SOCKSv5 server denies communication.

- Address resolution proxy. SOCKSv5's built-in address resolution proxy simplifies DNS administration and facilitates IP address hiding and translation. SOCKSv5 clients can pass the name, instead of the resolved address, to the SOCKSv5 server and the server resolves the address for the client.

- Proxy for UDP-based applications. SOCKSv5 supports UDP association by creating a virtual proxy circuit for UDP-based application data. Two differences exist between in TCP and UDP-based proxy circuits: The proxy circuit for UDP is a pair of addresses for the communication endpoints that send and receive datagrams. The UDP proxy headers encapsulate application data, including the destination address of a datagram.

There are two additional SOCKSv5-related standards to support authentication methods:

- Username/Password authentication for SOCKSv5 (RFC 1929)
- GSS-API (Generic Security Service Application Programming Interface) authentication for SOCKSv5 (RFC 1961)

Gauntlet

Two versions of Gauntlet are available from Network Associates: a version for Microsoft Windows NT/2000, and a version for UNIX. The UNIX version is the more mature of the two and has features yet to be made available for the Windows environment. Much of the functionality is the same between the two products.

Gauntlet can be thought of as a hybrid product that combines aspects of proxy server firewalls with stateful inspection packet-filtering capabilities. Network packets are routed dynamically between the proxy and dynamic packet filter layers based on user-defined security rules. Dependent on the security policy requirements that Gauntlet implements, more or less emphasis is directed toward the proxy or packet filter. For example, if stricter security measures are to be enforced, then more processing takes place at the Application Proxy layer. When security requirements are low, more processing takes place at the Packet Filter layer.

The basic difference between the Gauntlet implementation and other stateful inspection firewalls is what Network Associates calls its *adaptive proxy* by dynamically routing traffic to the appropriate proxy. Under a typical stateful inspection firewall, the stateful inspection kernel and the proxy have no interaction, so traffic is handled either by filtering or by the proxy. Adaptive proxying enables the proxy to communicate with the packet-filtering kernel. If a problem is detected during the proxy, a message can be sent to the packet filter to terminate the communication. Under a Gauntlet implementation, this type of inspection and communication are possible because of the proxy for each connection.

Gauntlet offers a wide range of proxied services. The traditional proxies are included, such as FTP, Telnet, SMTP, NNTP, and SSL. Gauntlet also provides proxies for other applications, including Microsoft SQL, NetMeeting, Oracle SQL*net, RealAudio/Video, Sybase, and VDOLive. Each of the proxies can be configured independently and permits a certain amount of customization. In addition to application proxies, Gauntlet supports authentication systems, such as RSA Security's SecurID, Remote Authentication Dial In User Service (RADIUS), and Telcordia's (formerly Bellcore) S/KEY.

The UNIX version of Gauntlet offers additional features and components. These tools offer capabilities for central control of the firewalls, further authentication, expanded support of third-party security products—including authentication servers—and intrusion detection systems.

PORTUS

From the PORTUS System Theory of Operation, the fundamental assumption behind Livermore's PORTUS firewall system is that "all functions are denied except those which are explicitly allowed. All unsafe functions and applications are disabled or removed from the firewall system. Options that could compromise system security are not offered."[1]

This approach makes available only those services that are necessary to perform required functions. It is similar to the "least access rule," which states that no one should have any more access than is required to complete their job function.

The security of access provided by PORTUS is based on strong user authentication. IP addresses are simply not trusted to accurately portray network communication. Taking this approach removes the reliance on packet filtering and the real possibility of IP spoofing. For a user to access the protected network, he is assigned a smart token via a smart card. The user then enters a personal identification number (PIN) for cryptographic authentication to the PORTUS system.

As with many proxy services, modified software clients, servers, and user procedures are necessary for security. The SOCKS server runs on the POR-TUS firewall, and SOCKS clients run on the protected hosts. For example, a user who needs FTP access should use the PORTUS FTP proxy. This FTP proxy performs cryptographic user identification and authentication before any other commands are accepted. System commands cannot be executed on the firewall.

PORTUS can allow or deny connections based on multiple criteria, in addition to user identification and authentication. Proxy filters can be based on other parameters, such as time of day, day of the week, and IP addresses/ports (both source and destination). All activity that passes through the firewall is logged.

In addition to Application level proxies for specific services, PORTUS provides a generic proxy (genproxy) to secure TCP/IP level services that do not have assigned proxies.

Genproxy is invoked by `inetd` with the name of the service supplied as a parameter. Based on its configuration file, genproxy determines whether to permit the execution of the requested service. Connections are permitted based on source and destination IP addresses and ports.

Summary

The use of proxy technology is strongly recommended for perimeter defense. Proxy firewalls are considered the most secure firewalls for networks. However, when they are implemented on firewall platforms, proxy servers generally reduce performance. Deciding what kind of firewall to implement boils down to a business decision and tradeoff among function, performance, and ease of use. The higher that security is, the lower the performance. The more difficult that a system is for general use, the more likely that users will find alternative means of using it.

Implementing a proxy firewall increases security for a number of reasons:

- Protecting against reconnaissance
- Protecting against protocol attacks

So-called reverse proxies can be deployed in front of an organization's servers for both performance and security gains.

Many applications and services can be employed together for additional security. Proxies and other filtering devices assist in perimeter protection, while securing protocols with encryption as implemented in SSL or IPSec adds protection to the underlying communication channels.

This chapter described the basics of proxy firewalls and identified products to assist in building more secure firewalls through the use of proxied services.

References

1 "PORTUS Tutorial 9." Livermore Software Laboratories. `http://www.lsli.com/ tut9.html`. December 2001.

5

Security Policy

WHEN YOU TALK TO VENDORS OR ATTEND a security course, they tell you to do this or that according to your site's security policy, but have you ever noticed that almost no one attempts to explain what the security policy is or how to write or evaluate it? This is why we have included this chapter in the book. Firewalls and other perimeter devices as well are active security enforcement engines. As we examine the material, we discuss the fact that organizations often have unwritten policies. In the first half of this chapter, we explore the task of mapping policy to perimeter architectures and translating policy to enforceable firewall rules. In the second half of this chapter, we consider an approach to develop policy that requires understanding authority, scope, expiration, specificity, and clarity. Developing and implementing policy is not easy, which is why we explicitly cover the hallmarks of good policy and examples of bad policy.

Note

"A security policy establishes what must be done to protect information stored on computers. A well-written policy contains sufficient definition of "what" to do so that the "how" can be identified and measured or evaluated."[1]

Firewalls Are Policy

The Yin and Yang of perimeter security policy can be referred to as access and control. When you come to fully understand these, it is hard to think of an access control list (ACL) in the same way. The point of a network is to provide access. *Access* pertains to accessibility, providing service, performance, and ease of use. *Control* focuses on denial of unauthorized service or access, separation, integrity, and safety. At one point as a community, we thought that two basic perimeter policy models existed:

- Everything is denied except that which is specifically permitted.
- Everything is permitted except that which is specially denied.

That sounds good, but it is bogus. In truth, one policy exists:

- Everything is denied except that which is specifically permitted or that which gets in anyway.

Let's illustrate this with the simple case of making the access control decision on the destination port. For example, if the destination is TCP port 27374, the default port for SubSeven 2.1, and 27374 isn't on the allow list, control is applied, and the packet is dropped. Internally, what is happening? The firewall scoots to the second 16-bit field in the TCP header and grabs the destination port to compare it to its access control policy. What if the packet is a fragment? Only the first fragment has protocol information. Let's say this is the runt, the last fragment of the original datagram, but it arrives first. We aren't going to make an access/control decision on 27374; it isn't there. To be sure, we can make many decisions when dealing with a fragment:

- Consult our state table to see if this is part of an existing connection.
- Buffer the fragment, reassemble the datagram, and then make the access control decision.
- Let the fragment through, but engage rate limiting to minimize harm.
- If outbound ICMP unreachables are disabled, let the fragment through.
- Drop the fragment and make the sender retransmit.

Firewall rules look simple when we are looking at a Check Point FireWall-1 GUI, but underneath might be many complex decisions and assumptions. Complexity is the enemy of enforceable, consistent policy. Sometimes, the result is that we are actually granting access when we think we are applying control. This is a case of unenforceable policy.

Access and Security Illustrated

Several years ago, I was talking with a perimeter analyst who was responsible for the site security policy for the Naval Space Command. He was overseeing the installation of a new application gateway firewall, a Sidewinder from Secure Computing. He wasn't sure what his organization should set for a security policy, so he decided to block everything and sit by the phone to see who called. This succeeded handily in providing security, but it fell a bit short in providing access. To this day when I am reviewing an architecture, I cannot help but remember this approach.

Active Policy Enforcement

You can argue with your security officer or your boss, but you can't argue with the firewall. The firewall is a genuine policy enforcement engine, and like most policy enforcers, it is none too bright. Much of this chapter is devoted to unenforceable policy. We are going to show that sometimes the problem is the firewall's limitations, but sometimes the firewall doesn't stand a chance. If you believe that a firewall can protect you, by the end of this section, you should have some serious doubt. Often, the firewall is unable to enforce the site's policy; if you do not have defense in depth, you are running at a high risk.

Unenforceable Policy

One thing that you should try to be sensitive to is unenforceable policy. We will first paint the picture clearly with non-technical organizational examples, but then show how it is possible to create situations in which policy is unenforceable with perimeter systems. At one time, the U.S. Government had a policy that mandated "no personal use of Government computers." During the time of mainframes (ancient computers that were the size of a house with less processing power than an Intel 386), that was probably enforceable.

Times changed. By 1985, almost all of us technical workers had at least one personal computer or workstation on our desktops. The world had changed, but the policy hadn't. When people have their own operating and file system, the rule of no personal use is unenforceable. Have you ever known you needed to finish that documentation, but on your way to bring up the word processor, clicked your email icon to check your mail for a second and neglected to get back to the document for an hour? Or brought up Google to look up one thing, saw something else that looked interesting, and never found the original fact? With tools like this, is "no personal use" possible? No way! That becomes an unenforceable policy, policy that is written, but cannot be enforced. Unenforceable policy, whether administrative policy, or failed perimeter policy enforcement is not a good thing.

Unofficial Official Policy

I still remember working for the Defense Mapping Agency, now NIMA. Just before the Christmas holidays, we used to load a game of *Star Trek* on the Digital PDP 1170s for about two days. The game was primitive by today's standards, but these were huge graphics terminals used to edit maps. Playing *Star Trek* on these computers was the coolest thing I had ever seen. After the Christmas party, we would remove the game and search the file system for any file that was the same size as the game in case it had been copied and renamed.

I asked the system administrator, "Why can't we leave it on there for slow nights when we get our work done early?" He informed me that the department head of the topography department was a powerful and authoritarian man and I really didn't want to cross him. He created an unofficial policy that we could play *Star Trek* for two days, but it had to be totally and completely removed after the Christmas party. This is known as an *administrative control.*

Administrative controls don't work. During the years I was at the Mapping Agency, the game would pop up now and again. We would find the game and remove it, but there was no way to actively and consistently enforce the *Star Trek* policy.

The Effect of Unenforceable Policy

If you have an unenforceable administrative policy, then people are encouraged to either ignore or push the rules. In fact, one of the reasons that hacking is so widespread is that any laws against it are virtually unenforceable, especially because many courts have ruled that the reconnaissance phase, scanning, is legal. Another classic unenforceable policy is the requirement that all computer virus infections are reported. After the problem is cleaned up, the tendency is to move on with life. The security office has no way of knowing how many infections the organization has. One Navy group went to an anti-virus console so that infections were automatically reported by the workstations. It went from seven reports the year before to more than 1,000 with the console. As a general rule, any policy that does not have a method to collect information and controls, the tools we use for enforcement, is probably unenforceable.

If You Were Told to Enforce "No Personal Use," Could You Do It?

I was once asked this question. It would be hard to get to a 100% solution, but I could block all incoming or outgoing traffic that wasn't to or from a .mil, .gov, or .int (NATO) address, and that would take care of a lot. This is some serious control!

In the case of no personal use though, just like our simple example of making the access control decision on the destination port, we have those complicated cases like fragmentation to deal with. Users might have the following types of questions:

- What if my wife sends me an email? Is it okay to read it?
- Can I check on my stocks at lunch?

The answer is "Yes, these things are okay." The U.S. government has retreated to a position called "limited personal use." Limited personal use is enforceable through a number of commercially available firewall or other perimeter tools. One of the better examples of a limited personal use policy can be found at `http://www.opm.gov/extra/itusepolicy.htm`. In essence, this says that you can use your Government computer for personal use. Don't ask, don't tell, and don't overdo the personal use. Don't send chain letters, do fundraising, or pass sexual, racist, or illegal files.

If you were assigned to enforce limited personal use, could you do it? Subscription-based services that have sets of banned URLs are available. You can load a set for sites that are banned because they have sexual content and another for hate speech and so on. These go by names like CYBERsitter and Net Nanny and are available for the desktop and the firewall. They are known to be inflexible; they tend to apply control when they should be allowing access. For a while, it was a common sport on the Internet to make these tools look bad because they stopped web queries for "breast feeding" and so forth. They also allow access when they should be applying control when they come across a URL they don't know and the site is a bit cagey. That is why you have to pay the money for the subscription; if you want the tool to work, you have to keep it up to date. Most K–12 school systems employ these tools on their perimeter, and there we see one of the most extreme examples of the harmful effect of unenforceable policy. Kids become heroes by going through an open proxy to download porn directly to the library workstations. The good news is that progress is on the horizon. We are just starting to see fairly useful next-generation content-aware tools such as WEBSweeper from Baltimore Technologies, but these are expensive and come with their own headaches. Are you starting to believe that complexity is the enemy of enforceable, consistent policy?

We have gone from administrative controls, such as manually searching for banned software, to perimeter tools that have protect-oriented security controls, such as blocking banned URLs. In our next section, we want to explore the ways we can create or find unenforceable policy in the perimeter. These problem vectors include coding errors, lack of understanding as to what the policy should be, web tunneling, email attachments, disks in briefcases, and every kind of backdoor you can imagine.

Vectors for Unenforceable Policy

If unenforceable policy is a problem because it enables people to access things that we would prefer to control, then we want to minimize it. On the organizational, administrative level, we can review our policies to see if they meet the criteria of good policy that we discuss later in this chapter. On the technical side, we can use tools, such as PacketX and hping2 to throw crazy packets at the perimeter and see what gets through. What kind of packets? Try short fragments, TCP packets with odd code combinations, or every possible option set. This can alert us to how the assumptions and design decisions that are underneath the rules that we are able to write are working. In addition to a firewalking-type assessment, it is a good idea to ask yourself what vectors might allow unenforceable policy to manifest itself. We are the most likely culprits. Sometimes we forget how firewall rules are processed, or we add them willy-nilly.

Unwittingly Coding Unenforceable Policy

Have you ever heard the saying, "I know it is what I asked for, but it isn't what I wanted!"? This happens to firewall administrators, the folks who write firewall rules, all too often. Many times we get what we asked for, but not what we wanted when our firewall has complex firewall rules. After all, a seemingly simple set of rules has underlying assumptions and rules, so a complex set of rules makes it pretty likely that a firewall administrator might accidentally arrange the rules in such a way that the firewall cannot enforce the policy that the administrator thinks he has defined. This is the reason you hear recommendations such as "Never have more than 20 rules." That sounds good, but what if you live in the real world? You might need a bit more than 20 rules.

Firewall administrators become aware of unwittingly coding unenforceable firewall policy when they run into their first case of self-inflicted denial of service. Such denial of service often happens simply because we fail to create a match before the default deny all style rule. The following are some examples of common errors you might make; the first example shows the incorrect way to allow HTTP and FTP:

```
allow tcp from any to any 80
allow tcp from any to any 21
deny tcp from any to any
```

The classic mistake here is forgetting FTP's data channel port 20. That is easy, and in a three-rule set, we pick it up in seconds. In a forty-rule set, it might not be so easy.

Another simple mistake that we make is to write a broad match before a deny. The administrator intends to stop HTTP and FTP, but he writes an allow rule first and the intended deny rules are never processed. This is easy to see in a three-rule set, but it is much harder in a large rule set.

```
allow tcp from any to any
deny tcp from any to any 80
deny tcp from any to any 21
```

If you have a fairly large rule set, pour a cup of coffee, sit down, pay close attention to the keyword any, and ensure that you know exactly what kind of matching your firewall has (is it best fit or the first rule to match wins), you are off to the races.

No Up-Front Policy

The simple mistakes that we just examined are why firewall books and instructors always stress that the first thing to do is to examine your site's policy and then create the rule set. If you just turn the firewall on and then start poking rules in, it is pretty easy to stuff an allow after a deny or vice versa. It really pays off to write a rule set from the ground up. If you are not comfortable with the policy first methodology that we show in this book, create your own rule set, test it, test it some more, and stick with it. Even with good rules that are properly organized though, our policy can be subverted or made unenforceable through those two Mack truck-sized holes living at TCP 80 and 25.

TCP Port 80

Most of us configure our firewalls to allow outbound port 80, HTTP, or the World Wide Web, and the rest of us are looking for employment. If you go to your favorite search engine and do a search on "tunnel port 80," you will find enough to curl your hair. From GNU httptunnel to custom web tunnels to emerging Internet standards, an abundance of tools and techniques is available to encapsulate any kind of network traffic imaginable in packets that appear to be HTTP. Many of these tools aren't just using port 80; they are actually encoding their traffic in HTTP with get, put, POST, and markup language tags. Can the fake or encapsulated traffic be detected? Sometimes it can, but it is pretty difficult, and keyword searches or content inspectors are the best shot. This is a case where your organizational policy really matters. Either you are going to allow HTTP tunneling or you are not. Tunneling is usually for the purpose of evading the firewall, so let's say you don't. If you do catch someone, then your organizational policy needs to clearly state that the individual's head will be mounted on a pole outside the main entrance of the building as a deterrent to others. Port 80 tunneling generally requires intent by someone on the inside; email, however, is the most amazing policy destruction technology of all time.

Email

The primary policy problems with email are users sending sensitive information, binary attachments, automated forwarding, and over-responsive email clients.

Sensitive Information

I did a project for the U.S. Military once whereby I collected nothing but the source, destination, and subject lines of outbound email for a month. I ran that through a keyword search for sensitive technologies. I will never forget watching the color drain from the face of a battle-tested senior officer as I showed him the results. Fortunately, it was only a 4.4 billion dollar-a-year weapons program; it would be a real shame if we were talking serious money. This organization had an unenforceable policy, "Never send sensitive information unencrypted over the Internet." However, these merry tricksters didn't give their employees any way to encrypt, they were against PGP, and they had been implementing PKI for about five years.

As email becomes a primary means of communication, we become more familiar with it and less aware of the risks. As a rule of thumb, before an employee has finished drinking his first cup of coffee, he will attach and send any file you ask for and never remember that he did it.

Don't you just love those cute greeting card programs that people send back and forth? Ever wonder if they might do more than whir or chirp? Content scanners at the perimeter are a good idea, especially for virus scanning. Some of my friends use two scanners, and they tell me time and time again that one scanner picked up the virus and the other missed it. The Royal Canadian Mounted Police has the handle on binary attachments. Whether word documents or programs, the Royal Canadian Mounted Police refuses them all and sends polite notes from its perimeter saying it doesn't accept attachments. Most of us lean way too far in the direction of access over control when it comes to email.

Outlook is the quintessential unenforceable policy engine; if it receives an email from some unknown party, it happily accepts the email's programming instructions. If someone is running Outlook internally, it is probably impossible to secure the perimeter.

Let's say you are in some super-duper secure place, such as the CIA or NSA. In the above-ground world, some whacky macro virus like Melissa variant two million and twelve is jumping from address book to address book, and suddenly the same behavior starts on your classified network that is air gapped from the Internet! What happened? I'd start looking for very large, very high-latency packets (VLVHLPs) immediately!

Lessons that Melissa Taught Us

Before Melissa and Lovebug, not everyone understood how dangerous Outlook's behavior was. I still remember the day I saw the future and shook my head in disbelief. A friend was testing a personal firewall. Someone had sent her an email message with a URL. Outlook kindly retrieved the URL as soon as she highlighted the message so she didn't have to wait for the picture of a flower to which the URL pointed. When Outlook tried to get the flower, her ZoneAlarm alerted. I asked myself, "If Outlook will do that, what else will it do?" Even today as I write this, years after many crazy security flaws and Microsoft Office macro exploits, the answer seems to be "Anything the sender wants it to." In this form-over-function world, I suppose organizations will continue to choose HTML-aware, macro-extendable programs such as Outlook, but I could live with plain, printable ASCII text in email if I had to.

Very Large, Very High-Latency Packets

When we do site security assessments, one of the things we like to do is the hurricane backup test. The idea is simple: a class five hurricane is expected to hit the site in 3–5 hours. Senior management directs that they get a backup of all the data out to a safe location in advance of the hurricane. After some initial scurrying, they start to run backups and load backup tapes. A classic old trick is to wait till they are about loaded and then ask, "Did you get all the data?" They usually nod yes. "What about the data on the user's local drives?" "That's the user's responsibility," they reply. "We back up the servers." "Ummm, and where will you be without your top salesman's contact list, or your CIO's notes?" In general, there is hopping around and a discussion of running to Costco to buy all the zip drives and disks they have. After some flapping, the hurricane only an hour away, we have to leave with whatever backups we have.

The first time we did this and watched the van loaded with all the tapes headed off to discover whether cold backup sites really work, the guy standing next to me commented, "Wow, when disks are in motion, you can think of them as very large, very high-latency packets!" As a security analyst, this is a significant vector to defeat our perimeter's active policy enforcement. VLVHLPs fit in shirt pockets, briefcases, any number of form factors. One thing is certain: every variation of sneaker net—physically moving data around on foot or by vehicle—has the capability to evade perimeter defenses. In fact, several of us on the team have worked in a number of secure facilities where disks are supposed to be registered as they go in any out, and they supposedly have spot checks, but in 20 years, we have never been stopped.

When the terrorists attacked the World Trade Center on 9/11/2001, several cold site vans were circling the blocks as administrators raced to get the VLVHLPs out of the trade center and surrounding buildings. We live in a time of increasing threat. If we are responsible for business continuity, we should think in a far smaller time horizon than 3–5 hours.

Backdoors

Backdoors make our security policy unenforceable by evading our perimeter defenses. Everyone knows that modems can breach perimeter defense, especially when they are connected to operating systems that support ipforwarding. Many countermeasures are available for this, ranging from communication or proactively scanning your phone lines to using digital phone lines. Wireless adds a whole new dimension of challenge; cell phones can surf the web, forward faxes, and connect laptops to the Internet. With 802.11 coming into wide use, organizations would be wise to walk their physical perimeters testing for signal. Don't be fooled by the box that claims they are only good for about a hundred meters. People with amplifiers and modified antennas can get significant range. You can run these tests yourself with a free copy of Network Stumbler (`http://www.netstumbler.com`) and a $200 Orinoco card from `www.wavelan.com`. We need to think about our perimeter as a physical bubble drawn around our physical assets and be ready to test for breaches in a number of ways, from physical access caused by disks moving across the perimeter to RF signal. Access and security does not just apply to the computer or network, but to the organization as a whole. This is why the one true firewall maxim is, "Everything is denied except that which is specifically permitted or that which gets in anyway."

At this point, you should have a lot to think about. If you think of other vectors for unenforceable policy, we would love to hear from you! It is important to be alert for the situations in which policy cannot be enforced. These situations have a tendency to lead to chaos; they encourage people to either ignore or push the envelope on the rules.

How to Develop Policy

Earlier, we pointed out the risks of trying to develop firewall rules without policy. The tendency is to do this willy-nilly, adding a rule here, modifying a rule there, until the rule set becomes difficult to maintain as it grows. Because we are in the active policy enforcement business, sooner or later, there will be controversy about why a certain service is either granted access or controlled. If the firewall administrator has a signed, approved, up-to-date policy to refer to, it can stifle the controversy. We need to have a policy on which to base our access and control decisions. Policy development can be approached in several ways, but in information security, we are probably best off to develop a risk-based approach. For this to work, we identify the risk, communicate what we have learned to authority, update or create security policy, and figure out how to measure compliance.

Identify Risks

It is time for a walkabout. Try not to let this stress you, but you will need to get out of your cubicle and go talk to some people. We realize that computer security types are a fairly introverted bunch, but users are a significant source of risk. Determine how your organization uses computers and networks in the conduct of business, both routinely and under emergency circumstances. You need to ask two questions:

- What data do you have or do you use from a different source that would really hurt the organization if it were not available?

- Do you use the Internet for anything other than email? (Of course if your organization doesn't have a presumption of privacy, you can pull the logs and know what answer to expect before you meet.) Keep in mind that if no policy exists, the users in your organization aren't doing anything wrong. Make sure they understand you are simply trying to establish a baseline, not cause anyone trouble.

These questions will provide insight into the risks that your organization faces. Odds are, this will not be pretty. Just because you are using a personal firewall and keeping your anti-virus up to date doesn't mean anyone else is. You might find that people download games and other untested software, and that they run chat programs that are capable of transferring files. You might even find a copy of Outlook or IIS if you look long enough. The next step will be to pass your findings on the areas of risk to management, the folks that are paid to approve or mitigate business risk.

Where Is It Written?

For many years, I believed that people were rational, and that any two reasonable persons could be expected to make the same decision in a given situation. That isn't so. Really intelligent people will ask questions like, "If we have a firewall, why should we have to patch our systems?" We all know the perimeter cannot guarantee that a system will be 100% protected, 100% of the time. But when people get a notion like that in their head, logic ceases to be the drug of choice. You can try to explain things to them and they just don't get it. What is phenomenal, though, is the power of the written word. When someone asks, "What instruction requires that we do it that way (or at all)?," if you show a written and dated policy signed by upper management, a surprising number of times the person nods and accepts the policy.

Communicate Your Findings

When communicating what you have learned to management, keep it simple, balanced, and fairly concise. If you mention an individual's name with respect to a problem or risk you have discovered at any point, management is likely to think of this as a personal attack and dismiss everything that you have done. Keep the general tone the types of problems that you found and the implications. When possible, give an example of where this type of behavior was financially damaging to an organization.

SirCam as an Awareness Tool

I worked with a group that was pretty lax about anti-virus, and nothing I said seemed to get them to understand the risks of malicious code. After SirCam hit in July 2001, I was at a restaurant with the group's senior manager. We were discussing a business deal, and I told him about a law firm that was hit by SirCam over the weekend. When the firm came in that Monday, the phones were lit up because sensitive documents of all sorts had been blasted over the Internet. It was fun to watch his face as he suddenly got it. Now the group has email screening on the firewall, and the workstations update their anti-virus signatures weekly.

Offer management a range of options for managing those risks. It's probably best to use two different anti-virus tools on the mail gateway, but if management decides to make the investment in only one, that is their choice. Our job is to give management the data in such a way they can make a reasonable decision. Don't try to do this by discussion only. Make sure you leave a written summary of your findings as well.

Create or Update the Security Policy as Needed

If no written policy is in place, write it and get it signed by upper-level management. Later in this chapter, we will cover the elements of policy and give you a few more tips for creating policy. However, life is too short to write policy from the ground up if you can avoid it. You don't write a makefile from scratch every time you build a new software distribution, do you? You usually modify an existing makefile. Many policy references are on the SANS web server (`http://www.sans.org/newlook/resources/policies/policies.htm`), and an Internet search should turn up plenty of additional resources. We went through a lot of trouble to build the case for avoidance of unenforceable policy. One way to prevent unenforceable policy is to build in methods that allow us to audit compliance.

Determine Policy Compliance

If you cannot measure compliance (conformance), the policy is unenforceable. If the policy is specific enough, it should be easy to determine if any item that we are testing is in compliance or not. For instance, if we are only allowed to play *Star Trek* two days a year, it is possible to audit the system for the presence of that software. If trading sound files is against policy, we can monitor logs for the default ports of tools like Gnutella, but also use Snort or a similar tool to look for the .mp3 file extension. One warning: If your plan is to spot check, make sure someone spot checks to see if the spot checks actually happen. The spot checks should be logged and should occur quarterly. Audit the spot check log. Again, if there are no metrics and no controls to ensure compliance, it is probably unenforceable policy. If security supposedly spot checks for disk media at secure installations and it really isn't happening, the security function will not detect violations of their policy. A word of warning though: most people will choose compromise over confrontation. Management might have the best of intentions. They might say all the right words, but make sure you do not run afoul of your corporate culture, or your policy experience might be a very unpleasant one.

Sound Out the Organization's Rules and Culture

Every organization has a particular style, an ethic or image. Many times, a senior manager maintains this style and the organization buys into it to some extent. Does the organization favor managers over technical people? Do they favor seniority over excellent performance? Do the rules apply to everyone, or only some people? Is the organization laid-back or aggressive? If you are writing policy, make sure it reflects the culture or it is certainly going to be unenforceable.

I like to ask a few questions to determine the security posture of the organization before looking at policy. Some of those questions include the following:

- What is the presumption of privacy, including phone and network monitoring? Do employees have a reasonable expectation that the files on their computer, what they say on the phone, and what they send on the Internet are protected communications?

- Are random physical searches permitted, and is there an active search program?

- Is the perimeter configured to allow all connections that are initiated from inside the organization?

- Are employees able to add software or modify settings on their desktop systems?

Are administrators able to make changes without going through a formal configuration management-approval program? The answers to these questions can really help you see the "tone" that you would expect their policy to have. Then you can continue to do an assessment of the culture by reading existing written policy and writing down unwritten policy.

Comparing Policy and Culture

Written policy can be found in a number of ways. It includes official policy, of course, but also directives from senior management, contracts, and other legal agreements, and even existing Human Resources cases. It can be an interesting experience to compare the official policy that is listed in documents with the other sources of policy we have described. The wise analyst examines the alternate sources and the cases of enforced policy to be alert for indications that the corporate culture does not completely agree with its stated policy. In a sense, this is just like Windows 2000 Active Directory: you have the group policy and the local security policy. These two might not totally agree. If you want your Windows system to be secure, you need to be aware of what the effective policy is at all times. This is the same principle at work when we consider official policy and corporate culture.

Note

Policy must be documented and consistently enforced. Humans have trouble with this, but perimeter devices do not. This is why it is imperative to consider the human side of the equation before engaging the perimeter.

Written Policy

The first place to start looking for your corporate culture is the Human Resources handbook that is given to every new employee. At some point, this document was almost certainly approved by senior management as the document they wanted new employees to see. Be sure to check that the same management team that approved the employee handbook is still in power. Also, directives and other standard policy information might be available. It can't hurt to check those, being sensitive to the date they were created. Checking these sources gives you an idea of what some combination of policy writers and management think they want the policy to be.

Directives

Senior management will have approved the primary policy documents of their organization, but they might have modified them afterward by issuing directives. Generally, an executive secretary or administrative officer serves as the organizational memory. Clearly, this person would not be comfortable sharing all email or directives with you, but you are only interested in directives that modify either access or control. Even informal emails from senior management can have a large effect on a corporate climate.

How do you ensure that the administrative officer takes this exercise seriously? We suggest a checklist that lists the proposed perimeter policy based to the extent possible on the written policy. This should be in English, not in a firewall rules language. This checklist can be done with bullets, for example:

- All internal systems are maintained according to the organization's best practice checklist.
- All connections that are implemented from the inside are considered trusted.
- Acme Corporation, a strategic partner, has implemented direct connection to us and is not blocked or monitored for the following services: file transfer, access to our product's database, or electronic mail.

Then you provide a place on the checklist for the administrative officer: "I have reviewed senior management directives, and the following directives and instructions indicate the proposed policy might need to be modified. If none, so state." This way if the CEO or president of the company is offended by the perimeter's active policy enforcement, you have a layer of protection, a firewall between the angry manager and yourself.

Contracts and Human Resources Rulings

Legal contracts can effectively modify corporate policy as can the hiring and firing disciplinary rulings from Human Resources. Many policies have a references section, and if you are aware of documents that modify the policy, you can include these in references as you update.

Unwritten Policy

If you immediately jumped to the conclusion, "No, policy *has* to be written," then we would ask you to consider the following:

- We have always done it that way!
- We have tried that five times and it always just dies.
- I wouldn't go there if I were you.

Every organization has hidden rules. Crossing these rules usually doesn't cause employment termination, but you can waste a lot of time. Every organization has wise folks who have been around for a long time, and these are the folks with whom to chat. Don't ask them to sign your checklist, but ask where the minefields are. You can always raise points with the senior manager who approves the implementation of the perimeter policy. Senior managers are paid to make the hard calls.

A chapter that is devoted to implementation of policy for perimeter devices cannot possibly cover all the elements of policy—that would be a book all by itself. That said, we do want to make sure that we discuss the most common elements.

Elements of Policy

You can think about the elements of policy as the outline or skeleton. When we learned to code, many of us were taught to build the main program and put in dummy function calls. The idea was to call the function and make sure we returned so that the flow of the program would work. This limits troubleshooting to one function at a time, so we would be able to build the program efficiently. The elements of policy serve the same purpose; you can think of them as function calls in a main program.

We are not going to provide an exhaustive list of the elements of policy. This policy is tailored to a perimeter situation, so it will not need everything that you find in more Human Resource-related policies. Keep in mind that we need to focus on access and control with the policy. We will discuss authority, scope, and expiration next. We will also cover the characteristics of good policy.

Authority

We need to consider levels of authority: the manager who is authorized to sign the paper, and the policy under which this policy might fall. Often, a higher-level ruling policy exists. For instance, a perimeter policy might reference the organization's information security policy, and that might reference the organization's security policy. If this is not policy at the highest level, then to whom does it apply? Everyone, or perhaps everyone in a particular department or group? This is why we need to explicitly define the scope of the policy.

Scope

The scope section of policy identifies the depth and breadth of coverage (to whom or what the policy applies). Is it for one element of the organization, or will it also apply to contractor agencies who work for your organization? It is worth paying careful attention to the scope. If the scope proves to be incorrect, you might end up having to support two firewall policies: one for group A and another for group B. Of course, things change, and the policy should be reevaluated periodically. This is the purpose of the expiration information.

Expiration

Some policy is only valid for a short period of time. If your organization merges with another, you might have a transitional policy for 30–90 days. Policy is fairly static, with the exception of perimeter policy, which needs to be reviewed at least yearly. Taking the time to craft good policy makes it easier to check periodically.

Hallmarks of Good Policy

Anything worth doing is worth doing well, and that certainly applies to policy. Let's take a few minutes to define what good policy is and is not. It does *not* have to be wordy, use obscure words, or use acronyms. It *does* need to state the issue, state what is expected, and be a tool that can be used to measure compliance. To best accomplish this task, the policy should be specific, concise, and realistic.

Specificity and Clarity

Specificity is one of the most important aspects of good policy. One of the best ways to avoid unenforceable policy is to reduce the ambiguity. Many times, people who write policy attempt to write in a formal tone that makes the policy hard to read. Just state the issue in plain readable language. It is imperative to be specific about the following:

- What needs to be done. Enough information should be available to create a checklist from the policy that is sufficient to ensure compliance.
- Why the policy exists and what the problem is designed to solve. Rational people need to understand what the problem is to fully buy into the solution.
- Who is responsible for accomplishing the tasks that are listed on the policy. This is particularly important if procedures are developed from the policy. It must be clear who is responsible for completing the procedures.

The policy should be reviewed for clarity to make sure the reader can understand the policy. One simple way to test for clarity is to have one of the individuals identified as being responsible determine whether he understands the responsibility. Ask this person to read the policy and describe in his own words what the policy requires to be done. One of the best ways to make a policy clear is to make it concise.

Conciseness

Rules of thumbs are dangerous, so this is meant to challenge you to say what you need to say in a reasonable length. A specific policy topic (such as antivirus signature updates) shouldn't exceed two pages. Many organizations limit them to one page.

Realism

Perhaps you have heard of the mnemonic SMART. It stands for specific, measurable, achievable, realistic, and time-based, and it is a good basis for effective policy. SMART also illustrates the importance of a realistic policy. Security policy shouldn't require people to try to implement things that can't be implemented. The *r* for realistic is such an important characteristic; if the policy is not realistic, it is unenforceable.

Perimeter Considerations

Next, we consider how policy can be implemented in our perimeter architecture. If good policy already exists, we simply need to assess our perimeter technology, asking the question, "Is it possible for us to implement our policy with the technology we have?" Now that we have a firm foundation in what policy is and we are sensitive to unenforceable policy, let's go back to the notion of active policy enforcement. We will discuss how to map our architecture to our policy, and how the limitations of technology sometimes force us to modify our policy.

Real-World Operations and Policy

All too often we have to bend policy to match our architecture. This doesn't have to be the guiding principle, however. As we close out this chapter, let's cover some of the technologies and consider their implications for our policy position. Because perimeters examine and log packets, privacy issues are associated with running a perimeter. In addition, as email bounces or gets sent back to us, we might see a user's private thoughts. Our policy needs to prepare us for these situations in which limitations in our technology throw us information we might not expect to see. Policy must provide guidance to administrators and to those who operate content-sensing devices about what is and is not appropriate when exposed to private information.

Note

Every time we buy a new product or upgrade a system, our goal must be to build an architecture that actively enforces our policy.

Presumption of Privacy

If you are a student at a university in the United States, you have a presumption of privacy. Certainly, some speech is not protected; for example, you can't threaten the President or threaten to take your own life and expect confidence. On the whole, however, custom, practice, and law protects your communications.

If you are a uniformed member of the United States armed forces, you tend to live on the other side of the spectrum. Every time you enter a military base, you are greeted by a sign letting you know that you and your possessions are subject to search. The telephones have stickers warning that they might be monitored. You know that you do not have a presumption of privacy.

In an earlier section, we gathered and evaluated both the written and unwritten policy, which gives us the groundwork to determine what the presumption of privacy policy is for our organization. This helps us make perimeter design decisions. If you are designing for a university, you probably shouldn't collect content of packets. One of the engineering requirements for the Shadow intrusion detection system was to be able to detect attacks without looking at content. Widely deployed anti-virus tools might be the "canary in the coal mine" that alerts us to a user who is circumventing the perimeter. Usually, we can use the information about the presence of a virus, but what do we do when we start getting arbitrary files from someone's hard disk courtesy of a W32.SirCam type infection? It depends on the presumption of privacy. Email handling is another sticky point.

Email Handling

Have you ever worked in an organization in which people were fairly certain that the postmaster read their email? Needless to say, it should be grounds for termination if someone intercepts and reads mail without cause or written permission, but bounced mail comes to the postmaster. Anyone who has been a postmaster for any length of time has a story to tell about bounced mail. A postmaster must try to handle this by giving a quick look at the mail headers and ignoring the content, but sometimes it is inevitable. If the mail to the postmaster is a complaint from an outsider who received mail from our organization, what then? We probably do need to respond and help in the investigation by collecting the logs that corroborate or disprove the complaint. This is just one of the ways that working with the perimeter defenses can vault us into the wonderful world of incident handling.

Incident Handling—Preparation, Containment

Consider the six stages of incident handling:

- Preparation
- Detection
- Containment
- Eradication
- Recovery
- Lessons learned

It quickly becomes apparent that the perimeter is a crucial player in the process. Building a perimeter that allows flexible active policy enforcement is one of the best ways to *prepare* for an incident. The event might well be detected by firewall or intrusion-detection logs. After detection, we can use the perimeter to assist in the containment phase, where we typically make a decision between two approaches: contain and clean or watch and learn.

If you have a system that you suspect is infected, your policy might be to contain and clean. You might choose to lock it down tight and prevent traffic from coming from the Internet to this system, and also prevent outbound traffic from the system to the Internet. In this book, we cover egress filtering, but it is worth emphasizing that a compromised box might be sending packets with spoofed source addresses. If you have a switched environment, you can often accomplish lockout right at the wall socket. Alternatively, you might decide to increase your instrumentation and see what you can learn about the motives and techniques of the hackers.

The watch and learn approach to incident handling takes access and control to the level of an art form. The Honeynet Project (http://www.honeynet.org/) has done more to advance the state of observing attackers in the wild who have been granted access, while maintaining control over the state of the system, than any other group. If you are considering this approach to incident handling, then you would be wise to visit Honeynet's web site, get on the mailing list, and get involved. Tools such as rate-limiting switches can be helpful with this approach. Instead of denying the attacker access to the suspected machine, you throttle the bandwidth to make the attacker's experience a longer wait. This gives you a little more time to analyze the situation. Watch and learn is a higher risk strategy than contain and clean, but the potential payoff is also much higher.

Incident Handling, Eradication—Lessons Learned

At some point, usually within 24 hours of a suspected compromise, the primary focus is to get the system back in business. The first step is to completely clean the system and then to restore operations. The perimeter systems can be used for additional monitoring and filtering. Often, the attacker comes back, and we must remain alert for this. In addition, the logs from the perimeter help tell the whole story and are useful during the lessons learned phase of the process. If you don't understand how you were attacked and make the appropriate changes, it is all too likely it will happen again tomorrow. In the final section of this chapter, we will consider policy that provides the security controls that apply to firewall administrators.

Rules of the Road

The perimeter sets the rules of the road. If we use active policy enforcement to manage access and control for various information assets, when and how do we have the authority to make changes in the perimeter? Who has the authority to request these changes, and under what circumstances? Who makes the final approval? Whatever your process is to approve changes, make sure that you document them. Often, an apparently small change in filtering policy can have unintended side effects. If a change log exists, it can be of great help to those who have to troubleshoot the system.

The Firewall Admin That Shouldn't Have

When I was working for the U.S. Department of Defense, I noticed some suspicious traffic on the Shadow Intrusion Detection System they had deployed. After considerable analysis, it was fairly clear that there was a complete TCP connection, stimulated from HTTP, but on a high port with a three-way handshake, a data exchange, and a graceful close. How could this be? A sandbox violation seemed impossible. The client system was behind an application gateway firewall, and things like Java and ActiveX were not permitted. How had the client been directed to open the connection from the inside of the facility? When I went to see the firewall administrator with the logs, I learned that the firewall admininistrator had turned off the HTTP proxy. My jaw dropped and I asked why. "I got a phone call and someone complained it was too slow" was the reply. Make sure you understand and follow the process in your organization for making changes to the perimeter's policy.

Summary

Policy is not something to be left to a non-technical administrative worker. Everyone who is involved in perimeter design and operations is involved in policy. The perimeter can be viewed as an engine or series of engines that actively enforces your organization's policy relating to access and control of traffic. For the perimeter to do a good job of enforcing the rules of the road, you need a comprehensive policy. Be sensitive to situations in which your stated policy cannot be enforced. Strive for a policy that is clear, specific, and concise so that any reasonable, technically educated person can look at the policy, and perimeter rules, and understand the relation between the two. Never forget your responsibilities in terms of maintaining the privacy and dignity of others. You are the keeper of the gate for your organization; don't let an organization down by misusing the information and authority that is available to you.

References

1 "Security Policy." SANS Security Essentials Course.

II

Extending the Perimeter

The Role of a Router

6

A ROUTER IS A DEVICE THAT INTERCONNECTS TWO or more networks. Because of its role as a gateway between networks, it becomes a focal point of your network's security. Just like any entranceway to a secured perimeter, efforts must be made to reinforce the router to ensure your environment's safety.

The role that the router plays in your security structure depends greatly on its placement and the networks that it joins together. The router might be a simple border router that joins your network to the Internet and relies on an internal firewall to take care of the majority of the security concerns. Or perhaps the router is used as the lone perimeter security device for a small- or low-risk network or a network subsegment. In either case, the main function of a router is the forwarding of packets from one network segment to another. Depending on the implementation you choose, you might strive to have the router focus on routing and perform routine security tasks as part of a larger defense in depth posture. Conversely, you could implement the router as an all-in-one perimeter security solution in an environment that has no other protection and reinforce this environment with additional defense in depth.

In this chapter, we discuss the router, its functions as a component of defense in depth, ways to implement it as an all-in-one security solution, and ways to protect the router through various hardening techniques. All examples use Cisco routers (Internetwork Operating System, or IOS, version 12.1 or greater), although the principles demonstrated could be applied to almost any brand of equivalent router.

The Router as a Perimeter Device

Simply stated, the main function of a router is the forwarding of packets between two network segments. This is often forgotten when it is time to implement a security structure. Many additional duties are thrust onto the router, and ultimately, performance suffers. Routers, like computers, have processors, memory, and storage space.

How Can You Tell Whether Your Router Is Overburdened?

When your router is overtaxed, many strange things can happen. Packets can be dropped, things can pass that shouldn't, and so on. To check whether your router is overburdened, look at its processor utilization. With a Cisco router, you can do this with the command `router#show processes cpu`.

This command shows the amount of Central Processing Unit (CPU, or another word for the processor) usage for each process. A command with even more interesting output is `router#show proc cpu history`.

Notice that this time, we abbreviated the word *processes* as *proc*. This command shows your CPU usage in a graphical format for the past 60 seconds, the past 60 minutes, and the past 72 hours. This can give you a much better idea of what kind of workload your router has had over given periods of time and when performing specific functions. If you are wondering how your router's memory is being dispersed, try the following command:

```
router#sh proc memory
```

This shows how much memory each of the running router processes is using. This can give you some major insight as to why you might need more RAM. With tools like these, the mysteries of an overworked router can be solved in record time!

You must consider these points when you're choosing a router for your specific network environment. Many of the features of expensive, high-power routers are also available in the lower power, more reasonably priced models; however, it is important to check under the hood. Make sure that the router you choose can handle enough bandwidth to fit your site's needs. Also be sure it has enough memory and storage available to handle the features that you plan to employ. Information is available from your router vendor on the amount of memory required for the features you need.

Routers usually don't have much storage space available, and storage upgrades are at a premium. When considering your design environment, think about the ramifications of implementing an external storage area for log files, configuration file backups, and operating software. Most likely, the router in question uses Syslog for remote logging and Trivial File Transfer Protocol (TFTP) for the transfer of configuration files and operating software updates. Therefore, ensure that you have systems that provide these services to the router to supplement its internal storage space.

Routing

To begin routing in a simple environment, a router needs little configuration. If you have two separate subnets that need to communicate, drop the router in and configure each connecting interface with an address for its attached network, make sure that routing is enabled, and *voilá*—instant communication! The router knows the IP address of its two interfaces and can apply this knowledge to forward traffic sent from one network to the other. Complexities begin to arise as the network segments the router isn't directly connected are added to the configuration. Because the router doesn't have direct knowledge of these segments, it must be told about them with statements in its routing table. Such statements can be added manually by an administrator (static routes) or dynamically by updates from other routers. Static routes are easy to configure in a small environment. On Cisco routers, configuration can be accomplished with a command such as `router (config)#ip route 10.10.10.0 255.255.255.0 10.1.1.1 1`.

In this command, `10.10.10.0` is the network address range you want to tell the router about, and `255.255.255.0` is its subnet mask. `10.1.1.1` is the address of the router or gateway device to which the router should forward information that is destined for the `10.10.10.0` network. The single number `1` at the end of the statement is a route metric. It can be any number between 1–255 and tells the router how far away the device in question is; if multiple choices are available, the router can make an informed decision about which route is the fastest.

The `ip route` statement can also be used in circumstances in which hundreds of networks might be unknown to our router, such as for a connection to the Internet. To forward all unknown traffic to an Internet router, we use the following form:

```
ip route 0.0.0.0 0.0.0.0 gateway IP
```

`gateway IP` is the address of the next hop Internet router. This statement is typically called a *default route*, or the gateway of last resort.

Static routes offer a secure routing method for configuring a small environment, but what happens when we have 100 routers in our corporation? Do we want to program all the necessary static routes manually? Of course not! This is when dynamic routing protocols come into play.

Dynamic routing protocols allow properly configured routers to learn from each other about available routing paths. Protocols such as Routing Information Protocol version 1 (RIPv1), Open Shortest Path First (OSPF), RIPv2, Interior Gateway Routing Protocol (IGRP), Enhanced Interior Gateway Routing Protocol (EIGRP), and so on, allow routers in a large environment to learn on-the-fly about one another. This process can simplify the configurations of what would be hundreds of static routing tables. This dynamic environment has its own set of problems, however. From a performance standpoint, all those updates travel around the network so that the routers can learn about each other. From a security standpoint, how do we know that the update that is being sent to our router is not from a nefarious outside party? Such updates could be sent in an effort to gain access to information on our network or sabotage its infrastructure.

Cisco Shorthand

Some of the examples throughout this chapter take advantage of Cisco router shorthand. On Cisco routers, you can use the fewest letters of a command that are different from all other commands. As long as the abbreviated form of the command cannot also represent another valid command, it will work. Otherwise, you will get this message:

```
% Ambiguous command:
```

This message is then followed by the characters you typed in framed in quotes. An example of this is the popular command `show configuration` being entered as `sh conf`. `show` is the only other command that begins with `sh`, and `configuration` is the only appropriate command-line option to follow `show` that begins with `conf`. If you tried to use the command `sh con`, you would receive the `ambiguous command` message because `con` could represent `configuration` or `connection`, which are both valid options.

The command `copy run star` actually represents `copy running-config startup-config`. You save a lot of time in typing, and if you are a bad typist, the less typing the better!

Secure Dynamic Routing

One important part of keeping an environment that uses routing safe is secure implementation of dynamically updated routing protocols, such as RIP (versions 1 and 2), OSPF, Border Gateway Protocol (BGP), IGRP, and EIGRP. Dynamic routing protocols are often a necessary part of a complex internetworking environment. However, if they are not configured correctly, dynamic routing protocols can be an easily exploited security hole. Some routing protocols use numbering schemes that require some knowledge of the specific details of your network's routing configuration to send acceptable routing updates. However, these numbers are transmitted in the clear (without encryption), so they can be sniffed. In addition, often the numbers chosen are guessed easily and might not provide adequate protection. Unless the configuration steps listed in the upcoming sections are taken, the use of these protocols might leave a gaping hole in what would be an otherwise secure network environment.

Route Authentication

Some dynamic routing protocols offer advanced protection known as *route authentication*. Despite its name, this process might not involve the use of a username and password combination to verify that updates are coming from a known friendly router. Actually, on a Cisco router, the process of route authentication involves the use of a secret keyword that is configured into all routers that are to share their dynamic routing information. This keyword, used in conjunction with the routing update information, generates a Message Digest 5 (MD5) hash signature to be sent with dynamic route updates. If this hash information is not included with the updates or is incorrect, contacted routers should ignore the provided route information. Protocols that support routing authentication include RIPv2, OSPF, EIGRP, and BGP. Two dynamic routing protocols of note that don't support this feature are RIPv1 and IGRP. Cisco routers have a feature that performs a simple check to help secure these two protocols. The `validate-update-source` command (which is configured by default) checks the source address of incoming RIP and IGRP updates to verify that they are from a neighboring device on the same network segment as the interface on which the update was received. This feature helps prevent false router updates from outside the network.

You could install route authentication on an OSPF routed network by using the `ip ospf message-digest-key 10 md5 secretkey` command.

You must enter this statement at the interface that will be propagating the routing updates. (For a refresher on the Cisco IOS interface, check out Chapter 2, "Packet Filtering.") `10` is the *keyid*, which is a number that represents the unique secret key that you define, and `secretkey` is the actual key used to create the MD5 hashes that protect your routing updates. The importance of the keyid value comes into play if you want to change keys in an active environment. You can simply add the new `secretkey` value in a similar statement with a different keyid number. The router identifies that it has a new key and starts sending two routing updates: one with the new key value, and one with the original key value. This behavior is by-design to allow a window of opportunity for you, the administrator, to change the keys on all other routers that share common routing information. After all routers have been updated, remove the original statement so that only one key is used. After all, using two statements simultaneously requires twice the bandwidth.

To activate the MD5 authentication, use the statement `area 0 authentication message-digest`.

This command is entered in global configuration mode. The 0 represents the OSPF area in which you will be using MD5 route authentication. It might differ depending on how OSPF is configured in your particular environment.

Implementation of router authentication varies slightly depending on the routing protocol, so be sure to check proper documentation before implementing in non–OSPF environments.

Other Dynamic Routing Defenses

Another way you can be sure to prevent tampering with your router tables is by blocking updates from networks that are deemed unsafe. For example, what if you had an extranet connection to a customer? You might not want their routers to have the ability to change the configuration of your routers (accidentally or on purpose). You can configure the interface that connects your router to theirs to deny routing updates. On Cisco routers, this is accomplished with the `passive interface` command, which prevents the interface from accepting *any* routing updates. Its syntax is as follows:

```
passive interface e1
```

In this case, `e1` is the interface that you want to keep from accepting updates. This command can have different effects with different routing protocols, and it is imperative that you keep this in mind when choosing to use it in your network infrastructure. For example, most routing protocols will still send out routing updates through the interface in question, although ignoring any updates inbound. However, with EIGRP, no routing information is allowed in or out of the interface in question.

Completely blocking all traffic coming into an interface might not fit many scenarios. What if trusted routers also existed outside this interface, and you only wanted to prevent certain routes from being accepted? Cisco routers use a `distribute-list` command that prevents the propagation or the acceptance of specified route updates through configured interfaces. For example, if you want to prevent outside routers from being able to make changes in routing information for a mission–critical network segment in your internal infrastructure, you can use `distribute-list 112 in e1`.

Here, `e1` is the interface that connects you to the outside routers, and `112` is an access control list (ACL) that defines the network address range of the mission–critical segment. The access list can define ranges of allowed or disallowed IP routing information (depending on whether it is a permit or deny ACL). In a similar manner, a `distribute-list out` command can be used to disallow the sending of a route update that includes information on how to route traffic to your top-secret lab. The syntax is `distribute-list 113 out e1`.

Again, *e1* is the interface you want to prevent routing information from leaving, and 113 is the access list number that defines the address range of the top-secret lab. Remember that the access list always defines the address range of the segment that you don't want to accept or propagate routing information. It does not represent the addresses of segments that you want to prevent from receiving or sending the information.

The Router as a Security Device

Because the router is traditionally the entranceway to a network, it plays an important part in network security. For this reason, routers have been designed with many built-in security features such as packet filters, stateful firewall features, Network Address Translation (NAT), and Virtual Private Network (VPN) support. The question is whether a router is utilized as your only security device or as a piece of a larger defense-in-depth security structure. In a perfect (secure) world, the answer would always be (as a part of a larger security structure), letting the router focus on its primary function, and allowing firewalls, intrusion detection systems (IDSs), and so on handle the burden of the security concerns. In this section, we look at scenarios that use a router as part of defense in depth and also as the primary security solution. We also explore the technologies that are often implemented when using a router as a lone security device, such as NAT, context-based access control (CBAC), ACLs, and so on. In addition, we look at the technologies that can be employed to make the router a complement to a greater security scheme.

The Router as a Part of Defense in Depth

In Chapter 11, "Design Fundamentals," we go into detail on the logistics of placing a router as part of the defense-in-depth structure and the functions that it should perform. In this section, we predominately focus on the technologies to make a router an effective part of defense in depth and ways to implement those technologies.

A router's role as part of defense in depth can vary depending upon the related pieces of the overall security scheme. For example, it would be foolish to implement a router with stateful inspection capabilities in conjunction with a stateful firewall. Typically, the rule of thumb is to keep the router from doing more than it has to, and let it focus on what it is good at.

Packet Filtering

As stated in Chapter 2, "Packet Filtering," blocking access from ranges of addresses is something that routers do well. It makes sense to take advantage of this strong suit when using the router as a role player in conjunction with a stateful firewall, by utilizing the router for ingress and egress filtering.

It is logical to implement ingress filters at the furthermost point on your perimeter, which is most likely your border router. Having the router perform this function offloads some of the burden from the firewall, allowing it to focus on the things for which it is better suited, such as the stateful inspection of defined protocols. Egress filtering is also a good choice for a router that is working in conjunction with other perimeter firewalls; blocking or allowing entire network ranges is something that packet filters are well suited for. Due to the structuring of the TCP/IP packet and the means by which matches are made with the standard packet filter, blocking a range of network addresses is simple bit matching that is difficult to circumvent on a router and that can be accomplished efficiently. For this reason, any time whole ranges of network addresses need to be blocked or allowed, the router is an excellent candidate for a point of implementation.

For more information on the best ways to implement egress and ingress filters and to utilize the packet-filtering features of a router, refer to Chapter 2.

Network-Based Application Recognition (NBAR)

Recently, routers have begun to be utilized in another way as a part of defense in depth. Cisco's network-based application recognition (NBAR) is a feature that was originally designed to help quality of service (QoS) issues (with full functionality available in IOS 12.1(2)e or later). With the onset of bandwidth-devouring streaming-multimedia applications and applications that require high QoS such as Voice over IP (VOIP), a method had to be created to allocate bandwidth based on the applications that were being used. NBAR can be used to allocate at least a certain amount of bandwidth to an activity or traffic type or to limit bandwidth for a given traffic type.

You might be wondering why QoS commands are being mentioned in a book about security. In today's world, security is more than disallowing or allowing access to resources. It also includes the protection of service demands and available bandwidth. Because of the increased threat of denial of service (DoS) attacks, protecting the bandwidth we have to offer our business or clients has become a major point of concern. A business relying on e-commerce whose storefront is inaccessible due to inadequate bandwidth can face a serious financial hardship. A lack of bandwidth equates to a DoS whether it is due to an outside malicious DoS attack or mismanaged use of internal bandwidth. Using solutions such as NBAR can prevent this mismanagement, keeping a "governor" on high-bandwidth activities that don't serve as an important resource for your business. For example, if your site relies on e-commerce to exist and you share bandwidth between e-commerce applications and Internet access for employees, NBAR would prevent a DoS condition caused from all of your employees simultaneously tuning in to the latest Victoria's Secret streaming fashion show.

NBAR can recognize traffic based on HTTP information—including MIME types, URLs, and host names. It can also search on static and dynamic port information. After the traffic is identified, it can be marked, and then a policy determining the amount of bandwidth allowed can be applied. This policy can be used in many creative ways to control QoS and protect application bandwidth.

For example, in a business environment, you might want to limit the bandwidth for multimedia applications to a fraction of your total Internet connection bandwidth so that they don't interfere with higher priority business applications. Using the following commands limits the bandwidth for all defined multimedia applications to 10 kilobits per second (kbps) total:

Tip

Cisco Express Forwarding must be enabled for NBAR to function.

```
router(config)#class-map match-any av
router(config-cmap)#match protocol http mime "audio/*"
router(config-cmap)#match protocol http mime "video/*"
router(config)#class-map match-any images
router(config-cmap)#match protocol http url "*.gif"
router(config-cmap)#match protocol http url "*.jpg|*.jpeg"
```

`av` and `images` are the unique names for the class maps, and `audio/*` and `video/*` are the MIME types for which we want to control QoS. With the `images` class map, we specifically limit the bandwidth for defined picture types as well.

Then both of these class maps can be combined into one all-inclusive class map:

```
router(config)#class-map match-any mmedia
router(config-cmap)#match class-map av
router(config-cmap)#match class-map images
```

Notice the use of the `match-any` keyword. The keyword `match-all` (not shown) requires that all of the listed criteria be met, whereas `match-any` allows a match if any of the listed criteria is the same. Because we want to affect traffic that matches either of the listed class maps, we must use `match-any`.

Now we will create a policy on how much bandwidth our `mmedia` class map will be assigned:

```
router(config)#policy-map mybusiness
router(config-pmap)#class mmedia
router(config-pmap-c)#police 10000 conform transmit exceed drop
```

`mybusiness` is a unique policy name that represents all class-maps for which we want to control QoS on an interface. Other class-maps could be applied in this same policy map. We apply the class-map `mmedia` that we created previously, and then allow no more than 10kbps of our 256KB bandwidth to it with the `police` command.

Finally, we apply the policy to an interface using the following command:

```
router(config-if)#service-policy output mybusiness
```

Here, *mybusiness* is the policy name previously defined, and `output` is the correct direction on the interface to which we choose to apply it.

NBAR has also become a method to prevent outside attacks from causing a DoS condition. With the advent of Code Red and Nimda worms, many sites that properly patched their servers still fell victim to the "noise" generated by other infected locations. They had no means to protect their bandwidth from the repeated assaults from outside infectors. By placing NBAR as a screening mechanism on border routers, you can effectively prevent just such a DoS condition.

The setup is similar to our previous example. We simply create another class map. This class map can be used to screen incoming malicious traffic that has a known uniquely identifiable structure, or *footprint*.

Note

Don't allow yourself to be lulled into a false sense of security. NBAR screening for malicious traffic is a dynamic process. As variants are discovered, the footprints that are used to screen content must be updated.

Our class map will include Cisco's suggested match information for Code Red, Nimda, and some current variants:

```
router(config)#class-map match-any web-attacks
router(config-cmap)#match protocol http url "*.ida*"
router(config-cmap)#match protocol http url "*cmd.exe*"
router(config-cmap)#match protocol http url "*root.exe*"
router(config-cmap)#match protocol http url "*readme.eml*"
```

This new class map can be added to an existing policy that is applied in the same direction on the same interfaces, or if you don't have a like policy, create a new one:

```
router(config)#Policy-map attacks
router(config-pmap)#class web-attacks
router(config-pmap-c)#police 10000 3000 3000 conform-action drop exceed-action drop
violate-action drop
```

Notice that the policy map looks similar to the last example, with the exception of the `police` command. Because of the addition of the `violate-action` keyword, we need to add burst speeds after the first bandwidth listing. However, the three numbers specified are meaningless because all defined actions will drop the identified traffic. Cisco has documented this as a solution for bandwidth issues in these situations, and can be found at `http://www.cisco.com/warp/public/63/nbar_acl_codered.shtml`.

> **Note**
>
> Realize that your border router will experience additional load from this NBAR screening process, and a seriously over-burdened router can also create a DoS condition.

Additional settings can be included on your router to limit the effect of DoS attacks. For an article on protecting against various other DoS attacks on Cisco routers, see `http://www.cisco.com/warp/public/707/newsflash.html`.

The Router as a Lone Perimeter Security Solution

In some environments, the router can be used as an effective perimeter security solution on its own. It can be used as a sole means of defense for a remote or home office, for an internal segment of your network, or as a security solution for a low-risk facility where it wouldn't be cost effective to add an additional firewall or other security device. No matter what the deployment, a properly configured router can provide a good base for a perimeter defense. However, it is still important to apply defense in depth principles beyond the router. Relying on any single perimeter device as your *only* security leaves you only one step from being compromised. An outsider needs to find only a single flaw to have access to your entire network.

Router Placement

The placement of your router might determine some of the security concerns that you should consider when deciding on the technologies that you can implement.

A border router that has to serve as an all-in-one security solution might have many duties to perform. Not only is it the router of network traffic between your network and the outside world, but it must also provide security. Depending on the environment, this might be accomplished with ACLs or stateful CBAC support. (For more information on CBAC, look at the "Technology Choices" section later in this chapter.) Also, since it is the border of your network, it may be necessary to implement NAT or Port Address Translation (PAT) to allow the use of a private addressing scheme internally. In turn it may be where VPN connections are decoded and information passed on to internal hosts. One important thing to remember when your border router is your sole security solution is that *it* is vulnerable. Many border routers are configured to securely protect internal hosts, and yet are open to attack themselves. In the section on router hardening, we discuss means to defend the lone router from being exploited.

Another way that a router can be placed is at internal subnetting points. IP networks are subnetted for various reasons, including performance and security. A router must be placed at the points where the subnetted segments join together to facilitate communication. Depending on environmental circumstances, a router might be a good device for enforcing resource separation on the network. For example, when subnetting off a research and development lab, you might want to consider preventing inbound access from other internal subnets, while allowing outbound access from the lab to the rest of the network and Internet. Again, this can be accomplished with ACLs or CBAC, depending on the segment's security level. If the internal network is based entirely on a private addressing scheme, it is unlikely that NAT would be implemented on a router joining such subnets.

No matter the placement, several security technologies can be used to secure the network. In the following section, we will discuss these technologies.

Technology Choices

With the advancement of technology, routers are becoming more feature-rich. Many options are available when implementing a router as a security solution, whether it is as part of an entire defense scheme or as a standalone device. All the technologies in the following list are discussed in depth in this section and can be used in either case, but they are often implemented as a lone solution:

- NAT/PAT
- CBAC
- Packet filtering and ACLs

NAT has long been a means to help solve the public IP address range shortage and help secure a network and its privacy. NAT allows the assignment of a public IP address on the "outside" of a device to a corresponding private IP address on the "inside." This way, the internal network addressing remains hidden from outside parties. As communication ensues, the NAT device is responsible for translating the traffic between the public outside and private inside addressing. Only the NAT device knows the internal addresses to which the outside public addresses relate. These translations can be statically assigned (to allow bidirectional communication) or dynamically assigned. When using dynamic assignment, a pool of available public addresses is created. This outside pool does not necessarily have to match one-to-one with the number of inside addresses, allowing many privately addressed stations to share a smaller group of public addresses. However, no more stations can make external connections at one time than there are available public addresses in the pool. When all available public addresses from this outside pool are in use, the next internal station that is attempting an outside connection will be unable to do so, unless a variation of NAT called *overloading* or *PAT* is also implemented.

Note

In the context of this section, we use the term NAT to define standard NAT using address-only translation. We use the term PAT to define NAT translation using port overloading.

The greatest conservation of addresses can be accomplished by using overloading or PAT (also called *NAPT*, or single address NAT). PAT maps multiple internal addresses to one external public address by tracking the communication sessions by the port number in use. As an example, an internal station at IP address 192.168.1.5 wants to contact an outside web server. It generates an ephemeral port of 1035 and sends the request to its gateway router, which happens to be a PAT device. The router translates the requesting station's address into the defined public IP address and assigns a new port number (1111 in this instance). This is accomplished by actually rewriting the packet's header information with the new IP address and port number information. It then enters this information as well as the station's original IP address information and the information of the server it is contacting into a table like this:

```
Source IP/port - Translated IP/port - Contacted IP/port
192.168.1.5.1035 - 200.200.200.2.1111 - 225.225.225.1.80
```

The PAT device attempts to assign the same port number on the outside that is being used on the inside. However, if another connection is already using the port number, the PAT device might reassign a new port number in approximately the same port range, as in our previous example.

When the traffic returns, the PAT device can refer to this table and translate the response for IP 200.200.200.2 port 1111 back to IP address 192.168.1.5, port 1035. Subsequent connections from inside stations would be translated to other ports on the same 200.200.200.2 address. This way, thousands of sessions can successfully take place with only one public IP address, and each will be able to be differentiated from the other. PAT does not have to be limited to a single IP address. Some implementations of PAT will allow multiple IP addresses to be translated.

On a Cisco router, a NAT configuration can be implemented as follows:

1. We start by applying the `router(config-if)#ip nat outside` command on the external interface. This command sets this interface as the outside NAT interface.

2. Next, we apply the `router(config-if)#ip nat inside` command to the internal router interface. For translation reasons, this command tells NAT that this is the inside interface.

3. We then have to configure a pool of addresses for NAT to use the following statement:

   ```
   ip nat pool natpool 171.16.1.208 171.16.1.223 netmask
   ➥255.255.255.240
   ```

   This statement defines the public address pool `natpool` with the IP addresses 171.16.1.208–171.16.1.223.

4. We follow with an access list to specify all internal addresses to be assigned public IP addresses from the NAT pool as follows:

   ```
   access-list 1 permit ip inside ip mask
   ```

   If you are using this device for a VPN as well, additional access lists will need to be created to allow the VPN traffic to bypass NAT. (For more information on VPN implementations on Cisco hardware, refer to Chapter 8, "Virtual Private Networks.")

5. The following command that is executed in global configuration mode is the bread and butter of the NAT implementation on a Cisco router:

   ```
   ip nat inside source list 1 pool natpool
   ```

   It starts by assigning the access list 1 as the addresses to be translated. Next, it defines the pool of public addresses to dynamically be assigned. This is a standard configuration for dynamic NAT, with a pool of addresses to be assigned.

   For PAT, the command would be changed as follows in the next example:

   ```
   ip nat inside source list 1 interface Ethernet0 overload
   ```

First, the definition of a pool of addresses is not needed because only one IP address will be used externally, although the definition of a pool would be allowable. The keyword `overload` is added to the end of the NAT statement, signifying that multiple outgoing connections can overload or share one external IP address. Notice that the following command doesn't use a pool name. Instead, the `interface` keyword assigns the external address followed by the listing of the external interface's name. This way, PAT and the router's external interface can share one public IP address. This statement would be entered in global configuration mode.

The entering of these commands can make almost any Cisco router into a NAT or PAT device. To view the NAT or PAT translation table at any point, use the command `router#sh ip nat trans`.

Note

NAT functionality was first available in IOS 11.2 plus images. The most up-to-date NAT and PAT versions are available in IOS version 12.1.

Although NAT can be considered a privacy method, it offers limited inherent security after a connection is established from the inside. After an inside IP address is added to the NAT table, the address it was contacting to can be accessed from the outside until the mapping is dynamically cleared. A standard Cisco NAT table contains no reference of port information, which leaves the inside station open to activity from the outside station (or from spoofed traffic) on protocols other than the one with which it had contacted. For example, if your internal web server contacted an outside DNS server for DNS information, and the DNS server replied to your server before the NAT table entry was automatically cleared, it would be allowed access to any services that your web server was offering. This makes a good case for the addition of ACLs or CBAC as a complement to properly secure NAT traffic. PAT offers more security because it also tracks the port numbers that are used for each connection and logs them in its translation table. As long as the source port that your internal station is using is a dynamically generated ephemeral port on which no services are hosted, your configuration should be rather safe. However, if an attacker has the ability to detect your IP address, then most likely he also will be able to detect the source and destination ports you are using. This means that if the translation table still holds the address/port combination in question, properly crafted traffic could pass. This assumes that the inside station is still listening on the port that it was contacting when the table entry was created.

Another problem with NAT is the lack of inherent outbound filtering. Any inside hosts can get out, which leaves an opening for Trojan software. The lack of granularity in the translation tables allows a greater likelihood of the occurrence of session hijacking or the infiltration of the network through an existing address translation. However, when used in conjunction with other technologies, such as static packet filtering, dynamic packet filtering, and even stateful inspection methods, NAT and PAT can provide an excellent privacy and security combination.

CBAC is a full-featured method of stateful inspection for Cisco routers. CBAC is available in the Cisco Secure Firewall Feature Set. (Some functionality was introduced in IOS version 11.2p, but many useful features have been added up to version 12.05t.) CBAC supports most popular protocols and keeps full track of the state of connections, dynamically creating access lists to allow return traffic from outside sources. The implementation of CBAC involves creating `inspect` statements that monitor the defined protocols. Following is an example of an `inspect` statement:

```
ip inspect name firewall http timeout 3600
```

`firewall` represents the name of the inspection set we will be applying to our interface. `http` is a keyword that defines the protocol that we are inspecting with this command, and the timeout option (which is not required) tells how long the dynamically generated access lists should exist after creation. This same formatting is applied to additional inspect statements for other protocols that you want to allow to exit your internal network. The set named `firewall` must be applied outbound on the external router interface with a command such as `ip inspect firewall out`. This command must be applied in interface configuration mode.

Because CBAC uses stateful inspection, not only does it make sure that ACLs are dynamically generated to allow return traffic, but it also verifies that the traffic that is being inspected is indeed what it claims to be at the application level. This prevents the use of well-known ports to facilitate possibly malicious activities (using port 80 for telnetting to a host instead of HTTP) and helps prevent session hijacking. For more information on stateful inspection and stateful filtering, see Chapter 3, "Stateful Firewalls."

Despite the fact that CBAC adds an extra layer of intelligence to the inspection of inbound and outbound traffic, it is not a security panacea. It is still wise to use ingress and egress filters in conjunction with CBAC. Despite CBAC's ability to inspect traffic, it will not provide NBAR type screening of malicious content. Although CBAC provides stateful inspection-level protection for communications channels, it is still only one segment of a total defense-in-depth deployment. In addition, CBAC uses more resources and is slower comparatively than the other technology choices. Despite the fact that CBAC might be the most secure method to protect traffic with a router, it might not be the best in all scenarios.

Another way to secure a router is through ACLs that use static and dynamic packet filtering. This is what the router does best, and it is a complement to any security configuration. An ACL can also be a facilitator. Often when other security solutions can't do something, a static packet filter is created to accomplish the task. This is often the way that a secure configuration can suddenly jump to insecure. ACLs are a power tool that must be carefully configured to prevent security holes. For more information on packet filtering with a router, see Chapter 2. For full example listings of ACLs, see Appendix A, "Cisco Access List Sample Configurations."

Regardless of which security technologies you choose for your router, it is important to remember that they all have their strengths and weaknesses, and no method is impenetrable. Also, each of these technologies can benefit from defense-in-depth methodology, even in the simplest of networks. Keep these points in mind when designing your network's security structure, and remember that even the most secure interior configuration can still leave the perimeter router at a point of vulnerability.

Router Hardening

Having the device that provides all of your network's security on the edge of the perimeter is like having an army's general placed ahead of his troops. The piece that is vital to your success or failure is in the most vulnerable position. When it comes to perimeter protection, we can use defense in depth to help, but in some environments, we might not have much support for our "general." This is why router hardening is so important to your network's security. In effect, it's like placing your general in a tank. We focus on protecting the protection device. This protection involves disabling all unneeded services and servers, blocking all unnecessary traffic types, locking down any methods we use to configure our security device, posting warning banners, and closely monitoring the device and the traffic that passes through it.

Operating System

Protecting a router isn't that much different from protecting a computer. (Hardening procedures applicable to hosts are described in Chapter 9, "Host Hardening.") One major concern that is often overlooked is patches for the operating system. The operating system for Cisco routers is called the IOS.

Keeping tabs on IOS updates and security flaws is imperative to defending your router from attack. Cisco's web site posts security issues as they are discovered, and it is a good practice to check such sites regularly. For a list of Cisco security advisories, go to
`http://www.cisco.com/warp/public/707/advisory.html`.

It is also wise to subscribe to an email/list such as SANS Institute's Security Alert Consensus, which automatically sends security advisory information to you as it becomes available. To subscribe, go to
`http://www.sans.org/sansnews`.

Cisco also has a security mailing list at `cust-security-announce@cisco.com`.

Information is available at
`http://www.cisco.com/warp/public/707/sec_incident_response.shtml`.

Locking Down Administration Points

One of the most important parts of securing a perimeter security device is locking down the ways it can be configured. Otherwise, it is like locking a door and leaving the key in the lock. Over the next few sections, we will discuss popular administration methods and some ways to secure them from outside attack.

Telnet

Telnet is probably the most popular way to remotely configure a router. Following are the two greatest concerns of Telnet:

- Properly securing the Telnet server from outside access to prevent remote nefarious users from reconfiguring your router.

- Ensuring that all information including login and password are sent in cleartext. This means that a sniffer could open access to your router configuration.

The Telnet server that is on board every Cisco router can be protected through username and password authentication. However, protection by authentication only might be insufficient for the securing of something as vital as a perimeter security device. For this reason, it is advisable to apply access lists that limit where Telnet sessions can originate. Following is an example of an ACL that allows an administrative station at IP address 192.168.1.1 to have Telnet access:

```
access-list 11 permit 192.168.1.1
```

This access list is applied to the virtual terminal lines (VTY) using the `access-class` command, which works similarly to the `access-group` command that applies ACLs to router interfaces. (For more information on ACLs or the `access-group` command, see Chapter 2.) This access list would be applied as follows:

1. To get into line configuration mode, enter normal configuration mode and type `router(config)#line 1 3`, where 1 through 3 is the range of VTY lines to which you want to apply the access list in question.

2. Enter the `access-class` command `router(config-line)#access-class 11 in`. One administrator's trick is to apply an ACL to the first several VTY lines (for example, 1 through 3) that allow access for the IP addresses of all administrators. Then, apply an ACL to the last VTY line, including only the IP address of the senior administrator's station. This way, the administrator can always get Telnet access, regardless of whom else is connected. These access lists don't only verify that you'll always have a free VTY session, but they also protect you from malicious outside users (and inside users for that matter).

3. Make sure that Telnet is the only input type your router will accept by using `router(config-line)#transport input telnet`. This command disables all other protocols from being used to access the VTY lines. (This is important to prevent access from alternate protocols such as `rlogin`.)

4. If you want to ensure that Telnet access is completely disabled at the router level, you can add the `login` keyword to the VTY line configuration of your router, and then add the `no password` command. This disables Telnet usage because a password is required for access.

The fact that Telnet transfers information in cleartext can only be corrected by using an alternative configuration method such as Secure Shell (SSH), which utilizes encryption.

SSH

SSH is a secure alternative to Telnet. Instead of passing login information in cleartext, SSH uses encryption to protect login names and passwords while authenticating. Since version 12.1 of IOS (only those that support encryption), SSH version 1 is supported only in most of the Cisco router platforms. If you remotely manage your routers, you are in a high-risk environment, and you have concerns about the security of your authentication information, consider using SSH as your Telnet replacement. To configure SSH server capabilities on your router, do the following:

1. Enter the command's hostname *host* and IP domain-name *domain*.

Telnet Trick

Sometimes you might want to separate VTY sessions on a Cisco router, such as when using lock and key access lists or other instances when you need to set different criteria for various VTY telnet sessions. You might want to have certain settings for VTY lines 1–3 and others for 4–5. How do you then log into lines 4 or 5? Using the default Telnet port (23) connects you to the first available VTY. If that doesn't happen to be lines 4 or 5, the alternatively defined criteria will not apply. access-class statements will not correct this problem. If your connection fails to one VTY line, you are simply denied access, not rolled on to the next line to see if its ACL will allow you.

I searched for a way to change this behavior to no avail. Then as I was perusing a firewall mailing list archive[1] one day, I found a workaround. A gentleman sent in the advice that you can use the rotary # command to allow VTY telnet access via an alternate port. This port is the number that is listed after the rotary command, added onto 3,000, 5,000, and 7,000. The result is that if you configure the option rotary 13 on your last VTY line with alternate criteria, you can initiate a Telnet connection to ports 3013, 5013, or 7013. You will also access the alternate criteria instead of what is configured for the other VTY lines. This can be great in situations where you have to execute an autocommand, such as with Lock and Key ACLs. Personally, I don't like having all of those ports available, so I lock down the line with an ACL such as access-list 117 permit tcp host *my IP* any eq 3013 and apply it with an access-class 117 on the VTY line in question. Not only does this verify that no one else will gain access, but it also ensures that I can only access port 3013. (Of course, this port is based on the rotary number that is used). Use this tip at your own risk—it is not the way the command was intended to be used, but it works!

2. Verify that the host and domain name information is entered before attempting to configure SSH. This information is required to enable key generation.

3. Our next goal is to create our RSA key with the statement crypto key generate rsa. This statement actually generates an RSA key and activates SSH. You can view generated RSA keys using the command show crypto key mypubkey rsa. You can verify that SSH is active by entering sh ip ssh.

Tip

Enter the crypto key generate rsa command at the global configuration command prompt. It is not part of your configuration file; therefore, it cannot be entered by editing and reloading the current configuration file.

4. We can set SSH options with the following commands:
   ```
   ip ssh time-out 50
   ip ssh authentication-retries 4
   ```
   If these options are not entered, the defaults for each are assumed.

5. Use the `login local` command to enable local authentication or use Authentication, Authorization, and Accounting (AAA) commands if authenticating through Remote Authentication Dial-In User Service (RADIUS) or Terminal Access Controller Access Control System (TACACS) servers.

6. Of course, you also have to include the command `username name password pass`, where *name* is the username for authentication and *pass* is the password of choice.

7. The `transport input ssh` command can be entered for the VTY lines in question. It disables Telnet remote configuration, allowing SSH to be the only connection method. (Multiple items can be listed for more than one input type.)

The Cisco router (IOS version 12.1(3)t and up) also includes an SSH client implementation so that other SSH-capable devices can be contacted from the router's console prompt. The command to start such a session is `ssh -1 user 10.0.0.1`, where *user* is the user ID that you will use to connect, and *10.0.0.1* represents the SSH server device to which you are connecting. Additionally, a `-p` option allows the use of an alternate port number, and a `-c` option allows the preferred encryption strength to be specified, either Data Encryption Standard (DES) or 3DES.

TFTP and FTP

TFTP is a dangerous protocol. It has the file transfer power of FTP, but with zero security. No login or authentication is needed—just point and transfer. You can imagine that if TFTP were running on any systems on your network, you wouldn't want anyone to have outside access to it. TFTP can be run as a server on some versions of Cisco routers, although it should be disabled by default. (For more information on disabling the TFTP server on Cisco devices, see the "Disabling Servers" section later in this chapter.) TFTP can also be run as a client on all Cisco routers, enabling transfer of configuration files, IOS upgrades, and so on.

Many experienced administrators use TFTP as their administration method of choice instead of Telnet or other command-line type utilities. This brings up the greatest TFTP security concern, which is not the router, but the TFTP server where configuration files are held. A place must exist for administrators to upload and download the configuration files that they edit, and these locations are a major point of concern. Many administrators use their personal or an administration station for this purpose and only run the TFTP server while in the process of updating configuration. This is the preferred method.

Having a TFTP server running all the time with former or current configuration files and IOS updates on is an outside attacker's dream. Those configuration files can be used as a map of your entire security structure. For this reason alone, it is imperative to block TFTP traffic that is coming in from the Internet. An access list to block traffic that is destined for a TFTP server using standard UDP port 69 would look something like this:

```
router(config)#access-list 110 deny udp any any eq 69
```

Of course, this wouldn't be necessary in an environment that only allows necessary traffic.

Since IOS version 12, FTP has also become available to transfer IOS and configuration information. Thankfully, FTP servers have the authentication controls that a TFTP server lacks. However, if you have administrative FTP servers running on your network, it is still advisable to verify that inbound FTP traffic is being blocked.

Configuration Management Tricks with TFTP

Anyone who has configured a Cisco router via Telnet or another command-line interface has wondered, "Isn't there a better way?" The order dependence of rules can make the reconfiguration of a long ACL via command line a chore of Herculean proportions. In addition, the retyping of key information for VPNs or other features that require encryption demands the utmost in accuracy. This is why many long-time Cisco administrators transfer config files to their station and use an editor to make router changes. Use the command `copy run tftp` and supply the details about where the TFTP server can be located. This will copy the running configuration from the Cisco device in question to your TFTP server. Then you can edit the document with an editor that can handle formatting, such as Wordpad in a Windows environment. (Other text editors might not be able to process the formatting, and the file will appear jumbled.) With Find and Replace, a changed IP address can be propagated throughout a complicated configuration with ease. Cut and Paste can allow the swift addition of ACL lines wherever you want them. When the process is complete, copy the saved file back to the router with the `copy tftp run` or `copy tftp star` command. If the update needs to be done without a reboot, you will need to copy to `run`. However, when copying to the running configuration, commands are appended rather than overwritten, which can be messy. A better way, in environments that can afford a few minutes down time, is to copy the config to star (or the startup configuration) and then do a reload to remotely reboot. Upon reload, the changed configuration will be loaded as typed. Watch for typing errors; with this method, you lose the error checking of the IOS until it's too late!

Simple Network Management Protocol

Simple Network Management Protocol (SNMP) is a popular way to manage network devices (including routers), especially in large, cumbersome, complex, or geographically dispersed networks. Many different management products and systems use it. However, allowing Internet access to SNMP, despite the fact that it enables an easy way for a distant administrator to help manage your network, still opens a potential security hole that outside malicious users can exploit. If an attacker can figure out your SNMP security scheme, or if the scheme isn't properly secured, the attacker could be the person managing your network. Because we strive to avoid this, it is highly advisable to simply block all SNMP traffic at the entrance to the network. SNMP devices may use several ports, but most typically operate on UDP ports 161 and 162. An access list to explicitly block such traffic would look like this:

```
router(config)#access-list 113 deny udp any any eq 161
router(config)#access-list 113 deny udp any any eq 162
```

Other SNMP-related ports that may need to be blocked in some environments are TCP ports 161, 162, 199, 391, 705, and 1993, and UDP ports 199, 391, and 1993. Of course, you would only use this access list if it were part of an existing access list that permits traffic by default. In other configurations, SNMP traffic would be most likely blocked by an implicit deny.

The most effective way to mitigate SNMP-related risks is to disable SNMP in environments where it is not required. You can accomplish this by applying the following command in the configuration mode:

```
router(config)#no snmp-server
```

> **Note**
>
> In February 2002, vulnerabilities were discovered that left many vendor's SNMP implementations open to exploit (http://www.cert.org/advisories/CA-2002-03.html). It is imperative that your product is patched to the level required to fix these vulnerabilities, or that a workaround is implemented to prevent external access to SNMP ports of your hosts and devices.

In Chapter 17, "Maintaining a Security Perimeter," we describe the benefits of using SNMP for monitoring the network devices on the internal network. If you want to take advantage of SNMP capabilities built into Cisco routers, here are some suggestions on best practices for securing SNMP. If your environment allows, implement at least SNMP version 3, which supports encryption and cryptographic authentication, and is significantly more secure than its predecessors. (SNMP versions 1 and 2c, which are also supported by Cisco IOS, are limited to using community strings for authentication, and transmit data in cleartext.) If you cannot use version 3, consider implementing IPSec encryption to protect the cleartext SNMP traffic if it absolutely must travel across the Internet. When you need to resort to using plain community strings, by all means, *carefully* pick community string names. Don't use the universal choices of public and private. The Cisco command for setting up a complex community name for SNMP version 1 reads as follows for read-only (RO) access:

```
router(config)#snmp-server community complex name RO
```

Substituting RO with RW (read–write) allows read–write access to the said community. It is in your best security interest to disallow read–write access from the outside network if possible. An IP access list number can be included to restrict access to certain stations by adding the number of a standard ACL to the end of the `snmp-server community` command as follows:

```
snmp-server community complex name RW ACL #
```

The standard ACL that is represented by the listed number includes the IP address range of stations that are allowed to access the agent.

Note

This is an SNMPv1 command. Do not use this command in an SNMPv3 environment, or the router will think you are using SNMPv1. For information about configuring SNMPv3 on Cisco devices take a look at http://www.cisco.com/univercd/cc/td/doc/product/software/ios120/120newft/120t/ 120t3/snmp3.htm.

Cisco Discovery Protocol

Another popular external protocol that is specific to Cisco routers is Cisco Discovery Protocol (CDP), which is a means by which Cisco routers discover specific details about each other. CDP can be a major security concern because detailed configuration information is propagated throughout the network. If you don't have a specific need for CDP, disable it. The command to do so by interface is `router(config-if)#no cdp enable`. To completely disable CDP, use `router(config)#no cdp run`.

Authentication and Passwords

When discussing the security of a managed device, it's imperative to mention authentication and passwording. In the Cisco router, each service has its own configuration options for the authentication method of choice (as mentioned in their individual sections). However, these options basically boil down to two types: remote or local authentication. Remote authentication is the preferred method, and relies on an external RADIUS or TACACS server. Both RADIUS and TACACS are remote server methods of verifying a user's name and password credentials. To set this up with the `login` command, specify the Cisco AAA options.

The advantage of remote authentication is not having all of your "eggs in one basket." If you use local authentication, your login and password information is accessible directly in the router. Moving this information to a remote location adds to its security. One negative point of remote authentication is that if your remote authentication source is down and you have no other authentication options available, you could be kept from logging in. However, remote authentication options can allow for many types of backups for just such circumstances, including the ability to use local or no authentication.

When a remote authentication server is not available, the only other option is local authentication. As mentioned previously, this is accomplished with the `login local` command. To configure a username and password, use the `username` command mentioned previously in the section on SSH. It is important to use best practice to select a username and password for configuration purposes. If you do remote configuration by Telnet or SSH, a good username and password might be all that stands between your network and an attacker.

For extra protection, passwords can be set to appear encrypted when listing configuration information on the router. This is accomplished with the command `service password encryption`. This command is simply a means to help sanitize configurations, preventing accidental exposure of passwords to "shoulder surfers." However, the encryption method employed is weak and will not protect the passwords from serious cryptographic analysis. Don't let this encryption give you a false sense of security and start leaving configuration files lying about!

Disabling Servers

Several servers can be run on most Cisco routers, and as with a PC, any running server is a point of vulnerability. Therefore, all unneeded servers should be disabled. Depending on the IOS version, these servers might be disabled by default; however, it never hurts to double-check. We already discussed the Telnet server and ways to defend it. Following are a few of the more common server programs and the commands to disable them:

- The Bootp server is a forerunner of DHCP that can be configured to hand out necessary IP information to configured clients. Bootp can be disabled with the command `no ip bootp server`.

- The tftp server on supported routers is disabled with `no tftp-server` *device-name*. Here, *device-name* is the device that is configured to receive files.

- The HTTP server offers alternative means to manage the router via a web browser. This can be a major security concern because web traffic is much more likely to be allowed into an environment than Telnet traffic is. You can disable HTTP by using the command `no ip http server`.

- If the HTTP server must be used for management, authentication can be enabled (much like the login local feature of Telnet) with the command `ip http authentication local`.

- For additional security, ACLs can be applied to allow only specified addresses access to the HTTP server with the command `ip http access-class ACL #`. `ACL #` refers to the standard access list that defines stations that can gain access.

- You can change the HTTP server's port address with the command `ip http port #`. `#` is the port that is used for HTTP access, numbered 0–65535. Picking an unusual port number helps promote "security through obscurity," making your Cisco router's web server harder to find.

Disable Unneeded Services

One key to securing any type of device is removing any services that are not needed. These services might not serve as a direct threat, but when maximizing security, any window that isn't needed should be boarded up. In this section, we will take a look at some services that are not used in some environments and that can be known troublemakers.

Small Services

Small services (ports below 20 TCP and UDP) and time (TCP and UDP port 37) are seldom used and are more of a liability than a value to you. These services can be disabled with the following commands:

```
router(config)#no service tcp-small-servers
router(config)#no service udp-small-servers
```

By typing these commands at the `config` prompt and saving the configuration, small services will be disallowed on the router. (These services are disabled by default on IOS version 12.0 and later.) Access to these services should be blocked at your perimeter. In an environment where inbound access is allowed until explicitly denied, access to these services running on internal systems can be blocked using an ACL as follows:

```
router(config)#access-list 101 deny tcp any any lt 20
router(config)#access-list 101 deny udp any any lt 20
```

The Time service should also be blocked. The rule of thumb in security is to block any service ports that you know you don't need. It doesn't matter whether this is regarding an unpopular service, such as Time, or one as popular as FTP. If your security policy states that a service isn't used on your network, block it. In an environment where you only block traffic that you don't want, the Time service can be filtered with two extended access lists:

```
router(config)#access-list 101 deny tcp any any eq 37
router(config)#access-list 101 deny udp any any eq 37
```

The following line is used to apply the access lists to the interface:

```
router (config-if)#ip access-group 101 in
```

This is applied with the rest of the deny statements on the external router interface to the Internet.

Network Time Protocol

Network Time Protocol (NTP) is used to allow synchronization of time sources on a network. If NTP is unneeded in your environment, Cisco includes a simple command to disable it on any router interface:

```
router(config-if)# ntp disable
```

NTP can be useful for doing things like synchronizing time sources when comparing log files from various sources and tracking time-sensitive update information. To prevent update information from unwanted sources, authentication can be enabled that requires all updates to be "signed" with a MD5 hash. If you are using a NTP source, verify that it is properly "hardened" and that you have these authentication mechanisms enabled.

Finger

Finger is a service that allows users to query a network device to discover information about a user by their email address, or about currently logged on users. Depending on the variation of finger server, you might find out only if the user is currently logged on, or more personal information including the last time the user retrieved his mail, his telephone number, full name, address, and so on. Cisco routers specifically can give information about users who are logged in currently to the router via services such as Telnet. Most ISPs now disable finger services for privacy reasons; we want to give out as little information as possible to prevent possible attacks. It is in your users' best interest to block the finger service at the furthest contact point from your private network, most likely your border router. To disable the finger server that is built into the Cisco router, use the command router(config)#no service finger.

An access list to specifically block the finger service would look like this:

```
access-list 122 deny tcp any any eq 79
```

It is unlikely that this access list would be used, however, because most environments only allow traffic they want.

Internet Control Message Protocol Blocking

Internet Control Message Protocol (ICMP) is a workhorse protocol in an IP-based environment. It is responsible for generating many of the error messages and informative messages that keep the Internet working. However, many popular attacks and reconnaissance techniques are based on this protocol. In this section, we will look at some ways to protect your router from these types of attacks.

Unreachables

We will now look at the filtering of "host unreachables" (ICMP type 3). A router sends this message when it can't find the listed host because it is down or it doesn't exist. This doesn't seem like such a bad thing, but if a malicious mapper compares the unreachables and other responses from an IP address range, she can determine which of the IP addresses represent valid, running hosts. This is yet another method for the devious to map out your network before an attack. A trace (using a product such as Tcpdump found at http://www.tcpdump.org) of communication between a sender and a non-existent recipient would look like this:

```
sender.com.31054 > receiver.com.23: S 3435678932:3435678932(0) win 8760
⇥<ms 1460> (DF)
router > sender.com: icmp: host receiver.com unreachable
```

The trace shows a Telnet send from sender.com to a non-existent host, receiver.com. Because the non-existent receiver can't respond for itself (obviously!), the router (called *router* in our example) replies to sender.com with the ICMP host unreachable message.

Because of these mapping concerns, host unreachables are another traffic type that is popular to block. Cisco has the following integrated command to disable them:

```
router(config-if)#no ip unreachables
```

After applying this in global configuration mode, all host unreachable messages will be disabled. To test this, telnet to an IP address that doesn't exist on your inside network, while running a network trace program to see what packets are returned to you. Be sure that Telnet traffic will pass through to your inside network by altering any access lists that would deny such traffic. After the command has been applied, you shouldn't receive host unreachables. You might wonder, "If it's not returning host unreachables, what would the traffic look like?"

The answer is simply that there would be no reply. The sender would give up on its own because it didn't receive a response in the allotted amount of retries.

Disabling such informative ICMP messages from your network or from being propagated by your router has consequences. The `packet too big` unreachable message (a subtype of the standard `ICMP unreachable`) is often necessary for proper network functionality. If you can't let outside parties know that they need to fragment their information or adjust their maximum transmission unit (MTU) size to communicate with you, you might not successfully communicate. For information on excluding the `packet too big` ICMP unreachable messages (type 3 code 4) from your ICMP filtering, as well as suggestions for the filtering of the various ICMP types from your network, look at the "Filtering TCP and UDP Ports and ICMP Types" section of Chapter 2. Blocking IP unreachables and other ICMP traffic types that facilitate smooth communications assumes that you either don't have any publicly accessible servers, or you do and aren't being a good Internet neighbor. If you have public servers, you might want to be a good Internet neighbor and allow certain ICMP interactions with them on your screened subnet. Apply all the ICMP filters to the router interface of the private network, protecting it, and allow chosen ICMP traffic to the screened subnet. This allows enhanced communications with outside parties who aren't familiar with your environment. Some allowed ICMP types might include outbound echo replies, time-exceeded messages, packet-too-big, administratively prohibited, and unreachables. Inbound, you might want to allow echo requests (perhaps just to a few particular servers' IP addresses). Your security policy and your ISP will decide the types you allow.

Most of these traffic types are security concerns because of an outsider's ability to map your network. This isn't as great of a concern on a publicly accessible segment. Echo replies and requests are of the most concern (due to exploits and covert channel concerns), but with properly patched, configured, and hardened servers, they shouldn't be a problem either. The proper logging of said traffic types is advised to verify that the traffic in question is not of a malicious nature. For more information on the logging and examination of malicious traffic, check out Chapter 7, "Network Intrusion Detection" and Chapter 18, "Network Log Analysis."

Directed Broadcasts

One command that is useful when securing Cisco routers against popular ICMP-based attacks is `router(config-if)#no ip directed-broadcast`.

This command disallows traffic to broadcast addresses, preventing amplification of Smurf-like attacks, where one echo request can generate hundreds of responses. For this reason, it is best to execute this command on all router interfaces on your network. As of IOS version 12.0, directed broadcasts are disabled by default. Although this command is popularly mentioned as a means to deter Smurf attacks that use the ICMP protocol, it is also effective against broadcast attacks using UDP, TCP, and IP.

Smurf Attacks

Smurfing is a type of denial-of-service attack that makes use of the broadcast behavior of IP networks. It is called smurfing because one of the first programs to implement the attack was named Smurf. The attack works by sending a series of spoofed ICMP echo packets to the broadcast address of a network. The attacker hopes that all the hosts on the network will send ICMP echo replies to the spoofed address. If the network segment is large, the attacker might be able to evoke hundreds of echo reply packets generated for every echo packet that he sends. This allows the attacker to magnify the bandwidth of the attack making it possible for a dial-up attacker connected at 56 Kbps to bring down sites connected using a T-1 line (1.544 Mbps).

Redirects

Another popularly implemented Cisco ICMP type command is `router(config-if)#no ip redirects`.

This command is often used in conjunction with anti-spoofing access lists and is applied to any router interface from which malicious traffic can enter your network. It is a means by which a nefarious user could manipulate the path of return traffic, and it should be disabled.

Spoofing and Source Routing

As introduced in Chapter 2, source routing and spoofing can be an effective and hazardous combination. This is why it is so important to apply ingress filters and disable source routing. As mentioned previously, the command to disable source routing on Cisco routers is `router(config)#no ip source-route`.

For a review of ingress filtering and source routing, refer to Chapter 2.

Router Logging Basics

Logging is an important feature of any firewall, especially one with a secured subnet. A router doesn't have much space onboard for logs, however. In addition, logging takes up extra resources on a possibly already taxed component of your network. Other logging solutions could involve installing an IDS or some other type of sniffer on your network to monitor and log the type of traffic that is roaming about on your network segments (A *sniffer* is a device that captures detailed packet information.) If you do a lot of logging on your router (with the log option appended to your access lists), you can set up or use an existing Syslog server on your network and redirect the log files to it. This way, you don't run into the space limitations of a router's onboard memory, and if you have more than one router, you can have all of the router's logs sent to one centralized location.

POSTED: No Trespassing—The Importance of Banners

When configuring a router, it is possible to configure a banner that will be displayed at the logon prompt when a user first accesses the router. The command to create such a login banner is `router(config)#banner login`

`,`

`scary approved message,.`

The commas in this command represent some (any) delimiter, and *scary approved message* represents a login message that your business has chosen to most effectively ward off evildoers. Posting a warning doesn't guarantee that if a bad person elects to trespass on your virtual property, you will be able to capture and convict him, but it can help improve the chances and help demonstrate the interloper's intent. More than one electronic trespasser has escaped conviction with the claim that "they didn't know that they weren't supposed to be there." It is a good idea to get counsel familiar with your area's legal specifics to help choose the wording for your banner to maximize its effectiveness. Don't include information about your site or its equipment because this can all be used against you.

Remember that a banner can work against you as well. Using a banner that says "Top Secret Government Site—DO NOT ENTER!" is just asking for trouble. Something along these lines might be preferable: "ALL ACTIVITY ON THIS DEVICE IS MONITORED AND WILL BE USED AS EVIDENCE IN THE EVENT OF PROSECUTION." Gives you a funny feeling, doesn't it? Again, the banner might have to be tweaked for your environment and local laws, but it does three things:

- It keeps your site completely anonymous.

- It lets trespassers know (without threats) that they are being watched.

- It states up front that the owner of this device will prosecute people who shouldn't be there.

The end result is that it makes the visitor think twice, and if bad things happen, it is a strong indicator of an attacker's intent.

Tip

When gathering logs from multiple sources, make sure that all devices are time-synchronized. Otherwise, integrating logs can be a logistical nightmare.

To configure a Cisco router to do logging, make sure that it is currently enabled with the command `router(config)#logging on`.

To send logging information to a local Syslog server, use the command `router(config)#logging` *ip address*.

ip address represents the IP address for the Syslog server in question.

After logging is successfully configured, the router sends its logging information to the Syslog server based on the "trap" level you configured. This is set using the command `router(config)# logging trap` *information level*.

information level lists the informational level of the messages that will be sent to the Syslog server. It sends all messages of the listed level or lower. The default level of the `trap` command is informational, which includes *all* message types except debugging information (which is generated by the Cisco debug commands). To log this information as well, change the trap level to `debugging`.

Tip

Warning! The debug commands can generate quite a lot of information and can fill up log servers quickly.

After logging is properly configured, messages like this one should magically appear on your Syslog server:

```
138: 1d06h: %SEC-6-IPACCESSLOGP: list 112 permitted tcp 10.0.0.3(4766)
-> 192.168.219.25(80), 5 packets
```

The message is an example of a standard Cisco log entry as generated by an access list, including the log keyword (`access-list 112` to be exact). The ACL was a permit rule, so this is reported as matching the permit and is allowed to pass. Most of the rest of the entry is pretty intuitive—address and port source and destination, except the cryptic Cisco labeling mechanisms. For more information on log files, take a look at Chapter 18.

Summary

The router plays a significant role in the security of your network. It can be configured as a role player in defense in depth, helping protect your QoS, defending against DoS attacks, or just taking some of the burden off your existing firewall by handling egress or ingress filtering. Your router might also be acting as your primary firewall, using technologies such as CBAC, NAT, and ACLs. With CBAC, your router might be supporting you as a truly stateful firewall. With NAT, your router might be shielding your addressing scheme from prying eyes and helping protect your network from unsolicited entrance. Finally, with access lists, your router might be defending your network using packet-filtering technology.

In any case, the router performs important security duties and must be sufficiently armored. Be sure to disable unused features and block unused services, use adequate passwording and authentication, secure configuration channels and methods, prevent the propagation of unneeded network information, and use logging to audit your success. A properly implemented and hardened router is the beginning of a secure network.

1 Firewalls Mailing List "RE: access-list on Cisco Routers." July 6, 1999. `http://www.shmoo.com/mail/firewalls/jul99/msg00078.html`. December 2001.

7

Network Intrusion Detection

A GOOD NETWORK INTRUSION DETECTION system (IDS) can have an enormous positive impact on the overall security of your organization. The focus of intrusion detection is identifying attacks and security incidents, but in this chapter, we see that intrusion detection can do so much more than that. After learning about the basics of intrusion detection, we discuss the critical role that IDS plays in a perimeter defense. Much of this chapter is devoted to determining where IDS sensors should be deployed in various environments. By the end of this chapter, you will have a strong sense of how you can use network intrusion detection to strengthen your organization's defenses.

Network Intrusion Detection Basics

Network intrusion detection systems are designed to examine network traffic to identify threats by detecting scans, probes, and attacks. One of the goals of intrusion detection is to assist you in ensuring that systems can handle those threats properly. By detecting malicious activity, network intrusion detection enables you to identify and react to threats against your environment, as well as threats that your hosts might be directing at other networks.

The focus of this chapter is network IDS. A network IDS sensor sniffs traffic and analyzes it, searching for various signatures that could indicate a scan or probe, reconnaissance activity, or an attempt to exploit a vulnerability. Traditionally, network intrusion detection systems don't interfere with traffic in any way. Unlike a firewall or packet filter, which makes decisions about what traffic to allow, an intrusion detection sensor is really a packet sniffer that also performs analysis. However, some sensors are starting to make active responses to suspicious traffic, such as terminating suspicious TCP connections. We'll discuss this more later in this chapter.

Besides network intrusion detection, a separate area of security, known as host-based intrusion detection, exists. Host-based IDS software focuses on detecting attacks against a particular host, such as a workstation or server. Log analyzers monitor operating system and application logs, looking for entries that might be related to attacks or security violations. File integrity software alerts you if particular files are altered, which might indicate a successful attack. You can learn more about host-based intrusion detection products in Chapter 10, "Host Defense Components."

The Need for Intrusion Detection

Many people have heard of intrusion detection, but they might not realize why they need to deploy it in their environment. Without intrusion detection, you are unaware of many attacks that occur. Because you don't have information about attacks, when a successful one occurs, you won't have the information you need to stop it from happening to that host again, or to other hosts. Most ominously, you will never know about an attack that doesn't damage your host, but simply extracts information, such as a password file, from it. Without intrusion detection, you will be unaware of these events until it's much too late. This is why intrusion detection can be beneficial in many environments.

Many attacks involve multiple steps or phases. For example, an attacker might start by launching a scan that sends a DNS query containing a `version.bind` request to each IP address in a range. Some DNS servers respond to such a query with their BIND version number. The goal of this scan is to identify which hosts are DNS servers and what versions of BIND they are using. Based on the results of the first scan, the attacker then sends a specially crafted DNS query to some of the DNS servers to exploit a buffer overflow vulnerability in a particular version of BIND. This second set of queries could occur hours or days after the first set—or it could occur within seconds. It depends on the tools being used and the attacker's methodology.

If any of the buffer overflow exploits are successful, the attacker might be able to perform unauthorized actions on one or more of the servers, potentially gaining root privileges. An attacker who gains root access to a server could do many things, including using that server to launch attacks against other hosts on your network and against external hosts. It is important to understand that this is not a hypothetical attack scenario we are describing. Various attack tools use this exact technique to scan, attack, and compromise servers; many worms also do this by spreading throughout the Internet on their own. Sometimes, it only takes seconds from the initial scan until the vulnerable host is compromised.

If you are not using intrusion detection, how will you know when a successful attack has occurred? Some attacks are immediately visible, such as a web site defacement; others are not. Perhaps you will look through a directory and see some strange files or directories. Perhaps your server's performance will decline and you will find many unknown processes running. Perhaps your server will crash and you won't be able to reboot it. Or perhaps no one will notice that anything has happened.

A properly configured, robust IDS can play more than one role in identifying typical attacks. Intrusion detection detects reconnaissance scans, notifying security personnel that such activity is taking place and that future attacks on the targeted systems are likely. It also generates alerts for the subsequent attempts to breach host security. Alerts are usually generated through one of two methods. The first method, *anomaly detection*, relies on statistical analysis to identify traffic that falls outside that which is normally seen in this environment. However, in part because anomaly detection solutions are still maturing, nearly every network IDS product relies primarily on another method, signature detection, which we will now study in more detail.

Network IDS Signatures

A *network IDS signature* is a pattern that you are looking for in traffic. When a signature for an attack matches observed traffic, an alert is generated, or the event is otherwise recorded. A simple signature example is the Land attack; the source and destination IP addresses in a packet are the same (http://cve.mitre.org/cgi-bin/cvename.cgi?name=CVE-1999-0016). Some older operating systems could not properly handle such packets, which violate standards, so attackers would send crafted packets with the same source and destination addresses.

Although some network traffic signatures, such as the Land attack, are quite simple, others are considerably more complicated. Many signatures are protocol or application specific; for example, many signatures pertain only to DNS traffic. Because DNS zone transfers traditionally use TCP port 53, a signature pertaining to a zone transfer vulnerability includes the TCP protocol, and also needs to look for destination port 53. Each signature specifies other characteristics that help to identify the vulnerability that the attacker is trying to exploit. Some IDS systems focus on long sequences of code from published exploits, whereas other IDS systems actually perform full protocol analysis, examining and validating the header and payload values of each packet. Although full analysis is more resource intensive, it tends to produce a much more robust signature solution.

Most intrusion detection vendors release new sets of signatures regularly. If a major new vulnerability is discovered or an exploit is widely seen, intrusion detection vendors quickly research the exploit or vulnerability, create new signatures for it (or determine that existing signatures already match it), and release the signatures to their users as soon as possible. This process is similar to the process that anti-virus software vendors follow when addressing threats from new viruses, worms, and trojans. When a major new threat emerges suddenly, such as the Nimda worm, IDS vendors typically have a signature that is available for their customers in a matter of hours.

How Signatures Work

Let's look at an example of a signature for the Nimda worm. When the worm tries to infect a web server, it sends a set of HTTP requests, including this one:

```
GET /scripts/..%c0%af../winnt/system32/cmd.exe?/c+dir
```

The purpose of this particular request is to exploit a Unicode-related vulnerability in certain unpatched Microsoft IIS servers to gain unauthorized privileges. %c0%af is the Unicode equivalent of a slash, so this command is actually trying to traverse the root directory to exploit the vulnerability. Although no damage is done to the server, success at this point tells the worm that the server is vulnerable. The worm can now launch a damaging attack to this server.

You want your network intrusion detection sensors to notify you when it sees this traffic. Many different possible signatures exist. A simple text-matching signature would look for /scripts/..%c0%af../ in a URL (more precisely, in the payload of a TCP packet that a client sends to a server's port 80). Because the Nimda worm issues several GET requests with slightly different values, you would need a separate signature for each one of them if you wanted to identify each attack attempt.

Some IDS sensors have a much more robust way of identifying these types of requests as attacks. Rather than doing simple text matching, they actually decode the request, substituting a slash for the %c0%af sequence, and then analyze the validity of the decoded URL. As a result of the analysis, the IDS sensor determines that the attacker is trying to go past the root directory, and it generates an alert. Although this method is more resource intensive, it provides a much better detection capability than the simple text-matching method because it actually examines traffic for the attack technique, not for specific known instances of that technique being used.

False Positives and False Negatives

Signature development is always a balancing act. A specific signature might be extremely accurate in identifying a particular attack, yet it might take many resources to do so. If an attacker slightly modifies the attack, the signature might not be able to identify it at all. On the other hand, a general signature might be much faster and require far fewer resources, and it might be better at finding new attacks and variants on existing ones. The downside of a general signature is that it also might cause many *false positives*—when a sensor classifies benign activity as an attack.

Every intrusion detection system generates false positives. When you first look at an IDS console and see dozens or hundreds of alerts, you might think that your systems are under massive attack. But those alerts are much more likely to be false positives. By selecting a solid IDS product and tuning your sensors, you can reduce false positives, but you can't completely eliminate them. No matter how precisely a particular signature is written, there's usually still a chance that some benign traffic will accidentally match that signature. False positives are a headache for an intrusion analyst because you have to spend time and resources determining that they are, in fact, false.

The Intrusion Detection System Is Possessed!
I will never forget the first time that I had to review and analyze intrusion detection alerts. I opened the IDS console to review the data, and my mouth dropped as I saw hundreds of alerts that all said *Devil*. I scrolled through screen after screen of Devil alerts, and I started to wonder if the IDS was possessed! The Devil turned out to be an alert for the Devil trojan. After several hours of research, I determined that the alerts were all false positives that were caused by a poorly written signature.

A *false negative* occurs when a signature fails to generate an alert when its associated attack occurs. People tend to focus on false positives much more than false negatives, but each false negative is a legitimate attack or incident that IDS failed to notice. False negatives get less attention because you usually have no way of knowing that they have occurred. Sadly, you're most likely to identify a false negative when an attack is successful and wasn't noticed by the IDS, or when a different network IDS sensor or host-based

IDS product notices it. In addition, if a signature generates many false positives, the analyst usually shuts off the signature altogether or ignores all the corresponding alerts. This means that the analyst doesn't review legitimate instances of the alert, and this also becomes a type of false negative. It's important to understand what causes false positives and negatives so that you can choose an IDS that minimizes them.

Developing Signatures that Minimize False Positives and Negatives

To better understand false positives and negatives, let's look at a simple example. Suppose that in your intrusion detection system, you write a signature that looks for `cmd.exe` anywhere in a URL. (`cmd.exe` is often used in root traversal exploits against IIS servers, such as the Nimda worm.) This is a general signature that matches many different attack attempts. Unfortunately, it also matches `cmd.exe-analysis.html`, a web page that contains an analysis of `cmd.exe` attacks. It matches against `nascmd.exe` as well, which is unrelated to these exploits. These are examples of false positives that are caused by an overly general signature.

Because of the false positives, you decide to rewrite your signature to use some contextual information as well. Now your signature is a URL that contains `/winnt/system32/cmd.exe`. Because this is a more specific signature, it triggers fewer false positives than the more general signature.

Unfortunately, reducing false positives often comes at the expense of increasing false negatives. If an attacker uses a URL that includes `/winnt/system32/../system32/cmd.exe`, the more specific signature misses it, causing a false negative to occur. However, the more general first signature would have sent an alert. And the more robust method described earlier, which decodes the entire URL and evaluates it for root traversals, would have sent an alert for both versions. More complex signatures are usually better than simple text-matching signatures, which are unable to identify most variations on attacks. In fact, some attackers purposely craft their attacks to avoid detection by simple signatures; this is known as *IDS evasion*.

Detecting IDS Evasion Techniques

As if developing an IDS signature that minimizes false positives and false negatives isn't difficult enough sometimes, you must also consider the effects of IDS evasion techniques on signature development. Attackers have many methods of altering their code to avoid IDS detection. Many are simple, such as the example discussed previously that obfuscated the path by including sequences. A common technique used in URLs is to replace a character with its hex or Unicode equivalent. Therefore, `cmd.exe` could become `cmd.%65xe` because %65 is the hex representation of e. Only IDS products that perform hex decoding before performing signature comparisons would determine that this string matches cmd.exe.

Some evasion techniques actually relate to the IDS sensor's core architecture, not specific signatures. One such technique is to fragment a packet so that it has a small initial fragment; the attacker hopes that the IDS examines only the first fragment, which looks benign, and ignores the remaining fragments, which contain malicious content. An IDS that does full-packet reassembly is not fooled by this evasion method.

Avoiding Unwanted Alerts

Besides false positives, you might also have alerts that address legitimate problems that you simply don't care about. Unwanted alerts seem to occur in just about every environment. For example, if your environment is an ISP or a wireless company, you are providing network services to customers. You probably have a lot of traffic passing on your networks between your customers and other outside hosts. If you are monitoring these networks with IDS sensors and you tune them to identify all possible scans and attacks, you are likely to be overwhelmed with a huge number of alerts that you honestly don't care about. Do you really want to know if one user sends another a FOOBAR.TXT.EXE file? This could trigger an alert because of the suspicious extension combination—and the alert would almost certainly be accurate—but the activity is outside the scope of your control.

Note

Tuning your sensors to produce only the information that is relevant in your environment is critical if you're going to get the best results from your IDS solution.

Alerting, Logging, and Reporting

When an intrusion detection system sees traffic that matches one of its signatures, it logs the pertinent aspects of the traffic or generates an alert, depending on the severity of the activity and the configuration of the IDS sensor. Alerts can be delivered to intrusion analysts in a variety of ways, including messages on the analyst console, emails, and SNMP traps, depending on the product being used.

Reporting is another key element of intrusion detection. If you have only one sensor, reporting should be simple. If you have dozens of sensors, you probably don't want separate reports from each of them. Instead, you want all data to be collected in one place because it's more convenient to view and easier to back up. It's also far easier to correlate events that all sensors see. Reporting formats vary widely among IDS products; many also permit sensor alerts and logs to be exported to databases for further queries and reporting.

Review IDS Sensor Status Regularly

I was helping an intrusion analyst tune the dozens of network IDS sensors that were deployed in his environment. He told me he had noticed recently that the number of alerts he was seeing on his analyst console had dropped significantly. After a few days of this, he noticed that several sensors weren't generating alerts. Puzzled, he finally checked the sensor status reports and discovered that none of them were seeing packets. An investigation revealed that a co-worker had reconfigured the switches to which the sensors were connected.

Check the status of your sensors regularly. Most IDS sensors provide some sort of status report that indicates how the sensor is functioning and what volume of traffic it is seeing. If you notice unexpected drops in traffic levels, you need to investigate the situation as quickly as possible; your sensor might no longer be seeing traffic.

Intrusion Detection Software

Many different network IDSs are available, each with its own distinct features. Some of the best-known and most popular products include Snort, Shadow, Cisco Secure, Enterasys Dragon, ISS RealSecure, and the NFR Security NID. They all provide alerting, logging, and reporting capabilities. Signature sets are available through a variety of means, depending on the product. Users of some products have written their own signatures and made them publicly available. Other products must be purchased to get signatures; some vendors hide the signature details, whereas others allow users to view and even modify their signatures.

Network IDS sensors have other helpful features. For example, some systems can perform network monitoring and traffic analysis, collecting statistics on connections, protocols in use, and the like. This ability can be invaluable in identifying policy violations, such as unauthorized services in use, and traffic oddities in general. We will discuss policy violations later in this chapter. Another feature that is covered in more depth later is that of *active response*, in which an IDS sensor works with other network devices to halt certain traffic from occurring.

Some IDS products provide tiered solutions, which typically involve deploying multiple IDS sensors on various network segments. Each sensor transmits its IDS data to a centralized server that stores all the data. The individual sensors or the centralized box, which is able to correlate events from all the sensors' data, can make alert decisions. Many IDS solutions also have separate analyst consoles that connect to the centralized system or the individual sensors; these enable analysts to view recorded data and alerts, as well as reconfigure the sensors and update signatures. Some software vendors, such as e-Security, offer console products that can process and correlate data from various brands of IDS sensors, firewalls, and other hosts.

IDSs

Besides intrusion detection products, some intrusion detection-related services might be able to assist you with the analysis of your intrusion detection data. Some organizations choose to outsource the analysis of their IDS sensor data to specialized monitoring services. Other organizations might elect to do their own analysis, but they also submit their data to distributed IDSs.

Distributed IDSs

A recent trend that has become quite popular is the use of distributed IDSs. The basic concept is that administrators from organizations all over the world submit logs to a distributed IDS service from their own IDS sensors, firewalls, and other devices. These services analyze the data from all the sites and perform correlations to identify likely attacks. Two of the best-known distributed IDS systems are Attack Registry & Intelligence Service (ARIS), located at `http://aris.securityfocus.com`, and DShield, located at `http://www.dshield.org`.

Using a distributed IDS service has a few benefits. Because the service receives logs from many environments, it has a wealth of data to use for its intrusion analysis. A distributed IDS service finds patterns among all the attacks that individual sites cannot see. Another great feature of some distributed IDS services is that if they conclude that a host at a particular IP address attacked a substantial number of sites, they will email the technical contact for that domain so that the activity can be investigated. Distributed IDS services can reduce some of the burden placed on intrusion analysis by analyzing logs, correlating events, and following up on highly suspicious activity.

Outsourced Intrusion Detection System Monitoring

Recently, some companies have started offering outsourced IDS management. These services generally provide 24-hour monitoring of your IDS sensors and alert your staff in case of attack. One advantage of using these services is staffing related; they can provide trained intrusion analysts to monitor your sensors at all times. Another advantage is that because these services collect data from so many networks, they can correlate attacks among them. The disadvantage is their lack of knowledge about your environment and their inability to correlate events unless they can access firewall and host log files in near real-time.

At best, outsourced IDS monitoring can identify serious attacks and help your organization respond to them quickly and appropriately. If your organization doesn't have the time or expertise to analyze its own IDS sensor data properly and promptly, outsourcing that work is important for maintaining a strong perimeter defense. At worst, such services add little or nothing to the existing IDS solution, while requiring substantial financial commitments.

The Roles of Network IDS in a Perimeter Defense

IDS sensors serve several purposes in a good perimeter defense. In some cases, they are uniquely suited to the task that they perform. Besides identifying attacks and suspicious activity, you can use IDS data to identify security weaknesses and vulnerabilities, including policy violations. IDS data is also an invaluable part of computer forensics and incident-handling efforts. Network IDS complements other perimeter defense components by performing functions that they cannot, such as full protocol and payload analysis. IDS sensors can also work with other defense components to halt active attacks. Network IDS is necessary in most environments to create and maintain a strong overall security solution.

Identifying Weaknesses

It is absolutely crucial that you identify vulnerabilities and weaknesses and reduce or eliminate them. If you don't take care of them, attackers will most likely find and exploit them, and hosts might be compromised. If a host is compromised, an attacker is likely to use it as a jumping-off point for attacks against other hosts in your environment. By preventing that host from being compromised, or by being alerted immediately after it has been, you can achieve a much better outcome. You can use IDS proactively to find vulnerabilities and weaknesses and identify early stages of attacks, and you can use it reactively to detect attacks against hosts and log what occurs.

Security Auditing

Network IDS can assist in security auditing. You can use the IDS logs and alerts to identify weaknesses in network defenses. For example, if a sensor sends alerts about suspicious Telnet activity from an Internet-based host and your firewall is supposed to be blocking all incoming Telnet activity, either your firewall is not blocking the traffic properly, or your network has an additional connection to the Internet that is not secured properly.

Policy Violations

Some IDSs enable you to receive alerts when certain protocols or well-known port numbers are used. For example, if your users are not permitted to use the Internet Relay Chat (IRC) protocol, you could tune your IDS to alert you whenever it sees IRC traffic on the network. Because many trojans such as SubSeven and other malicious code use IRC for communication, IRC traffic on your network could indicate that an incident has occurred. It could also indicate a user who is violating your security policy. Either way, it's activity that you're likely to want to know about.

Along the same lines, IDS sensors can be useful in finding misconfigured systems on your own networks, such as a host that isn't using your web proxy server and is reducing the overall security level of your environment. Sensors can also help you find rogue systems that unauthorized personnel are running; for example, a user might set up a web server for her consulting business on her corporate workstation. When reviewing your IDS logs, you would see port 80 traffic directed to this box. Identifying improperly configured hosts and addressing their problems is a key part of reducing the vulnerabilities in your environment.

Detecting Attacks from Your Own Hosts

Although many traditionally think of network IDS sensors as identifying suspicious activity that enters a network from the Internet, it's important to consider that you can also use IDS sensors to identify outgoing attacks. This use is particularly valuable in environments where outbound access is largely unrestricted. You certainly want to be aware of attacks that your internal hosts are performing on external entities; your users could be causing these attacks, or the attacks could signal that another party or a worm is using compromised machines to attack others.

In an environment where firewalls and packet filters are configured to let almost any activity out of your organization, an IDS is probably the only method you have of identifying such attacks. If your border devices place some restrictions on outbound activity, you might identify an attack by reviewing your firewall logs, but this is far less likely to happen because most firewalls have no signature capabilities and can't identify many attacks. Also, reviewing firewall logs is a much more resource-intensive process than reviewing the logs of an IDS sensor that checks outgoing traffic.

Incident Handling and Forensics

In an ideal world, your organization would have staff monitoring your IDS logs and alerts 24 hours a day and reacting immediately to suspicious activity. In the real world, it's more likely that you receive a page when the most serious alerts occur, and you probably review your IDS alerts and logs as often as you can, given all of your other duties. It's important that you review alerts as often as possible so that you can quickly identify serious attacks and react appropriately to them.

Even if you don't notice that an attack is occurring until the damage has been done, the IDS data can still be invaluable to you. It can show you what hosts were attacked and what attacks were used against them. This critical information can help you recover from incidents much more quickly and identify the likely source of an attack. It gives you the basic information you need when starting to handle an incident, and it indicates other hosts that might have related data, such as firewalls that the traffic passed through or other hosts that were attacked.

Along the same lines, many people do not consider the forensic uses of IDS. You can use IDS logs to investigate an incident. Also, some IDS products enable you to monitor and log specified types of traffic. For example, if you don't permit IRC to be used on your network, you might want to set your IDS to log all IRC traffic, which could then capture IRC communications between malware on one of your machines and a remote IRC server. Of course, you need to consider the privacy rights of your users before configuring your IDS this way; legitimate users might be chatting with each other using IRC, and the IDS might record their conversations.

Complementing Other Defense Components

Part of the purpose of network IDS is to correlate the activity that individual hosts might see. If 100 hosts each record one failed Telnet attempt, no one might notice; but if an IDS sensor records 100 failed Telnet attempts, it's much more likely to trigger an alert. Sometimes IDS sensors work with perimeter defense components to block active malicious connections. IDS sensors can also perform functions that other perimeter defense components, such as firewalls, generally can't.

Protocol and Application Analysis

Firewalls and packet filters have limited capabilities to examine traffic. Typically, they do not look at the contents of packet payloads, although some might do some basic protocol analysis. Firewalls generally look at some of the most basic characteristics of traffic and accept, deny, or reject it accordingly.

A firewall might try to stop certain services from passing through by blocking certain port numbers, but it generally does little or nothing to evaluate traffic that uses allowed port numbers. IDS sensors are designed to examine the contents of packets; some IDS sensors are even capable of doing full protocol analysis, which means that they can examine the contents of an entire session as it occurs and alert you if the traffic does not match its expectations, without matching the traffic against a known attack signature.

A simple example of this is the identification of applications that run on unexpected ports. For example, a trojan that is installed on a host might use TCP port 21 (usually associated with FTP control connections) for all communications with its trojan master. If your firewall is configured to let internal users FTP to external sites, the trojan could initiate a connection to its master, and your firewall would respond as though it were an FTP connection and permit it. However, the IDS sensor would actually analyze the content of the packets and alert you that the traffic was not FTP. You could then review the IDS logs for more information and investigate the host in question.

A more complex example of the value of protocol analysis is the identification of various known and unknown attacks. One of the most commonly used attack techniques is the buffer overflow, in which the attacker sets various fields or arguments to overly large or long values to attempt to overwrite memory locations. By performing protocol analysis—for example, validating the header and payload values in a DNS query—the IDS can identify anomalous values that are possible signs of buffer overflow attempts. Although stateful firewalls might do some protocol analysis, they are usually poor logging tools and have no signature capabilities. Other types of firewalls generally don't do protocol analysis at all.

Active Responses

Another task that some network IDS sensors can perform is that of active response. When a sensor determines that a serious attack is occurring, it changes its own configuration, or that of other network devices, to respond differently to traffic from the attacking host. Sensor responses include the following:

- Send crafted RST packets to the attacker that appears to be coming from the victim host's IP address to terminate the suspicious TCP connection.

- Send rule-set changes to a firewall or ACL changes to a packet-filtering device to temporarily or permanently block the attacker's connection attempts, or possibly all connection attempts to the victim.

- Monitor all traffic from the attacker more closely, either temporarily or permanently.

Although active responses can be useful for handling certain attacks, you must be cautious with them. IP addresses are often spoofed (although this is much less likely in the case of successful TCP connections), so the attacker might not be at the address that your sensor is seeing. In addition, your IDS sensor could be generating false positives, in which case the attacker isn't really attacking you at all. In either case, an active response against the apparent attacker could actually cause a denial of service to an innocent party, who might be unable to use your services and vice versa.

IDS Sensor Placement

Now that you're familiar with the basics of network intrusion detection, you're ready to consider how it fits into your environment from a network architecture standpoint. It can be difficult to balance your desire to monitor as much of your network as possible with financial and staffing limitations. This section looks at the need for having multiple IDS sensors and where they are typically placed in a network. We'll discuss some issues that can affect sensor placement, as well as the advantages of implementing a separate IDS management network. Finally, we'll take a brief look at firewall/IDS hybrid systems.

Deploying Multiple Network Sensors

In most environments, you should deploy multiple IDS sensors. Each sensor generally monitors a single network segment. In a small organization with a simple network architecture and limited traffic, a single sensor might be adequate, although more than one might still be advisable. In larger environments—particularly those with many network segments, those that offer substantial Internet-based services, and those with multiple Internet access points—multiple sensors are almost certainly needed to adequately monitor network traffic.

Deploying more intrusion detection sensors usually produces better results. By deploying sensors on various network segments, you can tune each of them to the traffic that you typically see on that segment—the type of hosts that use it and the services and protocols that are traversing it. You would probably tune a sensor on an Internet-connected segment much differently than you would tune one that is monitoring traffic between two tightly secured internal portions of your network. If you deploy only one sensor, the amount of tuning you can do is generally quite limited.

Another reason for using multiple sensors is the fault tolerance of your IDS. What if your single sensor fails, for any reason, or the network segment that it's monitoring is unexpectedly unavailable? If you have one sensor, you won't have a network intrusion detection capability until the failure is corrected. Having more than one sensor provides a more robust solution that can continue monitoring at least portions of your network during a sensor failure or partial network outage.

Placing Sensors Near Filtering Devices

Typically, you deploy IDS sensors, which are often paired with firewalls or packet filters, near Internet access points. Sometimes you place a sensor on one side of the filtering device, and sometimes on both sides. For example, an Internet firewall might have an IDS sensor on the external network segment to identify all suspicious activity, and a second IDS sensor on the internal network segment that can identify all suspicious activity that passes through the firewall from the outside.

If possible, deploy sensors on both sides of firewalls and packet filters. However, if financial or other resource constraints limit you to one sensor per filtering device, you have to decide on which side of the filtering device the sensor should be deployed. It's generally recommended that the sensor should be placed on the outside network so that it can detect all attacks, including those that don't get through the filtering.

However, in some cases, you might prefer to put the sensor on the inside network. Sensors on an outside network, particularly one that is connected to the Internet, are more likely to be attacked, and they're also going to process much more traffic than a sensor on an inside network. In addition, if your staff has limited time to perform intrusion analysis and can only address the most serious threats, putting the sensor on the inside network collects data and generates alerts only on attacks that get into the network. Another advantage to putting a sensor on the inside network is that it can help you determine whether your filtering device is misconfigured.

If you're limited to one sensor, your firewall policies might be relevant to its placement. We mentioned earlier that you should also consider issues involving outgoing traffic from compromised or malicious hosts within your own environment. If your firewall has a default deny policy for outgoing traffic, a sensor on the inside network is required to identify attacks that your internal hosts attempt against external hosts but that your firewall blocks. If your firewall has a default allow policy for outgoing traffic, the sensor's location is much less important (as long as there's one near your firewall).

Another factor in sensor deployment is the volume of data to be processed. If a network segment has an extremely high volume of data, you might want to deploy multiple sensors with different configurations to split the traffic. After a sensor starts dropping packets, you will almost certainly experience more false positives and negatives. If your external network sees extremely high volumes of traffic, consider putting a sensor outside the firewall that is tuned to identify only the most severe attacks, particularly flooding-type attacks that are meant to cause a denial of service for your Internet connectivity or firewall. Don't perform any sort of protocol or payload analysis with this sensor. Use a second sensor inside your firewall to do more detailed analysis; this sensor should see a significantly smaller volume of data than the first sensor.

Note

Wherever there is a link to the Internet or to other external networks or hosts, there should be an IDS sensor. This rule varies from environment to environment, of course. Another great place to put a sensor is where a filtering device should be but isn't.

Placing IDS Sensors on the Internal Network

In many environments, network IDS sensors are placed along the network perimeter only, typically around Internet firewalls and packet filters. However, some environments also benefit from the deployment of additional network IDS sensors. A classic example is a company's research and development division. The company might have established a firewall or packet filter that prevents users in other divisions from accessing the hosts in R&D. Because the information on the R&D hosts is valuable to external attackers and malicious insiders, it would be prudent to deploy an IDS sensor near the firewall or packet filter.

Some companies are so security-conscious that they deploy IDS sensors throughout their networks to monitor all traffic. Of course, this requires considerable financial and staffing resources, but it gives the intrusion analysts a great feel for what's happening throughout their environment. If you only look at the activity occurring on your borders, you're missing much of the picture. Remember that IDS sensors aren't limited to identifying attacks against servers; many can also find signs of trojans, worms, and other malware that is attempting to spread through a network, sometimes before anti-virus software can identify it.

Working with Encryption

When planning network IDS sensor placement, you must consider how to deal with encrypted network traffic, such as VPN connections. IDS sensors certainly don't have the capability to decrypt traffic, but that's a good thing! If all of the traffic on a certain network segment is encrypted, it still might be valuable to deploy a sensor to examine packet headers and look for unencrypted traffic. To monitor the content of the traffic that was encrypted, you should deploy IDS sensors at the first point in the network where the decrypted traffic travels. In addition, you should put host-based IDS software on the host that is decrypting the traffic because it's a likely target for attacks.

Processing in High-Traffic Situations

Consider the volume of network traffic. The amount of traffic that IDS sensors can process is dependent on many factors, including what product is being used, which protocols or applications are most commonly used, and for which signatures the sensor has been directed to look. Therefore, no simple answers exist as to what volume of traffic any particular product can handle. In general, IDS sensors reach their capacity before firewalls do, primarily because IDS sensors do much more examination of packets than other network devices do. Also, the field of IDS sensor and signature development and optimization is still fairly young, at least compared to other aspects of network security.

Configuring Switches

If portions of your network that you would like to monitor are switched, then ensure that you configured your IDS sensors and switches appropriately. Switches must have their spanning ports configured properly for network IDS sensors to see all the traffic that is passing through the switch. This critical configuration has adversely affected many IDS deployments. A sensor that tries to monitor traffic on an improperly configured switch might see no traffic at all—or it might see parts of the traffic, such as only one side of two-way TCP connections, which is only marginally better than seeing nothing. Thoroughly test sensors in switched environments to confirm that they are seeing all of the traffic properly.

Using an IDS Management Network

To improve the security of your network IDS sensors, you might want to create a separate management network to use strictly for communication between IDS sensors, a centralized IDS data collection box, and analyst consoles. In this model, each network IDS sensor has at least two NICs. One or more NICs sniff traffic from monitored networks as their sole function. These NICs do not transmit traffic. Instead, the last NIC is connected to a separate management network, which is only used for transferring IDS data and configuration updates.

By implementing such an architecture, you make it much more difficult for attackers to find and identify an IDS sensor because it will not answer requests that are directed toward its monitoring NICs. Because the management NIC is on an isolated network, attackers shouldn't be able to reach it. Also, some monitoring NICs are pure sniffers and do not use an IP address. If an IDS sensor uses an IP address and an attacker knows what that address is, the attacker could launch a DoS against it so that it couldn't see her attacks, or could otherwise try to hide or obfuscate her traffic from the sensor.

Implementing a separate management network has other advantages. It isolates management traffic so that anyone else who is monitoring the same network doesn't see your sensors' communications. It also prevents the sensors from monitoring their own traffic. A separate network might also be a good way to deal with potential problems that are related to passing sensor data through firewalls and over unencrypted public networks.

Maintaining Sensor Security

One important item that hasn't been addressed yet is that of sensor security. It's critical that you harden your IDS sensors to make the risk of compromise as low as possible. If attackers gain control of your IDS, they could shut it off or reconfigure it so that it couldn't log or alert you about their activities. Attackers might also be able to use your IDS to launch attacks against other hosts. However, if attackers can get access to your IDS management network, they might be able to access all your sensors. Maintaining the security of your sensors is key to creating a stable and valuable IDS solution.

Using Firewall/IDS Hybrid Solutions

Hybrid solutions that combine traditional firewall and intrusion detection capabilities are now available, although such solutions are not yet widely used to replace traditional network firewalls and IDS sensors. Some people feel that hybrid devices, such as Hogwash (`http://hogwash.sourceforge.net/`), are the wave of the future. Traffic that the hybrid device receives is checked against a firewall rule set, and also compared to an IDS signature set. Traffic that the firewall rule set permits might still be denied because of an IDS signature match. Such hybrid solutions are also known as *filtering IDS* or *gateway IDS*.

From an intrusion-detection standpoint, the advantage of implementing a hybrid solution is that you are getting an active response capability that is contained in a single box. Some attacks can be identified and stopped before they ever pass through the firewall. In a more traditional configuration, the network IDS sensor might identify the same attacks after they pass through the firewall. By the time the sensor asks the firewall to block the traffic, the attack might already have been successful. Combining the firewall and IDS sensor in one box can give you a slight time advantage that could reduce the chance of successful attacks. Of course, in the case of a false positive, the combination might also make your environment more prone to self-triggered denials of service.

The disadvantages of a network-based firewall/IDS hybrid are fairly obvious. It's often a bad idea to provide multiple services in a single box for reasons of security, performance, and fault tolerance. At this time, hybrid products are generally much less mature than traditional firewall and IDS solutions. They are certainly an interesting idea, and one that will probably become more significant in the coming years.

Case Studies

Now that we have discussed some of the factors that go into sensor placement, let's look at three different scenarios. Each one is shown through a simplified diagram of the relevant portions of the network. No right or wrong answers exist, only reasons why certain locations might be more beneficial than others.

Case Study 1: Simple Network Infrastructure

Figure 7.1 shows a network diagram for a small organization with a simple network infrastructure. It has only one connection point to the Internet. A firewall divides the network into three segments:

- An external DMZ segment that is connected to the Internet
- A screened subnet that contains servers that are directly accessed by Internet-based users or must directly access the Internet, such as email, web, web proxy, and external DNS servers
- An internal segment that contains servers that typically aren't directly connected to the Internet, as well as workstations, printers, and other host devices

In this environment, incoming connections from the Internet can only be made to hosts on the screened subnet; those hosts can then initiate connections to the internal network. Hosts on the internal network can initiate connections to hosts on the screened subnet or directly to Internet-based hosts. Although the firewall has a default deny policy for incoming traffic, it has a default allow policy for outgoing traffic. Little outgoing traffic is restricted.

IDS Deployment Recommendations

Figure 7.1 shows the IDS management network as a separate entity from the monitored networks. Each sensor contains two NICs: one sniffing packets on the monitored network, and the other transmitting IDS data on the management network. The management network is connected only to the sensors, a central IDS logging box, and the analyst workstations.

Ideally, all three network IDS sensors shown in Figure 7.1 should be deployed. IDS 1 (on the external segment) looks for any probes, scans, or attacks that are coming from the Internet. IDS 2 (on the internal segment) shows you which malicious traffic got through the firewall to your internal network. Both IDS 1 and IDS 2 can monitor outgoing traffic as well, looking for attacks from your internal hosts. IDS 3 focuses on identifying attacks against your externally exposed boxes, which are the most likely targets of attackers. The same sensor is also able to monitor network activity between your external servers that doesn't pass through the firewall. If one of your external hosts should become compromised, this is the only sensor that could see attempts from it to compromise other hosts on the same segment.

Figure 7.1   This is a simple network infrastructure that includes IDS sensors and a separate IDS management network.

Case Study 2: Multiple External Access Points

Figure 7.2 shows a more complicated network. This environment has multiple external points of access: a dedicated connection to the Internet, a dial-up modem bank for remote users, and multiple frame relay connections to remote offices and business partners. Firewalls have been deployed at each access point to restrict the traffic that enters the internal network.

Figure 7.2   A more complex corporate network has multiple external points of access, which each need to be protected with IDS sensors.

IDS Deployment Recommendations

This scenario follows the same general rule as before: Whenever practical, deploy network IDS sensors on both sides of firewalls and packet filters. The most interesting area to consider is that of the external networks that are connected through the frame relay connections. You will notice that no sensors monitor the connections on the external side. If your budget permits, you can add sensors to those connections as well, although they might not be needed. It depends on what is on the other side of the connection and what your firewall is supposed to be doing.

You might feel that a remote office poses little threat and that a separate sensor to monitor its connection is not necessary. Of course, you could also deploy a sensor at the remote location, which would monitor traffic before it was sent over the frame relay connection. If the remote site is a business partner's network, you might want to be more cautious; however, your firewall might only be permitting a small, well-defined set of traffic to pass through. The risk might be small enough that you can't justify the expense of an additional sensor. Perhaps the connection to your business partner is largely unrestricted, in which case you would want to monitor it much more closely. If you decide to deploy sensors for the external links that enter the firewall, and the firewall has several interfaces on separate network segments, you would probably want to deploy a sensor for each segment. Each sensor can then be tuned for the nature of that particular connection.

Another item to consider is the risk that outgoing attacks and probes pose. If you are not restricting outbound traffic very much, then sensor placement shouldn't be affected by it. But if you do restrict outbound traffic—for example, you block everything that is going to the modem bank—then having the sensor on the inside is necessary to detect attempted attacks. The question is, how much do you care about that? In your environment, is it sufficient for the firewall to report that a connection attempt was blocked, or do you need to know what the nature of that attempt was? How important is the resource on the other side of the connection? What are the consequences if you fail to notice an attack from one of your hosts against your business partner's systems?

Case Study 3: Unrestricted Environment

Our final case study, shown in Figure 7.3, is a greatly simplified view of a university network with three main groups of hosts: students, faculty and staff, and administration (registrar, bursar, and so on). As is typical of many university environments, no firewalls restrict traffic. A small amount of packet filtering might occur at routers throughout the network, but otherwise, virtually any sort of traffic is permitted. The only exception is some machines in the administration network that contain sensitive information, such as student grades and financial information; these machines are somewhat protected through router packet filtering. Because of the open nature of most universities, faculty and student machines are usually vulnerable to exploitation, in part because just about any sort of traffic is permitted. In addition, many servers are run by students or faculty, not centralized IT staff, and are almost certainly not kept fully patched and secured.

Figure 7.3 In a university environment with little network security,
it is not easy to determine where to deploy IDS sensors.

We can expect many student and faculty machines to use modems. We can
also expect that some of these machines run software, such as pcAnywhere to
allow external hosts to dial into them. In such an environment, it's impossible
to define the border of your network. It's also likely that the university offers
dial-in services for users and that these services require little or no authentication. (After all, why should you implement dial-in authentication when
anyone can walk into an on-campus computer lab and get the same access?)

IDS Deployment Recommendations

As you might imagine, the security requirements of the groups of hosts
shown in Figure 7.3 are quite different. In addition, staffing and financial
resources are probably quite limited, so you need to focus on the most
important areas. Your first priority is protecting the administrative computers,
which are at high risk of being attacked. You want to monitor these systems
as closely as possible, through a combination of IDS sensors that are deployed
to the segments where the hosts reside, and host-based IDS software running
on all of them. If you can do nothing else, you need to regularly monitor
IDS alerts and logs that are related to these sensitive hosts.

Even if you have the resources to deploy and monitor additional sensors, will you have the resources to react to what you see? These environments might contain tens of thousands of largely unsecured machines that can be infected with viruses, trojans, or other malware. This is a similar problem to that seen by ISPs, which carry customer traffic but have little control over what their customers do. In fact, portions of a university network can be thought of as an ISP for students. If network IDS sensors are deployed, they need to be carefully tuned to only send alerts on the most severe attacks. If the sensor sends an alert every time a port scan or host scan occurs, the intrusion analyst will quickly be overwhelmed with alerts. Sensors might also be unable to keep up with the high volumes of traffic if they are performing too much analysis.

You might be asking yourself, "Why should I bother trying to monitor this traffic at all? If users are permitted to do almost anything that they want to, why should I try to deploy sensors to the networks that they use?" Here's a scenario that explains why some level of network intrusion detection should be performed. Suppose that dozens of hosts throughout the university have been infected with the same trojan, and that these hosts are used to launch DoS attacks against other sites. Given the lack of other defense devices, your only chance of detecting such an attack and collecting enough information about it to identify the infected hosts is to deploy an intrusion detection sensor that monitors outgoing traffic.

Summary

In this chapter, you learned about the basics of network IDSs, particularly signatures and how they cause false positives and negatives. We took a close look at where IDS sensors and software can be located in various network environments and discussed the advantages and disadvantages of various deployment architectures. The goal of this chapter was not to teach you everything you will ever need to know about intrusion detection. Several good books focus on that topic, such as *Network Intrusion Detection: An Analyst's Handbook*, by Stephen Northcutt and Judy Novak, and *Intrusion Signatures and Analysis*, by Stephen Northcutt, Mark Cooper, Matt Fearnow, and Karen Frederick. Instead, we examined the role that IDS plays in a layered defense and how it has become a critical component of a good security solution.

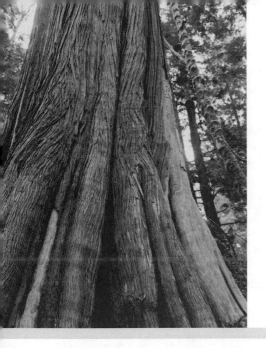

8

Virtual Private Networks

IN TODAY'S INTERCONNECTED WORLD, THE NEED to move information from site to site is becoming common. Whether this move is from one end of town to the other or across the globe, the basic challenge is the same: How can we securely transport our data? For many years, this transportation was accomplished with expensive proprietary links that were "leased" from communication vendors so that companies had a "private" segment for such communications. The longer the distance, the more these connections cost, making wide area networks (WANs) a luxury that many firms could not afford. At the same time, many firms could not afford to go without them. As broadband Internet connections became staples for many firms, the concept of using the existing structure of the Internet as WAN cabling became an intriguing concept. Costs could be greatly reduced using these already available public access points. The concern again was how to keep the data secure. Because we are sharing an international "party-line" with anyone else who connects to the Internet, how can we be sure that our data is protected from eavesdroppers? The solution is Virtual Private Networking (VPN).

In this chapter, we discuss the basic concepts of how a VPN works and is configured, the basic encryption technologies that a VPN uses, details of Internet Security (IPSec) Protocol (a standard for VPN networking), as well as other popularly implemented protocols for virtual networking. We also show example configurations that demonstrate practical applications for the theory we cover.

VPN Basics

A VPN is a connection that is established over an existing "public" or shared infrastructure using encryption or authentication technologies to secure its payload. This creates a "virtual" segment between any two entities that have access. This might occur across the shared infrastructure of a local area network (LAN), WAN connections, or the Internet. In this chapter, we focus predominately on VPNs that traverse the Internet as a means to create a secure channel over its public infrastructure. Such channels make for an inexpensive and effective remote networking solution that anyone with Internet access can take advantage of.

VPNs can be categorized into three basic configuration types: host-to-host, host-to-gateway, and gateway-to-gateway. Any of these scenarios could be used with a VPN that is traversing the Internet, although host-to-host VPNs are also popularly used as a means to communicate privately on local network segments.

Regardless of which media the VPN uses, which type of configuration it represents, or what shared infrastructure it crosses, the VPN is a powerful tool that can be used in many different ways to create a secure communication channel.

> **Note**
>
> If you would like to brush up on cryptography fundamentals, take a look at Appendix B, "Crypto 101," where we review key topics in cryptography that you need to know to effectively plan and implement VPNs.

Basic VPN Methodology

The basic concept behind a VPN is securing a communication channel with encryption. Communication can be safeguarded through encryption at many different layers of the network, such as the following:

- Application
- Transport
- Network
- Data Link

At the Application layer, encryption can be applied with programs such as Pretty Good Privacy (PGP) or through channels such as Secure Shell (SSH). In addition, remote single-session programs such as pcAnywhere and multi-session programs such as Terminal Server can be used with encryption to protect remote communications. Most of these programs work from host to host, meaning that they only offer protection for the packet's payload and not the packet. The exception is SSH, which can be used in a port-forwarding mode to create a tunnel. We will cover this in greater detail in Chapter 14, "VPN Integration."

At the Transport layer, protocols such as Secure Sockets Layer (SSL) can be used to protect the contents of a specific communication between two parties. This is typically used via web browser communications. Again the contents of the communication are protected, but the IP packets that carry this information are available for inspection. SSL can also be used as a tunneling facilitator for other communication session types using a product called Stunnel (`http://www.stunnel.org/`). SSL and its use are covered in greater detail in Chapter 14.

At the Network layer, protocols such as IPSec not only encrypt the payload of the packet, but they also encrypt the TCP/IP information. Although the IP address information for the parties that are encrypting and decrypting the packet is necessary to facilitate proper routing, higher-level information including transport protocols and associated ports can be completely obfuscated. Endpoint station IP address information can also be hidden if a gateway device such as a router, firewall, or concentrator is doing the encryption using a concept called tunneling. We will cover IPSec's implementation, its inner workings, and example configuration in detail in the "IPSec Basics" section later in this chapter.

Layer 2 Tunneling Protocol (L2TP) is an addition to Point-to-Point Protocol (PPP), which allows the encryption of packets sent over PPP on the Data Link layer (layer 2). We cover L2TP and its predecessor PPTP (Point-to-Point Tunneling Protocol) in greater detail later in this chapter, in the "Other VPN Protocols: PPTP and L2TP" section.

Despite the fact that these encryption technologies occur at many different network layers, they all could be part of a VPN. However, some might not be able to handle all the duties of a VPN without some help from other applications or protocols. In this chapter, we predominately discuss the use of Network and Data Link layer encryption technology for VPNs.

What Is Tunneling?

Tunneling is the process of encapsulating one type of packet inside another to facilitate some sort of transport advantage. For example, tunneling could be used to send broadcast traffic across a routed environment or NetBEUI traffic across the Internet, or to secure IP packets with encryption. One effective demonstration of tunneling as a means of encryption can be illustrated by using a gateway-to-gateway VPN example. Two networks in Figure 8.1 are interconnected via a VPN that is terminated at either end by a firewall.

Figure 8.1   A virtual tunnel is formed across the Internet connecting the two remote networks.

The firewall in our example translates any packet that is destined for the remote network into encrypted form and adds a new IP header to the resulting payload with its own IP address as the source address and the remote firewall's address as the destination IP address of the packet. Encryption hides the actual IP information of the original packet. When the remote firewall receives the packet, it decrypts it back to its original form and passes it to the host for which it was originally intended. The virtual segment that is being created between the two gateway endpoints is called a *tunnel*. The hosts have no knowledge of the fact that the packets are being encrypted or that they are being sent over a public network. No special software or configuration is required for the hosts. All that must be done is a packet destined for a host on the remote subnet and the process being handled completely by the gateway devices.

When using tunneling, even though host system IP addresses are masked from the outside world, they don't have complete anonymity. Because the IP addresses of the gateway devices are available, eavesdroppers can still determine who is communicating with whom. Maybe this won't give away communication streams on a host-to-host level, but it might on a network-to-network level, which could tell an outsider a lot. For example, what if it is rumored that Mr. X is a spy from Switzerland. The government immediately starts to monitor his Internet connection and determines that he is using a VPN. We can't tell what his communications are about. However, if we know Mr. X owns the source address and the destination is somewhere in Switzerland, we might want to investigate further.

Encryption, encapsulation, and tunneling do not make the packets that are being sent inaccessible. The packets can still be gathered and analyzed. However, if a properly implemented, adequately strong encryption algorithm is used, your payload should still be safe. In the next section, we take a closer look at what a gateway-to-gateway tunnel transaction looks like in packet form.

Packet Level View of Tunneling

The concept of tunneling can be more clearly understood by taking a look at it at the packet level. The following code, which uses Tcpdump, shows a packet as it would appear without going through an encrypted tunnel:

```
00:05:18.671517 192.168.44.129 > 172.16.1.128: AH(spi=580532459,seq=0x3):
➥1232 > 80: P 1:260(259) ack 1 win 17520 (DF)
```

This is actually an IPSec packet that uses the Authentication Header (AH) security protocol that we will cover in greater detail in the IPSec section of this chapter. This packet is sent in a mode that does not require tunneling. The packet traverses directly from one host to the other, without being translated in any way by the gateway devices. Make note of the IP addresses. They represent the addresses of two network hosts. In addition, notice that the Transport layer information is available and that this is an HTTP transaction, as signified by the use of TCP port 80. (It is actually the contacting of a web server.) Because the TCP flags are available, we can tell that this is actually the end of the three-way handshake. Host 192.168.44.129 is sending a lone ACK back to the web server at IP address 172.16.1.128.

The following code shows a similar packet that has been encapsulated. It is the same transaction as listed previously, but it is translated by a gateway-to-gateway VPN tunnel. Notice that the IP level information appears much the same. Also note the lack of Layer 4 TCP information:

```
00:01:30.057912 192.168.44.1 > 172.16.1.1: ESP(spi=1302500357,seq=0x3) (DF)
```

The source and destination IP addresses changed from the previous packet to this one. This address switch is because the tunneled packet took on the addressing of the source and destination VPN gateways. Layer 4 (in this case, TCP) information is missing because it, along with the original IP information and higher-level information, is actually encapsulated into the payload of this packet. All we have available is the IP information and the information of the protocol that is doing the encapsulation (ESP).

Advantages and Disadvantages of VPNs

When determining whether a VPN is the solution of choice for your business' remote connectivity needs, you must consider many factors. What is the confidence level of the data that you are sending? What value is placed on its secrecy? How important is it to know the source of the data? If the secrecy level is high enough, then even a VPN that uses strong encryption might be inappropriate. Only a dedicated point-to-point connection might be suitable.

You can describe all forms of remote connectivity as three different types:

- Dedicated point-to-point connections such as a leased T-1 line
- Standard unencrypted Internet communications
- Encrypted VPN Internet communications, which is a compromise between the first two types

Of the first two types, the security and performance advantages both go to a dedicated connection type. Why consider an alternative? The answer is that a third factor is involved: finances. Dedicated connections are expensive, especially when they cover great distances. To add to this expense, most sites are also already utilizing some sort of high-speed Internet connection. Because broadband Internet connections are becoming a common part of most networks, the ability to utilize this high-speed connection as a means of remote connectivity is attractive for most businesses. The monthly expense of leased T-1 lines can be a thing of the past.

However, the use of a shared medium such as the Internet makes security an even greater issue. Your data is literally traversing an infrastructure shared by millions of people around the world. The cost advantages of such public access connectivity must offset the value of your data's secrecy. Therefore, to be able to leverage the functionality of your existing Internet connection and increase the security level of your communications, the VPN is an excellent compromise. Encryption protects your data, but it adds a slight burden to your network and decreases bandwidth. Varying levels of encryption strength can add to the VPN's ability to protect your data, although greater encryption strength comes with a cost. More expensive hardware—or often, more expensive or additional software—might be required to use a stronger encryption algorithm. Because of the greater complexities of such an algorithm, additional overhead must be shouldered by the equipment you are using, decreasing overall bandwidth.

Note

Although some commercial VPN solutions might vary their prices based on the level of encryption that you choose, it should be mentioned that some excellent free VPN solutions are available. Many free Linux variants have exceptional IPSec implementations, and freeware VPN applications provide adequate protection as well.

Benefits of VPN

The main benefit of using a VPN for remote network access can be summed up as the price effectiveness of being able to utilize a public medium to transport private information as securely as possible. A VPN can supply many levels of security to a shared network medium, including the improvement of confidentiality, integrity, and authentication. Because a VPN utilizes existing infrastructures, it can be swiftly implemented, without having to wait for the establishment of a line or other factors that commonly hold up such implementations. If VPNs are used for remote users, they can offer a secure and more cost-effective "road warrior" solution. That way, people who need remote access can take advantage of local Internet access wherever they are, instead of making costly long-distance calls. The combination of security, quick setup, and cost effectiveness can make a VPN an excellent communication solution.

Security

VPNs offer many security features that make it a powerful method for securing information that is traveling across insecure territory. These features can be customized depending on the "hostility level" of the environment. This security level must be balanced against the value of the data.

Lower-strength encryption might be adequate for remote connections for many companies; the information that is being transmitted might be of little value to others. For example, if you owned a car lot with two locations, you might want to share inventory and pricing information between them. For obvious reasons, it might be a little too tempting for your competitors if you transmit this information in the clear, making it possible for someone else to read it. On the other side of the coin, it is unlikely that your competition will go to great lengths to break your encrypted traffic; they could easily drive by to count the inventory in your lot, and probably have a good general idea of what you are paying for your inventory. Utilizing a low-strength encryption VPN might adequately protect your information.

However, what if you are sending a top-secret formula for an item that was a matter of national defense or that was possibly the whole reason your company was in business? That data might be valuable enough that some outsiders would be willing to go to great expense and effort to defeat your protection. Therefore, stronger encryption would be needed.

Regardless of the strength of the chosen encryption technology used for your VPN, your VPN should still offer the requirements of a secure communication channel. The following three requirements are the most basic:

- Confidentiality is the guarantee that no one else is going to be able to peek at your information. The encryption algorithms that scramble your private data into meaningless segments of characters provide this for a VPN. If this encryption algorithm is not sufficiently strong enough to protect your data, then your confidentiality is compromised.

- Data integrity is the next issue that can be protected through encryption and VPN use. Integrity verifies that the information you are receiving is the same as it was when it was sent to you. Long ago, this was often accomplished by sealing a document with a wax seal emblem of the party who was sending the message. If the seal was broken, you could not be sure that the message wasn't altered in transit. In today's world, this same integrity assurance can be accomplished with digital signatures and hashes. Both are discussed in greater detail in Appendix B.

- Authentication verifies that the information has come from whom it is supposed to, and in turn, that it is received by whom is supposed to receive it.

Deployment Advantages

Anyone who has had to wait for the phone company to terminate or activate a line knows that the waiting can be the hardest part. When you need to have something done today, filling out requests and waiting for outside parties are not things that you want on your itinerary. Because VPNs can take advantage of existing infrastructure, many of these stumbling blocks can be avoided. Even in cases in which internal infrastructure needs to be patchworked, a VPN can shine. For example, imagine you are the network engineer at a college campus. You are told that the accounting office is having an audit tomorrow and you are responsible for setting up a place for the teams of auditors to work. The auditors have to be separate from the rest of the accounting office, and the only place you have for them to go is quite a distance away on the other side of the campus. Networks connect the whole campus, but none connect to the accounting office because it is on a separate segment from the rest of the campus. You could get out your handy spool of fiber-optic cable and trench digger and get ready to physically run the half-mile connection, or you could rely on securing the connection through existing infrastructure with VPN technology. This could either be accomplished by adding an additional hardware device and doing some fancy cable patching to tie the remote location to the accounting office, or relying on an existing VPN device that the accounting office already uses for remote connection and some already available Internet connections across campus. The end results are a lot less work, considerably less preparation time, and most likely, a savings cost of infrastructure changes.

Cost Effectiveness

A VPN can save you money in many ways, most of which involve the VPN replacing some type of high-cost, dedicated WAN link. Often, high-speed Internet access is already in place at these same locations. When pitching broadband Internet, you should see a bean-counter's eyes light up when you explain that the monthly Internet access charges will be offset by the removal of the dedicated T-1 link that they are currently using to connect to their branch office. Usually, same-speed Internet access offsets the price of a similar speed point-to-point T-1 within a year or two (this can vary greatly by region and location proximity), even considering the costs of additional firewall/VPN hardware.

VPNs can help pay for themselves in other ways as well. For instance, most VPN solutions can also offer an alternative to secure remote dial-in. This can add up to savings in long-distance bills for remote users who are accessing your network. It also removes the need for dedicated dial-in servers or modem pools for these same users, meaning lowered equipment cost, as well as a reduction in monthly dial-up phone charges. Regardless of the network setup, in most scenarios, a VPN can give an excellent return on investment and add up to considerable savings in the long run.

Disadvantages of VPN

Despite all of their positive points, VPNs are not all smiles and sunshine. You must weigh many disadvantages to confirm that a VPN is suitable for your environment. The use of encryption brings about an additional processing burden, most likely to be handled by your existing gateway devices or by equipment that must be purchased additionally. Fitting a VPN into an existing location can also be a challenge in some environments due to the additional packet overhead. A VPN has significant design issues that the novice (as well as some intermediates) will most likely not want to tackle on his own, and troubleshooting traffic that is encapsulated can be a real challenge for even the most experienced practitioners.

Processing Overhead

Encryption, the backbone of the VPN, involves incredibly complex mathematical computations. These must occur for every packet that is sent across and received by a VPN gateway device. These complicated computations take their toll not only on the gateway device, but also on the overall bandwidth of the VPN connection. This speed reduction intensifies with stronger encryption algorithms, which in turn require more mathematical complexity and more processing bandwidth. This problem has become such an issue over time that special "offload cards" have been created to help absorb some of the additional processing burden of VPN encryption. These hardware acceleration devices can improve the detriment of lost processing power, but at a hefty price. In turn, it is important to make this processing burden a part of your hardware and bandwidth determination requirements when deciding on a VPN.

Packet Overhead

Another interesting disadvantage of implementing a VPN is the additional overhead that is added to every packet. Because existing packets can be encapsulated, encapsulation requires the "wrapping" of the original packet in additional packet overhead. Even if you aren't using encapsulation, additional header information still adds to the packet size. In either case, this overhead, although not substantial, can be enough to become a design concern in some environments. In addition, adding size to every packet can negatively affect network bandwidth, not only due to the issues of sending a larger packet, but also because a larger packet is more likely to need fragmentation as it journeys across various gateways and routers. This fragmentation will negatively affect network performance.

Implementation Issues

Implementation is a concern when making a VPN part of your existing network infrastructure. Some of these implementation issues include VPN pass-through, the problems of VPNs and Network Address Translation (NAT), maximum transmission unit (MTU) size and design issues, and more. VPN design and implementation details are covered in greater detail in Chapter 14.

Troubleshooting and Control Issues

Troubleshooting a VPN can be a complicated process. Because the innards and payload of encapsulated packets are unavailable until they are decrypted, you can't see what is happening while the packet travels between two gateway devices. Tools such as Traceroute are ineffective when employed across a

VPN tunnel. For more information on Traceroute and VPN troubleshooting considerations, see Chapter 19, "Troubleshooting Defense Components."

Common means to examine the packet flow, such as network intrusion detection systems (IDSs), are less effective because the payload is unknown until *after* it passes through the perimeter VPN device. Not only can this make troubleshooting more difficult, but it also can punch a big hole in an otherwise secure network.

Note

Host based intrusion detection offers one way to effectively monitor encrypted traffic, as we discuss in Chapter 10, "Host Defense Components." Because the traffic is decrypted either before reaching the host at a perimeter device (tunnel mode), or on the host (transport mode), the host-based IDS can check the packets after they are translated. Therefore, in high security environments that use VPN, it is wise to implement host-based IDS on mission-critical systems.

It becomes a security concern when you don't have controls on entities that are remotely connected by VPN. For example, users who telecommute via VPN might become a backdoor to your network due to a lack of security on their home PCs. Also, smaller remote offices that lack an IT staff or even extranet connections to customers or vendors could be the source of back-door attacks or to the propagation of a trojan or worm.

Regardless of your environment, you must consider many issues when deciding the effectiveness of a VPN solution as your remote communication choice. If all issues are adequately considered beforehand, then the outcome will be a correct decision and a smooth implementation.

Internet Availability Issues

One final point that must be made about using the Internet as the backbone of your wide area network (WAN) are those communication glitches that can occur between you and your remote partner's networks. Technical problems at your Internet service provider's (ISPs) level, denial of service (DoS) attacks, or other infrastructure issues such as damage to outside cabling can cause outages to Internet service that most of us have experienced at one time or another. Because the Internet is redundant by design, hopefully these problems are few and far between. However, when your business relies on remote communications, any such outage can become a major financial burden and an unacceptable outcome. Designing in extra redundancy to your Internet connectivity can help alleviate such situations. Multiple Internet connections using multiple ISPs can lessen the chance that a problem at a single ISP will create a system-down situation for you. This, combined with the incorporation of screening routers or like products that can help prevent DoS conditions, can maximize Internet availability for your network. For more information on the use of such screening routers, check out Chapter 6, "Role of a Router."

IPSec Basics

Even though IP has become the most used communication protocol in the world and is the backbone technology behind the Internet, it still has many intrinsic flaws. Some of these issues are address space limitations, no auto-configuration of hosts, and a lack of intrinsic security. The main reason for these flaws is that IP wasn't designed for use by the masses. It was actually designed for a much smaller, self-sufficient, contained environment. Because IP has invaded most businesses and so many homes, many of these flaws have been patched with other protocols and programs.

In an effort to move IP forward, a new version of the protocol IPv6 (IP version 6) was born, with built-in functionality that took care of many of the issues of its predecessor. Because the adoption of a new version of IP in our constantly growing, current Internet environment has been difficult, the security measures that were incorporated into Ipv6 have also been ported to our current version of IP (version 4) as an optional protocol suite. This set of protocols is known as the IPSec Protocol Suite.

IPSec Protocol Suite

IPSec's goal is to facilitate the confidentiality, integrity, and authentication of information that is communicated using IP. This is accomplished through the use of several protocols, including Internet Key Exchange (IKE), Encapsulating Security Payload (ESP), and Authentication Header (AH). These three protocols combine to allow the secure exchange of information without fear of outside eavesdropping or tampering. A second goal of the security suite is a means for multiple vendors to have a set of standards by which they can interoperate securely. Industry-wide testing is being done to verify that the products of these vendors can all work together correctly. This security starts with the forming of a security association (SA) between two communicating parties.

SA

An SA is basically an agreement between two entities on how they will securely transmit information. One of the exceptional things about IPSec is the openness of its standard to support not only multiple protocols and communication modes, but also various encryption algorithms and hash types. All of these details must be prenegotiated before the secure exchange of user's data can begin. The resultant agreement is an SA. Each communication session has two SAs—one for each communication partner. Each partner negotiates a new SA for every IPSec connection he makes.

Before an SA is negotiated, the particulars that an IPSec partner is going to support must be configured for it locally. These settings are held in what is known as a security policy database (SPD).

After the SA has been negotiated, it is contained in a security association database (SAD). This is necessary because different communication rules can be configured for each of the sessions that a host or device might initiate. For example, look at Figure 8.2. A Cisco PIX Firewall can be set up to allow Data Encryption Standard (DES) or 3DES as the encryption algorithm for a VPN tunnel. When Host 1 connects, it might only support DES and would negotiate an SA with DES encryption. However, Host 2 behind another PIX might also attempt to create a tunnel with our PIX, and they might require a 3DES tunnel because of their own business and security requirements. In this case, only a 3DES tunnel could be negotiated. Each of these negotiated connections would require its own SA entry in the SAD, listing all the specific details of what was negotiated for each. These details will include such information as encryption algorithm negotiated (DES, 3DES, and so on), VPN mode, security protocol negotiated (ESP or AH), hash algorithm negotiated (MD5 or SHA-1), and so on.

Figure 8.2   IPSec connection parameters negotiated for VPN tunnels are maintained in the SAD.

Because multiple IPSec sessions are available per device (each with its own set of unique settings), for this process to function correctly, each SA session must have its own singular identifier. This identifier is made up of a unique security parameter index (SPI) that tells which SA database entry pertains to the connection in question, the destination address of the connection, and the protocol identifier for ESP or AH protocols, whichever is being used for the connection.

Listing 8.1 is an excerpt from a Cisco router's SA database for an inbound ESP connection.

Listing 8.1   **Cisco Router SA database**

```
inbound esp sas:
  spi: 0x71BB425D(1908097629)
  transform: esp-des esp-md5-hmac,
  in use settings ={Tunnel, }
  slot: 0, conn id: 2000, flow_id: 1, crypto map: mode
  sa timing: remaining key lifetime (k/sec):(4608000/3500)
  IV size: 8 bytes
  replay detection support: Y
```

This excerpt contains much information about this specific connection, such as the SPI number of the connection, the encryption and hash algorithms that are being used for this connection, the fact that it is working in tunnel mode, and the lifetime for this connection. This information is recorded in the SAD for each negotiated connection.

IPSec Tunnel and Transport Modes

An IPSec connection has two basic modes: transport and tunnel. Transport mode is a host-to-host form of communication and involves the encryption of a packet's payload only. Because of this host-to-host requirement, software needs to be loaded on all communicating hosts, which in large installations can be an administrative nightmare. However, this VPN mode is well-suited for encrypted communications between hosts on the same network, or in situations where it is important to be able to differentiate hosts by their IP address information. Transport mode lacks a means to do gateway-to-gateway communication and the ability to conceal host IP information, which can be a major concern when your data is traversing a public medium, such as the Internet. Transport mode communication can be coupled with other tunneling means for more a more secure communication channel.

The other IPSec mode takes advantage of tunneling. Tunneling mode is the method of choice for most VPNs because it encrypts not only the payload but also the entire original packet, partially or completely obfuscating the source and destination addresses of the communicating systems. Also, tunneling mode can occur host-to-host, host-to-gateway, or gateway-to-gateway, most popularly using the later. Gateway-to-gateway operation is another reason that tunneling mode is well-suited for VPN operation; it allows simplified network-to-network communications setup. Gateway devices, such as a router, firewall, or concentrator, need to be set up for VPN communication, but communicating hosts on the internal network need no special setup or additional software. Encryption of the entire packet and gateway-to-gateway setup combine to make tunnel mode an excellent choice for securing a communication channel. Most popularly, VPNs typically involve tunnel mode and at least one gateway device.

IKE

The IKE protocol is the authenticator and the negotiator of IPSec. It verifies that you are someone who should be allowed to start encrypted communication with the device in question and then negotiates the type of encryption that will be used. IKE is actually a combination of two protocols: Internet Security Association and Key Management Protocol (ISAKMP), which handles security negotiations, and Oakley (based on a variation of Diffie-Hellman), which is responsible for exchanging keys. Two phases of the IKE transaction precursor the creation of an SA between communication partners. In the following sections, we will explore these phases in greater detail.

Note

IKE is not the only key management solution for IPSec, although it is the standard. Key management can be done manually or by using IKE alternatives such as Secure DNS, Photuris, or Simple Key Internet Protocol (SKIP).

IKE Phase 1

If a remote user wants to begin a session with a VPN gateway device, the process begins with IKE Phase 1. Phase 1 serves two functions: authenticating the remote user and exchanging public key information that will be used for encryption in Phase 2.

IKE authentication can be done several different ways. The most common of these is with either pre-shared keys or with digital certificates. A pre-shared key simply means that some key value is preconfigured on all systems that want to communicate via the VPN. For an example configuration of a Cisco router using a pre-shared key configuration, see the pre-shared key example in the "Cisco Router VPN Examples" section later in this chapter.

In smaller, low-risk environments, a pre-shared key can be an easy and effective way to quickly set up authentication with little extra administrative overhead. It is by far the easiest means to configure VPN authentication, but with this simplicity comes several drawbacks. Sometimes the same pre-shared key is used on all communicating devices. This is not necessary (and definitely not recommended unless another choice is not available), but it is the easiest way administratively speaking. Using such a configuration is common when planning for dial-up remote systems because it is difficult to predict the IP addresses that they might use. The IP address could be anything, so a wildcard is used in place of an identifying address or host name and in conjunction with the pre-shared key value. Therefore, all stations dialing in must use the same key. Because this key value is configured locally on the devices, if *any* of them is compromised, the VPN's security is compromised as well. Of course, a pre-shared key can be reconfigured at any time if a compromise is known. However, if a pre-shared key is successfully captured and the thief is clever enough not to tip off the owner, the thief could have a backdoor into your system as long as that particular key is in use.

Because the pre-shared key must be manually configured, regularly changing them can be a headache that falls to the bottom of many busy administrators' lists. Using pre-shared key values with remote users is equivalent to giving them a password to your network. This is not a problem until they are no longer employed at your company. The effect is comparable to the re-keying of all of the locks in a building when an employee who had a key leaves, but in this case, you are the locksmith. Other key management issues occur as well, such as when trying to remotely configure sites. How do you send the key? Who at the remote site is trusted with keeping the value secret? Wouldn't is be nice if you could remotely manage keys for everyone who needs one on a connection-by-connection basis?

That brings us to a second popular way to authenticate users: digital certificates. Digital certificates can be assigned separately to each entity that connects to the VPN, and can be remotely managed and administered by a centrally located Certificate Authority (CA). This can ease administration problems, although it also adds an extra piece with which an administrator has to be concerned.

The CA is the centerpiece of a greater structure known as public key infrastructure (PKI). The whole concept behind PKI is a publicly available structure to distribute public key information. A popular way to do this in the enterprise is to combine the PKI with existing network directory structures, such as Microsoft's Active Directory or Novell's Network Directory Services. This way, the existing base of user information can be combined with the user's public key information, preventing duplication of user information databases. For an example of VPN authentication through digital certificates and a CA, look at the CA example under the "Cisco Router VPN Examples" section later in this chapter.

Other than authenticating that the parties who are conversing are supposed to be, the other function of the Phase 1 session is spent setting up the parameters for the communication session that will occur in Phase 2. Phase 2 is where the actual VPN's SA is negotiated. In other words, Phase 1's second purpose is the negotiation of the parameters for the connection (Phase 2) that will carry out the negotiation of the parameters for the actual VPN tunnel. This might sound redundant, but this is by-design to help ensure the security of the final VPN connection.

In Phase 1, two modes can be used when exchanging authentication information and security parameters for Phase 2: main mode and aggressive mode. The differences between them are in the number of packets that are exchanged and when the public key information is generated. Aggressive mode has a lower packet overhead, but main mode is the more secure of the two and the most popularly used. Some VPN implementations don't support the use of aggressive mode.

The important thing to remember is that the candidates who want to connect must both be using the same mode to negotiate successfully. Otherwise, errors will ensue.

Annotated IKE Phase 1 Example

Now you will see what one of these exchanges actually looks like under the packet microscope. The following example demonstrates a common exchange when doing an IKE Phase 1 negotiation. We can see the order in which the packets are actually transmitted and when the authentication and key exchange processes actually occur. The listing is actually from a log file generated by a SafeNet VPN client connecting to a Cisco PIX firewall. It is using main mode, as can be seen by the MM listings throughout. We start by exchanging proposed parameters for our IKE SA as follows:

```
Initiating IKE Phase 1 (IP ADDR=<MY IP ADDRESS>)
SENDING>>>> ISAKMP OAK MM (SA)
RECEIVED<<< ISAKMP OAK MM (SA)
```

Next, we exchange key information and what is known as a nonce. A *nonce* is the method used to confirm that the key information is coming from whom it is supposed to be coming from. A nonce is a random number that the initiator generates. The number is then digitally signed and sent back by the responder. This implementation also includes a vendor ID (VID) to allow participants in cross-platform interactions to make determinations on the capabilities and configuration of their partners that might be of a different manufacturer. The exchange of key information looks as follows:

```
SENDING>>>> ISAKMP OAK MM (KE, NON, VID, VID)
RECEIVED<<< ISAKMP OAK MM (KE, NON, VID)
```

In our final exchange confirming what we've negotiated, a hash is sent from each party to confirm that all are who they say they are. These are the first exchanges that are encrypted, using the negotiated information and keys exchanged in earlier messages. This is also where authentication of both parties finally takes place. The ID or identification value identifies the parties to each other. This value can be an IP address, host name, and so on as chosen when configuring the partners. Both hosts must use the same identification method or the connection will fail. The final exchange looks like this:

```
SENDING>>>> ISAKMP OAK MM *(ID, HASH, NOTIFY:STATUS_INITIAL_CONTACT)
RECEIVED<<< ISAKMP OAK MM *(ID, HASH)
Established IKE SA
```

The end result is an established IKE SA. This means that the two parties have agreed on the methods that they will use during Phase 2 IKE to exchange parameters for the actual VPN connection.

Note

Phase 1 of the IKE exchange creates the IKE SA, not an IPSec SA. The IKE SA states the parameters for Phase 2 communications. The IPSec SA states the parameters for the actual VPN communication. The IPSec SA is negotiated in IKE Phase 2.

If this had been an aggressive mode transaction, it would have only taken three packets instead of six. The first packet is sent to the responder with keys, nonces, and SA suggestions all in one. The responder then returns a similar packet, but with a hash appended for authentication. Finally, the initiator responds back with its own hash to confirm the IKE SA negotiation. Although aggressive mode obviously offers a speed advantage in that markedly fewer packets are exchanged, the lack of redundancy in the packet flow leaves it more open to exploit than its main mode counterpart.

IKE Phase 2

In IKE Phase 2, we are specifically negotiating the parameters of the IPSec SA. The exchange is similar to the one in Phase 1 aggressive mode. After Phase 2 is complete, the IPSec SA is formed and we have a VPN connection!

Phase 2 has one only exchange mode selection: quick mode. Quick mode is a brief exchange involving three packets. The security precautions of the Phase 1 exchanges aren't needed because of the protection given by the established IKE SA. Because the previous IKE SA was established, all of the exchanges in Phase 2 are encrypted using the negotiated protocols and encryption type. The only other protection is in the form of hashes and nonces that are included in the packets to confirm their origin.

Annotated Example

Now that we have discussed the principles of the Phase 2 exchange, it's time to look at an actual example. This is again, the log file from a SafeNet VPN client that is initiating a connection with a Cisco PIX 506 firewall. This time, because only internal private range IP addresses are listed, they don't need to be sanitized.

The first packets exchanged include hashes and nonce information as well as the proposed SA parameters. The responder returns a similar respondent packet. Both contain ID values, identifying each participant, as originally labeled in Phase 1:

```
SENDING>>>> ISAKMP OAK QM *(HASH, SA, NON, ID, ID)
RECEIVED<<< ISAKMP OAK QM *(HASH, SA, NON, ID, ID, NOTIFY:STATUS_RESP_LIFETIME)
```

Finally, the initiator confirms the agreement with a final hash. Notice that these transactions also use ISAKMP and Oakley, and that QM is used in the listings to represent quick mode (the only choice for Phase 2):

```
SENDING>>>> ISAKMP OAK QM *(HASH)
Loading IPSec SA (Message ID = 353EEA13 OUTBOUND SPI = B53E860B INBOUND
↪SPI = 3FAF771D)
```

A successfully established IPSec SA and the creation of unique inbound and outbound SPI information earmark the successful exchange. This last line tells us that we have successfully established a tunnel.

IPSec Security Protocols AH and ESP

Now that we have covered the creation of a security association using IKE, it's time to look at the security protocols. You have two security protocols from which to choose in the IPSec suite: AH and ESP protocol. When building an IPSec-based VPN you can elect to employ either one of these protocols or to use both AH and ESP at the same time. Each has its own functions, although in practical application, ESP is more popular for use on Internet spanning VPNs. In the following sections, we examine the inner workings of AH and ESP, and describe strengths and limitations of these protocols to help you set up an IPSec VPN that matches your needs.

AH Protocol

The AH protocol is IP protocol number 51. It offers authentication and integrity-checking capabilities, but it does *not* offer confidentiality for the packet's payload, limiting its effectiveness as a sole security method for most VPN implementations.

The AH protocol provides authentication and integrity protection by adding an additional header to the IP packet. This header contains a digital signature called an integrity check value (ICV) that is basically a hash value verifying that the packet hasn't been changed in transit. The IP information in the packet is guaranteed to be correct, but it is not hidden in any way. Because AH looks at the IP header when computing the digital signature, we can be sure that the source IP address on the packet is authentic and that the packet came from where it claims. AH also supports the use of sequence numbers that help prevent replay attacks. Because communicating devices track the stream of conversation using these numbers, an intruder who is attempting to gain VPN access can't re-send a captured packet flow.

The fact that AH authenticates the packet using its IP address information makes it incompatible with the IP header changes that are brought about by NAT. Since AH's ICV would be computed before the changes that NAT makes to the IP address for an outbound packet, when the packet arrived at its destination, the integrity check would fail.

On the other side of the coin, because AH offers no confidentiality of data for its packets, it does not possess the computational overhead of having to encrypt packets. Not only does the lack of payload encryption equate to smaller processing burden for the sending device, but it also means that the overall overhead of encapsulating packets is lighter. These factors combine to make AH a fine solution where only integrity and IP address authentication are needed and performance is highly valued.

Much can be learned about a protocol by taking a look at its packet header (see Figure 8.3). If a definitive source exists for what a protocol does or what information a packet carries, the header is it.

Figure 8.3   A graphical layout of what makes up an AH packet header.

The following lists the fields of information that are contained in the packet header:

- The next header field contains an identifier that specifies the protocol type of the next packet header following the AH packet header.
- The payload length field specifies the length of the AH header information.
- The reserved field is an area for the possible future expansion of the AH protocol.
- The security parameter index (SPI) value is listed next, showing of which unique SA's communication stream this packet is a part.
- The sequence number is the next field listed. It is simply a unique incrementing value that verifies that captured packets can't be re-sent to a victim's computer to extricate private information. This type of assault is called a *replay attack*.
- The authentication information is listed last. This field contains the ICV and digital signature, authenticating the packet in question.

Now that we know more about the packet structure, let's see an example of some AH packets. Listing 8.2 is a tcpdump trace of AH traffic. It is actually an example of a user accessing a web page. Notice that the payload of the packets contains cleartext representations of the information that they carry. (This is most noticeable in the last packet listed, seq=0x3.)

Listing 8.2 **AH Packet Trace**

```
00:05:18.645054 192.168.44.129 > 192.168.44.128:
↪AH(spi=580532459,seq=0x1): 1232 > 80: S 3631297390:3631297390(0)
↪win 16384 <mss 1460,nop,nop,sackOK> (DF)
0x0000      4500 0048 089a 4000 8033 1797 c0a8 2c81    E..H..@..3....,.
0x0010      c0a8 2c80 0604 0000 229a 38eb 0000 0001    ..,....."·8.....
0x0020      c118 fc19 0124 3688 d1b7 3e13 04d0 0050    .....$6...>....P
0x0030      d871 336e 0000 0000 7002 4000 57cd 0000    .q3n....p.@.W...
0x0040      0204 05b4 0101 0402                         ........

00:05:18.655236 192.168.44.128 > 192.168.44.129:
↪AH(spi=3951698033,seq=0x1): 80 > 1232: S 2981983731:2981983731(0)
↪ack 3631297391 win 17520 <mss 1460,nop,nop,sackOK> (DF)
0x0000      4500 0048 0080 4000 8033 1fb1 c0a8 2c80    E..H..@..3....,.
0x0010      c0a8 2c81 0604 0000 eb8a 2071 0000 0001    ..,....... q....
0x0020      24db fdd4 aaa4 0c89 16cf c00c 0050 04d0    $............P..
0x0030      b1bd 75f3 d871 336f 7012 4470 2b9b 0000    ..u..q3op.Dp+...
0x0040      0204 05b4 0101 0402                         ........

00:05:18.659869 192.168.44.129 > 192.168.44.128:
↪AH(spi=580532459,seq=0x2): 1232 > 80: . ack 1 win 17520 (DF)
0x0000      4500 0040 08a1 4000 8033 1798 c0a8 2c81    E..@..@..3....,.
0x0010      c0a8 2c80 0604 0000 229a 38eb 0000 0002    ..,....."·8.....
0x0020      cbf6 be88 73d7 97a6 a63b a092 04d0 0050    ....s....;....P
0x0030      d871 336f b1bd 75f4 5010 4470 585f 0000    .q3o..u.P.DpX_..

00:05:18.671517 192.168.44.129 > 192.168.44.128:
↪AH(spi=580532459,seq=0x3): 1232 > 80: P 1:260(259) ack 1 win
↪17520 (DF)
0x0000      4500 0143 08a2 4000 8033 1694 c0a8 2c81    E..C..@..3....,.
0x0010      c0a8 2c80 0604 0000 229a 38eb 0000 0003    ..,....."·8.....
0x0020      3521 0ef0 df8f 17db d87e 7477 04d0 0050    5!.......~tw...P
0x0030      d871 336f b1bd 75f4 5018 4470 0108 0000    .q3o..u.P.Dp....
0x0040      4745 5420 2f20 4854 5450 2f31 2e31 0d0a    GET./.HTTP/1.1..
0x0050      4163 6365 7074 3a20 696d 6167 652f 6769    Accept:.image/gi
0x0060      662c 2069 6d61 6765 2f78 2d78 6269 746d    f,.image/x-xbitm
0x0070      6170 2c20 696d 6167 652f 6a70 6567 2c20    ap,.image/jpeg,.
0x0080      696d 6167 652f 706a 7065 672c 202a 2f2a    image/pjpeg,.*/*
0x0090      0d0a 4163 6365 7074 2d4c 616e 6775 6167    ..Accept-Languag
0x00a0      > truncated for display purposes.
```

Not only is the payload of these packets in cleartext, but the Layer 4 (transport) information is also viewable. We can watch the three-way handshake as the first station attempts to contact the remote web server. We can also see other flags, window size settings, and TCP ports used (80 for the web server and 1232 as the ephemeral port chosen by the contacting station). SPI and sequencing information are also listed for each one-way connection.

ESP

The second security protocol that IPSec offers is ESP. The ESP protocol is IP protocol number 50. It offers full confidentiality by completely encrypting the payload of IP packets. Like the IPSec protocol suite, ESP is modular in design and can use any number of available symmetric encryption algorithms to encrypt its payload. Popular choices include DES, 3DES, and IDEA.

The way that ESP works differs slightly depending on the IPSec mode that is being used. In transport mode, ESP simply adds its own header after the IP header and encrypts the rest of the packet information from Layer 4 up. If ESP's authentication service is specified during the initial negotiation of the IPSec connection, ESP then adds a trailer that contains ICV information to confirm packet integrity and authentication, though unlike with AH, the ESP ICV is not computed using any of the IP header information.

In tunnel mode, ESP encapsulates the entire original packet, encrypting it fully and creating a new IP header and ESP header at the tunneling device. A trailer is also added for authentication purposes if ESP's authentication service is chosen.

In either mode, ESP offers sequence numbers in each packet that, like AH, provide protection against replay attacks.

ESP is often regarded as the IPSec protocol that works with NAT. Although this is usually the case for ESP used in tunnel mode, transport-mode ESP and NAT do not work together because of changes that NAT makes to the packet's header information. When NAT translates the packet's IP information, it also needs to recalculate the checksum located in the TCP header. This is because the TCP checksum is calculated not just using information in the TCP header, but is also based on information from the IP header, such as the source and destination IP addresses of the packet. Therefore, NAT must recalculate the TCP header checksum to keep the packet from failing its integrity check. In transport-mode ESP, the entire TCP header is encrypted, preventing the TCP checksum from being recalculated by the NAT device. (A similar problem occurs with UDP packets as well, when UDP checksums are used.) As a result, upon decryption the packet will fail its integrity check, keeping transport-mode ESP from successfully interoperating with NAT. This issue can be avoided in rare cases where TCP checksums are not used or can be disabled.

In tunnel mode ESP, traffic can successfully pass NAT because the entire original packet including both IP and Layer 4 information is encapsulated and therefore untouched by NAT. Since the IP and Layer 4 information and checksums are unaltered in tunnel-mode ESP, after the packet is decrypted it will still pass its TCP integrity check. However, even though ESP traffic in tunnel mode can pass through NAT, you may still encounter NAT-related problems when negotiating IPSec connection parameters. For instance, one-to-many NAT (frequently referred to as PAT) will rewrite the source port of an outbound IKE packet, causing it not to have the expected value of 500, and resulting in the failure to rekey IPSec session parameters.[1]

One great point of contention is the authentication capabilities of ESP. ESP has authentication services that can be used, but the hash that is generated is based on the entire packet with the exception of the IP header and authentication trailer. This is good in that any changes that might be made to the IP header (for example, by NAT) do not invalidate ESP's ICV value. However, this lack of IP header authentication is upsetting to some because it prevents the guarantee of identifying the originating IP address. In most implementations, however, the successful authentication of the packet's payload, as implemented by ESP, can be considered adequate proof that the packet actually came from the expected source.

Now that we have discussed the ESP protocol, let's take a closer look at the structure of it is packet header (see Figure 8.4).

Figure 8.4 A graphical representation of what makes up an ESP packet header.

Now we'll take a look at the individual fields in the ESP packet header.

- The SPI is the first field in this packet.

- The sequence number field follows it and is used, like the AH headers, to prevent replay attacks.

- The payload of the packet follows this information. This is where the encapsulated information is located.

- The Pad length field tells how much, if any, padding was needed to make the payload, pad length, and next header fields fit appropriately into the packet's bit-length requirements.

- The Next header shows the protocol number the type of information that is encapsulated inside the ESP packet.

- The Authentication information lists the optional ICV authentication option that is available for ESP packets.

Now that we have gone over the packet structure, let's look at a real-world example of ESP packets in transit. The following is a tcpdump trace of ESP encrypted traffic. Notice that no identifiable commands or information exists in the payload of the packets, because of the encryption of the packet's payload (in this particular case, with 3DES). Despite its obscure appearance, Listing 8.3 is actually an example of a user checking a standard web page, like in the AH trace seen previously.

Listing 8.3 **ESP Packet Trace**

```
00:01:30.031 192.168.44.128 > 192.168.44.129: ESP(spi=1728941913,seq=0x1) (DF)
0x0000    4500 0050 0061 4000 8032 1fc9 c0a8 2c80    E..P.a@..2....,.
0x0010    c0a8 2c81 670d 8f59 0000 0001 0262 5e96    ...,.g..Y.....b^.
0x0020    d238 3af3 c90e c385 fca7 09cf 693a b6cc    .8:.........i:..
0x0030    6d88 5400 d417 a0c4 6f5b df7f 5e96 994f    m.T.....o[..^..O
0x0040    cb03 1624 6668 d10d cf89 f6b0 e4e7 46a9    ...$fh........F.

00:01:30.038 192.168.44.129 > 192.168.44.128: ESP(spi=1302500357,seq=0x2) (DF)
0x0000    4500 0048 06a7 4000 8032 198b c0a8 2c81    E..H..@..2....,.
0x0010    c0a8 2c80 4da2 9405 0000 0002 f22d 2ce7    ...,.M.........-,.
0x0020    4dc6 ba58 11e3 333f 0cd5 8079 62d7 7128    M..X..3?...yb.q(
0x0030    0590 3056 085a dd96 3653 ef97 35e1 593c    ..0V.Z..6S..5.Y<
0x0040    8213 a0e7 2516 835b                         ....%..[

00:01:30.105 192.168.44.128 > 192.168.44.129: ESP(spi=1728941913,seq=0x2) (DF)
0x0000    4500 01a8 0062 4000 8032 1e70 c0a8 2c80    E....b@..2.p..,.
0x0010    c0a8 2c81 670d 8f59 0000 0002 5e96 994f    ..,.g..Y....^..O
0x0020    cb03 1624 7da5 0ecb 392f a703 6f53 aa21    ...$}...9/..oS.!
```

One point of interest on this ESP trace is that you might have noticed the changing SPI numbers. The SPI numbers change depending on which partner initiates the communication, since each end of an IPSec connection has its own SPI value assigned. You might also notice that each packet has an incrementing sequence number to help prevent the use of replay-type attacks. Layer 4 (TCP or UDP) transport information is blatantly missing because any such information is encapsulated into the encrypted payload of this packet. Other than these points, this trace looks much like any other IP traffic exchange.

The existence of two IPSec protocols—AH and ESP—offers the flexibility of selecting the configuration that is appropriate for your security requirements and can operate under the constraints of the existing network infrastructure. AH is great at providing authentication and integrity services, but does not protect the confidentiality of the packet's payload. ESP is more computationally expensive, but is able to encrypt data while also offering limited authentication capabilities.

Combined Use of ESP and AH

If your environment requires address authentication capabilities of AH and the confidentiality provided by ESP, then the two protocols can be combined into a single IPSec implementation. In this configuration, not only are the strong points of both AH and ESP combined, but the weak points are as well. Therefore, you have a configuration that has all of the NAT problems of AH and the additional processing burdens of ESP, which are added on the AH processing for an even greater overall workload. Such extra security comes at a high price, and in the real world, such configurations are relatively uncommon.

IPSec Configuration Examples

Now that we have journeyed through the creation of a VPN, let's take a look at some practical examples of VPN configuration on some popularly used devices that you might even find on your own network.

Cisco Router VPN Examples

Most Cisco routers have the potential (with the correct IOS software version) to be a gateway device for a VPN. The only other consideration is the processing power of the router, which could become heavily taxed by the additional burden of traffic encryption and decryption. However, if you have the horsepower, we provide a sample configuration of a Cisco router VPN with a pre-shared key.

A Cisco router can be configured as part of a VPN in many ways. In this example, we allow the creation of a tunnel from one Cisco router to another, using ESP as the IPSec security protocol and SHA-1 as the hashing algorithm. A pre-shared key provides the authentication. This configuration and all commands are based on IOS version 12.1.

The first section of the code involves the ISAKMP settings for the IKE part of the VPN configuration as follows:

```
crypto isakmp policy 10
authentication pre-share
crypto isakmp key <s3cr3t!> address 199.199.199.199
```

In the isakmp policy section, the authentication type is specified as using a pre-shared key, and the key (<s3cr3t!>) is set up for the address in question (199.199.199.199) in the line that follows it.

The next code shows all of the security options that this router will require when negotiating an SA. In Cisco's world, these security configuration options are called a *transform-set*:

```
crypto ipsec transform-set secure esp-3des esp-sha-hmac
```

The transform-set secure is set up with the listed encryption capabilities. Other transform sets, using other unique names, can be set up as well, each defining other security options that the router would also accept during the negotiation process.

> **Note**
> A VPN device must be set up with security parameters that are acceptable to its communication partner; otherwise, a connection will not be established.

The next command is used to assign a crypto map to an interface:

```
crypto map cmap local-address Ethernet1
```

In this example, the crypto map name is cmap. A *crypto map* is a set of configuration information to define traffic that should traverse the VPN and the details of how that connection can occur.

In the next section of the listing, we define the crypto map cmap, from the last example:

```
crypto map cmap 10 ipsec-isakmp
set peer 200.200.200.200
set transform-set secure
match address 101
```

These statements tie together all of the VPN configuration components. They give the peer address of the entity to which the tunnel will be constructed, list any transform sets that will be allowed, and specify an access list that will match any traffic that should be directed across the VPN.

The following access lists are the ones defined in the crypto map `cmap`:

```
access-list 101 permit ip 192.168.2.0 0.0.0.255 192.168.1.0 0.0.0.255
access-list 101 deny ip 192.168.2.0 0.0.0.255 any
```

They are specifically used to match the VPN traffic, and in turn, encrypt those packets and direct them to the VPN peer.

Now we will look at the interface configuration section of the router:

```
interface Ethernet1
description external interface
ip address x.x.x.x
crypto map cmap
```

The only setting that is specifically needed for a VPN configuration is the crypto map `cmap` command. With Cisco routers, it is necessary to apply a crypto map to the interface where the tunnel will be initiated.

The following line is typically used to configure NAT service on a router. It is listed here because a Cisco router that is running NAT must be explicitly configured to allow VPN traffic to bypass NAT translation:

```
ip nat inside source route-map nonat interface Ethernet1 overload
```

When you configure the route-map that defines the traffic that should be NAT translated, it should exclude VPN traffic. In this example, the route-map is called `nonat`.

In this section, we define the route-map `nonat`:

```
route-map nonat permit 10
 match ip address 102
```

This route-map allows the traffic that is denied in the listed ACL to bypass NAT, while NATing the permitted traffic.

Following are the access lists that are defined in the previously listed route-map `nonat`:

```
access-list 102 deny ip 192.168.2.0 0.0.0.255 192.168.1.0 0.0.0.255
access-list 102 permit ip 192.168.2.0 0.0.0.255 any
```

These access lists are used to bypass translation by NAT and allow the IPSec-related traffic that will initiate the VPN tunnel:

```
access-list 112 permit udp any any eq isakmp
access-list 112 permit esp any any
```

The access lists are configured to allow in the ISAKMP (UDP port 500) and ESP (IP protocol 50) traffic involved in the creation and use of the VPN tunnel. If you will be using AH protocol (IP protocol 51), you will need an access list that allows it.

Cisco Routers VPN and Access List Rules

When using a Cisco router as a VPN device, it is important to understand how the rules that apply to access lists work, specifically in a VPN environment. For example, after a VPN-encrypted packet initially passes through the access list that allows IKE, AH, or ESP traffic and is unencrypted, it will be tested a second time by the inbound access list. Creating an access list that allows traffic from the private IP address range used by the partner VPN to the private IP address used by the local network solves this issue. You should have no fear of this access list being a security hole; if someone fabricated traffic that would be able to pass it, the responses would be encrypted and sent to the VPN peer and would never be returned to the originator.

When traffic leaves the inside network, it is encapsulated in a new packet with a source address of the gateway device and a destination address of the peer gateway. This has to be considered when creating outbound access lists on the external interface. For example, if you are creating an egress filter that is applied outbound on the outside interface, it typically reflects the inside IP address range. Encapsulated VPN traffic does not pass this egress filter. For this reason, egress filters work better inbound on the inside router interface.

Next, we provide an in-depth example of a Cisco Router with Certificate Authentication. Using pre-shared keys appears to be such a simple solution that some question exists on why you would choose an alternative. Setting up two VPN peers is as simple as typing in a few commands and a single secret piece of information. However, when your environment grows from 2 peers to 2,000, the concept of a centralized key-handling authority becomes more attractive. This concept becomes more appealing when you consider the scenario of having to change keys. Being able to make these changes through a centralized CA is why PKI is a buzzword among the IT elite. To show the differences between a pre-shared key and a CA configuration, we will use the same Cisco router example we used previously, only changing settings that are needed for certificate authentication. All commands that remain the same will not be re-listed; we will only list new commands and commands that would need to be changed. This section will assume that you have an accessible CA already configured in your environment and available to you.

Let's start our look at CA authentication by seeing what must be changed from our previous configuration. Because we are discussing authentication specifically, we know that this falls into the IKE section of the VPN; therefore, only our ISAKMP settings will need to be affected. Crypto maps, transform sets, encryption types, and everything else will remain the same. We only need to change the authentication type under our ISAKMP policy and then make the changes necessary to prepare our router for such authentication.

The first statement in this section is identical to the one listed in the pre-shared example section:

```
crypto isakmp policy 10
authentication rsa-sig
```

The change is reflected in the second line of the section. The authentication command must reflect the use of RSA digital signatures, or `rsa-sig` for short.

Because a certificate-based authentication scheme requires the querying of an entity outside the router for its keys, key storage and CA accessibility become important issues. If the CA is inaccessible, your router might accept an expired certificate or you might suffer an offline condition on your VPN. Storing certificates locally can help offset this problem of downtime, but at the price of taking up some of the precious router NVRAM storage. To configure your Cisco router to request a certificate whenever necessary, use the following command:

```
MyRouter(config)# crypto ca certificate query
```

This command prevents the storage of certificates or certificate revocation lists (CRLs) from using any of your router's NVRAM. Because these items wouldn't be found in local NVRAM, the router must take a performance hit to make a request.

The next commands are probably already configured on your router. However, they are listed here because they are essential for operation with digital certificates:

```
MyRouter(config)# hostname <MyRouter>
MyRouter(config)# ip domain-name <domain.com>
```

Host and domain names must be present in the router configuration because certificates are named with a fully qualified domain name. This means that the certificate's name is actually the host name of the router followed by its domain name. For example, in this example, our router's certificate would be named `MyRouter.domain.com`.

Before we go any further, we must generate the RSA key pair that we will use to request a certificate for our router. The following command is entered only once to generate the keys and is not a saved part of the configuration:

```
MyRouter(config)# crypto key generate rsa
```

To verify that your keys have been generated, you can use this command: `show crypto key mypubkey rsa`.

Now we must configure the specifics so that our router knows where and how often to collect certificates:

```
MyRouter(config)# crypto ca identity <CA.COM>
```

This line specifies the domain name of the certificate authority and drops you into CA configuration mode.

The following line is the last required line in this section. The rest are optional or used only in some environments:

```
MyRouter(ca-identity)# enrollment url <http://ca_4u>
```

This line simply specifies the URL of the CA. In this example, it is `http://ca_4u`.

These next two lines are needed only in environments that use a Registration Authority (RA). An RA is an extra entity that caches certificates and CRLs in case the CA is down or otherwise unavailable.

```
MyRouter(ca-identity)# enrollment mode ra
MyRouter(ca-identity)# query url <ldap_url>
```

If you have an RA in your environment, specify the first command. The second is also only used in an RA environment, but one that also support LDAP. `<ldap_url>` in this example is the URL of the LDAP server.

The next two optional lines specify how often in minutes the router will retry to get a certificate and how many times it will retry:

```
MyRouter(ca-identity)# enrollment retry period <5>
MyRouter(ca-identity)# enrollment retry count <100>
```

The default number of minutes for the first command is 1, and the default number of retries is infinite.

This last entry that can be configured in the CA configuration mode is regarding whether CRLs must be available to accept a certificate:

```
MyRouter(ca-identity)# crl optional
```

When this line is entered, if a given CRL is not available, the router still accepts the certificate in question. This could be a security concern because the certificate might have been previously revoked. However, it can keep authentication functioning even if the CA is temporarily unavailable.

Now we are ready to request the CA's certificate. This is done with the following command:

```
MyRouter(config)# crypto ca authenticate <CA.COM>
```

Requesting the CA's certificate is necessary for authentication before receiving a certificate for your router. As a best practice, you might want to manually confirm this certificate after downloading it from the CA. The information used in this command should match the information that is specified in the crypto ca identity command:

```
MyRouter(config)# crypto ca enroll <name>
```

The previous command is used to receive a certificate for your router. After this command has been issued, you should be ready to initiate a VPN connection.

Following are a couple of useful commands for auditing your router's CA capabilities:

```
MyRouter# show crypto key pubkey-chain rsa
```

The previous command shows details of available RSA public keys on your router.

The following command lists all certificates that are stored on your router if you are not using query mode, which disallows certificate storage:

```
MyRouter# show crypto ca certificates
```

It is plain to see that setting up the use of digital certificates is more complicated than using pre-shared keys in the short haul, but in the long run, the time spent can pay back many times over, especially in a large environment.

Windows 2000 IPSec Configuration Example

Windows 2000 can also effectively handle IPSec duties if properly configured. Doing so requires the addition of the IP Security Policy (ipsecpol) snap-in to your Microsoft Management Console (MMC) and monitoring with the IP Security Monitor (Ipsecmon) utility. This integrated capability lies at the operating system level and its Windows 2000's prevalence in many businesses will most likely make it an important player in the future of VPNs.

IPSec VPN policy is configured on a Windows 2000 system using the IPSec snap-in for MMC. The console appears in Figure 8.5.

Figure 8.5 MMC can be used to configure local and remote Windows 2000 IPSec policies via the ipsecpol snap-in.

As listed in the right pane, several default security policies can be used for quick setup of Windows 2000 is system-to-system VPNs. However, to set up an IPSec policy that will work well with other VPN products, we need to create a custom policy. This is primarily because the default authentication used for these policies is the Windows Kerberos authentication protocol. To create a new security policy, follow these steps:

1. Right-click the desired IP Security Policies object in the left pane of the window, and select Create IP Security Policy. This opens the IP Security Policy Wizard. Click Next to continue.

2. Name your security policy. You might also want to include a description of its purpose. When you are finished, click Next to continue.

3. On the following window, remove the check from the Activate the Default Response Rule check box. Click Next to continue.

4. Verify that the Edit Properties check box is selected because we will be customizing this policy. Then click Finish.

5. This brings up the *policy* Properties box (see Figure 8.6) where *policy* is the name of the policy you specified in step 2. Make sure that the Use Add Wizard check box is checked, and then click the Add button to continue. This opens the Security Rule Wizard. Click Next to continue.

Figure 8.6 The Security Policy Properties box is used to define IPSec rules for the currently selected policy.

5. Choose whether or not to use a tunnel. In this example, we will use a tunnel, so click the option button to specify the tunnel endpoint and type in its IP address. Click Next when you're finished.

6. Choose the type of network connections you want to effect (most likely All Network connections) and click Next.

7. In the Authentication Method window, we pick the authentication we want to use: Kerberos, certificates, or a text string to use as a pre-shared key. If you are creating a connection to be used with another Windows 2000 system, you should probably use the default Kerberos authentication. Otherwise, for interoperability, you will most likely have to use certificates or pre-shared keys. For our example, we will use the latter. To use a pre-shared key, choose the appropriate option button and specify the pre-shared key value used in the text box below it (see Figure 8.7). Click Next to continue.

Note

Microsoft discourages the use of preshared keys for IPSec authentication on production systems, stating that it was implemented primarily to achieve RFC compliance. Furthermore, the confidentiality of the shared key is difficult to protect because it is stored in a format viewable from the local computer.[2] Whenever possible, use Kerberos or certificate authentication methods for IPSec.

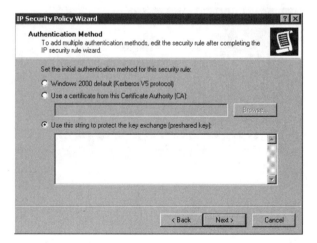

Figure 8.7   In the Authentication Method window, we specify which authentication method should be used for the IPSec policy.

8. In the IP Filter List tab, click the Add button. In the next window, make sure the Use Add Wizard box is checked, specify a name for the filter you are creating, and click the Add button.

9. This opens the IP Filter Wizard. Click Next to continue.

10. For Source Address, choose My IP Address. This assumes that you are using this system directly to contact the peer VPN device and not using it as a gateway or proxy device. If you were using your Windows 2000 system as a gateway, you would most likely choose A Specific IP Subnet and specify the IP addresses and subnet mask settings. Click Next to continue.

11. For destination address, choose the appropriate type from the drop-down menu. A Specific IP Subnet is usually the correct selection for a VPN. Then specify the subnet range of the network that is protected by the gateway VPN device. Click Next when you're finished.

12. Unless you have a specific change needed, leave the protocol type as Any and click Next. With tunnel traffic, it would be inappropriate to specify a setting other than Any because tunnels can't filter on port information or protocol type.

13. Make sure that the Edit Properties box is checked so that we can verify settings. Then click Finish.

14. Verify that the Mirrored check box is checked in the Filter Properties window, under the Addressing tab. The Mirrored check box ensures that the policy applies to both incoming and going traffic. Click OK when you're finished.

15. Click Close on the IP Filter list screen.

16. On the resulting window, choose the filter list that you just created from the ones listed, and then click Next.

17. On the Filter Action screen, make sure that the Use Add Wizard check box is checked and click the Add button.

18. This opens the IP Security Filter Action Wizard. Click the Next button to continue.

19. Create a new name and optionally a description for your filter action and click Next.

20. Choose Negotiate Security for Standard IPSec Operation. You could otherwise create a specific permit or block rule in this section. When you're finished, click Next.

21. Check Do Not Communicate with Computers That Do Not Support IPSec to support only IPSec communications. Then click Next.

22. In the IP Traffic Security window, choose the security level you desire based on the settings of the peer device with which you are communicating. Although High for ESP Support would seem like a good choice, it supports DES and MD5 as its defaults. Use Custom to allow you to set exactly the encryption and hash algorithm combination that you want to use. Click Next when you're finished.

23. You have come to the end of the wizard. Verify that the Edit Properties check box is checked so that we can make final settings changes. Then click Finish.

24. This drops you into the Properties window for the action that you just created. Be sure to uncheck the Accept Unsecured Communication, But Always Respond Using IPSec check box for highest security. You should end up with a screen similar to the one in Figure 8.8, but reflecting your security choices.

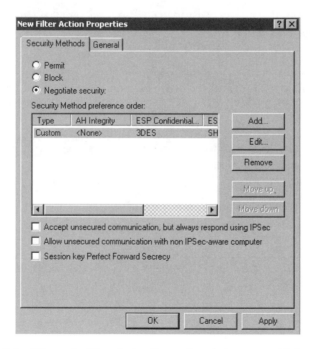

Figure 8.8   We use the Filter Action Properties window to specify how IPSec properties should be negotiated for traffic that matches the current IP filter.

25. Choose the new filter action you just created on the Filter Action screen. Click Next.

26. Make sure the Edit Properties check box is unchecked because we are now done. Click Finish.

27. Click Close on the Policy Properties box, and your new policy should appear in the right pane of the window. Right-click the policy and choose Assign. This changes the Policy Assigned column from No to Yes. The policy is now active.

28. Run the `ipsecmon` command from the run line. Next, open a command prompt and try to ping a host on the remote subnet in question. After security is negotiated, the pings will get through if everything is configured correctly. This can be confirmed by checking the IP Security Monitor screen (see Figure 8.9) to show active security associations after the device is successfully pinged.

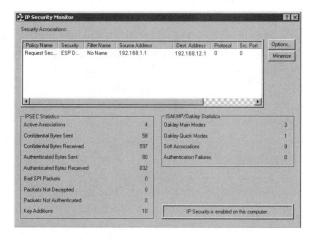

Figure 8.9   We can use IP Security Monitor to observe statistics regarding the host's IPSec operations.

Other VPN Protocols: PPTP and L2TP

As stated previously, IPSec is not the only tunneling set of protocols that can offer VPN type service. At layer 2, PPTP and L2TP are both popularly implemented VPN protocols. The greatest reason for this is that both are included with Microsoft Windows operating systems, which enjoy the greatest distribution of any operating system to date. This means that a large portion of the deployed computer base has built-in VPN capabilities using PPTP and L2TP. For this reason (and that popular VPN software often goes for as much as $100 per seat), both protocols, especially the newer L2TP, can be effective for VPN solutions in Windows environments. An interesting thing to keep in mind is that neither has inherent encryption capabilities. Encryption must be added to make either a true VPN protocol. Let's take a look at each.

PPTP

PPTP is an outgrowth of PPP, which appeared in computers everywhere with the advent of dial-up Internet access. PPTP, although popularized by Microsoft, was actually designed by a consortium of computer technology vendors, including the likes of US Robotics, Ascend, and 3com. Microsoft's original implementation of PPTP was highly criticized as being insecure by cryptography gurus industry wide, which left a bad taste in the mouths of many IT people. For encryption, PPTP relies on Microsoft Point-to-Point Encryption (MPPE), which uses the RC4 cipher. However, most of the security issues were due to the insecurity of its authentication method—the Microsoft authentication protocol Microsoft Challenge/Reply Handshake Protocol (MSCHAP). PPTP has PPP's capability of user authentication using all associated protocols, such as MSCHAP, Password Authentication Protocol (PAP), Challenge/Reply Handshake Protocol (CHAP), or Extensible Authentication Protocol (EAP). Later PPTP implementations from Microsoft that included MSCHAP version 2 actually resolved most of the aforementioned security issues, making it a much safer bet (although not as well regarded as IPSec) as a VPN protocol.[3]

PPTP operates through two channels that work together. The first is a control channel that operates on TCP port 1723. This channel sends back and forth all the commands that control the session management features for the connection. The second is an encapsulated data channel that uses a variant of the Generic Routing Encapsulation (GRE) protocol IP protocol 47, that uses UDP as its transport protocol.[4] PPP frames are encapsulated and sent using this method. This is the "tunnel" of PPTP. An advantage of the GRE tunnel over a standard IPSec tunnel is that it can encapsulate and carry protocols other than IP. For this reason, GRE tunnels can find their way into environments that are otherwise completely IPSec.

PPTP does have some interesting attributes that can make it useful in particular environments. First, it works without a hitch through NAT because NAT-related changes to the IP layer have no effect on Layer 2 PPTP. Second, it comes integrated with many hardware devices and is available in operating systems; with such high availability, it is more easily deployable in environments that use such products. However, on the downside, because PPTP uses PPP to initiate communications, it can be vulnerable to spoofing and man-in-the-middle type attacks.

L2TP

L2TP is defined by RFC 2661. It is, as its name implies, a layer 2 tunneling solution. L2TP is actually a hybrid of two previous tunneling protocols, Cisco's Layer Two Forwarding (L2F) protocol and PPTP, combining the best attributes of both. It replaces PPTP as the VPN protocol of choice included with Microsoft Windows operating systems as of Windows 2000.

L2TP, like PPTP, uses PPP's user authentication capacities (MSCHAP, CHAP, EAP, PAP, and so on). Also like PPTP, L2TP has two communication method types: control messages and data transmission "tunnel" messages. The first bit in the PPTP header differentiates these message types (1 for a control message, 0 for a data message). Control messages are given precedence over data messages to ensure that important session administration information gets transmitted as effectively as possible. The concept behind L2TP's operation is similar to PPTP. A control connection is set up for the tunnel, which is then followed by the initiation of an L2TP session. After both are completed, then information in the form of PPP frames can begin to traverse the tunnel.[5]

Comparisons of PPTP, L2TP, and IPSec

L2TP most commonly uses UDP port 1701 as its transport medium for all its packets. Because UDP is a connectionless protocol, it can actually require less communication overhead (it doesn't require TCP's response traffic to confirm connection) than PPTP, which transports control messages (only) on connection-oriented TCP.

An advantage of L2TP over both PPTP and IPSec alone is that it can create multiple tunnels between two hosts. However, its disadvantage is that it relies on PPP and can be victimized by spoofing and man-in-the-middle attacks. Also, like PPTP, it supports the transmission of non-IP protocols, which is an advantage over IPSec. However, unlike PPTP, it does not require IP and TCP as its transmitting protocols. It can use other options such as x.25, Frame Relay, and ATM.

Although L2TP lacks its own encryption capability, it has the potential as a Layer 2 protocol of working in conjunction with IPSec. L2TP can be used to provide a tunnel for transport-mode IPSec traffic. For example, Windows 2000 relies on IPSec as the encryption method for its L2TP tunnels. Conversely, Windows 2000 does not have a well-developed tunnel implementation of IPSec, so it relies on L2TP for tunneling. This combination of IPSec and L2TP can be mutually agreeable because it allows IPSec to supply packet authentication for L2TP control messages, which lack such protection. L2TP offers IPSec multiprotocol transmission capability and multiple tunnel support. Also, the advantage of L2TP's user authentication protocols can be applied to IPSec, which has no such ability of its own.

Note

When user-level authentication is needed, L2TP can be employed as the tunneling method for IPSec, allowing the utilization of the user authentication protocols that L2TP has to offer, such as PAP, CHAP, and MSCHAP.

PPTP and L2TP Examples

Now that we've discussed the details of how PPTP and L2TP tunnels work, let's look at some practical examples of how the technologies can be implemented in common network devices: a Windows 2000 system and a Cisco PIX firewall.

Client Windows 2000 Setup

Because L2TP support is integrated by default in Windows 2000, setting up client software to support an L2TP VPN is not difficult as the following steps prove:

1. Double-click the Make New Connection icon under the Network and Dial-Up Connections window to start the Network Connection Wizard.

Note

You can open the Network and Dial-Up Connections window by right-clicking My Network Places and choosing Properties.

2. After receiving the splash screen, click Next to continue. For L2TP VPN client access configuration, you will choose the Connect to a Private Network Through the Internet option button. Click Next to continue.

3. On the Public Network window, you can specify a dial-up connection if necessary, or choose Do Not Dial the Initial Connection If Communicating Through a Direct Network Connection or Broadband Internet. Click Next to continue.

4. On the Destination Address window, type the host name or IP address of the entity to which you are connecting. Click Next to continue.

5. On the Connection Availability window, you can choose whether the connection that we are creating will be available to everyone or just to the user who you are logged in as. Make your selection and click Next.

6. The Internet Connection Sharing window allows you to specify that the system that you are working on should act as a gateway for other network systems. That way, other systems can gain access to the entity you are connecting through your system. Unless you have a specific need for this type of sharing, do not check the check box. Click Next to continue.

7. Finally, you can type a new name for this connection into the text box at the top of the window. If you would like a shortcut for this connection placed on the desktop, you can check the check box in the lower section of the window before clicking the Finish button to close the wizard.

8. You will immediately be on the Logon window for your newly created connection. Here is where you will need to specify the logon and password information to authenticate with the L2TP device you are connecting to. Before going any further, we need to click the Properties button to do some final configuration.

9. Although the default settings are fine for most situations, you should take a look at a couple of places for your own reference. First, on the Networking tab at the top is a drop-down box that specifies the type of VPN you are calling. It defaults to Automatic, which should work fine for most connections, but you can specifically choose PPTP or L2TP instead.

10. On the Security tab, the Typical setting again works fine in most circumstances, but it can be tweaked for your specific environment. In addition, the Advanced selection allows even greater granularity in the security specifics that you can choose for your individual connection, including allowed authentication protocols.

After your settings are tweaked and your authentication information is entered, you are ready to connect. Simply click the Connect button, and the system will attempt to contact the remote system. If the connection fails, it returns an error and waits a predetermined time before redialing. This connection can be reached any time through the Network and Dial-Up Connections screen.

Note

The VPN connections that are created as explained in this section are for PPTP or L2TP connections specifically. They do not necessarily support IPSec as listed. For IPSec support, see the example in the IPSec Examples section.

Cisco PIX VPDN Setup for PPTP Traffic

In this example, we will specify the specific commands of interest in a Cisco PIX configuration that is running software version 5.1 or later. We will not go over all of the standard configuration commands, just those that pertain to Virtual Private Dial-Up Network (VPDN) support for PPTP connections. VPDN is basically Cisco's way to support non-IPSec, dial-up type protocols. The protocols are most popular incarnations of PPP: PPTP, L2TP, and Point-to-Point Protocol Over Ethernet (PPPOE), which is popularly used with DSL connections.

To begin our PIX configuration, we need to specify an access list to describe the traffic leaving our network that will need to bypass NAT. PIX firewalls have NAT integrated at the lowest level, and to keep VPN traffic from "breaking," we need to make sure that it isn't translated. Here is the access list we will be matching:

```
access-list 101 permit ip 10.0.0.0 255.255.255.0 192.168.1.0 255.255.255.0
```

This access list simply says that it will match or allow any IP traffic that has a source address in the 10.0.0.x subnet and a destination address in the 192.168.1.x subnet.

The next section does not specifically relate to VPDN, but is of interest because it lists our inside and outside interface addresses. This can shed some light on other IP address selections in the rest of this listing:

```
ip address outside 172.16.1.2 255.255.255.0
ip address inside 10.0.0.1 255.255.255.0
```

The outside address or external address in this case is 172.16.1.2 and is using a Class-C subnet mask. The inside address also uses a class-C subnet and is 10.0.0.1.

Our next statement creates an address pool to assign all connecting PPTP clients:

```
ip local pool pool4pptp 192.168.1.1-192.168.1.50
```

The pool name is pool4pptp and the address range is 192.168.1.1-50.

Only one of the next lines is of consequence in our VPDN configuration. They are the NAT settings that will be used on our PIX. The global command lists the range of external addresses that will be used for our NAT pool:

```
global (outside) 1 172.16.1.3-172.16.1.4
nat (inside) 0 access-list 101
nat (inside) 1 10.0.0.0 255.255.255.0 0 0
```

The nat (inside) 1 command shows all IP addresses that should be NAT translated. The command of interest is the nat (inside) 0 command. This command shows what addresses should bypass NAT. In this case, the addresses are specified by the 101 access list that we looked at previously. Therefore, traffic that has the source address of our internal network and is being sent to the addresses that are being used by connected PPTP clients (as stated in our pool) should bypass NAT. Otherwise, if the source address is in our network address range (as stated in the nat (inside) 1 command), NAT it.

The next command simply states that all PPTP traffic should be uniformly allowed access.

```
sysopt connection permit-pptp
```

VPDN will not work without this command.

The next group of settings shows specific configuration options for our VPDN clients. The first line shows the protocols that we will allow access through our VPDN configuration. L2TP could also be specified:

```
vpdn group 1 accept dialin pptp
```

The next group of authentication settings shows acceptable protocols to use for PPTP authentication. Only specify the protocols that you want to allow:

```
vpdn group 1 ppp authentication pap
vpdn group 1 ppp authentication chap
vpdn group 1 ppp authentication mschap
```

The next line is what assigns our IP address pool mentioned previously to the connecting PPTP clients:

```
vpdn group 1 client configuration address local pool4pptp
```

The following line chooses where the authentication information is held:

```
vpdn group 1 client authentication local
```

In the example, it will use local configuration settings on the PIX. This is not a best practice. Ideally, it is best to have authentication information held outside of the PIX on a separate authentication system like a RADIUS or TACACs server.

The username line then specifies the local information we alluded in the last statement:

```
vpdn username <user> password <secret>
```

<user> refers to a username as defined by the person configuring the PIX, and <secret> refers to a well-chosen password.

Finally, the `enable outside` command says that the outside interface can accept VPDN traffic. With this final statement, PPTP traffic will be allowed to traverse our PIX firewall:

```
vpdn enable outside
```

Summary

In this chapter, we discussed the basics behind how VPNs work and the process of tunneling. We discussed the advantages of VPNs, including security, deployment, and cost benefits. We also looked at some disadvantages, including bandwidth considerations, design and implementation issues, and troubleshooting and control issues.

We also covered the popular VPN protocols IPSec, L2TP, and PPTP. IPSec is a suite of security protocols that includes IKE, AH, and ESP. IKE is used in two phases to negotiate and authenticate VPN partners. Next, one or both AH and ESP protocols are used as the main security protocol for data transmission. AH is used to authenticate and verify integrity of data flow, whereas ESP completely encapsulates the packet or its payload (depending on SA mode), offering full confidentiality of data flow.

Finally, we covered L2TP and PPTP and saw the advantages of a layer 2-based tunneling protocol, including the transmission of non-IP protocols, and its ability to pass NAT without issue. The downside is that because both protocols were built on PPP, they have communication session vulnerabilities that aren't found with IPSec.

Regardless of your choice of VPN hardware or tunneling protocol, the concepts of VPNs are universal. Correctly identifying and weighing the disadvantages and advantages for your particular environment is a necessary part of designing remote communications. After a VPN is decided upon as the choice communication for your situation, a full understanding of the principles of cryptography and their incorporation into the VPN will help facilitate a smooth implementation.

Understanding VPNs, IPSec, cryptography, and other tunneling protocols will be advantageous to anyone who is involved in the upkeep and implementation of network security.

References

1 Microsoft, Inc. "How to Configure a L2TP/IPSec Connection Using Pre-shared Key Authentication (Q240262)." `http://support.microsoft.com/default.aspx?scid=kb;EN-;q240262`. 15 March 2002.

2 Bernard Aboba. "IPSec-NAT Compatibility Requirements." May 30, 2001. `http://www.ietf.org/internet-drafts/draft-aboba-nat-ipsec-04.txt`. January 2002.

3 Bruce Schneier and Mudge. "Cryptanalysis of Microsoft's PPTP Authentication Extensions (MS-CHAPv2)." August 1999. `http://www.counterpane.com/pptpv2-paper.html`. January 2002.

4 Kory Hamzeh, Gurdeep Singh Pall, et al. "Point-to-Point Tunneling Protocol—PPTP" June 1996. `http://www.phptr.com/solomon/html/drafts/draft-ietf-pppext-pptp-00.txt`. January 2002.

5 W. Townsley, A. Valencia, et al. "RFC 2661—Layer Two Tunneling Protocol 'L2TP'." August 1999. `http://www.ietf.org/rfc/rfc2661.txt`. January 2002.

9

Host Hardening

THE TERM *HARDENING* DESCRIBES TAKING A typical or default installation of an operating system (OS) or application and making modifications to decrease its potential exposure to threats. The extent of hardening depends on the host's role on the network. Hardening allows systems to contribute toward building a reliable network security perimeter.

This chapter focuses on principles of host hardening, with the goal of helping you devise standards and procedures for locking down system configurations in your organization. We examine several weaknesses that are inherent to host devices; attackers seek out these flaws, and we show you how to armor against them. We discuss vulnerabilities located in the OS and techniques that can exploit these vulnerabilities locally or remotely. We complete the discussion of host hardening by looking at weaknesses in systems at the application level. The topic of host-level security continues in Chapter 10, "Host Defense Components," where we build on host hardening guidelines by explaining how to use hosts to help detect and isolate attacks on the network security perimeter.

Levels of Hardening

How many people believe that simply placing a firewall between the Internet and their internal network protects their internal systems from potential attackers? Unfortunately, if the firewall software and OS have not been locked down according to hardening principles presented in this chapter, a false sense of security might have been established.

Any application that is installed on a non-hardened OS has an increased chance of being successfully exploited due to vulnerabilities in the underlying OS. Of course, application-specific vulnerabilities are equally important. A design flaw or a coding error in an application can provide access to the underlying host and give the attacker an internal "island" from which to proceed with the attack. For example, buffer overflow exploits against an application can allow an attacker to execute privileged commands on the targeted system. When building a house, you want to make sure that high-quality concrete is used to provide a robust foundation for the structure built upon it so that the concrete will not crack under stress. In a network security system, each level that we strengthen allows us to build a quality host that is suitable to support applications and users. Operating systems and applications contain vulnerabilities that attackers can exploit, even though some of these vulnerabilities might not have been discovered yet or have not been publicly announced.

When devising hardening procedures for hosts on your network, keep in mind the cost you incur from applying the hardening techniques and maintaining the systems that have been locked down. Not all hosts should be hardened to the same extent—it is up to you to find and incorporate appropriate levels of security hardening, depending on the criticality of the host's role in the network. Hardening a host so that it is as secure as possible yet can still perform its functions is a challenging task, in part because custom scripts or applications often fail when hardening techniques are applied. You need to weigh the fine line that exists between security and functionality to determine what exposure to threat is acceptable while still providing critical business services.

As we increase the level of security in the host, we generally decrease the level of convenience that is offered to its users. That might be one of the reasons that systems are not shipped to us secure by default. For example, Microsoft ships its product with user–friendly default settings for ease of setup and use; however, such settings are often poor from a security standpoint. Another reason why hosts aren't secure by default is that the same OS or application might be deployed in various environments, such as an individual's home computer or at a large corporation. The functional requirements and security needs vary widely, depending on the role of the host. If an end user workstation, a web server, and a VPN server have different responsibilities on the network, their extent of appropriate hardening is different as well.

In this chapter, we define three levels of hardening techniques to protect against local, network, and application exploits. Figure 9.1 demonstrates how these levels work together to provide defense in depth for the host. Classifying hardening steps into these categories can help you lock down the systems in a controlled manner and determine the extent of hardening that is appropriate for a particular host. The layered approach to perimeter security that we have been applying to network devices is also appropriate for increasing the security of an individual host.

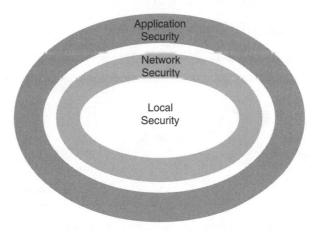

Figure 9.1   The three levels of host armoring work together to accomplish defense in depth for the host.

Level 1: Hardening Against Local Attacks

Hardening the host's configuration against local attacks is fairly straightforward. At this level, we concentrate on restricting the use of powerful utilities, such as those used for disk and user management. We also implement proper file system permissions to assist with "least privilege" access methods to ensure that users have only the minimum rights that are necessary. Proper planning of user accounts and groups assists with managing access restriction and eases system administration tasks. Therefore, at this level, we also modify user account settings and restrict group membership.

Restrict Use of Administrative Utilities

Administrators often use powerful tools to create user and group accounts or configure the system's services. Rather than using many different commands or manually editing various files to make system changes, some tools provide a user-friendly interface that covers many administrative functions. Examples of such programs include the Windows 2000 Computer Management utility, which is a snap-in to the Microsoft Management Console (MMC); the Sun Solaris admintool; and the Linux linuxconf utility, which is pictured in Figure 9.2.

Figure 9.2   The linuxconf utility provides an easy way for Linux system administrators to make host configuration changes, but it also can be an attractive target for attackers.

These management tools are considered virtual frontends because they redirect commands to underlying files and executables. For example, Figure 9.2 depicts the ability to enable or disable services using linuxconf. When the FTP service is enabled, the inetd.conf file is modified to start this service through Inetd. However, although some attackers might seek utilities, such as linuxconf, many attempt to modify the underlying files directly when compromising a host system.

By restricting access to tools so that only administrators can access them, we decrease the likelihood that a compromised user account will be able to use these tools to modify the host. As part of the lockdown process, you should review the tools that are installed on the host and remove those that are not required. For example, a C compiler might be installed on a Linux-based web server by default, but it is unlikely to be required for the web server to operate properly. When a system is compromised and these utilities are available to the attacker, the attacker is more likely to use the utilities to compile additional attack tools or to install a backdoor to the system that will allow future access.

After compromising a system, attackers frequently attempt to hide the files they placed on it, such as a toolbox of exploits, backdoors, and sniffer logs. To hide these files from an administrator, an attacker might alter administration tools such as ls, dir, du, ps, and fsck to conceal the existence of certain directories, files, and processes. As we discuss in Chapter 10, it often makes sense to monitor the integrity of critical system tools so that you can detect whether they have been replaced.

Use Correct File Permissions

To protect system management tools as well as other applications and data on the host, we must apply correct file and directory permissions. The first step in implementing correct file permissions is to make sure the host uses a file system that supports security permissions. File systems, such as DOS, FAT16, and FAT32, do not restrict file access, granting all local users complete access to any file on the file system.

Modern file systems, such as the NT file system (NTFS) and the UNIX file system (UFS), allow administrators to restrict access to files based on the user's identity. To take advantage of this functionality, we must tighten the default permissions that are assigned during OS installations; for example, Windows NT gives Full Control privileges to the group Everyone for many files and directories by default. This is a bad combination. Attackers love to take advantage of file permissions that allow everyone full access. When assigning proper permissions to specific users and groups, we should give only the minimum access that is required to perform the user's tasks.

As we alter file system permissions from Full Control to a properly restrictive level, we need to be cautious and aware of the minimum requirements for applications to function. For example, if we modify the file permissions in %SystemRoot% and %SystemRoot%\system32 directories to limit access from the Everyone group, we might create a problem when a user attempts to print. The *%SystemRoot%\system32\spool\printers* folder requires read and write access for users to be able to print successfully. After restricting file permissions, be sure to test application compatibility; many applications no longer function correctly due to dependencies on specific file permissions. UNIX does not grant file permissions as freely as Windows, but it is still possible to exploit vulnerabilities because of incorrect file permissions.

One type of vulnerability that is frequently associated with incorrect file permissions as well as coding errors is a race condition, which requires precise timing to be exploited. In this attack, during a brief window of opportunity, files are temporarily assigned file permissions that allow anyone to access them. Attackers can then manipulate these files. For example, a race condition in FreeBSD's `rmuser` script allows a local user to extract all password hashes from the system while the administrator removes a user (`http://www.securityfocus.com/advisories/3544`). This attack is possible because `rmuser` created a temporary file that was world-readable.

Manage Users Properly

After an attacker chooses a host to target, he might want to find out what user accounts he can use to gain access. An attacker frequently tries to access privileged accounts, such as root or administrator, because they possess the greatest access permissions. In many cases, if an attacker encounters a host that is difficult to compromise, she will move on to look for a less hardened host. We can secure administrative accounts by limiting access to these accounts to as few individuals as possible. For Windows systems, we recommend renaming the administrator account. For UNIX systems, we recommend restricting root logon except from the console, which requires that a system administrator must log in with his own username and then `su` to root. These steps can make it considerably more difficult for an attacker to compromise administrative accounts and can help provide an audit trail for the use of privileged accounts on the system.

Renaming administrative accounts is just one step in improving the host's defenses. Even if such accounts are renamed, attackers have methods of identifying accounts with privileged access. User accounts are generally associated with a unique ID number; in Windows this is called a security identifier (SID), and in UNIX it is called a user identifier (UID). Because this ID does not change even when the account is renamed, it can be used to determine which account possesses the administrative privileges. The UNIX root account's UID is 0, and the Windows NT and 2000 administrator account's

SID ends with 500. If additional levels of hardening are not applied, someone could search the /etc/passwd file for UID 0 or use the sid2user utility (`http://www.securityfocus.com/tools/544`) to locate the account name that corresponds to the SID suffix 500. Either process allows an attacker to locate the renamed administrative account or other accounts that are root equivalents.

Tip

You might want to consider creating a dummy local account named Administrator or root that has no privileges and an extremely long and complex password. This should keep the script kiddies busy for a while. If you create a dummy administrative account and enable auditing, you will know when someone is attempting to use the account.

Every hardening technique we apply to a host takes it one step further from a compromise. Attackers tend to focus on exploiting known vulnerabilities and basic configurations. By renaming the administrative accounts and restricting root logons, we make exploits more difficult for attackers.

Perform Effective Group Management

Now that we have the user accounts hardened, we will place them into specific groups and assign access permissions to those groups. We should only grant groups the minimum permissions that their members need to perform required tasks. A common mistake when placing users into groups is having too many users in administrator-level groups.

Note

One reason for assigning access permissions to groups instead of individual users is that group permissions automatically apply for each user in the group. By managing permissions for groups and assigning users to groups, administrators can keep much better control of security in their environments.

Although it's natural to think of placing users who need to perform certain administrative functions in the Domain Administrators group under Windows or in the UNIX sys group, you should determine whether another administrative group has lesser permissions that are still adequate for performing the required tasks. For example, if you have to change the time on a host, what would be the preferred group membership? The recommended groups for Windows NT and 2000 would be Server Operators or Power Users. It's important to determine which group would provide the most restrictive level of permissions while still supporting the task. (See

http://www.microsoft.com/technet/treeview/default.asp?url=/TechNet/
prodtechnol/winntas/proddocs/concept/xcp02.asp for more information.)

UNIX groups such as sysadmin, sys, or root should also have a controlled
membership. The permissions we have applied to these groups might allow
their members to access sensitive files and executables. Some groups, such as
root, should be strictly limited to the root account only. Instead of adding
user accounts to these critical groups, consider using tools, such as Sudo
(http://www.courtesan.com/sudo/), to allow specific users to execute privileged commands without having full root privileges. Sudo is an effective
security measure because it restricts administrative privileges and records the
invocation of Sudo privileges into a log; this is terrific for determining
accountability for restricted tasks.

Attackers strive to locate a user account with a weak password that can
easily be compromised to gain the identity of the user. After an attacker
obtains access to a user account, he often seeks to elevate the user's permissions to administrative permissions. This is sometimes accomplished by
associating the user account to an administrative group. Windows NT
has an infamous exploit called GetAdmin (http://www.insecure.org/
sploits/NT.get-admin.kernal.hole.html) that adds the user's account to the
Administrators group, thereby granting full access to the local machine.
Other exploits obtain elevated privileges by exploiting a local vulnerability
that allows the attacker to directly run commands with administrative
privileges.

Log Security-Related Information

Security logs are invaluable for verifying whether the host's defenses are
operating properly. Another reason to maintain logs is to ensure that forensics
evidence is available when we need to figure out what happened, even if we
already determined that something went wrong. Of course, each security
safeguard is only as good as the actions taken upon it. A log file is of minimal
value if you never look at it. As we discuss in Chapter 10, it is often wise to
utilize software, such as host-based intrusion detection systems (IDSs), that
can notify the administrator when a suspicious event occurs. This helps provide effective responses to potential security threats. A common alternative to
having in-house staff monitor logs for signs of malicious activity is outsourcing this task to a company that provides security-monitoring services.

Windows Logging

Microsoft Windows NT and 2000 offer built-in tools that help perform logging and auditing. By default, Windows systems log only typical system events aimed at resolving system and application faults. To log security-related activity, you must enable auditing settings, such as account logon events or object access, as illustrated in Figure 9.3.

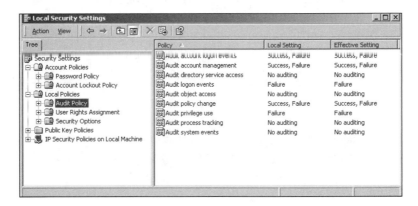

Figure 9.3   Windows NT and Windows 2000 provide several audit policies that can be extremely useful for logging system and security-related information.

Be aware that after an attacker has compromised a Windows NT host, he might use a tool such as WinZapper (`http://ntsecurity.nu/toolbox/winzapper/`) to clear event log files so that the record of how he compromised the host will be deleted.

UNIX Logging

UNIX has several files that keep track of significant user activities and record information such as logon and logoff times, failed logons, the use of privileged accounts, and even the commands that the user executes. Although the configuration of UNIX logging facility is flexible and varies across systems, some of the more standard UNIX log files are as follows:

- sulog—Maintains a historical record for each time the `su` command is used on the system.
- utmp—Maintains a snapshot listing of users who are currently logged in.
- wtmp—Maintains a historical record of users' login and logout activity.

UNIX systems generally use the Syslog facility to centralize logging of security and other system events. Syslog records messages from the UNIX kernel, user processes, the mail system, and the user administration process and supports locally defined events. System log files should be audited regularly because attackers typically focus on these files to cover their tracks; besides, it's impossible to track activity if you don't log. Much more information on logging is available in Chapter 18, "Network Log Analysis."

By following best practices when configuring the host's security on the local level, we provide a solid foundation for applying additional hardening layers. Placing users into groups and establishing proper file system permissions for those groups helps secure the host at its core. Potential attackers will have a more difficult time trying to gain access to administrative accounts that have been concealed and to which access has been restricted. Logging security-related activity offers invaluable information for detecting attacks at an early stage and helping determine what happened in the event of a successful compromise. Now we are ready to extend security into the network level, where we eliminate dangerous services to help harden the system's OS and applications.

Level 2: Hardening Against Network Attacks

At the network security level, we focus on practices that help to protect systems against attacks that are launched across a network. Some of the steps in hardening the system at this level include eliminating unused user accounts that can be accessed remotely, setting the minimum requirements for password complexity, and disabling network-accessible services that are not required for the system to perform the system's business tasks. This level is critical to the overall security of the host because the majority of system compromises occur over the network.

Eliminate Unnecessary Accounts

One of the most effective ways to prevent unauthorized access to a system over the network is to eliminate unnecessary accounts on the host. For example, the Windows NT and 2000 Guest user, if enabled, can be used to remotely obtain full control over the system's file. It's important to verify regularly that unused user accounts are disabled or deleted to ensure that they are not accidentally reactivated. Attackers can use enabled but unused accounts without a legitimate user noticing odd activity on her account.

Although disabling such accounts is a good administrative practice, we don't want to fall into the habit of leaving accounts disabled for a long time. Disabled accounts can be accidentally re-enabled. There are also reasons unrelated to security for deleting accounts, such as disk space usage and software licensing costs. In addition, the fewer accounts you have to maintain, whether disabled or active, the easier account management is. As we harden the host at the network layer, we want to minimize the number of disabled accounts by removing them after a reasonably short time. Some of the most vulnerable accounts on a host are service accounts. Background services run with privileges of these "users," without requiring someone to log in locally. Service accounts are often created with more privileges than they need; a classic example is backup software. Products, such as Backup Exec and ARCserve Backup, usually create service accounts so that they can back up devices over the network or launch scheduled backups. Accounts such as these should have complex passwords to prevent an attacker from remotely accessing the system using the service account. For instance, *arcserve* is not a good password for the arcserve account.

If possible, service accounts should be disabled in a way that logs attempts to access the account over the network. In Solaris, this is easily accomplished by setting the shell of service accounts to `noshell`, which logs out the user who logs in interactively and creates an appropriate entry in the system's log. (The noshell utility is part of the Titan hardening package, and can be downloaded free from `http://www.fish.com/titan/`.) Service accounts on Solaris include daemon, bin, adm, lp, uucp, nobody, and noaccess. Of course, we don't want to disable service accounts that provide critical business functions.

Enforce Strong Passwords

Knowing a user's password can provide an entry point to launch further attacks against the host, as well as to access information that is available through the user's account. User accounts with poor passwords are one of the most commonly exploited security weaknesses. This includes administrative accounts, such as root and administrator, with generic or default passwords. The system's users need to be educated to understand that they are responsible for safeguarding their passwords. Knowing that even security-conscious people have a tendency to select easy-to-remember passwords that are easily guessable, administrators should implement mechanisms that enforce the desired password selection guidelines.

Default Passwords on Network Devices

While performing a network assessment, I found several devices that used default passwords, such as Cisco routers with their enable passwords set to *cisco*. Does that sound a little like Cisco's basic training 101 configuration? I also located a Nortel Accelar switch. Curious to find out what the default password was, I performed a search of the Internet and was directed to http://www.securityparadigm.com/defaultpw.htm. I found that the default password for the Accelar switch might be *rwa*; when I typed that in, I gained full access to the switch. Imagine what could have happened if an attacker had tried the same thing!

An end user might have a difficult time remembering cryptic passwords required by a system that has strong password requirements. At the same time, increasing the complexity of a user's password makes it much harder for an attacker to compromise the user's account with a password-cracking tool that guesses passwords based on a dictionary file. A few such tools include L0pht Crack (http://www.atstake.com/research/lc/), Crack (ftp://ftp.cerias.purdue.edu/pub/tools/unix/pwdutils/crack/), and CrackWhore (http://www.subreality.net/). Establishing an effective password policy and educating the users about proper ways to select and remember strong passwords goes a long way toward helping to prevent unauthorized system access. Another way to help ensure the integrity of the authentication process is to use devices, such as RSA's SecurID. SecurID is a small hardware or software device that generates a different access code every 60 seconds and works in conjunction with RSA's ACE/Server. When logging in, users are asked to supply a password that they remember, as well as the access code that the SecurID token generated.

Another challenge in securing access to user accounts is the administrative complexity of assigning initial passwords to new user accounts. Many organizations use the same default password for all new users, and many individuals in the organization generally know this password. Using a random initial password is an effective way to protect new user accounts. Many attackers, especially insiders, attempt to compromise newly created accounts by trying typical first-time passwords such as *password*, *test*, or the username of the user. Other important password policies include a minimum password length of eight characters, password aging, password history, and account lockout after a certain number of consecutive failed login attempts.

Note

Enforcing the account lockout policy might open your organization to a denial of service (DoS) attack if attackers can attempt to log into your system over the network as the user whom they want to lock out.

Many system administrators do not implement *password aging*, which sets the amount of time the password is valid before the user must select another password. This option is critical for preventing an attacker who knows an account's password from being able to access the host months later because the user doesn't want to and doesn't have to change the password. Password history is important because users often inadvertently circumvent security policies. Password history will remember the prior *n* number of passwords used for an account and prevent the passwords from being used again.

Although password history is helpful, users can frequently bypass this restriction by incrementing the number that they add at the beginning or the end of the password. If possible, consider implementing mechanisms that require that a new password differ from the previous password by a certain number of characters.

Password Games Users Play

In some environments, password aging only sets the maximum age for a password, not a minimum age. A *minimum age* says that after a password has been set, a user cannot change it for a certain number of days. If you do not establish a minimum password age, but you require passwords to be changed regularly, some of your users will play a fun password game. For example, a user might change his password *raiders* to *newpass* and then immediately change it back from *newpass* to *raiders*. If you have password history enabled, some users will rapidly change their password several times, then change it back to what it originally was. Change the rules of the game by implementing a minimum password age of at least a few days.

We can help ensure that users select stronger passwords by implementing tools, such as Npasswd (`http://www.utexas.edu/cc/unix/software/npasswd/`) for UNIX and passfilt.dll (`http://support.microsoft.com/support/kb/articles/Q161/9/90.asp`), freely available from Microsoft for Windows NT. Strong password functionality is also built into Windows 2000 through the use of Group Policy (`http://support.microsoft.com/support/kb/articles/Q225/2/30.ASP`). These tools require that new passwords meet specific complexity requirements. These include creating passwords that are dissimilar to the account's username and forcing each password to contain at least one lowercase letter, one uppercase letter, and one digit.

A compromise of the password's confidentiality might grant a remote attacker local access to the system, whether the password belongs to user or a service account. Password-related issues can be mitigated through user awareness and through enforceable policies that encourage good password practices. By developing and implementing a password policy that balances security needs with user demands, you can alleviate many of the risks that are associated with password misuse.

Disable Unused Network Services

Most operating systems have services installed by default that are not required for the host's business function. The system administrator should disable all services that are not needed, especially if they can be accessed over the network. Attackers frequently scan networks in search of systems listening on commonly used ports, especially those that are associated with services known to have exploitable vulnerabilities. Leaving unnecessary services running on the system increases the risk that the system might be compromised. Even if the host is located behind the firewall, attackers can gain access to the host's services by connecting over ports that the firewall doesn't filter, or by finding ways to bypass the firewall altogether.

Disabling the service decreases the likelihood that it will be used as a doorway into the system, but it might complicate the task of remotely administrating it. For example, file-sharing services might not be directly related to a business function of an Internet-accessible web server, but they might be helpful for administrators when uploading or downloading the server's files. The more critical the system, the more likely you will be willing to forego some administrative convenience for the sake of hardening its configuration.

The first step to disabling unnecessary services is determining which services are currently running on your hosts. For example, the Code Red worm exploited a vulnerability in Microsoft Internet Information Server (IIS), but it also infected workstations that were running Microsoft Personal Web Server. In many cases, users were unaware that Personal Web Server was even on their PCs.

By proactively checking services running on all hosts, you can help ensure that only the necessary services are configured to accept network connections. One way of automating this procedure is to create a script that routinely captures the output of the `netstat -na` command to see whether unexpected ports are open on the system. You can use a file comparison tool, such as fc.exe under Windows or diff under UNIX, to detect deviations between the expected port listing and the one that the script reports. If you detect that a host is listening on port 80, somebody might have started a web server on the system. If you see the host listening on port 8787, it might have become infected through Back Orifice 2000.

Change Default SNMP Strings

An oversight of many system administrators involves not resetting the Simple Network Management Protocol (SNMP) community strings, which frequently have the default values of *public* and *private*. These strings are similar to passwords; they are used to provide primitive authentication when retrieving system information using SNMP tools. SNMP generally supports the use of the public community string when authenticating to obtain read-only access to host's statistics and configuration information. The private community string is used to obtain read/write access to host's information. For example, an attacker who obtains read/write access to the system's SNMP parameters can modify the host's configuration or runtime environment. Change the default values of SNMP community strings on your devices, and treat them like you would treat a system password. Numerous SNMP tools can be used to retrieve a wealth of information about the host that is running SNMP services, much more than information leakage that is frequently associated with null sessions on Windows systems.

Disable Resource Sharing Services (Windows)

Unhardened Windows systems have a tendency to offer too much information to anyone looking for it. One of the largest weaknesses of this type is known as the *null session* connection, where a host attempts to establish a communication channel with another Windows system anonymously. Unless null sessions are disabled, Windows does not require such connections to be authenticated. One of the legitimate ways to use null sessions is to list shares that are available on the remote Windows NT server when browsing through Network Neighborhood. Unfortunately, an attacker can use the same mechanism to query the remote system for usernames, services, network shares, and other data, and use this information to direct future attacks. Because null sessions have legitimate uses when administrating Windows domains, certain functions might no longer work without them.

Note

One of the problems inherent in the use of the Everyone group to enforce restrictions is that users who access the system via a null session are considered to be part of the Everyone group. To help administrators get around this problem, Microsoft introduced the Authenticated Users group that does not include null session users.

Windows file and print services do not hesitate to advertise shared resources to other systems on the network. Depending on the host's role, consider disabling server and related service on the system, or turning off support for NetBIOS altogether. If business needs require that you leave NetBIOS enabled, you might still be able to turn off "hidden" administrative shares, such as C$, ADMIN$, or WINNT$. Leaving these shares enabled without a valid reason provides the attacker with another opportunity to access the system.

Disable Remote Access Services (UNIX)

UNIX systems support numerous services that can be used for remotely accessing the host and that can be misused by an attacker. The most vulnerable of such programs are the so-called r-commands, which include rsh and rlogin. These two programs allow users to execute remote commands, but do not encrypt the communications. Telnet is another popular mechanism for remotely accessing UNIX systems. Much like the r-commands, Telnet is gradually being phrased out in favor of Secure Shell (SSH), which encrypts the session and provides stronger authentication options.

You can set up a trust relationship between systems so that a remote UNIX user can execute a command on another host without providing a password. Such trust relationships are useful and might be required for the system's business purpose. Most r-commands use IP addresses as the basis of verifying the identity of the trusted system; therefore, it is relatively easy to spoof the trusted host's identity. Remote access mechanisms, such as SSH, support the establishment of trust relationships based on cryptographic keys, which are much more dependable for authenticating users and systems. With all trust relationships, keep in mind that if it is easy for a legitimate user to jump from host to host, it is just as easy for an attacker who compromises just a single trusted host to do the same.

TCP Wrappers

TCP Wrappers (ftp://ftp.porcupine.org/pub/security/) is a time-tested mechanism for letting the UNIX server restrict and log access to its network-accessible services. In basic terms, TCP Wrappers works by checking whether a remote system is allowed to connect to a specific service before the connection is passed to the application. Hosts that are allowed to connect are listed in the hosts.allow file, and hosts that should be blocked are specified in the hosts.deny file. In a way, this resembles the functionality of host-centric firewalls that we discuss in Chapter 10.

TCP Wrappers has been used primarily to control access to services that are launched through Inetd; however, TCP Wrappers functionality can also be compiled into many standalone daemons. For example, SSH servers from OpenSSH (http://www.openssh.org) as well as from SSH Communications (http://www.ssh.com) can be configured via a compile-time option to use TCP Wrappers libraries. (The SSH version of the daemon also supports the use of AllowHosts and DenyHosts tags in the server's configuration file.)

TCP Wrappers can provide access control functionality at a level that is independent of the application's internal authentication mechanism. As a result, TCP Wrappers can be used to block undesired networks or hosts before they have an opportunity to target the application. This functionality contributes to defense in depth by reinforcing the application's internal access control mechanisms.

Network-level vulnerabilities offer attackers numerous exploit opportunities against hosts. Attackers can take advantage of weak passwords to usurp a user's identity or to access a service account. Attackers can also acquire confidential information and obtain elevated access to the host by finding unsecured or vulnerable network services on the targeted system. Protecting against such attacks involves enforcing good system maintenance and usage practices, disabling unnecessary services, and monitoring the system's logs for suspicious activity.

Level 3: Hardening Against Application Attacks

With the host's local and network levels more secure, we can address applications as the final level of host hardening. Each level of security builds on the other ones. We have created a strong foundation with files, users, and groups from the local security level and applied network level security by securing passwords and disabling potentially vulnerable users and services. Our outermost level of hardening focuses on application security, which protects the host against application-specific attacks that might be unrelated to the configuration of the host's OS. The principles we review in this section can be applied to many different applications. We want to harden each application by defining access and authentication methods to best satisfy our needs.

The most common application weaknesses can usually be resolved fairly easily. For example, the application should use the most recent security patches, and it should communicate on as few ports as possible. Vulnerabilities based on insecure default configurations allow someone with a little knowledge to create a big problem. Such weaknesses are what attackers look for. Two of the application characteristics that attackers most often exploit are poor default configurations and buffer overflows.

Buffer overflow exploits are a common way to take advantage of vulnerability in the application's code to gain unauthorized access to the system. A *buffer overflow* happens when a program does not properly check the size of data that it receives and tries to put too much data into a memory buffer. The additional data overflows the end of the buffer and can overwrite other memory locations, executing arbitrary code that the attacker supplies. Consequently, the exploited application might execute instructions that damage files, elevate user privileges, or cause a denial of service. To limit the impact of buffer overflows, keep applications updated and implement sound access and authentication methods.

Defining Access Methods

Applications often use internal access control mechanisms to define who can use various application functions. For example, Oracle has an internal database to authenticate usernames, passwords, and roles. This validation is completely separate from the OS. Database administrators rely on users and roles defined in the database to enforce who can do what with the application's data. Just as we limited host file permissions on the local level, we want to ensure that each application provides the equivalent level of security for its data and functions.

When installing an application, first examine the recommended procedure that the vendor supplies. Vendors are becoming increasingly security conscious and often provide valuable documentation on best practices for their applications, which can help you fine-tune the application's default configuration according to your security needs and policies. Many administrators install applications to run as the service user, who has more privileges than he needs. For example, an application might be using the administrator or root account instead of a dedicated account that possesses only those OS access rights that are required for the application to function. Additionally, the use of the dedicated account can help alleviate maintenance issues later, when patches need to be installed and the only account that can do it is the account used for the original installation.

Within many applications, a *user privilege* is a right to execute a particular function, or a right to access certain data. One way to handle privileges is by defining *roles*, which group several privileges and grant them to selected users. System privileges can be powerful, so they should be cautiously granted to roles and users. Doesn't this sound like setting up OS users and groups? It should—the principle is similar. As we determine whom is given responsibility for managing the data, we should focus on determining the appropriate rights that are required to perform those tasks. As we grant role permissions for tasks, we also need to determine when to revoke or drop the role permissions when they are no longer required.

Application Passwords

Applications that have their own passwords should also have password policies enforced, particularly password aging, lockout, complexity, and especially logging of access attempts. Databases are attractive targets for attackers because they centrally store valuable data, such as customers' contact or credit card information. Many attackers are aware of the default passwords for application and database system accounts. These accounts are often created automatically during installation and might go unnoticed by administrators. After an application or database is installed, be sure to change the account passwords or disable the accounts if they are not needed. Restricting access to system accounts and limiting application roles to specific tasks helps protect the application's data.

OS and Application Patches

Vendors routinely release OS and application patches to address vulnerabilities that are discovered during the lifetime of the system. Patch installation is a critical component for hardening hosts against known vulnerabilities. Keeping up-to-date with vendor's patches can be time intensive, but it is required to allow a system administrator to address the vulnerabilities before an attacker exploits them. At times, a serious vulnerability is known but the patch is not yet available; you must be prepared to compensate for this exposure by temporarily adjusting other components of your security perimeter.

Note

In most cases, applying appropriate patches from the application's vendor could have thwarted attacks that have been exploited by buffer overflow vulnerabilities.

Patch installation resolves several security issues, but it can also create larger issues. Install patches with caution. Although a patch typically corrects the faulty OS or application code, resolving the security issue, a patch could have side effects that prevent your custom scripts or applications from working properly. Test any patches prior to deploying them to your production hosts. By testing in a controlled environment, you can verify that the patch will resolve your security issues without breaking critical functions.

Security Announcement Notifications

Be sure to monitor security announcement forums used to post notices about discovered vulnerabilities and released patches that impact your computing environment. Some of the more popular forums are listed here:

Microsoft Products

- Subscribe to the Microsoft Security Notification Service by sending an email message to securbas@microsoft.com.

- Subscribe to the SANS Security Alert Consensus weekly bulletin by selecting Windows and Cross-Platform at http://www.sans.org/sansnews.

- Subscribe to the Security UPDATE newsletter by sending an email message to Security_UPDATE_Sub@lists.win2000mag.net.

continues ▶

Sun Products

- Subscribe to the Sun Customer Warning System by sending an email message to `security-alert@sun.com` with the subject *subscribe cws*.

- Subscribe to the SANS Security Alert Consensus weekly bulletin by selecting SUN and Cross-Platform at `http://www.sans.org/sansnews`.

Oracle Products

- Monitor alerts posted to the Oracle Security Alerts site at `http://technet.oracle.com/deploy/security/alerts.htm`.

All Products

- Subscribe to the SecurityFocus News mailing list by sending an email message to `sf-news-subscribe@securityfocus.com`. This newsletter provides weekly summaries for vulnerabilities that are discussed on the Bugtraq mailing list.

- Subscribe to the CERT Advisory mailing list by sending an email message to `majordomo@cert.org` with the body *subscribe cert-advisory*.

Additional Hardening Guidelines

Hardening the host by using the three levels presented in this chapter helps to armor the system against potential attackers. We have reinforced this concept several times as we have moved from the operating system to the application level. So far, we have addressed several of the major key components of hardening the host.

To conclude this chapter, let's look at some valuable resources that provide hardening guidelines and checklists. Such documents, offered by industry leaders, such as CERT and SANS, can assist in implementing the hardening best practices described here. Using a checklist or a script to harden hosts helps ensure that they are built in a consistent manner every time, and that the extent of hardening that is applied to the systems is properly documented.

Common Security Vulnerabilities

The 20 Most Critical Internet Security Vulnerabilities list (`http://www.sans.org/top20.htm`) produced by the SANS Institute and the FBI provides a wonderful summary of the most often compromised vulnerabilities. The purpose of creating the Top 20 list was to help administrators start securing their hosts against the most common threats, without feeling overwhelmed by the task. We recommend that you review this list to verify that your hardening procedures account for the top 20 weaknesses, and that your hosts' configurations do not match this "most wanted" list. Understanding the vulnerabilities in the system's configuration goes a long way toward helping to arm the host against them.

Hardening Checklists

Many great resources on the Internet contain detailed information on hardening various operating systems. For example, numerous software vendors provide security guidelines or step-by-step instructions on their web sites. A general resource with many papers related to operating system, network, and application security is the SANS Reading Room, located at `http://rr.sans.org/`.

You can also find the following free OS hardening documents helpful for defining procedures for securing your own hosts:

- The "Armoring" series of papers by Lance Spitzner does an excellent job describing how to harden the configuration of Linux, Solaris, and Windows NT servers (`http://www.enteract.com/~lspitz`).

- NSA publishes well-researched security recommendation guides for Windows NT and 2000 systems (`http://nsa.www.conxion.com/`).

- Wamala Paul Mubanda demonstrates how to harden a Windows NT server (`http://rr.sans.org/win/cant_hack.php`).

- For help creating a Windows hardening checklist, try the Out-of-the-Box NT Security Checklist (`http://www.windowsitlibrary.com/Content/121/18/toc.html`).

- Todd Jenkins wrote a concise whitepaper regarding "Hardening Bastion Hosts." You can find the paper at `http://rr.sans.org/securitybasics/hard_bastion.php`.

- The Center for Internet Security offers several checklists and benchmarking tools to rate security of Windows and UNIX hosts (`http://www.cisecurity.org/`).

Several well-regarded resources are available free that can help you automate hardening procedures for your hosts:

- NSA security recommendation guides for Windows systems contain INF files that can help automate several hardening steps (`http://nsa.www.conxion.com/`).

- Sun offers an excellent toolkit called JASS to automate the hardening of Solaris systems (`http://www.sun.com/security/jass/`).

- Solaris hardening scripts that offer similar functionality to JASS are YASSP (`http://www.yassp.org/`) and Titan (`http://www.fish.com/titan/`).
- The Bastille Linux project offers scripts to automate the hardening of Linux systems (`http://www.bastille-linux.org/`).

Summary

Hardening the configuration of host computers allows us to reinforce the security of the network perimeter by following the principles of defense in depth. As with all components of a defense infrastructure, we rely on multiple security layers to protect resources against attacks. This notion can be applied at the network and at the host level. The extent to which a system should be hardened depends on its role on the network, and also accounts for resources that you have available to maintain the locked down configuration. As we discussed in this chapter, default OS and application installations rarely implement hardening best practices that allow us to build systems that are highly resistant to attacks.

To ensure that we design and apply hardening procedures in a controlled and reliable manner, we have defined three levels for locking down the system: local, network, and application. When defending against local attacks, we focused on restricting the use of administrative tools, restricting file permissions and group membership, and activating logging of security-related events. To protect the host against network-based attacks, we eliminated unnecessary accounts, enforced password restrictions, and locked down dangerous services that were accessible over the network. We also looked at application-specific issues that result in security breaches by restricting access to application components and ensuring that patches are routinely applied. To further assist you in defining hardening procedures that are appropriate for your environment, we also pointed out trustworthy guidelines and tools that implement hardening steps for Windows and UNIX operating systems.

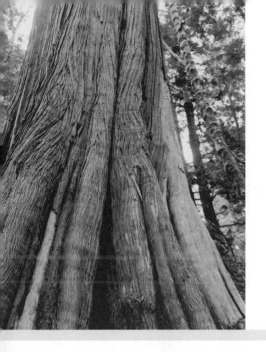

10

Host Defense Components

THE HOST'S PERIMETER, OPERATING SYSTEM (OS), and applications are our last line of defense against network attacks. If an attacker manages to get through or around your firewall, or if you are defending against malicious code or an insider, it is up to the host to limit the scope of the potential compromise. In Chapter 9, "Host Hardening," we explained how to configure the system's OS and related applications to help the host withstand local and network-based attacks. We locked down the file system, disabled unnecessary accounts and services, enforced strong passwords, fine-tuned group membership, and applied patches. This chapter builds on the concepts of hardening by demonstrating how hosts can play an active role in protecting data and services. In a layered security architecture, hosts that are configured according to the risks they might face and to the task they need to fulfill reinforce perimeter components such as routers, firewalls, and network intrusion systems.

In the following pages, we explain how to use hosts to help detect and isolate attacks, and we discuss tools and approaches that will help you strengthen the system's defenses. We look at differences in needs of several host categories and describe best-fit roles for anti-virus software and host-based intrusion detection products. We also talk about host-centric firewalls and how they compare to gateway firewalls that you have seen in the book so far. We examine strengths and weaknesses of each type of host defense component to allow you to effectively incorporate them into the design of the overall network security perimeter.

Hosts and the Perimeter

Any system that is operating as part of a network infrastructure has the potential of falling victim to a remote attack. A successful compromise might come as the result of a system misconfiguration or might be possible due to vulnerabilities in the OS or installed applications. As you know, administrators can help mitigate risks that are associated with known vulnerabilities by routinely applying software patches. To effectively protect systems against attacks that might yet be unknown to us, we have been using the defense-in-depth approach, relying on multiple layers in the defense perimeter's architecture to reinforce its resilience.

Red Hat and the WU–FTPD "File Globbing" Vulnerability

An unknown vulnerability and one that has been announced to the world are different. At the end of November 2001, Red Hat issued a security advisory about a bug in Washington University File Transport Protocol Daemon (WU-FTPD).[1] The vulnerability could allow a remote attacker to obtain root access to the server that is running WU-FTPD, which is bundled with many Linux distributions. Unfortunately, the statement was erroneously published days before the date on which Linux vendors had agreed to issue the advisory and release appropriate patches. Red Hat's announcement accidentally undermined efforts to coordinate the announcement with the availability of the fix, leaving thousands of users of non-Red Hat distributions vulnerable.[2]

Of course, the WU-FTPD vulnerability existed before Red Hat's announcement; those who were aware of its technicalities might have been quietly exploiting it. The security advisory, albeit unfair to Red Hat's competitors, allowed administrators to consider ways to protect against the vulnerability, possibly by disabling the vulnerable daemon until the patch became available. On the other hand, by prematurely publicizing the information, Red Hat increased the chances that a skilled attacker could develop an exploit to take advantage of the vulnerability before administrators could protect their hosts against it.

The nature in which the system is being used impacts the risks that it might need to be protected against and ways in which the host's defense components need to be deployed and configured. To help you understand the applicability of host-centric security software, we have classified systems into two general categories: workstations and servers. Although the distinctions between these types of hosts are often intuitive, let us formalize the security challenges that are associated with each category to lay groundwork for subsequent discussions.

Workstation Considerations

Workstations, which can include laptops and desktops, are used by end users to interactively run local applications and to access services on the network. Workstations routinely interact with potentially unsafe resources on the

Internet as users connect to external sites that provide services such as web, FTP, and instant messaging. Because of the unpredictable nature of human behavior, it is difficult to foresee the problems that might arise when a user connects to an external system that is not under your control. The same workstations are also used to connect to resources that are more trusted: internal file and mail servers, human resources systems, and other applications that are specific to your organization's business. Interactions with partner and supplier networks carry a degree of risk as well. In these cases, although you cannot directly control the security of third-party resources, you can often define accountability and liability through the use of legal agreements with your partners and suppliers, as well as by inquiring about their security posture when formalizing the business relationship.

Workstations are not always located behind the reinforced security perimeter of your network. This is especially true of laptops because traveling and telecommuting users might dial in to an ISP to connect to the Internet. In these cases, the workstations do not have the protection that security components offer, such as network firewalls and intrusion detection systems (IDSs).

The Qaz Worm and Microsoft

Around October 2000, an attacker was able to gain unauthorized access to Microsoft's internal systems and, reportedly, view source code for upcoming product releases. Investigators surmised that the attacker succeeded at compromising Microsoft's perimeter defenses by first infecting an employee's home workstation with the Qaz worm by emailing him a trojanized attachment.

Qaz propagates by scanning the subnet for Windows shares that are not password protected. When a vulnerable system is found, it copies itself to its Windows directory via NetBIOS as notepad.exe, while renaming the original notepad to note.com. The worm also modifies the infected system's registry key to ensure that the host automatically launches the worm upon startup. The worm also establishes a backdoor on TCP port 7597 on the infected system, allowing the attacker to run arbitrary commands, upload a new files, or terminate the worm's program. To announce the IP address that the attacker can use to access the backdoor, the worm sends an email message to 202.106.185.107, which corresponds to a system that is located in China.[3]

The attacker probably used the backdoor that the trojan established to access Microsoft's systems when the employee connected to the company's internal network. If Microsoft's corporate firewall did not block inbound connections on TCP port 7597, the attacker also could have waited for Qaz to infect the company's internal systems and connected to them directly.

One of the challenges in maintaining workstations is the sheer number of them, generally one per employee in a company. This makes it difficult to effectively monitor workstations for suspicious events, install OS and application patches, update virus definitions, and enforce security policies.

A useful tool for determining the current patch level of systems distributed throughout your network is Microsoft Network Security Hotfix Checker (HFNetChk), available as a free download from `http://www.microsoft.com/technet/security/tools/hfnetchk.asp`. HFNetChk is a command-line utility that can remotely determine which patches are missing from Windows NT and 2000 OS, as well as the Internet Information Server (IIS), SQL Server, and Internet Explorer. By default, HFNetChk operates by downloading from the Microsoft web site a digitally signed file that contains information about available patches and queries the registry and the file system of remote machines to see whether the patches have been applied. Figure 10.1 shows the output of running `hfnetchk.exe -s 2 -i 192.168.1.201,192.168.1.202` to scan two workstations. As you can see, HFNetChk provides a Microsoft Knowledgebase article number for service packs or hotfixes that are not installed.

Figure 10.1 HFNetChk scans remote systems and establishes which patches for selected Microsoft products have not been applied.

The data file that HFNetChk uses to check the status of installed patches is XML based, which means that it is possible to create your own HFNetChk data file manually to check for the presence of arbitrary files and registry settings. In fact, during the outbreak of the Nimda worm, a customized version of the data file was made available through the NTBugtraq mailing list to remotely check workstations for Nimda infections.[4] You can use the `-x` parameter to run HFNetChk with your own data file when searching for specific system anomalies. Unfortunately, as of this writing, Microsoft has not formally documented the format of the data file for HFNetChk.

Server Considerations

Server systems are frequently dedicated to running services that are accessed by client systems over the network; they do not allow users to directly execute local processes. In such cases, only the server's administrators can log on to the system. This decreases the likelihood that a user who is logged on to the server will launch a local copy of Internet Explorer and start browsing through dubious web sites. Your security policy should restrict the kind of actions that administrators can take when maintaining such servers.

Dedicating a server to a particular task allows you to strip the system of many components, leaving only software that is required for the server to perform its business task. In this case, security of the local system can be improved because the usability of the server does not need to be as full featured as that of a workstation. For example, a Solaris 8 server with 64-bit support running Check Point FireWall-1 requires only 83 packages[5], out of hundreds that would be needed if the system were used as a workstation.

Multiuser hosts form another class of servers, which allow multiple users to be simultaneously logged into and running interactive processes on the system. For example, such servers can be implemented by deploying Windows Terminal Services or by creating multiple accounts on a UNIX system and allowing users to log in using SSH. Universities frequently offer such services to students and faculty by allowing them to log in to the multiuser server and run shell-based as well as X Window System applications.

When defending against vulnerabilities that can be exploited over the network, you can deploy multiple firewalls, fine-tune packet filters on your routers, and configure network IDSs to detect the attacks. These measures are not effective, however, at defending the multiuser server against a user who already has local access to the system. For instance, a buffer overflow vulnerability in the Point to Point Protocol (PPP) utility `pppattach` under Caldera UnixWare 7 and OpenUnix 8.0.0 could allow a local user to execute arbitrary commands with elevated privileges (`http://cve.mitre.org/cgi-bin/cvename.cgi?name=CAN-2001-0858`). This condition could not be directly exploited over the network without first obtaining local access to the server. System hardening, patch management, host-based intrusion detection, and security policy are probably your best bets for protecting multiuser servers.

Servers are usually considered to be more sensitive than individual workstations. Whether the attacker compromises a multiuser or a dedicated server, she is likely to have an immediate impact on numerous users who rely on the services of that host. Consider the influence an attacker might have if she manages to compromise a primary domain controller (PDC) in a Microsoft Windows domain. Another prominent attack of this sort is a web server defacement that announces to the world that the company's public web server has been compromised. Attacks on the more sensitive servers located within a company are likely to inflict larger financial harm to the victim, but are generally not widely publicized.

Defacement Without a Compromise?

On November 29, 2001, a message distributed through Attrition's Defaced Commentary mailing list reported that the web site of SecurityFocus, a highly regarded source of information security research and intelligence services, had been defaced. The defacement was an uncommon one because the actual servers that were hosting the SecurityFocus site were not compromised. Instead, the attacker altered an image that was stored on the server of an external company that provided banner ads to the site. As Attrition's message pointed out, "The SecurityFocus 'defacement' consisted of an alternate banner at the top of their site, replacing the normal rotating banner ad. Instead of seeing an advertisement for a legitimate company or product," visitors saw the image that was hosted at the following URL: `http://adj18.thruport.com/banners/Client11/sf468.gif`. Nothing else was altered on the `www.securityfocus.com` site.[6] Figure 10.2 presents the crafted banner ad featured in this incident. In this rather unusual hack, the SecurityFocus site was defaced without their web server being compromised.

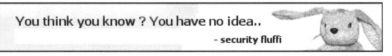

Figure 10.2 The crafted banner ad, shown to visitors of `www.securityfocus.com`, suggests that the defacement can be attributed to Fluffi Bunni (a.k.a. Fluffy Bunny).

Anti-Virus Software

Anti-virus software is the most widespread mechanism for defending individual hosts against threats that are associated with malicious software, or *malware*. Malware threats are posed by viruses that are carried via infected files, worms that spread autonomously over the network, and humans who use malicious software as agents to remotely control the victim's system. Many established vendors, such as Symantec, McAfee, Trend Micro, and F-Secure, offer products that detect and, in many cases, eradicate malware from the system. This is accomplished by monitoring the local host's boot sector, memory, and file system for signatures of known viruses, trojans, and worms. Another detection mechanism that is often used in conjunction with the database of malware signatures monitors programs for behavior patterns that are frequently associated with malware. When properly deployed, anti-virus software can be effective at helping to establish an in-depth security architecture.

Note

Software for defending hosts against malicious software is called *anti-virus* primarily for historical reasons, even though it protects the system against several categories of malware, including viruses, trojans, and worms.

Strengths of Anti-Virus Software

Anti-virus software establishes a significant layer in a reinforced security perimeter. Just like all defense components, anti-virus software has its strengths and weaknesses. Some of the core strengths of anti-virus software are listed next:

- Anti-virus software is effective at numerous popular malware specimens. Anti-virus companies enjoy the benefit of significant research investments and can analyze malicious software relatively quickly to the extent that it allows them to produce a signature for a specific virus, trojan, or worm.

- Anti-virus software is unobtrusive partly because it has a relatively low rate of false positives. Even when configured to operate in a "real time" protection mode, anti-virus software runs in the background, rarely drawing attention to an event that should not require the user's attention. As a result, end users do not mind having virus protection enabled on their workstations.

- Anti-virus software is affordable and has been accepted as a necessity by many budgetary decision makers. It is not easy to find a person who is unaware of the dangers associated with malicious code. Anti-virus software has been around long enough that it has become an accepted part of a corporate lifestyle.

The EICAR Test File: The Ultimate False Positive

While conducting a security assessment, I discovered that although anti-virus software was installed on all critical servers, it was not actually enabled, to the surprise of the systems' administrators. Take care to verify that virus protection is active on your systems and that it operates as expected. One of the quickest ways to check this is through the use of the EICAR test file. Most anti-virus products are programmed to recognize this file's content as a virus, even though it does not actually contain malicious code. The file, which can be downloaded from http://www.eicar.org/anti_virus_test_file.htm, consists of 68 ASCII characters. If saved with the .com extension, it actually executes on Windows platforms to print the message "EICAR-STANDARD-ANTIVIRUS-TEST-FILE" to standard output. Of course, if your anti-virus software is active, it should not let you execute this file in the first place.

In addition to protecting individual hosts, anti-virus software is also effective when integrated with gateways that process SMTP, HTTP, and FTP traffic. Trend Micro has a significant market share in such configurations and offers malware-blocking software that runs on Windows NT, Solaris, HP-UX, and Linux-based gateways. For example, you can integrate Trend Micro's InterScan VirusWall with a Sendmail-based mail relay so that malicious code is stripped out of SMTP messages before they enter into the heart of your network.

A relatively new class of anti-virus software is meant to provide malware protection services to custom server-side applications. Symantec's CarrierScan Server is one such product. It decouples the virus-scanning engine used in Symantec's GUI-based products and runs it as a service on a dedicated server. Developers can query the CarrierScan Server, asking it to determine whether a given file contains malicious code. The server can also attempt to clean the file at the programmer's request. Developers can program their applications to serve as clients to CarrierScan Server, interacting with it in two ways:

- By taking advantage of the C-based application programming interface (API) using libraries that Symantec provides.

- By making direct network connections to the server and using a text-based protocol that Symantec defines. By default, CarrierScan server listens to such connections on TCP port 7777.

Note

Yahoo! Mail uses CarrierScan Server to give its users the option of having their email attachments scanned for malicious code before downloading the files to the workstation.[7] The flow of the back-end process for this request probably involves Yahoo's servers programmatically contacting the CarrierScan engine, asking it to scan and clean the attachment. This server-centric approach allows end users to take advantage of virus-scanning software without having it installed locally.

As you can see, malware protection can take place at several different locations on the network. You do not need to limit yourself to any one of these. In fact, it is generally advantageous to perform such scans on individual workstations, as well as on file servers and Internet gateways. If malware is a large concern for your business, consider deploying one vendor's anti-virus product on your hosts and another vendor's product on the gateways. This configuration increases the likelihood that a malware specimen will be blocked. Such redundancy can be justified because anti-virus software has many significant limitations that impact the design of the security perimeter.

Limitations of Anti-Virus Software

In most cases, the effectiveness of the anti-virus product depends on the extensiveness of its malware signatures. When the Nimda worm appeared, it spread so rapidly that most organizations were aware of its existence by the end of the business day, but leading anti-virus vendors did not provide Nimda signatures until that night or the following morning. Even then, not all companies were capable of automatically distributing the latest signatures to their hosts. As you might recall, we discussed some of the ways of preparing for such incidents at the end of Chapter 1, "Perimeter Security Fundamentals." As one of the measures, be sure to set up your systems to routinely poll the signature distribution server for updates. Most anti-virus products allow you to configure the software to automatically download the latest signature database from the vendor's web or FTP site. Enterprise versions of such software allow you to distribute signature updates from your own server within the organization. This approach allows you to centrally monitor infection-related alerts across many systems and allows you to force remote hosts to retrieve the latest updates outside of the routine schedule, especially when you know about a worm outbreak.

Another limitation of current anti-virus products focuses on their effectiveness at detecting mutations of known malware specimens. For instance, if you receive an email attachment with a little-known SRVCP trojan, your anti-virus software is likely to detect it and display a warning similar to the one in Figure 10.3. Unfortunately, it is sufficient to modify a particular byte in the trojan's executable using a plain text editor to prevent Norton AntiVirus from recognizing it as malicious software. This change, if you know what you are doing, would not affect the trojan's core functionality. By modifying the executable in a relatively trivial manner, you might alter one of the characteristics that anti-virus software uses for the trojan's signature.

Figure 10.3   Norton AntiVirus has no problems detecting the original variant of the SRVCP trojan.

Another way of mutating a malware specimen is to use one of the many *packers* that compress and often encrypt the compiled executable. The encoded version of the executable is self-contained and contains a small decoding routine that is triggered during runtime to extract the original program into memory. For example, another way of mutating the SRVCP trojan without changing its functionality would be to use a freely available packer called UPX. When the trojan's original executable is compressed, as shown in Figure 10.4, Norton AntiVirus no longer flags it as malicious code. By encoding the executable, UPX decreased its size, prevented Norton AntiVirus from detecting the trojan, and complicated analysis of its functionality.

Figure 10.4   UPX is a popular packer for compressing and encoding executables.

Of course, individuals who possess the source code for malicious software have the luxury of modifying it directly with the specific goal of bypassing signature-matching anti-virus engines. Malware mutations are not as effective against behavior-based scanners, but behavior-based techniques are not yet adopted as widely as those that rely on the database of known malware signatures.

Packers for Executables

Many packers are available for compressing and possibly encrypting executables. Some of these allow you to reverse the packing process to recover the original executable; others purposefully do not make such a facility available. In some cases, anti-virus software might be able to automatically reverse the encoding to compare the original version of the program to malware signatures. Some of the more popular packers include these:

- UPX (http://upx.sourceforge.net/)

- NeoLite (http://www.neoworx.com/products/neolite/)

- Petite (http://www.un4seen.com/petite/)

- ASPack (http://www.aspack.com/)

Polymorphic malware, which changes itself on-the-fly, is another challenge that anti-virus vendors have been working to overcome with a varying degree of success. One of the first mechanisms that facilitated the creation of polymorphic malicious code was created in 1993 under the name Dark Avenger's Mutation Engine (DAME).[8] Although modern anti-virus products easily uncover polymorphic tricks that DAME performs, other techniques can significantly complicate the detection of malware. The evolution of malicious software is running its course in parallel with advancements in anti-virus technologies. Ways to bypass controls enforced by anti-virus software will probably always exist.

Anti-virus applications, just like any other software, can have vulnerabilities that expose its host to attacks while helping to combat malware. For example, a version of Trend Micro OfficeScan anti-virus client allowed a remote attacker to perform denial of service (DoS) attacks against its host (CAN-2000-0203, CAN-2000-0204), as well as modify the program's configuration settings (CAN-2000-0205). To make the matter worse, such attacks were relatively difficult to pick out from the stream of network probes because the vulnerable program listened on port 12345, which has traditionally been used by the NetBus trojan.[9]

Despite the limitations, anti-virus software remains one of the most effective ways to control the spread of common malware specimen across multiple systems. Viruses, worms, and trojans are difficult to block using traffic-filtering devices alone because they can enter the network through open channels, such as email, web browsing, or floppy disks. After malware is inside, it can be programmed to communicate with its author via outbound connections that are often allowed to pass through the firewall unchallenged, whether to announce its presence via SMTP or to retrieve additional instructions through an HTTP request. An attacker can use malware as an agent working inside the targeted network, facilitating further, more directed attacks on internal resources. Host-centric firewalls, deployed on systems throughout the network, are another part of an in-depth security architecture that can mitigate some of the risks that anti-virus software doesn't cover.

Host-Centric Firewalls

The firewalls that we have been discussing in this book so far are network-centric. We placed them on the borders between subnets to regulate how network traffic crosses from one segment to another. Similar processes can be applied at the host level to control how packets enter and leave the system that the host-centric firewall is protecting.

Most host-centric firewalls enforce access policies bidirectionally by monitoring packets that enter and leave the system. Controlling network access at the host level is effective, whether the host is located behind layers of traffic-screening devices or is directly connected to the Internet. Host-centric firewalls reinforce the system's defenses by addressing threats that anti-virus products don't cover:

- Unrestricted access to the system's file shares
- Anonymous access to the system
- Undetected malicious code
- Port scans and other types of reconnaissance probes
- Vulnerable network services running on the system

Host-centric firewalls are often referred to as personal firewalls because they aim to protect individual systems instead of whole networks. We would like to use the term *personal firewall* solely when discussing traffic screening functionality on workstations. Although such software can be installed on servers, referring to it as *personal* might be misleading because server systems are rarely used just for personal computing.

In this section, we examine a number of popular host-centric firewall software choices, some of which are available for free. To help you plan and deploy appropriate host-level defenses, we discuss capabilities of firewalls that are optimized to run on workstations and compare them to features of products that are more suited to protect individual servers.

Firewalls for Workstations

Host-centric firewalls are often geared to run on workstations, especially on roaming laptops that cannot always enjoy the protection of the firewall at the network's border. The number of products that fit into the category of such personal firewalls has been increasing, and in this section, we discuss only a few of them to illustrate important concepts. Some of the more popular products in this sector are listed next:

- ZoneAlarm (`http://www.zonelabs.com/`)
- Tiny Personal Firewall (`http://www.tinysoftware.com/`)
- Norton Personal Firewall (`http://www.symantec.com`)
- Sygate Personal Firewall (`http://www.sygate.com/`)
- ConSeal PC Firewall (`http://www.consealfirewall.com/`)
- VPN-1 SecureClient (`http://www.checkpoint.com/products/secureclienttour/`)

Many of these products are inexpensive; in fact, they are often available free of charge for non-commercial use. Many other products provide host-centric firewall functionality for the workstation. Some of these can be used on servers as well. Firewall functionality is sometimes built into host-based intrusion detection systems (IDS), as is the case with BlackICE Defender, which we look at in the "Host-Based Intrusion Detection" section of this chapter.

The majority of personal firewalls that run on Windows-based workstations are capable of imposing access restrictions based on the local application that is attempting to send or receive packets. Before an application is allowed to connect to another host, or before the host is allowed to accept a network connection, the personal firewall must consult its rule set to determine whether access should be granted. For example, Figure 10.5 illustrates how you can use Tiny Personal Firewall to allow iexplore.exe, the executable file used by Internet Explorer, to make outbound network connections to any system on TCP ports 80 (HTTP) and 443 (HTTPS).

Figure 10.5 Tiny Personal Firewall allows users to define filter rules for specific applications—in this case, Internet Explorer.

Early versions of personal firewalls associated an access rule solely with the name of the local executable to which the rule applied. If an attacker or a malicious agent were to change its name to iexplore.exe, for example, it would be able to usurp connection privileges of that program. To counteract this threat, personal firewalls can now examine the one-way hash of the connecting executable to look up applicable access rules. As you can see in Figure 10.6, Tiny Personal Firewall uses the Message Digest 5 (MD5) algorithm for automatically computing such hashes. The firewall can alert the user if the file's hash has changed or if an executable that is trying to connect has not been fingerprinted yet.

Figure 10.6   Tiny Personal Firewall automatically computes MD5 hashes for executables known to the firewall and allows the user to verify whether the executables are still intact.

Host-centric firewalls, such as Tiny Personal Firewall, allow you to define access restrictions using the same parameters as traditional network firewalls: protocol, destination IP, and port number. Others products, such as ZoneAlarm, take a more simplistic approach that might not be as intuitive for firewall administrators, but are aimed at simplifying firewall configuration for less tech-savvy users. As you can see in Figure 10.7, ZoneAlarm allows users to group external systems into those that are trusted (Local) and those that are not (Internet). Each of the two zones can have its own set of access restrictions, which are applied depending on the remote host's category. For example, you can allow NetBIOS traffic going to, and possibly from, systems in the Local zone. By placing the internal subnet into the Local zone, you allow the workstation to connect to a Windows-based file and print services on the internal network. Other networks would be placed in the Internet zone, which is generally much more restrictive and does not allow NetBIOS connections.

Figure 10.7 ZoneAlarm groups network resources into Local and
Internet zones, depending on how trustworthy the resources are.

Most personal firewalls ship with a default rule set that improves the security
of the workstation compared to its state without a firewall, but is still overly
permissive. We suggest customizing the default firewall policy by backing it
up and then clearing the original rule set. Personal firewalls that do not have
a rule set usually default to prompting the user for every new communication attempt to or from the host. Figure 10.8 shows such a prompt as presented by ZoneAlarm, asking whether Internet Explorer should be allowed
to access the Internet. This allows you to build the rule set by letting the
firewall "remember" your responses to communication attempts. When going
through the initial "learning" period, you might become frustrated by a
seemingly unending stream of questions regarding applications that seem to
want to initiate network connections. Don't worry: The rule set tends to
reach a stable state after a couple of days.

Keep in mind that although you might be willing to answer the firewall's
questions while it "gets to know" your system, other users at your organization might not be as patient or might not know how to answer some of the
firewall's questions. This is a major obstacle to the adoption of host-centric

firewalls by the general population of users. As we discuss in the section "Controlling Distributed Host Defense Components" at the end of this chapter, personal firewall vendors offer software that centralizes the creation and distribution of the firewall policy across the organization's workstations. Deploying host-centric firewalls on servers is not as dependent on the product's user friendliness and carries its own set of advantages and challenges.

Figure 10.8 ZoneAlarm can be configured to prompt the user if an unfamiliar application attempts to initiate a network connection.

Firewalls for Servers

Host-centric firewalls are also effective at helping to protect individual servers; they function similarly to firewalls that run on workstations. Although servers are often located behind traffic-screening devices, the critical nature of their data and services might warrant this additional layer of protection that does not usually come at a large expense. Host-centric firewalls are also useful for protecting servers that cannot be located on a screened subnet or a DMZ, or that are at an increased risk of insider attacks. In many cases, the same software used to protect workstations can be used for servers. The major differences in requirements between firewalls for workstations and for servers are as follows:

- The performance impact of installing the host-centric firewall is more critical for servers. Network latency is generally not as high of a concern on a workstation as it is on a server.

- The need to focus on inbound connections to the system is more critical for servers. Outbound connections made by servers are usually not as unpredictable as those exhibited by workstation users; this often eliminates the emphasis on controlling outbound activity on a per-application basis.

- The need to eliminate interactions between the firewall software and the system's user is more critical for servers. Host-centric firewalls installed on servers cannot be expected to prompt the user for rule set questions or alerts because most of the time, no one is logged into the server locally.

Because you have already seen host-centric firewalls that are optimized to protect workstations, this section examines products that address server-specific requirements. Instead of focusing on protecting whole networks, host-centric firewalls are tuned to provide protection for a single system. This section discusses the following methods of protecting individual servers:

- IPFilter
- SunScreen Lite Firewall
- FireWall-1 SecureServer
- Packet filtering via IPSec in Windows 2000

As you may recall, in Chapter 9, we mentioned TCP Wrappers as one of the tools used for controlling inbound connections to individual systems. TCP Wrappers is an effective way to control access to the server's network services, especially those that were started through `Inetd`. However, TCP Wrappers lacks some of the features that are available in full-fledged firewalls that we can install on the network as well as on a host. One such "true" firewall that we discuss next is IPFilter, which is available free and runs on numerous UNIX platforms.

IPFilter

In Chapter 3, "Stateful Firewalls," we discussed IPTables, which is a stateful firewall that can be installed on UNIX hosts. IPFilter (`http://www.ipfilter.org/`), sometimes referred to as IPF, is a robust stateful firewall package that has actually been in use longer than IPTables. Although IPFilter is most commonly seen on BSD systems, it can run on Solaris, IRIX, HP-UX, QNX, FreeBSD, OpenBSD, NetBSD, BSD/OS, and some versions of Linux. Features offered by IPFilter are similar to those of IPTables, and they make

IPFilter an excellent firewall for protecting whole networks, as well as individual hosts. Let us see how to use IPFilter for implementing some of the tasks that are typical for host-centric firewalls that run on servers.

IPFilter obtains its rule set from a plain-text configuration file. By default, IPFilter reads through all entries in the file before making a final decision about whether to block a packet. This differs from the default behavior of most firewalls that we encountered, which stop processing the rule set after locating the first rule that is applicable to the packet in question. To force IPFilter to stop iterating through the rule set as soon as it makes a match, we need to use the `quick` keyword in the rule's definition. For example, when deciding whether to let a small TCP fragment into the system, IPFilter stops processing the rule set after encountering the following rule:

```
block in quick proto tcp all with short
```

The `short` keyword is used to block small fragments that are often indicative of an attack. Attackers might split the packet's header such that some TCP flags are located in one fragment, and some in the other; this might confuse a firewall that tries to determine whether the fragment belongs to an existing session, or whether the fragment matches a particular rule. The preceding rule is useful when you do not want to block all fragmented packets because they might carry valid traffic. To block all inbound fragments, regardless of the protocol or their size, you could use this:

```
block in quick all with frag
```

Like most modern firewall packages, IPFilter is a stateful firewall. It can monitor the state of TCP sessions, and, to a limited extent, the "state" of UDP and ICMP connections. Use the `keep state` keyword in the rule to specify that IPFilter should keep track of a session's state. For example, when running IPFilter on a web server, you could use the following statements to allow inbound HTTP and HTTPS traffic in a stateful manner:

```
pass in quick on fxp0 proto tcp from any to <host.ip.addr> port = 80 keep state
pass in quick on fxp0 proto tcp from any to <host.ip.addr> port = 143
↪keep state
```

In this case, `fxp0` is the server's NIC where inbound requests will be originating, and `<host.ip.addr>` represents the web server's IP address. Of course, these web server rules assume that at the end of the rule set, you have specified the following rule that blocks (and probably logs) all traffic that has not matched any other rule in the policy:

```
block in quick on fxp0 log all
```

We can fine-tune HTTP and HTTPS rules presented previously by ensuring that IPFilter creates a state table entry only for TCP packets that have a `SYN` flag set. Packets with any other TCP flags should not be allowed to initiate a connection, and could constitute attempts to mangle the system's state table. To account for such packets, we would use the `flags` keyword like this[10]:

```
pass in quick on fxp0 proto tcp from any to <host.ip.addr> port = 80
⮡flags S keep state keep frags
pass in quick on fxp0 proto tcp from any to <host.ip.addr> port = 143
⮡flags S keep state keep frags
```

Notice that we also added a keep frags tag to the rules to ensure that IPFilter accounts for fragments that might be part of a valid connection initiation packet but do not have a SYN flag in the headers. If IPFilter is configured to block and log all inbound packets that are not explicitly allowed, then the revised web preceding server rules can help detect port scans against the server that manipulates TCP flags in an attempt to avoid detection.

> **Note**
>
> Additional intricacies are involved in using the `flags` keyword with a flag mask to account for the presence of TCP flags, such as URG and PSH, in session initiation packets. For information regarding the use of the flag mask in IPFilter, please see the IPFilter "Howto" document at `http://www.obfuscation.org/ipf/ipf-howto.txt`.

Even though UDP packet exchanges are effectively stateless, a UDP request is expected to have a reply with inverse port and IP address parameters. This can allow IPFilter to offer basic stateful protection for UDP packets that are targeting a DNS server:

```
pass in quick on fxp0 proto udp from any to <host.ip.addr> port = 53 keep state
```

To control outbound connections made by the server, you could use the following rule that blocks and logs outbound traffic that has not been explicitly allowed:

```
block out log quick on fxp0 all
```

Because inbound traffic is controlled through the use of stateful rules, it is wise to keep outbound connections made by the server to a minimum. This is more challenging on a workstation, which tends to make outbound connections much more often than it accepts inbound traffic. As a result, host-centric firewalls that are optimized for workstation usage generally pay more attention to offering a granular and user-friendly approach to controlling outbound connections.

Responding to Ident Requests

By default, when blocking a connection, TCPFilter does not return a response to the sender to let it know that the packet was not allowed through. As mentioned in Chapter 3, this behavior is often advantageous for defending the system against reconnaissance probes. In some cases, however, lack of a response from your server might introduce delays as the peer's system waits for the timeout or attempts to re-send the packet. For example, if your server is configured to send outbound email, the recipient's mail server might try to connect back to your Ident daemon in an attempt to confirm the identity of the user who is connecting from your system. If your server is hardened, it is probably not running the Ident daemon and blocks all packets that are destined to Ident's port 113. However, the delivery of your outbound email mail is likely to be suspended until the recipient's mail server's Ident request times out. To speed up this process, you could configure your server to respond with a TCP RST packet to all connection attempts to Ident's TCP port, or with an ICMP "port-unreachable" packet to its UDP port. (UDP connections rely on ICMP for the equivalent of a TCP RST.) The following IPFilter rules cause your server to block connections to TCP and UDP port 113 and respond with an appropriate "error" packet.

```
block return-rst in quick on fxp0 proto tcp from any to <host.ip.addr>
➥port = 113

block in quick on fxp0 return-icmp(port-unr) proto udp from any to
➥<host.ip.addr> port = 113
```

IPFilter is effective at protecting networks when it is installed on a gateway system. When installed on an individual server, it offers robust protection against network-based attacks that target the individual host. This can also be said for other UNIX firewalls in IPFilter's class, such as IPTables, which we covered in Chapter 3, and SunScreen Lite, which we discuss in the following section.

SunScreen Lite

SunScreen Lite (`http://www.sun.com/software/securenet/lite/`) is a stateful firewall that is bundled, for no additional charge, with Solaris 8. Sun markets SunScreen Lite as the product "designed to protect individual servers or very small workgroups."[11] Sun also offers a commercial product called SunScreen, which is better suited for protecting networks and was used as the code-base for its slimmed-down cousin SunScreen Lite. SunScreen Lite is appropriate for protecting individual systems in a manner similar to the way we can use IPFilter. SunScreen Lite is particularly attractive to organizations with Solaris expertise for the following reasons:

- SunScreen Lite can be installed similarly to other Solaris packages through the use of the pkgadd utility. (GUI-based installation is also available.)

- Installing SunScreen Lite does not require the administrator to compile code.

- SunScreen Lite is free for Solaris 8 users and is supported by Sun.
- SunScreen Lite software can be easily updated during routine patch roll-outs together with other Solaris components.

In many aspects, both the commercial and the free version of SunScreen resemble the functionality and the look of Check Point FireWall-1. SunScreen allows administrators to group servers and networks into objects with the goal of easing the manipulation of the firewall's rule set. The objects are used to define network parameters of rule set components so that these details do not need to be hard-coded into each rule. SunScreen Lite can use a GUI application to build the firewall policy, and it supports a command-line firewall configuration tool. Administrators can define a firewall rule to include elements such as these:

- Source object. The group of source hosts to which this rule applies.
- Destination object. The group of destination hosts to which this rule applies.
- Service object. The group of protocols to which this rule applies.
- Firewall action. The action (deny or allow) that the firewall should take if a packet matches this rule.
- Track option. The way the firewall should log the event that matches this rule.

If you are familiar with Check Point FireWall-1, you should have little trouble setting up SunScreen Lite on your critical Solaris systems, without purchasing additional software. Organizations with an investment in Check Point software or those that need to protect servers that are not based on Solaris might prefer to use FireWall-1 SecureServer, which is useful for providing host-centric firewall services for individual systems.

FireWall-1 SecureServer

Check Point FireWall-1 SecureServer (`http://www.checkpoint.com/ products/security/secureserver.html`), formerly known as the Host Inspection Module, is a version of FireWall-1 that is licensed to run on an individual system instead of a gateway host. SecureServer is administered in the same way as the other Check Point FireWall-1 products, and is an especially good choice for organizations that have FireWall-1 expertise. You can specify that you want to install SecureServer by selecting the VPN-1/ FireWall-1 SecureServer option when the Check Point installer asks which component you want to install. (Of course, the software also requires that you supply the license that matches your selection.)

Because of the fees that are associated with purchasing SecureServer, selecting it as the host-centric firewall makes the most sense to companies that have already deployed other Check Point products. Some of the key advantages of SecureServer in such environments are as follows:

- It's not necessary to train administrators in a new firewall package.
- Technical support for SecureServer can be received through the channels that are used for other Check Point products.
- Multiple SecureServer installations can be centrally administered through the FireWall-1 Management Server, together with other FireWall-1 products.

We have numerous choices when it comes to installing firewalls on servers. We can use products that are marketed for use on workstations, as well as software that is not as user friendly and is catered more toward the needs of a server. As the last mechanism in the discussion of host-centric firewalls for servers, let us examine an inexpensive way of achieving packet-filtering functionality on Windows 2000 through the use of IPSec policies.

Packet Filtering Via IPSec on Windows 2000

One of the most powerful network security components built into Windows 2000 is IPSec. In Chapter 8, we described how to use IPSec to secure communications between remote systems. We used the Microsoft Management Console (MMC) to define IPSec policies on VPN endpoints. In this section, we show how to use IPSec policies, supported natively by Windows 2000, to filter out unwanted network traffic that is targeting the Windows 2000 server. Packet-filtering capabilities built into the Windows 2000 IPSec driver allow us to specify which local ports can be accessed without authentication and encryption, and which should be limited to valid Authentication Header (AH) or the Encapsulating Security Payload (ESP) peers, or blocked altogether. This technique allows us to mimic basic functionality that is offered by many host-centric firewalls for servers, without deploying additional products.

Note

Packets that are blocked by the Windows 2000 IPSec driver are dropped silently, without an RST or an ICMP unreachable packet being sent to the connecting host. This behavior is different from the basic TCP/IP filtering built into Windows 2000 and Windows NT, which returns an RST to blocked packets.[12]

Consider the scenario in which the system acts as a publicly accessible web server that offers HTTP services on TCP port 80. We can use IPSec policies to block IP packets targeting all ports other than 80. Let us begin by defining two IP filter lists:

- The `All Inbound Traffic` filter matches all inbound packets targeting the server. We need this filter to later specify that this traffic should be blocked.

- The `Inbound HTTP Traffic` filter matches all inbound packets that are targeting the server on TCP port 80. We need this filter to later specify that this traffic should be permitted.

The necessary traffic filters can be created by right-clicking the IP Security Policies on Local Machine object in MMC and selecting Manage IP Filter Lists and Other Filter Actions. In the Manage IP Filter Lists tab, use the Add button to define the filters to use as selection criteria when applying the IPSec policy. Table 10.1 displays the settings to use to define the IP filters.

Table 10.1 **IP Filters for the IPSec Policy**

Filter Name	Source Address	Destination Address	Protocol	Destination Port
All Inbound Traffic	Any IP Address	My IP Address	Any	N/A
Inbound HTTP Traffic	Any IP Address	My IP Address	TCP	80

After defining the two traffic filters, the filter listing should resemble the one displayed in Figure 10.9. You can use the `Inbound HTTP Traffic` filter as the template for defining other criteria that specify protocols and port numbers that should be accessible to the public. The IPSec driver uses these filters for determining which actions to take on packets that it processes. When defining filters, be sure to leave the Mirrored check box enabled; this tells the IPSec driver to automatically match responses to packets that match the original filter (by reversing IP addresses and port numbers).

Windows 2000 has several default actions built in, such as those that can permit IPSec drivers' traffic to pass through, or can require the use of ESP or AH. To block undesired traffic, we need to define one more action by going into the Manage Filter Actions tab of the Manage IP Filter Lists and Filter Actions dialog box. We can call the new action `Block` and specify `Block` as its security method. The resulting action list should resemble the one displayed in Figure 10.10.

Figure 10.9 Windows 2000 uses IP filter lists to define the criteria for selectively applying IPSec policies.

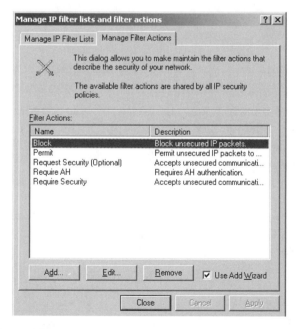

Figure 10.10 We need to define a `Block` rule before configuring IPSec policies to block undesired traffic.

We are now ready to define an IPSec policy that blocks all traffic that matches the `All Inbound Traffic` filter and permits packets that match the `Inbound HTTP Traffic` filter. Right-clicking the IP Security Policies on Local Machine object in MMC and selecting Create IP Security Policy can do this. Let us call the new policy `Local Defense (Only Inbound HTTP)`. We will not be using the default response rule, so be sure to disable it when prompted. Here, we will define two IPSec rules so that the policy resembles the one shown in Figure 10.11. The first rule applies to packets that match the `Inbound HTTP Traffic` filter and associates the filter with the Permit action. This is also where we would tell the server to use specific IPSec parameters if we wanted to take advantage of VPN capabilities of the IPSec driver.

Figure 10.11 When defining IPSec policies, we associate previously created traffic filters with actions and IPSec connection settings.

The second rule in our IPSec policy specifies that all traffic that matches the `All Inbound Traffic` filter should be blocked, as shown in Figure 10.12. This policy uses the `Block` rule that we created a few steps earlier. When prompted for the authentication method to use for each of the two IPSec policy rules, we can specify Kerberos even if we do not have Kerberos on the network. This is because the authentication method is ignored unless the rule specifies the use of AH or ESP for the connection.[13]

Figure 10.12 We use the previously defined filter action Block to specify that packets that match the `All Inbound Traffic` filter should be blocked.

After IPSec rules are defined, we can begin enforcing the policy by right-clicking its object in MMC and selecting Assign. IPSec policies become effective as soon as they are applied, without requiring that the system be rebooted. When the policy is active, the server's IPSec driver examines all IP packets that leave and enter the system and applies specified access rules. In our scenario, all packets to TCP port 80, as well as applicable response packets, will be allowed through, and all other packets will be blocked. We can use the same mechanism to selectively filter traffic based on source IP addresses, such as if only traffic from a specific address range is allowed to access the web server.

Dropping all non-HTTP traffic makes it difficult to maintain the system remotely. We can use built-in IPSec filtering capabilities to permit administrative traffic from authenticated remote systems. We could, for instance, create a new IPSec rule that accepts ESP-protected administration traffic from specific hosts. If worried about the added load on the server, we could use AH instead of ESP to remotely authenticate the host without encrypting the administrative traffic. Of course, we would need to configure IPSec policies on administrative workstations to match IPSec connection parameters on the hardened server.

Tip

Remotely administrating a Windows-based bastion host is often a challenge because it frequently opens the server to attacks on native Windows protocols. One of the ways to address such concerns is to configure the Windows 2000 server to block all administrative connections that are not secured with ESP. This provides a way to easily tunnel traffic across the firewall without using native and potentially vulnerable Windows protocols if the server is located on a screened subnet.

Configuring IPSec policies on numerous servers that need to be protected is a time-consuming and error-prone process. Environments that have deployed Active Directory can use Group Policy to centrally distribute IPSec policies to multiple systems. Additionally, Microsoft provides a command-line tool called IPSecPol, which can be used to automate all aspects of IPSec policy creation and modification. You can download IPSecPol free from `http://www.microsoft.com/windows2000/techinfo/reskit/tools/existing/ipsecpol-o.asp`. (IPSecPol works regardless of the presence of Active Directory.)

IPSec-based filtering is prone to similar limitations as other on-stateful traffic-filtering devices that we described in Chapter 2, "Packet Filtering." Additionally, the Windows 2000 IPSec driver does not log packets that it blocks, which significantly complicates troubleshooting. Lack of logging also prevents us from performing intrusion detection tasks that would be possible with the majority of host-centric firewalls. Although filtering based on Windows 2000 IPSec policies is much more configurable than the basic TCP/IP filtering mechanism built into Windows NT and 2000, the Windows 2000 IPSec driver cannot block certain traffic. As a result, IPSec-based filters are not effective against the following IP communications[14]:

- The Windows 2000 IPSec driver does not block broadcast packets.
- The Windows 2000 IPSec driver does not block multicast packets, which are in the range of 224.0.0.0–239.255.255.255.
- Windows 2000 uses Resource Reservation Protocol (RSVP) to provide quality of service (QoS). The Windows 2000 IPSec driver does not block RSVP packets, which are IP protocol 46.
- IPSec uses the Internet Key Exchange (IKE) protocol to negotiate connection parameters, and cannot be matched via IPSec filters. The Windows 2000 IPSec driver does not block UDP packets with the source and destination port of 500.

- Windows 2000 uses Kerberos as the core for its domain authentication. The Windows 2000 IPSec driver allows TCP and UDP packets with the source or destination port of 88.

You can use packet-filtering capabilities of the Windows 2000 IPSec driver to add an extra layer of defense to Windows 2000 servers with relative ease. Other server-centric filtering mechanisms that we discussed in this section are either more expensive or do not natively integrate with the existing Windows 2000 infrastructure. At the same time, full-fledged firewall products generally have more robust traffic-filtering capabilities and come with thought-out logging facilities.

So far, we have discussed two primary defense components that we can use to reinforce the security of individual systems: anti-virus software and host-centric firewalls. As we have shown, each component category, as well as each tool within the categories, is optimized for different environments and is best at mitigating different risks. In the next section, we examine host-based IDS products, which are optimized for detecting and investigating malicious behavior on the host.

Host-Based Intrusion Detection

As you saw in the previous section, firewalls can be used to defend whole networks, as well as individual servers. Similarly, IDSs exist in two varieties: network and host based. We introduced the notion of intrusion detection in Chapter 7, "Network Intrusion Detection," where we examined optimal uses of IDS components for monitoring a network for malicious events. We deployed network IDS sensors in a way that allowed us to sniff traffic going between hosts and network devices. Network IDS enabled us to apply certain criteria to captured traffic to single out events that were likely to be indicative of an attack. Much like their network counterparts, host-based IDS sensors also exist primarily to detect and examine malicious activity at various stages of an attack, but they are optimized for monitoring individual hosts. Additionally, host-based IDS sensors can be configured to integrate their findings to provide a unified view of multiple systems throughout the network. In this section, we examine key aspects of the host-based intrusion detection process and look at several categories of host-based IDS products.

The Role of Host-Based IDS

At its core, host-based intrusion detection involves monitoring the system's network activity, file system, log files, and user actions. A host-based IDS should generate an alert when it detects escalation of privileges for a user or system account. For example, you would want to see an alert if accounts such as guest or nobody suddenly possessed administrative privileges. This kind of behavior is difficult to monitor at the network level because a network IDS sensor cannot usually see or interpret actions that take place on a host. Specifically, host-based IDS has the following key advantages over their network counterparts:

- Host-based IDS sensors can monitor user-specific activity on the system. Host sensors can observe the user's local activity because they have access to such host-specific information as the process listing, local log files, and even system calls. Network sensors, on the other hand, have a hard time associating packets to specific users, especially when they need to determine whether commands in the traffic stream violate the specific user's access privileges.

- Host-based IDS sensors can monitor data exchanges of encrypted network streams by tapping in at the connection's endpoint. Running on the VPN's endpoint allows host sensors to examine packets in their clear-text form, before the host encrypts outbound packets, or after it decrypts inbound packets. A network IDS sensor, on the other hand, cannot examine the payload of an IPSec packet or the contents of a packet that is part of an SSL session. The need to perform content analysis of network traffic at the host continues to increase as companies continue to deploy VPN solutions.

- Host-based IDS sensors can help detect attacks that utilize network IDS evasion techniques. As we discussed in Chapter 7, such techniques exploit inconsistencies in the way a network IDS interprets the packet's intentions from the effect that the packet might have on the targeted host.[15] For example, a vulnerability in leading commercial and freeware network IDS products allowed attackers to evade detection by formatting HTTP requests with a non-standard Unicode encoding (`http://cve.mitre.org/cgi-bin/cvename.cgi?name=CAN-2001-0669`). However, Internet Information Server (IIS) was able to decode such requests and execute potentially dangerous commands that the network IDS would not detect. Host IDS sensors operate on the targeted host and have a chance to detect attacks that might have eluded the network IDS.

Host-based intrusion detection is also useful for correlating attacks that are picked up by network sensors. If a network IDS sensor detected an attack that was directed at one of your hosts, how do you know whether the attack was successful? The host's IDS software can help you determine the effect of the attack on the targeted system. Of course, if the host is compromised, its logs might be altered or deleted. But if you are automatically relaying all host IDS data to a central, dedicated log server, then you can use that data instead of the original IDS logs if they are unavailable or untrusted. From an incident-handling perspective, host-based IDS logs are also vitally important in reconstructing an attack or determining the severity of an incident.

Ideally, you would deploy host-based IDS sensors on every host in your organization. However, that might not be a viable option for your company, considering the amount of resources involved in deploying and maintaining numerous IDS sensors. When deciding whether to deploy host-based IDS sensors on a system, consider the host's risk level. Critical servers that store sensitive data and are accessible from the Internet will surely benefit from an extra layer of protection that host-based IDS provides. You might consider deploying such products on workstations as well, depending on the nature of threats to which they are exposed.

Host-based IDS products can watch over the channels that need to remain open for the host to perform its business function. If a host needs to function as a public web server, its firewall cannot block inbound connection attempts to TCP port 80, but its IDS can be tuned to monitor HTTP traffic or other host attributes for malicious activity. Additionally, some host-based IDS products can interact with the firewall software that is installed on the system and can be configured to shun the attacker if an intrusion attempt is detected.

Host-Based IDS Categories

Now that we understand the roles that host-based IDS plays when operating as part of a network's security perimeter, let us examine different types of host-based IDS solutions. As you know, multiple sources for data can be used to perform intrusion detection at the host level. The primary reason for wanting to look at the host's file system, log files, and network connections is because the malicious activity on a host can exhibit itself in multiple ways. Some commercial products, such as ISS RealSecure Server Sensor and Enterasys Dragon Squire, can monitor several data sources on the host. Other products are optimized to perform host-based intrusion detection based on a specific data source:

- The host's file system: Tripwire, AIDE
- The host's network connections: BlackICE, PortSentry
- The host's log files: LogSentry, Swatch

Checking the File System's Integrity

Host-based IDS tools, such as Tripwire and AIDE, aim at detecting unauthorized changes to the host's file system. They operate by taking a "snapshot" of the file system in a trusted state, when all the files are considered to be valid. During subsequent scans, these tools compare the system's files to the initial baseline and report noteworthy deviations. To tune the integrity-checking mechanism so that it only monitors relevant aspects of files, you can specify what file attributes are allowed to change, or what files can be ignored altogether. For example, applications frequently create temporary files in C.\WINNT\Temp or /tmp directories; alerting the administrator every time a new file appears or disappears from these directories would generate too many false positives. On the other hand, contents of core system libraries rarely change, and it is normal for the host's log files to grow in size while retaining initial ownership and access permissions.

Note

AIDE software that we discuss in this chapter is a free integrity verification tool meant to offer an alternative to Tripwire. This is different from commercial AIDE software that carries the same name, but is an intrusion detection tool for correlating log information from different firewall and IDS products. Litton PRC developed the commercial AIDE program; it has no relation to the freeware AIDE utility discussed here.

Integrity-checking tools such as Tripwire are able to detect changes to the file's contents by calculating the file's checksum or cryptographic hash during the scan and comparing it to the file's "signature" that was obtained when creating the baseline. An alternative method, which is impractical in many situations due to space requirements, would have been to make an actual copy of each file to be monitored. Increasing the difficulty of tampering with the database of baseline signatures can be accomplished in several ways:

- Obfuscate the contents of the baseline database by using a proprietary binary format instead of plain text when saving the database to disk. Although this mechanism makes it more difficult to tamper with the database, it hardly prevents the attacker from discovering the obfuscation scheme or from using the integrity checker to update the baseline.

- Place the baseline database onto a read-only media, such as a write-protected floppy disk or a CD-ROM. This method requires that the disk or the CD be accessible to utilities when it performs the verification scan. This method is reliable and is most useful for hosts whose baseline does not need to be frequently updated. Keep in mind, though, that even if the attacker is unable to modify the baseline database, he might be able to change the scanning utility or modify its configuration to use an unauthorized baseline. Placing the scanning utility onto the read-only media helps defend against some attacks of this nature, but having access to the host might allow the attacker to modify the system's kernel or file system drivers to conceal his presence on the host anyway.

- Digitally sign the baseline database. In this scenario, updating the program's baseline typically requires that the administrator presents the appropriate cryptographic keys and supplies the necessary passwords. This technique achieves a good balance between the first two approaches. It is frequently used in environments that need to be able to remotely update the baseline periodically, such as when installing system patches or otherwise updating the host's configuration.

Tripwire is the most well known among system integrity-checking utilities. In many ways, Tripwire is a benchmark against which other tools in this category are measured. The original version of Tripwire was developed in 1992 at Purdue University, and it is still available free under the name of Tripwire Academic Source Release (`http://www.tripwire.com/products/tripwire_asr/`). This version of Tripwire runs only on UNIX platforms. Despite its age, this version of Tripwire is still effective at detecting unauthorized changes to the host's files, although it is no longer being actively maintained. A full commercial version of Tripwire is not free, but it boasts a number of improvements over the initial version:

- The commercial version of Tripwire runs on Windows as well as UNIX hosts. The Windows version of the tool can monitor the system's registry in addition to the file system.

- The commercial version of Tripwire can monitor the integrity of configuration files on routers and switches.

- Multiple hosts and devices monitored by the commercial version of Tripwire can be controlled centrally through a unified configuration and reporting interface called Tripwire Manager.

Note

An open source version of Tripwire for Linux is available free at `http://www.tripwire.org`. This version was derived from the commercial product, but unlike the academic version, it is actively maintained. Tripwire Open Source Linux does not offer centralized management features that are present in the commercial version of the product.

Tripwire Manager is a console that is available with the commercial version of Tripwire that offers the ability to centrally manage multiple Tripwire "agents" that are deployed on remote hosts and devices across different operating systems. Tripwire Manager is the key difference between the commercial version of Tripwire and free tools that exist in the same category of host-based IDS products. When you need to support many Tripwire instances, this feature alone can help justify purchasing Tripwire instead of using the freeware alternatives.

AIDE (`http://www.cs.tut.fi/~rammer/aide.html`), which stands for Advanced Intrusion Detection Environment, is a free integrity checker that functions similarly to Tripwire. AIDE offers features that closely resemble the capabilities of the academic release of Tripwire. Some of the key differences between AIDE and various Tripwire versions are listed next:

- AIDE is free, just like the academic version of Tripwire and the Linux version of Tripwire Open Source.

- AIDE is maintained through a steadier development cycle than the academic version of Tripwire, which is no longer maintained. At the same time, the commercial version of Tripwire is being developed much more actively.

- AIDE runs on a wide range of UNIX platforms but, unlike the commercial version of Tripwire, it does not run on Windows.

- AIDE can be used with a Perl script called ICU (`http://nitzer.dhs.org/ICU/ICU.html`), which offers limited capabilities for centrally controlling remote instances of AIDE "agents" but is far from being as comprehensive as Tripwire Manager.

- AIDE does not cryptographically sign its baseline database, making it more difficult to ensure the integrity of its findings. (The academic version of Tripwire does not do this either.)

Overall, organizations that cannot justify paying for the commercial version of Tripwire will probably benefit from installing AIDE instead of the academic version of Tripwire. Those who need to perform file system integrity verification for critical Windows systems will not find many robust alternatives to the commercial version of Tripwire, but they might consider taking advantage of similar features that are built into generalized host-based IDS products, such as RealSecure Server Sensor and Dragon Squire.

One inexpensive way to identify environment changes on Windows platforms is to use the sysdiff utility that detects added or deleted files and identifies changes to configuration files and registry entries. Sysdiff does not use cryptographic techniques enjoyed by tools such as AIDE and Tripwire, but it is handily available with the Windows NT and 2000 Resource Kit. A more powerful alternative to the sysdiff tool is a relatively inexpensive monitoring utility for Windows called Winalysis (`http://www.winalysis.com/`). Winalysis has a graphical interface, supports the collection of SHA-1 digital signatures, and can be scheduled to observe remote hosts from a central location.

Note

For information regarding configuring and running AIDE, take a look at the AIDE manual at `http://www.cs.tut.fi/~rammer/aide/manual.html` and a paper titled "AIDE: Poor Man's File Integrity Checker" at `http://rr.sans.org/audit/aide.php`.

Both AIDE and Tripwire expect the administrator to supply a policy file that defines which attributes of which files need to be monitored for changes. One of the ways to go about defining this policy is to list a limited number of critical files on the system that you know are supposed to change infrequently. A more comprehensive approach, applicable primarily to hardened server systems, calls for monitoring all files on the host with the exception of those that change frequently. Defining such a policy is a time-consuming process because each server is configured slightly differently and can modify different files during normal operation.

When defining a comprehensive file-monitoring policy, it is recommended that you start by specifying that the program should monitor all files and directories recursively from the root of the file system. You can then run the integrity checker, see which attributes of which files changed during the system's normal operation, and modify the policy appropriately. After several iterations, you should be able to achieve a stable state that will save you from having to constantly update your policy and the baseline database, while monitoring as many aspects of the host's file system as possible.

Network Connection Monitors

Now that we know how to detect unauthorized changes to the host's file system, let's switch our attention to monitoring another critical aspect of the host's operation: its network connectivity. Specifically, we want to use available data about network connections that attempts to initiate or terminate on the host to detect malicious behavior. The impetus behind connection monitoring is similar to the one in network IDS products that run in promiscuous mode to examine network streams for multiple hosts and devices. A host-based IDS, however, can also associate network sockets with specific processes and users on the system. Additionally, host-based network-monitoring software is less likely to be overwhelmed by the voluminous network traffic that continues to push the limits of network IDS performance.

One popular host-based IDS product for monitoring the system's network connections is BlackICE Defender (`http://www.networkice.com/products/blackice_defender.html`), produced by Internet Security Systems (ISS). BlackICE Defender runs on Windows-based operating systems and comes in two versions: one optimized for protecting a workstation, and another with attack signatures that are optimized for servers. To ease the burden of maintaining BlackICE Defender instances on many systems in the organization, ISS also sells a version of BlackICE Defender as part of a product called ICEpac Suite. ICEpac Suite allows administrators to centrally control and monitor BlackICE Defense instances (called BlackICE agents when part of ICEpac) that are distributed across the enterprise. ICEpac Suite offers BlackICE agents that run on Windows as well as Solaris hosts.

Whenever BlackICE observes a suspicious network connection that targets its host, it creates a log for this event. A firewall would typically create an individual record for each blocked packet. The IDS mechanism in BlackICE is able to group events that are associated with multiple offending packets into a single log entry that identifies the attack. For example, Figure 10.13 shows that BlackICE detected several suspicious events, one of which was identified as a TCP port scan. Instead of logging each packet that comprised the scan, BlackICE created a single entry in the log. However, BlackICE can be configured to capture full packets that it identifies as belonging to an attack sequence and log them for future analysis. In addition to performing IDS services, BlackICE comes with a built-in host-centric firewall that can block unauthorized inbound connections to the system. Unfortunately, although the IDS component of BlackICE monitors traffic bidirectionally, its firewall mechanism cannot block outbound connections.

Host-based IDS products that monitor network connections frequently have the option of responding to detected attacks by blocking the attacker's host from accessing ports on the protected system. This capability is sometimes referred to as *active response* or *active defense*, and we described it in the context of network IDS sensors in Chapter 7. Host-based IDS products, such as BlackICE, can implement active response by automatically reconfiguring the host's traffic-filtering software to shun the attacking IP address for some time period. (BlackICE can only do this by interacting with its own firewall components, actually.) This capability is useful for blocking an attack at an early stage, such as during a port scan, before it escalates into something more forceful, such as a buffer overflow attempt.

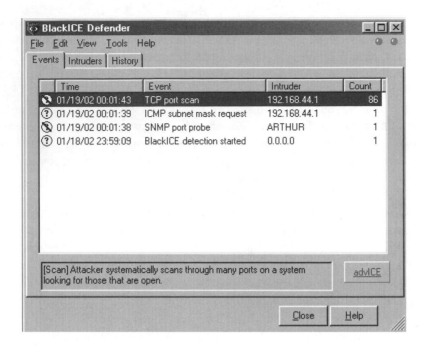

Figure 10.13   BlackICE Defender can detect and log network-
based attacks that target the host on which it runs.

Psionic PortSentry (http://www.psionic.com/abacus/portsentry) is another
host–based IDS product that can detect port scans and other unauthorized
connection attempts to the system. PortSentry is free and can run on most
UNIX operating systems. When PortSentry detects a network-based attack, it
can block the attacking host by automatically reconfiguring the compatible
firewall on the local host or by placing an appropriate entry into the
hosts.deny file used by TCP Wrappers. For example, the following are
Syslog records that document PortSentry actions when it detects a port
scan coming from 192.168.44.1:

```
Jan 19 10:35:57 localhost portsentry[1252]: attackalert: TCP SYN/Normal
➥scan from host: 192.168.44.1/192.168.44.1 to TCP port: 13
Jan 19 10:35:57 localhost portsentry[1252]: attackalert: Host
➥192.168.44.1 has been blocked via wrappers with string: "ALL: 192.168.44.1"
Jan 19 10:35:57 localhost portsentry[1252]: attackalert: TCP SYN/Normal
➥scan from host: 192.168.44.1/192.168.44.1 to TCP port: 21
Jan 19 10:35:57 localhost portsentry[1252]: attackalert: Host:
➥192.168.44.1/192.168.44.1 is already blocked Ignoring
```

In this example, PortSentry detected an unauthorized connection to TCP port 13 on the local host. It responded by reconfiguring TCP Wrappers in an attempt to block subsequent connections from the offender.

As useful as active response capabilities can be in a host-based IDS, they are also dangerous because the supposed offender might get blocked based on a false positive. As a result, this functionality is much more appropriate for workstations than it is for servers. Workstations are not accessed via inbound connections as often as servers are, and they are less likely to receive a slew of benevolent inbound connections that look like a port scan.

Log File Monitors

So far, we have examined host-based intrusion detection techniques that involve examining the system's network connections and its file system. Another core data source for useful security information is the host's log files. Log file monitors observe contents of critical logs and alert administrators when suspicious events are detected. One such host-based IDS product is called Swatch (its name stands for "simple watcher") and is available at `http://www.oit.ucsb.edu/~eta/swatch/swatch.html`. Swatch is free and runs on most UNIX operating systems. We could use Swatch, for example, to stay abreast of attacks that PortSentry detects. To set this up, we would configure Swatch to email the administrator when it locates a line with the string `attackalert` in a Syslog record.

Another free UNIX-based tool for monitoring log files is Psionic LogSentry (`http://www.psionic.com/products`). Unlike Swatch, LogSentry does not monitor logs in real time; it runs periodically and emails alerts in batches. This helps the administrator to limit the number of email messages that he receives, but it might also delay the administrator's response to an attack.

Log file monitoring utilities are available for Windows platforms as well. The following represent a couple of the products worth your look:

- TNT Event Log Monitor (`http://www.tntsoftware.com/`)
- LANguard Security Event Log Monitor (`http://www.gfi.com`)

Log file monitors have the benefit of being able to observe events that are generated by multiple security components on the host. Moreover, in scenarios in which logs from several systems are submitted to a single host, log file monitors can perform intrusion detection based on data from multiple perimeter security hosts and devices. This is a powerful technique that transcends the boundaries of defense components of a single host, and we discuss it in greater detail in Chapter 17, "Maintaining a Security Perimeter," and in Chapter 18, "Network Log Analysis."

Challenges of Host Defense Components

We have examined host defense components that help provide defense in depth at the level of an individual host and allow us to treat the host as an active member of the overall security perimeter. We have discussed individual strengths and weaknesses of each component type. In this section, we look at major challenges that face host defense components as a unified product category. Some of these challenges, which impact the deployment of anti-virus software, host-centric firewalls, and host IDS components, are listed next:

- Ensuring the component's effectiveness and trustworthiness after a system is compromised
- Configuring and monitoring host defense components that run on systems

Let us take a closer look at these challenges so that we are prepared to adjust the design of the overall security perimeter accordingly.

Defense Components on Compromised Hosts

As you probably realize, systems that are protected by host defense components can still be compromised. The attacker can deploy a malicious agent that is not recognized by the anti-virus software or can bypass the host's firewall protection via an open port or through another compromised route. As a result, an attacker can delete security logs, create new accounts, install backdoor programs, and disable locally installed security components. To minimize the likelihood that such an attack will succeed, we deploy multiple security components that work in unison, but we need to be prepared for the possibility that our controls will be bypassed.

Host hardening procedures that we discussed in Chapter 9 offer an effective way to limit the scope of the attacker's influence on the compromised host. Additionally, software such as Tiny Trojan Trap (`http://www.tinysoftware.com/`) further protect a Windows host by severely restricting which system resources can be accessed by locally installed applications. Another constraining mechanism, which we mention in Chapter 12, "Separating Resources," calls for the use of Chroot to create a "jail" around an application on a UNIX system. Additionally, a host-centric firewall on the compromised host has not necessarily outlived its usefulness: It can still assist the administrator in detecting the compromise, and it can help restrict a host's access to other systems on the network.

Although these measures can help dampen the attacker's progress, the effectiveness of host defense components drastically decreases after the intruder has gained access to the system. Having access to the host gives that attacker the capability to target the system's defense components from within. Malware specimens, for example, have been known to proactively fortify their positions on the infected system. When the Gokar worm infects a host, it kills processes of common anti-virus products.[16] This particular action was most beneficial for the worm when it first appeared and anti-virus software could not yet detect it; that made it made it more difficult for the victim to begin using updated virus signatures. The Goner worm, released around the same time as Gokar, contains code that not only knows how to disable and remove common anti-virus products, but can also affect a large number of well-known personal firewalls.[17]

Controlling Distributed Host Defense Components

Another challenge to deployment of host defense components lies in the ability to centrally manage large numbers of them. Any participant of the security perimeter, whether it is a router, a firewall, or an IDS, needs to be watched over after it has been installed. This often involves fine-tuning its configuration, installing software updates, reviewing activity logs, and responding to alerts. The more security components we have to manage, the more challenging it is to do so effectively. Manually maintaining a limited number of servers is something that is possible with a relatively small staff, but the challenges increase as we consider deploying host defense components on workstations throughout the organization.

Note

Attackers have developed effective mechanisms for centrally controlling thousands of victimized computers in an efficient manner. Copies of the Leaves worm, for example, knew to retrieve encrypted instructions for operation from a network of publicly accessible web sites. Instances of the SRVCP Trojan, which we mentioned in the beginning of this chapter, were programmed to log in to specific Internet Relay Chat (IRC) channels and sit there waiting for instructions from the attacker.

Anti-virus products are the oldest among host defense components that we discussed in this chapter. As a result, their means of effectively operating in large numbers are the most mature. Built into most anti-virus products is the ability to automatically retrieve virus signature and anti-virus software updates from the vendor's site, without special modifications to the organization's existing infrastructure. This helps ensure that anti-virus software is up to date, but it does not really assist the company's system administrators in keeping an eye on effectiveness of virus protection. Major anti-virus vendors offer products that centrally manage distributed anti-virus software installations. For example, Symantec System Center allows the administrator to use

Microsoft Management Console to see what, if any, viruses were found on Norton AntiVirus installations throughout the company, obtain copies of infected files, and remotely install and update anti-virus software on multiple hosts.

Makers of commercial host-centric firewalls and host-based IDS software also offer products for centrally managing their defense components that are installed on multiple hosts. These enterprise-centric products are typically structured to consist of the following major tiers:

- The policy enforcement agent, such as the host-centric firewall or the host-based IDS sensor.

- The central management server, used by administrators to control remote instances of policy enforcement agents. This server pushes software and configuration updates to enforcement agents and collects events that enforcement agents report.

- The back-end database, used by the management server to archive events that enforcement agents submit to the server. Some products rely on a built-in data store for this functionality, whereas others can interoperate with external relational databases.

- A client application, such as a web browser, that the administrators can use to communicate with the management server.

Most of the commercial products that we discussed in this chapter follow this architecture. Tripwire can be centrally managed with Tripwire Manager; BlackICE is a component of the ICEpac Suite; Tiny Personal Firewall can be purchased as part of the Centrally Managed Desktop Security (CMDS) product; and ZoneAlarm acts as an enforcement agent for Zone Labs Integrity. AIDE, even though it does not have an enterprise-ready management component, can be centrally managed with the ICU utility or with the collection of custom-built scripts.

Summary

In this chapter, we looked at reinforcing the security of the network perimeter by equipping hosts with defense components of three types: anti-virus products, host-centric firewalls, and host-based IDS software. We examined strengths and weaknesses of each category of host defense components and learned to take them into account when designing and implementing a defense-in-depth architecture.

We rely on anti-virus products to defend hosts against malicious software, with the understanding that they cannot detect every malware specimen that can find its way onto the system. We use host-centric firewalls to protect the system from network attacks that are not blocked by traditional network firewalls. Host-centric firewalls are configured based on the business requirements of the individual host on which they run, and they can usually block inbound as well as outbound network traffic. Some potentially vulnerable channels might need to remain open for the host to perform its function; these can be watched over with the use of a host-based IDS. Host-based intrusion detection further complements network IDS by monitoring the host's internal parameters such as critical files, logs, and local user activity.

Host-defense components, as a category of security tools, possess several limitations that need to be accounted for in the overall design of the network perimeter. We examined some of these at the end of the chapter. We learned what to expect from a host-defense component running on a compromised system, as well as how to manage host-defense components that are installed on systems throughout the organization. We will take advantage of our knowledge of strengths and weaknesses of host and network defense components in Part III, "Perimeter Design," where we concentrate on architecture considerations of the network security perimeter.

References

1 "Updated wu-ftpd Packages Are Available." Red Hat. November 20, 2001. `http://www.red-hat.com/support/errata/RHSA-2001-157.html`. December 2001.

2 ARIS Incident Analyst Team Wu-Ftpd Report. "Wu-ftpd Incident Alert." November 28, 2001. `http://aris.securityfocus.com/alerts/wuftpd/`. February 2002.

3 "W32/QAZ.worm." McAfee Virus Information Library. October 27, 2000. `http://vil.mcafee.com/dispVirus.asp?virus_k=98775`. December 2001.

4 Russ Cooper. "Re: Nimda Checker—Now Available." September 24, 2001. `http://www.ntbugtraq.com/default.asp?pid=36&sid=1&A2=ind0109&L=NTBUGTRAQ&P=R3498`. December 2001.

5 Lance Spitzner. "Armoring Solaris: II." November 5, 2001. `http://www.enteract.com/~lspitz/armoring2.html`. December 2001.

6 Jay Dyson, Simple Nomad, et. al. "SecurityFocus Defaced? Kind Of." Attrition's Defaced Commentary Mailing List. November 2001.

7 Symantec Press Center. "Symantec Announces Network-Available Anti-Virus Scanner for Internet Providers." December 5, 2000. `http://www.symantec.com/press/2000/n001204a.html`. January 2002.

8 Mikko Hypponen. "F-Secure Computer Virus Information Pages: DAME." `http://www.europe.f-secure.com/v-descs/dame.shtml`. December 2001.

9   Nicole Bellamy. "Port 12345: Hacker Haven or Internet X-File?" January 21, 2002. http://www.zdnet.com.au/newstech/security/story/0,2000024985,20263054,00.htm. February 2002.

10 Brendan Conoboy and Erik Fichtner. "IP Filter-Based Firewalls HOWTO." July 21, 2001. http://www.obfuscation.org/ipf/ipf-howto.txt. January 2002.

11 Sun Microsystems. "SunScreen 3.1 Lite." http://www.sun.com/software/securenet/lite/. January 2002.

12 Steve Riley. "Using IPSec to Lock Down a Server." August 28, 2001. http://www.microsoft.com/serviceproviders/columns/using_ipsec.asp. January 2002.

13 Steve Riley. "Using IPSec to Lock Down a Server." August 28, 2001. http://www.microsoft.com/serviceproviders/columns/using_ipsec.asp. January 2002.

14 Microsoft, Inc. "Traffic That Can—and Cannot—Be Secured by IPSec." August 16, 2001. http://support.microsoft.com/directory/article.asp?ID=KB;EN-US;Q253169. January 2002.

15 Thomas H. Ptacek and Timothy N. Newsham. "Insertion, Evasion, and Denial of Service: Eluding Network Intrusion Detection." January 1998. http://secinf.net/info/ids/idspaper/idspaper.html. January 2002.

16 F-Secure Virus Descriptions. "Gokar." December 13, 2001. http://www.f-secure.com/v-descs/gokar.shtml. January 2002.

17 Internet Security Systems Security Alert. "Goner/Pentagone Mass-Mailer Worm." December 4, 2001. http://xforce.iss.net/alerts/advise104.php. January 2002.

III

Perimeter Design

11

Design Fundamentals

IF YOU ARE NOT CURRENTLY THE LEAD DESIGNER for your organization, we assume that becoming one is your goal. You might be laying out a network from scratch, assessing the strength of an existing infrastructure, determining where to place a new security device, or deciding whether to deploy one at all. You know of many defense components that you could incorporate into your security infrastructure, and you know of countless ways of arranging them. This chapter concentrates on the do's and don'ts of security perimeter design and covers some of the more common scenarios.

Before jumping into a design session, you need to have the right tools for making design-related decisions. In the world of network security architecture, these tools are bits of information about your environment and your business goals. You need to figure out the following:

- What resources need to be protected
- Who you are protecting against
- What your business needs are
- What your policy constraints are

In this chapter, we review the factors that you need to consider when designing the network's perimeter. We analyze several building blocks that are useful for crafting more complex architectures. These scenarios will incorporate firewalls, routers, and VPN devices in various permutations.

Deciding on a particular defense architecture is a rewarding and complicated task that requires making tough choices in the world where functionality and security tend to be at odds with each other. It is understandable to want to delay making such decisions as long as possible. After all, it is easier to avoid confrontation than fight an uphill battle for budget and resources. Making security design decisions involves resolving conflicts that incorporate many aspects of the network and application infrastructure, such as usability, reliability, manageability, and cost. Principles that are presented in this chapter are meant to help you make hard decisions early in the process of setting up a security perimeter; that way, you can save sleep, time, and money in the implementation and maintenance phases of your deployment.

Tip

The later you make a decision that modifies your design, the harder it is to properly implement the change. You should put extraordinary effort into the design phases of your engagement to minimize the chance of making significant changes later in the process.

Gathering Design Requirements

Whether you are designing a new network or working with an existing infrastructure, it helps to treat components and requirements of your environment as elements of a unified perimeter security architecture. Doing so allows you to identify scenarios in which devices might be configured in an inconsistent or even conflicting manner, and lets you tune the design to match your needs. Based on specifics of your environment, you will decide, for instance, whether a single packet-filtering router on the edge of your network will provide sufficient protection, or whether you need to invest in multiple firewalls, set up one behind another, to properly segment your network. A good place to start designing your perimeter architecture is determining which resources need to be protected.

Determining Which Resources to Protect

In the realm of network security, we focus on ensuring confidentiality, integrity, and availability of information. However, the notion of *information* is too general and does not really help to make decisions that account for specifics in a particular situation. For some organizations, information that needs to be protected is credit card and demographics data; for others, it might be legal agreements and client lists. Information can also take the form of application logic, especially for web sites that rely on dynamically generated content. To decide what kind of network perimeter will offer adequate protection for your data, you need to look at where the information is stored and how it is accessed.

Servers

Modern computing environments tend to aggregate information on servers. This makes a lot of sense because it is much easier to keep an eye on data that is stored centrally; some of the problems plaguing peer-to-peer file-sharing systems such as Gnutella demonstrate difficulties in providing reliable access to information that is spread across many machines. Because all of us face limitations of overworked administrators and analysts, we often benefit from minimizing the number of resources that need to be set up, monitored, and secured.

The Case of a Missing Server

InformationWeek once published a story about a missing server that had been running without problems for four years. System administrators, unaware of the server's whereabouts, had to resort to manually tracing the network cable until it led them to a wall. Apparently, "the server had been mistakenly sealed behind drywall by maintenance workers."[1] (Alas, some claim that this is just an urban legend,[2] but there is some truth to all tales.) Do you know where *your* servers are?

Make sure you know what servers exist on your network, where they are located, what their network parameters are, and what operating systems, applications, and patches are installed. If you have sufficient spending power, you might consider taking advantage of enterprise system management software such as HP OpenView, Microsoft Systems Management Server (SMS), and CA Unicenter to help you with this task.

If the infrastructure you are protecting is hosting multitier applications, you need to understand the role of each tier, represented by web, middleware, and database servers, and their relationship to each other. In addition to documenting technical specifications for the server and its software, be sure to record contact information of the person who is responsible for the business task that the system is performing. You will probably need to contact him when responding to an incident that is associated with this system.

Workstations

End-user workstations serve as an interface between the technical infrastructure that powers the computing environment and the people who actually make the business run. No matter how tightly you might want to configure the network's perimeter, you need to let some traffic through so that these people can utilize resources on the Internet and function effectively in our web-dependent age. To create a perimeter architecture that adequately protects the organization while letting people do their work, you need to make sure that the design reflects the way in which the workstations are used and configured.

For example, if your Windows NT workstations never need to connect to Windows servers outside the organization's perimeter, you should be able to block outbound NetBIOS traffic without further considerations. On the other hand, if your users need to access shares of a Windows server over the Internet, you should probably consider deploying a VPN link across the two sites.

Similarly, evaluating the likelihood that your system administrators will routinely patch the workstations might help you decide whether to segment your environment with internal firewalls. Organizations that have the ability to remotely distribute OS and application updates to users' systems are less likely to be affected by an attacker gaining access to a workstation and then spreading to other internal systems. At the same time, if the centralized control channel is compromised in this configuration, the attack could affect many systems.

When examining your workstations, look at the kind of applications and operating systems they are running and how patched they are. Is data stored only on your servers, or do users keep files on their desktops? Don't forget to take into consideration personal digital assistant (PDA) devices; corporate users don't hesitate to store sensitive information on their Handsprings, Palms, BlackBerries, and iPAQ Pocket PCs. You also need to make special provisions for traveling and telecommuting users; by going outside of your core network, telecommuters will unknowingly expand your defense perimeter.

Networking Gear

Bridges, switches, and routers interconnect your computing resources and link you to partners and customers. In earlier chapters, we talked about the role of the router and explained the need to secure its configuration. Modern high-end switches offer configuration complexities that often rival those of routers, and should be secured in a similar manner. Moreover, virtual LAN (VLAN) capabilities of such switches might require special considerations to make sure attackers cannot hop across VLANs by crafting specially tagged Ethernet frames.

Note

Is this process beginning to look like an audit of your environment? In many respects, it is. Given budget and time limitations, you need to know what you are protecting to determine how to best allocate your resources.

Make sure you know what devices are deployed on your network, what function they serve, and how they are configured. Hopefully, you will not keep finding devices that you did not think existed on the network. It is not uncommon to see an organization with "legacy" systems that were set up by people who are long gone and that everyone is afraid to touch for fear of disrupting an existing process. Be mindful of network devices that terminate private or VPN connections to your customers or partners inside your network. You need to evaluate your level of trust with the third party on the other end of the link to determine the impact of such a device on your network's perimeter.

Modems

When looking for possible entry points into your network, don't forget about modems that might be connecting your servers or workstations to phone lines. Modems offer the attacker a chance to go around the border firewall, which is why many organizations are banishing modems from internal desktops in favor of VPN connections or centralized dial-out modem banks that desktops access over TCP/IP. With the increasing popularity of VPNs, the need to connect to the office over the phone is gradually decreasing. Yet it is common to find a rogue desktop running a remote control application such as pcAnywhere over a phone line.

Sometimes, a business need mandates having active modems on the network, and your security policy should thoroughly address how they should and should not be used. For example, modems that accept inbound connections might need to be installed in data centers to allow administrators out-of-band access to the environment. In such cases, your security architecture should take into account the possibility that the modem might provide back-door access to your network. To mitigate this risk, pay attention to host armoring, consider deploying internal firewalls, and look into installing hardware authentication devices for controlling access to the modems. (Such devices are relatively inexpensive and block calls that do not present a proper authentication "key.")

Telephone Firewalls

Several vendors offer devices that control access to telephone lines in a manner that is similar to regular firewalls. Instead of keeping track of protocols and IP addresses, telephone firewalls look at call type (voice, data, or fax) and phone numbers to determine whether to let the call through. These products also provide logging and alerting capabilities that allow administrators to monitor phone-related activity in the organization.[3] Examples of such products are SecureLogix TeleWall and Phonewall by Sentry Telecom Systems.

Other Devices

When looking for devices that can be used to store sensitive data or provide access to information, private branch exchange (PBX) systems often slip people's minds. However, even back in the era when voice communications were completely out of band with IP networks, attackers knew to tap into organizations' voice mail systems over the phone, fishing for information and setting up unauthorized conference calls and mail boxes. With the growing popularity of IP-based telephony systems, the distinction between voice and data is beginning to fade. For instance, in a hybrid system offered by Shoreline Communications, traditional analog phones are employed, but the dialing process can be controlled using a desktop agent over TCP/IP, and voice mail messages are stored as .wav files on a Windows-based server.

Tip

If it can be accessed over the network, it should be accounted for in the design of the perimeter.

Don't forget to consider other devices that comprise your computing infrastructure, such as modern printers and copiers. Manufacturers of these systems often embed advanced services into these devices to ease management without regard for security. Don't be surprised if your Sharp AR-507 digital copier comes with built-in FTP, Telnet, SNMP, and HTTP servers, all with highly questionable authentication schemes.[4]

Indeed, modern networks are heterogeneous and support communications among a wide range of resources. We need to understand what servers, workstations, and various network-aware devices exist on the network to determine what defenses will provide us with adequate protection. Another factor that contributes toward a properly designed security architecture is the nature of threats that we face. Potential attackers who could be viewed as a threat by one organization might not be of much significance to another.

The next section is devoted to determining who it is we are protecting ourselves from, and is meant to help you assess the threat level that is appropriate for your organization.

Determining Who the Potential Attackers Are

We think we know who our enemy is. We're fighting the bad guys, right? The perception of who is attacking Internet-based sites changes with time. Sometimes we look for attackers who are specifically targeting our sites, from inside as well as outside, to get at sensitive information. In other situations, we feel inundated with "script kiddy" scans where relatively inexperienced attackers are running canned scripts in an attempt to reach the "low hanging fruit" on the network. Lately, automated agents such as remote-controlled trojans and worms have been making rounds and threatening our resources in new and imaginative ways that we will discuss in this section.

In reality, only you can decide what kind of attacker poses the greatest threat to your organization. Your decision will depend on the nature of your business, the habits and requirements of your users, and the value of the information that is stored on your systems.

Each category of attacker brings its own nuances to the design of the network's defenses. When operating under budget constraints, you will find yourself assigning priority to some components of your security infrastructure over others based on the perceived threat from attackers that worry you the most.

Determined Outsider

Why would anyone be targeting your network specifically? Presumably, you have something that the attacker wants, and in the world of computer security, your crown jewels tend to take the form of information. A determined outsider might be looking for ways to steal credit card numbers or other sensitive account information about your customers, obtain products at a cost different from what you are offering them for, or render your site useless by denying service to your legitimate customers. The threat of a denial of service (DoS) attack is especially high for companies with relatively high profiles.

The Egghead Crack

On December 22, 2001, a popular e-commerce retailer Egghead announced that the security of its site had been breached, and an intruder might have accessed millions of credit card numbers stored in its customer databases.[5] The extent of the damage has been difficult to determine, and there are still speculations regarding Egghead's subsequent claim that customer data was not actually accessed. After an intruder has obtained administrative access to your systems, it is usually difficult to tell what information he has accessed.

If your organization provides services that are accessible over the web, a determined outsider might be interested in obtaining unauthorized access to such services, instead of specifically targeting your information. In some cases, you might be concerned with corporate espionage, where your competitors would be attempting to obtain your trade secrets, important announcements that have not been released, your client lists, or your intellectual properly. Such an attack is likely to have significant financing, and might even incorporate the help of an insider.

The difficulty of protecting against a determined outsider is that you have to assume that with sufficient money and time to spare, the attacker will be able to penetrate your defenses. To counteract such a threat, you need to estimate how much the potential attacker is likely to spend trying to penetrate your defenses, and build your perimeter to withstand such an attack. Additionally, intrusion detection presents one of the most effective ways of protecting against a determined attacker because it offers a chance to discover an attack in its reconnaissance state, before it escalates into a critical incident. A properly configured intrusion detection system (IDS) also helps to determine the circumstances of an incident if an attacker succeeds at moving beyond the reconnaissance state.

Determined Insider

The threat of a determined insider is often difficult to counteract partly because it is hard to admit that a person who is working for the organization might want to participate in malicious activity. Nonetheless, many high-profile criminal cases involve a person attacking the organization's systems from the inside. With a wave of layoffs hitting companies in 2001, disgruntled ex-employees have been causing something of a stir at companies that have not recognized this as a potential risk.

Insiders at Cisco

On August 20, 2001, two former Cisco accountants admitted to exploiting an internal "Sabrina" system, used by the company to manage stock options, to illegally issue themselves almost $8 million of Cisco shares. They used access to the system to "identify control numbers to track unauthorized stock option disbursals, created forged forms purporting to authorize disbursals of stock," and "directed that stock be placed in their personal brokerage accounts."[6]

The insider does not need to penetrate your external defense layers to get access to potentially sensitive systems. This makes a case for deploying internal firewalls in front of the more sensitive areas of your network, tightening configurations of corporate file and development servers, limiting access to files, and employing internal intrusion detection sensors. Note that because an internal attacker already knows your environment, it is much harder to detect an insider attack early on, as opposed to an attack from the outside.

Even without getting into the argument of whether insider attacks are more popular than the ones coming from the outside, the ability of an internal attacker to potentially have easy and unrestricted access to sensitive data makes this a threat not to be taken lightly.

Script Kiddy

The term *script kiddy* is at times controversial due to its derogatory nature. It typically refers to a relatively unsophisticated attacker who does not craft custom tools or techniques, but instead relies on easy-to-find scripts that exploit common vulnerabilities in Internet-based systems. In this case, the attacker is not targeting your organization specifically, but is sweeping through a large number of IP addresses in hopes of finding systems that are vulnerable to published exploits or that have a well-known backdoor already installed.

Scanning for SubSeven

In 2001, SubSeven was one of the most popularly probed for trojan horse programs on the Internet. Knowing that SubSeven often listens on TCP port 27374 by default, attackers who are looking for easily exploitable computers scan blocks of IP addresses in hopes of finding a computer with an already-installed instance of SubSeven. The scanning tool then tries to authenticate to the trojan using common backdoor passwords that are built into SubSeven. After the attacker is authenticated, he has virtually unrestricted access to the victim's system.

The nature of script kiddy attacks suggests that the most effective way of defending against them involves keeping your system's patches up to date, closing major holes in network and host configurations, and preventing trojans from infecting your internal systems.

A hybrid variant of the "script kiddy" attack might incorporate some of the elements of a determined outsider threat, and would involve an initial sweep across many network nodes from the outside. This activity would then be followed up by a set of scripted attacks against systems that were found to be vulnerable to canned exploits. In such scenarios, IDSs are often effective at alerting administrators when the initial exploratory phrase of the attack begins.

In one example of a hybrid script kiddy attack, Raphael Gray, a.k.a. "Curador," harvested tens of thousands of credit card numbers in March 2000. He started the attack by using a search engine to locate potentially vulnerable commerce sites, and then exploited a known vulnerability to gain unauthorized access to the site. Referring to the attack, Raphael said, "A lot of crackers don't like what I did. They consider me to be a script kiddy, someone who can't program in any language, because I used an old exploit instead of creating a new one. But I've been programming since I was 11."[7] By the way, one of the credit card numbers that Ralph obtained belonged to Bill Gates.

Automated Malicious Agents

The beginning of the century shifted the spotlight away from attacks performed directly by humans to those that were automated through the use of malicious agents. Worms such as Code Red and Nimda demonstrated the speed with which malicious software can spread across the Internet and our inability to analyze and respond to these threats early in the propagation process. By the time we had detected and analyzed the Nimda worm, it had infected an enormous number of personal and corporate systems.

Worms and Script Kiddies

The Nimda worm had several propagation vectors that allowed it to spread across a large portion of the Internet in a matter of hours. One such mechanism allowed the worm to scan Internet hosts for vulnerable IIS servers and infect machines that it came across.

This technique closely resembles actions of a script kiddy because the worm was preprogrammed to scan for several well-known exploits and backdoors. The advantage that the worm had over a script kiddy is that by infecting a corporate system via one vector, it could continue spreading internally to hosts that were not accessible from the outside.

Maintaining a perimeter that is resilient against worm-based attacks requires keeping abreast of the latest vulnerabilities and applying patches as soon as they are released. To further limit the scope of the agent's potential influence, you should consider segmenting your infrastructure based on varying degrees of security levels of your resources. Anti-virus products can also be quite effective at dampening the spread of malicious agents. Unfortunately, as we have learned from the earlier worm experiences, virus pattern updates might not be released in time to prevent rapid infection of vulnerable systems.

Defining Your Business Requirements

When designing the perimeter security infrastructure, we need to keep in mind that the purpose of addressing information security issues is to keep the business running. Considering that security is a means, not an end, the design must accommodate factors such as services that are provided to your users or customers, fault tolerance requirements, performance expectations, and budget constraints.

Cost

Cost is an ever-present factor in security-related decisions. How much are you willing to spend to protect yourself against a threat of an attack or to eliminate a single point of failure? For instance, SANS spent three months and significant resources putting all their servers in a highly secure NOC. Then when Code Red hit, they experienced 50 times more traffic in 24 hours than during any previous peak. They were secure against intrusions, but the architecture became a single point of failure.

How much should you spend? As we discussed earlier, this depends on the perceived value both for access and control of the resources you are protecting. Making informed choices regarding the need to spend less on one component of a defense infrastructure allows us to spend more on another layer that might require additional funding. When looking at the cost of a security component, we should examine the following cost factors:

- Initial hardware
- Initial software
- Initial deployment (time to deploy)
- Annual software support and updates
- Maintenance and monitoring of the component

Cost and Risk Mitigation

When considering whether to invest in a set of intrusion detection sensors at a financial institution, I had to present a detailed cost analysis report that included all factors outlined in the preceding list. Each sensor cost around $7,000 to obtain (software and hardware), $3,000 to deploy (let's say three days of work at the rate of $1,000 per day), and $2,000 per year for technical support and software upgrades. I also had to take into account the "hidden" cost of having the device monitored and supported by system administrators or intrusion analysts. Associating specific numbers with risk mitigation options allowed us to make an informed decision regarding our ability to purchase the IDS.

When calculating the cost of adding a perimeter security component, you might conclude that mitigating the risk that it would protect you against is not worth the money it would cost to deploy and maintain it. In that case, you might consider employing a less thorough but more affordable solution. For example, alternatives for purchasing a relatively expensive commercial IDS product might include obtaining open source packages such as Snort, an outsourced security monitoring solution, or an additional firewall. (An additional firewall might mitigate the same risk in a less expensive manner, depending on your environment.) Even when using "free" software such as Snort or an academic version of Tripwire, be sure to take into account the cost of your administrator's time that will be spent installing and maintaining the new system.

Business-Related Services

Of course, when setting up your network's perimeter, you need to know what services need to be provided to your users and customers. In a typical business, you will probably want to block all non-essential services at the network's border. In a university, you might find that unrestricted access is one of the "services" that is provided to the university's users. In that case, you will probably be unable to block traffic by default; instead, you will filter out only traffic that is most likely to threaten your environment.

Protecting your resources against threats that come through a channel that needs to be open for business use is not easy. For instance, if you decide to allow ICMP through your network for network troubleshooting purposes and are fighting an ICMP flood attack, blocking ICMP traffic at your ISP's upstream routers is likely to free up some bandwidth for services that absolutely must be accessible. If, on the other hand, you are being flooded with SYN packets that are targeting TCP port 80 and you are a web-based e-commerce site, asking the ISP to block this traffic at their routers is probably not an option. (You can try blocking traffic from specific sources, but in a distributed DoS attack, you might have a hard time compiling a complete list of all attacking addresses.) Only a defense in depth architecture has a chance of protecting you from attacks that might come through legitimately open channels.

Performance

When analyzing your business requirements, you need to look at the expected performance levels for the site that are protected by the security infrastructure. As we add layers to perimeter defense, we are likely to impact the latency of packets because they might be traversing through multiple filtering engines, sanity checks, and encryption mechanisms. If performance is a serious consideration for your business, you might be able to justify spending money on equipment upgrades so that the impact of additional security layers is minimized. Alternatively, you might decide that your business hinges on fast response times and that your budget does not allow you to provision appropriately performing security hardware or software. In the latter case, you might need to accept the risk of decreased security for the sake of performance.

Establishing performance expectations in the design phase of your deployment, before the actual implementation takes place, is a difficult but necessary task. Indeed, it's often hard to estimate how much burden an IPSec encryption tunnel will put on your router, or how many milliseconds will be added to the response time if a proxy server is in place, instead of a stateful firewall. If your design goes over the top with the computing power that is required to provide adequate performance, then you might not have much money left to keep the system (or the business) running. At the same time, not allocating proper resources to the system early on might require you to purchase costly upgrades later.

Inline Security Devices

Consider the architecture that incorporates multiple inline firewalls located one behind another. For a request to propagate to the server located the farthest from the Internet, the request might need to pass through the border router and several firewalls. Along the packet's path, each security enforcement device will need to make a decision about whether the packet should be allowed through. In some cases, you might decide that the security gained from such a configuration is not worth the performance loss. In others, you might be willing to accept the delay in response to achieve the level of security that is appropriate for your enterprise. Or you might devise alternative solutions, such as employing a single firewall, to provide you with a sufficient comfort level without employing inline firewalls.

The Use of Encryption

Other significant effects on performance are associated with the use of encryption due to the strain placed on the CPU of the device that needs to encrypt or decrypt data. You might be familiar with SSL and IPSec accelerator cards or devices that you can employ to transfer the encryption duties to a processor that is dedicated and optimized for such tasks. These devices are not cheap, and the business decision to purchase them must take into account the need to provide encryption, the desired performance, and the cost of purchasing the accelerators.

For example, most online banking applications require the use of SSL encryption to protect sensitive data as it travels between the user's browser and the bank's server. Usually, all aspects of the user's interaction with the banking application are encrypted, presumably because the bank was able to justify the expense of purchasing the computing power to support SSL. Cost is a significant factor here because you need to spend money on SSL accelerators to achieve the desired performance.

At the same time, you will probably notice that SSL encryption is not used when browsing through the bank's public web site. This is probably because information that is provided on the public site is not deemed to be sensitive enough to justify the use of encryption.

Detailed Logging

Among other considerations relating to the site's performance is the system's ability to handle large amounts of log data. Availability of detailed logs is important for performing anomaly detection, as well as for tuning the system's performance parameters. At the same time, enabling verbose logging might inundate a machine's I/O subsystem and quickly fill up the file system. Similarly, you must balance the desire to capture detailed log information with the amount of network bandwidth that will be consumed by logs if you transport them to a centralized log archival system. This is an especially significant issue for situations in which you need to routinely send log data across relatively slow wide area network (WAN) links.

Fault Tolerance

The amount of fault tolerance that should be built into your environment depends on the nature of your business. The reason we discuss fault tolerance in an information security book is because eliminating single points of failure is a complex task that strongly impacts the architecture of your network.

When designing fault tolerance of the infrastructure, you need to look at the configuration of individual systems, ways in which these systems interact with each other within the site, and, perhaps, consider offering geographic redundancy to your users.

Intra-System Redundancy

Looking at a single system, you examine its disk subsystem, number of processors, redundancy of system boards and power supplies, and so on. You need to decide how much you are willing to pay for the hardware such that if a disk or a system board fails, the machine will continue to function. You will then weigh that amount against the likelihood that this will happen and the extent of damage that it will cause.

You might also ask yourself what the consequences will be of a critical process on that system failing, and what is involved in mitigating that risk. The answer might be monitoring the state of that process so that it is automatically restarted if it dies. Alternatively, you might consider running a program that duplicates the tasks of the process; for instance, you might want to run both LogSentry and Swatch to monitor your log files. Keep in mind that many applications were not designed to share the host with multiple instances of themselves. Moreover, running multiple instances of the application on the same system does not help when the host fails and eliminates all processes that were supposed to offer redundancy. When running a duplicate process on the same host is not appropriate or sufficient, look into duplicating the whole system to achieve the desired level of redundancy.

Intra-Site Redundancy

Redundant components that are meant to fulfill the same business need are usually considered to be operating in a *cluster*. We might set up such clusters using hardware and software techniques for the most important systems in the environment, such as the database servers. Similarly, network and security devices can operate in a cluster, independently of how other components of your infrastructure are set up.

If a clustered component is actively performing its tasks, it is considered to be *active*; if the component is ready to take on the responsibility but is currently dormant, it is considered to be *passive*. Clusters in which all components are active at the same time provide a level of load balancing and offer performance improvements, albeit at a significant cost. For the purpose of achieving intra-site redundancy, it is often sufficient to deploy active–passive clusters where only a single component is active at the same time.

Redundancy of the network is a significant aspect of intra-site redundancy. For example, if Internet connectivity is very important to your business, you may need to provision multiple lines linking the network to the Internet, possibly from different access providers. You may also decide to cluster border routers to help ensure that failure of one will not impact your connection to the Internet. Cisco routers usually accomplish this through the use of the Hot Standby Router Protocol (HSRP). With HSRP, multiple routers appear as a single "virtual" router. Many commercial firewalls also provide clustering mechanisms that you can use to introduce high availability to that aspect of your perimeter, should your business justify the added cost. Also, consider how the availability of your systems will be impacted if one of the internal switches goes down. Some organizations address this risk by purchasing a standby switch that they can use to manually replace the failed device. If the delay to perform this manually is too costly for your business, you may decide to invest in an automatic failover mechanism. High-end Cisco switches such as Catalyst 6000 can help to achieve redundancy in the switching fabric, although at a significant expense.

Geographic Redundancy

Sometimes, achieving intra-site redundancy is not sufficient to mitigate risks of system unavailability. For example, a well-tuned DoS attack against a border's routers or the ISP's network equipment might not allow legitimate traffic to the site. Additionally, a disaster might affect the building where the systems are residing, damaging or temporarily disabling the equipment. To mitigate such risks, consider creating a copy of your data center in a geographically distinct location.

Much like clusters, the secondary data center could be always active, sharing the load with the primary site. Alternatively, it could be passive, activated either manually or automatically when it is needed. In addition to considering the costs that are associated with setting up the secondary data center, also look at the administrative efforts involved in supporting and monitoring additional systems. You might also need to accommodate data sharing between the two sites so that users have access to the same information no matter which site services their requests.

Design Elements

One of the reasons we have so many choices when architecting network perimeter defense is because resources differ in the sensitivity of their information and the likelihood that they will be successfully exploited. For example, a web server that is running Apache and hosting static HTML pages is generally subject to fewer risk factors than an Oracle database that is storing order information for the organization's customers.

Risk Versus Vulnerability

Risk that is associated with an event is a function of how likely an event is to occur and the extent of the damage that it can cause. *Vulnerability* refers to the likelihood that the resource can be compromised. Risk takes into account vulnerability as well as the importance of the resource in question. Thus, a resource can be vulnerable but not risky if little is at stake.[8]

In the world where we are free to permute security components in any imaginable manner, some design elements are seen more often than others. We cover some of the more basic patterns here to put you in the right frame of mind, and discuss more specialized architectures in subsequent chapters.

Firewall and Router

The firewall and the router are two of the most common perimeter security components. In Parts I and II of this book, we described different types of these devices and explained what roles they play in defending the network. In this section, we concentrate on the relationship between the router and the firewall and go over several configurations that you are likely to encounter when setting up and securing your network.

Figure 11.1 illustrates one of the most common ways to deploy a router and a firewall together. The Corporate Subnet hosts "private" systems that are used by the organization's internal users, and the Screened Subnet hosts "public" servers that need to be accessible from the Internet. In this scenario, no internal server can be accessed from the Internet; for example, instead of opening TCP port 25 on the firewall to the internal mail server, we route SMTP traffic through mail relay that is hosted in the Screened Subnet.

Figure 11.1 Deploy a router with a firewall behind it.

Basic Filtering

In the configuration that was described previously, the router is responsible for performing routing functions that it was designed to perform—it links the site to the Internet. It often makes sense to use the router's packet-filtering capabilities to filter out some of the "noise" that we might not care to see in the firewall's logs or that we want to stop at the very edge of the network. We described a similar setup in Chapter 2, "Packet Filtering," and Chapter 6, "Role of a Router," where the router was configured to perform basic egress and ingress filtering, as well as to disable dangerous routing options, control the flow of ICMP messages in and out of our network, and so on.

Generally, we do not want to block too much at the router because in this configuration, most of the monitoring efforts will be focused on the firewall. By blocking the majority of network traffic at the router, we might not have a complete view of the denied packets in the firewall's logs, and correlating events that are logged at the router and the firewall might be too draining for many organizations.

Access Control

In the scenario that was described in the previous section, the firewall has primary access control responsibilities. This is where we will implement the policy of blocking all traffic by default and explicitly allowing only those protocols that our business requires. In this case, the firewall becomes the manifestation of the business rules that your security policy defines. By this point of the design, you should have a good understanding of what your business needs are (see the first half of this chapter if you are not sure), so implementing the firewall rule set should not be too daunting of a task.

> **Note**
>
> Even if your hosts are located in a screened subnet behind a firewall, they should be armored to withstand attacks that the firewall might let through or that might be launched if the firewall is bypassed. The extent to which you need to tighten the systems' configuration depends on sensitivity of their data and the likelihood that they will be compromised.

Note that in some cases, placing systems onto the Screened Subnet might not be appropriate. Perhaps this is because the firewall is too much of a bottleneck, or because the system is not trusted to be located on the same subnet as the servers in the Screened Subnet. In this case, you might consider placing this system into the DMZ, between the border router and the firewall. You will need to use the router's packet filtering capabilities to control access to this system from the Internet. You will also need to configure the firewall to regulate communications between this system and the Corporate Subnet.

Router Under the ISP's Control

ISPs can provide you with an Ethernet connection to their networking equipment, eliminating the need to set up your own border router, but not giving you control over how their router is maintained and configured. You would then typically place your firewall behind the ISP's router. In some respects, this simplifies the task of setting up and administrating your network because you have to maintain one fewer component. At the same time, you cannot trust that the ISP configured the router in the same way that you would have configured it.

Note

Lack of control over the border router might conflict with the business requirements of your organization. In such cases, you might need to devise technical solutions or make business arrangements that give you greater control over the router's configuration.

This architecture is not very different from the one discussed previously. Not having control over the router simply means that you might not have the level of defense in depth that you could have had if you had tightened the router's configuration yourself.

One of the major limitations of such a configuration could be lack of detailed information about blocked traffic. If the ISP relies on the router to block unwanted traffic, your firewall never gets a chance to log it. If this is the case, consider asking your ISP to lax access control restrictions that the router enforces or to share the router's logs with you.

Router Without the Firewall

In Chapter 6, we saw the configuration in which the border router was the only device that separated the internal network from the Internet. This might be appropriate for organizations that decide that risks associated with the lack of the firewall are acceptable to their business. When properly configured, routers can be quite effective at blocking unwanted traffic, especially if they implement reflexive access lists, or if they use the firewall feature set that is built into high-end Cisco routers.

It is also common to find routers at various other points on the internal network, not just at the border of the perimeter. After all, the router's primary purpose is to connect networks, and a company might need to connect to networks other than the Internet. For instance, if your organization has several geographically distinct sites, you will use routers to connect them. In such cases, the routers will probably be decoupled from the firewall.

Even when you are using routers with private WAN connections, such as T1s or frame relay links, lock down the devices, tightening their configuration by disabling unnecessary services and setting up required access control lists. This approach is compatible with the defense in depth methodology that we've been discussing, and helps protect the network against a multitude of threats that we might not be aware of yet.

Firewall and VPN

Firewalls and VPNs are often discussed in the same context. Firewalls are generally responsible for controlling access to resources, and VPN devices are responsible for securing communication links between hosts or networks. Examining how VPNs interact with firewalls is important for several reasons:

- Network Address Translation (NAT) might be incompatible with some VPN implementations, depending on your network's architecture.

- VPNs might create tunnels through your perimeter that make it difficult for the firewall to enforce access restrictions on encrypted traffic.

- VPN endpoints have access to data in clear text because VPN devices are the ones that decrypt or authenticate it; this might warrant special considerations for protecting the VPN device.

- VPNs, by protecting confidentiality of the encrypted data, can be used to pass by IDSs undetected.

When deciding how to incorporate a VPN component into the network architecture, we have two high-level choices: maintaining the VPN module as its own device, external to the firewall, or integrating the VPN with the firewall so that both services are provided by the same system. Each approach has its intricacies, strengths, and weaknesses. We will present the general overview here, leaving a detailed discussion of VPN integration for Chapter 14, "VPN Integration."

Firewall with VPN As External Device

Many design choices allow us to set up a VPN endpoint as a device that is external to the firewall. Some of the placement options for VPN hardware include these:

- In the DMZ, between the firewall and the border router
- In the screened subnet, off the firewall's third NIC
- On the internal network, behind the firewall
- In parallel with the firewall at the entry point to the internal network

NAT is the cause of some of the most frequently occurring problems when VPN equipment is deployed separately from the firewall. For example, outbound packets that pass through the VPN device before being NATed by the firewall might not pass the integrity check at the other end of the VPN connection if using an authentication scheme, such as IPSec's Authentication Header (AH). This is because AH takes into account the packet's headers when it calculates the message digest signature for the packet. Then the NAT device modifies the source address of the packet, causing the message digest verification to fail on the other end of the VPN connection.

Another issue with VPN devices that are located behind the firewall is address management; some VPN specifications require that VPN devices are assigned a legal IP address. For example, when authenticating VPN devices using X.509 certificates, the IKE phase of IPSec might fail if the certificates were bound to each gateway's IP addresses that were then rewritten by NAT.[9]

Placing VPN hardware in front of the firewall, closer to the Internet, helps avoid potential NAT and address management problems, but it might introduce other concerns that are associated with all NAT deployments. As you probably know, many applications—such as those that use Microsoft's Distributed Component Model (DCOM) protocols—do not work with some NAT implementations. This is because generic NAT processors translate addresses only in the packet's header, even though some application-level protocols embed addressing information in packet payload as well.

Another disadvantage of placing VPN devices in front of the firewall is that then they cannot enjoy the protection that the firewall offers. If the system that is serving as the VPN endpoint is compromised, the attacker might gain access to information whose confidentiality is supposed to be protected by the VPN.

Firewall and VPN in One System

When deploying a device that integrates VPN and firewall functionality into a single system, you will most likely recognize some cost savings over the solutions in which the two devices are separated. Most of these savings will not come from the cost of initial deployment because VPN functionality on a firewall is likely to require additional software licenses and possibly a hardware upgrade. An integrated solution is generally less expensive to maintain, though, because you have fewer systems to watch over. Additionally, commercial VPN solutions, such as Check Point VPN-1, integrate with the GUI that is used to manage Check Point's firewall. Most integrated solutions do not have NAT-related problems that we discussed earlier, and enjoy robust access control capabilities offered by the firewall component of the device.

One of the biggest drawbacks of an integrated solution is that you might be limited in the choices that you can make with regard to optimally deploying your VPN and firewall components. Firewall products that match most closely to your business needs might not be as well suited to their VPN components. Similarly, under some situations, you will benefit from deploying an external specialized VPN device, and purchasing an integrated solution might lock you into having VPN and firewall components on the same system.

Hopefully, we gave you an idea of some of the choices and dilemmas you will face when integrating a VPN component into your perimeter architecture. Further discussion about VPN placement scenarios can be found in Chapter 14.

Multiple Firewalls

Some designs call for the use of multiple firewalls to protect the network. This makes sense when you want to provide different levels of protection for resources with different security needs. Such scenarios might involve deploying firewalls inline, one behind another, to segment resources with different security requirements. Firewalls can also be deployed in parallel, next to each other and equidistant from the Internet.

Using multiple firewalls provides the designer with the ability to control access to resources in a fine-grained manner. On the other hand, costs of setting up and maintaining your network increase dramatically as you add more firewalls. Some products, such as Check Point FireWall-1, provide an intuitive interface for controlling multiple firewalls from a single system. Others, such as NetFilter, might require more significant efforts for keeping firewall configurations in sync with the organization's security policy.

Inline Firewalls

Inline firewalls are deployed one behind another, and traffic coming to and from the Internet might be subjected to access control restrictions of multiple firewall devices. This is not as unusual of a configuration as you might think. Consider the typical architecture in which a single firewall is located behind the border router. If you use the router's access list functionality to control access to resources instead of doing only basic packet filtering on it, the router is acting very much like a firewall. The idea here might be to have redundancy in your access enforcement points; that way, if one device doesn't stop malicious traffic, the one behind it might.

If locating one firewall-like device right behind another seems wasteful to you, another inline configuration presented in Figure 11.2 might make more sense. Here, we take advantage of the subnets with different security levels created by multiple firewalls. The closer the subnet is to the Internet, the less secure it is. In such architecture, we could place web servers behind the first firewall, while keeping more sensitive resources such as database servers behind the second firewall. The first firewall could be configured to allow traffic to hit web servers only, whereas the second firewall would only allow web servers to talk to the database servers.

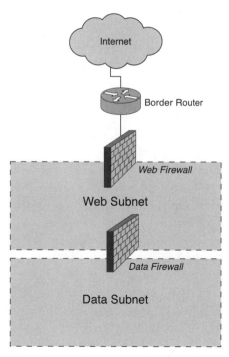

Figure 11.2 When employing multiple inline firewalls, the most sensitive information should be kept behind the second firewall.

One of the biggest problems with environments incorporating inline firewalls is that of manageability. Not only do you need to set up, maintain, and monitor multiple firewalls, but you need to support multiple firewall policies. If, for example, you need to allow a system behind multiple firewalls to connect to the Internet, you need to remember to modify rule sets of both firewalls. Commercial firewalls, such as Check Point FireWall-1 and Cisco PIX, provide software solutions for managing multiple firewalls from a single console, and allow you to ensure that all inline firewalls are properly configured. If you determine that a device that is protected by inline firewalls needs to communicate directly with the Internet, you might also consider restructuring the network's design to minimize the number of firewalls to be traversed.

The Cost of Maintaining Inline Firewalls

One company where I worked realized the difficulty of maintaining inline firewalls after deploying three clusters of two PIX devices one behind another. The solution was robust from an architecture perspective, but it took forever to modify and troubleshoot access control restrictions when more than one cluster of firewalls was involved. After much deliberation, the company ended up investing in Cisco Secure Policy Manager (CSPM) to automate firewall policy management. CSPM is expensive software, and it added significantly to the cost of the infrastructure.

Firewalls in Parallel

Many times you might be compelled to set up firewalls in parallel with each other. In this configuration, the firewalls typically protect resources with different security needs. When firewalls are set up inline, as discussed in the previous section, packets that are destined for the hosts deep within the organization's network might be delayed because they need to go through several access control devices. With parallel firewalls, this is not a significant concern because the firewalls are equidistant from the Internet.

In a parallel configuration, we can deploy firewalls that are each tuned specifically for resources that they are protecting. One such scenario is shown in Figure 11.3. Here, we use an application gateway and a stateful firewall, each protecting a different set of systems.

In this example, we assume that our business requires the use of robust proxy-level capabilities of an application gateway to protect Internet-accessible systems such as web, SMTP, and DNS servers. We were okay to the generally slower performance of the proxying firewall for this purpose. At the same time, we needed the flexibility of a stateful firewall for the corporate network, which hosted internal workstations and servers. By deploying two different firewalls in parallel, we were able to take advantage of best of breed functions that were offered by each type of device. At the same time, we did not have the luxury of placing a system behind multiple layers of firewalls, as would be the case with the inline configuration.

We can design architectures that incorporate firewalls in parallel in many other ways, and we will cover several more of them in further chapters.

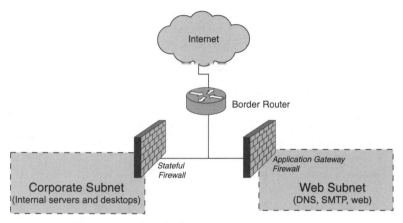

Figure 11.3 When employing parallel firewalls, delays are avoided because the firewalls are equidistant from the Internet.

Summary

This concludes our discussion of the fundamentals of perimeter design. In the course of this chapter, we talked about the need to carefully examine our environment before jumping into design, and that by spending time in the planning stages of the deployment, we minimize late changes to the network's architecture, thus saving time and money. Business needs drive all security requirements in the real world, and we must understand our goals and requirements before deciding what traffic should be blocked at the border and how many firewalls should be deployed. Recognizing that organizations differ in their business needs, we discussed several building block patterns that are popular and explained their advantages and disadvantages. We will use these principles in the upcoming chapters to empower you to create a robust network perimeter that meets your security and business needs.

References

1 John Rendleman. "Server 54, Where Are You?" InformationWeek. http://www.informationweek.com/story/IWK20010409S0001. September 2001.

2 "University of North Carolina Denies They Are Looking for Solaris 'Server 54'." Sun Microsystems. http://www.sun.com/smi/Press/sunflash/2001-05/sunflash.20010521.3.html. September 2001.

3 Archie Woodworth. "Securing the Wile Modem." April 30, 2001. http://www.sans.org/infosecFAQ/telephone/sec_modem.htm. September 2001.

4 Kevin Smith. "Do You Copy? Security Issues with Digital Copiers." September 16, 2000. http://www.sans.org/infosecFAQ/threats/copy.htm. September 2001.

5 "Egghead Hacked and Cracked." E-Commerce Times. December 22, 2000. http://www.ecommercetimes.com/perl/story/6286.html. October 2001.

6 "Osowski and Tang." August 20, 2001. US Department of Justice. http://www.usdoj.gov/usao/can/txt/press/html/2001_08_20_osowski_and_tang.html. October 2001.

7 "The Hacker Who Sent Viagra to Bill Gates." July 12, 2001. BBC News. http://news.bbc.co.uk/hi/english/uk/newsid_1434000/1434530.stm. October 2001.

8 Bruce Schneier. Crypto-Gram Newsletter. September 15, 2001. http://www.counterpane.com/crypto-gram-0109.html. October 2001.

9 Craig Biggerstaff. VPN FAQ. "How Does IPsec Work with Network Address Translation (NAT)?" http://kubarb.phsx.ukans.edu/~tbird/vpn/faq.html. September 2001.

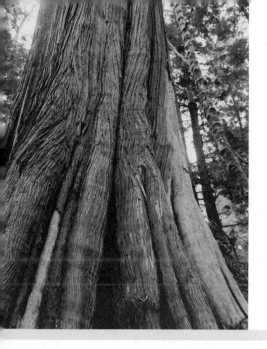

12

Separating Resources

Resource separation is one of the core network defense principles, and it is evident in many security-conscious designs. Grouping resources based on similarities in security-related attributes allows us to limit the attacker's area of influence if he gains access to a system inside the perimeter. The way that we group resources depends on their sensitivity, on the likelihood that they will be compromised, or on whatever criterion you choose as the designer.

We have applied the principle of resource separation throughout this book, perhaps without formally stating so. For example, we used screened subnets to host servers that were accessible from the Internet, presumably because their sensitivity and acceptable exposure differed from systems on the internal network. In addition to segmenting the network, resource separation can be accomplished by dedicating servers to specific tasks, and even by splitting the site into geographically distinct hosting centers. Resource separation also influences the design of software architecture, as we demonstrate in Chapter 13, "Software Architecture."

By the end of this chapter, you will understand practical means of achieving the desired extent of segregation on your network. We present several ways to separate resources within servers and networks, and explore examples that incorporate such separation. We also discuss Chroot, mail relays, split DNS, and wireless networks, and examine the merits and dangers of using VLANs when implementing security zones.

Security Zones

As you have already witnessed, in one of the basic network design patterns, we might place external web servers onto the same network as public DNS servers and mail relays. This makes sense because we want to limit which resources an attacker can access directly if he succeeds at compromising one of the systems. We can use many techniques to achieve resource segmentation on different layers of defense, all of which share the underlying principle of security zones.

A *security zone* is a logical grouping of resources, such as systems, networks, or processes, that are similar in the degree of acceptable risk. For instance, we might place web servers in the same security zone as public DNS and mail relay servers because all these systems have to be accessible from the Internet and are not expected to store sensitive information. If, on the other hand, we use the mail server to host data that is more sensitive than what is stored on the public web and DNS servers, we would consider placing it into a separate network, thus forming another security zone. Organizations have also been known to place critical systems, such as the company's Human Resources servers or the university's grade databases, behind internal firewalls.

The notion of a security zone is not limited to networks. It can be implemented to some extent by setting up servers that are dedicated to hosting similar applications. To create an effective design, we need to understand how to group resources into appropriate security zones. This approach mimics the design of a large ship that is split into multiple watertight compartments to resist flooding. If one of the sections is compromised, other areas retain a chance of maintaining their integrity.

A Single Subnet

Let's look at how we can create security zones within a single subnet by using servers that are dedicated to particular tasks, as well as those that are shared among multiple applications. In an attempt to minimize the number of systems that need to be set up and maintained, designers are often tempted to create servers that aggregate hosting of multiple services. This configuration is often effective from a cost-saving perspective, but it creates an environment that is more vulnerable to intrusion or hardware failure than if each service were running on a dedicated server.

Consider a scenario in which a single Internet-accessible Linux box is used to provide DNS and email services. Because both of these services are running on the same server, an exploit against one of them could compromise security of the other. For example, if we were using BIND 8.2.2, an unpatched "nxt overflow vulnerability" would allow a remote attacker to execute arbitrary code on the server with the privileges of the BIND process (`http://cve.mitre.org/cgi-bin/cvename.cgi?name=` `CVE-1999-0833`).

Hopefully, in this scenario, we already configured the BIND server to run as the limited user *nobody*; that way, the attacker would not directly gain root privileges through the exploit. Having local access to the system gives the attacker an opportunity to exploit a whole new class of vulnerabilities that would not be triggered remotely. For instance, if the mail processing part of our server relied on Procmail, the attacker might have been able to exploit the locally triggered "unsafe signal handling" vulnerability in Procmail 3.10 to gain root-level access to the server (`http://www.securityfocus.com/` `bid/3071`). Had we not had the vulnerable BIND application on this system, the attacker would not have been able to take advantage of the Procmail vulnerability because only a local user could exploit it.

Security Zones Within a Server

What should you do if you do not have the budget to purchase servers that are dedicated to performing each task? In the previous example, the organization segments BIND from the rest of the server in a primitive manner by running BIND as the user nobody, instead of root. That is a good start because it doesn't allow the attacker to immediately obtain administrative access to the system by compromising BIND. This technique of dedicating limited access accounts to applications is appropriate in many circumstances on UNIX as well as Windows-based systems.

A more robust way of separating a daemon such as BIND from the rest of the system involves the use of the Chroot facility, which is available on most UNIX operating systems. In a way, Chroot allows us to set up multiple security zones within a single server by creating isolated subsystems within the server, known as the *chroot jails*.

How Chroot Works

Relative isolation of the chroot jail is accomplished by changing the perspective of the "jailed" process on what its root directory is. Most applications that run on the server locate files with respect to the system's root file system identified as /. A chroot'ed process considers its / to be the root directory of the jail, and will not be able to access files above the jail's root directory. For example, BIND's core executable often resides in `/usr/local/sbin/named` and loads its configuration file from `/etc/named.conf`. If BIND is set up to operate in a chroot jail, located in `/usr/local/bind-chroot`, the named process will be started from `/usr/local/bind-chroot/usr/local/sbin/named`. This process will think it is accessing `/etc/named.conf` to load its configuration, although in reality it will be accessing `/usr/local/bind-chroot/etc/named.conf`.

A chroot'ed application is typically not aware that it is operating in an isolated environment. For the application to function properly, we need to copy the required system libraries and devices into the chroot jail because the application will not have access to OS components outside the jail. An attacker who exploits a chroot'ed process will have a hard time accessing resources outside the chroot jail because file system access will be severely limited, and the environment will not have most of the tools that are necessary to cause serious damage. Procedures for setting up Chroot are available throughout the web and are often specific to the application that you are trying to isolate.

Some applications rely on too many OS components to make setting up a chroot jail for them practical or beneficial. Additionally, in numerous documented cases, problems with the implementation or the configuration of a chroot'ed environment allowed an attacker to break out of the chroot jail. (For examples of such vulnerabilities, search for *chroot* in the Common Vulnerabilities and Exposures (CVE) database at http://cve.mitre.org.) Finally, not all operating systems provide Chroot facilities. Such caveats make it difficult to set up fault-proof isolation for security zones within a single server. However, dedicated system accounts and Chroot-like facilities are effective at complementing other zoning techniques on the server and network levels.

Security Zones via Dedicated Servers

A more effective method of reliably separating one application from another involves dedicating a server to each application. (This technique is often considered to be among information security's best practices.) As in most designs that incorporate security zones, the purpose of dedicated servers is to help ensure that a compromise of one infrastructure component does not breach the security of the other. If an attacker exploits vulnerability on one server, either in an application or an OS module, the other server still has a chance of withstanding an attack. This configuration slows down the attacker's progress, giving the system's administrator more time to detect and respond to the attack.

For example, many organizations need to maintain web and mail servers that are accessible from the Internet. Such web servers are often used to host the company's public web site, which typically combines static and dynamically generated content. The mail server is usually used to accept email messages via SMTP, which are then delivered to the company's internal users. Many companies use web servers like the one in this example primarily for marketing purposes, and do not store confidential information on the web server's file system. The mail server, on the other hand, might store confidential data in the form of sensitive email messages from the company's partners and clients. Therefore, it makes sense to split the two services into separate security zones to provide a degree of isolation for applications that differ in the degree of acceptable risk. In many cases, business needs might allow us to purchase multiple servers, but prohibit us from placing them on separate networks because of budget constraints. Setting up an additional network costs money and time that some organizations cannot justify spending.

Even if the company does not consider the mail service to be more confidential than the web service, it can justify splitting them into separate servers because web services tend to be more vulnerable than mail services. Functionality offered by web server applications tends to be more feature-rich and less predictable than functionality of mail applications. As a result, history shows that web services are exploited more frequently than mail services.

Note

As you might recall from Chapter 11, "Design Fundamentals," risk is a function of the resource's data sensitivity and of the likelihood that it will be compromised. Because risk is the primary driving force behind the need for security zones, we must look at both sensitivity and vulnerability when deciding how to separate resources. Even if data sensitivity of two services is the same, differences in the likelihood of a compromise can warrant placing them into different security zones.

Providing resource isolation solely through the use of dedicated servers is often sufficient when differences in acceptable risk of resources are not significant. Under more varying conditions, however, we might need to increase the extent of isolation that the design provides. In the next section, we explore situations in which the nature of resources, along with business needs, require us to separate systems by using multiple subnets.

Multiple Subnets

Multiple subnets provide a reliable means of separating resources because communications between systems on different subnets are regulated by devices that connect the subnets. Tools and expertise for implementing such segmentation are widely available. After all, much of perimeter defense concentrates on using routers and firewalls to control how traffic passes from one subnet to another.

In addition to creating security zones by enforcing access control restrictions on traffic across subnets, routers and firewalls limit the scope of network broadcast communications. Broadcasts can have significant effects on network performance as well as on resource security.

Broadcast Domains

A *broadcast domain* is a collection of network nodes that receives broadcast packets and typically matches the boundaries of a subnet. Subnets have traditionally been used in network design to limit the size of network broadcast domains. Splitting a network into two or more subnets decreases the number of hosts that receive network broadcasts because routing devices are not expected to forward broadcast packets. Broadcasts have security implications because they have a tendency to send data to all local hosts that care to listen. Decreasing the size of a broadcast domain also brings significant performance advantages because network chatter is localized to a particular subnet.

A Doomed Network?

When Doom first came out, it quickly showed up on LANs throughout the world, from corporate networks to college computer labs. Doom was one of the earliest multiplayer shoot-em-up games. The game allowed players to easily establish game sessions over the network. Network administrators quickly discovered detrimental effects that Doom v1.1 had on the LAN's performance. It turned out that, probably in an unbridled enthusiasm to release the first version of Doom, its coders programmed the game to use broadcasts for all communications among players. In tests (yes, someone performed such tests), a four-player Doom session was shown to generate an average of 100 packets per second and increase the network load by 4 percent.[1] If administrators couldn't ban Doom from the network, they had to rely on broadcast domain boundaries to prevent Doom communications from engulfing the whole network.

We mentioned network broadcasts in Chapter 6, "Role of a Router," in the context of disabling propagation of broadcasts through a router. This was done primarily to prevent Smurf-type attacks, which could use a single packet sent to a broadcast address to elicit replies from multiple hosts on the network. ARP uses the ability of broadcasts to deliver packets to all hosts in the broadcast domain when a system on the Ethernet segment does not know the MAC address of the host to which it wants to send an Ethernet frame. In this case, the sender typically issues an ARP request to the MAC address ff:ff:ff:ff:ff:ff, which is always the Ethernet broadcast address. The Ethernet media delivers this discovery packet to all hosts on the segment; the exception is that the system that holds the sought-after IP address replies with its MAC address.

Because ARP traffic travels without restraints within a broadcast domain, a malicious system could manipulate MAC to IP address mappings of another host with relative ease. Most ARP implementations update their cache of MAC to IP address mappings whenever they receive ARP requests or replies.

As illustrated in Figure 12.1, an attacker who is on the broadcast domain could poison system A's cache by sending it a crafted ARP packet that maps host B's IP address to the attacker's MAC address. As a result, all traffic that system A tries to send using host B's IP address is redirected to the attacker. Tools such as Dsniff (http://www.monkey.org/~dugsong/dsniff/) and Ettercap (http://ettercap.sourceforge.net/) are available free and are effective at automating such attacks. One way to defend against ARP cache poisoning is to enforce proper authentication using higher-level protocols, such as Secure Shell (SSH). Controlling the size of broadcast domains also limits a site's exposure to such attacks.

Figure 12.1   When performing an ARP cache poisoning attack, the attacker convinces System A to use the attacker's MAC address instead of System B's MAC address.

As you can see, IP communication in Ethernet environments is closely tied to MAC addresses. Systems can send network-layer broadcasts by destining IP datagrams to broadcast addresses such as 255.255.255.255, *NET.ADDR*.255.255, and so on. In this case, the underlying Data Link layer, such as the Ethernet, is responsible for delivering the datagram to all hosts in the broadcast domain. Ethernet accomplishes this by setting the destination address of the Ethernet frame to ff:ff:ff:ff:ff:ff.

Note

On Ethernet-based TCP/IP networks, IP broadcasts are translated into Ethernet broadcasts to the ff:ff:ff:ff:ff:ff MAC address. As a result, all hosts in the broadcast domain receive broadcast datagrams, regardless of the operating system or the application that generated them.

Network-layer broadcasts are frequently seen in environments that host Windows systems because Windows often relies on broadcasts to discover services on the network. The following network trace demonstrates such NetBIOS over TCP/IP (NBT) packets directed at all hosts on the local subnet 192.168.1.0. (We used Tcpdump to capture this traffic.)

```
192.168.1.142.netbios-ns > 192.168.1.255.netbios-ns:NBT UDP PACKET(137):
↪QUERY; REQUEST; BROADCAST
192.168.1.142.netbios-ns > 192.168.1.255.netbios-ns:NBT UDP PACKET(137):
↪QUERY; REQUEST; BROADCAST
192.168.1.142.netbios-ns > 192.168.1.255.netbios-ns:NBT UDP PACKET(137):
↪QUERY; REQUEST; BROADCAST
```

If you fire up a network sniffer even on a relatively small subnet that hosts Windows systems, you are likely to see similar NBT broadcast datagrams at the rate of at least one per second. Because all nodes in the broadcast domain must process such datagrams, a system devotes CPU resources to processing broadcasts whether it needs to or not. We talk more about performance implications of network broadcasts in Chapter 15, "Tuning the Design for Performance." From a security perspective, broadcast communications are likely to leak information about the application that generated them because all hosts in the broadcast domain will be "tuned in." One purpose of splitting networks into smaller subnets is to limit the amount of traffic that each node processes due to broadcasts.

Security Zones via Subnets

In perimeter security, the most powerful devices for enforcing network traffic restrictions are located at subnet entry points and usually take the form of firewalls and routers. As a result, we frequently use subnets to create different security zones on the network. In such configurations, communications that need to be tightly controlled are most likely to cross subnets and be bound by a firewall's or a router's restrictions.

Consider the example illustrated in Figure 12.2. We separated the network into three security zones, each defined by a dedicated subnet.

In this scenario, we group resources based on their primary purpose because that maps directly to sensitivity levels of the data that the system maintains. The border firewall and the internal router allow us to control access to and from network resources based on the business requirements for each zone. The zones are defined as follows:

- The Public Servers zone contains servers that provide information to the general public and can be accessed from the Internet. These servers should never initiate connections to the Internet, but specific servers might initiate connections to the Corporate Servers zone using approved protocols and ports.

- The Corporate Servers zone contains the company's internal servers that internal users can access from the Corporate Workstations zone. The firewall should severely restrict the servers' ability to initiate connections to other zones.
- The Corporate Workstations zone contains internal desktops and laptops that can browse the Internet using approved protocols and ports and can connect to the Corporate Servers zone primarily for file and print services.

Figure 12.2 Here, subnets create three security zones: the Public Servers zone, the Corporate Workstations zone, and the Corporate Servers zone.

Access control lists (ACLs) on the internal router are set up to let only NetBIOS traffic from corporate workstations access the servers. (In this example, the servers are Windows based. For UNIX, you would allow Network File System (NFS), Line Printer (LPR), and related protocols.) In this scenario, we do not have business requirements for the corporate servers to initiate connections to the Internet. If the servers have peering relationships with external partner sites, the router's ACLs need to be tuned appropriately. Additionally, the organization's security policy in this example does not allow servers to download OS and software patches from external sites. Instead, patches are retrieved and verified in the Corporate Workstation zone before they are applied to relevant servers.

The firewall is configured to allow from the Internet only inbound traffic that is destined for systems in the Public Server zone on HTTP, DNS, and SMTP ports. These servers are not allowed to initiate connections that cross security zone boundaries except when relaying mail to the internal mail server.

Systems on the Corporate Workstations zone are allowed to browse the web using approved protocols, such as HTTP, HTTPS, FTP, and so on. (For tighter control, we might want to set up a proxy server to help enforce restrictions on outbound traffic.) Corporate users can also connect to the Corporate Server zone in a manner that is controlled by the internal router. The workstations can connect to hosts in the Public Servers zone for remote administration using the SSH protocol.

So far, this example has focused on the high-level requirements for defining security zones and associated access control rules. Some additional details need to be addressed before you implement this design. Specifically, you need to pay close attention to how corporate and public systems resolve domain names and how inbound and outbound email relaying is configured.

What would happen if we hosted all corporate and publicly accessible systems on a single subnet, without defining multiple security zones? We would still be able to control how traffic traverses to and from the Internet because the Internet is considered a security zone, and we know that we have control over traffic that crosses zone boundaries. However, we would have a hard time controlling how internal systems interact with each other, primarily because internal traffic would not be crossing zone boundaries. (You can control intrazone traffic if the subnet is implemented as a VLAN, which we discuss in the "Private VLANs" section of this chapter.)

The reality is that setting up multiple security zones on the network is expensive. It requires additional networking gear, such as routers and switches, and it significantly complicates ACL maintenance on all access enforcement devices. That is partly why we are rarely able to provision a dedicated subnet for each core server of the infrastructure.

Also, it is generally much easier to justify separating publicly accessible servers from internal systems than splitting internal systems into workstation and server-specific zones. In terms of risk, public servers are accessible to everyone on the Internet and are more likely to be compromised than internal servers. This difference in vulnerability levels often serves as the primary factor for separating public and internal resources into different security zones. The distinction between internal servers and workstations is often not as clear-cut, but it still exists because workstations are more likely to be infected with malicious software as a result of a user's actions. Each organization must decide how much it is willing to invest into resource separation given its budget and business objectives.

Common Design Elements

We would like to spend a few pages discussing design elements that are not only commonly used, but are also representative of architectures that take into account resource separation. This section talks about setting up a mail relay to help you secure your organization's email link to the Internet. We also explore a DNS configuration known as Split DNS, which is very useful for mitigating risks that are associated with running a publicly accessible DNS server. Finally, we discuss ways of applying resource separation techniques to secure a wireless infrastructure, which is likely to come soon to a network near you. These scenarios are meant to demonstrate practical uses of resource separation. They will help you make decisions regarding the extent of separation that is appropriate and feasible for your organization.

Mail Relay

In Chapter 4, "Proxy Firewalls," we briefly described the *store and forward* configuration of a mail server, which uses a mail forwarding agent to relay inbound messages to an internal mail system. In that scenario, we installed mail-relaying software on a bastion host that was accessible from the Internet. We configured the relay to forward all inbound messages to the internal mail server, which, in turn, delivered them to the organization's internal users. Splitting the mail server into two components allowed us to place them into separate security zones.

Justifying Mail Server Separation

Instead of implementing a store and forward configuration to separate mail functions into two components, we could have used a single mail server to attend to internal users and accept email from the Internet. This setup eliminates the cost of deploying and maintaining an additional host, but increases the risk that an external attacker might get access to the company's sensitive information. As we have seen throughout this chapter, it often makes sense to separate public systems from the internal ones to sandbox an attacker who gains access to an Internet-accessible server. Additionally, modern mail systems, such as Microsoft Exchange, which are commonly used within a company, are complex and feature rich. Hardening such software so that it is robust enough to be accessible from the Internet is often difficult.

Splitting the public-facing component of the server from the internal mail distribution system allows us to place these resources into separate security zones. This offers many benefits over a configuration that integrates the two components into a single system:

- We can use different software for each component in a manner that is optimized for the component's tasks and risk factors.

- We can isolate the most vulnerable component in a way that limits the extent of a potential compromise.

- We can have higher confidence that we tightened the relay's configuration appropriately because its software is relatively straightforward.

- We can allow ourselves granular control over how tightly each component is configured and how it can be accessed over the network.

Implementing a Mail Relay

A common configuration for implementing a mail relay is illustrated in Figure 12.3. As you can see, we have placed the mail forwarding agent into the Public Servers zone, which was set up as a screened subnet. The internal mail server was placed on the Corporate zone to be used by internal users when sending and receiving email messages. To ensure that messages from the Internet are delivered to the mail relay server, the organization's DNS server set the mail exchange (MX) record for the company's network to point to the relay server.

The primary function of the mail relay is to receive messages from the outside and forward them to the internal mail server. To further isolate the internal mail server from the Internet, you might want to route outbound messages through the mail relay as well. Making outbound connections is not as risky as accepting inbound ones, but fully separating the internal server from the outside helps decrease the likelihood that it will be adversely affected by a system on the Internet. In this configuration, the internal mail server accepts messages from internal workstations and servers and forwards those that are Internet-bound to the mail relay in the Public Servers zone.

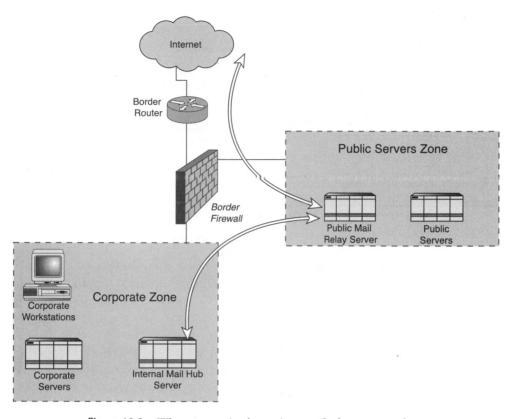

Figure 12.3 When you are implementing a mail relay, you can place the mail forwarding agent in the Public Servers zone.

One of the advantages of splitting Internet-facing mail functionality away from the internal mail server is that it allows us to use different software packages for each component of the mail infrastructure. For instance, a Microsoft Exchange server might have the desired functionality for an internal server, but you might consider it be too feature loaded for a simple mail forwarding agent. In that case, you might want to use software that you feel more comfortable locking down, such as Sendmail, Postfix, and Qmail, to implement the mail relay.

Note

Using products from different vendors for public and internal servers decreases the chances that vulnerability in one product affects all systems. At the same time, it increases the number of software packages that you need to maintain and watch over.

Specifics for configuring a mail relay to forward inbound messages to the internal server and outbound messages to the appropriate system on the Internet differ with each software vendor. In most cases, you need to specify the following parameters on the mail relay:

- The name of the domain for which the forwarder is relaying mail. If you don't specify this, the mail relay might reject inbound messages, thinking they are destined for somebody else's domain.

- The name or addresses of internal systems from which you accept outbound mail messages. To prevent internal SMTP clients from accessing the relay directly, you should consider limiting this to include only your internal mail server.

- The name or address of the internal mail server to which inbound messages will be forwarded.

You should also consider implementing masquerading features on the relay server, especially if multiple internal servers need to send outbound mail through the relay. *Mail masquerading* rewrites headers of outbound messages to remove the name of the originating host, leaving just the organization's domain name in the From field.

The Enterprise edition of the Microsoft Exchange 2000 Server supports a distributed topology that allows you to set up a front-end server that acts as a relay for mail-related communications, and forwards them to the back-end server that actually maintains users' mailboxes. Specifying that the Exchange server should be a front-end server is a matter of going into Properties in the desired server object in Exchange System Manager and selecting the This Is a Front-End Server option.

Microsoft recommends that the front-end server be fully configured before placing it into the DMZ or a screened subnet. "Configuring settings on the front-end server in Exchange System Manager requires the System Attendant (MSExchangeSA) service to be running so that the configuration information can replicate to the metabase. The MSExchangeSA service requires RPC access to the back-end servers, and RPCs often are not allowed across an intranet firewall in a perimeter network."[2] Future changes to the front-end server might, therefore, require temporary changes to the firewall's policy to allow RPC traffic for the period when the front-end server is being reconfigured. Alternatively, you can set up an IPSec channel between the administrative workstations and the front-end server to tunnel the RPC traffic in a secure manner.

Tip

If you are setting up an Exchange front-end server, be sure to follow the Exchange lock-down instructions described at `http://www.microsoft.com/exchange/techinfo/deployment/2000/E2KFrontBack.asp`.

If you are interested only in relaying SMTP and do not require POP, IMAP, and Outlook Web Access (OWA) functionality of Microsoft Exchange, you could use the SMTP Virtual Server built into Microsoft's Internet Information Server (IIS) as the mail relay. Such configuration will generally cost less to deploy because you are not required to purchase the Enterprise Edition of Microsoft Exchange 2000 server. As shown in Figure 12.4, the SMTP component of IIS offers highly configurable mail relaying functionality, and it can be set up with most of the other functionality built into IIS disabled. (Be sure to lock down IIS appropriately; it has a history of security compromises.)

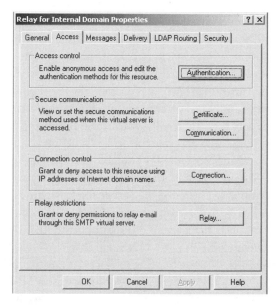

Figure 12.4 When configuring an IIS SMTP Virtual Server, you can set options that specify how the system relays mail, authenticates users, and communicates with other network components.

Administrators who are not experienced in hardening Windows-based servers will probably prefer to use a UNIX system as the mail relay server. However, if you specialize in setting up and maintaining Microsoft Windows servers, you will probably benefit from using the operating system you know best. You need to strike a balance between using software that you know best and deploying software from multiple suppliers across your security zones. If your organization is relatively small, you will probably benefit from not over-loading your support staff with maintaining mail software from multiple vendors. Larger enterprises are more likely to benefit from using specialized software for different components of the mail system.

Splitting email functionality into two servers allows us to apply different levels of hardening to each system. The mail relay should be configured as a bastion host, stripped of all OS components and applications that are not required for forwarding SMTP messages. The internal mail server does not need to be hardened to the same degree because it does not communicate with hosts on the Internet. This is often advantageous. The internal mail server might need to integrate with the internal user management system, such as Microsoft Active Directory, whereas the mail relay does not need to be aware of any such nuances of internal infrastructure.

Split DNS

The DNS service, which maps hostnames to IP addresses and vice-versa, is a principal component of many networks. In this section, we examine a *Split DNS* configuration, which is also sometimes called *Split Horizon DNS*. This is a relatively common design pattern that calls for separating the DNS service into two components: one that is available to external Internet users, and another that is used internally within the organization.

One of the purposes of Split DNS is to limit what information about the network's internal infrastructure is available to external users. If an Internet-accessible DNS server hosts your public and internal records, an external attacker might be able to query the server for hostnames, addresses, and related DNS information of your internal systems. The attacker can issue targeted lookup requests for a specific domain, hostname, or IP address, or attempt to retrieve the complete DNS database through a zone transfer.

Another purpose of Split DNS is to decrease the likelihood that critical internal resources will be affected by a compromised DNS server. Earlier in the chapter, we looked at how buffer overflow vulnerability allowed an attacker to gain shell access on the server running BIND. Many such attacks have been found in DNS software over the past few years, as evidenced by postings to vulnerability forums and databases.

BIND and the Lion Worm

The Lion worm, which spread across vulnerable UNIX servers in early 2001, exploited the TSIG vulnerability in BIND 8.2.x (`http://cve.mitre.org/cgi-bin/cvename.cgi?name=CVE-2001-0010`). The buffer overflow vulnerability in the portion of BIND's code that handled transaction signatures allowed Lion to execute its payload with the privileges of the user who was running the BIND daemon (`http://www.securityfocus.com/bid/2302`). If the worm succeeded at exploiting the TSIG vulnerability, it attempted to download a copy of itself from a web site at `coollion.51.net`.[3]

After Lion infected the server, it attempted to replace many frequently used programs and set up a shell listening for inbound connections as a backdoor into the system. It also emailed contents of local `/etc/passwd` and `/etc/shadow` files to huckit@china.com. The worm continued to spread by scanning random IP addresses for vulnerable BIND servers until the site from which it was hard-coded to download itself was disabled.[4]

Justifying DNS Server Separation

When deciding where to place DNS servers and whether to split DNS servers into multiple security zones, consider two primary types of users of DNS services:

- Users on the Internet who need to be able to obtain DNS information of publicly accessible systems that are hosted on your network. In addition to being able to resolve hostnames of your public systems, external hosts frequently use DNS to obtain the name and address of the MX server.

- Internal users within your network perimeter who need to be able to obtain DNS information of hosts on the Internet, as well as of hosts on the intranet. If a DNS server does not know the answer to the internal user's query, it can connect to external DNS servers to find out the answer; this action is known as a *recursive query*. Alternatively, the DNS server can simply forward the request to a predefined DNS server that will perform the necessary recursive queries and return the final answer to the initial DNS server.

DNS servers that are catering to different audiences vary in sensitivity of data that they require for useful operation. Specifically, publicly accessible DNS servers do not have to be aware of hostname to IP mappings of systems that cannot be reached from the Internet. Also, DNS servers differ in the likelihood that they will be compromised, depending on whether they can be accessed from the Internet. Differences in risks associated with different types of DNS servers point to the need to separate DNS resources into multiple security zones.

DNS Spoofing Attacks

DNS is an attractive target for spoofing, or *poisoning* attacks through which attackers attempt to propagate incorrect hostname to IP address mappings to the DNS server. Such attacks, in various forms, have been known to affect DNS software from most vendors.

Because DNS queries are typically submitted over UDP, servers cannot rely on the transport protocol to maintain state of the DNS connection. Therefore, to determine which response matches to which query, DNS servers embed a numeric query ID into the DNS payload of the packet. If an attacker is able to predict the query ID that the DNS server used when directing a recursive query to another DNS server, the attacker can craft a spoofed response that might get to the asking server before the real one does. The DNS server usually believes the first response it receives, discarding the second one as a duplicate. Consequently, the host that uses the DNS server to look up the spoofed domain record is directed to the IP address of the attacker's choice. Predicting DNS query IDs was relatively easy in older versions of DNS software because it tended to simply increment the IDs by one after each query.

Another variation of the DNS spoofing attack is effective against servers that happily cache a DNS mapping even if they received it as additional information in response to a query that was completely unrelated to the spoofed record. By default, DNS server software that comes with Windows NT and 2000 is vulnerable to this attack unless you explicitly set the following registry key to the `REG_WORD` value of `1`: `HKEY_LOCAL_MACHINE\System\CurrentControlSet\Services\DNS\Parameters\SecureResponses`.[5] On Windows 2000, this registry value also can be defined using the DNS Management Console by checking the Secure Cache Against Pollution check box in properties of the server's object.[6] As shown in Figure 12.5, this check box is not set by default. Microsoft DNS is not the only software that might be vulnerable to such attacks; older versions of BIND were vulnerable to such spoofing attacks as well.

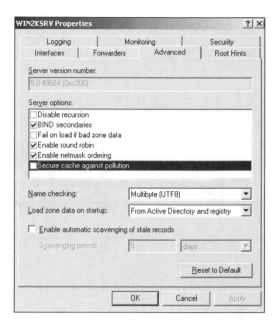

Figure 12.5   The Secure Cache Against Pollution check box is not enabled by default.

Implementing Split DNS

The implementation of Split DNS is relatively straightforward when it comes to servicing inbound DNS requests from the Internet. As shown in Figure 12.6, the external DNS server is located in the Public zone, which is typically set up as a screened subnet or a DMZ. The external server's database only contains information on domains and systems of which the outside world should be aware. Records that need to be accessible only by internal users are stored on the internal DNS server. This design decreases the possibility that an attacker can obtain sensitive information by querying or compromising the external DNS server.

The internal DNS server, in addition to maintaining authoritative records for internal systems, needs to handle requests from internal hosts for DNS information about systems on the Internet. How does the internal server answer queries about external systems for which it does not have authoritative information? We can configure the internal server to forward such queries to another DNS server that performs the recursive query. Frequently, the DNS server that is located in the Public zone plays this role. Alternatively, we can configure the internal DNS server to perform recursive queries.

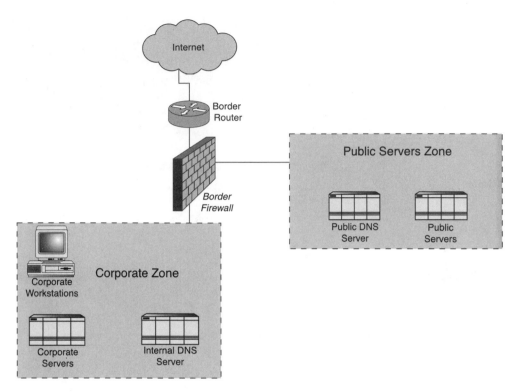

Figure 12.6 In Split DNS configurations, public and internal DNS records are hosted using two servers, each located in different security zones.

Consider a scenario in which the internal DNS server forwards queries for Internet records to our external server. In this case, the internal DNS server is maximally isolated from the Internet because in addition to never accepting connections from external hosts, it never initiates connections to systems on the Internet. The external DNS server, of course, needs to be configured to accept recursive queries only if they come from the internal DNS server. Unfortunately, in this scenario, the internal server relies on the server in the Public zone to handle such requests. That is the same server that we deem to be under increased risk because it accepts DNS requests from external hosts. If an attacker compromises the external DNS server or manages to spoof its DNS records, the internal DNS server might receive fabricated answers to its queries.

An alternative configuration permits the internal DNS server to perform recursive queries, in which case it initiates DNS connections to hosts on the Internet. In this scenario, the queries do not have to go through a server in the Public zone, which bypasses a potentially weak link in the DNS resolution process. Unfortunately, by allowing the internal server to make connections to systems on the Internet, we increase the possibility that the internal server is directly affected by an external system. For example, a malicious DNS server could exploit a buffer overflow condition by carefully crafting a response to a DNS query. An attacker could use the server's ability to initiate connections to the Internet to establish a covert channel for communicating across the network's perimeter.

Note

The server that makes outbound connection requests is under the increased risk that it will be directly affected by an attack. Besides exploiting vulnerabilities such as buffer overflows, attackers could exploit DNS-specific weaknesses of the server, for example, by poisoning the server's DNS cache in response to a query. You can protect yourself against known vulnerabilities of this sort by properly configuring the latest version of DNS software. You also need to ensure that additional defense mechanisms are in place to mitigate risks that are associated with unknown attacks.

If you use a server in the Public zone to process outbound DNS requests, you are not protected against attacks such as DNS cache poisoning because spoofed information might be propagated to the internal DNS server. After all, a DNS server in the Public zone is more likely to be compromised because it accepts requests from external hosts and is located on a subnet with other publicly accessible servers.

If you are willing to accept the risk that a compromise to the external DNS server might impact the ability of your internal users to resolve Internet hostnames, consider relaying outbound DNS requests through the server in the Public zone. In a best-case scenario, you would actually use three DNS servers: one for servicing external users, one for answering queries for internal domains, and one for performing recursive queries about Internet systems. Unfortunately, this alternative is relatively expensive to set up and maintain and is quite uncommon.

Wireless Networks

Wireless networks, such as those defined by 802.11 specifications, are beginning to augment traditional wire-based LANs within companies. The pervasive nature of wireless communications forces a security perimeter designer to reexamine some of the underlying principles of traditional network architectures. In a wireless world, we can no longer assume that physical infrastructure (walls, doors, guards, and so on) will reliably protect the network against unauthorized external access on OSI layer 2 (Media Access) and layer 1 (Physical). To access wireless resources, the attacker only has to be in the proximity of the wireless network, often without even having to enter the building of the potential victim. In this section, we cover common vulnerabilities of wireless networks and discuss the role that resource separation plays in mitigating risks that are associated with wireless deployments.

802.11 Fundamentals

802.11 is a family of specifications adopted by the Institute of Electrical and Electronics Engineers (IEEE) for implementing wireless LANs. 802.11 is similar to the IEEE 802.3 Ethernet standard in that it maps to OSI layer 2 and layer 1 protocols and services.[7] Much like in Ethernet, wireless nodes address each other using MAC addresses, which are typically embedded into the compatible network cards. Unlike Ethernet, 802.11 does not rely on wires for carrying signals on layer 1. This means that 802.11-compliant nodes can wirelessly communicate with each other within a range that is defined by the specifications and supported by their wireless equipment. Because the wireless aspect of communications is limited to the Media Access and Physical layers, higher-level protocols such as IP, TCP, and UDP do not need to be aware that datagrams are transported without wires.

802.11 networks that are most frequently deployed within companies require the use of one or more *Access Points*. An Access Point is a device that facilitates wireless communications between 802.11 nodes and bridges the organization's wireless and wired networks. In this configuration, known as the *infrastructure mode*, wireless nodes must go through the Access Point when communicating with each other and with nodes on the wired network. Alternatively, wireless networks can be deployed using an *ad hoc* topology, in which case participating 802.11 nodes communicate directly with each other on a peer-to-peer basis.[8]

Although Ethernet-based networks do not incorporate encryption at Media Access and Physical layers, 802.11 designers developed specifications for the Wired Equivalent Privacy (WEP) mechanism to allow authentication and encryption of communications between wireless nodes on layers 1 and 2. WEP is meant to limit access to the wireless infrastructure, thus protecting against the inherently "public" nature of wireless communications that allows them to pass through walls and other physical barriers.[9]

Justifying Wireless Separation

Wireless infrastructure components have historically been vulnerable to attacks that could allow a determined attacker to access data on the wireless network as well as on the wired network that is bridged through the Access Point. Such attacks have an increased threat level because 802.11 allows the attacker to connect to the wireless network at the Media Access layer without having to infiltrate the organization's physical facility. All that is needed to communicate with an 802.11 network is a compliant network card and the appropriate proximity to the target. The attacker is more likely to gain access to the wireless network if the organization has not enabled WEP or related access-control mechanisms in its 802.11 deployment. An inexpensive "war driving" experiment by security enthusiasts in the Boston area detected hundreds of 802.11 access points, only 44% of which had WEP enabled.[10]

Even if WEP or related security mechanisms are enabled, the attackers might gain unauthorized layer 2 access to the wireless and the neighboring wired networks by exercising a range of attack types. Wireless attacks, such as those in the following list, have been successful under relatively inexpensive circumstances:

- Cryptographic attacks on underlying encryption protocols and implementations
- Interception of authentication keys and shared secrets
- Monitoring of broadcast 802.11 messages
- Impersonation of a wireless Access Point

Cracking WEP with AirSnort

AirSnort, freely available from `http://airsnort.sourceforge.net`, is a Linux-based sniffer that intercepts and decodes WEP-encrypted packets. AirSnort can be used by promiscuously capturing wireless packets. After approximately 100MB–1GB of wireless data has been gathered, AirSnort can "guess the encryption password in under a second."[11] AirSnort accomplishes this by exploiting a vulnerability in the key scheduling algorithm of RC4, discovered by Scott Fluhrer, Itsik Mantin, and Adi Shamir. (`http://www.securityfocus.com/data/library/rc4_ksaproc.pdf`)

AirSnort needs to collect wireless packets before cracking the WEP password because, according to the program's documentation, out of 16 million 128-bit WEP keys that wireless cards can generate, about 3,000 are considered "weak." After the program gathers enough "weak" WEP key packets, it is able to decipher the WEP password and decode WEP-protected packets.

Because an Access Point typically acts as a bridge between wireless and wired networks, nodes that are located on networks on both sides of an Access Point participate in the same broadcast domain. Under these circumstances, a wireless attacker can use techniques that apply to wire-based networks, including attacks such as ARP cache poisoning, exploiting the loquacious nature of broadcast domains.[12] Such an attack would impact other wireless nodes that are connected to the Access Point, as well as devices on the wired side of it.

Because of the number of vulnerabilities that have been associated with wireless deployments, it makes sense to treat nodes that are located on 802.11 networks as more vulnerable than those on an isolated wired network. The justification for separating wire-based and wireless resources is further reinforced by unrestrained layer 2 access that a wireless node might have to wired hosts on the other side of the Access Point. Under some circumstances, it might also make sense to logically separate wireless nodes from each other, using techniques that apply to wire-based networks.

Implementing Wireless Separation

We have described several 802.11 vulnerabilities that could allow a wireless attacker to compromise security of other wireless nodes, as well as of neighboring wired systems. Depending on your requirements, you might consider limiting the way that every wireless node communicates with each other or, in a more cost-effective manner, group wireless nodes with similar security risks into security zones. In the scenario illustrated in Figure 12.7, we group all wireless laptops into a single security zone because for the purposes of this example, our laptops do not significantly differ in acceptable risk exposure. (For this example, each laptop is as likely to be compromised as the other because of its use and configuration, and each laptop contains data of similar sensitivity.) At the same time, we consider wireless nodes to be more vulnerable to attacks than hosts on the wired segment, and we decided to separate wireless and wired systems by placing them into different security zones.

In this scenario, wireless and wired machines are hosted on different subnets, one representing the Corporate zone, and another representing the Wireless zone. We use an internal firewall to control the way that traffic passes between the two subnets. The firewall ensures that even if an attacker is able to gain Layer 2 access to the Wireless zone or its hosts, her access to the Corporate zone will be restrained by the firewall's rule set. (Additional defense mechanisms will still need to be in place to protect against attacks that will use protocols that the firewall doesn't block.) We could have used a router instead of a firewall, which would also segregate broadcast domains and dampen the attacker's ability to perform attacks against systems in the Corporate zone. We elected to use a firewall because its access restriction mechanisms are generally more robust than those of a router; however, if your budget does not allow you to deploy an internal firewall, a properly configured router might provide a sufficient level of segmentation. As always, this decision depends on requirements and capabilities of your organization.

Note that wireless Access Points typically have hub-like characteristics. This means that any wireless node that gains Layer 2 access to the Access Point might be able to promiscuously monitor network traffic on all ports of the Access Point. Placing a firewall between wireless and wired hosts does not protect you against such attacks because the firewall can only control traffic that crosses security zones that we defined. To mitigate risks of wireless-to-wireless attacks, you would probably need to employ personal firewalls—coupled with robust VPN solutions such as IPSec to encrypt and authenticate wireless traffic—in a manner similar to protecting wired traffic that travels across potentially hostile networks.

Figure 12.7 To accommodate differences in risk, we isolate wireless systems by placing them into a dedicated security zone.

VLAN-Based Separation

VLANs were created with the primary purpose of allowing network administrators to define broadcast domains flexibly across multiple switches. VLANs are a useful isolation tool, especially for the purpose of improving the network's performance. Using VLANs to implement security zones carries additional security risks that we examine in this section.

From a performance perspective, it makes sense to place devices that frequently communicate with each other into the same broadcast domain, especially if the systems rely on broadcast-rich protocols such as NetBIOS or IPX's SAP advertisements. Often, systems that are physically separated from each other should logically belong to the same subnet; for example, your Accounting users might be sitting on different floors but accessing the same file and print servers. VLANs allow you to logically group devices into broadcast domains without tying the domain's boundaries to a particular switch, or in some cases to a single geographic location. Properly configured VLANs can also help you group resources according to their risk exposure and function, even if systems in question are located on different floors of the building and cannot be interconnected using a single switch.

In server farm deployments, where servers tend to be in close proximity to each other, VLANs are increasingly used to define multiple virtual switches within a single high-end switch. A VLAN-enabled switch can host multiple VLANs, each representing a specific broadcast domain. Using VLANs to structure subnets is often enticing because it frees administrators from deploying dedicated switches for each subnet and allows them to add ports to VLANs by simply reconfiguring the master switch without purchasing additional hardware. Using only one physical switch to represent multiple subnets also minimizes the number of devices that need to be maintained and monitored. The flexible nature in which VLANs can be configured, and a slew of intra- and inter-VLAN communication options available in high-end VLAN implementations, makes VLANs an attractive tool for network administrators.

Unfortunately, using VLANs to define boundaries of security zones is less reliable than using dedicated switches for each subnet. The distrust for reliability of VLAN isolation stems from vulnerabilities in some VLAN implementations and the ease with which a misconfiguration might allow an attacker to "jump" across VLAN boundaries. In the next few pages, we discuss risks that are associated with VLAN deployments to help you assess the applicability of VLANs to the design of your perimeter. Along with the potential dangers, we examine security-enhancing features of VLANs that could allow you to control how traffic travels *within* a single VLAN.

VLAN Boundaries

Even though subnets that are defined by VLANs might be considered virtual, they still require a router to forward network traffic from one VLAN to another. Intra-VLAN routing can be performed using a traditional router and can be controlled via ACLs much just like traffic that is crossing regular subnets. Vendors of high-end switches, notably Cisco, also offer hardware modules for their VLAN-enabled switches that can perform inter-VLAN routing at high speeds within the switch. For example, Cisco's high-end Catalyst switches support Multilayer Switching (MLS) through the use of add-on cards, which function like virtual routers within the switch and can route traffic across VLANs. MLS supports access lists that we can use to control how network traffic crosses VLAN boundaries.

> **Note**
>
> The ability to perform routing within a switch is sometimes called *Layer 3 switching.* Cisco implements this using MLS-enabled cards such as Multilayer Switch Feature Card (MSFC) for Catalyst 6000 switches.[13] Practically, Layer 3 switching is different from traditional routing only in implementation; instructions to perform Layer 3 switching are hardwired into the dedicated module that is part of the switch, whereas traditional routing is implemented in software that runs using the router's CPU. Because Layer 3 switching is hardware assisted, it tends to be faster than traditional routing.

Because VLANs are meant to create isolated broadcast domains, we could use VLANs within a single switch to implement security zone subnets in network designs that are presented throughout this chapter. As with physical LANs, we would rely on routers (or their MLS equivalents) and firewalls to transport packets across subnet boundaries in a controlled manner. For this implementation to work, we would need to ensure that the switch that hosts the VLANs does not allow an attacker to "jump" across VLANs and avoid the router or firewall.

Jumping Across VLANs

According to the IEEE 802.1q standard, Ethernet frames traversing through VLAN-enabled switches can be identified as belonging to a particular VLAN through the use of a *tag header* that is inserted into the frame immediately following the source MAC address field.[14] Frame tagging is used when multiple switches are *trunked* together to function as a single switch that can host multiple VLANs. Tag headers defined in the 802.1q standard carry identifying VLAN information across trunked switches and identify a frame as belonging to a particular VLAN.

Note

Switch trunking requires the configuration of *trunking ports* that are used when wiring participating switches together.

Under certain conditions, it might be possible to craft custom 802.1q frames that the switch will direct to the desired VLAN, avoiding the Layer 3 routing mechanism that is generally required for intra-VLAN communications. Specifically, Cisco Catalyst 2900 switches were found vulnerable to such attack when multiple VLAN switches were trunked together.[15] For this attack to work, the attacker needs to have access to the VLAN that contains an active trunking port (http://cve.mitre.org/cgi-bin/cvename.cgi?name=CAN-1999-1129). By connecting to a VLAN that contains a trunking port, the attacker could craft Ethernet frames destined for arbitrary VLANs on the other switch.

Tip

To decrease the risk of VLAN hopping attacks in trunked environments, place trunking ports onto dedicated VLANs.

This is just one type of an attack on a switch that could allow attackers to "jump" across VLANs, avoiding access restrictions of a routing device. The vulnerability described in the previous paragraph has been carefully researched and resulted in a specific recommendation for mitigating the risk associated with trunking configuration options. Considering the complexities of VLAN implementations, it is likely that other, presently unknown, vulnerabilities can be exploited in a similar manner.

The primary reason for remaining skeptical toward VLANs as security-zone enforcement mechanisms is that VLANs were created specifically to optimize performance, not to ensure security. Perhaps then, it is not surprising that Cisco's "Security Blueprint for Enterprise Networks" warns customers against using VLANs for securing access between subnets: "The capability for human error, combined with understanding that VLANs and VLAN tagging protocols were not designed with security in mind, makes their use in sensitive environments inadvisable."[16]

It is often difficult to withstand the lure of using VLANs to represent security zone subnets, especially in enterprise environments that have already deployed high-end switches and only require a configuration change to create a new "virtual" subnet. When deciding whether to use VLANs, consider the likelihood and the implications of a compromise to the VLAN boundary on layers 1 or 2. For high-security environments, you might benefit from employing simple, non-manageable, "dumb" switches to represent each subnet. By dedicating simple switches to each subnet, instead of relying on VLANs, you physically ensure that the attacker is unable to communicate across subnets without passing through a routing device. With simple switches, you do not have to worry about configuration intricacies of trunking, or consider other possibilities that might result in the switch ignoring VLAN boundary restrictions.

Tip

You might be able to justify using VLAN-enabled switches to segment the internal network, where the convenience of VLANs outweighs the risk of deploying them in a relatively low-threat environment. You might then consider using dedicated "dumb" switches for high-threat segments, such as the DMZ or the screened subnet.

Private VLANs

The appeal of modern high-end switches makes it increasingly difficult to resist using VLANs to define subnet boundaries. VLAN implementations are becoming more robust, and network engineers are becoming more familiar with the configuration and maintenance of VLANs. Some Cisco switches support an attractive VLAN security feature called Private VLANs, which you should weigh against the risks associated with VLAN deployments. A *Private VLAN* is a grouping of ports that is specially configured to be isolated from other ports on the same VLAN.

Private VLANs can help you restrict how hosts communicate with each other within the primary VLAN. As we discussed earlier in this chapter, firewalls and routers allow you to control network traffic only when it crosses subnet boundaries. Private VLANs are helpful for isolating systems within the subnet. The ability to enforce such restrictions is most relevant in server farm deployments, where servers are frequently placed on the same subnet but rarely require unrestrained access to each other. If you are able to justify the use of VLANs in your environment, Private VLANs will improve your design by adding another layer of security to the network's defenses.

When configuring ports that belong to a Private VLAN, you can specify whether the device connected to a particular port can communicate with other ports of the Private VLAN. *Promiscuous ports* have the ability to communicate with all other ports and are typically assigned to routers or firewalls. *Isolated ports* are completely shielded from all other ports of the Private VLAN, except with promiscuous ports. *Community ports* can communicate among themselves and with the promiscuous ports.[17]

Despite features that might enhance security, Private VLANs can be subverted if they are not properly configured. Private VLAN restrictions can be bypassed by routing intra-VLAN traffic through the router connected to the VLAN. Normally, hosts that are located on the same VLAN communicate with each other directly because they are on the same subnet. An attacker with access to one host on the Private VLAN could purposefully route packets to a neighboring system through the router. Because the router is usually connected to the promiscuous port, it will be able to forward traffic on layer 3 to the targeted system despite layer 2 isolation that the Private VLAN creates. To prevent this from happening, you can configure ACLs on the primary VLAN to deny traffic with the source and destination of the same subnet.[18]

As you can see, VLANs offer numerous features that allow network designers to separate network resources in a very flexible manner. At the same time, VLAN-based subnet boundaries are more likely to be compromised than if they were implemented using simpler, physically separate switches. At this point, we hesitate to recommend using VLANs for defining high-risk security zones, especially those that are in close proximity to the Internet. However, administrative advantages that VLAN-capable switches offer might justify using VLANs to segment internal network segments, depending on their security requirements and VLAN expertise in your organization.

Summary

This brings us to the end of the chapter on separating resources. Our discussion focused on ways to isolate systems and processes based on their security requirements, and tried to take into account budgetary and administrative overhead of segmenting resources in an overly granular manner. In the process, we discussed the advantages of limiting how resources interact with each other when crossing security zone boundaries. This approach to the design of the security perimeter allowed us to limit the scope of the influence that an attacker would have if the network were compromised. We also examined some of the merits and disadvantages of employing VLANs to segregate systems. As you have seen, resource separation is an important technique for fortifying the layers of your defense in depth strategy. The extent of the appropriate isolation depends on your goals and capabilities, which are articulated when assessing your business needs and documented as part of your security policy.

References

1 Laura Chappell and Roger Spicer. "Is Your Network Doomed?" NetWare Connection. http://www.nwconnection.com/jan-feb.96/doomed/. December 2001.

2 "Exchange 2000 Front-End and Back-End Topology." Microsoft Corporation. October 31, 2001. http://www.microsoft.com/exchange/techinfo/deployment/2000/E2KFrontBack.asp. December 2001.

3 "Lion Internet Worm DDoS Targeting Unix Systems." National Infrastructure Protection Center. Advisory 01-005. March 23, 2001. http://www.nipc.gov/warnings/advisories/2001/01-005.htm. December 2001.

4 "Lion Worm." Global Incident Analysis Center. April 18, 2001. http://www.sans.org/y2k/lion.htm. December 2001.

5 "Microsoft Windows NT and 2000 Domain Name Servers Allow Nonauthoritative RRs to Be Cached by Default." CERT Coordination Center. Vulnerability Note VU#109475. http://www.kb.cert.org/vuls/id/109475. December 2001.

6 "How to Prevent DNS Cache Pollution (Q241352)." Microsoft Corporation. September 10, 1999. http://support.microsoft.com/support/kb/articles/Q241/3/52.ASP. December2001.

7 "Introduction to IEEE 802.11." Intelligraphics. http://www.intelligraphics.com/articles/80211_article.html. December 2001.

8 Jim Zyren and Al Petrick. "IEEE 802.11 Tutorial." http://www.wi-fi.net/downloads/IEEE_80211_Primer.pdf. December 2001.

9 "802.11b Wired Equivalent Privacy (WEP) Security." Wireless Ethernet Compatibility Alliance. February 19, 2001. http://www.wi-fi.net/pdf/Wi-FiWEPSecurity.pdf. December 2001.

10 Craig Ellison. "Exploiting and Protecting 802.11b Wireless Networks." ExtremeTech. September 4, 2001. http://www.extremetech.com/print_article/0,3428,a%253D13880,00.asp. December 2001.

11 AirSnort Homepage. http://airsnort.sourceforge.net/. December 2001.

12 Bob Fleck and Jordan Dimov. "Wireless Access Points and ARP Poisoning." http://www.cigitallabs.com/resources/papers/download/arppoison.pdf. December 2001.

13 Cisco. "System Requirements to Implement MLS." http://www.cisco.com/warp/public/473/55.html. December 2001.

14 "IEEE Standards for Local and Metropolitan Area Networks: Virtual Bridged Local Area Networks." IEEE Std 802.1Q-1998. http://standards.ieee.org/reading/ieee/std/lanman/802.1Q-1998.pdf. December 2001.

15 David Taylor. "Are There Vulnerabilities in VLAN Implementations?" July 12, 2001. http://www.sans.org/newlook/resources/IDFAQ/vlan.htm. December 2001.

16 Sean Convery and Bernie Trudel. "Cisco SAFE: A Security Blueprint for Enterprise Networks." June 25, 2001. Cisco Systems, Inc. `http://www.cisco.com/warp/public/cc/so/cuso/epso/sqfr/safe_wp.htm`. December 2001.

17 "Configuring VLANs." Cisco Systems, Inc. June 1, 2001. `http://www.cisco.com/univercd/cc/td/doc/product/lan/cat4000/rel6_2/config/vlans.htm`. December 2001.

18 "Securing Networks with Private VLANs and VLAN Access Control Lists." Cisco Systems, Inc. `http://www.cisco.com/warp/public/473/90.shtml`. December 2001.

13

Software Architecture

SOFTWARE ARCHITECTURE IS A CRITICAL CONCEPT that is frequently overlooked when thinking about network security. Essentially, *software architecture* refers to where and how the components of an application should be deployed in order to make it as secure as possible while preserving its usability and maintainability. Many people are unaware that many functionality and security issues are related to where application components are deployed on a network. If these issues are not addressed, the application is at increased risk of encountering serious functionality or security-related problems, which could also impact other applications or even the entire organization's security. In this chapter, we review various software architecture issues, focusing on the effects that software architecture and network defense components, such as firewalls and routers, have on each other.

After examining the basics of software architecture, we review several issues involving how to configure software to be more secure. One of the features of this chapter is an extensive discussion of what characteristics to look for when purchasing software or when designing a solution. We also talk about the importance of testing software in a secure environment before deployment and implementing your network security in a way that will make future application deployments easier. Finally, we look at case studies of two application deployments to see how they can be made more secure by following the principles of good software architecture.

Software Architecture and Network Defense

When we speak of software architecture, we are talking about where each component of an application should be deployed on a network. Application components include user interfaces, databases, and middleware, which can be thought of as the back end of the application, providing functionality behind the user interface and connecting the user interface and the database. Application users can be considered another "component" of the application. In this chapter, we focus on applications whose users are on Internet-based hosts. Such applications are often at high risk of being attacked because, by definition, they must be accessible from the Internet. These applications often contain sensitive data, such as credit card numbers, that attackers want to access.

The Importance of Software Architecture

To clarify what software architecture does and doesn't involve, let's consider a simple example. You work for a company that wants to deploy a web-based application so that customers can buy widgets online. The users of this application access it from various hosts on the Internet. The application has a web interface for the users, which interacts with a database server through a middleware component. When you are planning the deployment of this application, you must consider where to place the web interface, middleware, and database on your network so that business needs for functionality and security are met. This is the core of software architecture.

Deciding where to deploy components is a much more complicated issue than you might realize. Many applications do not work properly when you pass their traffic through firewalls; for example, a common problem is that an application is incompatible with Network Address Translation (NAT). Applications also often fail to provide adequate encryption for sensitive network traffic. Some applications require extensive network defense changes to be made in order to run properly and securely, depending on how you deploy them and how insecure their design is. When applications need to interact with hosts on the Internet, software architecture and network defense components are often at odds with each other. Two viewpoints must be considered:

- Many applications are not designed to follow best security practices and, in fact, might not work properly if you try to secure them. For example, an application might require root privileges to run properly on a host. You will be required to weaken your network and host defenses in order to use the application; therefore, applications that cannot be secured adequately should not be used.

- The whole purpose of having the network is to meet business needs, and that network defenses should not "get in the way" of providing needed services and functionality to users. Security measures should be flexible and robust enough to provide adequate protection without hampering application functionality.

So which point of view is correct? Both are. The purpose of security is to support business needs by allowing accessibility to applications and data while protecting them against unauthorized activity. If your network defenses are so rigid that they cannot accommodate a new, critical application, then you should reconsider your defense design. It does no good to have a secure network if it can't meet your organization's needs. On the other hand, if an application is so insecure that it is prohibitively difficult or expensive to secure properly, it's likely in the best interest of your organization not to implement it. Your decisions should be based on a combination of your organization's needs and your security policy.

The Need to Evaluate Application Security

If security were a major concern during the selection of a software solution, potential conflicts between software characteristics and network defense would be mitigated because security would be considered from the beginning of the software selection process. However, it's far more typical for security to be largely ignored until well after the software has been purchased. Often business users in the organization who know nothing about networks, security, or computing in general are the ones who choose the software. These users know what business needs must be met, and they choose the software solution that they feel best meets those needs. Unfortunately, the business users are unaware that the solution that they are choosing might be completely insecure, violate your security policies, and in some cases, be impossible to run with your present network defenses and configuration.

The Value of Assisting with Software Evaluations

I worked at a large company where well-meaning people from various business units were selecting applications without considering security and then were upset when the IT department raised objections to deploying these applications. We found an easy solution for this problem: a few of us who were knowledgeable in security and application deployment approached the business units and offered to attend meetings with the business unit employees and software vendors. We watched the product demonstrations and had the opportunity to ask various security questions. We then evaluated the products and documented our security concerns with each product. The business unit employees used our reports as one factor when deciding which solution was the best.

Of course, we would be happiest if they chose the product that we felt had the best security. But even if the product with the most serious security shortcomings was the one chosen, we would have adequate time to plan how to compensate for them, and we would already know what the potential issues would be. We strongly felt that our participation in product selection was a win-win situation—the business unit employees and IT staff would have far fewer headaches and surprises to deal with.

How Software Architecture Affects Network Defense

In the course of planning or deploying a software solution, you often have to make adjustments or changes to your network defense. Firewalls and packet filtering devices are often affected by new applications, particularly those that use more than one static port. Issues with network configurations and architectures also occur frequently, including poor reliability and performance. Ensuring that connections carrying sensitive data are encrypted is very important too. Finally, you might have to face an application that uses an operating system that isn't usually deployed in your environment. The following section considers all these potential problems.

Firewall and Packet–Filtering Changes

Probably the most common issue involving software architecture and network defense is that of changing firewall rule sets and router ACLs. Many applications that are either accessed through the Internet or access the Internet themselves might need to pass traffic through your firewalls or routers. In many cases, these applications use protocols or port numbers that you normally do not permit to pass through your firewall. Although on the surface it sounds like it should be easy to just open the required port on the firewall, it's a much more complex issue than that.

Many applications require more than one port to be opened; in fact, some applications require several. This might be because the application uses more than one service; in such a case, it might be acceptable to open each of those ports on your firewall. Unfortunately, some applications or protocols require a range of ports to be opened—sometimes dozens or hundreds of port numbers. Examples of this include many instant messenger programs, games, and multimedia and streaming protocols, such as RealAudio. As if that isn't bad enough, some applications assign ports dynamically and use any one of hundreds or thousands of possible port numbers at any time.

If your organization requires the use of these types of applications, you do not have many options. Certain firewalls, such as Gauntlet (`http://www.pgp.com/products/gauntlet/default.asp`), provide proxy services for commonly used protocols, particularly multimedia-related ones. As we discussed in Chapter 4, "Proxy Firewalls," these proxies can be extremely helpful in handling application ports securely. Some applications also enable you to restrict the number of ports they use, for example, opening only a small range of ports instead of hundreds. If you have no other option but to open many firewall ports, be sure to strictly limit which internal hosts can be accessed through those ports, and of course, harden those hosts as strongly as possible to limit the risk posed by attacks on them.

Handling Unexpected IP Protocols

It's always possible that an application might use an IP protocol other than TCP, UDP, or ICMP. I was once testing a VPN client application, but my co-worker and I could not get it to work. When we realized that the firewall was blocking the traffic, we were confused because we thought the rule set should be allowing the traffic. We banged our heads on our desks for a while until we found a casual reference in the application manual to the fact that the application used the Generic Route Encapsulation (GRE) protocol, IP protocol 47. Then we did some research on our firewall and found out that although it blocked GRE packets by default, this was not shown in the firewall rule set. After we learned about the GRE protocol, decided it was acceptable to use, and reconfigured the firewall to accept GRE packets, the application was able to communicate properly.

Internet Application Components

Over the past several years, various protocols have been developed to facilitate communications among distributed application components in an Internet or intranet environment, regardless of the language that each component uses. Two of the best-known architectures are the Distributed Component Object Model (DCOM) and the Common Object Request Broker Architecture (CORBA), which have been used to design many distributed applications. Unfortunately, their designs conflict with network security practices and network configurations in many environments.

DCOM (`http://www.microsoft.com/com/tech/DCOM.asp`), which was created by Microsoft, dynamically assigns a TCP or (optionally) a UDP port at runtime to each DCOM process. In order for clients to connect to the correct process, they must first connect to the DCOM Service Control Manager (SCM) at port 135 to get the dynamic ports for the process. If this sounds like RPC, that's because DCOM is based on RPC. By default, DCOM uses any available ports for processes, although this can be restricted. Additionally, DCOM does not work in environments using Network Address Translation (NAT) or proxying. We'll look at this problem further in the next section.

CORBA is an industry standard for designing distributed application objects. IIOP[1] is part of the CORBA standard that was created to ease the implementation of CORBA-based solutions over the web. IIOP does not have a fixed port number, and various implementations of IIOP use different port numbers. It is difficult to characterize the issues in deploying an IIOP-based application. However, IIOP is known to have problems with NAT. Also, many IIOP-based applications often require connections to be implemented from client to server and from server to client, which is unusual compared to most application protocols, which make unidirectional connections.

Note

You might be wondering why one web application would use HTTP and another would use a protocol such as IIOP. HTTP is designed to transfer text only; IIOP can transfer many types of data other than text, such as arrays.

Fortunately, some firewalls have proxying capabilities for protocols such as IIOP, as well as NAT implementations that can handle them properly. Such firewalls are able to process the application traffic securely by accommodating dynamic port assignments and compensating for NAT-related issues. Also, newer protocols such as the Simple Object Access Protocol (SOAP), which is part of Microsoft .NET, provide similar functionality to DCOM and IIOP while working within HTTP. IIOP can be tunneled over HTTP as well. By using HTTP as a transport mechanism, application components can communicate with each other using TCP port 80.

Note

The SOAP specification is available at http://www.w3.org/TR/SOAP. Microsoft has additional information on SOAP at http://msdn.microsoft.com/library/default.asp?url=/nhp/Default.asp?contentid=28000523.

If you only consider firewall port numbers, then tunneling applications over HTTP might sound like a great idea because you are probably already permitting port 80 traffic through your firewall. However, doing this has definite disadvantages. Port 80 is intended to carry HTTP traffic for web page access; this application protocol is embedding itself inside HTTP so it can be carried by it. Now you have multiple types of traffic being sent using the same port number. As this trend continues and more applications use HTTP as a transport mechanism, port 80 traffic might become a jumble of applications and protocols that will be extremely difficult to monitor and control properly.

Conflicts with Network Configuration

Another problem that occurs with some applications is that they do not work properly with your existing network configuration. A typical example of this is that some applications are incompatible with NAT. We've already mentioned that DCOM and IIOP have problems with NAT; many VPN solutions also cannot work with NAT.

So why do so many applications have problems with NAT? Many applications and application protocols embed the client's actual IP address and port within their data. Remember that with NAT, the IP address and port that the client is actually using are different from the IP address and port that the server sees. In addition, the client's IP address is usually a reserved address, such as 10.1.2.3. Some applications insist on sending data to the client's real IP address, rather than the NAT address assigned by the firewall. When the Internet-based application server tries to communicate with your host at 10.1.2.3, instead of the NAT address, it will be unable to do so.

Application Incompatibilities with NAT

One of my former colleagues was recently involved in the deployment of a business-to-business e-commerce application. The application worked great until it was tested in the production environment, where it wouldn't work properly at all. After several conversations with technical support, she finally reached a support engineer who was able to diagnose the problem: the application was incompatible with NAT. (The application vendor had previously assured them that the software worked just fine with NAT.) The deployment was delayed for weeks while additional network hardware was deployed and new subnets that did not use NAT were created. After much additional work, the application was transferred to the new network addresses, and it was able to work properly.

You might find that you have problems between applications and other network components, such as firewalls. These are issues to be particularly cautious about; if the application conflicts with these components, you might need to drastically modify parts of your infrastructure in order to accommodate the application. A great example is a firewall that is not able to handle a particular IP protocol that your application uses. Can you imagine what would happen if a critical application that was about to be deployed in your environment failed to work because your firewall couldn't support the protocol?

Tip

Make sure to document the components of your network infrastructure and review them with the vendor for potential trouble areas before deploying the software.

Encrypting Connections

Many applications do not encrypt data that is sent between the user and the application server. The significance of this depends on your organization's security policy. Generally, if the application is running on an internal network and the data is not sensitive, then this is not usually a problem. However, if public networks are being used or the data is sensitive, then encryption usually needs to be used. If the application can't encrypt the data, then you need to consider using SSL, VPNs, or other methods of encrypting the connections.

Although it's important to protect connections between users and servers, it's also important to make sure that traffic between servers is protected. For example, you might have a publicly accessible server that accepts information from users and then transmits that information to a database server. The application designers might have assumed that both servers would be on a private network and didn't encrypt the data going between them. If you are deploying a multitier application, be sure to consider the need to secure data connections between the tiers.

Performance and Reliability

An often-overlooked issue is the effect that network security can have on application performance and reliability. For example, firewalls, especially proxies, can add considerable delay to connections. Encrypting traffic usually adds substantial overhead as well. In many cases, these delays won't drastically affect the usability of the application, but they could. As we describe in Chapter 15, "Tuning the Design for Performance," performance and security are often inversely related.

Reliability is another interesting area of software architecture. The more devices that host components of the application or pass traffic among the devices, the less reliable the application will tend to be. For example, if you are deploying a multitier application and have put each tier on a separate host, each separated by firewalls, you need to consider how reliable the overall solution will be. This is not to say that you should use as few devices as possible; rather, you should ensure that proper redundancy and fault tolerance measures are implemented as needed to keep the overall reliability at an acceptable level. For more information on dividing components among hosts, see Chapter 12, "Separating Resources."

Atypical Operating System

Most environments tend to support a few operating systems, such as certain versions of Windows, Solaris, and Linux. Some applications might require the use of a particular operating system that is not normally used in your environment. Of course, the biggest issue is probably that of support. How will your organization be able to support and maintain this operating system?

Another important issue is that of host security. If the application requires the use of an operating system with which your staff is not familiar, they aren't likely to have much knowledge of how to secure and maintain it properly. Substantial financial and personnel resources will be required in order to gain and maintain such knowledge; in many cases, these resources are unavailable. Such an operating system is likely to be excluded from standard security maintenance measures due to lack of expertise, making it much more vulnerable to attacks. Whenever possible, it's a good idea for support and security reasons to stick with operating systems with which your technical staff is familiar.

Software Component Placement

At the heart of software architecture are issues involving where to deploy various components of each application. The architecture will vary greatly depending on whether the application and its data must reside on a single system or whether they can be run on multiple systems. We will discuss this in more detail as we look at single-system and multitier applications, including those used by internal users only. We will also look at issues surrounding administrator access to application components.

Single System Applications

An application and its associated data are often designed to reside on a single host, and it might not be possible to split them among multiple hosts. In this situation, your major design decision is where the system should be located. Assuming that the system has external users, you will want to put it either on a screened subnet or possibly on your internal network and deploy a proxy server for it on a screened subnet. In both cases, external users are connecting to the system on your screened subnet and are unable to initiate a connection to your internal network. You will just need to alter your firewall rules to allow external hosts to initiate a connection to only the screened subnet host using only the necessary port numbers.

Multitier Applications

Multitier applications present much more complex design issues than single-system applications. A multitier application consists of distributed components that can sometimes reside on the same system, but usually reside on separate systems. Multitier applications often have a user interface, a middle-ware component, and a database component. Sometimes the middleware and database components are combined, and sometimes several tiers exist. You will want to follow the same basic strategy when designing a secure architecture for multitier applications that you do for single system applications, regardless of the number of tiers.

Generally, with multitier applications, the most sensitive tier is the one that contains the data, such as financial or personal information. This is the tier that should be the most isolated from users. If the application is designed with security in mind, users should never access the data directly; instead, they should interact with the application, which then accesses the data on their behalf. Therefore, avoid placing servers that contain application data on publicly accessible networks. Instead, such servers should be placed on private networks, and access to them should be tightly restricted.

Likewise, the tier that contains the user interface is the one that the users directly contact. This tier should be on a screened subnet (which is close to the external network), or perhaps accessible only by a proxying firewall. In any case, it's important to separate the top tier, with which the users interact, from the lower tiers, which contain the data and middleware. By keeping the tiers on separate machines and implementing each tier securely, you greatly reduce the risk that data will be compromised or that middleware code will be accessible if the top tier is compromised.

Administrator Access to Systems

Another important thing to keep in mind when designing an application architecture is that others beside users will need to access your applications and data. Database administrators, software developers, backup operators, and technical support personnel will all likely need to have access to components of the application. Therefore, you will need to consider their needs when designing your application architecture.

User-Unfriendly Security

If you create a security architecture that becomes too unwieldy, IT staff members may try to circumvent security. Human nature is to do things easily and quickly. If you make tasks too complicated and time-consuming, people will look for ways to do them differently. Unfortunately, the alternative methods are likely to be less secure. Educating your staff about why the security measures are necessary should help. Always consider usability versus the risks in your environment.

Too Much Security Can Be a Bad Thing

Here's a simple example of how too much security can be a bad thing. I've seen instances in which a web developer needed to follow several steps to update a single page. In some environments, the standard way to update a web page was to log on to a staging server and transfer the code to that box. Then you could initiate an additional connection from that box to the production box and transfer the code again, one file at a time. The purpose of doing this was to have the intermediate server log all connections and page updates.

The web developers quickly grew tired of having to do all of these logins and remember the complex passwords, so they instead copied their code onto a floppy, walked into the server room, and copied the code from the floppy to the server. By implementing a solution that was great from a network security standpoint but lousy from a usability standpoint, the solution failed to provide the level of security that the network administrator had been seeking.

External Administrative Access to Applications

Another problem that is difficult to handle is that of people from other companies who need administrative access to your application. Most typically, this is a developer or technical support person from your application vendor. This person can create a whole new set of security concerns. You will have to find a way to give this person access to your systems. This person might be using completely different protocols or accessing different hosts than those used by your application's users.

Although the application might be on a screened subnet that is directly accessible from the Internet, the development or staging systems that external personnel might need to access are traditionally located on your internal network. You might want to think of alternative ways to give access to external personnel, rather than permitting them to enter your internal network from the Internet. An example is a modem connection that gives outsiders access to limited resources on a single development server and no network access at all.

Applications for Internal Users Only

Throughout this chapter, we have focused on applications that are used by Internet-based hosts. However, you should keep a separate category of applications in mind: those that are used exclusively by internal users. Although most of these applications do not have any connectivity to external networks such as the Internet, some of them do. A good example would be an application that downloads weather data from a site on the Internet, stores it locally, and presents it to users on the internal network. Another example is the SETI@Home screen saver, which downloads data from the SETI project's servers at UC-Berkeley and uploads results back to that server. Although such applications can present a security risk, generally that risk is much lower than that of applications that external users access.

Many of the security principles that we discuss throughout this chapter still apply to applications that only internal users use. However, there are usually very few architectural decisions to make with such applications. They will normally be deployed to your internal network. The biggest architectural item to consider is whether the application can "pull" updates by initiating connections to the Internet host, or whether it is forced to accept "push" updates initiated by the Internet host. In the latter case, you should seriously consider placing the application on a screened subnet so that the external host can't connect to your internal network. It's almost always better to pull updates rather than to push them because you are in control of the operations when you're pulling. If you need to get updates for internal users, it's best to push or pull the updates to an intermediate box on your network; users can then interact with the intermediate box.

Identifying Potential Software Architecture Issues

To avoid a range of potential problems when implementing an application, it's a great idea to be proactive and evaluate the security of an application before it's purchased or written. A key component of this is to talk to vendors at length about their products so that you can do a thorough evaluation of them and make solid recommendations to the potential application owners as to which product would be the best from a network configuration and security standpoint. The trick is knowing what information to get from the vendors and how to get it.

Software Evaluation Checklist

Many people who work in information security are involved with choosing enterprise software solutions. When you are talking with software vendors or application developers, you might be unsure what questions you should be asking. Following is a list of questions that can help you evaluate the security of application architectures. Besides these general questions, ask specific questions that are related to your environment and security policy:

- How will this application interact with the rest of your environment? With what other resources on your network, or other networks, will it work? Do special requirements exist that have security implications; for example, does the application's host need to be a member of the same Windows domain as other servers?

- Who will be using this application: external or internal users or both? Who will be administering or updating this application: external or internal users or both?

- What protocols will be used, and what ports will need to be open? Be sure to find out which direction the traffic will be going and which components initiate which connections.

- If network traffic should be encrypted, does the application perform that encryption? If so, what encryption algorithm choices are available? Are these industry standards or proprietary methods? If encryption is not available, can the traffic easily be "wrapped" in another application or protocol that can provide adequate encryption?

- Does this application work with our current network security and network configuration (that is, proxy servers, firewalls, Network Address Translation)?

- Does security seem to be a fundamental part of the product, or an afterthought? Does the vendor incorporate good security practices into its product design? When a security flaw is found, does the vendor act quickly to inform its customers and release a patch?

- Does the vendor have security recommendations? Does the vendor supply default architecture recommendations? Will the vendor support the application if you deploy it in a different architecture than what is recommended?

- Does this application violate your network security policies?

Sources of Application Information

It's often helpful to test a working demo copy of the product. Sometimes this is not possible due to the complexity of the application, but in some cases it's trivial. If possible, install a demo of the product and look at its behavior. Another option is to talk to other organizations that are running the software to find out what problems they have encountered involving security or application architecture. This can give you a different point of view and provide valuable information that you cannot find elsewhere.

When you are attempting to evaluate the security of a product that you don't have access to, you have to rely primarily on the vendor for information. Don't be afraid to ask detailed technical questions and demand specific answers, preferably in writing. Don't settle for a general assurance that an application will work in any environment because it simply isn't true. Every environment is different, and vendors certainly can't be expected to create a product that is going to work in each one. In addition, look for other sources of information on the security of the product: reviews, security advisories, and the like.

Just the Facts, Please

I've been in many meetings with vendors where I asked fairly simple technical questions and received very vague answers. For example, during a product demonstration, I asked a vendor which firewall ports would need to be opened. The vendor said that some would need to be and that we could work all that out during final implementation. Obviously, that is not an acceptable answer. Insist on getting specific answers to your questions to prevent problems for both sides in the future.

How to Handle an Unsecurable Application

At times, an application's characteristics are such that you feel it cannot be deployed with sufficient security in your environment or where it clearly violates your organization's security policy. You have a few options at this point: replacing the application, modifying it, or deploying it with less than ideal security. In the latter case, you and the application owners will need to discuss the severity of the security issues and the risks of deploying the application.

If the application owners are considering replacing or changing the application, they need to consider the time and resources necessary to make that happen. Of course, they should also consider security more strongly during product selection or modification so that other security or network problems do not occur again.

Software Testing

Time and time again, applications have worked great in a test or staging environment, but failed miserably when deployed in the production environment. Usually this is because the testing environment and production environment have major differences, often involving network and host security.

Host Security

The application might have been tested on a server that had not been secured or hardened at all, and it broke in production when it couldn't perform the same actions on the secured system that it could on the unsecured test server. When you are testing an application, do so on a server that is as close to the production configuration as is possible. The application and associated services should run with the correct privilege levels, and file and directory rights should be set properly. Many, many applications aren't designed or intended to run following your security standards; this sort of testing might be the only way to identify those problems before putting the application into production.

Too often, applications are tested successfully on a test system with full administrator privileges, and then the application support person is surprised that the application does not function properly when it runs with limited privileges. It is amazing how many applications are written to require root-level access when running. Although it's normal for applications to require many privileges during installation, nearly all should run with reduced privileges. If an application such as DNS runs as root in production and it is compromised, an attacker could potentially gain root access to your server through the vulnerability in that application. Other applications require wide-open file sharing rights, such as shares, directories, or files set to Full Control privileges on Windows 2000 boxes, for example.

In some cases, you can coerce an application that expects such privileges into working properly without them. You might be able to get the application to run with limited administrator rights. Alternatively, you might be able to set directory rights that are more restrictive than it supposedly requires, but less restrictive than what you would normally use. Just because the manual for an application claims to need certain privileges doesn't mean that it really does. For example, an application might need Full Control to a directory on a Windows 2000 workstation, but only for one function which the users didn't need. Hopefully the application can be deployed with limited rights while still giving the users the functionality that they need. Unfortunately, this isn't always possible.

Ultimately, you and the application owners must decide if the application is so critical to meeting business needs that it's necessary to deploy it even though it introduces substantial vulnerabilities. You should implement additional network security measures to further monitor activity and restrict access to the machine in question. If the application has multiple tiers and the security weakness exists in a single tier, you might be able to isolate that particular tier so that only the other tiers of the application can access that box and no other host can contact it directly. It's vitally important to do everything that you can to protect this box.

Network Configuration and Security

Another problem that happens repeatedly is that applications are tested without production network security measures in place. During testing, all the components of the software solution are often on servers on the same subnet; firewalls or packet filters aren't involved. Then the application is transferred to a production environment, and the application owner quickly discovers that the network configuration and security measures prevent the application from working.

In an ideal world, the production environment would be duplicated in the test environment; however, this is typically not done due to resource limitations. Still, it can be costly not to discover a major architecture problem until the application is deployed to production. Delaying the rollout of a system for days or weeks while a firewall is upgraded or replaced, or the application architecture is otherwise redesigned, could cost a company substantial revenue. In such situations, it's certainly advisable to test in advance with a duplicate of your production firewall and other perimeter security components. Perhaps you can justify the purchase of spare equipment to your organization because that equipment can be used both for application testing and for a spare should your production equipment experience a failure.

If your organization simply cannot afford additional network equipment, another possible option is to do application testing using the production network. A separate screened subnet can be established for the test servers to shield them from all but your test traffic. This is a reasonable solution in some cases, particularly with applications that you fully expect to work without making changes to your network configuration. However, if you test the application and discover that it's not working in your production network environment, how easily will you be able to troubleshoot the problem and adjust your network? For example, changing rules on the production firewall on-the-fly to fix such a problem can be extremely dangerous. Such work should be done only in a test environment.

Network Defense Design Recommendations

Establishing a network defense that can handle the needs of applications in a secure manner is important. It's one thing to design a defense that meets your current needs, but it's quite another to design one that can handle future needs. Obviously, you can't anticipate everything, but you can take some proactive steps:

- Choose firewalls and border routers that are sophisticated and robust enough to securely support various types of applications. For example, some devices have built-in capabilities to support multimedia protocols, dynamic port allocation, multicasting, and other methods that applications might use. If you choose a firewall that cannot support multicasting, for example, what will you do when your business requires an application that uses it?

- Business needs often occur unexpectedly, especially from the perspective of IT staffs. It's a good idea to have extra interfaces in your firewalls, not only so you can quickly recover from an interface failure, but also so that you can create additional subnets quickly if an application requires it. In addition, plan for future growth.

- Understand the basics of various areas of security—including host, network, application, and database security—well enough to evaluate a design, identify the security weaknesses, and recommend ways to reduce or eliminate them. Staying current with the latest security technologies and products is also very important.

If you will need to make major changes to your network defense to accommodate an application, you should answer the following questions and present them to the application owners for consideration:

- What impact will these changes have on the security of this application? On the security of other applications? On overall network security?

- How will these changes affect application performance, reliability, and usability?

- What is the cost of making these changes, in terms of time and resources?

Case Study: Customer Feedback System

Now that we have learned about software architecture, let's examine a case study that shows how software architecture and network security fit together. Company Z wants to deploy a simple web-based application that allows its external customers to fill out a series of forms in order to provide feedback on their new line of widgets. None of the data is confidential or sensitive. The feedback is supposed to be anonymous; therefore, no usernames, email addresses, or other data that might be sensitive from a privacy standpoint is transmitted or stored.

The perimeter network configuration at Company Z is pretty simple; it is shown in Figure 13.1. The configuration has an Internet firewall with three interfaces. One interface connects to the Internet, and a second interface connects to the internal corporate network. The third interface connects to a screened subnet that external users can access; it provides external email connectivity, DNS resolution, and web services. The firewall does not perform NAT, and no proxy servers are in use.

Figure 13.1   This perimeter network is simple; a basic firewall passes packets between the Internet, the hosts on a screened subnet, and the internal network hosts.

Company Z has selected an application that meets its business requirements. All components of the software must run on the same host, and the data must be located on that host as well. You have been asked to recommend where in the network the application should be deployed, and what adjustments or changes need to be made to network security in order to implement it securely.

Deployment Locations

In this case, the application could be placed in a few possible locations. Let's consider the benefits and drawbacks of each of them:

- Using the existing screened subnet. Because other services that are accessed by external users are located on the existing screened subnet, it is a logical place to add another host that offers services to external hosts. The firewall rule set would need to be slightly adjusted to permit the appropriate traffic to and from this host. Deploying the application to this location would require the least work of the three options.

- Deploying a new screened subnet. If an evaluation of risk indicates that this application requires a different level of security than hosts on the existing screened subnet, then a new screened subnet can be created for it. This requires using an additional interface on the firewall and creating new firewall rules.

- Using the internal network. If the Internet firewall does not have strong proxying capabilities, consider deploying a reverse proxy server to a screened subnet and only allowing that server to contact the application. This directly limits connections from external hosts that enter the internal network and might provide better host protection. However, unlike the first two solutions, using the internal network might require an additional host to be created and secured if a suitable proxy server isn't already deployed.

Architecture Recommendation

Because this is a one-system application, your primary areas of concern should be potential conflicts between the application and the border firewall and router, as well as anything that contradicts your organization's security policy. But in general, any of these options should provide an adequate solution. Because the data is not sensitive, the consequences of an application compromise are not as high as they would be for many other applications.

This is not to say that you shouldn't be concerned about security, but that you should keep in mind that security is only one factor in creating a design. A proxy-based solution might be somewhat more secure, but the additional costs and resources required for it might be unreasonable given the nature of this application. Performance and reliability might also become unacceptable due to certain network security components. Although it's good from a security standpoint to deploy the host on the existing screened subnet, you will need to consider business needs and resources when choosing the best solution for your environment.

Case Study: Web-Based Online Billing Application

Company X has decided to deploy a web-based online billing application so that its customers can view and pay their bills through the Internet. This application must be able to use the data in the existing billing database so that the company continues to have one source of billing information. Because customers will be providing their credit card or checking account numbers as part of the payment process, the company is particularly concerned about protecting that information, as well as respecting the privacy of its customers.

The perimeter network configuration at Company X is somewhat complex. As shown in Figure 13.2, Company X has an Internet firewall with four interfaces. One interface connects to the Internet, and a second one connects to the internal corporate network and provides NAT capabilities for all internal addresses. The third interface connects to a screened subnet that both internal and external users frequently access. That subnet provides external email connectivity, DNS resolution, and web services; it also hosts web proxy servers used by internal hosts that want to access Internet web sites and reverse proxy servers used by external hosts that want to access internal web resources. The final interface connects to another screened subnet that provides VPN capabilities for telecommuting employees.

Company X has completed the software selection process based on its business requirements and has chosen an application to be deployed as quickly as possible. The application has three components: a web-based user interface, the application server to run the core components of the application, and a database. Because the company wants to use its existing online billing database, it wants to modify and expand this database rather than establish a new one.

You have been asked to research the application and determine how it can be deployed smoothly into the Company X environment. You should be most interested in identifying any potential network defense changes and problems that the application might pose to the current network configuration.

Deployment Locations

You have several options for where to put each component of the application. You want to use the existing database, which is currently located on the internal network; conceivably, you could move this host, but the company doesn't want to move it unless it's absolutely necessary. Because you want to keep the lower tiers (containing data) on protected networks, you might choose to keep the database on the internal network. Let's think about where the other systems could be deployed and what the strengths and weaknesses of each architecture are.

Figure 13.2   This perimeter network has a firewall that connects two screened subnets with the Internet and internal network; it also provides NAT capabilities for internal hosts that access the Internet.

Web Interface on Existing Screened Subnet

Company X already has a screened subnet established for hosting services that are used by external hosts. You could locate the web interface on this subnet, perhaps on an existing server that already delivers web pages. Users would connect to this server. The server would then make requests on their behalf to the application and database servers, which would be located on the internal network. Potential problems with this architecture are as follows:

- The firewall might not be able to handle the protocols used between the web server and the application server.

- The data that is passed between the web server and application server might need to be encrypted because it is passing on a publicly accessible network.

- External hosts would directly access the web server.

Web Interface and Application on the Same Screened Subnet

Another option is to deploy the web interface and the application server to the same screened subnet and leave the database server on the internal network. Although it is certainly preferable to leave the application server on an internal network if users do not need to contact it directly, it might be necessary to have the web server and application server on the same subnet if the firewall cannot securely and efficiently pass traffic between them.

If sensitive data is passed between the web and application servers and it is prohibitively difficult to encrypt it, you can largely circumvent this problem. You can create a separate screened subnet, deploy only these two servers to it, and use strong network security measures to tightly restrict access to this subnet.

All Components on the Internal Network

The web interface, application server, and database server could all be located on the internal network. As mentioned in the previous case study, in this case, you would want a reverse proxy server on a screened subnet that handles web requests on behalf of the web interface. If that's not feasible, external users could potentially be allowed to enter the internal network, but that creates a much higher level of risk.

Architecture Recommendation

Of the options presented here, you should recommend placing the web server on a screened subnet and the application and database servers on the internal network as the best overall solution. This solution is the least expensive and least resource-intensive, while providing a good level of network security.

If it were impossible to separate the web and application servers due to protocol or firewall issues, then placing them on separate hosts on the existing subnet or a new subnet would be an acceptable alternative. Avoid deploying all components to the internal network unless all other alternatives have been eliminated.

Summary

In this chapter, we examined many issues surrounding software architecture design and deployment. The goal of this chapter was to give you the knowledge to evaluate applications and determine how they can be deployed in your environment with their functionality intact and their code and data safeguarded from malicious activity. Although software architecture and perimeter defenses are sometimes in conflict with each other, in most cases you can design and deploy software in such a way that it and your perimeter defenses both maintain a proper level of security. However, in many cases, issues between software and network and host defenses are not discovered until the application is already placed into production because software architecture design is not evaluated properly in advance. By being proactive and somewhat aggressive in terms of software architecture evaluation, you can help your co-workers design and deploy solutions much more easily, efficiently, and securely.

References

1 Object Management Group. "CORBA/IIOP Specification." September 2001. `http://www.omg.org/technology/documents/formal/corba_iiop.htm`. December 2001.

14

VPN Integration

I N CHAPTER 8, "VIRTUAL PRIVATE NETWORKS," we addressed the basics of VPN technologies. This chapter discusses VPN integration, which refers to how these VPN technologies can be integrated with other perimeter security components. VPN integration is a complex subject because so many types of VPN solutions are available, and each one has many potential implementation issues. Without a good understanding of VPN integration, you will be ill prepared to design or deploy VPN in your environment.

In this chapter, we look at several VPN options:

- Standard SSH connections and SSH tunnels
- Standard SSL connections and SSL tunnels
- Single session and multiple session remote desktop software
- IPSec

For each type of VPN, we examine the following:

- What services it can provide
- Under which circumstances it is most useful
- How it should be installed and configured
- How it can be integrated with other defense components

We also discuss other advanced VPN integration topics. Finally, we look in depth at a case study that presents a real-world scenario and demonstrates the advantages and disadvantages of three potential solutions.

Secure Shell

The first VPN method that we examine in this chapter is Secure Shell (SSH). It has become a popular and secure replacement for Telnet, rlogin, and other inherently insecure remote utilities. SSH can be used to provide strong encryption for remote shell access, file transfers, and other application usage. Another nice feature of SSH is that it offers multiple authentication methods, including username/password-based and public key-based. In this section, we look at the two main types of SSH usage: standard SSH connections and SSH tunneling.

Standard SSH Connections

The most popular use of SSH is to provide a strongly encrypted connection to a remote server in order to gain shell or command-line access on that server, to transfer files between the client and server, or to remotely execute commands. We refer to these types of usage as *standard connections*.

SSH Client Integration

Installing SSH client software is simple. Actually, in most UNIX operating systems, installing SSH is not necessary because it's already included in the default OS install. If it's not, then downloading, building, and installing freely available SSH client code, such as OpenSSH (`http://www.openssh.org`), is easy. However, Windows boxes do not include SSH client software, so you need to download SSH client software and install it. One of the most popular, free Windows SSH clients is PuTTY, available at `http://www.chiark.greenend.org/uk/~sgtatham/putty`. OpenSSH has also been ported to Windows (`http://www.networksimplicity.com/openssh`). Installing just about any SSH client should be easy because they are typically simple software packages that do not make changes to a machine's network configuration. It's as simple as installing the SSH client and running it.

SSH Server Integration

SSH server software installations are also straightforward. Many UNIX systems have an SSH server daemon (sshd) installed by default. If not, it's usually simple to install sshd by compiling it from the source code. The only special note is that you may need to set sshd to start automatically so that it's available after a server reboot. Of course, it's important to keep all sshd installations and their servers' operating systems current with patches and upgrades.

Each SSH server implementation has its own default configuration. Many different SSH server configuration options are available, and it's highly likely that you will want to change some of the options to fit the needs of your environment. These settings not only affect the security of your installation, but may also impact the functionality of your SSH solution. The exact options that you set are based on several factors, including the capabilities of your sshd implementation, the characteristics of your environment, your security needs, and the capabilities and characteristics of the SSH clients. Examples of options that you should carefully consider include the following:

- How many failed logins should be allowed in a single session
- Which SSH protocols to allow: SSH1 or SSH2
- Which types of authentication to permit

The Dangers of SSH

You should be aware that, like any other program, SSH can be dangerous if it is not deployed, maintained, and upgraded properly. Multiple serious vulnerabilities exist in various implementations of SSH, and weaknesses have been identified in the SSH1 protocol. If you are going to use SSH in your environment, be sure to use the latest software versions and to keep it current with all patches. Also, configure your SSH servers to only permit the use of the SSH2 protocol instead of SSH1, unless a specific need exists for backward compatibility. SSH servers have become popular targets for attackers, so you must take great care to protect and harden such servers as much as possible.

SSH Perimeter Defense Adjustments

Minimal changes need to be made to most perimeter defenses in order to accommodate standard SSH connections. SSH servers typically listen on TCP port 22 only; this means that perimeter defenses only need to be adjusted to permit traffic to the SSH server's TCP port 22. Where in your environment should SSH servers be deployed? You may have many servers to which you want to enable external users to SSH, and it's both logical and easy to set up SSH server daemons on each of those servers. From a perimeter defense perspective, however, it's unwise to allow external users to directly SSH to each of those servers. You are opening too many holes in your perimeter and allowing unauthorized external users to have access to too many internal hosts.

From a security perspective, it would be much better to have an SSH server deployed on a screened subnet at the edge of your perimeter and to permit external users to initiate an SSH connection to only that server. After external users have successfully authenticated to that server, they can then SSH from that box to other SSH-enabled hosts on your internal network. This does require external users to perform an extra step in order to access the internal hosts, but it provides much greater control over your perimeter defenses and provides a much more secure solution.

The Hidden Value of Using SSH for File Transfers

As mentioned earlier, SSH has file transfer capabilities. One major advantage of using SSH instead of FTP is that whereas FTP establishes one connection as a control channel and an additional connection for each data transfer, SSH only needs a single connection for all control functions and data transfers. SSH not only provides encryption for file transfers, but it also causes much less of an effect on perimeter defenses than FTP.

When to Use Standard SSH Connections

Standard SSH connections have a well-defined usage: to facilitate remote shell access, remote command execution, and file transfers. Each connection provides access to a single host; therefore, if a user needs to access several hosts at a time, he needs to establish several separate connections. Standard SSH connections are handy for external users who simply need SSH access to particular internal hosts. However, for more sophisticated or complex needs, other VPN methods should be considered because a standard SSH connection has limited capabilities. One alternative that may provide a good solution is SSH tunnels.

SSH Tunnels

SSH has a powerful capability called *port forwarding*. In port forwarding, an arbitrary local port is chosen and linked by an SSH connection to a particular remote host and remote port. After the connection is established, the SSH client listens for traffic on the specified local port. Any traffic that is sent to that port is then sent through the tunnel to the remote SSH server. This technique is known as *SSH tunneling*.

Tunneling can be used for many services and applications; however, it's important to realize that because tunnels are remote-port specific, you need a separate tunnel for each remote host/port combination to which you want to tunnel traffic. For example, if you want to tunnel Hypertext Transfer Protocol (HTTP) and Internet Message Access Protocol (IMAP) traffic to and from host X, you need to establish a tunnel to host X's port 80 and another tunnel to its port 143. If you need to use six different protocols, you need to establish at least six tunnels—or possibly more than that if a particular protocol uses more than one port number. Another limitation of SSH tunnels is that they can only transfer TCP packets; therefore, other protocols, such as UDP cannot be used within SSH tunnels.

SSH Tunnel Client Integration

The same SSH client software that is used for standard SSH connections can often be used for tunneling as well, although not all SSH clients support tunneling. If you want to do SSH tunneling, verify that your client supports it. The installation and configuration procedures for preparing for SSH tunneling are nearly identical to those for standard SSH connections, with one important exception: If you are configuring tunneling, you usually want to tell the SSH client to accept local connections only. This means that other hosts cannot connect to your local port that is being used for port forwarding and then pass traffic through your tunnel. If your SSH client accepts connections, attackers can contact your local port and gain access to the remote network.

After you have installed and configured your SSH client software to facilitate tunneling, you must reconfigure all the software packages on your local host that need to utilize the tunnel. For example, if you had a POP3 client on your system, you would set it to contact the local port that you have configured to perform SSH port forwarding to the remote server's TCP port 110 instead of trying to contact the remote server's TCP port 110. When you ask your POP3 client to retrieve your mail, it would contact your local port, which would then forward the request through the tunnel to the remote mail server. The mail would then be returned through the tunnel to the local port and given to the POP3 client.

SSH Tunnel Server Integration

Setting up an SSH server for tunneling is nearly identical to setting it up for standard connections. The only difference is that most SSH servers have some sort of configuration setting that allows tunneling to be enabled or disabled. Of course, you would need to set this to enable tunneling. The exact details of the setting are server-dependent, so consult your SSH server's documentation for information on how to configure tunneling.

SSH Tunnel Perimeter Defense Adjustments

Unlike standard SSH connections, which require minimal perimeter defense changes, SSH tunneling can require many perimeter changes to be made.

Remember that each tunnel may have a different destination port; therefore, if external users are establishing tunnels on a variety of ports to many internal hosts, perimeter security can become a nightmare. Such a scenario opens far too many holes, allowing external users to attack many different internal hosts and their services. However, it's easy to eliminate this problem.

One nice feature of SSH tunnels is that you can put a tunnel within another tunnel. To implement this securely, you place an SSH server on a screened subnet on your perimeter, just as is recommended for standard SSH connections. After a user establishes a tunnel from her local host to this SSH server, she could then establish additional tunnels that pass through this tunnel to connect to other hosts on the remote network. In this scenario, the perimeter configuration needs to be modified to permit tunnels to be established to this single server, and then to pass additional tunnels between that server and other hosts. Although this still weakens the perimeter somewhat, it is more secure than permitting dozens or hundreds of different tunneling connections to be made directly between external hosts and various internal hosts.

Note

When you place an SSH tunnel inside another SSH tunnel, you suffer a performance impact due to the two layers of SSH processing required and keying. Depending on the bandwidth available to users, the overhead involved in running a tunnel inside another tunnel may be significant.

When to Use SSH Tunnels

SSH tunneling can provide an inexpensive solution for remote users who need to run one or more insecure protocols over public networks in a secure manner. A major advantage of tunneling over most other VPN methods is that it can generally be deployed extremely quickly and at minimal cost. However, configuring and using tunneling requires a certain level of technical knowledge that many end users might not have. Also, because a separate tunnel needs to be established for each port, it can become cumbersome to establish several different tunnels, one or more for each protocol. Another factor is that some SSH clients do not support tunneling; therefore, users might have to find a client that does. Therefore, SSH tunneling is recommended for technically proficient users who want to use a limited number of protocols.

Secure Sockets Layer

The Secure Sockets Layer (SSL) protocol and its successor, the Transport Layer Security (TLS) protocol, can be used to provide strong encryption for transmitted data. In this section, we will generically refer to both protocols as SSL. Like SSH, SSL-based solutions fall into two categories: standard connections, which provide protection for a single SSL-enabled application, and tunnels, which allow one or more applications, SSL-enabled or not, to be passed through public networks securely. However, as we shall see, SSL is far different from SSH.

SSL Standard Connections

Without a doubt, the most widely used VPN method is web-based SSL. Countless web sites use SSL to provide secure connections between web browsers and web servers. Most users are unaware of SSL other than seeing a little lock or other "secure" symbol at the bottom of their browser window. All major web browsers, such as Microsoft Internet Explorer, Netscape Communicator, and Opera, are SSL-enabled. SSL has become the standard method of providing encryption for web communications. Standard HTTP traffic uses TCP port 80; SSL-encrypted HTTP (better known as HTTPS) uses TCP port 443.

Although SSL is most commonly associated with HTTP, it can be used to provide encryption for other protocols. In fact, default port numbers have been assigned to various protocols that can be performed over SSL, such as Simple Mail Transfer Protocol (SMTP) over TLS/SSL (SMTPS), Net News Transfer Protocol (NNTP) over TLS/SSL (NNTPS), Lightweight Directory Access Protocol (LDAP) over TLS/SSL (LDAPS), IMAP over TLS/SSL (IMAPS), and Post Office Protocol version 3 (POP3) over TLS/SSL (POP3S). (More information on these assignments is available at http://www.iana.org/assignments/port-numbers.)

Note

Many standard desktop applications also have web-based versions that are easily integrated with SSL to provide secure connections. A classic example is web-based email, which allows remote employees from anywhere on the Internet to get secure email access through an SSL-enabled web browser. However, as we'll discuss later, deploying such applications securely is more complicated than it might first appear.

SSL Client Integration

SSL is easy to enable on a client if the software that needs to use it is SSL-enabled. For example, nearly all web browsers are SSL-enabled by default. Although most browsers also allow users to configure certain SSL settings, such as using only certain SSL versions, users who leave the settings at the defaults should be able to use web-based SSL without problems.

Other applications that support SSL tend to require some basic configuration changes to enable SSL. For example, an email client, such as Eudora, is probably set by default not to use SSL because most email users do not need to. However, Eudora versions 5 and higher have an option that can be set to either require SSL to be used or to use SSL only if it is supported by the email server and to connect without SSL otherwise. Configuring an SSL-enabled client to use SSL is generally a fairly simple process. If a program does not provide SSL support, however, it is probably prohibitively difficult to try to integrate that application with SSL. An alternative method, such as SSL tunneling, could be used instead.

SSL Server Integration

Enabling SSL support on an SSL-capable server program, such as a web server, is a fairly straightforward task. SSL uses a signed digital certificate on the server, so the major task in establishing SSL on a server is usually getting the proper certificate created and installed. Many SSL-capable server programs make this process fairly easy. First, the administrator is prompted to enter passwords or pass phrases, and the program generates a public key pair and a certificate signing request (CSR), which contains the public key. Next, the administrator sends the CSR to a reputable Certificate Authority (CA), who reviews the CSR and supporting information to confirm that the request is legitimate. The CA generates a digital certificate by signing the public key and sends the certificate to the administrator. Finally, the administrator installs the certificate by following the directions for that particular server program. Now the server software is SSL enabled.

Note

Administrators are free to use any CA that they would like, or even to establish their own CA. The value of a certificate is largely dependent on how it has been signed. If SSL is needed for an application that external customers will use, you will want to use a well-known and dependable CA; if you just need SSL for an internal-only application, then creating and using your own CA might be a better option.

When setting up SSL for a server, you should keep in mind several configuration issues. Although configuration options vary among programs, one issue that you should consider is what level of encryption to require. Historically, the most common problem with web browser-based SSL is that the maximum encryption strength of SSL connections has varied among browser implementations. For years, due largely to U.S. encryption regulations, many web browsers were distributed in two versions: one with only 40-bit or 56-bit strength encryption, and another with much stronger 128-bit or greater encryption.

Most users either were unaware of the security advantages of downloading the latter version or were not legally permitted to use it, so they installed the one with weaker encryption.

Nowadays, most new browsers have 128-bit or greater encryption by default, but a sizable base of users still have browsers that cannot support 128-bit encrypted SSL connections. On most SSL-enabled servers, you can require a minimum encryption level. If your users will be transferring sensitive data, you should be using strong encryption levels, such as 128-bit. However, if you configure your server to require clients to use at least 128-bit encryption, then your users who have older browsers that cannot support 128-bit encryption will be unable to use your application. Over time, this will become less of a problem, but you should always keep in mind what capabilities your users have.

Along the same lines, it is important to remember that in most cases, you will not have control over your external users or their hosts. Assume that your clients will act as insecurely as possible, and establish your SSL security accordingly. If you don't establish a sufficiently strong minimum encryption level, or if you don't require users to run SSL, you can be sure that some connections will be made with less than desirable security. Carefully consider your organization's security policies when determining what levels of encryption your systems should support and require.

SSL Perimeter Defense Adjustments

Adding SSL-enabled services to your environment usually requires some perimeter changes, depending on which services are being used. Because SSL-enabled services use different ports from their standard equivalents, firewalls and other filtering devices need to be modified to allow traffic involving those ports to be passed through. You also can choose to implement web proxy services, either on a firewall or on a separate dedicated proxy server. It might be possible to put a digital certificate on that device and have it provide SSL capabilities for web-based applications. Of course, you probably want to place these proxies on your perimeter, not on your internal network. See Chapter 13, "Software Architecture," for more information on where to deploy application servers, particularly web interfaces.

When to Use SSL

The most obvious case to use SSL is to provide encryption for HTTP sessions. However, this concept can be extended to make web-based SSL even more useful. For example, the Microsoft Outlook email client has a web-based equivalent: Outlook Web Access (OWA). By adding SSL support to a server that provides OWA, VPN-based email can be provided for remote users. Web-based SSL might be able to facilitate various applications being delivered securely—both web-native applications and those with alternative web-based interfaces. And you're usually pretty safe in assuming that your end users have SSL-capable web browsers already installed. Web-based SSL is often transparent to users.

A Note of Caution on SSL and Outlook Web Access

Be cautious when implementing web-based SSL solutions. You might want to just enable SSL on servers and call it a solution, but always consider perimeter defenses. For example, if you utilize Microsoft Outlook and Exchange, then OWA users might need to be authenticated to the corporate domain. Assuming that you deploy your OWA server to a screened subnet and put it in its own domain, you need to implement a trust relationship between that server and internal domains. Carefully consider the perimeter defense implications of your designs; don't be tempted just to enable SSL on servers and consider the architecture complete and sound.

Choosing to implement SSL for non–web–based traffic, such as POP or IMAP, is a more difficult decision. Although many POP and IMAP clients support SSL, some do not. In general, client programs that support SSL do not automatically use it; settings and options need to be adjusted to facilitate this. Still, these changes are minor and only need to occur during initial client configuration. SSL can provide an easy way to give clients VPN capabilities for certain applications or protocols without requiring major client changes to be made.

SSL Tunnels

A lesser-known way of utilizing SSL is by generating an SSL tunnel, which is similar to an SSH tunnel. After an SSL tunnel has been established, many other protocols can be sent through that tunnel. To use SSL tunneling, an SSL tunnel server must be set up, and SSL tunneling software must be installed on each client. The best-known software for SSL tunneling is called stunnel. More information on stunnel, including directions on its installation and configuration, is available from `http://www.stunnel.org`. SSL tunneling utilizes the same port-forwarding methodology as SSH tunneling: Stunnel clients designate a local port to listen for traffic and forward it through the tunnel to a particular port on the remote server. Applications on the client are reconfigured to point to the local port. The stunnel server software runs on the same server as the remote application and listens at a particular port. When the server receives traffic through the tunnel, it decrypts it and forwards it to the local port where the remote application is listening.

SSL Tunnel Perimeter Defense Adjustments

Like SSH tunneling, SSL tunneling might require many perimeter defense changes because SSL tunnels can be established to many hosts and multiple ports on those hosts. This can severely degrade the integrity of your perimeter defenses. A better alternative is to create an SSL tunneling server and have users generate a tunnel to it. Then generate additional tunnels inside that tunnel. This method limits the impact of tunneling on the perimeter defenses, although it makes tunneling more complicated and also has a negative impact on performance because of the overhead in running all traffic through two levels of tunneling.

When to Use SSL Tunnels

Overall, SSL tunneling provides similar functionality to SSH tunneling. The most significant difference is that SSL tunneling can be somewhat more expensive and not deployed as rapidly if you need an external certificate authority to sign digital certificates for the servers. On the other hand, this also provides a hierarchical trust capability that SSH tunneling does not. Another factor is that certain operating systems might not have an SSL tunneling client available, although most do. Generally, SSL tunneling is recommended in the same scenarios as SSH tunneling: for a group of technically savvy users who need to access a small number of protocols remotely.

Note

Many other tunneling solutions are available besides the ones mentioned in this chapter. Although some products might work great in your environment, others might have serious issues, such as poor performance and instability. Thoroughly test any tunneling software before deploying it to users, and when in doubt, go with a well-known, proven solution.

Remote Desktop Solutions

Another class of VPN methods utilizes remote desktop software to provide remote users with some of the same capabilities as local workstation users. Remote desktop software allows an external user to have access through the Internet to an internal host's graphical interface, such as a Windows 2000 workstation. A remote user can access applications, files, and other host and network resources through the remote desktop software. Such software packages fall into two general categories: single session for one user at a time, and multiple session for concurrent users.

Single Session

Single-session remote desktop software allows one user at a time to have access to the GUI of a particular host. The best-known single session software package is pcAnywhere, although many different remote desktop products are available. Many people do not think of software like pcAnywhere as a VPN option, but it can easily be configured to provide useful VPN capabilities. pcAnywhere, and some other remote desktop software packages, have encryption capabilities that can provide a strongly encrypted "wrapper" through which many applications can be run, files can be transferred, and other resources can be utilized. Other remote desktop software does not natively provide encryption but could possibly be through an SSH or SSL tunnel to provide VPN capabilities. For example, VNC (`http://www.uk. research.att.com/vnc/faq.html`) does not provide encryption in its client software, and it recommends that tunneling methods be used to protect connections.

The Risks of Do-It-Yourself Remote Desktops

For many years, users have covertly installed packages, such as pcAnywhere, onto their corporate workstations to remotely access them from their home computers. Originally, this was done primarily through modem connections, but this has increasingly changed to Internet-based connections. Encryption capabilities were only recently added to pcAnywhere, and many users probably do not use them. Therefore, these connections and their hosts are often completely unprotected. Even if a user does enable encryption, he might not set it to be strong enough or he might not use sufficiently strong authentication (or any authentication, for that matter).

Don't permit remote desktop packages to be implemented for usage between internal and external hosts if you do not have the utmost confidence in the security of the internal host. Do not permit users to implement and configure their own solutions because that is just an accident waiting to happen. Block traffic that is used by such packages as your firewall, and only permit such traffic to particular internal hosts whose security you can verify and maintain.

Single-Session Remote Desktop Client Integration

The appropriate remote desktop client software that corresponds to the remote desktop server software must be installed on the end users' workstations. Most products, such as pcAnywhere, can only be installed on Windows hosts. Remote desktop products usually install like any other software and do not make changes to the network configuration of the host.

Single-Session Remote Desktop Server Integration

As mentioned previously, the same brand of remote desktop software must be installed on the client and the server. In general, you want to configure an internal host to have any necessary applications or resources, and install the remote desktop server software onto that host. Of course, you want to harden this host strongly to reduce the risk of it being compromised because external users will be connecting directly to it. You also want to take prudent measures to authenticate users properly, such as by requiring strong passwords to be provided for authentication, and in the case of pcAnywhere, using a shared secret-like mechanism between the client and server software to further authenticate the external host. pcAnywhere also can be configured to only accept connections from certain IP addresses, which might be helpful in certain situations.

It is absolutely critical that the server software be configured to require a sufficiently high level of encryption and to use a cryptographically strong encryption protocol. Avoid using proprietary encryption methods because their cryptographic strength has usually not been verified through peer reviews and research. Proprietary methods often turn out to be flawed, which means that your traffic could be decrypted much more easily than you expect. For example, pcAnywhere 8.0 offers three encryption levels: symmetric encryption and public key encryption, both of which rely on the Microsoft CryptoAPI, and pcAnywhere encryption, which is a proprietary method that provides a weak level of encryption. Thoroughly research the available encryption options for all remote desktop products; do not assume that just because the product offers encryption, the encryption is sufficiently strong for your needs.

Single-Session Remote Desktop Perimeter Defense Adjustments

Each remote desktop software package uses one or more specific TCP or UDP ports for its communications. Perimeter defenses need to be modified to permit traffic for these ports to pass. Determining where to deploy the remote desktop host can be difficult, depending on the purpose of the host. For example, if this solution is needed so that a particular user can access his corporate workstation from home, it's unlikely that you would move that user's workstation to a screened subnet; you would leave the workstation on the internal corporate network. However, this would mean that you would have to allow external traffic to directly contact the internal host. Host security, particularly host-centric intrusion detection and firewalls, is important in such a situation because external parties could target the host.

One way around this is to use SSH tunneling to connect the external host to an SSH server on a screened subnet, and then tunnel the remote desktop software traffic through it. Another possibility is to use a product that can be proxied by a firewall, which adds at least a better degree of perimeter security than just allowing a pure direct connection between an external and an internal host. The applications and protocols that can be proxied vary widely among firewalls, so make sure to verify your firewall's capabilities.

When to Use Single-Session Remote Desktop Software

A VPN solution based on remote desktop software provides a capability that no other VPN method can offer. When a user needs to run graphical applications that cannot be installed on the client system, or he needs to interface graphically with an application that manipulates huge amounts of data (too much to transfer from the server to the client), remote desktop software might provide the only feasible VPN option.

Obviously, single-session remote desktop software is not very scalable. Multiple session products, discussed in the next section, provide a more robust implementation. But for an isolated use—one external user who absolutely needs VPN capabilities to a particular host on the network—such a solution is inexpensive and easy to deploy. Note that single session connections might be slow due to the amount of graphics that are being transmitted over the public network. However, when a graphical application must be run on an internal host and have its results sent to an external host, nothing can be done to alleviate the problem.

Multiple Session

Multiple-session remote desktop software is more commonly referred to as a *terminal server*. A terminal server, such as Citrix Metaframe or Windows 2000 Terminal Services, establishes a desktop standard and allows multiple users to receive virtual copies of the same host desktop at the same time. Because a terminal server grants access to virtual interfaces, not the server's actual interface, none of its users has access to the others' sessions or data. Terminal servers provide a much more robust and scalable solution than single-session software. In addition, popular terminal servers have encryption capabilities;

for example, Citrix SecureICA can be added onto a Citrix Metaframe installation to provide 128-bit encryption for its users' sessions. This section uses Citrix Metaframe as an example, but other products, such as Windows 2000 Terminal Services, have similar capabilities and requirements.

Multiple Remote Desktop Client Integration

To use a terminal server, each host must have the appropriate client software installed. The Citrix Metaframe client is called Citrix ICA; it is available for various Windows versions, handheld devices, UNIX, and Macintosh clients. Citrix ICA is also available in three web-based versions: ActiveX, Java, and a Netscape plug-in. All Citrix ICA client software is free of charge and available from the Citrix web site at http://www.citrix.com.

Multiple Remote Desktop Server Integration

A terminal server should have its own dedicated host. The host should be strongly hardened to reduce the risk of system compromise, of course; this is particularly important because external users will be connecting to this server, so it will be directly exposed to attacks from the outside. After the terminal software has been installed, it should be configured to require all clients to connect using sufficiently strong encryption and strong passwords. Then all desired user applications should be installed on the terminal server.

Multiple Remote Desktop Perimeter Defense Adjustments

Most terminal servers require multiple TCP or UDP ports to be used. Some firewalls have proxying capabilities for services, such as Citrix ICA, but many do not. In most cases, you will probably just have to open holes in firewalls and packet filters to allow such traffic through. Of course, you should place your terminal server on a secured subnet, not your internal network, if at all possible.

When to Use Terminal Server Software

Terminal server software can provide a great VPN solution. Because the only traffic that is passing between the terminal client and server is graphics, keystrokes and mouse movements, a terminal server can handle virtually any application and any protocol because the applications and protocols are not passing their traffic across the VPN connection. Unlike the other methods we have discussed, which could not handle UDP-based applications, a terminal server-based VPN would not know or care that UDP was being used on the internal network.

Any time that you have graphical applications that must run on a host but be accessed by remote users, terminal servers should be strongly considered. Many applications might not be portable due to resource issues, platform requirements, data volumes, software licensing issues, or excessive costs, among other reasons. The only feasible way to access these applications remotely and securely is by implementing a remote desktop solution.

However, if you want to use a terminal server-based VPN across the Internet, you should consider the risks that are associated with doing that. The terminal server's native encryption might not be strong enough, or the encryption implementation might contain serious security flaws. In addition, terminal servers might have authentication issues. Remember that a terminal server is designed primarily to provide remote application usage on a local network, not to secure data that is traversing public networks. Consequently, you might find that to achieve a sufficiently secure solution for Internet usage, you will need to tunnel terminal server traffic inside a standard VPN solution, such as IPSec, rather than rely solely on the terminal server's encryption and authentication mechanisms.

IPSec

In Chapter 8, we discussed many of the characteristics of IPSec. Before we examine how IPSec can be implemented optimally, let's review the three types of IPSec architectures:

- **Host-to-host.** The entire connection between the client and the server is encrypted. This is comparable to the encryption that standard SSH or SSL connections provide.

- **Host-to-gateway.** The entire connection is encrypted except for the portion between the gateway and the remote server. The gateway is usually located on the perimeter. Host-to-gateway provides protection similar to SSH or SSL tunneling from a host to a remote SSH or SSL server.

- **Gateway-to-gateway.** The connection between the two gateways is encrypted, but the connections from the client to the client-side gateway and from the server to the server-side gateway are unencrypted. Both gateways are typically located on their respective network perimeters. A gateway-to-gateway IPSec VPN provides similar encryption to SSH or SSL tunneling between a client gateway and a remote SSH or SSL server.

What's the difference between using SSH or SSL and using IPSec? Although SSH, SSL, and IPSec might provide similar encryption capabilities, they are different from a functional standpoint. For every additional application that you use through SSH or SSL, you have to establish additional connections and tunnels. IPSec makes one connection from a client to the remote VPN gateway or host, and it tunnels all application traffic through that one connection. Certain IPSec architectures can also conceal IP addresses, which is a significant security consideration in some environments. From a perimeter defense perspective and from a usability perspective, implementing VPNs using IPSec instead of SSH or SSL has many advantages. Let's look at how IPSec-based VPNs fit into perimeter defenses.

IPSec Client Integration

Various IPSec clients are available, which differ most significantly in how they affect the operating system. IPSec clients need to modify networking functions; because networking is usually a part of the operating system, most IPSec clients actually need to modify portions of the operating system. In the early days of IPSec, all IPSec clients were add-on programs, but as IPSec has increased in popularity, several operating systems, including Windows 2000, Windows XP, and OpenBSD, have included IPSec support. However, many operating systems in use today still do not natively support IPSec and require a separate IPSec client program to be installed and configured.

Most non-native Windows-based IPSec clients fall into one of two categories:

- Clients based on shim technologies, such as the Nokia VPN client, actually add a new layer between the existing network adapter and the TCP/IP protocol that is normally bound directly to the network adapter. This new layer is responsible for processing all traffic and implementing IPSec for all appropriate traffic. Because the shim is part of the existing network configuration, no routing changes are necessary for it to work properly.

- Clients that create a new network adapter, which is in addition to existing network adapters. Because this IPSec-specific network adapter is separate from the regular network components, the host requires routing changes so that traffic that needs IPSec processing goes through that adapter, and non-IPSec traffic goes through the other adapter.

A few implementation methods also exist for UNIX-based IPSec clients. IPSec support can be added directly to the kernel, added as a new device driver that is recompiled into the kernel, or added as a loadable kernel module. Examples of UNIX-based IPSec software include FreeS/WAN and the BSD IPSec implementation. Other UNIX flavors, such as HP/UX and Solaris, also include IPSec capabilities.

As already mentioned, IPSec clients sometimes require routing changes to be made on the host. This is particularly true when a client needs to contact internal hosts and external hosts; only the traffic that is destined for the internal hosts must be handled using IPSec, although all the traffic could be. This isn't just because of the way the client software works; often it is due to the organization's security policy. It might be desirable to route all traffic through the VPN connection and then permit the remote VPN gateway to route traffic to external or internal hosts as appropriate. Of course, this causes a significant performance hit as compared to allowing the VPN client to make direct requests to other external hosts without utilizing the VPN connection to do so.

You need to know one other important note regarding IPSec client software. If you are making a connection between a single external host and a VPN gateway, you should configure the client software so that other hosts cannot use the tunnel. If you want to connect a remote network to your VPN gateway, of course, you have to configure the IPSec software on the client side as a gateway, to pass through traffic only from the authorized hosts on that local network.

IPSec Server Integration

IPSec servers can be deployed to different types of devices. Chapter 11, "Design Fundamentals," contains a good discussion of VPN basics. To quickly review, the three most commonly used systems are as follows:

- **VPN concentrators.** These dedicated boxes are used solely for VPN functions. Besides handling the establishment, maintenance, and termination of VPN connections, they might also perform functions, such as firewalling, packet filtering, and network address translation (NAT). The advantage of using a concentrator is that it is a single-function device, dedicated to VPN.

- **Firewalls.** Some firewalls, such as Check Point FireWall-1, provide support for IPSec. Using a firewall for VPN functionality is possible as long as the VPN overhead does not adversely affect the firewall's other operations. This solution is generally less expensive than a dedicated VPN concentrator.

- **Routers.** Certain routers have IPSec capabilities. The advantage of this is that a VPN can be established between two IPSec-capable routers, which provides an inexpensive gateway-to-gateway VPN.

Note

Although some devices implement IPSec according to standards, others have proprietary IPSec implementations that deviate from standards. If a VPN server runs a proprietary IPSec implementation, its users might be required to use a particular IPSec client.

IPSec Perimeter Defense Adjustments

IPSec requires some interesting changes to perimeter defenses. Encapsulating Security Payload (ESP) mode uses IP protocol 50, whereas Authentication Header (AH) mode uses IP protocol 51. The Internet Security Association Key Management Protocol (ISAKMP) negotiation uses UDP port 500. However, IPSec implementation can result in other things as well. NAT is often incompatible with IPSec. Because AH mode makes authentication value calculations based on the entire packet, which includes the source and destination IP addresses, any NAT must occur before IPSec is used on the packets. ESP mode does not have the same problem because it does not include the entire header when it makes its authentication value calculations. In general, if you want to use AH mode, you should not use NAT; however, ESP mode and NAT should be fine together.

This issue becomes more complicated when port address translation (PAT) is used instead of NAT. PAT relies on the use of port numbers. Remember: These are TCP and UDP port numbers, stored within the TCP or UDP payload portion of the packets. If the payload is encrypted, the port numbers are encrypted too, and the PAT devices are unable to process the packets because they cannot access the port number. Even if the payload is not encrypted, the structure of IPSec packets is different from that of non-IPSec packets, and many PAT devices can't correctly parse the IPSec packet structure. Therefore, it is generally recommended that IPSec not be used in PAT environments, regardless of whether AH or ESP mode is being used.

Note

VPN passthrough refers to the concept of successfully allowing VPN traffic to go through a perimeter defense device, even when that device performs NAT, PAT, or other actions that could adversely affect VPN traffic. VPN passthrough is often achieved by allowing VPN traffic to bypass functions, such as NAT.

Whether you are implementing IPSec services on a VPN concentrator, a firewall, or a router, you have several options on where to place the IPSec services. This is discussed in detail in Chapter 11. Likely places for standalone VPN servers are on your perimeter, such as your DMZ or a screened subnet, or in parallel with your Internet firewall. Your design decision also depends on which IPSec architecture you want to implement.

IPSec Architectures

As we discussed earlier in this chapter, three types of IPSec architectures exist. Each is appropriate to meet certain types of needs.

- Host-to-host is most appropriate when external users need to access a single host. This requires software installation and configuration on the target host, as well as each client that needs to access that host. Of course, installation is not necessary if the host operating systems have built-in IPSec support.

- Host-to-gateway is the best option for remote access, when many external users need to access a variety of internal hosts and resources. Each user's system must be IPSec-enabled (if it is not already) and configured appropriately. On the remote network, only the gateway needs to be configured; no changes are necessary for each host on the network that the external users will contact.

- Gateway-to-gateway is most commonly used to provide VPNs between separate external networks, such as two business partners, or to provide VPN capabilities within a single network, also known as an intranet VPN. The biggest advantage of this architecture is that no changes need to be made to the VPN clients or the hosts that they contact.

Other VPN Considerations

We have already discussed several aspects of VPN integration. Other VPN issues also need to be considered when designing a VPN architecture. Two issues that are particularly important are the usage of proprietary VPN systems, and issues caused by compromised or malicious VPN clients.

Proprietary VPN Implementations

In the "IPSec Server Integration" section, we mentioned that some IPSec implementations do not strictly adhere to the IPSec standard and might be considered proprietary. A much larger class of VPN solutions implement proprietary VPN protocols or proprietary versions of standard VPN protocols. Such solutions require users to install a particular VPN client on their workstations. You must be particularly careful when evaluating a proprietary VPN product to ensure that it has client software available for all of the operating systems that your users might utilize. Also, keep in mind that as new versions of operating systems are released, a significant lag might be present before the proprietary client software is available for that operating system.

Note

In the early days of IPSec, vendors often stated that their products implemented standard IPSec, yet administrators would encounter significant incompatibilities between such products. Although this problem has lessened as IPSec solutions have matured, it still occurs in some cases.

Compromised or Malicious VPN Clients

Because VPN client hosts are usually external and are typically not under the control of your organization, your environment might be at serious risk if one or more of the client hosts is compromised or is acting maliciously. When a VPN connection is established between a client and your network, you can consider that client to be on an extended portion of your network. If trojans have compromised the client hosts, then remote attackers might be able to connect to that host and pass through the VPN connection onto your network. Depending on your VPN architecture and perimeter defenses, attackers might be able to enter your internal network and do serious damage to your resources.

To make this situation even worse, VPNs complicate the monitoring of network activity. Because by definition VPNs encrypt traffic, they can interfere with the normal operation of network intrusion detection systems (IDSs), anti-virus software, content-monitoring software, and other network security measures. When you are planning a VPN implementation, you should pay particular attention to where your network security systems currently reside. Either your VPN should be designed so that decrypted traffic from it passes through your regular network security systems, or you might have to move or add network security measures so that the traffic is monitored. For example, an additional network IDS sensor might need to be deployed, or a host IDS software might need to be added. If you do not monitor the traffic that has been sent through the VPN, you greatly increase the risk of incidents from external clients occurring through your VPN.

VPN Design Case Study

Now that we have examined many different aspects of VPN integration, let's tie all of the VPN concepts together by reviewing a case study. By analyzing a real-world situation, you will gain a much better understanding of the importance of VPN integration issues. We start with a list of requirements and business needs, and then we describe and critique various potential VPN architectures. This gives you some great examples of how to evaluate the strengths and weaknesses of a VPN design.

Case Study: Home Users and Multiple Applications

A network engineer at your organization has designed a VPN architecture. The purpose of the VPN is to provide limited access to a few corporate applications from employees' home computers, for occasional access primarily on nights and weekends. The user community for this VPN has been fairly well defined, as follows:

- Approximately 500 remote users exist, who will have an estimated maximum of 20 concurrent connections.

- Users will access the VPN from their personal computers only, not from corporate computers.

- Most users will connect to the Internet through dial-up ISP access, with a smaller but growing number connecting through higher speed methods.

Management has determined which applications and resources must be accessible through the VPN, as follows:

- The corporate intranet server, which includes many static web pages, as well as several web-based applications. The web pages and some of the applications do not utilize sensitive data, but a few of the applications contain information on personnel and operations that must remain confidential.

- Microsoft Exchange email, which is accessed through a Microsoft Outlook interface. All users have received training on Microsoft Outlook; therefore, management has mandated that Outlook is the only permitted email client. Because many emails between internal employees contain sensitive, unencrypted data, it is vital that the content of these emails does not pass across the Internet in plaintext format. Also, it is desirable that end users not be able to easily download and store corporate emails on their home computers, primarily for data retention and liability reasons.

- The corporate mainframe, to which users connect using TN3270 emulation. Only a small percentage of the remote users need mainframe access; however, the data that they will be accessing is sensitive.

Now that we have reviewed the user community characteristics and the business requirements, let's look at a few designs that attempt to meet these needs.

Terminal Server

Using a terminal server for VPN services has some advantages:

- Because users need secure access to a variety of applications—Microsoft Outlook, plus multiple web-based and mainframe-based applications—a terminal server would provide a single method of accessing all of these resources, without requiring changes to the resources.

- Because all application components are available through the terminal server, users do not need to install business applications, such as mainframe terminal emulators or email clients, on their home computers.

- One or a few terminal servers could meet the needs of 20 concurrent users during peak times.

- External users would only directly connect to the terminal server. The terminal server would then initiate its own connections to other hosts as needed.

However, the terminal server-based design does have some disadvantages:

- Because users' home computers are being used, the chosen terminal server would need to have clients for several different operating system types and versions. In most cases, the users would have to install terminal server client programs on their home computers, which could require massive technical support resources, not to mention the possibility of significant software licensing expenditures.

- Performance for these users, who are primarily connected to the Internet through dial-up connections, is likely to be sluggish at best and unacceptably slow at worst. Because the screen graphics are transmitted from the server to the client, users with slow network connectivity are likely to become frustrated at times with the performance.

Although a terminal server could be used to create a VPN solution, some significant issues are associated with it. Let's look at another likely option: an IPSec-based VPN.

IPSec

An IPSec-based design has several positive features:

- One IPSec-enabled firewall, or a dedicated IPSec concentrator, should have no problem handling 20 concurrent VPN sessions.

- External users would be directly connecting to the IPSec-enabled server. Decrypted traffic would then be passed from that host to other hosts. This allows direct connections to internal hosts through the VPN only; therefore, non-VPN users cannot make such connections.

- Compared to a terminal server solution, performance for IPSec users should be much better over slow connections.

However, IPSec also has some definite disadvantages:

- As with the terminal server solution, multiple issues are possible with users' home computers. IPSec clients will need to be acquired, distributed, installed, or configured for most of the client hosts' operating systems. This is certainly not a trivial undertaking.

- Users need to have access to the client interfaces for all applications that they use. The web-based applications should be fairly easy because nearly every computer has a web browser installed on it, but the other applications will be considerably more difficult. If users can utilize OWA instead of the full Microsoft Outlook client, then they will not need to install Microsoft Outlook on their home computers. However, OWA only has some of Microsoft Outlook's functionality, so more information is required before making a decision. Finally, the users who need mainframe access will have no choice but to install and configure terminal emulator software.

Microsoft Outlook Email Security

Over the years, many vulnerabilities in the Microsoft Outlook email client have been well publicized. Countless viruses have taken advantages of these vulnerabilities, often with disastrous results. An alternative to using the full Outlook email program is deploying OWA instead. You can think of OWA as "Outlook Lite." It provides the core Outlook functionality, yet it is a completely separate program that is completely web based. Therefore, the vulnerabilities that Outlook has generally do not apply to OWA, although it has vulnerabilities of its own. Viruses that are targeted toward Outlook are nearly always targeted at the full client and not at OWA.

Another, less obvious advantage exists for using OWA instead of Outlook for remote users. I used to work at a company that had stringent data retention policies. All email was automatically deleted from corporate systems after a certain number of days. Also, employees were forbidden by corporate policy from downloading emails or any other corporate data to non-corporate workstations. If users were permitted to connect to corporate Exchange servers using the full Outlook client, they would have been downloading emails to their personal computers' hard drives. By using OWA, they were able to retrieve their emails, but because OWA is web-based, there was no easy way to download the emails onto their workstations. OWA was helpful to us in meeting corporate data retention requirements and in ensuring that sensitive data was not stored on unsecured non-corporate computers.

From a purely technical perspective, IPSec is an elegant, robust, and efficient VPN method that definitely meets the needs and requirements as outlined at the beginning of the case study. However, when you consider the potential user and support-related issues, an IPSec-based design might be resource intensive to deploy and maintain. If one of your goals is to minimize user interaction and technical support costs, then you might want to consider an alternative VPN method, such as SSL.

SSL-Enabled Applications

It is obvious that SSL could be used to provide encryption for the web applications and pages on the corporate intranet server. And as previously mentioned, Microsoft's OWA is available to provide a web-based interface to Outlook. OWA traffic can easily be encrypted using SSL because it is based on HTTP. But what about the mainframe access? Well, a little research on the Internet turned up dozens of Java-based TN3270 emulators, several of which have SSL support built in. You can set up a dedicated server that acts as an SSL-enabled TN3270 proxy; users connect to it and are forced to authenticate themselves before then being connected through the proxy to the mainframe.

As we did with the first two designs, let's look at the advantages and disadvantages of relying on SSL-enabled applications:

- The cost of SSL-enabling a server is low, especially when compared with the cost of deploying a terminal server or a VPN concentrator.

- The performance of the applications should be good—certainly much better than with a terminal server.

- To provide sufficient encryption, some users would need to upgrade their web browsers to use 128-bit encryption rather than 40-bit or 56-bit. Because most newer browsers already have 128-bit encryption, this should not affect many of the users.

- Besides the browser updates, no other installations or configuration should be necessary, with the exception of the small group of users who require mainframe access. Limited resources will be needed to assist them with downloading and configuring the chosen TN3270 emulator.

- Various changes would need to be made to the required resources. The corporate intranet server would need to be SSL enabled. More significantly, OWA would need to be deployed, which can be a major project. The TN3270 proxy would also need to be set up, requiring a significant effort.

- External users would be directly connecting to the intranet and OWA servers. One potential workaround for this is the implementation of a reverse proxy server, which would add at least some degree of separation between external users and internal resources.

The most important unanswered issue at this point is how to authenticate users. If we are allowing users to connect to the intranet server and other resources using SSL, how are we authenticating them? One possibility is to issue digital certificates to all home-based users and then activate checks for SSL client-side certificates, but that might be complex and difficult to support. However, after a user has been authenticated to a particular server through a client-side certificate, the user can run multiple applications on that particular server, if you have configured the server to permit that. This solution provides SSL-based authentication while being relatively convenient for users.

Case Study Conclusion

Of the three options we have reviewed (terminal server, IPSec, and SSL), which is the best? Although all three can provide the required functionality and meet the identified needs, each has serious weaknesses that must be carefully considered. The best method in this case really depends on what the organization's security policies are, how much risk the organization is willing to incur, and how much money and time they are willing to spend on deploying and maintaining a solution. Unfortunately, there is no "magic answer" as to which method is clearly the right choice.

Summary

In this chapter, we examined the topic of VPN integration and learned how VPN technologies can be integrated with other defense components. The potential VPN methods that we reviewed include standard SSH and SSL connections, SSH and SSL tunneling, remote desktop software, and IPSec. Each of these types has advantages and disadvantages, of course, and each is best suited to certain types of usage. To choose the best solution, you must consider several factors, including the characteristics of end users and their systems, which applications will be used, and what effect everything will have on perimeter defenses. By gathering and evaluating all the pertinent information on the need for a VPN, you can choose an optimal method that secures your organization's data and resources.

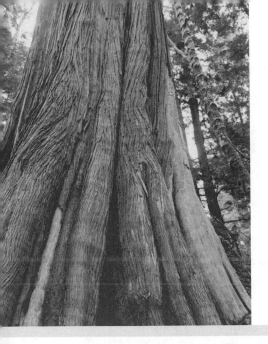

15

Tuning the Design for Performance

As was discussed in Chapter 11, "Design Fundamentals," performance is an important element to include in the design of a network. Networks that do not offer acceptable performance to their users are frequently not used. It is also important to consider performance when designing the security infrastructure for a network because many techniques that are used to protect networks have performance impacts. Managing these impacts in your design is essential if you hope to deliver a secure network that is acceptable to its users. This can be difficult because performance issues can be hard to quantify prior to implementation, and adding security might decrease performance. This chapter discusses performance issues as they apply to security. We provide you with guidance on how different elements of your security infrastructure can contribute to performance problems and how you can reduce or eliminate the performance impacts of your design decisions.

Performance and Security

Performance and security are not necessarily directly competing design goals. Although many of the steps you must perform to secure a network do have performance costs, it is your job to identify the design elements that add the required security while allowing the network to meet its performance goals.

Defining Performance

When your users complain of poor network performance, they could be referring to several distinct problems. For example, they could be experiencing long download times from their favorite FTP site, or they might be experiencing slow processing of their commands on a remote server. Different types of performance issues can cause each of these problems. Therefore, we begin our discussion of performance with a few definitions.

Network Bandwidth and Latency

Network bandwidth is a measure of how fast information can flow across a network segment. It is typically measured in bits per second. A network that can transfer 500KB of information in 16 seconds would have a bandwidth of 256kbps (500 * 1024 * 8 / 16). This is a measure of how much information "fits" in the network in a given second. Bandwidth is shared among the different devices that are hooked up to a network segment. Wide area network (WAN) links are normally limited to two devices, which means that all of the bandwidth is available to transfer data between them; however, LANs can have hundreds of hosts competing for the network's bandwidth. On a LAN, the available bandwidth between two hosts might be much lower than the total network bandwidth if many other hosts are trying to transfer data at the same time. Fortunately, LAN bandwidth is cheap. Common LAN technologies have large bandwidth capacities. 100BASE-T Ethernet networks are extremely common, and they are rated for 100Mbps. This is in direct contrast to WAN links. A T1 circuit is relatively slow (1.544Mbps) compared to 100BASE-T Ethernet, and it can cost thousands per month.

> **Tip**
>
> Because bandwidth is shared between the devices that need to communicate across a network, when determining bandwidth requirements, it is important to factor in the number of simultaneous network conversations that will be occurring. The easiest way to control this is by limiting the total number of computers attached to the network.

Network latency is a measure of how long it takes for a packet to travel from one point in a network to another. It is frequently measured by sending a test packet to a host, which it then returns to the sender. The round-trip time is then calculated to determine the latency. Several contributing factors can add latency to a packet:

- Propagation. This is the time it takes for the packet to travel from the start to the end of a particular transmission medium and is largely a function of distance. For example, neglecting other factors, a packet traveling from New York to California is going to have a larger propagation delay than a packet traveling from Manhattan to Queens.

- Gateway processing. This is the time taken by each device between the transmitter and the receiver that must process the packet. As a packet travels between network segments, it might have to pass through routers, switches, firewalls, network address translations (NATs), VPNs, and other types of network devices. Each of these devices takes time to process the packet.

- Available bandwidth. A packet might have to travel across many network segments to reach its destination. The time it takes for the packet to travel across each segment is directly affected by each network segment's available bandwidth.

- Packet size. Larger packets take longer to transmit than smaller packets. This time becomes more pronounced when available bandwidth is low or when a gateway-processing device is required to examine the entire packet.

> **Note**
>
> The `ping` command is frequently used to measure network performance, but it is important to note that it is a measure of latency and not bandwidth. By default, `ping` transmits a small packet and then waits to receive it from the destination device. This correctly determines the round trip time between the two devices, but does not tell you anything about the bandwidth between the two devices. Correctly measuring bandwidth requires that a much larger amount of data be transmitted between the two devices to attempt to completely use up all available bandwidth between them. Ping can be told to transmit larger packets, but this is still insufficient to reach the transmission rates that are normally necessary to saturate the network. Other available tools, such as `ttcp`, are specifically designed to test network bandwidth. Cisco IOS 11.2 and above implement a version of `ttcp` that is available as a privileged command. `ttcp` is also available free on many UNIX distributions.

Response Time

Response time is the amount of time it takes a response to be received after a request is made. Response time is a function of the latency between the requester and the responder plus the processing time needed by the responder to calculate the response. Interactive protocols that require frequent bi-directional conversations, such as Telnet, are affected by response time. Response time is primarily what determines whether users perceive a service to be fast or slow. Because of this, when a request is received that will take a long time to calculate, some services immediately return an intermediate response to the user to indicate that they are working on the problem.

Throughput

Throughput is the measure of how much information can be reliably transmitted between two devices on a network. Throughput is principally a function of bandwidth, but it also is affected by protocol overhead. Protocols that are required to transmit large amounts of data in a timely manner are more affected by throughput restrictions. These include applications, such as file transfer protocols, video-conferencing, and Voice over IP (VoIP).

Understanding the Importance of Performance in Security

It is worth spending some time discussing why we should care about performance when designing our security infrastructure. Remember, for a network to be secure, it must maintain confidentiality, integrity, and availability to its users. When performance is too low, the network fails to maintain availability. This can be true even when the service is still responding to requests. The performance of network services can directly impact the acceptability of those services. If we offer services securely, but at a service level below the users' tolerance, the services will not be used. Can we really consider the services secure when the users cannot or will not use them?

Of course, different applications have different performance requirements. It is an important part of the security-design process to identify the acceptable performance levels for the services on the network. This requires that you establish metrics to use to measure performance and determine acceptable values for each of these metrics. The following lists some commonly used metrics:

- Response time
- Throughput
- Maximum simultaneous users
- Minimum availability (for example, 24×7×365)
- Maximum downtime
- Mean time between failure (MTBF)

Keep in mind that acceptable levels for each of your metrics will vary depending on the type and context of the request. For example, it is a commonly held rule of e-business that a visitor typically waits no longer than eight seconds for a web page to download. However, when placing an order, visitors are frequently willing to wait much longer than eight seconds to receive an order confirmation.

Network Security Design Elements that Impact Performance

Almost every decision you make concerning a network's security infrastructure impacts its performance. From the choice of which firewall to field, to the architecture of the network, many factors combine (sometimes in complex ways) to affect the network's overall performance. When designing your network, you need to understand what the individual performance impact of each design element is so that you can predict what the cumulative impact will be for the resulting network.

The Performance Impacts of Network Filters

Because perimeter defense relies so heavily on packet filters and firewalls to protect networks, it makes sense to start our performance discussion with them. Network filters perform the important job of determining which packets should be allowed to enter our networks. The process they go through to make this decision takes time, and the amount of time taken directly impacts the latency of the packet. Assuming similarly performing hardware, the more complex the decision that needs to be made, the longer it will take to reach the decision. From a performance point of view, we should prefer algorithms that can make simple, quick decisions. However, substantial security advantages result from performing more complex analysis of incoming packets. The following four filtering techniques demonstrate this security/performance tradeoff:

- Packet filters
- Stateful firewalls
- Proxy firewalls
- Content filters

Packet Filters

As was discussed back in Chapter 2, "Packet Filtering," packet filters are one of the most basic forms of network filters. All decisions are made based on the contents of the packet header with no reference back to previous packets that have been received. The most common fields on which to filter are source IP address, source port, destination IP address, destination port, and status flags. A typical filter rule might be to allow connections to TCP port 80 on a web server. Assuming the web server is at IP address 192.168.1.5, the Cisco ACL would look like this:

```
access-list 110 permit tcp any host 192.168.1.5 port 80
```

To make the filtering decision, the packet filter need only examine the packet's header for the destination IP address (192.168.1.5) and destination port (80). No other information is required. This is a simple operation that takes little processing time to complete, resulting in little added latency to the packet. Be careful when adding access lists to routers that already have high CPU utilization. The added load, minor as it might be, could cause the router to start dropping packets.

Tip

Apply access lists on incoming interfaces to minimize the performance impact. When applied on an incoming interface, the router does not need to make redundant routing decisions on packets that are being rejected.

When security decisions can be made based on small amounts of information, performance impacts are small. Unfortunately, as was shown in Chapter 2, several problems exist with packet filters, including problems protecting against spoofed packets and the difficulties allowing return traffic back into the network without opening up unintended holes in the filter. To address these deficiencies, the filtering device must perform additional work.

Stateful Firewalls

Stateful firewalls (covered in Chapter 3, "Stateful Firewalls") address some of packet filtering's shortcomings by introducing a memory to the packet filter in the form of an ongoing connections table. Performance is impacted due to two additional tasks that the firewall must perform on this table. First, when a new packet is allowed through the firewall, the firewall determines whether the packet is the start of a new network conversation. If it is, an entry is added to the ongoing connections table. Second, when the firewall receives the return packet, a lookup must be performed to find the corresponding entry in the ongoing connections table before access can be granted. As you could imagine, on a busy firewall, this table can grow large. As the table grows, the time necessary to locate entries also grows, increasing the time necessary to make the access decision. Stateful firewall vendors employ hash algorithms to attempt to reduce this overhead, but it cannot be completely eliminated.

Tip

Most stateful firewall vendors allow you to tune the firewall by increasing the size of the connection table and corresponding hash table. Increasing these settings can noticeably increase performance and is recommended if your firewall can support the increased memory requirements.

If performance is still unacceptable, most products allow you to disable the memory feature on a per-rule basis. On Check Point FireWall–1, this is called FAST Mode. Using this feature increases performance, but at the cost of reduced security.

Proxy Firewalls

Proxy firewalls have the potential to make the best security decisions, but they are the worst performing of the three types of network filters we have discussed. Why use them? As we described in Chapter 4, "Proxy Firewalls," proxy firewalls place themselves in the middle of network conversations. Clients connect first to the proxy firewall, and the proxy firewall makes the request to the server on the client's behalf. To accomplish this, the proxy firewall must maintain two network connections for every ongoing network conversation. Every ongoing connection requires its own data record that records the source and destination of the connection and the current protocol state. When a packet is received, the proxy must examine the data portion of the packet and determine whether it is making a valid request based on that protocol state. This enables the proxy to deny requests that are invalid or out of sequence for the current protocol. For instance, according to RFC 921 (the RFC for Internet mail), during an SMTP session, a `mail from:` command should precede a `rcpt to:` command. By understanding the normal states that a protocol should support, the proxy can reject requests that would break the state model of the protocol—in this case, by rejecting any `rcpt to:` commands that are issued prior to a `mail from:` command being received. Although this approach has a substantial security benefit, it comes at the expense of high memory and CPU requirements. Careful consideration should be given to the choice of the firewall's hardware platform, especially when filtering high-bandwidth traffic.

Content Filters

Content filters protect a network by attempting to detect malicious activity in the content of a packet. Email filters are the most common type of content filters, but they also exist for other types of network traffic. As described in Chapter 10, "Host Defense Components," most of these tools are signature based. They contain a large database of malicious activity signatures. When a new message is received, the content filter must search the message to determine whether it contains malicious signatures. The amount of time this takes is dependent on the size of the signature database, the size of the message, and the speed of the computer performing the filtering.

Signature databases are guaranteed to grow over time. Little benefit would result from removing signatures from these databases. The outcome would be known attacks that the filter would not be able to detect. As the size of the signature database increases, performance of the content filter decreases. It is important to remember this when determining the appropriate hardware on which to host your content filter.

Another important factor to consider is the percentage of malicious traffic to normal traffic. When a malicious message is detected, most content filters need to perform additional work, such as sending out an alert or writing a log entry. This extra work is not an issue when most messages are normal. However, when the number of malicious messages becomes large, this extra work can undermine the ability of the content filter to function. It is possible for an attacker to exploit this problem by sending a large volume of malicious messages to induce a denial of service.

Network Architecture

Because a network that starts out slow will only become slower if we add security devices, it is useful to discuss ways that network design affects network performance. The following four network design issues that can directly impact the overall performance of a network are discussed in depth in the subsequent sections:

- Broadcast domains
- WAN links
- TCP/IP tuning
- Routing protocols

Broadcast Domains

Broadcast messages are the most expensive type of packet in terms of performance that can be transmitted on a network. Two reasons explain this. First, when a normal packet is sent out on a network, most hosts can ignore the packet if it is not being sent to them. However, every host in the same broadcast domain must process a broadcast packet, even if the packet is not relevant to it. As discussed in Chapter 12, "Separating Resources," each host in the same broadcast group must take a small performance hit for every broadcast packet received. Second, broadcast messages consume some of the network bandwidth from every host in the same broadcast domain, even when the network is implemented using network switches. Normally, network switches are able to intelligently direct packets to the intended recipient without consuming network bandwidth from other connected hosts. However, this is not possible with broadcast packets because they are supposed to be sent to all hosts.

Tip

To minimize the performance impact of broadcast messages, keep the number of hosts in a broadcast group as small as practical and try to eliminate or replace protocols that generate many broadcast messages.

WAN Links

WAN links allow geographically distributed networks to be connected. They are normally implemented using circuits that are provided by common carriers, such as telephone companies, which charge a recurring fee to provide the WAN service. WAN services are sold in a wide variety of capacities, and the fee for service can grow large for high-bandwidth connections. Table 15.1 lists some of the most common circuit types.

Table 15.1 **Bandwidths for Common Circuit Types**

Circuit Type	Bandwidth
Dial-up modem	9.6–56kbps
Switch 56	56kbps
ISDN BRI	128kbps
Cable modem	Approximately 1Mbps
Digital Subscriber Line (DSL)	256–768kbps
T1	1.544Mbps
T3	45Mbps
OC3	155Mbps
OC12	622Mbps
OC48	2.45Gbps

When establishing a WAN connection, it is essential that the bandwidth requirements for the connection be carefully analyzed. If you order too small a circuit, the network performs unacceptably. If you order too large a circuit, you waste your company's money. Finding an appropriate balance can be tricky, especially when large price increases exist between levels of service. If circuit prices are reasonable in your area, always opt for more bandwidth than you think you will need. You will always find a use for it later. If larger circuits are too expensive, though, you will need to make a careful price versus performance analysis that will require a detailed understanding of your WAN performance requirements.

After the appropriate circuit has been set up, it is important not to waste bandwidth over the connection. Following are some tips to help you avoid unnecessary WAN usage:

- Do not bridge the networks because this forces all broadcast traffic on both networks to flow over the WAN link. Route between them instead.

- Do not make one network reliant on the other for basic network services. For example, if you are running Windows NT, place a domain controller on each side of the circuit.

- Use network filters to restrict WAN traffic to essential connections.

- Cache frequently referenced materials locally. Just as Internet providers use web caches to improve performance, any frequently referenced materials should be cached locally to prevent redundant WAN usage to retrieve the same information.

- Try to schedule batch jobs that send large amounts of data over the WAN link for periods of low activity.

TCP/IP Tuning

Many TCP/IP stacks are not set up to perform optimally by default. To get the most performance possible, examine some of the specific controls that are available for your servers to optimize TCP/IP performance for your environment. Following are some specific issues for which you should look:

- Maximum transmission units (MTUs). If you transmit a packet with too large an MTU, it might have to be fragmented to reach its destination. This adds substantial latency to the packet, and in some cases, it might prevent delivery. To address this, many manufacturers set the MTU to the smaller of 576 or the MTU of the outbound interface. This is normally small enough to avoid fragmentation, but it can significantly reduce transfer efficiency. RFC 1191 describes a method to dynamically discover the MTU. It works by sending out packets with the do not fragment bit set. When a compliant router receives one of these packets but cannot forward the packet because the next link has a smaller MTU, it sends back an Internet Control Message Protocol (ICMP) error message that includes a new recommended MTU size. This allows the transmitting host to reduce the MTU to the largest value that will still permit the packet to reach its destination without being fragmented. Most manufacturers support RFC 1191, but it might not be turned on by default.

Note

Some networks block all ICMP messages at the network's border. This can break several TCP/IP protocols, including the mechanism on which RFC 1191 relies to function. For an RFC 1191-compliant operating system to determine a correct MTU, it must be able to receive ICMP type 3 (destination unreachable) and code 4 (Fragmentation Needed and Don't Fragment was Set) packets. If all ICMP messages are filtered, the sending host assumes that the current MTU is supported, which might cause unnecessary packet fragmentation. In some implementations, it might disable communications entirely if the do not fragment bit is set on all outgoing packets. For this reason, it is important to carefully consider what types of ICMP messages should be allowed into and out of your network instead of just creating a generic deny all ICMP rule.

- Window size. The TCP window value determines how much TCP data a host can transmit prior to receiving an acknowledgement. This is part of TCP's error-correction mechanism. When the value is small, errors in transmission are quickly detected. This is good if the circuit is unreliable. For reliable circuits, a larger TCP window size is more appropriate. TCP is designed to dynamically vary the window size to adjust for circuit quality. This mechanism works well for reasonably high performance circuits. When circuit speeds are extremely high (>800Mbps), the maximum window size is exceeded and performance suffers. To address this, RFC 1323 was proposed. RFC 1323 adds extensions to TCP to support extremely high-performance networks, including an increase in the maximum window size.

Tip

When working with extremely high-performance networks, you should use operating environments that support the RFC 1323 extension. Examples of operating systems that support RFC 1323 include AIX 4.1, HP-UX, Linux (kernels 2.1.90 or later), Microsoft Windows 2000/XP, and Sun Solaris (versions 2.6 and above).

- Socket buffer size. The send and receive socket buffers hold data during transmission until an acknowledgement for the data has reached the transmitting host. At this point, the acknowledged data can be flushed from the buffer, allowing new data to be transmitted. When these buffers are too small, performance suffers because the connection between the two hosts cannot be filled up completely with data. The amount of data that will fit between two hosts is directly related to the bandwidth and latency between the hosts. It can be calculated by the following formula:

amount of data = bandwidth $\star$ round-trip time delay

The resulting value is the optimum size for the transmit and receive buffers for communication between the two hosts. Of course, different values would be obtained for conversations between different hosts. Currently, TCP does not support calculating this value dynamically, so a reasonable maximum should be chosen. Some applications allow the users to specify the buffer sizes, but this is uncommon. For most applications, the only way to increase the buffer sizes is to increase the system-level defaults. This should be done with care because it causes all network applications to use additional system memory that they might not require. Keep in mind that you will only gain a performance increase if both hosts are using sufficiently sized buffers.

Routing Protocols: RIP Versus OSPF

Routing is the process of deciding how to deliver a packet from one network to another. To deliver a packet, each router between the source and destination devices must know the correct next-hop router to which to send the packet. Routers maintain routing tables to make these decisions. These tables can be configured in two ways: by manually entering routing information into each router, or by using a routing protocol. Routing protocols are designed to automatically determine the correct routes through a network by exchanging routing information with neighboring routers.

Two of the most common routing protocols in use on LANs are Routing Information Protocol (RIP) and Open Shortest Path First (OSPF). RIP is included as a standard routing protocol on most routers and was the first major routing protocol for TCP/IP. RIP is easily implemented and normally works just by turning it on. For this reason, many manufacturers use it as the default routing protocol. This is unfortunate because RIP suffers from many deficiencies, including substantial performance problems.

RIP has two major performance problems. First, it cannot make routing decisions based on bandwidth. RIP uses hop-count as its metric to determine the shortest path between two networks. Paths with smaller hop-counts are preferred over paths with higher hop-counts even if the bandwidth of the lower hop-count path is much lower. For an extreme example, see Figure 15.1. Router A has a 100Mbps connection to Router B, which has a 1000Mbps connection to Router C. In addition, Router A has a 300Mbps connection to Router C. If Host 1 attempts to send a packet to Host 2, the preferred path from a performance standpoint would be A–B–C, but RIP would choose A–C, forcing the packet to travel across the extremely slow link.

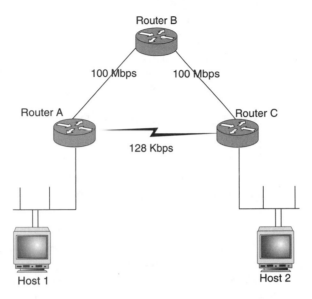

Figure 15.1   RIP networks occasionally make poor routing choices.

RIP's second problem is that it has an inefficient method of sharing routing information across a network. Every 30 seconds, routers that are running RIP must broadcast their entire routing table to each neighboring router. On large networks, these tables are big and can consume a substantial amount of network bandwidth. If the network includes slow network links, this route information can bring performance across the link to a crawl. In addition, RIP has other deficiencies that can make it a poor choice as your routing protocol. The most significant of these is that it takes a relatively long time for RIP routes to propagate throughout the network. In some cases, this can mean that RIP might not stabilize when routes are changing rapidly.

OSPF was created to provide a non-proprietary routing protocol that addressed the deficiencies of earlier routing protocols, such as RIP. OSPF includes the ability to represent a cost for each interface, which allows it to make decisions based on the bandwidth differences between paths. OSPF is significantly more efficient when sharing routing information across the network. It transmits routing changes only when they occur instead of broadcasting them at fixed intervals. The improvements that OSPF brings do come at the cost of implementation complexity. OSPF networks are more difficult to implement than RIP networks.

Case Studies

Following are two case studies to illustrate some of the concepts covered so far. In the first, we examine performance issues that might occur when connecting a field office to corporate headquarters. In the second, we examine performance problems that can crop up when packet latency becomes high.

Case Study 1: Two Networks Connected Using 128K ISDN

The network presented in Figure 15.2 is a classic example of a field office connection to corporate headquarters. This office is responsible for processing sales orders for its local region, and its network has been connected to corporate headquarters over an ISDN BRI WAN circuit. The network's main resource is a fileserver. It contains product information, customer lists, and other materials that the field office uses to sell the company's products to its clients. Most of the sales transactions can be performed locally; however, when processing a new sale, real-time inventory quantities must be queried from a server at corporate headquarters. Every hour, collected sales order information is uploaded to the corporate database. The field office network is modest and is organized as a single network subnet, which contains a dozen PCs, three network printers, and the fileserver. The network used to be a collection of different operating systems, including Windows 95, Windows NT, NetWare 4, and Mac OS 7. This changed when all systems, including the fileserver, were swapped out for Windows NT systems. The corporate headquarters network is large with dozens of subnets. It is mainly a TCP/IP network, but IPX is also in use due to some infrequently used Novell file-servers. In addition, the marketing department has a few Mac OS systems that are running AppleTalk.

The field office has been complaining for months about sporadic performance problems on its network. The workers are concerned with slow response time when checking inventory levels because it makes it difficult for them to respond appropriately to their customers. This problem is intermittent, but it is frequent enough to affect business. The company has asked you to determine what is causing the performance problem.

Given this information, what type of questions should you ask? You should focus your attention on several clues. The field office has a small bandwidth connection back to corporate headquarters. It would not take much unnecessary traffic to affect performance. What could some of the sources of unnecessary traffic be? Look for unnecessary protocols. In addition to TCP/IP, the corporate network is running IPX and AppleTalk. Because the field office used to have NetWare and Mac OS systems, it is possible that IPX and AppleTalk were once in use. It is reasonable to assume that the routers might be configured to pass this traffic. Now that the field office has standardized on Windows NT, these extraneous protocols are no longer needed.

Figure 15.2   Case Study 1 discusses the performance issues in low-bandwidth WAN connections.

Another potential source of traffic is the routing protocol. The example did not mention which was being used, but it is highly possible that the office is using RIP. Because corporate headquarters has a large number of networks, RIP routing announcement packets will be large. Should you have the field office switch to something more efficient, such as OSPF? In this case, that might be overkill. Because the field office router has only two possible places to send packets, it might be better to use a static route.

Why is the problem sporadic? Could it be the hourly transmission of sales information to corporate headquarters? If this information does not need to be available immediately, perhaps it would be better to hold off transmission of the sales information until after business hours.

The last issue you might look at is the size of the circuit. Perhaps the office has outgrown its current bandwidth. In this case, the best course of action would be to purchase additional circuits or to upgrade to a faster type of circuit.

Case Study 2: Satellite-Based Network

The network shown in Figure 15.3 collects weather data at several remote sites across the continental United States. Each collection site consists of a Solaris 2.5 workstation connected serially to a weather data collection unit, and a router connected to a satellite radio. The workstations send data on weather conditions whenever a change from the last transmitted value is detected. When conditions are stable, the rate of transmission is low. However, when conditions are variable, the data rate can be high. The equivalent of T1-sized circuits has been purchased to address this problem. However, even with the large satellite circuits, the scientist working on the project still experiences packet loss during rapidly changing weather conditions. You have been asked to determine what the problem is. Where do you begin?

Figure 15.3 Case study 2 discusses performance issues with large latency applications.

One of the major attributes of a satellite-based network circuit is that it has high latency. It takes a long time for a signal to travel the distance to geosync orbit (45,000 kilometers) and then return to Earth. Even when bandwidth is high, this added time could cause performance problems if the network protocol is not set up to handle the added delay. If TCP is the protocol being used to transmit the data, it is possible that the packet buffers are too small, or the maximum window size has been reached. Either or both of these issues could cause reduced performance.

To determine this, we must calculate the amount of data needed to fill our satellite pipe. Based on the given circuit speed bandwidth of 1.544Mbps and the roundtrip time of 1 second for a satellite circuit, our bandwidth $*$ delay product is 1544Kb, or close to 200KB. It turns out that Solaris 2.5's default packet buffer size is 256K. This is large enough to prevent delays; however, Solaris 2.5 is not RFC 1323 compliant. The maximum window size for non-RFC 1323 systems is 64K. This is more than likely the problem because it would prevent us from making maximum use of the bandwidth of our circuit. To address the problem, we would need to upgrade our Solaris system to a version that does support RFC 1323. Solaris systems from 2.6 on are RFC 1323 compliant.

Impact of Encryption

Encryption provides powerful security advantages when used appropriately. It is also one of the most computationally expensive protection measures available in our security toolkit. In this section, we will discuss cryptography from a performance standpoint, including the differences in ability and performance between public key and symmetric key cryptographic systems.

> **Note**
>
> If you would like to learn more about cryptographic services, see Appendix B, "Crypto 101." It provides a basic introduction to the subject and its terminology.

We will also discuss performance characteristics of network cryptographic protocols at the network layer, such as IPSec, and transport layer, such as SSL.

Cryptographic Services

As discussed in Chapter 8, "Virtual Private Networks," cryptography is often used to provide four important security services: confidentiality, integrity, authentication, and non-repudiation.

Each of these services uses particular cryptographic techniques, and each has varying impacts on the performance of your systems. Confidentiality and integrity services affect performance for as long as they are in use. Because of this, they are normally provided using symmetric key cryptography. Efficient symmetric key algorithms exist that allow high-performance systems to be built using relatively low-end equipment. Public key cryptography can also be used in theory to provide confidentiality and integrity services, but this is not common because public key cryptography requires significantly more work and time to encrypt and decrypt data than symmetric key cryptography.

Public key cryptography makes up for its performance problems by offering the ability to authenticate users and uniquely identify the creator of a message. Because authentication and non-repudiation are typically only performed once per session, the additional work needed for the public-key algorithm does not unduly affect the performance of the entire session. Protocol developers frequently combine the best aspects of both types of cryptography when designing their protocols. It is common for public key techniques to be used to authenticate users and then exchange session details, including a shared secret. This shared secret is then used to generate a key used to encrypt the rest of the conversation using symmetric key cryptography. In this way, the strengths of both techniques are maximized while their weaknesses are minimized.

Understanding Encryption at the Network and Transport Layers

Cryptographic services can be added to almost any layer of the network stack. The decision of which layer to implement your cryptographic services on is dependent on the specific security goal you are trying to accomplish. In the following section, we will discuss cryptography at the network and the transport layers.

Network Layer Cryptography

Network layer cryptography allows private conversations to occur across untrusted networks. They can be organized as network-to-network, network-to-host, or host-to-host links. The major cryptographic service offered is confidentiality. Performance impacts are driven primarily by the increased CPU utilization of the sending and receiving devices. This impact grows with traffic volume; high bandwidth circuits use more CPU cycles than low bandwidth circuits.

Assuming sufficient network bandwidth, performance of a VPN is mainly determined by the choice of algorithm and the hardware platform. A variety of popular algorithms are in common use, including Digital Encryption Standard (DES), Triple DES (3DES), Advanced Encryption Standard (AES), and Twofish. However, the choices available to you will frequently be limited by your choice of VPN device. Most VPN providers offer a limited selection of algorithms. For instance, VPNs that are implemented using Cisco routers are limited to DES or 3DES, whereas Check Point FireWall-1 offers DES, 3DES, RC4, CAST-40, and its own proprietary algorithm FWZ-1. In general, algorithms that use larger keys are more secure, but they also perform significantly worse. Table 15.2 shows some common algorithms and the key sizes that they support.

Table 15.2 **Symmetric Key Algorithm Key Sizes**

Algorithm	Key Size
RC4	40 bits
FWZ-1 4	8 bits
DES 4	0 or 56 bits
3DES	112 bits

Algorithm	Key Size
Twofish	128 bits
AES	Variable in 32 bit increments; typically 128, 192, or 256 bits

Even though algorithms with key sizes of 56 bits or lower, such as DES, have been decrypted using brute force methods, you should not immediately discard their use. If immediate discovery of the contents of your messages is your primary concern, a 56-bit key algorithm might be more than enough to provide the necessary security while allowing you to use much higher performing encryption algorithms.

The speed of the hardware platform is the other major determinant of VPN performance. Encryption is a CPU-intensive operation. Because of this, platforms with faster processors perform better. Some hardware vendors also support hardware cryptographic accelerators. These are co-processors that are optimized to perform cryptographic operations.

Tip

Be wary of manufacturer performance claims. Performance claims are often highly optimistic. If possible, test the performance of a device in your environment prior to committing to it.

When implementing a VPN in your environment, it is tempting to use pre-existing equipment to implement the VPN service. Most firewalls and routers offer this ability either as a standard feature or a low-cost option. The major performance impact of Network layer encryption is CPU utilization on the encrypting and decrypting devices. You should be careful when adding a VPN to an existing router or firewall. If the CPU utilization is already high, then adding the VPN might cripple the device's ability to perform its other duties.

Tip

If CPU utilization is too high but a hardware upgrade is not possible, consider reducing the amount of network traffic that is being encrypted. Most VPN devices allow you to set filters that specify a subset of the network traffic to encrypt. Using this feature can dramatically reduce CPU load.

Secure Socket Layer

Chapter 4 describes Secure Socket Layer (SSL) in detail, so it's not necessary to explain how SSL sessions are established here. However, it *is* important to discuss some of the performance characteristics of SSL. As was mentioned earlier, SSL is composed of two different protocols: the record protocol and the handshake protocol. The record protocol carries the traffic of the SSL connection and can support several encryption protocols, including RC4, DES, 3DES, and Fortezza. The encryption protocol that is used is determined during session negotiation, which is conducted using the handshake protocol. The handshake protocol authenticates the server to the client, optionally authenticates the client to the server, and negotiates session details, including the exchange of a master secret that will be used to generate the symmetric keys used by the record protocol.

The SSL performance cost is a combination of the one-time session setup costs performed by the handshake protocol, followed by the continuous cost of the record protocol as it encrypts the session traffic using the chosen encryption protocol. Of the two, the record protocol would seem to be the more dominate of the two because its performance impact lasts for the entire session, whereas the handshake protocol's impact is limited to once per session. This turns out not to be true. There are two main reasons for this. First, web sessions tend to be short, with an average data transfer of approximately 4000 bytes. This limits the amount of time over which the handshake costs can be amortized. Second, the SSL handshake, at least from the point of view of the server, turns out to be an expensive operation.

We went over the steps for establishing an SSL session in Chapter 4, but let us quickly review them while looking at performance implications of the handshake protocol. During the SSL handshake, both the client and the server are asked to perform public key cryptographic operations. However, the server performs the majority of the work. During the handshake, the client receives the server's certificate, which it uses to extract the server's public key. It uses this key to encrypt a secret, which the server eventually uses to generate the shared secret upon which the record protocol relies. Before the server can make use of this secret, it must decrypt it. This decryption operation requires roughly two to three times more work than the encryption operation. During a typical SSL web transaction, the server might have to perform 100 times more work to negotiate the session than it would use to encrypt the data to be transferred.

The designers of SSL were aware of this problem. To help alleviate it, they included an ability to cache session details so that subsequent SSL sessions could resume the previous session without performing any of the public key operations. During the initial communication between client and server, the client can present a session ID that it received during the previous handshake. If the session details are still in the cache, the session can be resumed.

Performance improvements as cache hits increase are impressive. Netscape reports the ability to handle 2.5 times more operations per second when session reuse is at 100%.[1]

Tip

If SSL performance is low, try increasing the size of the session cache and the length of the session timeout. This increases the chances of cache hits.

If performance is still too low, try limiting the sections of the web site that require SSL protection. Most e-commerce sites do not switch to SSL protection until a financial transaction is about to occur. This limits the amount of SSL sessions that the site must accommodate.

Using Hardware Accelerators to Improve Performance

Another method you can use to boost performance is to offload the CPU workload to a coprocessor that is specifically designed to perform cryptographic operations. This provides two performance benefits. First, it significantly reduces the load on the main CPU. Because the main CPU does not have to perform the cryptographic operation, its time can be spent performing its normal activities. Second, because hardware accelerators are designed specifically to perform the mathematical operations that cryptography requires, they can perform cryptographic operations more efficiently than general-purpose computers.

Hardware accelerators are available for a wide variety of platforms, including Cisco PIX firewalls, HP-UX servers, Sun Solaris servers, Windows NT and 2000 servers, and Linux Servers, and a variety of protocols, including SSL and IPSec. When considering the purchase of one of these devices, keep the following details in mind:

- Support for the appropriate protocol (IPSec, SSL).
- Support for your hardware platform.
- Performance when executing session encryption.
- Performance when negotiating a session. This is especially important for SSL accelerators.
- Cost.

Accelerator Cards and Performance Bottlenecks

Be careful that you understand what an accelerator accelerates before you purchase one. In a site where I worked, a CryptoSwift eCommerce Accelerator card was added to an under-performing secure web server. It made a noticeable improvement in the use of the secure web site. The page had many hits from many different users, obviously generating a new session negotiation for every visitor. When the same card was added to another secure web site, the performance didn't improve. In this case, only 5–6 users were on the web site at a time, causing few key negotiations. The performance issue in this case turned out to be problems in the backend database.

Whether you should consider a hardware accelerator depends on your performance goals and the availability of a product that supports your environment and your budget. The price of hardware accelerators can be high. If your current hardware can support the workload, then hardware acceleration is wasted money.

Case Studies

These two case studies illustrate some of the cryptographic performance concepts we have covered so far. The first case study examines link encryption performance between two networks. The second case study looks at performance of web servers when encrypting http sessions.

Case Study 3: Link Encrypting Between Two Routers

A large organization (ALO) has purchased a 768kbps frame-relay connection between its main headquarters and one of its business partner's field offices (BFO). A Cisco router, as shown in Figure 15.4, terminates each side of the connection. The ALO side has a Cisco 3640 router, and the BFO side has a Cisco 2611 router. Because the ALO is not in control of the security policy of the BFO network, it has placed a firewall between its network and its Cisco 3640 router. Rules have been established on the firewall to prevent unauthorized network traffic from entering the ALO network. In addition, due to the sensitivity of the information that needs to be sent between the two networks, an IPSec encrypted tunnel has been set up between the two edge routers. Cisco's documentation shows that the 2611 router would not be able to provide sufficient performance when using the 3DES algorithm. DES performance, however, looks acceptable. Because of this, a business decision has been made to use the less secure but faster 56-bit DES algorithm. Performance between the two networks is acceptable, but it is slower than expected given the relatively large bandwidth connection that was purchased. The ALO management has asked you to look into the problem.

Figure 15.4 Case study 3 examines the link encryption performance issues.

In this case, the problem is more than likely the performance hit from the encrypted tunnel. Running a tool such as ttcp between the two sites can verify actual available bandwidth.

Tip

Never run ttcp during normal production hours. To measure the bandwidth, ttcp has to consume it all. Not only would running ttcp during business hours cause its results to be wrong, but it would also bring the network to its knees while it was running.

In this case, ttcp reports performance in the 260kbps range. This is far below the bandwidth of the WAN link, so we need to look further into our configuration to determine the problem. An examination of the CPU utilization of both routers taken during the ttcp test will reveal the problem. The Cisco 3640 will more than likely be reporting CPU utilization rates at or below 50%. This will not be the case of the Cisco 2611. This router has a much slower CPU and will likely be reporting utilization rates above 85%. At this level, packet forwarding performance is affected, increasing latency and potentially causing packets to be dropped. With encryption, the weakest link sets the overall performance—in this case, the Cisco 2611.

Now that we have identified the likely cause of the problem, what can we do about it? Because performance is acceptable, the easiest answer might simply be to ignore it. This is somewhat unsatisfactory though, because the ALO is paying for WAN bandwidth of which it is not able to take advantage. Reducing the bandwidth of the circuit—if it substantially reduced the price—might be a compensation for this, but be careful not to reduce the bandwidth too low or it will become the bottleneck. Another solution might be to reduce the key size of the encryption protocol. Forty-bit DES might reduce the load sufficiently to allow full performance to be achieved, although this would come at the expense of a substantial weakening of the confidentiality of the connection. An alternative solution might be to look at another tunneling protocol. Cisco routers support a proprietary tunneling protocol called Cisco Encryption Technology (CET). CET performs better than IPSec, so when your VPN consists entirely of Cisco products, CET might be a viable option. Your last option is to upgrade the hardware. If you have the budget, you could solve the problem by upgrading the Cisco 2611 router or adding a crypto accelerator card to it.

Case Study 4: SSL Web Server

A company maintains a server that has a web site that it uses to provide private company information to its large traveling sales force. After a recent embarrassing defacement of their public web site, they became much more security conscious and have configured an SSL version of the web site on the server. Client certificates have been installed on all of the sales force laptops, and the web site has been configured to require client-side SSL authentication. Almost as soon as the SSL web site went online, the complaints started to come in. The sales force stated that the web site was almost unreachable, and when it did respond, it took forever for a page to download. You have been asked to help eliminate the performance problems while still maintaining the security of the site.

By reusing the existing server, it is likely that the company did not consider the additional load that the SSL protocol would add to the server. CPU performance is more than likely the cause of the problem, and CPU utilization measurements bear this out. To reduce the load, you might look at SSL session reuse. If the session timeout values or session cache sizes are too low, the server performs unnecessary full SSL handshakes. Increasing these values might reduce the magnitude of the problem. If performance is still too slow, a hardware upgrade might be appropriate. Assuming that the budget is available, a faster computer or an SSL accelerator could be used to decrease the performance hit that SSL is causing. If this is not possible, the only remaining option is to limit the required number of SSL sessions. If some data on the site were less sensitive than other data, then removing it from the SSL side of the web server would reduce the work that the server needed to perform.

Using Load Balancing to Improve Performance

Sometimes the amount of work that must be performed exceeds the capabilities of any single device that is available to us. In this case, the only way to increase performance is to divide the work between multiple devices. By dividing the work in such a way that many devices can work on it, you create a much more scalable and potentially reliable solution. These benefits come at the expense of added complexity and cost. When deciding to use load balancing, you will have to weigh the need for performance against the added costs in equipment, staff, and time needed to build and maintain the system.

Load balancers use various methods to direct requests to a pool of mirrored servers. One of the simplest methods to distribute the workload is DNS round robin. This system works by having the DNS server provide the IP address of a different server from the pool every time a DNS request is made. Although simple, this solution does not work well for high-performance systems. This is due to many factors, but the largest is the problem of client networks caching the results of the first DNS query for the server. This causes all clients on a network to send their requests to a single server in the pool. If the number of users on the network is large, this can completely undermine DNS round-robin's ability to balance the traffic.

More sophisticated solutions such as F5's Big IP controller and Cisco's Local Director rely upon a dispatch controller to distribute the requests to the pool as they arrive. These products perform two important functions. First, when a dispatcher receives a packet that is the start of a new network conversation, it must deliver the packet to a server in the pool that has the capacity to handle the new request. Second, when a packet arrives at the dispatcher that is part of an ongoing conversation, the dispatcher must have the intelligence to deliver the packet to the server that has been previously assigned to handle the request. The sophistication used to make the first decision is the major difference between the various products on the market.

Load balancing can also be used to increase availability. If one of the devices in the group breaks down, the other systems can take up the load and continue operation. If you are going to rely on this to maintain availability, keep in mind the loss of performance that your solution will experience when it loses a system. You will need to make sure that a minimum number of systems is always available, even if one of the systems fails. Also, if you are truly concerned about redundancy, don't forget to have a redundant load balancer. Without one, a load balancer failure will bring down the entire system.

Problems with Load Balancing

Load balancing does not improve all situations. Certain types of problems are difficult to divide among various servers. If a problem cannot be divided or if the work necessary to divide it would exceed the performance gained from distributing it, then load balancing will not help. Another problem with load balancing occurs if the hand-off of a request from one server to another requires the second server to perform expensive setup operations. SSL is a classic example of this. As we discussed earlier, SSL handshakes are so expensive that the SSL servers cache session details so that new sessions do not have to go through the entire handshake. When using some load balancing systems, it's not guaranteed that a returning client will be redirected back to the server that handled the previous request. This might actually result in performance lower than before the load balancing solution because almost every request will be forced to make a full SSL handshake. More sophisticated load balancing devices (such as the Alteon Content Director) include the ability to redirect SSL session requests back to the original server. This is accomplished by tracking the session ID in the header of the packet and sending successive packets from a client (with the same session ID) to the same back end server.

Layer 4 Dispatchers

Two major types of dispatcher products are on the market: Layer 4 dispatchers, such as the previously mentioned F5 Big IP Controller, and Layer 7 dispatchers, such as Radware's Server Director Pro. The layer numbers are taken from the Open System Interconnection (OSI) reference model.

Layer 4 dispatchers make delivery decisions based on information that is contained within the Layer 4 (Transport) header and Layer 3 (Network) header of the TCP/IP packet. This information includes the source and destination IP addresses, source and destination protocol addresses (ports), and other session information such as whether the packet is the start of a session or a continuation. Because the different pieces of information in the header of the packets are always in the same locations within the packet, Layer 4 dispatchers do not have to perform much work to locate the information on which they will make their delivery decision. This enables fast decisions and fast switching.

When a packet arrives at a Layer 4 dispatcher, the dispatcher determines whether the packet is the start of a new session or the continuation of a previously started session. If it is a new session, the dispatcher chooses a server to handle the new connection and forwards the packet to it. The way this decision is made varies depending on the load sharing algorithms that the dispatcher supports. Common algorithms include round-robin, weighted round-robin, least connections, least load, and fastest response. If the packet is a continuation of a session, then the dispatcher looks up the connection details and forwards the packet on to the server that is handling the session.

Layer 7 Dispatchers

Layer 7 dispatchers look above the Transport layer into the Application data (OSI Layer 7) to make their delivery decisions. This allows them to make more intelligent decisions when delivering packets. One major advantage with Layer 7 dispatching of web servers is that different web servers in the pool can serve different types of content. Layer 4 dispatchers are unable to make decisions based on content. This means that when using a Layer 4 dispatcher, all servers in the pool must have identical content. This is not a major issue if your site is fairly static. However, it *is* a major issue if your site content is changed dynamically. Keeping all of your servers up to date can be a major undertaking requiring significant network, storage, and computational resources. Having a shared file system eliminates the synchronization problems, but it introduces significant load on the servers. The servers must fetch a copy of the requested information from the common file server before the page can be returned to the client.

Content-based (Layer 7) dispatching provides an alternative to full replication or common file systems by making use of information that is contained within the http request to route the packet. The dispatcher can look inside the web request to determine what URL has been requested and then use that information to chose the appropriate server.

The cost of this ability is a significant increase in the complexity and required resources for each delivery decision. Because the application data is pretty freeform and not structured into the rigid fields typified by the packet header, a substantially more expensive search must be conducted within the application data to locate the information from which the delivery decision will be made. Because of this, high-performance Layer 7 dispatchers tend to be more expensive than similarly performing Layer 4 solutions.

Summary

This chapter highlighted some of the more important issues involved in performance tuning your perimeter security. Performance and security often seem at odds with each other, but careful design can help minimize the impact that security has on performance. Remember that almost any security feature you want to implement will come with varying levels of performance impacts. You should be especially careful when implementing encryption in your design. Cryptographic techniques offer tremendous security advantages, but they are expensive from a performance standpoint. Try to identify as early as possible the performance requirements of your network, prior to building or revising your network structure. Performing this initial analysis will help you choose appropriate security measures that permit the security policy to be enforced while still allowing the network users sufficient performance to carry out their work efficiently. Security and performance must be in balance for the ultimate objectives of the network to be met.

References

1   Netscape Corporation. Performance Tuning, Scaling, and Sizing Guide, Netscape Enterprise Server. `http://enterprise.netscape.com/docs/enterprise/60/perf/perf60.pdf`, page 80.

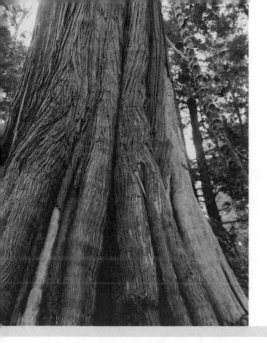

16
Sample Designs

Let's put together all the security design information we have presented to you in Part III, "Perimeter Design." Each chapter has presented a substantial amount of material that you must incorporate into your designs to ensure that they reflect the needs of your organization. As we have discussed, designing a defense perimeter requires you to achieve a balance between conflicting factors, such as security, performance, and usability. For example, deciding to use inline firewalls might have provided the best protection for your network, but the performance impact caused when information must flow through both devices might have been too great. In other instances, it might have been difficult to determine when to follow a particular piece of design advice. To help integrate all this material, this chapter provides case studies to illustrate how network designs vary depending on the unique needs of the organization. The case studies were chosen to highlight several distinct design situations:

- A telecommuter who is using a broadband connection to access the corporate network via the Internet
- A business that has only a basic Internet presence
- A small e-commerce site that has a corporate network as well as several systems accessible from the Internet

As an example of a more complex architecture, we also discuss a multizone design that was presented by a candidate for a GIAC Certified Firewall Analyst (GCFW) certification. This design was submitted as part of a GCFW practical assignment that received an honors status. We begin with a review of core design criteria for a network security perimeter.

Review of Security Design Criteria

Before we start our discussion of the case studies, let's review what we have covered so far in the design section of this book. In Chapter 11, "Design Fundamentals," we described the factors that must be considered when designing your network's perimeter. Put simply, this means that you must incorporate the answers for each of the following three questions in every design you create:

- What needs to be protected?
- What are the threats?
- What are the business requirements?

Before embarking upon the design of the perimeter, you must establish what it is that you are protecting. At one level, this will be the servers, workstations, databases, and other network devices that are located on the network. At a deeper level, though, it is the information contained on the network along with the services that the network must offer. To begin your design, you must determine what will compose your network. If you are starting from scratch, this is relatively easy, but when adding security to an existing network, the discovery process can be difficult. This is especially true when the network is large and not well documented.

Where Does This Wire Go?

During an assignment to add a private WAN link between two government organizations, I discovered an unlabeled T-1 line in one of the network closets that was connected directly to the first organization's backbone network. No one in the organization seemed to know what is was being used for. The management of this organization was concerned with security and had spent a small fortune on the installation of firewalls and other perimeter security devices, so I was a bit surprised that they allowed this line to exist. When I asked the IT group why they allowed the connection, they told me that it had been installed before any of them had joined the organization; and they were afraid that if they disconnected it, someone might complain. For the record, they did eventually unplug the line, and no one ever complained.

Next, you need to determine what threats you are worried about. All networks attached to the Internet need to worry about the random attacks that script kiddies perform, but other organizations need to consider more directed attacks. If your organization is famous in any way (or has a name that is close to someone who is) or has information that would be useful to an attacker (such as credit card data), you will almost certainly come under attack from determined outsiders. These attackers will spend significant time analyzing the security of your network. Protecting against these attackers requires significantly more effort than preventing access by amateurs. Even more difficult to protect against, though, is the determined insider. Preventing individuals who have been already granted some access to your network from gaining more can be extremely difficult and requires you to consider significantly more internal security controls than you would need to defend against purely external attack.

When designing the security perimeter, you must also determine what the business requirements for the network are. As we have emphasized throughout the book, network security is a means to an end, not an end to itself. It is important that the business reasons and business constraints are taken into account as you design your security architecture. To begin with, you need to know what services need to be provided to your users and customers. You also need to determine how reliable and accessible these services need to be. A network that provides a basic web site describing a company's services might not need to be as reliable and fast as a network that hosts an e-commerce site that processes all the sales requests for a large company.

You must also consider the amount of resources in terms of money and time that should reasonably be spent to secure the network. We would like every network we build to have every security control that we can think of, but we must always be cognizant that the purpose of the network is to support the business. A network design that is unaffordable but securely designed will never be implemented.

As we go through the case studies that follow, try to keep in mind these three basic design criteria. To focus your attention, ask yourself the following questions as you review each design:

- Does the design sufficiently protect the major resources of the network?
- Does the design place the emphasis on protecting the right resources?
- Does the design sufficiently account for the likely ways that it might be attacked?
- Does the design support the business goals, or are the security controls likely to impact business operations negatively?

Case Studies

Presented next are four security designs to address four different business situations. Each was chosen to illustrate the need to vary your designs based on the specific business needs of an organization.

Case Study 1: Telecommuter Who Is Using a Broadband Connection

The situation presented in Figure 16.1 shows an increasingly common way for users to access private corporate network resources. The user has subscribed to a cable company's broadband Internet service and is using this connection to work from home. These types of connections are becoming increasingly popular and represent a significantly different security problem than the slow dial-up connections they are replacing.

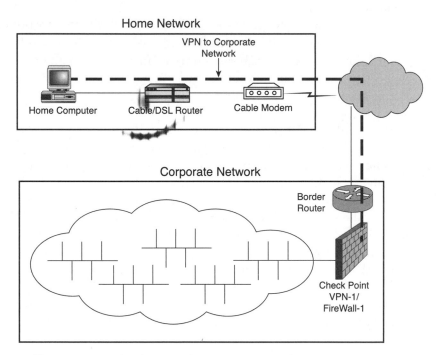

Figure 16.1   In this design, a telecommuting user relies on a Virtual Private Network (VPN) to tunnel across the Internet to reach the corporate network.

Previously, home computer users had limited exposure to Internet attacks because they were only accessible while they were dialed-in to the Internet. A potential attacker would need to time his attack to coincide with the time that the user was using the Internet. This is not true with broadband services, such as cable and DSL. These types of connections, much like typical office Internet connections, are always on, making it much easier for the attacker to access the home computer.

Because of this problem combined with the low security awareness of the typical home computer user, broadband-connected home computers have become a frequent target of computer attackers, which has resulted in many home user systems becoming compromised. These systems have then been used to commit other acts of cyberattack, including participating in denial of service (DoS) attacks.

The problem of home computer security has become important to companies as they begin to allow their employees to access private network resources from home. If home computers become compromised, the attacker can use them to circumvent the network's perimeter security.

The user's company—in this case, Stuffy—is concerned about these security problems but wants to allow the employee the flexibility of working from home on a high-speed connection. The company has asked us to create a secure home network design for the user.

The following is the design criteria the company provided to us:

- The user's home computer is the primary resource that must be protected.

- The company is specifically worried about the outsider threat. It recognizes that by allowing the home user to log in remotely, it is extending its security perimeter to include the home user's computer system. If the user's computer becomes compromised, it could be used to access the corporate network.

- From a business need perspective, this company views this service as a nice-to-have but not a business essential. High redundancy is not needed, and the solution must be reasonably inexpensive.

The company is also specifically worried about the following issues:

- The always-on connection subjects the home computer to direct network attack.

- Malicious code could be introduced onto the home computer through the receipt of an email attachment or the downloading of software that contains malicious code.

- The user's browser might contain vulnerabilities that are exploitable if the user visits a malicious web site.

- The user's connection to the corporate network might be monitored or altered as it travels across the Internet.

To address these concerns, this design uses several perimeter security techniques to secure the home network. To start, a cable modem/DSL router has been placed between the home computer and the cable modem. These devices have become popular because they allow multiple home computers to share a broadband account, but most also include basic firewall functionality. For this case study, a SpeedStream 2614 4-Port DSL/Cable Router has been chosen.

Because this home network is only used to access the Internet and does not host public network services, no externally initiated connections are needed. This enables us to use the default configuration of the cable/DSL router, which only allows connections that are initiated from the internal network to proceed. This defense measure prevents a broad range of attacks from proceeding.

In addition to the cable/DSL router, the design also calls for the personal firewall product Tiny Personal Firewall to be installed on the user's home computer (`www.tinysoftware.com`). This product is free for personal use. Tiny Firewall enables you to specify which applications are allowed to send and receive information over the network. For instance, we can tell Tiny Firewall to only allow connections that are destined to hosts on port 80 from Internet Explorer or Netscape Communicator.

To enable the home user to securely access private corporate resources, the Check Point SecuRemote client is installed on the user's home computer and is configured to establish a 3DES IPSec VPN connection to the corporate firewall whenever a packet needs to be sent to the corporate network. Basic username/password authentication is used whenever the VPN is established. The SecuRemote client supports stronger, certificate-based authentication but requires a public key infrastructure (PKI).

The last element of this security architecture is the installation of the Symantec Norton AntiVirus product on the home computer. With the cable/DSL router and personal firewall products preventing most forms of direct attack, the next most likely way of gaining access to the home computer is the introduction of some form of malicious code. If the user downloads a program from the Internet that contains a Trojan horse or receives an email with a virus attached, the computer can still become compromised. To help prevent this, the Norton AntiVirus tool has been configured to scan each downloaded file and each received email message for known malicious code patterns. Because these types of products are only as good as the content of their malicious code signature database, the anti-virus tool has also been configured to check the Symantec web site for new malicious code signatures on a daily basis.

As you can see from this description, even with small networks, you still need to consider all the design criteria when building the security perimeter. Understanding what you need to protect, how it might be attacked, and how much effort you should spend to secure it are fundamental issues that affect every design you create. In this network, what we needed to protect was narrow and consisted of a single workstation. We were specifically concerned with direct attack from the Internet plus the indirect attack from malicious code. Because our budget was small, we had to limit ourselves to inexpensive measures. Given these constraints, we were still able to come up with a design that should be highly effective at protecting the user's home computer while allowing secure access to the corporate network.

Case Study 2: A Small Business That Has a Basic Internet Presence

In this case study, a small sales company wants to set up an Internet connection but does not intend to sell products directly over the Internet. The owner of the business has read several horror stories about companies being taken over by attackers and has specifically asked for as secure a design as possible, but he does not have a large budget. Following are the specific design requirements and business needs that the company has established:

- The workstations and Windows NT servers are the primary resources that must be protected. The company needs to establish an information web site for its customers, but the site is not considered essential to the businesses operations.

- The company does not know of any individuals or organizations that would specifically want to do them harm, but it does store customer information, including credit card data, on Windows NT servers.

- Employees must be able to send and receive email.

- Employees must be able to browse their suppliers' web sites.

- The company web site is not expected to get a large volume of traffic.

- The design must be secure, but the budget for security devices and software must be kept as low as possible.

- The external connection that has been arranged with the ISP is a burstable T1 line provisioned for a continuous usage of 256Kbps.

Note

Burstable T1 lines allow the full 1.544Mbps of the T1 line to be used some of the time, but the ISP only guarantees the continuous bandwidth level that has been agreed upon.

The resulting design is shown in Figure 16.2. The IT resources of the company are limited to a dozen PCs running Windows 2000, two Windows 2000 servers acting as primary and backup domain controllers, and a network printer. The following features have been added to the network to meet the design requirements.

Figure 16.2 In this design, a small business outsources the hosting of Internet-accessible services to a third party.

- A Nokia IP330 device has been added to act as both the border router and the external firewall.
- A web cache proxy, located in a screened subnet, is being used to control and protect the users' web sessions.
- A network intrusion detection system (IDS) is monitoring the local network.
- The web site and email services have been outsourced to a web hosting company.

The first line of defense for the network is the Nokia IP330, which runs a version of the Check Point FireWall-1 security software. We have installed a T-1 card in the Nokia to allow it to act as both the border router and the external firewall. Of course, if the Nokia were to become compromised, the entire network would be exposed to the Internet. This is a design compromise that has been made to reduce cost; the money that would have been spent on the router can now be spent on a more sophisticated firewall. Other security measures, such as the IDS, will be counted on to provide the defense in depth that is necessary to back up the Nokia. The rulebase for the Nokia is shown in Table 16.1.

Table 16.1 **Rulebase for Nokia IP-330**

Source	Destination	Service	Action
Workstations	Web cache server	HTTP, HTTPS, FTP in service	Allow
Web cache server	Internet	HTTP, HTTPS, FTP, DNS	Allow
Firewall	All	All	Deny, Log
All	Firewall	All	Deny, Log
Local network, web cache server	All	Ping	Allow
Any	Any	Any	Deny, Log

This rulebase has three main features. First, there are no rules with the Internet as a source, which prevents external attackers from initiating a connection to the company's internal computers. Second, all web and FTP connections from the LAN must be proxied through the web cache server before they can reach the Internet, which allows us to configure the web cache server to restrict which web sites the employees can visit and provides the additional security benefit of terminating the external web site connection at the web cache server instead of a workstation's browser, thereby preventing some malicious web site attacks. Last, the rulebase makes no allowance for remote management or monitoring for any of the security devices. This network is sufficiently small, so a decision has been made to administer and monitor each system from its respective console.

The next device that needs to be discussed is the web cache server. To keep the cost down, this server has been implemented entirely from open-source products. A PC that is running a hardened version of Red Hat Linux server hosts the open-source Squid Web Cache Proxy software (www.squid-cache.org). This process is the only one running on the server that is listening to network ports.

Squid supports proxying of HTTP, HTTPS, and FTP connections and can limit by IP address the computers that are able to make use of its services. In this case, the proxy has been configured to allow hosts in the IP range of the workstations to connect to it. Squid also can limit which web and FTP sites users can visit. Currently, this company's users are allowed to surf to any site, but it has reserved the right to block access to any sites that it deems inappropriate or unsafe. In addition to the workstations, the IDS has been allowed to use the web cache server, but Squid has been configured to allow it to connect to only the Snort web site (www.snort.org) and the company's web site.

The last specific security device to talk about is the IDS. Like the web cache server, the IDS is implemented using only open-source software. Red Hat Linux is again used as the operating system to host the Snort IDS software. Snort is a highly capable IDS, especially when its signature database is kept up to date. Luckily, the Snort community is active, and it continually updates the Snort signatures. It is not uncommon for a new Snort signature to be available for a new attack before any of the commercial providers has been able to update its signature databases. The reason the web cache has been configured to allow the IDS to connect to the Snort web site is to allow the latest Snort signatures to be conveniently downloaded.

You might notice that no web, mail, or DNS servers are on the network. All these services have been outsourced to NTT/Verio, a web-hosting company. For a small monthly fee, NTT/Verio provides space on one of its web servers to host the company's web site. Administration of the web site is performed using Microsoft FrontPage. In addition to the web site, NTT/Verio provides WebMail, a web-based email system, which allows employees to send and receive email using their web browsers. By outsourcing these services, the design eliminates the need to handle externally originated connections, reducing the risk of network compromise substantially. However, it does require that the company trust NTT/Verio to secure the web and email services. To provide one additional level of protection, a small shell script has been placed on the IDS sensor that checks whether the home page of the web site has been modified. If it has, the shell script generates an alert, providing a limited amount of protection should the NTT/Verio-maintained web site become corrupted.

This case study shows some of the compromises you might have to make due to the business needs of the organization. Not every site requires three layers of firewalls with a full-time security administrator. In this case, it made more sense to outsource the harder elements to secure. It is unlikely that this company would dedicate the effort to properly administer the security of its public services. Outsourcing these services to a firm that provides them full-time was a more secure solution. Always remember that each design must be attentive to the needs of the situation.

Case Study 3: A Small E-Commerce Site

In this case study, a small organization has decided that it could dramatically boost sales by accepting orders over the Internet. At the same time, it is concerned with some of the news reports about cybercrime and the possibility that private customer data might be stolen, opening up the potential for law suits. The company asked us to create a design that allows it to sell products over the Internet while protecting customer data. It has provided a reasonable but not overly large budget for the design. These are the design guidelines that the company has established for the assignment:

- The primary resource that must be protected is customer data, but the design must provide reasonable protection for the other devices on the network, such as user workstations.

- It is important that the site be available to customers, but a highly redundant design has been rejected as too expensive.

- The company is specifically concerned with attack from determined outsiders.

- The company expects only a moderate number of visitors and estimates approximately 1,000 visitors per day with fewer than 5 percent of these visitors actually ordering anything.

- The company wants to maintain control of all equipment and rejected the idea of outsourcing any part of its network.

- Employees need to be able to send and receive email.

- Employees need to be able to access external web sites.

The resulting design is shown in Figure 16.3 and shows a fairly classic network security design, although certain security design features are not visible from the diagram.

Figure 16.3 In this design, a small e-commerce site uses
several defensive measures to protect customer data.

Here is a quick description of the major features of the design:

- A border router connects the network to the Internet and provides some basic filtering.

- Just behind the router, a proxy firewall enforces the majority of the access control for the network.

- Public services and private services have been separated by putting them on different network segments that are separated by the firewall. The firewall also maintains a special segment for management systems.

- The web server holds only transaction data for a short period of time. Periodically, the order server removes all current transactions from the web server for processing.

- Inbound email is cached on the email relay server until the Internal email server retrieves it.

- Split DNS is being used. The public DNS server provides name resolution for public services only. The private DNS server contains records for all systems, but external users cannot access it.

- Intrusion detection sensors are located on the public, private, and management network segments to watch for unusual activity.

- The workstations that are located on the Internal network can connect to the proxy firewall to gain access to external web and FTP servers. No other internal systems are allowed to connect to the outside.

- All security log entries are sent to the log server, which generates alerts when suspicious activity is detected.

- All configuration of security devices is performed from the management console.

Traffic that is entering the network must first pass through the border router; therefore, it is the first device that we can use to enforce access control for our network. A thorough discussion of how to securely configure routers is included in Chapter 6, "Role of a Router," so we will not go into depth about how this router should be configured. However, it is worth mentioning that ingress filters have been installed on the router to block packets that have illegal addresses. In addition to the ingress filter, an egress filter has been put in place to block outbound packets if they do not have a valid source IP address. The purpose of this egress filter is to make it harder for the site to be used to attack other sites should one of our servers be compromised.

The primary security device for this network is the Symantec VelociRaptor 500 firewall appliance. This device is based on Symantec's enterprise firewall software and runs on a specially hardened version of Linux. The VelociRaptor comes with four Fast Ethernet interfaces, which we have used to create four security zones for this network:

- The Internet zone connects the network to the Internet and is completely untrusted.

- The Public Services network holds all servers that must provide service to users from the Internet.

- The Internal network holds private servers and workstations that external users do not need to directly access.

- The Management network holds the log server and the management console.

The rulebase on the firewall controls what traffic can flow between each of these zones. Table 16.2 shows the rules we are using to secure the network.

Table 16.2 **VelociRaptor Rulebase**

Incoming Zone	Outgoing Zone	Source	Destination	Service	Action
Internet	Public	Any	Web Server	HTTP, HTTPS	Allow
Internet	Public	Any	Mail Relay	SMTP	Allow
Internet	Public	Any	DNS Server	DNS	Allow
Internal	Public	Order Server	Web Server	SSH	Allow
Internal	Public	Int. Mail Server	Mail Relay	SSH	Allow
Internal	Internet	Int. Mail Server	Any	SMTP	Allow
Internal	Internet	Int. DNS Server	Any	DNS	Allow
Internal	Internet	Workstations	Any	HTTP, HTTPS, FTP	Allow
ALL	Management	All Devices Group	Log Server	Syslog	Allow
Management	Any	Management Console	Security Devices Group	SSH, SRMC	Allow, Log
Management	Internet	Management Console	snort.org	HTTP, HTTPS	Allow
Any	Any	Any	Any	Any	Deny, Log

A lot is going on in this rulebase, so let's go over it step by step. The first three rules are designed to allow the public to access the public servers. The fourth rule allows the order server to retrieve customer transactions from the web site. The company has built a custom e-commerce application that takes the following steps to protect customer information. When the web server accepts a customer transaction, it writes the details of the transaction to a file, which it then places in a special directory. This directory is only accessible to two accounts on the web server: the account that the web software is running as, and an account created for the order server. The web server is running a Secure Shell (SSH) daemon to allow the order server to periodically log in and retrieve the customer transaction files. In this way, the customer details are swept off the more exposed web server to the order server where they can be better protected. Using this arrangement, even if an attacker did gain control of the web server, he would only be able to capture a few customer transactions.

The fifth rule on the firewall allows the internal email server to retrieve inbound mail messages from the mail relay server. Normally, a mail relay server would use Simple Mail Transfer Protocol (SMTP) to transfer inbound messages to an internal mail server, but a security decision was made not to allow traffic to originate from the Public Services to the Internal network, which should block an attacker from accessing the Internal network even if she manages to compromise one of the public servers. Still, we need to allow the network's users to receive mail. To accomplish this, the internal email server periodically retrieves queued messages from the mail relay using the same method that the order server uses to retrieve information from the web server. It logs onto the mail relay using the SSH protocol and downloads the queued messages.

To allow outbound email, the sixth rule allows the internal mail server to send SMTP information to the Internet. In some situations, this might open up the internal mail server to attack from a malicious mail server. However, in this case, the risk is minimized due to our choice of firewall. The VelociRaptor is a proxy firewall, and it will be making the SMTP request on behalf of the internal mail server.

The seventh rule allows the internal DNS server to resolve DNS requests for external sites. Just like with SMTP, the VelociRaptor provides a proxy to protect the DNS server from direct attack.

The eighth rule allows the workstations to access web and FTP services on the Internet. Again, the VelociRaptor provides proxies for these services to protect the workstations as they go out on the Internet.

The ninth rule allows any device on the network to send syslog traffic to the log server. This rule allows all security log entries to be consolidated on a single server and is especially important for consolidating the log entries for the multiple IDS sensors that are deployed on the network. Consolidating the logs simplifies their analysis and makes it easier to defend against log modification. When an attacker gains control of a server, one of the first things he will do is modify the log files to erase evidence of his attack.

Moving the log entries to the log server prevents this from happening. It also makes it easier to detect malicious activity. By centralizing all the log entries, it becomes possible to look for attack behavior across systems. A special process runs on the log server to look at the incoming log entries for these signs of attack. The log server has a modem attached to allow it to dial a beeper service to notify administrators when an attack has been detected.

The tenth rule allows the management console to log into all the security devices on the network, including the IDS systems and the border router using the SSH protocol; this, in turn, allows each of these systems to be remotely administered. The firewall can also be remotely administered, but it does not support SSH. Instead, it uses a proprietary protocol; it calls Secure Remote Management Console (SRMC). Like SSH, SRMC encrypts all network traffic.

The last rule is the standard deny all rule. If none of the other rules match, this rule denies and logs the traffic. This rule enforces the design concept of least privilege.

The firewall and router do a good job of limiting access to the network, but it is still possible that an attacker might figure out a way to gain access, especially to the public servers. To provide additional protection to the network, each network segment has an IDS installed on it. As with the previous case study, we have opted to use Snort as our IDS. This is the purpose for the rule just before the deny all rule. The management console needs to be able to download the latest signatures for the Snort sensors on a regular basis. In addition to the standard signatures, we are also adding a few custom signatures to detect traffic that is specifically unusual to our network, instead of relying purely on the default signatures.

To understand how this might be useful, let's look at the sensor that is located on the management network. Only a limited amount of traffic should be traveling across this network segment. By deciding which traffic is allowed, we can set up signatures to look for traffic that is abnormal. If we limit our discussion to TCP traffic, the following packets should be allowed:

- TCP packets that are leaving the Management network use only HTTP, HTTPS, SRMC, and SSH.

- TCP packets that are entering the Management network are replies to previous Management Console requests.

- TCP traffic that is local to the Management network is only the Management Console logging into the Log Server or the IDS using SSH.

Any traffic that does not match one of these conditions is invalid and might indicate that an attacker has gotten past our other defense measures. To detect this, we can add custom signatures to our Management network Snort sensor. For example, to detect invalid TCP packets leaving the Management network, we add the following rules to the sensor. Assume that the Management network has been allocated the IP range 192.168.10.0/24:

```
var MgmtNet 192.168.10.0/24
alert tcp $MgmtNet any -> any 1:21 (msg: "Invalid TCP Packet destination on Management
➥Network";)
alert tcp $MgmtNet any -> any 23:79 (msg: "Invalid TCP Packet destination on
➥Management Network";)
alert tcp $MgmtNet any -> any 81:417 (msg: "Invalid TCP Packet destination on
➥Management Network";)
alert tcp $MgmtNet any -> any 419:442 (msg: "Invalid TCP Packet destination on
➥Management Network";)
alert tcp $MgmtNet any -> any 444: (msg: "Invalid TCP Packet destination on Management
➥Network";)
```

The combination of these five signatures triggers if any TCP packet is sent out of the management network that is not destined to a HTTP, HTTPS, SSH, or SRMC server. Additional rules would need to be added to alert on unauthorized UDP and ICMP traffic.

These types of signatures would produce many false positives if placed on a typical network. However, in the special case of the Management network, if any of these rules were to trigger, it would be possible that an attacker had gotten past the firewall. This idea can be extended to any network segment where it is convenient to enumerate legitimate traffic.

Unlike our previous case study, this organization made the decision to rely heavily on e-business. Breaches in security could easily put the company out of business, which justified a larger investment in security but still did not free us up to spend money on security indiscriminately. We had to balance the need to protect the network resources (especially the customer data) while keeping the need for security in balance with the other business requirements. The design that resulted provides defense in depth for the critical elements while keeping the overall expense of the design to a minimum.

Case Study 4: A Complex E-Commerce Site

In this last case study, we review the design produced by Rita Will as part of the requirements for her GCFW certification. As part of a practical assignment, GCFW students were asked to create a secure network for a fictitious entity named GIAC Enterprises (GIACE), which is in the business of selling fortune cookie sayings. The requirements for the assignment included the following details:

- The business will be run entirely over the Internet.
- Expected sales are $200 million per year.
- Three classes of external users must be accommodated: customers who purchase the sayings, suppliers who provide the sayings, and business partners who translate and resell the sayings for the foreign market.
- GIACE management considers security a fundamental requirement of its business. It is willing to spend significant funds to ensure that a secure system is developed.

Reading a bit into the assignment, we can extract the following design criteria:

- The most important resources that this network must protect are the fortunes, which constitute GIACE's intellectual capital, and the customer, supplier, and business partner records that GIACE must maintain.
- All GIACE revenue is generated from its web site. Due to this, it is essential that the web site be up 24 x 7.
- Suppliers must be able to securely provide new fortunes.
- Business partners must be able to securely access fortunes.
- The network must protect itself against determined outsiders. In addition, there is some concern about attacks launched by business partners and suppliers.
- Based upon the sales projections, GIACE expects to be a high-volume site, which must be accounted for in the design.

The design that Rita submitted to meet these requirements was awarded honors by the GCFW Advisory Board and is shown in Figure 16.4. It can be downloaded at `http://www.giac.org/practical/Rita_Will_GCFW.zip`. It is a good design for securing the proposed network, but it is by no means the only way that the network could have been secured. You need only look at the hundreds of student practicals posted at `http://www.giac.org/practical/GCFW.php` to see just how many different ways this problem can be approached.

Rita's design uses two firewalls to break the network into five major security zones. These are the Internet, the DMZ, the Proxy layer, the Security network, and the Internal network. As a way of organizing this discussion, we describe the security features of each zone security separately.

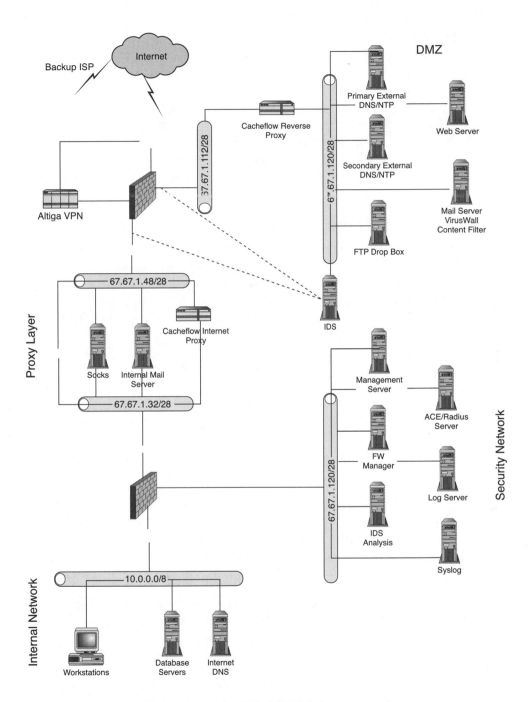

Figure 16.4   Rita Will's GCFW design uses several
security zones to enforce security across the network.

The Internet

This zone is unlabeled on the diagram, but it is the network formed between the border routers and the external firewall. Access to the Internet is provided by a pair of Cisco 3660 routers, which are using Hot Standby Routing Protocol (HSRP) to allow one of the routers to take over for the other, should one of them fail. This is the first example of the redundancy features that have been included to make sure that availability of the network is high. The routers are also being used to provide some packet filtering, including ingress and egress filters that are similar to the ones described in the previous case study.

Located just in front of the routers are the border firewalls and two Cisco VPN 3000 concentrators. The concentrators allow suppliers, vendors, and employees to establish secure VPN connections to the network from the Internet and have been set up to failover to each other should one stop working. The concentrators can use hardware accelerator cards to provide high performance and support several authentications systems. For this design, the token-based RSA SecurID system is being used to authenticate users prior to granting access.

The border firewalls are a pair of Nokia IP650s that are also set up to failover to each other. Like the IP330 that was chosen in our second case study, the IP650 runs Check Point FireWall-1. The firewalls provide the first major access restrictions for the network. The rulebase is largely due to the complexity of the design, so we will not go over it in detail. Here are the highpoints:

- Allow external visitors to browse to the cacheflow reverse proxy. This rule allows visitors to access the GIACE public web site.
- Allow the public web sites to connect to the internal database servers.
- Allow the Internet proxy to connect to external web sites. This allows internal users to browse web sites on the Internet.
- Allow mail into and out of the external mail server.
- Allow DNS queries between the DMZ and the Internet.
- Allow the suppliers, partners, and employees who have established VPNs with the Cisco VPN concentrator to reach the FTP drop box server.
- Allow employees who have established VPNs with the Cisco VPN concentrator to reach the internal GIACE network.
- Drop all other unnecessary traffic.

Using this rulebase, the firewalls effectively block all but the bare essential traffic from entering the GIACE network. This is a good implementation of the design concept least privilege.

The DMZ

Strictly speaking, this zone should be referred to as a screened subnet because it is a network segment protected by a firewall; however, it is not an insecure area located between two secure areas. As Chapter 1, "Perimeter Security Fundamentals" mentions, these two terms are often used interchangeably.

The zone holds all the servers that are accessible to external users. This includes the Cacheflow reverse proxies, the public web servers, the external DNS servers, the external mail server, and the FTP drop box server. Each of these servers plays a public role for the GIACE network.

This zone is considered a high-risk network segment. Because of this, extra security precautions have been implemented. To start with, all servers have been hardened by removing all unnecessary services and making sure that all the remaining services are as up to date as possible. Next, a Snort IDS sensor has been located in the zone to watch for suspicious activity. If an attacker manages to circumvent some of the security controls that are in place, it is hoped that this sensor will provide a sufficient warning for the onsite staff to respond appropriately.

The most important servers in the zone are the web servers. The web servers provide the primary interface between GIACE customers and GIACE. All sales transactions are conducted on these systems and then recorded on the Internal network database servers. To enable the web servers to keep up with the volume of traffic that is expected, all external web requests first pass through one of the cacheflow servers.

The cacheflow servers are being used as reverse proxies for all connections from the Internet to the public web sites. Cacheflow servers are designed to protect web servers while accelerating SSL connections. Because of the reverse proxies, external users never directly access the public web servers. Because many attacks against web servers require a direct TCP connection to the web server, placing the proxy between the Internet and the web server provides a substantial security improvement. By using the cacheflow servers, this design maximizes performance and availability of the GIACE public web site.

Other servers on the network include the DNS, mail, and FTP servers. Each has some specific security controls that are worth mentioning.

The DNS servers provide name resolution for external users. This network uses the split DNS concept, so these servers only contain records for publicly accessible servers.

The external mail server sends and receives email from the Internet. It is implemented using a Sun Solaris server that is running Sendmail. To prevent malicious code from entering the network via email, the server runs Trend InterScan's VirusWall software. This software scans each incoming or outgoing email message for viruses. Scanning incoming mail for viruses is a powerful way of protecting the network from malicious code. Keep in mind though, that scanners are only as good as their signature databases.

The last server on the DMZ is the FTP drop box server. Suppliers, partners, and employees use this system to exchange files. Due to the rules in place on the border firewalls, this server is only accessible to internal users or to users who have established VPNs through the Cisco VPN concentrator. In addition, a username/password authentication is required, adding a second layer of defense to protect the server.

The Proxy Layer

The proxy layer protects internal and security network systems while allowing these systems to access network services located on other networks. Because it is directly on the path to the rest of the GIACE network, another Snort IDS sensor has been placed in front of it to watch for suspicious traffic. This provides some extra defense should an attacker get by the border firewalls.

The proxy layer uses four devices to form a kind of proxy firewall. These include a cacheflow server, the internal mail server, a SOCKS server, and a bypass router. Each device allows different types of communications.

Probably the most used from a traffic volume point of view is the cacheflow server. Similar to the cacheflow server used on the DMZ, this server proxies web requests for the internal and security network zones. Any internal system that needs to communicate to a web server must pass the request through the cacheflow server, which allows GIACE to restrict the web sites that employees can access while protecting the requesting system from malicious web sites.

The internal mail server passes email into and out of the internal networks. By allowing only this system to send and receive email from the external mail server, this design limits the server's exposure to attack.

In addition to the web proxy that the cacheflow servers provide, two SOCKS servers have been used to provide proxy services for SOCKS-aware applications. SOCKS is a standards-based protocol that performs network layer proxies at the transport layer. It is used in this design to provide external access for some proxy-aware applications, such as RealAudio.

The last device is a Cisco 3660 router that allows network traffic that SOCKS or cacheflow servers cannot proxy.

Located just behind the proxy layer is the internal firewall, which creates the remaining two security zones. Following is a summary of the proxy layer's rulebase:

- Allow the Internal network to make use of the cacheflow web proxies.

- Allow the internal network to send and receive email from the internal mail server.

- Allow web site maintainers to log into systems in the DMZ. This requires that the maintainer authenticate to the firewall to prove his identity.

- Allow the internal network to FTP to the FTP drop box server.

- Allow remote employees who have VPNd into the Cisco VPN concentrator to gain access to the internal network.

- Allow systems on the security network to manage the security devices that are located throughout the network.

This rulebase puts in place the access restrictions that form the two remaining security zones: the internal network and the security network.

The Internal Network

The internal network holds all the internal systems, including employee workstations and GIACE databases. This network contains a broad amount of information that is valuable to GIACE. This is why it has been protected with so many layers of defense.

The Security Network

The security network contains the systems that manage and monitor the security of the network. Two servers on the network manage the GIACE security devices. These servers must be carefully protected because they would grant an attacker the ability to circumvent almost all security controls on the network if one of them were to be compromised.

Another system on the security network is the RSA ACE server, which provides the authentication service for the SecurID tokens. The ACE server is accessed when users VPN into the Cisco VPN concentrator. It is also used by the internal firewall to authenticate the web site maintainers prior to allowing them to log into the DMZ.

Next, this network holds a system that analyzes the results from the Snort IDS sensors. All alerts that the sensors generate are forwarded to this system. When a critical alert is received, the security network alerts a security administrator.

The last two servers on the security network centralize and protect all security log data that is generated on the network. As we mentioned in the third case study, attackers like nothing better than to erase the evidence of their attacks. By moving log data into a protected place, we can prevent attackers from erasing their footprints.

This design is pretty involved, so it is somewhat difficult to get your hands around all its security features. To recap, let's summarize some of the design's better qualities:

- Extensive redundancy is used throughout the network. No single point of failure will bring down a critical network service.

- Performance and security concerns at the web servers are addressed using a reverse proxy server to accelerate SSL content while protecting the web servers from direct Internet attack.

- Multiple layers of firewalls create distinct security zones. These zones group systems at similar risk levels. This makes it easier to enforce appropriate security controls in each zone.

- Mail is virus scanned before it enters or leaves the network. Assuming the virus signatures are kept up to date, this is a powerful way to prevent network compromise.

- VPN technology allows partners, suppliers, and employees to gain remote access to appropriate internal resources. This, in combination with the firewalls, allows appropriate individuals into the network while restricting them to just the set of services that they should get access to.

- All remote access is strongly authenticated through the use of SecurID tokens. This is a substantial improvement over username/password authentication and provides a high level of confidence that you know the identity of the person that you are granting access.

Summary

In this chapter, we provided four security designs for you to review. The first three were chosen to highlight the requirement to match the needs of the business with the design of the perimeter security. In each case, we started with a description of the business needs for the network and moved from there to a design to meet those needs.

We followed these case studies with an example pulled from the practical assignment of a GCFW honors student. This example was substantially more complicated than the previous case studies and provided an interesting assortment of security techniques. Studying other professional's designs is one of the best ways to discover new ways to protect the networks that you are responsible for.

Now that we have learned how to design secure networks, it's time to learn how to administer, test, and improve them. The next and final part of this book is on perimeter assessment. In it, you will learn how to maintain your security perimeter, monitor it for unusual activity, troubleshoot it when problems crop up, and test it to make sure it is functioning. Chapter 21, "Design Under Fire," builds on the principles of creating and maintaining a security perimeter by presenting a lesson on improving the security of the network through adversarial review. This chapter uses two more GCFW practicals to demonstrate how even good security designs can be improved by looking at their design through the eyes of an attacker.

IV

Perimeter Assessment

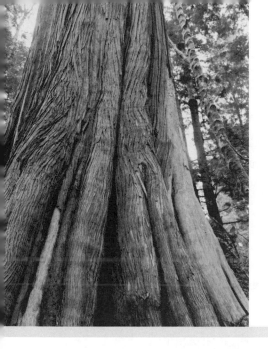

17

Maintaining a Security Perimeter

Welcome to Part IV, "Perimeter Assessment." In Part I, "Perimeter Fundamentals" and Part II, "Extending the Perimeter," we talked about primary components of the network security perimeter, such as firewalls, routers, hosts, intrusion detection systems (IDSs), Virtual Private Networks (VPNs), and policies. In Part III, "Perimeter Design," you learned how to deploy these elements according to their strengths while taking into account their weaknesses to create a unified defense architecture. After your security perimeter has been set up, two processes must continuously take place: administration of the perimeter's components and evaluation of its effectiveness. Mastering these concepts is the final step on the path to defense in depth.

This chapter discusses core principles of maintaining a security perimeter. One of the requirements for effective perimeter maintenance is awareness of the operating environment, which is why we begin with a section on system and network monitoring. In this chapter, you learn how to gather monitoring requirements and see how to implement them using free or relatively inexpensive software. We build upon monitoring processes by examining ways to respond to system fault events and malicious incidents. We also talk about the process of managing changes to the infrastructure throughout the evolution of the security perimeter so that the infrastructure's components stay effective in the face of changing threats and business requirements.

System and Network Monitoring

In the context of perimeter security, the primary goal of system and network monitoring is to provide administrators with the awareness of the state of a protected environment. We discussed monitoring in the context of intrusion detection in Chapter 7, "Network Intrusion Detection" and Chapter 10, "Host Defense Components," where we tuned IDS sensors to automatically detect events that are frequently indicative of misuse. System and network monitoring also involves anomaly detection but concentrates on availability and performance parameters of resources. Security professionals should be interested in seemingly mundane issues, such as server uptime, network utilization, and disk space availability for numerous reasons:

- Monitoring helps detect interruptions in availability of the services that the security perimeter is meant to protect. A host's partition might have filled up, a critical process might have died, or a denial of service attack might have taken a system offline. Ensuring availability, as you might recall, is one of the key objectives of information security.

- Monitoring helps detect changes in performance and availability of the system, which might be indicative of misuse. Administrators who routinely monitor their systems are able to sense even the slightest change in the behavior of the host or device and are wonderful intrusion detection sensors.

- Monitoring helps detect bottlenecks and shifts in performance of the infrastructure, which might indicate that the design or the implementation of the security perimeter is not properly tuned. For example, a web-based application might function too slowly over HTTPS if its servers cannot cope with the load that SSL imposes on them. Monitoring can help determine which aspects of the security perimeter need to be fine-tuned and in what way.

- Monitoring helps detect unexpected changes in the environment that might adversely impact effectiveness of the security perimeter. For example, a new server might have been brought online without proper hardening, or hasty changes to the firewall rule set might have unintentionally blocked access to a critical service.

A well-defined monitoring process allows administrators to detect problems at an early stage—hopefully before the problems escalate into critical incidents. One of the most powerful ways to increase effectiveness of this process is to perform monitoring centrally, which generally involves configuring a server—or a cluster of unified servers—to observe multiple resources throughout the network. A centralized monitoring infrastructure often benefits from the use of client modules that report to the central server information gathered from remotely monitored systems. You should already be familiar with such a configuration because it is frequently used to manage multiple firewalls, VPN nodes, or IDS sensors centrally.

Throughout this section, we look at one way of implementing a centralized monitoring infrastructure through the use of a popular monitoring application called Big Brother. After we introduce you to the basic capabilities of this program, we use Big Brother in examples to demonstrate monitoring concepts throughout this section.

Big Brother Fundamentals

Big Brother is a flexible software tool for performing network and system-monitoring functions (http://www.bb4.com). Numerous products can fulfill monitoring needs; a small sample of these includes BMC Patrol (http://www.bmc.com), HP OpenView (http://openview.hp.com), and NetSaint (http://www.netsaint.org). Unlike several other contenders, Big Brother focuses solely on monitoring aspects of system maintenance, without offering features to remotely manage devices. This makes it a lightweight application that is particularly well suited for illustrating monitoring concepts. As a result, we use Big Brother in examples throughout this section for many of the reasons we would consider using it on our networks:

- It is free for non-commercial use.
- It is relatively inexpensive for commercial use.
- It runs on Windows and UNIX-based operating systems.
- It is relatively easy to set up and maintain.
- It supports a wide range of monitoring and alerting requirements.
- It is expandable through the use of custom scripts.
- It has been around since late 1996 and has established itself as a trustworthy monitoring tool.

Big Brother is able to track the status of remote nodes by attempting to connect to monitored systems over the network. In this role, Big Brother can detect the availability of a system via ping packets, as well as by attempting to elicit an expected response from specific TCP services. Big Brother also supports the use of agent modules that run on remote nodes as Big Brother clients and gather local information, such as CPU performance, disk space utilization, and process status.

Big Brother's architecture consists of four core components that are integrated into a unified application. These components, described in the following list, can run on distributed systems to achieve the desired extent of scalability or can co-exist on a single server:

- The BBNET host probes remote systems to determine availability of monitored network services.

- The remote client agent runs on a monitored system and gathers performance and resource availability data local to its host.

- The BBDISPLAY host generates and displays web pages that administrators can look at to determine the status of monitored devices.

- The BBPAGER host issues notification alerts and processes event escalation measures.

If Big Brother determines that a monitored parameter has exceeded an acceptable threshold, it alerts administrators by displaying a warning on the BBDISPLAY's web page. Figure 17.1 shows how Big Brother consolidates status information regarding multiple systems onto a single summary page. Icons on Big Brother's summary matrix represent the current status of monitored parameters for each system. A green square represents the normal state of the system, which is the case for more services in this figure. A flashing star icon for the HTTP service on "lemon" indicates that Big Brother experienced problems connecting to the web server on "lemon" over the network. Administrators can obtain additional information regarding the problem by clicking on the icon. Additionally, Big Brother can send the alert via email, pager, Short Message Service (SMS), or a custom script.

Now that you know a little about fundamental capabilities of monitoring software, the next section covers how to determine which resources should be observed in the first place and how to set up such monitoring.

Figure 17.1   Big Brother presents a unified view of monitored
resources by using icons to represent the status of observed attributes.

The Capabilities of HP OpenView

Of course, Big Brother isn't the only game in town when it comes to monitoring networks and systems. A wide
variety of offerings are available to suit different requirements and budgets. HP OpenView is a product that is at
the higher end of the price and functionality spectrum. The foundation of the OpenView family of products is the
OpenView Network Node Manager. This application provides the framework for performing basic monitoring and
discovery functions by using SNMP, ping, and other network probes, as well as for collecting historical data and
handling event notification.

An extension of Network Node Manager, but more full featured and expensive, is a product called OpenView
Operations. This application is aimed at enterprises that require more extensive managing and monitoring features,
along with native support for additional devices and applications. OpenView Operations also supports programmable actions that can respond to system events, such as by automatically restarting a crashed process. A core component in OpenView Operations, called Service Navigator, allows administrators to "teach" OpenView about
relationships between particular services that are distributed throughout the network. For example, if a router
goes down, Service Navigator (if appropriately configured) can flag all services that this event might affect, such
as email or a mission-critical database. This functionality can help to assess the event's impact, determine its root
cause, and assist in the troubleshooting process.

HP OpenView isn't for everyone due to its high price and significant implementation complexities. However, if a
particular feature is important to your business and slimmer or less expensive tools do not support it, then look at
enterprise-centric solutions, such as HP OpenView.

Establishing Monitoring Procedures

Be sure to define your goals and priorities before rolling out a monitoring solution. For example, if you are maintaining an e-commerce site that makes a significant portion of its revenue via the Internet, you might be interested in focusing on the following data points:

- Bandwidth utilization
- Server load
- Where your hits are coming from
- What percentage of site visitors proceed to a sale

Considering that most of us operate under the constraints of limited staff, it is impractical to treat all changes in the state of the environment with the same urgency. Moreover, monitoring all aspects of performance and availability on each system is likely to produce so many alerts that those that are truly important will be drowned out by the noise of inconsequential events. Knowing when a firewall process dies is likely to be more important than receiving notifications every time a user's workstation is rebooted.

We have been using risk analysis to define the extent of hardening and segregation for security perimeter components throughout the book. Similarly, we can define monitoring requirements based on the resource's importance and the likelihood that its availability might be disrupted. For example, if email communications are a critical business function for your company, you might consider monitoring numerous aspects of the mail server's availability and performance, such as the accessibility of the host over the network, the status of the mailer's processes, and the state of file system utilization. If that same mail server has been acting flaky, you might be interested in adjusting monitoring criteria to help track down the cause of the problem or to enable yourself to react to problems more quickly. In that case, it might help to adjust the thresholds for alerts or to monitor additional attributes, such as auxiliary system processes, as well as CPU and memory utilization.

Note

Monitoring and alerting go hand-in-hand. It is not uncommon to monitor more devices and attributes than we want to be alerted about. We then configure alerting thresholds so that we are notified of events that warrant immediate attention. Events that are less critical might not require a real-time response. Additionally, historical information that is collected through the monitoring process will be available for when we need to troubleshoot problems or to determine the relationship between events that we were alerted about.

Monitoring applications, such as Big Brother, can keep track of multiple attributes for resources throughout the network and offer you the flexibility to drill down into specific parameters of individual systems that need to be observed. Let us see how to establish monitoring procedures to track aspects of the environment that are most likely to require a watchful eye:

- Hosts and devices
- Accessibility of network services
- Local system attributes

Hosts and Devices

One of the first steps in setting up a monitoring system is to define which hosts and devices should be watched over. As we discussed a few paragraphs earlier, you need to strike the balance between your ability to handle information and the number of systems that warrant your attention at this stage. So that you see what's involved in configuring core aspects of a monitoring system, let's take a look at how to accomplish this with Big Brother. Big Brother uses a text file called bb-hosts to list systems that it should observe. The bb-hosts file follows the format of the regular hosts file, with the addition of directives that are specific to Big Brother.

For every system that you want to monitor, you can specify which attributes should be observed. A good starting point is ensuring that the host or device is accessible over the network. This can be defined for Big Brother by using a bare-bones bb-hosts file like this:

```
#
# THE BIG BROTHER HOSTS FILE
#
192.168.214.132 apple    # BBPAGER BBNET BBDISPLAY
192.168.214.17  lemon    #
192.168.214.97  peach    #
```

In this bb-hosts file, we defined apple as the host that houses Big Brother components that centrally monitor other systems. (Note that the apple host will be monitored as well.) Because we did not define directives for "lemon" and "peach," Big Brother only checks whether it can access them over the network via ping.

Specifying IP addresses for hosts, as we did in the bb-hosts file, makes the monitoring system more self contained and decreases the possibility that a domain name resolution problem will skew monitoring results. However, maintaining IP address-to-hostname mappings specifically for the monitoring system creates additional administrative overhead. Furthermore, defining IP addresses within the monitoring system might be impractical when observing hosts that dynamically obtain IP addresses from a DHCP server. To address this, you can configure Big Brother to use the host's native domain name resolution mechanisms, such as DNS or the host's file. You can accomplish this by simply specifying 0.0.0.0 for IP addresses in the bb-hosts file.

Some systems are configured not to respond to ICMP echo requests, or a firewall between the monitored system and the monitoring host will not let such traffic through. You can use the noping directive to prevent Big Brother from performing the ping test. In such cases, you will probably want to check accessibility of specific services on the monitored host instead.

Accessibility of Network Services

One of the most useful features of monitoring programs is the ability to determine whether a remote service is accessible over the network. After all, a service might have crashed or have gotten disabled even if its host maintains network connectivity. You can use one of two primary methods to determine accessibility of a TCP-based service:

- Check whether the monitored port is open by initiating a plain TCP connection with the service without exchanging data. You can do this with a half-connect, in which the monitoring server does not complete a three-way TCP handshake. Most monitoring systems, however, complete the handshake and close the connection as soon as it is established.

- Attempt to initiate a conversation with the remote service using the application-level protocol that is appropriate for the monitored service. For example, we could check accessibility of a POP service by attempting to access a mailbox.

Port probes that are based on plain TCP connections obtain information without requiring us to program the monitoring system with knowledge of the protocol that is specific to the observed service. However, this technique does not help us detect problems with remote applications that accept TCP connections but do not respond properly. By programming the monitoring system to know the application-level protocol of the monitored service, we allow it to detect problems with greater accuracy and granularity. Another advantage of the application-level approach is that it can work with TCP as well as UDP-based services.

Monitoring systems usually come with built-in support for determining accessibility of popular network services, such as SMTP, Telnet, FTP, POP, SSH, and IMAP. For example, the following line in Big Brother's bb-hosts file can be used to determine whether SMTP and SSH services run on the remote system `plum`:

```
192.168.214.101 plum   # smtp ssh
```

Big Brother usually attempts to evoke a response from the application when testing its availability, instead of simply verifying that it can establish a TCP connection. In most cases, Big Brother accomplishes this by sending the string `quit` to the remote service. Big Brother can handle some services in a slightly more intelligent manner by attempting to follow their protocols to make the test less obtrusive. For example, it sends `ABC123 LOGOUT` to IMAP services and sends an identifying string with the prefix of `Big-Brother-Monitor` when connecting to the SSH service.

Tip

Sometimes, it makes sense to check whether a particular service is *not* running on a remote system. For example, if you transfer files only through Secure Shell (SSH), you might want to be alerted if a particular host suddenly starts accepting FTP connections. You can set up Big Brother to do this by using an exclamation mark (!) prefix when specifying directives in bb-hosts:

```
192.168.214.101 plum   # smtp ssh !ftp
```

When testing accessibility of remote services, do not be surprised to see error messages in logs on the systems that are being observed. Monitoring tools often do not bother exercising all options of the remote service; they close the connection as soon as they receive some data in return or without exchanging data at all. For example, the Sendmail daemon records a message like the following one whenever Big Brother verifies accessibility of the SMTP service:

```
Feb 24 16:50:02 apple sendmail[23130]: NOQUEUE: apple [192.168.214.129] did not issue
➥MAIL/EXPN/VRFY/ETRN during connection to MTA
```

Big Brother has provisions for verifying service accessibility through plain TCP-based connections instead of exchanging data through a simplistic application check. To configure Big Brother to perform such probes, you can append `:s` to the applicable directive in bb-hosts like this:

```
192.168.214.101 plum   # smtp:s ssh
```

Unfortunately, this approach does not eliminate spurious log messages in many cases because Big Brother often confuses the monitored service by establishing a full TCP connection and not exchanging meaningful data. For example, using the `:s` suffix to test the SMTP service does not prevent Sendmail from issuing the alarming message shown previously. However, using :s might be effective for eliminating errors in the logs for certain software, so you might want to give this option a shot if the need arises.

Logging Incomplete OpenSSH Connections

The OpenSSH daemon creates the following log entry when a client initiates a connection to its port and closes the socket without going through the full SSH connection negotiation process:

```
Feb 24 16:51:03 apple sshd[19925]: Did not receive ident string from 192.168.214.129.
```

This message might indicate that a monitoring system is configured to observe the SSH service via plain TCP connections. The message is different when the system attempts to exchange data with the remote SSH service, for example:

```
Feb 24 16:52:46 apple sshd[1295]: Bad protocol version identification 'Big-Brother-
➥Monitor-1.8d4  ' from 192.168.214.129
```

Of course, similar messages might appear in the logs when the SSH server is subjected to a port scan, so be careful not to blindly disregard these messages when examining the logs.

Monitoring web servers often warrants special considerations because web-based services are ubiquitous and are frequently critical to company operations. As a result, monitoring applications frequently offer you the ability to retrieve specific web pages. To set this up with Big Brother, you can use the bb-hosts file to specify which URLs to monitor:

```
192.168.214.17  lemon   # https://lemon/cart/order.jsp
192.168.214.97  peach   # http://peach/
```

The preceding configuration lines set up Big Brother to verify the availability of the /cart/order.jsp page on server lemon via HTTPS and to check the root page on server peach via HTTP. Clicking the HTTP icon on Big Brother's summary page enables you to see details of the established HTTP connection, as shown in Figure 17.2.

By monitoring applications, you can determine the accessibility of network services without installing additional software on monitored systems. However, obtaining detailed information about local attributes of the monitored resources often requires the further cooperation from the monitored system.

Figure 17.2 Big Brother can capture details of the HTTP response when connecting to the desired URL—in this case, to http://peach/.

Local System Attributes

Several attributes that are local to the monitored host might warrant your attention not only because they are critical to the host's function, but also because they can serve as an early warning system. Detecting the following conditions might help you discover problems before a host's network service stops being accessible over the network:

- File system is almost full
- CPU utilization has exceeded an acceptable threshold
- Critical processes are failing to run

One of the most effective ways to observe these attributes is through the use of a monitoring agent that reports its findings to a monitoring server. Figure 17.3 shows a configuration screen of such an agent for Big Brother, with the client module running under Windows. Typical of such configurations is the need to define the central server to which notifications will be sent—in this case, 192.168.214.132.

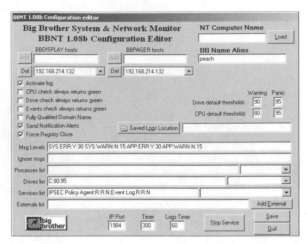

Figure 17.3   A GUI-based configuration utility defines monitoring
settings for Big Brother clients that are running under Windows.

In this example, we set up the Big Brother client to monitor the state of two
local services: IPSec Policy Agent and Event Log. Also, the client is set to
issue a warning-level alert when the C: partition becomes 90% full and a
panic-level alert when the partition's utilization reaches 95%. Even when the
system is functioning normally, you can obtain useful information about the
state of its resources. For instance, Figure 17.4 shows a status page displayed
on Big Brother's central server when the remote host's file system utilization
is below alarming thresholds. Status green means everything is OK with this
particular attribute of the monitored host.

Figure 17.4   Monitoring systems can offer useful diagnostics
information even when remote nodes operate below alarming thresholds.

Another way to obtain detailed information about a monitored system is via Simple Network Management Protocol (SNMP). The use of application-specific monitoring agents that we've discussed so far requires that client software be deployed on systems that need to be observed. One of the biggest advantages of using SNMP is that it is already built into numerous devices and applications. An SNMP-compatible monitoring server can periodically *poll* remote SNMP agents for performance and availability attributes, such as configuration parameters, network statistics, and process details. For instance, here are some of the many attributes that Cisco routers natively expose via SNMP:

- MAC and IP address accounting
- CPU utilization
- Memory availability
- Startup and running configuration
- Network interface status

Note

Universal support for SNMP is one of the biggest advantages of this protocol, as well as a potential weakness. The SNMP vulnerability announced in February 2002, which we mentioned in Chapter 6, "Role of a Router," simultaneously affected SNMP implementations of numerous vendors. Don't assume that an implementation of an established protocol is bug-free. Even if the software has been around for years, you never know what dormant vulnerabilities lie within.

SNMP agents can also issue alerts to the monitoring system when a predefined condition occurs on the local device. These *traps* are generated asynchronously, regardless of the regular polling schedule that the monitoring system implements. Traps can notify the monitoring system of an event that threatens performance or availability of the device. You can use the following command to enable all supported SNMP traps on a Cisco router. (You will also need to use the `snmp-server host` command to specify where the traps should be sent.)

```
router(config)#snmp-server enable traps snmp
```

One of the notifications that is enabled by using this command is the authentication trap, which alerts administrators when a remote host fails to properly authenticate when attempting to access the SNMP agent. This notification can help detect SNMP network scans and brute force attacks targeting the device over SNMP. If you are not interested in enabling all SNMP traps that the router supports, consider activating at least the authentication trap using the following command:

```
router(config)#snmp-server enable traps snmp authentication
```

> **Tip**
>
> Big Brother offers limited support for SNMP polling and trap handling through the use of add-on modules that can be downloaded from www.deadcat.net.

> **Versions of SNMP**
>
> SNMP has been around since 1988 and has been exposed to scrutiny by standards bodies, network engineers, and system administrators. As a result, numerous revisions have been made to the original SNMP protocol, but some of them failed to gain the community's acceptance and phased away. One of the more popular phased-out SNMP provisions was the party-based authentication specification of SNMPv2 (now called SNMPv2p or SNMPv2 classic), which attempted to provide a more secure alternative to SNMPv1's community string authentication. Cisco routers used to support party-based authentication through the use of the `snmp-server party` command, but stopped supporting it after release 11.2 of IOS.[1] Instead, Cisco followed the example of many other vendors in limiting itself to handling only SNMPv1-style community string authentication defined by SNMPv2c.
>
> Additionally, Cisco adopted a full implementation of SNMPv3, which includes a rich set of cryptographic security mechanisms. One of the few major vendors that still supports enhanced security framework of the SNMPv2 generation is Sun, which uses user-based authentication mechanisms defined by SNMPv2u in its Sun Management Center product. (Sun seems to refer to this protocol as SNMPv2usec.)[2]

Another method of obtaining detailed information about remote system attributes is available, in addition to using SNMP or custom monitoring agents. This third method involves remotely executing commands that are native to the monitored host. For example, SiteScope (http://www.sitescope.com) obtains data from remote Windows machines through the PerfMon API, which Microsoft designed to gather performance-related information. To obtain detailed information from UNIX hosts, SiteScope executes commands, such as ps and uptime, on the remote system via Telnet and SSH. When it comes to remotely executing commands or obtaining potentially sensitive information from the observed systems, you must take care to prevent attackers from exploiting the monitoring channel. We examine such considerations in the next section.

Security Considerations for Remote Monitoring

Attackers can exploit monitoring mechanisms, just like any other service operating on the network, to obtain sensitive information or to gain unauthorized access to remote systems. When selecting and configuring a monitoring solution, consider the following factors relating to its defenses:

- How sensitive are the monitoring communications that traverse the network, and should they be encrypted? You might not be concerned about the confidentiality of CPU statistics carried across the internal network, but you might not want to use clear-text SNMP to retrieve a router's running configuration across the Internet.

- How strong is the authentication scheme that prevents unauthorized entities from accessing monitored resources? Many monitoring solutions rely solely on IP addresses for access control. Additionally, SNMPv1 and SNMPv2c support only the use of community strings, which can be intercepted over the network or brute-forced via tools such as SolarWinds (`http://www.solarwinds.net`).

- Do monitoring mechanisms provide write access to observed resources? Even though we have been focusing on read-only aspects of system monitoring, SNMP can also be used to modify settings on remote devices. For example, an attacker with write access to a resource might be able to manipulate a router's ARP table or otherwise change the configuration of the system.

- Can the monitoring infrastructure be exploited to grant attackers elevated access to the systems? For example, a vulnerability in Big Brother allowed execution of arbitrary commands on the monitoring server with the privileges of the Big Brother user (`http://cve.mitre.org/cgi-bin/cvename.cgi?name=CAN-2000-0450`). Even if the server were restricted to accept status information from only specific IP addresses, systems hosting Big Brother agents could have been used to obtain access to the monitoring server.

Unauthorized access from monitoring agents to the central server is a particularly significant concern because the server is often located in a more secure area than the agents. Consider the configuration in Figure 17.5, where the server on the internal network collects performance and availability information from hosts on the screened subnet. If this scenario were implemented using Big Brother, then client modules that run on public servers would be sending notifications to the monitoring server's TCP port 1984 and could exploit the CAN-2000-0450 vulnerability described earlier. (IANA officially assigned port 1984 for Big Brother's client-to-server communications.)

Figure 17.5   The central monitoring server could be exposed to attacks coming from a host on the screened subnet if agents can initiate connections to the server.

To minimize the risk of such attacks, run monitoring services as user accounts with constrained access. Big Brother, for instance, should be set up as a dedicated user without administrative privileges. If possible, also config-ure the hosts so that connections are initiated from the more secure subnet to limit the possibility of privilege escalation across network security zones. In the case of SNMP, for example, this would involve using the polling mechanisms when observing hosts across subnets as well as limiting trap communications to a single subnet. Monitoring applications might allow you to set up dedicated servers in each subnet for collecting status reports and then link them together; this way, the amount of traffic that is crossing subnet boundaries is minimized.

Perhaps one of the safest ways to monitor devices is by remotely probing their ports from the central server as we discussed in the "Accessibility of Network Services" section. This method does not provide detailed information about the local state of the observed machines, but it also does not require that additional software be enabled on remote systems. Moreover, monitoring services that need to be accessible over the network, such as HTTP, DNS, and SMTP, often can be tested over channels that are already open. When a packet filtering device blocks access to remote services from the network where the monitoring server is located, be sure to open access only to and from IP addresses that are required for monitoring to take place.

Monitoring products out of the box rarely provide many options when it comes to restricting which systems can obtain status information from a remote agent, or who can submit status reports to the central server. Most products support restrictions based on IP addresses. To set this up in Big Brother, for example, you need to edit its security file to list addresses of hosts that should be able to communicate with the monitoring server.

Note

Monitoring products can provide supplementary modules that enhance the security of communications between the monitoring components. For example, you can purchase an add-on to HP OpenView Operations, called Advanced Security, to support encryption and cryptographic authentication.

IP-based restrictions form a useful layer for improving the security of the monitoring infrastructure and are most effective when combined with strong authentication in client-to-server communications. Cryptographic authentication is supported in SNMPv3; you should take advantage of it when setting up your monitoring infrastructure. SNMPv3 can also encrypt its messages, which helps to protect their confidentiality. As SNMP agents are beginning to adopt security mechanisms of SNMPv3, it is becoming easier to find a monitoring system that can support them. Here is a list of some of the products that are able to securely communicate with SNMPv3 agent modules:

- HP OpenView via a commercial add-on called SNMP Security Pack (`http://www.snmp.com/products/snmpsecpack.html`)
- Castle Rock SNMPc Network Manager (`http://www.castlerock.com`)
- AdventNet SNMP API for implementing SNMP support in Java-based applications (`http://www.adventnet.com/products/snmp`)
- MG-SOFT SNMP management software (`http://www.mg-soft.com`)
- Lorot, a free SNMP node manager for Windows (`http://www.llecointe.com`)

- Net-SNMP, a popular set of free SNMP utilities for UNIX, utilized by applications such as Big Brother (`http://net-snmp.sourceforge.net/`)

By this point in the chapter, we have discussed fundamental principles of setting up system and network monitoring in a secure and reliable manner. After such infrastructure is in place, administrators can connect to a central server to view the status of the network's hosts and devices. The next step in maintaining a security perimeter is ensuring that administrators are alerted when critical conditions occur and empowering administrators to quickly respond to such events.

Incident Response

An *incident*, in the context of this chapter, is an anomalous event that can impact confidentiality, integrity, or availability of the infrastructure. The anomaly might be malicious, or it might be an indicator of a system fault. In either case, we need to know how to set up alerts that warn us about a potentially threatening condition. Both IDS and system-monitoring mechanisms are useful for detecting suspicious events, but they are not of much help if administrators are not actually aware of conditions that these systems observe.

One way to remain apprised of the state of your resources is to periodically check status screens of the monitoring system or the IDS console. Relying solely on this approach, however, does not allow detection and reaction to problems as soon as they occur. This is an especially significant concern for organizations that need to respond to incidents around the clock but cannot afford to hire personnel to observe the alert screen of the monitoring system 24 hours a day. Configuring IDS and monitoring systems to send out alerts and knowing how to respond to alarm conditions is an integral part of effective security perimeter maintenance. In this section, we discuss how to configure notification options in a way that is consistent with your security policy and monitoring requirements. Additionally, we examine considerations for responding to detected system faults and malicious events.

Note

Relying solely on automation of IDS or of the monitoring systems to detect all suspicious events in real-time is dangerous. We illustrated limitations of this approach in Chapter 7 in the discussion of false positives and false negatives. Therefore, be sure to combine automated alerting with manual examination of data that such systems collect.

Notification Options

An old slogan of a New York telephone company reminded people that "We're all connected." Accessibility of system administrators, wherever they are, allows systems to get in touch with them in close to real-time whenever a device requires attention. When evaluating or deploying an IDS or a monitoring system, consider the following aspects of its notification functionality:

- What means of alert notification do you require? Some of the more popular options are email, pager, and SMS-based messages. It might also be possible to integrate the notification mechanism with other applications that are already in use in your organization.

- What alert acknowledgement options do you find useful? If a critical alert is sent to multiple administrators, you might want to have the ability to let your colleagues know that you are working on the problem so that your efforts do not overlap.

- How configurable is the notification logic? You might want to send alerts to different people depending on the day of the week or the time of the day, or issue alerts to different devices depending on the event's severity. Also, plan for outages in your notification scheme because the primary notification mechanism might fall victim to a system fault or an attack.

> **Tip**
>
> Keep in mind that some of the cheaper paging devices, especially those that are purely numeric, do not guarantee that a message will be delivered. To ensure that an alert eventually reaches the administrator when he is back in the communications range, you might want to subscribe to paging services that can queue messages to guarantee their delivery. Alternatively, or in conjunction with this, consider configuring the monitoring system to periodically re-issue alerts until one of them is acknowledged.

One of the advantages of having a centralized alerting configuration is that only a single host needs to have the ability to generate alerts destined for mailboxes or pagers of system administrators. This eliminates the need to set up dial-out modems on every observed system for dialing a numeric pager, or from allowing each server to send email when its business purpose does not require such functionality. In Big Brother, for example, a central server consolidates performance and availability information, and only the host that is designated as BBPAGER issues notification alerts. To eliminate a single point of failure, you might consider setting up multiple alert-generating systems or configuring them to operate in a failover mode.

General Response Guidelines

Make sure that your company's policies and procedures clearly explain what an administrator should do when responding to an alert. Creating and distributing a document that answers the following questions will help you make sure that problems are resolved in a consistent and thought-out manner that has the support of management and technical personnel:

- Who is responsible for responding to alerts? Defining this in advance helps ensure that the qualified staff members are available, according to relevant policies and business requirements. Also, this helps prevent administrators from failing to respond because they think somebody else will react to the alert.

- Whom should the administrator notify of the problem? As we already discussed, it is often worthwhile to let other administrators know that someone is responding to the alert. Additionally, the company's management should probably be notified of severe or prolonged conditions.

- What troubleshooting and investigative steps should the administrator take when resolving a problem? Consider creating a document that explains how to handle problems that are common to your infrastructure. (Chapter 19, "Troubleshooting Defense Components" addresses this aspect of perimeter maintenance.)

- How should the administrator connect to the troubled system? VPN access might come in handy when the administrator is away from the hosting facility. You might also want to define transportation options if she needs to travel to the hosting facility.

- When should the administrator call for help? It's possible that the person who is responding to an alert might not be the best person to resolve a particular problem. Specifying in advance when to involve a colleague or even an external vendor and empowering the administrator to do so even during off-hours helps to expediently resolve problems.

- How should the administrator document the cause of the problem and its resolution in a way that might help the company learn from this experience?

It is not uncommon for the administrator who is responding to the alert to perform preliminary examination and then to call in the heavy artillery for in-depth troubleshooting. One such scenario, perhaps most relevant to our book, is when the administrator suspects that the event is malicious in nature. Your security policy should account for the need to investigate such situations and define roles and responsibilities for staff who is involved in responding to malicious incidents.

Responding to Malicious Incidents

Any anomaly, whether reported by an IDS, a monitoring system, or recognized by a human, might turn out to be a malicious incident. After the event is deemed to be malicious, then specialized procedures that were created for handling such situations should guide your staff's response. These procedures can be broken into several phases, as defined in "Computer Security Incident Handling Step by Step," published by the SANS Institute.[3] The following list presents a high-level overview of these phases:

1. Preparation. Tasks in this phase need to take place before actually responding to a malicious incident. They involve formalizing policies and procedures, training team members, and preparing communication channels for contacting people inside and outside your organization.

2. Identification. In this phase, a primary handler is assigned to the incident. He begins the investigation by determining whether the incident is, indeed, malicious. If it is, he assesses its scope, establishes a chain of custody for collected evidence, and notifies appropriate personnel.

3. Containment. The purpose of this phase is to set the stage for further analysis while preventing the incident from escalating. Here, the handler creates a backup of the affected systems to make sure that pristine evidence is available for later use. He also assesses the risk of continuing operations by reviewing logs, interviewing observers, and consulting with system owners. Determining the extent of the compromise and either taking appropriate systems offline or attempting to otherwise block attackers' access achieves containment.

4. Eradication. At this point in the response effort, the handler determines the cause of the malicious incident, reinforces the system's defenses, and closes vulnerabilities that might have allowed the attack to succeed.

5. Recovery. This phase is devoted to restoring and validating affected systems, returning to business as normal, and continuing to closely monitor systems that were compromised. At this point, the organization needs to decide whether it is ready to resume operations.

6. Follow up. In this phase, the incident handler creates a report that consolidates the team's experiences that relate to the incident. This "lessons learned" process helps improve the organization's defenses by addressing factors that allowed the compromise to occur. At this stage, the team implements follow-up actions that management approved.

As you can see, responding to alerts, whether they relate to a system fault or a malicious event, is no easy matter. As we discuss in the following section, you might be able to automate responses to some of the simpler events that require immediate action and that can be addressed without directly involving the administrator.

Automating Event Responses

Automating responses to events that are unlikely to be false alarms helps to expedite problem resolution. For instance, a monitoring system might detect that a critical process on the observed host died, issue an alert to the administrator, and automatically start a new instance of the process. When configuring such functionality, you might want to set limits on the number of times the systems attempts to take corrective action in a given time period. If the process repeatedly dies soon after being restarted, chances are good that the automated recovery mechanism cannot help in this situation, in which case an administrator should become directly involved. Even if the fault was automatically resolved, the administrator should still follow up to assess the scope of the problem, determine its cause, verify that the corrective action was acceptable, and attempt to prevent the fault from reoccurring.

Another type of automated response can take place when an IDS detects a malicious event. IDS products frequently offer the ability to respond to an attack directly, or they can dynamically reconfigure firewalls to block the attack. As we discussed in Chapter 7, such *active response* carries the advantage of shunning the attacker as soon as malicious actions are observed, but it is often dangerous because it might deny service to a legitimate user. When deciding whether to enable active response on a particular sensor, weigh the risk of mistakenly blocking an authorized user against the risk of not blocking a particular attack right away.

One of the more interesting examples of active response techniques combines the functionality of an IDS with a firewall to create a filtering device that blocks not solely based on a predefined rule set, but also according to attack-recognition patterns. Freely available Hogwash (`http://hogwash.sourceforge.net/`) is one product that offers this capability. It is an inline traffic-filtering device that uses an IDS engine of Snort to determine which packets to allow into the network.

In our discussion about maintaining a security perimeter, so far we have looked at monitoring the infrastructure for faults and malicious events and discussed how to efficiently respond to alarming conditions. An effective way of decreasing the rate at which anomalies occur in the first place is to ensure that perimeter components are updated in a controlled manner. We examine the process of managing changes to the environment in the following section.

Accommodating Change

The reality of maintaining a security perimeter built perfectly in tune with the organization's business needs is that at some point it will need to change to accommodate new requirements and emerging threats. The ability of the infrastructure to handle change in a controlled manner is one of the main attestations to the quality of its design, implementation, and maintenance. This section discusses rolling out patches, reconfiguring systems, and detecting environment changes without compromising the security of your network.

Fundamentals of Change Management

The general concept of *change management* refers to the ability to handle changes in business or technical areas of the organization. In the confines of this chapter, we focus on processes that support changes to network infrastructure and applications. One example of a process that might require change management is the rollout of a critical patch to web server software that needs to take place without causing prolonged downtime, crippling its applications, or exposing new security weaknesses. Similarly, a change to a firewall's rule set should take place without inadvertently denying authorized traffic or exposing internal systems to new threats. To accommodate such adjustments to the infrastructure, a robust change-management process should incorporate the following elements:

- Buy-in from management and technical personnel
- Communications regarding proposed changes
- Prevention and detection of unauthorized changes
- Ability to test changes before deployment
- Procedures to verify proper system operation
- Ability to roll back undesired changes

The majority of change-management situations benefit from the process that incorporates these steps. However, the extent of each phase might differ, depending on how complicated or risky the change is. For example, migrating a mail server from Microsoft Exchange to Lotus Notes is likely to require more planning and testing than adding a routine security patch to a server. Next, we examine these elements in greater detail so that you are better positioned to set up a change-management program that matches your needs.

Buying-In from Relevant Personnel

Obtain buy-in from relevant parties regarding reasons for implementing the change before rolling it out. For instance, you might have valid reasons for wanting to block all outbound SMTP access from your screened subnet, but you might not realize that several servers hosted there might have valid business reasons for generating email. We recommend formalizing the change-approval process so that management and technical personnel have a chance to voice objections to upcoming modifications. This procedure helps prevent making rushed choices that cause adverse side effects. The process should also define individuals who are authorized to make final decisions regarding proposed changes; this eliminates unending discussions and resolves potential conflicts.

Communicating About Proposed Changes

Keep business and technical personnel apprised of proposed modifications so that they are not caught off guard when the change occurs. Establish a procedure for notifying appropriate parties of scheduled changes and verify that all relevant parties have a way of obtaining necessary information. Also, do not forget to notify end users that systems might be inaccessible for a certain time period. To help alleviate inconvenience caused to end users by potential service disruptions, consider scheduling the change to take place during off-time hours.

Tip

To make notification to relevant personnel of planned service disruptions easier, consider preparing template documents that describe some of the more common downtime scenarios. The templates should explain when the event will occur, which services will be impacted, and when systems are scheduled to resume normal operation. You might also want to explain how users or the organization will benefit from upcoming changes so that they are more supportive of your plans.

Preventing and Detecting Unauthorized Changes

You need to be well versed in enforcing access controls by this point in the book. Implementing such controls will help prevent unauthorized or inadvertent changes to your systems. Also, integrity-assessment tools, such as Tripwire, are useful for detecting unapproved changes or for tracking authorized changes that mold your system during its lifespan. To prevent unpleasant situations in which administrators' actions are second-guessed, your security policy should clearly define who is authorized to make changes and what approval and communication process they need to follow.

Testing Changes Before Deployment

All changes to be introduced into a production environment should be tested first on a separate, staging network. Granted, you might not be able to afford to create a full replica of your production infrastructure for this purpose. However, you might still be able to introduce the proposed change into a scaled-down laboratory environment to help you assess the risk of rolling it out to production. When testing, be sure to go through the process of regression testing, which tests the new environment for all bugs. Often, by fixing an open problem, you might reopen an issue that was fixed previously. Regression testing will help you find these problems before they are reintroduced into the production environment. Your effort in testing the change before deployment should be proportional to the impact that the change is likely to have on the production environment. In most cases, adding an entry to a system's hosts file is likely to require less testing than upgrading the version of the firewall software.

Verifying Proper System Operation

Having a detailed plan for verifying that the infrastructure functions properly after the change is rolled out allows you to limit the impact of problems and makes it easier to track down their causes. The plan should incorporate a standard suite of tests that are performed after any change and should include specific tests to verify that the intended change has been implemented. Be sure to test access to relevant services and exercise core aspects of applications after upgrading software, reconfiguring hosts, or tweaking access control rules.

Rolling Back Undesired Changes

Even after all the planning and testing, your change might cause problems that you are unable to correct right away; in that case, you will need to roll back to the previous configuration. You save yourself and those around you a lot of anguish by preparing (and testing) a rollback plan before implementing the change. A time-tested method of reversing the effects of a change to a system is to restore it from the most recent backup. Of course, be sure to verify that such a backup exists and that you are able to restore data from it before implementing the change. A tape backup might come in handy even if you are applying a patch that has an uninstall function because such rollback mechanisms have been known to fail. If the scope of your change is relatively narrow, for instance if you are just modifying a configuration file, a rollback plan might be simply a matter of creating a copy of the file before editing it.

When making changes to the infrastructure, you are often faced with making tough choices, even if your change-management process incorporates principles mentioned earlier. In the next section, we go over several mechanisms that can help you make such decisions.

Implementing Change-Management Controls

The process of change management, described in the previous section, focuses on making sure that changes to the environment happen in a controlled and deterministic fashion. The cornerstone of this process is a documented change-management procedure that explains how things should be done, when, and by whom. There are also techniques that can make it easier for your organization to follow this procedure. In this section, we examine ways of using tools and procedures to assist in implementing change-management practices for some of the more common scenarios:

- Applying patches
- Discovering new services and devices
- Determining configuration changes

Let's start by looking at an age-long problem that you've most likely faced in your career already: applying patches.

Applying Patches

On several occasions throughout this book, we've emphasized the need for regularly patching your OS and applications to prevent attackers from exploiting known software vulnerabilities. Unfortunately, sometimes this is easier said than done. It is not always easy to keep track of patches that vendors release for all the products that you need to maintain. More importantly, some of the more urgent patches do not undergo regression testing, so the vendor does not guarantee that they will work well in all permutations of system configurations.

To make it harder to forget applying necessary patches, clearly designate individuals who are responsible for monitoring patch and vulnerability announcement forums. It often makes sense to assign this responsibility to system administrators who maintain respective products, but do not assume that they are already subscribed to relevant mailing lists. Consider handing out a list of applicable announcement forums. As a security professional, you should monitor them as well to help ensure that a vulnerability does not go by unnoticed.

As a stream of vulnerability announcements flows through your mailbox, you need to decide whether they apply to your environment and how urgent it is for you to react. You need to weigh the risk of delaying a patch rollout, perhaps to perform more thorough testing, against the risk of having a vulnerable network resource. For instance, if a patch prevents an exploitable compromise of your DNS server, you might want to deploy the fix as soon as it comes out. A patch that is, perhaps, less urgent might be one that aims to correct a theoretical vulnerability in a print server deep within your network. If the print server is not your most critical resource, you might decide to wait until the vendor provides a more comprehensive upgrade or until your peers share their experiences pertaining to this patch. In some cases, patches might not be available or might be too risky to apply, and you will need to consider other workarounds to address critical vulnerabilities.

Whatever decisions you make regarding applying, testing, or delaying the installation of a patch or a workaround, be sure to document them. Such journals will help you remember reasons for making certain decisions, and if you chose not to apply the patch, the journals will allow you to revisit the decision at a later date. We suggest including the following fields in each journal entry:

- The date the patch or the vulnerability was announced
- The list and description of systems to which the patch or the vulnerability applies
- The decisions made regarding the patch or vulnerability
- The names of persons who made the decision
- If corrective action was deemed necessary, who is responsible for implementing it
- The date on which the decision was made, or when the corrective action was taken

In large environments, it might be difficult to know versions of applications that are installed throughout your organization, or even which services are running on remotely accessible systems. Our next section focuses on techniques for keeping track of new systems and services that come online on your network.

Discovering New Services and Devices

You need to know which systems and services are available on your network to be able to assess risks and correct potential vulnerabilities. To help achieve this awareness, you might establish a policy that new network services have to be registered with and, possibly, approved by information security person-nel. However, environments change quickly, and before too long, your net-work is likely to contain resources that you were not notified about. One of the most effective ways to discover the presence of unauthorized or inadver-tent network resources on your network is to compare periodic snapshots of the state of your network.

We already described one mechanism for discovering new services offered by your systems in Chapter 9, "Host Hardening." There, we mentioned that you can schedule each host to periodically run the `netstat -na` command to list ports that the system listens on. You can then create a script that com-pares the output of each successive run by using `fc.exe` under Windows or `diff` in UNIX. This technique focuses on individual systems, but it might not be practical for monitoring the state of workstations, servers, and devices on a mid-to-large size network.

Network and vulnerability scanners, which we describe in greater detail in Chapter 20, "Assessment Techniques," offer a way to remotely test for the existence of network services. To locate newly set up systems or unautho-rized port listeners, you would compare the output of successive network scans and flag the differences. Nessus, a popular vulnerability scanner, and Nmap, one of the most powerful network scanners, make this a relatively painless task.

Nessus, freely available from `http://www.nessus.org`, does a great job of scanning networks for accessible hosts or open ports, and it specializes at probing systems for known vulnerabilities. One of the ways to detect changes in your environment is to regularly scan your network with Nessus and compare the results. To simplify this task, Nessus can perform *diff scanning*. If this function is enabled, Nessus includes only those findings in its report that are different from the previously executed scan. To take advantage of this function, you need to activate the knowledge base saving feature and then enable the setting marked as Only Show Differences with the Previous Scan, as illustrated in Figure 17.6.

Tip

To build in support for diff scanning in Nessus, you need to explicitly compile it with the `--enable-save-kb` configuration option, as specified in `http://www.nessus.org/doc/diff_scan.html`.

Figure 17.6 Nessus can be configured to only discover hosts, services, and vulnerabilities that differ from the previous scan.

If you are not interested in scanning for vulnerabilities or you prefer to use a tool other than Nessus, you can take advantage of scanning capabilities of Nmap. Nmap (http://www.nmap.org) is a wonderful tool for locating hosts and open ports, and it's invaluable for performing security assessments. You can also schedule Nmap to periodically scan your network and compare differences in the network's state. To perform diff scans with Nmap, you can use an add-on utility called NDiff, available for free from http://www.vinecorp.com/ndiff.

To use NDiff, you first scan your network with Nmap and then save the output into a file by using an -m option, like this:

```
# nmap -m snapshot.nm 192.168.1.0/24
```

In this example, Nmap port-scans all hosts on the 192.168.1.0/24 network and saves the output into a file called snapshot.nm. The next time you run Nmap, you would save its output into a different file, say newsnapshot.nm. You would then use NDiff to compare contents of the two files, like this:

```
# ndiff -b snapshot.nm -o newsnapshot.nm -format minimal
new hosts:
192.168.1.100
```

```
missing hosts:

changed hosts:
192.168.1.204
80/tcp/http (unknown -> open)
443/tcp/https (unknown -> open)
```

In this example, NDiff detects that a new host appears on the network, and that another host begins listening for HTTP and HTTPS connections. To simplify the task of running Nmap, storing its output, and then comparing the results of the scan, NDiff comes with a wrapper utility called nrun.

Using diff scanning, you might detect services that should not be present on your network and react by disabling them. On the other hand, your investigation might show that a new service has a legitimate need, in which case you will need to understand what it is about to determine how it should be configured. In Chapter 13, "Software Architecture," we presented a Software Evaluation Checklist with questions that you can ask when assessing how an application fits in with the rest of the security perimeter. We suggest asking such questions not only of your third-party providers, but also of your colleagues. Understanding the application's technical and business requirements will help you assess its risks and devise appropriate mitigations.

Summary

This chapter discussed core principles of maintaining a security perimeter and examined the fundamentals of system and network monitoring, incident response, and change management. A reliable monitoring process is essential to knowing the state of your infrastructure and allows you to rapidly detect problems and react accordingly. We also covered considerations for centrally monitoring remote resources without exposing them to additional vulnerabilities.

Next, we examined incident response procedures to prepare you for responding to alerts that are generated by monitoring and intrusion detection systems. We emphasized the need to define a detailed plan for handling malicious and fault-related incidents so that you can focus on investigating and eliminating the problem when the need arises.

Recognizing that even the most thought-out infrastructure is bound to evolve along with the organization, we described the significance of sound change-management practices. This aspect of perimeter maintenance focused on applying patches, deploying new applications, enforcing controls, and detecting infrastructure changes in a deterministic manner.

The next chapters are meant to help you apply some of the practices discussed in this chapter while incorporating design concepts from earlier parts of the book. We also examine the process of assessing the effectiveness of architecture and implementation of the security perimeter. Stay tuned!

References

1 Cisco Systems, Inc. "Configuring SNMP Support." 1998. `http://www.cisco.com/univercd/cc/td/doc/product/software/ios121/121cgcr/fun_c/fcprt3/fcd301.htm`. February 2002.

2 Sun Microsystems, Inc. "Sun Management Center 3.0: General FAQ." `http://www.sun.com/solaris/sunmanagementcenter/faq/faq-general.html`. February 2002.

3 Stephen Northcutt. "Computer Security Incident Handling Step by Step." SANS Institute. 1998.

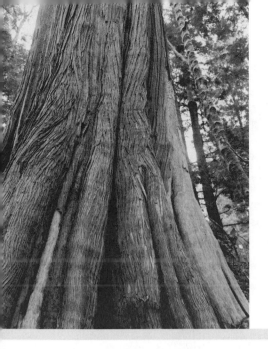

18

Network Log Analysis

ONE OF THE MOST CHALLENGING, yet rewarding, aspects of perimeter security is network log file analysis. This process involves trying to identify intrusions and intrusion attempts through vigilant monitoring and analysis of various log files, and correlating events among those files. There are many different types of network log files to review, from devices that include network firewalls, routers, and packet filters to host-centric firewalls and host-centric intrusion detection systems (IDSs). Although analyzing log files might sound like a dreary chore to you, the techniques that are presented in this chapter help you to gain a great deal of value from your files in a short amount of time.

This chapter discusses several important topics that demonstrate why log file analysis is so critical to establishing and maintaining a strong perimeter defense:

- Purpose of and characteristics of log files
- Basics of log file analysis, particularly how to automate as much of the analysis as possible
- Examples of how to analyze router, packet filter, network, host-centric firewalls, and host-centric IDS logs

By the end of this chapter, you should be well-prepared to perform your own analysis of network log files in your environment to accurately identify suspicious and malicious activity and to respond to it quickly. As a first step toward that goal, let's talk about why you should care about log files and what they can tell you if you listen.

The Importance of Network Log Files

In many environments, system administrators completely ignore network log files; the administrators are constantly putting out fires and don't have time to devote to log file review. Actually, it's more accurate to say that the files are ignored until a major incident occurs. Then there's a mad scramble to find out what happened, which typically includes a check of log files, often done by an administrator who isn't very familiar with the log file format or the proper procedures and steps for performing good log file analysis. Sometimes the administrator discovers that detailed logging was not enabled, so no record of the event exists. After the crisis has ended, the log files are again ignored until the next catastrophe occurs.

Log files have many things to tell you, if you only stop to listen to them. Log files have several purposes of which you might not be aware, which will be reviewed in the "Purposes of Log Files" section later in this chapter. They are incredibly helpful in meeting a range of needs, such as intrusion detection, incident handling, event correlation, and troubleshooting. Each log file contains many pieces of information that can be invaluable if you know how to read them and, more importantly, if you know how to analyze the data from a perimeter defense viewpoint to identify scans, intrusion attempts, misconfigured equipment, and other noteworthy items. Before you can learn how to analyze the data, you first have to understand what sort of data you will likely have.

Characteristics of Log Files

Many different types of log files exist, and they are generated by various sources. Most operating systems, including all flavors of UNIX and some versions of Windows (such as 2000 and NT), perform extensive logging of events as they occur. Also, many applications log events of significance, such as authentication attempts, application errors, and configuration changes. For our purposes, we are most interested in analyzing network log files; to understand the events that occur on a network, you want to focus on log files that record network-related events, such as successful and failed connections. Many other logs (such as operating system log files) also contain valuable information, which can be used to correlate the network activities, although the primary focus in this chapter is the examination of network logs. Devices such as firewalls, routers, and network intrusion detection systems generate network logs.

Note
Although operating systems and many applications have great logging capabilities, they are often disabled by default. System administrators must take care to ensure that logging is enabled and that the logs are sufficiently detailed.

If you have ever looked at log files from several different devices or applications, you have surely noticed that the logs are typically in completely different formats. Later in this chapter, starting with the "Analyzing Router Logs" section, we will review some of the most commonly encountered log formats. Although it's important to realize that log formats differ, it's far more important to understand that different devices and applications might log very different information. Some logs contain little useful data, perhaps only a timestamp and the source and destination addresses and ports, whereas others contain just about everything you would possibly want to know about the event in question. Some logs record virtually every IP and TCP or UDP characteristic of traffic, plus interpretation of the significance of that traffic. The two main factors—various log formats and different log information—are what make network log analysis a bit intimidating at first. Let's work through that by examining what data you might find in network log files.

Information That Log Files Usually Record

Most systems that utilize network log files record several core pieces of information about each connection or packet that they deem to be of interest:

- Timestamp, which typically includes the date, as well as the time in seconds or fractions of a second, when the event occurred or when the event was recorded to the log
- Basic IP characteristics, such as source address, destination address, and IP protocol (TCP, UDP, ICMP, and so on)
- TCP or UDP source and destination ports, or ICMP type and code

Additionally, most log entries contain some sort of reason why the event was logged. However, this varies widely among log formats:

- Descriptive text explanation
- Rule number that matched traffic
- Action that was performed, such as accepting, dropping, or rejecting a connection

Although this might not seem like much data, you can do a lot with just this information. For example, you can analyze it to identify port scans, host scans, or other failed connection attempts. You can also do basic traffic analysis, but with just these elements, the amount of analysis you can do is quite limited. You need more data on events to perform a more in-depth analysis.

Information That Log Files Sometimes Record

Many network logs do record more information than just the core items. Other types of data that might appear include these:

- Other IP characteristics, particularly the IP identification number and the time to live (TTL)
- More TCP-specific characteristics, such as flags (SYN, ACK and the like), TCP window values, and TCP sequence numbers
- The interface that saw the event
- The beginning of the payload's content, although this is much more the exception than the rule

These additional fields can be beneficial in terms of log analysis. For example, the time to live and TCP window values can be used to perform OS fingerprinting to determine the likely OS of the attacker (although a smart attacker can modify tell-tale values such as the TTL). TCP flags might indicate the intent of an attacker; certain flag combinations tend to mean that the packets are trying to evade firewalls or IDSs. Some of these extra fields can also help determine what tool or malware is generating the attack. Most tools have a unique signature, and these data elements can help you to find that signature so that you know exactly what the attacker is trying to do. Unfortunately, even with this extra information, you still might not have enough data to perform as detailed of an analysis as you would like to do.

Information That Log Files Rarely Record

Most devices that perform network logging do not closely examine or even record the full payloads of the traffic that they see. Doing so is generally outside the capabilities of the device, and it is incredibly resource-intensive. Most network logging is based on examining the core characteristics of the packets and connections, and making decisions based on those characteristics alone. There's little need, from the perspective of that device, to examine or record all the packets in a connection.

However, it's often beneficial to have more information on traffic and to be able to do more careful evaluations of payloads. It's often useful to record full packet headers as well to capture all of the pertinent information, not just the header values that are stored in the log. If full packets are recorded for connections or packets that are deemed suspicious, you could then perform a deeper examination as needed and have all the packet's information available. Unfortunately, most logs do not support packet recording; in these cases, you might be able to set up a dedicated packet sniffer or use a program such as tcpdump to perform packet captures; in most environments, however, the volume of traffic will be too high to record all packets, and organizational policies might forbid the recording of all traffic for privacy or liability reasons.

Most devices that perform network logging do not also perform protocol decoding at the application layer. A good example of this would be a DNS request. A network log might report that host 10.20.30.40 sent a packet to UDP port 53 on host 172.30.128.12. You see port 53 and think "DNS," but you really have no idea whether this was a DNS request. Even if it were a DNS request, you have no information about the request. With the exception of a proxying firewall, devices that perform network logging usually don't do protocol decoding or verification. You must rely on stateful network IDSs and proxies to perform protocol verification.

Note
One great feature of proxying firewalls is that a web proxy can log URLs. If a new worm that exploits HTTP is spreading, other perimeter devices may log port 80 connection attempts, but the web proxy will actually log the URL that the worm uses, which can be invaluable in determining what is occurring.

Purposes of Log Files

Now that you have looked at the types of data that log files record, let's step back for a minute and think about the purposes that log files serve. Of course, the main purpose of a log file is to record events of significance or interest. But what you would really like to know is how these records can be useful to you and your organization. As you will see, log files have several important roles to play and can assist you in such areas as incident handling, intrusion detection, event correlation, and general troubleshooting.

Incident Handling

Probably the most obvious use of network log files is to provide data that can be used for incident handling. For example, if a network administrator receives a report that a device has been compromised, she might use network log files to determine which host or hosts might have been responsible for the attack and what methods of attack might have been used. When a web page is defaced, the sysadmins are likely to consult the web server's logs, but also the logs of other devices through which the malicious traffic might have passed, which could provide additional information about the attack and the attacker. Network log files are an invaluable component of incident handling.

During incident handling, you will need to preserve evidence should you want to perform disciplinary actions against someone within an organization or pursue legal actions against an external party. Under those circumstances, log files are extremely important for forensic purposes. When properly preserved, network log files provide evidence of activity—evidence that might be admissible in legal proceedings. The procedures you need to follow for evidence handling vary widely depending on where you are located, but a general guideline is that the original, unaltered log files should be preserved, preferably both electronically and on paper. Contact your local law enforcement agency for advice on how to preserve log file evidence. For additional information on incident handling, see Chapter 17, "Maintaining a Security Perimeter."

Intrusion Detection

Although log files are invaluable during the handling of many incidents, this is a purely reactive use of log files. A related proactive use is that of intrusion detection. By automatically and continuously monitoring log file entries, you can be notified when someone is scanning your network or performing reconnaissance or when an actual incident is in progress. This will also help with incident handling; when a significant intrusion is detected and reported to you, you already have much of the data you will need to perform incident handling for that event.

Note

Even the simplest firewall and router logs can be used for some basic intrusion detection. For example, blocked packets or connections can be counted by source or destination IP address or by destination port, which is useful in identifying scans, probes, and reconnaissance attempts.

Event Correlation

Event correlation is useful in performing both incident handling and intrusion detection. When we speak of event correlation, we mean that it's possible to use multiple logs from various devices or applications together. Event correlation can be done to confirm what has occurred. For example, you see a suspicious entry on an internal router's log that involves an external host, and you search the logs of the Internet firewall for entries that provide more information on the action. Another use of event correlation is to relate events to each other. If your email server is compromised, you would search through various network logs from routers, firewalls, and other devices to look for any evidence relating to the compromise, such as other connection attempts made to the email server, or other hosts on your network that have been targeted by the same attacker.

General Troubleshooting

A final use of network log files is to assist in general troubleshooting, particularly those involving connectivity issues. For example, a user complains that application XYZ can't download data from an external server. By getting the IP address of the user's machine and finding out what time he tried to use the application, you could quickly search your firewall's logs to look for denied attempts to make the required connection. If your firewall also logs all permitted connections, you could look for a valid connection to the remote site, which would indicate that the problem most likely involves the remote server or the application, not your perimeter defense configuration. More information on troubleshooting is presented Chapter 19, "Troubleshooting Defense Components."

Note

In most environments, configuring your firewall to log all permitted connections is not possible due to the negative impact on performance and resources. However, temporarily configuring your firewall to log all connections is often helpful when troubleshooting a problem.

Log Analysis Basics

Now that we've discussed the basics of network log files, let's dig in to the really interesting material—how to analyze the log files after you have them. Log file analysis is an incredibly important area of network security that is often overlooked. If network log analysis is not being performed regularly and thoroughly in your environment, your organization's perimeter defenses are significantly weakened because you and other administrators are missing a large part of the overall security picture.

Getting Started

When you're just starting to perform log analysis, you might find it difficult. Let's be honest—looking at page after page of cryptic log entries probably isn't how you want to spend your time. You have many other tasks to do, and most of those tasks are attached to people who are calling you, wanting to know when you're going to be taking care of them. Log files don't yell at you or beg for your attention, so it's easy to ignore them or forget about them altogether. And when you first start analyzing your logs, it's bound to take a significant amount of your time.

But after you have been reviewing your logs on a regular basis for a while and you have automated the log analysis (as described in the "Automating Log Analysis" section later in this chapter), you will find that it doesn't take as much of your time as you might think, and it can actually save you time and headaches down the road. The hardest part is getting started. Here are some tips that will help you start analyzing your logs:

- Establish a set time each day to review your logs, and stick to that schedule. Preferably, you can do your review at a time of the day when you will have minimal interruptions. If you start making excuses for skipping your log file review, you will most likely stop reviewing them altogether. Just hang in there—it will become easier and faster over time.

- Choose a reasonable length of time to do your daily log review and analysis session. Of course, this is highly dependent on how many log entries you will be reviewing and the security needs in your environment. An hour a day is probably a good starting point; adjust accordingly as needed. Of course, if you find that the amount of time doesn't work for you, you can always change it later.

- Decide in how much depth you want to analyze your logs. There is value in doing an overall review of all the log files, but also in doing an in-depth analysis of log excerpts. When you're starting, it's probably good to try both techniques to get a better "feel" for your log files.

> **Note**
>
> One method that might help you to "break the ice" and start analyzing your logs is to do searches on them using keywords such as "blocked," "denied," and "refused." With many log files, this is a quick and easy way to identify log entries that might need further review.

This brings up a critical point: the concept of "feel." Much of the motivation for reviewing your log files regularly is that you will get a feel for what your log files normally look like. The only way to achieve this is through regular reviews. After you have a sense of the baseline, it should be easy for you to spot most deviations from that baseline in the future. If you know what entries are normally recorded in your logs, and one day you see an entry that you have never seen before, then you will naturally target that as something to be investigated further. If you didn't have that feel for your logs, you probably wouldn't even notice such an entry. That's the hidden value in performing regular analysis—the ability to sense when something unusual has occurred. After you have that feel, you can increasingly rely on automation to perform the basic log analysis for you, selecting only those items that are of particular interest to you.

Fun with Log Files?

You might think that reviewing log files is the most boring thing you could possibly do with your time. Personally, I find log analysis to be a fascinating area of network security, and it's actually become a hobby of mine. Honest! When I am reviewing a potential incident, I think of log file analysis as a jigsaw puzzle, with some pieces that don't look like they fit at all, and other pieces that seem to be missing. Each piece has something to contribute to the picture, and figuring out how they fit together is really quite addictive.

When I first started doing log analysis, I found it to be rather boring and difficult. I didn't understand most of the log formats, and I usually didn't realize the significance of the data that I was reviewing. Over time, my knowledge grew, and trying to decipher the activity behind the log entries became a welcome challenge. Try log file analysis—you might be surprised at how much you like it.

Automating Log Analysis

After you have been manually reviewing and analyzing your log files for a while, you will be able to glance at many log entries and immediately understand their significance. Most log entries will probably be of little or no interest to you. Over time, you will notice that fewer of the entries merit your attention. This is where automated log analysis becomes so helpful to you. By now, you know what log entries you really want to see—or, more correctly, you know what log entries you really *don't* want to see. By automating parts of the log analysis process, you can generate a report of only the unusual activities that you would like to investigate further, which will save you a great deal of time.

Log analysis automation can be a bit tricky, depending on the format of the log files. Many log files, such as Cisco router logs, are in a text format, which means that they are typically easy to review using automated techniques. However, other log files, such as Check Point FireWall-1 logs, are in binary or proprietary formats that cannot be automatically reviewed in their native form. In some cases, you can export the log file to a text file, either through the application that recorded the log file or through a separate log conversion utility. In other cases, you might not be able to access the log file information unless you use a viewer that the application provides; in this example, you probably can't automate the review of that log file. Whenever possible, it is best to handle log files that are in some sort of text file format, such as tab-delimited or comma-separated values (CSV). This will make the rest of the automation process far easier for you.

Another potentially difficult aspect of log analysis automation is handling the volume of the logs. Depending on the amount of traffic that is being monitored and what events are being logged, a single log could contain millions of entries a day. Remember, you might be reviewing dozens, hundreds, or even thousands of logs, depending on the size and composition of your environment. In such a case, you will need to choose an automation method that cannot only process that number of entries in a timely manner, but that also has adequate storage space. Some of the possible automation methods are discussed in the next section, "Getting the Right Data from Log Files."

As you do network log analysis, you will discover that reviewing the "bad" log entries is often insufficient. Sometimes you will also want to look through the original log file to see other entries from the same source IP address, for example, or to look for other activity that occurred immediately before or after the event in question. If you save only "bad" log entries and do not preserve the raw logs, you lose the ability to analyze such events. Raw logs are sometimes required for evidentiary purposes, so saving them is often important.

Getting the Right Data from Log Files

As mentioned earlier, it's best to convert your binary log files to a text format such as tab-delimited or comma-separated values. After you have your log files in a suitable format, you want to find the pertinent log entries and generate a report. You can do this in two ways:

- Use a searching utility such as `grep` or `sed` to look through a log file for records that match or do not match particular strings or regular expressions.
- Import some or all of the data from the log files into a database, and then search and analyze the data.

Determining which method to use depends on several factors, including your own preferences. Performance is a major consideration; if you have to process enormous numbers of records, you need to choose a method that can handle it. This is dependent on the number of log entries, the complexity of the searches and analysis that you want to perform, and the tools and databases that are available to you. Databases have a distinct advantage because you can import logs into a database, store the data there, and run reports over days, weeks, or even months of data and significant events. This can identify suspicious activity that occurs over long periods of times, which might never be found by processing a day's worth of data at a time. It is also invaluable when performing incident handling because you can review previously logged events involving particular hosts or protocols.

Many different tools can be used to assist in log file processing. `grep` and `sed` are two useful text searching tools from the UNIX world that have Windows equivalents. Programming languages such as Perl can be extremely powerful in parsing log files, selecting entries, and generating reports. If you have a small volume of logs, you might be able to import them in a spreadsheet and analyze them through macros, sorts, and searches. Microsoft Excel has a feature called AutoFilter that allows you to quickly sift through numerous rows of data. For larger volumes of logs or more complex logs, a full-fledged database might provide a robust and powerful solution that can analyze log entries and generate reports of suspicious activities.

Note

If you are a UNIX administrator who needs to perform log analysis on Windows systems, you might find that the task is much easier if you use a collection of cross-platform tools such as Cygwin (`http://www.cygwin.com/`), which provides a simulated UNIX environment, complete with many UNIX utilities, for Windows machines.

Be aware that it might take considerable time and resources to create a log analysis automation solution. You might need to write programs or scripts to perform the analysis and to generate reports based on the results of that analysis. For every hour that you spend creating and testing a strong automation solution, you will save yourself many more hours in analysis time, and you will be able to react much more quickly when an incident occurs.

Automating Check Point FireWall-1 Log Analysis

After spending hours each day looking through FireWall-1 logs, I realized the need for a system to automate some of the mundane tasks of correlating and flagging suspicious records. Unfortunately, we did not have the budget to purchase a commercial log analysis solution, so I decided to do what I could with a custom Perl script. The script that I wrote operated as follows:

- It extracted records from FireWall-1 log files.
- It parsed each entry to pull out relevant fields for all blocked packets.
- It counted the number of log entries for each source IP address, destination IP address, and destination port.
- It added record counts to numbers saved from previous runs.
- It generated a report that specified the top 20 addresses and ports that the firewall blocked.

This relatively simple script made it easier for me to get a quick sense for activity that was present in each day's logs, and helped me detect low and slow scans that would not have come to my attention without maintaining a historical record of events.

Designing Reports

This might seem to be a silly question, but what do you want to report? Of course, you want to know what suspicious activity is occurring. But in many cases, it's ineffective to generate a single report of all suspicious activity. Some events are going to be much more significant than others in your environment by default, so you might want to emphasize them in your report and summarize the less interesting events. For example, if your daily logs typically include entries for a thousand port scans and two or three DNS exploit attempts, you probably want to see some details on the DNS attacks but only a summary of the port scan activity.

A key issue to consider is who will be receiving the report. If the report is just for you, then by all means, design it however you would like to. Perhaps, however, you are designing reports that will list suspicious activity for all of your organization's firewalls. Some system administrators might like a report of all events that involve their hosts that were logged by the firewall. The person who is responsible for web server security might like a report of suspicious web-related activity. It would also be nice to be able to do custom reports on demand, such as quickly generating a report of all events that were logged in the past two weeks involving a particular IP address. Such a capability would be extremely helpful when investigating an incident.

Using a Third-Party Analysis Product

Writing programs or scripts to analyze log files and generate reports might sound like a lot of work. Many times, it is, although it does give you a highly tailored solution. If creating your own automation system is not feasible, you might want to consider using a third-party product that will perform some log analysis and reporting for you. Or you might want to combine your own custom scripts with third-party products to create a solution.

Vendors such as NetForensics (`http://www.netforensics.com/`) and Intellitactics (`http://www.intellitactics.com/`) offer software products that can be of great assistance to you in automating network log analysis. These products are designed to accept logs from various sources, including many brands of firewalls, network and host-centric intrusion detection systems, and operating systems. They process all the log entries to perform event correlation and identify likely intrusion attempts. Third-party log analysis products offer other useful features, such as log archiving and extensive reporting functionality. You can save yourself many hours by using a third-party analysis product as the heart of your network log analysis solution.

Timestamps

The importance of timestamps in log files cannot be emphasized strongly enough. If an incident ever requires legal action and the timestamps in your log files are out of sync with the actual time, you might have difficulty proving that the incident occurred at a particular time. In many courts, you must be able to prove that your time source is reliable. A much more frequent problem is that you will have an extremely difficult time correlating activities among different log files if all of the log files are not synchronized to the same time. It's easy to compensate for this if two boxes are in adjacent time zones and are synched to be exactly an hour apart, but if you are dealing with 20 devices that are each seconds or minutes apart from each other, it becomes nearly impossible to correlate events effectively between any two logs, much less several of them.

The Network Time Protocol (NTP) can be used to perform time synchronization between many different devices on a network, as well as synchronizing the clocks on a network with a highly accurate NTP public time server. A detailed discussion of NTP is outside the scope of this book, but more information on it is available at many sites on the Internet, with the primary page hosted by the University of Delaware at `http://www.ntp.org/`.

Hopefully, the logs that you will be working with will have synchronized timestamps. However, if you are forced to work with logs that have unsynchronized timestamps, you can make the necessary adjustments to manually synchronize the logs. For example, you might be able to write a script that requests the current time from each logging device at the same time. It could then determine with a reasonable degree of accuracy (a few seconds) how far out of sync each box is. When the log files for that day are analyzed, the timestamps could be adjusted as necessary to bring all log entries to within a few seconds of being correctly synchronized. Of course, if you have a device that is drifting badly out of sync on a daily basis, you should probably be more concerned about taking care of its clock issues than synchronizing its log timestamps!

Note

It is generally recommended that if your organization's systems cover multiple time zones, you configure your systems to log everything using Greenwich Mean Time (GMT) to avoid confusion.

So far in this chapter, you have learned about the basics of log files and some of the fundamental concepts of log analysis. Now it's time to look at some real-world analysis examples. For the rest of this chapter, you will examine classes of devices: routers, network firewalls and packet filters, and host-centric firewalls and intrusion detection systems. You will go through several log examples by studying a particular log type's format, reviewing a real example of that log format, and explaining how it can be analyzed. By the time you reach the end of the chapter, you will have a great exposure to how to analyze logs and identify suspicious and malicious activity. Let's start our journey by looking at router logs.

Analyzing Router Logs

Compared to other log files that you will look at in this chapter, router logs tend to contain only the most basic information about network traffic. That makes sense because routers are typically processing high volumes of traffic and only examine the most basic characteristics of packets and connections when making routing decisions. However, this doesn't mean that router logs are not valuable; on the contrary, they can be extremely helpful in identifying certain types of activity, such as unauthorized connection attempts and port scans. Although the focus in this section will be on Cisco router logs, you will also briefly look at what information other routers log, which tends to be roughly the same.

Cisco Router Logs

In Chapter 2, "Packet Filtering," we discussed Cisco routers in depth, including how their logging capabilities can be configured. All Cisco routers use the same basic log file format. The following is an entry from a Cisco router log:

```
Jan 28 03:15:26 [10.20.30.40] 265114: %SEC-6-IPACCESSLOGP: list 105 denied tcp
➥172.30.128.12(1947) -> 10.20.1.6(80), 1 packet
```

The format of the log entries requires a bit of explanation. After starting with a date and timestamp, the entry lists the router IP address and the message sequence number. The next entry, `%SEC-6-IPACCESSLOGP`, requires a bit more explanation. The `SEC-6` indicates that this is a security-related entry of severity level 6; the `IPACCESSLOGP` refers to the specific message type. The remaining fields are the ACL that matched this activity, the action performed, the IP protocol, the source IP address, the TCP source port, the destination IP address, the TCP destination port, and the number of packets.

> **Note**
>
> If you're already familiar with Cisco router logs, you might look at this example and think that the format doesn't match your Cisco router's logs. That's entirely possible; aspects of the log format are configurable. For example, many logs contain an additional time value, which indicates the router uptime. Some logs also have a GMT offset value at the end of each entry.

As you can see, only the most basic information is logged. In this example, you know the IP addresses and the TCP ports that were used, but that's about it. This entry tells us that an attempt to initiate a connection to port 80 on host 10.20.1.6 was blocked. Port 80 is most commonly used for HTTP.

By itself, this router log entry doesn't give us much information, just that someone probably tried to connect to the host for HTTP and that the router blocked the connection. However, think about what it would mean if you saw thousands of entries like this one in our router log, each one targeting TCP port 80 on a different destination host. Then, based on these log entries alone, you would have strong reason to believe that someone was scanning your entire network, looking for web servers.

Other Router Logs

Other brands of routers tend to log approximately the same information that Cisco routers do. For example, Ascend routers log all the same pieces of data that Cisco routers do, plus two others that are helpful in performing analysis: the packet size and the TCP flags (if applicable). In most cases, though, you will not have that additional information in router logs—just the most fundamental characteristics of the packets.

Although all of your router logs will contain important information, the most significant logs to check are probably your Internet routers, particularly any that are on the edge of your network, such as outside your firewalls. If an Internet router denies a request from an external host, only that router can contain a corresponding log entry; devices that are further inside your network will never see the traffic. Therefore, that router's log is the only place that you can see evidence of the denied request. Internet router logs are a rich source of information on failed scans, probes, and attacks that never reach other areas of your network. Your network firewall logs are another great source of intrusion data.

Analyzing Network Firewall Logs

Dozens of different network firewall solutions are available, each with a unique logging format. Some such devices log little information about traffic—approximately the same information that most routers log. Other firewalls are capable of recording a great deal of detail about traffic that they monitor. As you will see in the examples that follow, the variety in the amount of information logged has a large impact on how deeply you can analyze incidents and suspicious activity. We have chosen to review the log formats of the three firewalls that were discussed in Chapter 3, "Stateful Firewalls": the Cisco PIX, Check Point FireWall-1, and IPTables.

Cisco PIX logs

The Cisco PIX firewall logs events of interest in the following format:

```
Jan 28 03:10:04 [10.20.30.50] %PIX-2-106001: Inbound TCP connection denied from
➥172.30.128.12/1938 to 10.20.12.34/53 flags SYN on interface outside
```

Take a moment to compare the format of this entry with that of the Cisco routers. Although the two have some similarities, they are different in certain ways as well. Whereas the Cisco router logs simply refer to the rule number that caused the entry to be logged, the Cisco PIX provides a detailed text-based explanation as to why this traffic was recorded. Also, note that the Cisco PIX records the TCP flags in its log entry, but the Cisco router does not. Because you're already familiar with the Cisco router log format, the rest of the Cisco PIX log format should be self-explanatory.

Let's practice log analysis a little more formally by examining the Cisco PIX log entry excerpt. What can be determined about the nature of this event based solely on the log entry? Of course, you know what date and time the event occurred. You can see which of your hosts was the target of the event and what the IP address of the potential attacker is. You know which firewall logged the activity, which might be helpful in determining why the traffic was blocked because you can examine that particular firewall's rule set. In addition, the log shows that the traffic was blocked trying to enter the firewall from an external interface. All of this information helps you investigate the event and correlate it with logs on other devices.

One of the reasons that correlation is so important is that it's difficult to determine the nature of this event based on just this log entry. You can see that the blocked connection attempt had a destination of TCP port 53, which is typically associated with DNS traffic. Attackers often target TCP port 53 to get information from DNS servers or to attack vulnerabilities in those servers. However, there's not enough data here to make that assumption; a misconfiguration or another benign reason could cause this activity. By correlating this log entry with other logs—particularly a network intrusion detection sensor that saw this attempt—you can make a better determination as to the significance of this event.

Check Point Firewall-1 Logs

Check Point's FireWall-1 product is another popular network firewall product. Some of the fields included in FireWall-1 logs are listed next:

- The log entry number
- The date
- The time
- The interface that saw the activity
- The device that saw this activity
- The type of log entry
- The action that was performed (such as "block")
- The destination port number or service name
- The source IP address or hostname
- The destination IP address or hostname
- The protocol of the logged packet (such as "udp")
- The rule in the firewall's rule base that is associated with the log entry
- The source port number or service name
- Additional information that might be applicable to the log entry

You might look at the order of these fields and think that it's rather peculiar. Most devices list the source IP address and port together, and then the destination IP address and port together; the FireWall-1 format is quite different. However, there's a good reason for this. FireWall-1 administrators typically view the log files through a GUI interface, which shows the log entries in a table format, with the columns in the order just reviewed. Figure 18.1 shows a screen capture of the Check Point Log Viewer as it displays information about several packets that the firewall blocks.

Figure 18.1 The Check Point FireWall-1 Log Viewer shows the default display order for log entries.

Note

The FireWall-1 Log Viewer can decode the FireWall-1 binary log file format and export the log entries to a text file.

Now think of what information you, as a log analyst, are typically most interested in. You want to know what the target was; that is listed in the destination port address and port, which in most cases will correspond to a particular protocol, such as HTTP or DNS. From an analyst's point of view, it makes a great deal of sense to pair the action with the destination service because they are often related. The source port, which is often not a factor when analyzing traffic, is not listed with the more pertinent data. Although this arrangement might be confusing at first, at least now you understand why it might be done that way.

IPTables Logs

In Chapter 3, we discussed IPTables, a great firewall solution. As you will see, IPTables log much more comprehensively than the other firewalls that are reviewed in this section.

```
Jan 28 03:09:31 mybox kernel: Packet log: IN=ppp0 OUT=
➥MAC=xx:xx:xx:xx:xx:xx:xx:xx:xx:xx:xx:xx:xx:xx SRC=172.30.128.12
➥DST=10.20.1.121 LEN=80 TOS=0x00 PREC=0x00 TTL=55 ID=13492 PROTO=UDP
➥SPT=1907 DPT=27374 LEN=60
```

Here's a quick interpretation of the fields in this log entry: date, time, IPTables host name, syslog level, incoming and outgoing interfaces, MAC addresses, source IP address, destination IP address, packet length (LEN), type of service (TOS), TOS precedence (PREC), time to live (TTL), IP identification number (ID), IP protocol, source port, destination port, and IP payload length (LEN).

Not only does IPTables log all the information that the Cisco PIX and FireWall-1 do, but it also logs several other fields that are helpful in performing advanced log analysis. If you are highly experienced with network intrusion detection, you probably already know how valuable this data can be when identifying the nature of an attack, as well as the characteristics of the attacker.

Analyzing Host-Centric Firewall and IDS Logs

So far, we have discussed performing analysis on logs from network firewalls, packet filters, and routers. These devices are monitoring connections to and from many different hosts. Now let's turn our attention to host-centric firewalls and intrusion detection systems, which also record suspicious network activity, but only involve a single host. Such systems are most often installed on workstations. They are discussed in Chapter 10, "Host Defense Components."

Host-centric firewall and IDS software often records activity that is otherwise unnoticed by network devices. For example, a firewall that only logs denied or rejected traffic won't keep a record of a connection that it permits to an internal host. In such a case, the internal host is the only device that might record the activity if it is using a firewall and/or IDS that is configured to reject and log such an attempt. Also, in many environments, few restrictions are placed on connections between hosts on the internal network; host-centric network logs might be the only way that some malicious activity between internal hosts is recorded.

ZoneAlarm

The format of ZoneAlarm logs is easy to understand. ZoneAlarm records all of its information in a comma-separated value format in text files. Following are sample log entries for blocked TCP, UDP, and ICMP activity, respectively:

```
FWIN,2002/01/28,03:47:43 -6:00 GMT,172.30.128.23:15384,10.20.84.167:80,TCP
➥(flags:S)
FWIN,2002/01/28,03:57:46 -6:00 GMT,172.30.128.23:3283,10.20.84.167:3283,UDP
FWIN,2002/01/28,04:06:30 -6:00 GMT,172.30.128.23:0,10.20.84.167:0,ICMP
➥(type:8/subtype:0)
```

By now, this format should be pretty easy for you to decipher. The first address and port number are for the source; the second pair is for the destination. The FWIN label indicates that the firewall blocked traffic in the entry, and that it was incoming. Lines that begin with FWOUT indicate that outgoing traffic was blocked. Finally, lines that start with PE indicate that the ZoneAlarm user has permitted a particular application's traffic to pass through the firewall.

Note

The ZoneAlarm GUI allows you to enable or disable logging and specify where the log file should be stored, but it does not permit you to view the log entries. You must manually open the ZAlog.txt log file in a program such as a text editor or spreadsheet.

Although you don't see much detailed information in each entry, remember that these entries are being recorded on a particular host. If ZoneAlarm is being run on a user's workstation, odds are good that the workstation offers few or no services, and that there are only a few ports on which it might legitimately be contacted. ZoneAlarm should be configured to permit those connections and to reject and record any other connection attempts, which are almost certainly caused by misconfigured or unauthorized equipment or software, mistakes such as a typo in an address, or malicious activity.

Each ZoneAlarm log by itself can contain valuable information. These logs become much more useful when they are gathered together from many different hosts. If most or all of your workstations are using host-centric firewalls and you can monitor all of their firewall logs, you can get a great picture of what suspicious activities are occurring within your network. The ZoneAlarm Pro version can be administered remotely; also, Zone Labs, the manufacturer of ZoneAlarm, sells a product called Integrity that facilitates centralized logging and has other features that are extremely helpful to analysts.

Note

If you will be analyzing ZoneAlarm logs, a free utility that might help you is VisualZone Report Utility (http://www.visualizesoftware.com), which performs intrusion analysis and generates reports based on ZoneAlarm log data.

Here's an interesting entry from a ZoneAlarm log:

```
FWIN,2002/03/01,22:30:51 -5:00 GMT,172.30.128.198:22,10.20.84.94:22,TCP
➥(flags:SF)
```

You can see that this blocked connection was intended to target TCP port 22 on host 10.20.84.94. SSH usually utilizes this port, so this looks like an attempt to find or use an SSH server. Can you tell whether this is a benign or malicious activity?

There are two telltale signs in this log entry. The more obvious one is that the SYN and FIN flags are both set, which is a classic sign of malicious activity. The less obvious one is that the source port is also set to 22. In a normal SSH connection, you should see a high source port and destination port 22. Because the source port is also set to 22, this is almost certainly crafted traffic that is malicious in nature. Just through this single log entry, you can determine that an attacker is hoping to exploit SSH vulnerabilities on this host.

Tiny Personal Firewall

Tiny Personal Firewall records similar information to ZoneAlarm. Although it does not use a comma-separated or tab-delimited format, Tiny does have a consistent, structured format and it does use a text file for logging. The log excerpt shown next is clear and easy to understand without additional explanation.

```
1,[28/Jan/2002 04:08:37] Rule 'Packet to unopened port received': Blocked:
↪In TCP, wks-172-30-128-23.someisp.foo [172.30.128.23:18509]->
↪localhost:27374, Owner: no owner
```

This entry shows an attempt to connect to port 27374 on the local workstation, which is not an available port on this host. Tiny Personal Firewall log entries can be forwarded from individual hosts to a central location via Syslog, which might be important in large environments.

Here's a great example of a potential incident that has been recorded in a Tiny Personal Firewall log. Take a few minutes to review these entries and to get as much information about the incident from them as you can.

```
1,[28/Jan/2002 04:28:10] Rule 'Packet to unopened port received': Blocked:
↪In TCP, 172.30.128.23:2246->localhost:8080, Owner: no owner
1,[28/Jan/2002 04:28:10] Rule 'Packet to unopened port received': Blocked:
↪In TCP, 172.30.128.23:2247->localhost:80, Owner: no owner
1,[28/Jan/2002 04:28:10] Rule 'Packet to unopened port received': Blocked:
↪In TCP, 172.30.128.23:2248->localhost:3128, Owner: no owner
1,[28/Jan/2002 04:28:10] Rule 'Packet to unopened port received': Blocked:
↪In TCP, 172.30.128.23:2249->localhost:1080, Owner: no owner
```

Are you finished with your review? Let's take another look at the log entries to see what they're trying to tell us. Here are the key pieces of information and their significance:

- All four log entries show the same source IP address. If you saw one attempt from the source address, it could be an accident; however, four separate attempts is much more likely to be malicious activity than an accident.

- All four connection attempts occurred within the same second. This indicates that the activity was almost certainly automated or scripted. It also gives you more proof that this activity is purposeful, not accidental.

- The destination ports—8080, 80, 3128, and 1080—might not look familiar to you. A quick check of a known ports list shows that all four of these ports are web server- or web proxy-related.

Based on these three points, it appears that this log has recorded a scan by a single host for web-related services. If the source address is external, you might want to consider restricting incoming traffic to block such attempts in the future, only permitting incoming traffic on the necessary ports to those hosts that are authorized to provide web services to external hosts.

It's also likely that other hosts on your network were scanned; therefore, correlating this activity by checking your other network log files for similar events is highly recommended.

Tiny Personal Firewall and ZoneAlarm have limited IDS capabilities. Although they can show blocked connections, that's really about it; they do no analysis of the activity that they see and cannot determine the likely intent of a connection attempt or packet. A similar software package that can provide much stronger IDS capabilities is BlackICE Defender.

BlackICE Defender

BlackICE Defender goes a step further than the other host-centric firewalls we examined; although they all block unauthorized connections, BlackICE Defender also applies basic intrusion detection principles against the traffic to attempt to identify the intent of the connections. It's much more of a firewall/intrusion detection system hybrid than ZoneAlarm or Tiny Personal Firewall. As you can see in the following log entry, BlackICE Defender not only reports a connection attempt to port 111, but it also labels it as an RPC port probe. The IDS capability of the product assists you in analyzing the logs.

```
39,2000-04-15 13:22:09,2003402,RPC port
➥probe,10.10.20.142,scan.com,10.4.6.123,target.net,port=111,1
```

This log format is a bit more difficult to decipher than the others in this chapter. From left to right, the fields are severity, date, time, signature number, signature description, source IP address, source host name, destination IP address, destination host name, additional information about why this traffic is suspicious (such as the destination port), and the number of occurrences. As you can see, BlackICE Defender stores each event in a comma-separated value format in a text file.

By adding IDS capabilities to the host-centric firewall, BlackICE Defender saves you time when you perform an analysis. For example, in this case, BlackICE tells you that port 111 corresponds to RPC. That's something you would need to look up, if you weren't already aware of it. The text descriptions that explain why the event was logged also facilitate easy searching and log automation. From an analysis standpoint, it's definitely advantageous to have an intrusion detection capability on hosts such as workstations and servers, rather than simply relying on host-centric firewalls.

BlackICE has some other noteworthy features. Imagine that an attacker performs a host scan by attempting to connect to 100 different TCP ports on a particular host. The host's ZoneAlarm firewall is configured to reject all incoming TCP connection attempts. ZoneAlarm would log 100 entries, one for each failed attempt, and if set to alert, would also generate 100 alerts. Meanwhile, BlackICE would realize that all the attempts were part of one large host scan and would generate one alert and one log entry. Although consolidating the activity into one alert is helpful, not recording a log entry for each attempt might significantly hinder any network log analysis you want to perform for the scan.

On the other hand, BlackICE has a capability that most other host-centric products do not: It can log raw packets. This means that BlackICE stores the entire packet—including headers and payload—for your later review. Various network protocol analyzer utilities, such as Ethereal (`http://www.ethereal.com/`), can process these recorded packets and will greatly assist you in performing an in-depth analysis of a particular incident.

Summary

Throughout this chapter, you learned of the many valuable roles that network file log analysis plays in a strong perimeter defense. By automating most of the log analysis and reviewing the reports that are generated by the automation, you can quickly gain insight into activity on your network and respond much more quickly to events that have just occurred or are in progress. Network log analysis can be of great assistance in such diverse areas as intrusion detection, incident handling, and problem troubleshooting. With an initial investment of time to familiarize yourself with typical log entries and to establish log analysis automation, you can make network log analysis an integral part of your perimeter defenses.

19

Troubleshooting Defense Components

TROUBLE HAPPENS. WE ALL KNOW IT. It doesn't matter how much time and effort your team has spent researching, designing, implementing, and maintaining your world-class network security architecture. Something is going to break. That's why troubleshooting skills are so important.

Troubleshooting is simply a diagnosis process—one you apply to learn enough about a problem to fix it. As with a medical diagnosis, you will work with symptoms when troubleshooting a network security problem. These symptoms usually start out at a very general level, such as "It hurts" ("I can't connect to the server"). Much of your work will be to gather more specific symptoms by asking questions such as "Where does it hurt?" ("Which server?") until you can discover the root cause of the problem and fix it.

This chapter serves you best by focusing on a general troubleshooting methodology in the context of example problems, instead of trying to cover a subset of network security products and hoping they apply to your environment. You have already learned a lot about security technologies in the other chapters. Now, you will improve your troubleshooting skills by learning about the process. The bulk of this chapter is spent showing you how to apply a set of tools to gather input for the process. This is a hands-on approach to help you develop a methodology and toolkit that works for you, based on your strengths, weaknesses, and work environment.

The Process of Troubleshooting

Troubleshooting is a problem-solving process that many find rewarding. In general, troubleshooting revolves around proving or disproving hypotheses. The following steps are part of the troubleshooting process:

1. Collect symptoms.
2. Review recent changes.
3. Form a new hypothesis.
4. Test the hypothesis.
5. Analyze the results.
6. Repeat if necessary.

You probably already apply some form of this process whenever you sit down to solve a problem. You gather information and formulate a hypothesis, whether consciously or not, by simply thinking of a pertinent question to ask. The answer either strengthens or weakens the proof and helps you move on to the next question.

Let's describe these steps in the context of an example whereby Internet users can no longer access our company's web site. We learn of this after getting a call from an outside user saying that she can no longer remotely connect to the site. It's time to gather some facts to see if we can get to the root of the problem.

Collecting Symptoms

Collecting symptoms seems like an obvious step, but sometimes it's easy to jump into solving a problem before you even understand what the problem is. You can often save a lot of time by slowing down and making sure you know the symptoms before proceeding further. Take a little time and try to re-create the problem (unless the symptoms are catastrophic, of course). If you can re-create the problem, you will have an easier time later determining whether your solution actually fixes it. Also, check whether your client or server software includes debug options that might help you collect more specific symptoms.

After talking to the outside user, the main symptom we have for our web site problem is that the browser just times out after a while and presents a message saying that the server is unavailable. We also know that other calls have been received from outside users, so this isn't a contained problem for one user. To verify this symptom, we try to connect to the troubled server from the outside as well, using a dial-up Internet connection. We are unable to connect to the site as well, so this appears to be a problem that affects all outside users. In addition, we try to access the server locally. It works fine, which suggests that this is probably not a server problem. Because our symptoms haven't given us a definitive answer yet, let's consider things that might have recently changed in our environment that could shed some light on the situation.

Reviewing Recent Changes

We include this as a separate step because it so often results in problems. Obviously, you must suspect any recent changes if they coincide with the problem timeframe. In fact, you should consider these changes even if they don't seem to relate to the problem. Often, a change uncovers problems that existed before, but didn't manifest themselves because the conditions weren't quite right, such as server changes that don't present themselves until the first time you reboot. Depending on the circumstances and your environment, you might want to exercise your judgment in considering whether to remove the change immediately and worry about understanding the real cause later. As far as our example problem goes, we do some research and determine that a firewall that is protecting the web server's network segment was replaced with a new firewall about the time that the problem started. We need more information before we can fix it. To get more information, we need to formulate a hypothesis to pursue.

Forming a Hypothesis

If you like puzzles, you might enjoy this part of troubleshooting unless you are under severe pressure to fix the problem. This is where the troubleshooting gurus really shine. Your mission is to combine all your observations, experience, intuition, and prayers to come up with a fix for the problem. You do this by first hypothesizing the cause of the problem and then working to prove it. If you can't guess a specific cause, try the reverse approach. Form a hypothesis, and then work to disprove it. This is a good way to collect additional symptoms or other pertinent information.

Let's continue the example whereby our users can't access the web site after a firewall upgrade. An obvious hypothesis is that we somehow configured the firewall rule set incorrectly, and it's blocking inbound HTTP. The next step is to test that hypothesis.

Testing the Hypothesis

Ideally, you test your hypothesis by implementing a fix for the problem, which is the most direct way to prove or disprove it. However, you might still be working to narrow the possible causes of the problem, in which case a fix is not yet apparent. In that event, you might design and execute a series of tests for the purpose of gathering information until a specific fix presents itself or until you're forced to try a different hypothesis.

Our firewall problem isn't in the "fix-it" stage yet because we're still investigating whether the rule set is the problem. Perhaps the easiest way to test that hypothesis is to look at the firewall configuration and logs to see whether they are blocking the traffic. A quick check shows that the configuration is correct, and the log shows that HTTP traffic is being allowed through.

Analyzing the Results

After you have executed your test, the next step is to analyze the results. If your test involved implementing a fix, such as rearranging the firewall's rule set, then all you need to do is check whether the problem is resolved. In that case, you will have an easier time with this step if you were able to reproduce the problem while you were collecting symptoms. If the problem isn't fixed yet, you will need to analyze the test results to determine what to do next.

We tested our hypothesis that our firewall rule set was incorrect and found that nothing was wrong with it. We might not have completely disproved the hypothesis, but we should look at other possibilities. We will have to continue troubleshooting the problem to get to its root cause and fix it.

Repeating If Necessary

If the problem is solved, your work is done. Otherwise, you will have to perform another iteration of the process. If your test disproved your hypothesis, you must continue by forming and testing another hypothesis. Otherwise, you will have to design another test whose results you can analyze to further narrow the possible causes. This is the nature of most problems, which are rarely solved by the first pass through the troubleshooting process.

We have completed one iteration for our sample firewall problem without solving it. Maybe you would have started with another hypothesis, or you already have another test in mind for gathering more information. To learn whether you're right, however, you have to read more of the chapter to finish the diagnosis!

Troubleshooting Rules of Thumb

Before moving on to describe troubleshooting tools, we want to present a few favorite rules of thumb. These can't be classified as steps in the troubleshooting process, but they will help keep your hypotheses focused on the problem. You probably already have a few rules of your own, and you undoubtedly will develop more as you find other tricks to keep you on track.

Make Only One Change at a Time

This is perhaps the most important rule, and it can be the hardest to follow when you're in a hurry. You can look at multiple sources of information, but don't make multiple changes. Otherwise, you will end up not knowing for sure how you fixed a problem. Worse, you might mask the solution with another problem.

While troubleshooting our firewall example, we moved the client between external and internal locations and, while we examined the firewall configuration, we didn't change it. As a result, we know that the problem depends on the client location. We wouldn't have proved that if we had changed the firewall rule set at the same time; we might have incorrectly focused our attention on the rule set change.

Keep an Open Mind

We can't overstress the importance of an open mind when working on a tough problem. Most people, especially experienced troubleshooters, tend to reason through many problem aspects at an almost unconscious level. Have you ever had trouble explaining a conclusion to someone who is trying to understand how you arrived at it? Sometimes those conclusions are sound, born of past experiences that aren't easily recalled but have been internalized in your own rules of thumb. Sometimes, though, these conclusions are influenced by inaccurate perceptions, false assumptions, personal motivations, and a host of other human traits. If you believe you made no mistakes configuring the firewall—a natural assumption—you might not do a good job of examining the configuration. If you can, work with another troubleshooter to help keep each other honest.

Get a Second Opinion

Sometimes when you can't see the solution to a problem, you need a second set of eyes. Bouncing a situation off of a peer can be a great help when you think that you hit a dead end while troubleshooting a problem. Just the process of methodically explaining to someone else the steps you have gone through can be enough to help you find holes in your own troubleshooting methodology. In any case, brainstorming can be a powerful troubleshooting tool, and it is indispensable when a solution is difficult to find.

Stay Focused on Fixing the Problem

If you subscribe to our philosophy, a problem isn't truly fixed until you understand what caused it. If you don't understand a problem, it's likely to reappear in the future. Obviously, the way that you apply this philosophy should be based on the context of the situation. It's often easier to fix a problem than explain how it happened. If the problem is causing your users pain, fix it and finish debugging it later.

We might easily fix the firewall problem, for example, by hooking back up the original firewall. If the outside caller was a paying customer who was complaining about the web server being inaccessible, we would certainly choose that route. In that case, the quick fix would justify the extra difficulty we might face in trying to finish the diagnosis offline or with a different network configuration.

Don't Implement a Fix that Is a Source of More Difficulties Than the Original Problem

This is usually worth some thought. Hopefully, you wouldn't diagnose a fiber-optic problem by staring at the end of the cable. Also, the pain that is associated with a fix doesn't always arrive immediately, especially when you're fixing security problems. All too often, in an effort to get something working, security is put on the back burner. In the long run, this can be a greater liability than the original issue was. For example, you shouldn't fix a firewall problem by installing a "permit everything" at the top of the rule set.

Remember that the Hardest Problems to Diagnose Are Often Those that Are So Obvious They Are Overlooked

How much time have you wasted diagnosing connectivity problems when you have accidentally grabbed a crossover cable? Start with the simplest hypotheses first, and work your way up to the most complex.

Develop a troubleshooting methodology that works for you. Your methodology will depend on your own responsibilities, strengths, and weaknesses. We have provided some food for thought to help you develop or improve your personal methodology, but so far we have omitted a core component: the tools. We rectify that situation in the next section.

The Troubleshooter's Toolbox

In this section, we present some of our favorite tools and techniques to troubleshoot security-related and network problems.

The tools in this section are organized by the TCP/IP layers to which they apply; that way, you can pick and choose between them depending on the kind of problem you are addressing. You will see that some of the tools apply to multiple layers, which represents the nature of most troubleshooting efforts. You will also learn how the tools can help you zero in on a particular layer depending on the problem symptoms.

UNIX and Windows Tools Differ

Many of the tools that we examine in this chapter are available for Windows as well as UNIX-based operating systems. When tools aren't included in a default installation, we include URLs where you can download them.

If you see a UNIX tool that you do not think exists under Windows, don't despair; open source UNIX environments are available for Windows. One of the most popular ones is Cygwin, which was developed by Red Hat and uses a DLL to provide a UNIX emulation layer with substantial UNIX API functionality (according to the web site). You can download Cygwin from `http://www.cygwin.com`. A user guide is provided at `http://www.cygwin.com/cygwin-ug-net/cygwin-ug-net.html`. You might find that some tools have been ported to Cygwin that would otherwise be unavailable under Windows.

Application Layer Troubleshooting

We like to work our way down the TCP/IP reference model when troubleshooting, so we start at the top with some tools that apply to the Application layer. This layer primarily addresses issues that arise on the local machine, such as configuration file locations and missing link libraries. Another area that can be problematic, though, is the Domain Name System (DNS). Applications query DNS to resolve host names to IP addresses so that, if the DNS server isn't responding for some reason, applications that use hostnames as opposed to IP addresses cannot function.

Sometimes the application clients can be useful in debugging problems. Most email clients, for example, include menu items to view all the message headers, which can be invaluable in determining where the email came from, to whom it was addressed, and so on. You might use a client combined with other tools to dig into the actual network traffic that is associated with the application. A couple of tool classes that are especially worth mentioning, though, are DNS query tools and system call trace utilities. Nslookup is a common DNS query tool, whereas common trace utilities include strace, ktrace, and truss. A couple of other useful tools in this category are strings and ldd.

Nslookup

Many application communication problems are associated with DNS. Applications query DNS through the resolver, which normally occurs transparently to the end user of the application. DNS is always a good place to start troubleshooting when your application can't connect to a remote host by its name. First, make sure that IP address connectivity is successful, and then verify that the host name you are attempting to contact maps to the IP address it is supposed to. You can do this by using a tool to query the DNS. Perhaps the most common DNS query tool is nslookup, which is available on both UNIX and Windows NT/2000. It can be most helpful in diagnosing application layer connectivity problems involving your secure network architecture.

Note

Although we have focused on the cross-platform tool nslookup in this section, UNIX platforms also offer another tool called dig. Dig provides more information with fewer keystrokes after you get used to its syntax, and it's a fine substitute for nslookup if it's available.

UNIX-based operating systems provide a Network Name Switch (NSS), whereby the functions that are used to query the resolver can first check a local file before issuing a DNS query. The search order is configurable on most UNIX variants through the use of the /etc/nsswitch.conf file, and the local file is in /etc/hosts by default. You must consider this when you're doing DNS troubleshooting.

Windows does not have a configurable NSS capability, so the nsswitch.conf file does not exist. The local file is always searched before DNS and, if both of those fail, NetBIOS name resolution is attempted. The local file is located in %SystemRoot%\hosts on Windows 9x, or in %SystemRoot%\system32\drivers\etc\hosts on Windows NT/2000. For new installs, you will find a hosts.sam (sample) file at that location that you will have to rename or copy to hosts, without the extension. Don't edit the hosts.sam file and expect it to work!

For example, suppose that you're trying to ssh to an external server, and the command simply hangs without establishing a connection. This could indicate a problem with DNS or with your NSS configuration. Use nslookup to bypass the NSS and query DNS directly as follows:

```
$ ssh www.extdom.org
never connects, no error messages, nothing
^C
$ nslookup www.extdom.org
Server:        192.168.1.2
Address:       192.168.1.2

Non-authoritative answer:
Name:   www.extdom.org
Address: 192.100.2.100
```

The nslookup query puts www.extdom.org at 192.168.2.100, which in this case is correct.

If you're working from a UNIX host, check /etc/nsswitch.conf, as follows, to determine which name resolution facility the host uses:

```
$ grep hosts /etc/nsswitch.conf
hosts:    files nisplus nis dns
```

The hosts line indicates that local files are checked before other name services, including DNS. This means that if an entry exists in /etc/hosts for www.extdom.org, it will be used in preference to DNS. Check /etc/hosts, as follows:

```
$ grep www.extdom.org /etc/hosts
192.168.2.111               www.extdom.org
```

Because the entry doesn't match the DNS information we obtained earlier, we clearly have the wrong address in the /etc/hosts file. The administrator might have switched the web server to a different host, justifiably thinking that he could notify the world of the change through DNS. Although you could modify /etc/nsswitch.conf to change the NSS search order, it's often handy to override name resolution through local files. The best fix for this problem is probably to delete the entry in /etc/hosts.

Tip

A quick way to determine which address an application is using, without examining the /etc/nsswitch.conf and /etc/hosts files, is to ping the target host. Ping does not query DNS directly like nslookup does, so it goes through the NSS to get the destination IP address and then prints it to the screen even if a firewall blocks its packets. If you're executing it on Solaris, you will have to specify the -n switch to see the IP address. Also, remember that the NSS operates differently on Windows, where it checks the local file and DNS and then tries to resolve the NetBIOS name.

System Call Trace Utilities

System call trace utilities simply monitor the OS calls that an application executes and print the details to the console or a specified output file. This can be a great way to find out, for example, where an application looks for its configuration files. Suppose that you install the binary OpenSSH distribution for Solaris from `http://www.sunfreeware.com` and can't find in the documentation where it hides its sshd_config file. Just run `truss` on the `sshd` executable:

```
# truss -o sshd.truss sshd
# grep conf sshd.truss
open("/usr/local/etc/sshd_config", O_RDONLY) = 3
open("/etc/netconfig", O_RDONLY)      = 3
open("/etc/nsswitch.conf", O_RDONLY)    = 3
```

Here, we saved the `truss` output (which is usually voluminous) to sshd.truss and then searched for anything that looked like a configuration name. This example shows sshd trying to open the file at /usr/local/etc/sshd_config. If you browse the `truss` output, you will see a wealth of other information about the application.

> **Tip**
>
> SGI IRIX includes the par utility that produces system call activity. HPUX admins can download the tusc program at `ftp://ftp.cup.hp.com/dist/networking/tools/`.

For non-Solaris operating systems, you can get the same type of information from strace or ktrace tools. Strace is usually distributed with Linux, and ktrace with BSD.

> **Tip**
>
> Look for an open source version of strace for Windows NT and 2000 at `http://razor.bindview.com/tools/desc/strace_readme.html`. Take note of its shortcomings, however. To install strace, copy the strace.exe and strace.sys files from the zip archive to %SystemRoot%.

Other Useful Utilities

Other useful utilities for debugging problems at the Application layer include the strings and ldd utilities for UNIX. Strings prints everything from a binary file that looks like a printable string, which you can browse or search for interesting stuff. For example, the following command executed on a Linux machine shows the sendmail version to be 8.11.0. (We use the sed utility to filter out lines before the `version.c` string and after the next line beginning with @.) Tricks like this one can let you quickly gain access to information that you might have otherwise had to spend a considerably longer time researching.

```
# strings /usr/sbin/sendmail | sed -e '/version.c/,/^@/!d'
@(#)$Id: version.c,v 8.43.4.11 2000/07/19 20:40:59 gshapiro Exp $
8.11.0
@(#)$Id: debug.c,v 8.2 1999/07/26 04:04:09 gshapiro Exp $
```

Note

BinText is a Windows-based tool that does pretty much the same thing as the UNIX strings utility. It's free and can be downloaded from

http://www.foundstone.com/knowledge/termsofuse.html?filename=bintext.zip.

The `ldd` command prints shared library dependencies, which can come in handy when installing or copying executables. The following output shows all library dependencies are met for the TCP Wrappers daemon on an IRIX 6.5 machine.

```
$ ldd /usr/freeware/bin/tcpd
    libwrap.so.7 =>       /usr/freeware/lib32/libwrap.so.7
    libc.so.1 =>  /usr/lib32/libc.so.1
```

Transport Layer Troubleshooting

The Transport layer encompasses many of the problems with which you're likely to deal. The Transport layer is the first layer (we're counting down from the top) that directly addresses connectivity issues that are associated with network services. In this section, we will describe the following tools:

- Telnet
- netstat
- lsof
- Fport
- hping
- Tcpdump
- Netcat

Case Study: Troubleshooting Check Point FireWall-1 SMTP Security Server

I once worked for a company that implemented a Check Point FireWall-1 as its main perimeter security device. Sometimes, taking advantage of the full potential of such a powerful piece of equipment can have a real learning curve! Check Point FireWall-1 includes an SMTP Security Server that enables firewall administrators to filter incoming mail or pass it off to a virus checker. The SMTP Security Server acts as a proxy, and it is invoked by defining a resource and rule to associate TCP port 25 (SMTP) traffic with the host that handles email. It offers a powerful mechanism for screening email messages and attachments before they enter your network.

At the time, I was not completely familiar with FireWall-1, and I simply defined a rule that allowed SMTP connections to our publicly accessible mail server. Later, I decided to define a resource and do some filtering on inbound mail. This worked fine. Then I decided to hide the publicly accessible server by changing the associated rule to accept SMTP connections to the firewall's external interface. Unfortunately, the firewall started blocking all inbound SMTP when we implemented the change. The reason was immediately apparent. I forgot to consider the DNS MX record for the domain. Here's how you can query an MX record with nslookup:

```
$ nslookup
> set type=mx
> zilchco.com
Server:  ns.s3cur3.com
Address:  192.168.111.1

zilchco.com …, mail exchanger = mail-dmz.zilchco.com
> exit
```

Here, nslookup operates in interactive mode, allowing the user to set the query type for MX records. We see that the domain MX record points to `mail-dmz.zilcho.com`, which is the original email server. This means that everyone on the Internet will continue to send email for `zilcho.com` to the old server, which the firewall will now block. The solution is to add an A record for the external firewall interface and point the domain MX record to it. I chose to name it mail-gw, as shown in the following example:

```
$ nslookup
> set type=mx
> zilchco.com
Server:  ns.s3cur3.com
Address:  192.168.111.1

zilchco.com …, mail exchanger = mail-gw.zilchco.com
> exit
```

Our goal is to show you how to effectively use these tools to troubleshoot problems at the Transport layer. As a result, most of the tools in this category test Transport-layer connectivity. A few tools display connection information on the local host. We have selected these tools because their usability will likely lead you to use them over and over again.

Telnet

Telnet and its underlying protocol were developed so that local users could start a shell session on a remote host. Telnet uses TCP port 23 by default, but it's incredibly handy simply because it takes an optional command-line argument to specify the remote TCP port to which to connect. In addition, the client is available on almost every platform, including many routers.

Telnet prints a message after the connection is established, as well as any header information that the server cares to return. These combine to provide a quick way to check whether the remote service is accessible. For example, suppose that you're having trouble connecting with ssh to a remote server. To test whether the service is available, telnet to port 22 on the server:

```
# telnet mail-dmz.zilchco.com 22
Trying 192.168.1.20...
Connected to mail-dmz.zilchco.com (192.168.1.20).
Escape character is '^]'.
SSH-2.0-OpenSSH_2.9
^]
telnet> quit
```

After the `Escape character is '^]'` message appears, you know that the connection is established, which is useful for services that don't return greetings. In this case, a banner announces some details about the secure shell server. To break the connection, type ^] (Ctrl+]) to get a `telnet>` prompt, from which you can end the session gracefully by typing `quit`. Now let's see how Telnet behaves when the remote service isn't available:

```
$ telnet mail-dmz.zilchco.com 21
Trying 192.168.1.20...
telnet: Unable to connect to remote host: Connection refused
```

FTP (port 21) is obviously not running on the server. Bear with us for one more example, and we will stop beating this dead horse; we have been going into all this detail for the grand finale, for which we pose the following puzzle:

```
# telnet mail-dmz.zilchco.com 143
Trying 192.168.1.20...
Connected to mail-dmz.zilchco.com (192.168.1.20).
Escape character is '^]'.
Connection closed by foreign host.
```

What happened? We established a connection to the IMAP service on port 143, but we never got a greeting before the connection terminated. This is almost always indicative of a service that is protected by TCP Wrappers. The tcpd daemon accepts the connection and then validates the client IP address against the /etc/hosts.allow and /etc/hosts.deny files to determine whether it's allowed to connect. If it's not, the tcpd daemon terminates the TCP session.

netstat

If you aren't already familiar with it, you will find the netstat utility invaluable in debugging several types of connectivity problems. It is distributed with all UNIX and Windows variants, but its command-line options vary greatly, unfortunately. You will have to become familiar with it on your platform by looking at the man page or typing `netstat /?` in Windows.

Use netstat to display information about Transport-layer services that are running on your machine and about active TCP sessions. We will show other uses for netstat in subsequent sections. For now, use the `-a` switch to get Transport-layer information; with UNIX, you might also want to use the `-f inet` switch to restrict the display to TCP/IP sockets. Use the `-n` switch to prevent host name resolution and display IP addresses. As an example, here's the output from a hardened OpenBSD web server:

```
$ netstat -anf inet
Active Internet connections (including servers)
Proto Recv-Q Send-Q  Local Address          Foreign Address    (state)
tcp       0      0    192.168.111.99.22      192.168.111.88.33104    ESTABLISHED
tcp       0      0    192.168.111.99.22      *.*     LISTEN
tcp       0      0    192.168.111.99.80      *.*     LISTEN
tcp       0      0    192.168.111.99.443     *.*     LISTEN
```

We see the TCP and UDP port numbers displayed as the final "dot field" (for example, .22) in the Local Address column. Only three TCP services are running on the machine, as identified by the LISTEN state: SSH on TCP port 22, HTTP on TCP port 80, and HTTPS on TCP port 443. The SSH session has been established from 192.168.111.88.

The Linux netstat command-line options are significantly different from those of most other UNIX variants. For example, use `--inet` instead of `-f inet`. Windows doesn't include an `inet` option because that's the only address family that its netstat can display.

Lsof

The UNIX lsof utility can display everything that is covered by netstat and much more. Unfortunately, lsof isn't part of most distributions.

If you can't find a trusted binary distribution for your platform, you can get the source at `ftp://vic.cc.purdue.edu/pub/tools/UNIX/lsof/`. We include lsof in our toolbox primarily because of its capability to list the process ID (pid) and command name that are associated with a socket. This is useful if you're investigating a possible break-in on your machine or verifying that a service is running on it. (The Linux version of netstat can provide the same information using its -p option.) For example, here's the output of lsof that is running on a Linux machine:

```
# lsof -i -n -V -P
COMMAND      PID    USER    FD   TYPE   DEVICE SIZE NODE NAME
portmap     1209    root    3u   IPv4    18068      UDP  *:111
portmap     1209    root    4u   IPv4    18069      TCP  *:111 (LISTEN)
rpc.statd   1264    root    4u   IPv4    18120      UDP  *:1016
rpc.statd   1264    root    5u   IPv4    18143      UDP  *:32768
rpc.statd   1264    root    6u   IPv4    18146      TCP  *:32768 (LISTEN)
ntpd        1401    root    4u   IPv4    18595      UDP  *:123
ntpd        1401    root    5u   IPv4    18596      UDP  127.0.0.1:123
ntpd        1401    root    6u   IPv4    18597      UDP  129.174.142.77:123
X           2290    root    1u   IPv4    23042      TCP  *:6000 (LISTEN)
sshd        7005    root    3u   IPv4   143123      TCP  *:22 (LISTEN)
```

The lsof utility, by name, lists all of the open files on a system. (As you might have guessed, lsof stands for LiSt Open Files.) With the -i command-line switch appended, lsof lists only open files of the type IP (version 4 or 6), which basically give us a list of files that are running IP processes. The -n option removes the listing of host names, and the -V guarantees a verbose output. -P is used to force lsof to display port numbers, rather than the popular service name for the port in question. The result of the command is a list of programs that are running that have a TCP or UDP port open. Listings with (LISTEN) following them are actually accepting traffic on the port in question. Anyone who has ever tried to figure out whether a back-door service is installed on his machine can recognize the value in this! Of course, lsof won't magically find a backdoor if the attacker has taken advanced steps to hide it, such as replacing the lsof utility with a trojan version or installing a cloaking kernel module.

Fport

Foundstone's Fport, available at `http://www.foundstone.com/rdlabs/ proddesc/fport.html`, is a Windows NT/2000 tool that reports open TCP and UDP ports and maps them to the owning process, similarly to lsof. Listing 19.1 shows the output from running Fport on a Windows 2000 machine, edited slightly to shorten the length of a couple of lines.

Listing 19.1 **Running Fport on Windows 2000**

```
C:\>fport
FPort v1.33 - TCP/IP Process to Port Mapper
Copyright 2000 by Foundstone, Inc.
http://www.foundstone.com

Pid   Process          Port  Proto Path
392   svchost     ->   135   TCP   C:\WINNT\system32\svchost.exe
8     System      ->   139   TCP
8     System      ->   445   TCP
588   MSTask      ->   1025  TCP   C:\WINNT\system32\MSTask.exe
8     System      ->   1031  TCP
8     System      ->   1033  TCP
920   mozilla     ->   1090  TCP   ...\Mozilla\mozilla.exe
920   mozilla     ->   1091  TCP   ...\Mozilla\mozilla.exe
420   spoolsv     ->   1283  TCP   C:\WINNT\system32\spoolsv.exe
392   svchost     ->   135   UDP   C:\WINNT\system32\svchost.exe
8     System      ->   137   UDP
8     System      ->   138   UDP
8     System      ->   445   UDP
220   lsass       ->   500   UDP   C:\WINNT\system32\lsass.exe
208   services    ->   1027  UDP   C:\WINNT\system32\services.exe
872   MsFgSys     ->   38037 UDP   C:\WINNT\System32\MsgSys.EXE
```

You can see a number of NetBIOS and other services that are running on
the machine. You might consider eliminating some of them if you're hardening the system. You can also use Fport when you're investigating a possible
break-in or verifying that a service is running.

Hping

UNIX program Hping has several capabilities, some of which we will touch
on later in this chapter. With hping, you can control which flags and options
are set in the packets. You can set the SYN flag as another way to determine
whether a TCP port is open on a machine, as shown in Listing 19.2.

Listing 19.2 **Checking Firewall TCP Rules with Hping SYN Packets**

```
# hping --count 1 --syn --destport 80 www.extdom.org
eth0 default routing interface selected (according to /proc)
HPING www.extdom.org (eth0 192.168.2.100): S set, 40 headers + 0 data bytes
46 bytes from 192.168.2.100: flags=SA seq=0 ttl=53 id=24080 win=16384 rtt=17.0 ms

--- www.extdom.org hping statistic ---
1 packets transmitted, 1 packets received, 0% packet loss
```

```
round-trip min/avg/max = 24.8/24.8/24.8 ms

# hping --count 1 --syn --destport 443 www.extdom.org
eth0 default routing interface selected (according to /proc)
HPING www.extdom.org (eth0 192.168.2.100): S set, 40 headers + 0 data bytes
46 bytes from 192.168.2.100: flags=RA seq=0 ttl=53 id=42810 win=0 rtt=20.2 ms

--- www.extdom.org hping statistic ---
1 packets transmitted, 1 packets received, 0% packet loss
round-trip min/avg/max = 20.2/20.2/20.2 ms
```

We sent a SYN packet to port 80. We can see that HTTP is open because
the server returns a SYN+ACK (`flags=SA`). However, a similar packet that
was sent to port 443 returns a RST+ACK (`flags=RA`) packet, which means
that HTTPS is not open.

Note

Although it doesn't show it, hping sends a RST packet when it receives a SYN+ACK response. That way, we can't
accidentally cause a SYN flood denial of service!

Hping's control over individual flags makes it particularly useful for testing
firewall filtering capabilities and configuration. Consider the following output, where we send two SYN packets to a randomly chosen destination port:

```
# hping --count 2 --syn --destport 3243 www.extom.org
eth0 default routing interface selected (according to /proc)
HPING www.extom.org (eth0 192.168.2.100): S set, 40 headers + 0 data bytes
--- www.extom.org hping statistic ---
2 packets tramitted, 0 packets received, 100% packet loss
round-trip min/avg/max = 0.0/0.0/0.0 ms
```

We don't receive responses to the SYN packets, so we know the firewall
silently drops disallowed traffic. We can verify that by looking at the firewall
logs. Now look at the results in Listing 19.3, where we send ACK packets
instead of SYN packets.

Listing 19.3 Checking Firewall TCP Rules with Hping ACK Packets

```
# hping --count 2 --ack --destport 3243 www.extom.org
eth0 default routing interface selected (according to /proc)
HPING www.extom.org (eth0 192.168.2.100): A set, 40 headers + 0 data bytes
46 bytes from 192.168.2.100: flags=R seq=0 ttl=53 id=8060 win=0 rtt=17.1 ms
46 bytes from 192.168.2.100: flags=R seq=0 ttl=53 id=2472 win=0 rtt=17.3 ms

--- www.extom.org hping statistic ---
2 packets transmitted, 2 packets received, 0% packet loss
round-trip min/avg/max = 17.1/17.1/17.1 ms
```

The firewall allows ACK packets to come through! This firewall most likely does not support stateful filtering and is configured to allow outbound TCP connections; otherwise, this simulated response packet would have been silently dropped like the SYN flagged packet was. Allowing unsolicited ACK packets can be exploited as a reconnaissance method or as a means to successfully mount a denial of service (DoS) attack.

Tcpdump

Tcpdump is one of the most common sniffer programs; it has many uses, including diagnosing Transport-layer issues. We have used Tcpdump throughout this book to look at network traffic. The program came out of the BSD environment and runs on other platforms, including Linux, Solaris, and Windows. It is a critical component for debugging almost any network problem, and many experienced troubleshooters begin with it unless they're obviously not dealing with a network problem.

Try a Graphical Alternative to Tcpdump

Although Tcpdump is a command-line tool, other more graphical programs use the same programming interfaces and file formats, so you can get the best of both worlds. One of our favorite graphical tools is Ethereal, which is available for many UNIX variants and Windows at http://www.ethereal.com. One of the benefits of using a tool such as Ethereal is that it depicts both the raw data and a context-sensitive translation of header fields, such as flags, port numbers, and so on. In other words, this tool is closer to a protocol analyzer, so it's more user friendly. On the other hand, it's hard to wrap Ethereal in a shell script or run it on a machine that doesn't run a GUI like Windows or X, which is where Tcpdump comes in.

You will probably run Tcpdump often as you realize the power it gives you. The ability to see whether traffic is even being transmitted is often enough to solve a problem or at least isolate it. For example, suppose a client at a small company is complaining that he is unable to connect to web sites on the Internet. You watch him attempt a connection and, sure enough, his Internet Explorer just hangs whenever he types in a URL. Many factors, including DNS issues, a routing problem, or problems with the web site, could cause this behavior. You could spend a lot of time working through this list, or you can fire up a laptop and run Tcpdump. In this case, you might see something like the following when the user tries to access http://www.yahoo.com. (The ellipses indicate where we truncated the long lines.)

```
# tcpdump -i eth0 -n host 192.168.11.88 and tcp port 80
tcpdump: listening on eth0
17:59:26.390890 192.168.11.88.33130 > 64.58.77.195.80: S ...
17:59:29.385734 192.168.11.88.33130 > 64.58.77.195.80: S ...
17:59:35.385368 192.168.11.88.33130 > 64.58.77.195.80: S ...
```

Now we know that the user's machine is transmitting the SYN packets successfully (which means that it already has successfully queried DNS for the remote IP address), but isn't receiving responses. We now hypothesize that something is filtering the responses, so we pursue that by connecting the laptop outside the border router. Now Tcpdump prints something like the following:

```
# tcpdump -i eth0 -n tcp port 80
tcpdump: listening on eth0
18:28:10.964249 external_if.53153 > 64.58.77.195.80: S ...
18:28:10.985383 64.58.77.195.80 > <external if>.53153: S ... ack ...
18:28:10.991414 <external_if>.53162 > 64.56.177.94.80: S ...
18:28:11.159151 64.56.177.94.80 > <external_if>.53162: S ... ack ...
```

The router is performing network address translation (NAT), so *external_if* represents the router's external IP address. The remote site is responding, but the SYN+ACK responses aren't making it through the router, or we would have seen some in the previous output. This is indicative of a filtering problem on the router. You might hypothesize that someone modified the ACLs incorrectly, and test your theory by looking at the router configuration. Imagine how long we might have spent isolating this problem without Tcpdump!

Netcat

We doubt that you will ever see a TCP/IP network troubleshooting discussion that doesn't include Netcat. The Netcat program, usually named nc, has several capabilities, but its core feature is probably the most useful. This feature includes opening a socket and then redirecting standard input and standard output though it. Standard input is sent through the socket to the remote service. Anything that the socket receives is redirected to standard output. This simple capability is unbelievably useful, as we will show in a moment. For now, you can become familiar with Netcat's other options by executing nc -h. You will see a source port (-p) option, a listener option (-1), and a UDP option (-u).

Note

Take notice of Netcat's support for UDP. This is one major advantage of its functionality over Telnet because Telnet only supports TCP.

You might also try connecting to a TCP service by executing nc -v *rmt host port*, as in the example in the Telnet section, earlier in the chapter. Note that you break a Netcat connection with Ctrl+C rather than Ctrl+].

Note

Although Netcat started out as a UNIX tool, it has been ported to Windows. Netcat is included with most Linux and BSD distributions, but it might not be installed by default. You can download the UNIX version at `http://www.atstake.com/research/tools/nc110.tgz` and the Windows version at `http://www.atstake.com/research/tools/nc11nt.zip`. The Windows version includes a compiled executable.

Let's consider a situation in which an administrator is unable to query an external DNS server while troubleshooting another problem. You decide to investigate. You know that the organization uses a Cisco router to restrict Internet traffic, and you hypothesize that it's been configured to accept only DNS queries that originated from port 53. How do you find out? You choose a test case based on Netcat.

Note

DNS servers are sometimes configured to forward queries from source port 53, so router filters can be constructed to allow query responses without opening inbound UDP to all non-privileged ports. Of course, this wouldn't be necessary if the router supported reflexive ACLs, as described in Chapter 2, "Packet Filtering."

Most DNS queries are encapsulated in UDP datagrams. UDP, being a stateless transport protocol, does little validation of received datagrams and simply passes them on to the application. This means that the application must decide whether to respond to datagrams that don't make sense. DNS silently drops most such datagrams. We have to send a valid DNS query to receive a response and prove that source port 53 filtering is in place. Nslookup can't use source port 53, so we have to find another way. First, capture a query using Netcat and save it in a file. (If you're on UNIX, as in the following example, you have to be logged in as root to bind port 53.)

```
# nc -u -l -p 53 >dnsq &
# nslookup -timeout=5 www.yahoo.com localhost
^C
# kill %1
```

The background Netcat command listens on UDP port 53 (we assume this isn't a DNS server, which would already have port 53 bound) and redirects anything that is received to a file named dnsq. Then, Nslookup directs a query to localhost, so it's intercepted by Netcat and written to the file. Press Ctrl+C before the specified 5 second timeout to terminate nslookup before it issues a second query. Then kill the background Netcat, which causes it to print the punt! message. If you have a hex editor, the contents of file dnsq should look something like this:

```
00000000    00 43 01 00   00 01 00 00   00 00 00 00   03 77 77 77   .C..........www
00000010    05 79 61 68   6F 6F 03 63   6F 6D 00 00   01 00 01      .yahoo.com.....
```

Finally, execute Netcat again to send the captured query using source port 53 to the remote DNS server and save any response to another file:

```
nc -u -p 53 -w 10 <dns_server> 53 <dnsq >dnsr
```

The `-w` option specifies a timeout of 10 seconds; therefore, you don't have to terminate Netcat manually. If a response is received, the dnsr file will have a non-zero size and you will know that your hypothesis is correct: The router allows outbound DNS queries if the source port is 53.

Network Layer Troubleshooting

Security device problems at the Network layer usually fall into one of the following categories:

- Routing
- Firewall
- NAT
- Virtual Private Network (VPN)

We will show you some tools to help troubleshoot problems in each of these areas.

NAT Breaks Some Application Protocols

We discussed that NAT breaks some VPN implementations in Chapter 14, "VPN Integration." VPN is not the only application that NAT breaks. This is usually because the associated protocols embed Transport or Network-layer information in their payloads. Perhaps the most notable of these is H.323, which is used in videoconferencing applications, such as Microsoft Netmeeting. NAT devices change IP and Transport-layer header information, but they know nothing about what ports are stored in the application payload for a remote peer to work with. To make a long story short, such protocols simply will not work through NAT devices unless they have proxy support. In the case of H.323, a complex protocol, the proxies are few and far between. Don't expect your video conferencing setup to work if the traffic goes through a NAT device.

You have already seen some of the tools that we present at this layer, but here we show how to use them for Network-layer problems. Some display information on the host, and some test network connectivity. Many have multiple uses and were introduced earlier.

Ifconfig and Ipconfig

Both ifconfig and ipconfig utilities display host information that helps you verify that the IP address, subnet mask, and broadcast address are configured correctly. There's nothing magic here, but it's probably one of the things you'll check most often.

The UNIX ifconfig utility configures network interfaces and displays network interface details. Use the -a option to display all interfaces when you don't know the name of the interface you're trying to look at. The -v option might show additional information such as the speed and duplex of the interface, as in the following display from an SGI IRIX box:

```
# ifconfig -av
ef0: flags=415c43<UP,BROADCAST,RUNNING,FILTMULTI,MULTICAST,
➥CKSUM,DRVRLOCK,LINK0,IPALIAS>
inet 192.168.114.50 netmask 0xffffff00 broadcast 192.168.114.255
speed 100.00 Mbit/s full-duplex
lo0: flags=1849<UP,LOOPBACK,RUNNING,MULTICAST,CKSUM>
inet 127.0.0.1 netmask 0xff000000
```

The Windows NT and 2000 ipconfig utility primarily displays IP configuration information, although you can also use it to release and renew DHCP configurations. Use the -all option to print the IP address, subnet mask, and broadcast address of each interface. Ipconfig also displays the IP addresses of the DNS servers and, if applicable, the DHCP and WINS servers that are configured on the host. Windows 9x users might not know that they also have access to ipconfig's functionality because they might use the winipcfg GUI program to obtain the same information. Listing 19.4 shows the type of information you get from ipconfig.

Listing 19.4   **Sample Ipconfig Output**

```
C:\> ipconfig -all

Windows 98 IP Configuration

        Host Name . . . . . . . . . : TELLUS.intdom.org
        DNS Servers . . . . . . . . : 192.168.111.2
        Node Type . . . . . . . . . : Broadcast
        NetBIOS Scope ID. . . . . . :
        IP Routing Enabled. . . . . : No
        WINS Proxy Enabled. . . . . : No
        NetBIOS Resolution Uses DNS : Yes

0 Ethernet adapter :

        Description . . . . . . . . : Novell 2000 Adapter.
```

```
Physical Address. . . . . . : 18-18-A8-72-58-00
DHCP Enabled. . . . . . . . : Yes
IP Address. . . . . . . . . : 192.168.111.130
Subnet Mask . . . . . . . . : 255.255.255.0
Default Gateway . . . . . . : 192.168.111.1
DHCP Server . . . . . . . . : 192.168.111.1
Primary WINS Server . . . . :
Secondary WINS Server . . . :
Lease Obtained. . . . . . . : 12 19 01 4:09:39 PM
Lease Expires . . . . . . . : 12 20 01 4:09:39 AM
```

From a security device troubleshooting perspective, you will most often focus on a few items in this output. The DNS server IP address in the configuration section can help you diagnose some Application layer problems. The IP address and Default Gateway addresses, in the Ethernet adapter section, are useful for routing or other connectivity problems. The DHCP server and Lease information might also be useful for troubleshooting connectivity problems. The other lines might be of interest for troubleshooting Windows domain or workgroup issues, such as file sharing or network neighborhood problems.

Netstat

As we mentioned in the section "Transport Layer Troubleshooting," the netstat utility exists in all UNIX and Windows distributions. We usually apply its -r option at the Network layer to display the host routing table. Most of the time, we're looking for the default gateway, which is displayed with a destination IP and subnet mask of 0.0.0.0. The following Linux output shows two networks, 10.0.0.0 and 129.174.142.0, accessible through the vmnet1 and eth0 interfaces, respectively. Both are Class C sized, with subnet mask 255.255.255.0. The default gateway is 129.174.142.1. Almost all TCP/IP devices include a loopback interface, named lo in this case, serving network 127.0.0.0:

```
$ netstat -rn
Kernel IP routing table
Destination     Gateway         Genmask         Flags Iface
10.0.0.0        0.0.0.0         255.255.255.0   U     vmnet1
129.174.142.0   0.0.0.0         255.255.255.0   U     eth0
127.0.0.0       0.0.0.0         255.0.0.0       U     lo
0.0.0.0         129.174.142.1   0.0.0.0         UG    eth0
```

When troubleshooting Network layer issues, you will usually focus on the default gateway line in netstat output. Many routing problems are caused by missing or incorrect gateway entries in the routing table. Every TCP/IP device, unless you're working on a standalone LAN or a core Internet router, should have at least a default gateway entry. The routing tables can become long when you're running a routing protocol, such as the Routing Information Protocol (RIP) on your network, but routing updates are automatic in such environments, which could eliminate the need to run netstat.

Ping

The venerable `ping` command, which is included in all UNIX and Windows distributions, employs the Internet Control Message Protocol (ICMP) to test whether a remote host is reachable. It sends an ICMP echo request packet and listens for the ICMP echo reply from the remote host. This is a great test of end-to-end connectivity at the Network layer; however, unfortunately, most firewalls block ICMP these days. The protocol has been used one too many times in ICMP flood and other attacks. If you want to test end-to-end connectivity, you might have to move up a layer and use the hping utility that was described in the section "Transport Layer Troubleshooting."

Traceroute

Traceroute is another classic utility that is available on all UNIX and Windows machines, although it's called tracert on Windows. It manipulates the IP header time-to-live (TTL) field to coerce the gateways between your machine and the destination into sending back ICMP messages. Each gateway decrements the TTL and, if it's zero, returns an ICMP time-exceeded message to the sender. By starting with a TTL of 1 and incrementing it, traceroute detects the IP address of each router along the way by examining the source addresses of the time-exceeded messages. Traceroute also inserts a timestamp in each packet so that it can compute the round-trip time, in milliseconds, when it gets a response. This is possible because the ICMP response messages include the original packet in their payloads. These capabilities make traceroute an excellent tool to help determine where traffic fails as it traverses the Internet.

Traceroute is also useful in diagnosing performance problems. If you see the route change frequently, you might hypothesize that you have a route flapping problem somewhere. Unfortunately, proving that might be impossible because the loci of such problems are usually on the Internet, outside of your jurisdiction.

By default, UNIX traceroute sends a UDP datagram to a high-numbered port on the destination. The port is almost always closed on the destination. Therefore, an ICMP port-unreachable message is sent back when a packet finally makes it all the way, which tells traceroute when to stop.

Unfortunately, this won't work when your firewall blocks the outbound UDP packets or when the high port is actually open on the destination (in which case it will probably be discarded, with no response). Traceroute also breaks when the target organization blocks inbound UDP (for UNIX traceroute) or inbound ICMP (for Windows traceroute), or if your firewall won't allow inbound the ICMP traffic replies. Windows uses ICMP echo request packets instead of UDP. Many UNIX distributions now support a -I option to use ICMP instead of UDP.

Of course, traceroute won't work if your firewall blocks outbound UDP or ICMP echo-request messages (as the case may be) or inbound ICMP time-exceeded messages. The `hping` command includes `--ttl` and `--traceroute` options to specify a starting TTL value that is incremented like a real traceroute. Applying these options to an HTTP SYN packet, for example, will get the outbound packets through your firewall. However, if it blocks inbound ICMP, you will never see the time-exceeded messages sent back by external gateways.

The ouput in Listing 19.5 shows a typical traceroute. You can see that three packets are sent for each TTL value. No packets were lost in this example (we don't see any * values in place of the round-trip times), so we don't see performance problems on this route.

Listing 19.5 **Sample Traceroute Output**

```
# traceroute -n www.yahoo.com
traceroute: Warning: www.yahoo.com has multiple addresses; using 64.58.76.224
traceroute to www.yahoo.akadns.net (64.58.76.224), 30 hops max, 38 byte packets
 1  63.212.11.177  0.675 ms  0.474 ms  0.489 ms
 2  63.212.11.161  1.848 ms  1.640 ms  1.636 ms
 3  172.20.0.1  26.460 ms  17.865 ms  40.310 ms
 4  63.212.0.81  24.412 ms  24.835 ms  24.488 ms
 5  198.32.187.119  33.586 ms  26.997 ms  26.715 ms
 6  216.109.66.4  33.570 ms  26.690 ms  27.066 ms
 7  209.185.9.1  33.576 ms  26.932 ms  26.811 ms
 8  216.33.96.161  20.107 ms  20.097 ms  20.181 ms
 9  216.33.98.18  24.637 ms  26.843 ms  26.901 ms
10  216.35.210.122  35.771 ms  28.881 ms  27.052 ms
11  64.58.76.224  33.452 ms  26.696 ms  27.020 ms
```

Tcpdump

We have to include Tcpdump at this layer, at least to help debug VPN problems. The latest versions print much useful information about the Internet

Key Exchange (IKE) service (UDP 500) that establishes and maintains IPSec authentication and encryption keys. Tcpdump also prints some information about the IPSec Encapsulation Security Payload (ESP) and Authentication Header (AH) protocols (50 and 51, respectively. These are protocol numbers, not port numbers.)

If you have users who are unable to establish an IPSec tunnel with a device that you are administering, you could successfully troubleshoot possible issues by tracing the traffic arriving at the device in question with Tcpdump. You can verify that IKE exchanges are occurring correctly, and that the proper ESP traffic is getting to the device in question. This is especially helpful because IPSec lacks good logging facilities of its own.

Keep Tcpdump in Your Toolbox

As you might have noticed by now, Tcpdump is one of our favorite tools. It can put you on a fast track to solving almost any network problem, and many experienced troubleshooters will go straight to it rather than trying to understand all the problem symptoms, eyeball configuration files, and so on.

Performance issues represent one of the hardest classes of problem on which to get a handle. One time, I was at a client's office when she happened to complain that logging in on her Windows 2000 desktop took forever. She attributed this to a lack of available bandwidth on the network because everyone had the same problem. She was unconvinced when I pointed out that it would be hard for the 30 or so users on her Windows domain to exhaust the bandwidth of the corporation's 100Mbps switched network. I pulled out my laptop, connected both machines to the network through a hub I always carry, and ran a Tcpdump while she logged in. The Tcpdump output immediately pointed to a DNS problem. Her machine was issuing many queries for a non-existent DNS domain. It turned out the local admin, still unfamiliar with Windows 2000, had configured her machine identity properties with membership to a non-existent domain, apparently without realizing the DNS relationship. A quick test with my laptop acting as the DNS server for her machine convinced her that network bandwidth constraint was not the problem.

Revising the Example Firewall Problem with Transport Layer Techniques

We have verified that something is blocking the HTTP traffic over our dial-up laptop connection to the web server because we installed a new firewall. We wonder whether they're even making it to the firewall. We run Tcpdump on the web server and see no HTTP traffic. We run Tcpdump on another machine that is connected to the external network and see our laptop's SYN packets addressed to the web server; we don't, however, see response packets. Now we wonder if the firewall is blocking HTTP traffic, despite what we found in our earlier examination of its configuration and logs. From the external machine, we telnet to port 80 on the web server and discover that it works fine. Therefore, the firewall is not blocking HTTP from the external machine. However, the firewall doesn't seem to receive HTTP packets from the Internet at all; we would see log messages if they were blocked, and we would see response packets from the server if they weren't blocked.

We have presented a few tools for Network-layer troubleshooting and have provided a few examples of their use. NAT and VPN problems probably represent the bulk of the problems you're likely to deal with in this layer. Next, we will move down to the bottom of the TCP/IP reference model: the Link layer.

Note

Although we discuss running Tcpdump on many machines throughout this chapter, be careful if you're tempted to install it on your servers. Doing so can be a serious security problem in the event that a server is compromised, especially if the intruder executes with super user privileges (such as suid root under UNIX). It's better to keep a CD handy that contains Tcpdump and other troubleshooting programs. In fact, you might want to include copies of netstat, ifconfig, ipconfig, lsof, Fprot, ls, and other common utilities that attackers might replace on penetrated servers to hide their activities.

Link Layer Troubleshooting

This layer can present you with some of your toughest problems. These problems will be a lot easier to solve if you master a couple of key topics:

- The Address Resolution Protocol (ARP)
- The differences between non-switched and switched networks

ARP is the Link layer protocol that TCP/IP devices use to match another device's Media Access Control (MAC) address with its IP address. MAC, not IP, addresses are used to communicate with other devices on the same network segment. When a device determines that a given IP address resides on the same segment that it does (by examining the address and its own subnet mask), the device uses ARP to discover the associated IP address. Basically, the device sends a link-level broadcast asking who has the IP address. Every device on the segment examines the request, and the one that uses the enclosed IP address responds. The original device stores the source MAC address of the response in its ARP table; that way, subsequent transmissions don't require the broadcast process. ARP table entries eventually expire, which necessitates periodic re-broadcasts, to facilitate moving IP addresses between devices without manual reconfiguration of all the other devices on the network segment.

In a non-switched network, a network segment usually maps directly to the physical network medium. In a switched network, a network segment's boundaries become a little vague because the switches might be configured to break the physical network into logical segments at the Link layer. In general, the set of devices that can see each others' ARP broadcasts delineates a network segment.

You can find out more about these topics and their security ramifications elsewhere in this book and at many locations on the Internet, including `http://www.sans.org/newlook/resources/IDFAQ/switched_network.htm`. With an understanding of these subjects under your belt, all you need are a couple of tools to diagnose almost any problem at this layer.

You will find Link layer tools that are similar to those that apply to the other layers. Most of them display host information. Once again, you will find Tcpdump useful for displaying what's happening on the network.

Ifconfig and Ipconfig

We already covered these tools in the "Network Layer Troubleshooting" section, but you might not have noticed that they can also display the MAC address associated with the Link layer. Look back at the `ipconfig -all` output and you will see the MAC address displayed as the Physical address. On UNIX machines, the method for determining the address varies greatly. On Linux and FreeBSD machines, it shows the address by default, as seen in the following Linux output, as the `HWaddr`:

```
# ifconfig eth0
eth0      Link encap:Ethernet  HWaddr 00:10:5A:26:FD:41
...
```

Try one of the following methods to display the MAC address for your system:[1]

- Solaris: `arp `hostname``
- OpenBSD: `netstat -ai`
- IRIX: `netstat -ai`

`arp`

The `arp` command, naturally, displays information that pertains to ARP. It exists in all UNIX and Windows distributions, and it is most often executed with the `-a` option to display the ARP table, as follows:

```
# arp -an
? (123.123.123.123) at 00:02:E3:09:D1:08 [ether] on eth0
? (192.168.126.88) at 00:D0:09:DE:FE:81 [ether] PERM on eth0
```

```
? (192.168.126.130) at 00:D0:09:DE:FE:81 [ether] on eth0
? (192.168.126.127) at 00:10:4B:F6:F5:CE [ether] PERM on eth0
? (192.168.126.1) at 00:A0:CC:7B:9C:21 [ether] PERM on eth0
```

You can glean a lot of information from this table, in which ARP stores its IP/MAC pairs. If you ssh to another machine on the same LAN, you can see your own MAC address in case the other methods that we showed you failed. It shows static entries (tagged with PERM) that were added manually with the arp -s option, which can help mitigate vulnerability to some dev-astating Link layer attacks. The ARP protocol discovered the other entries and added them dynamically. You can also see that two logical networks are accessed via the eth0 interface, and that this is probably a Linux box given the interface name.

> **Note**
>
> Some Windows versions have trouble maintaining static ARP entries (see http://www.securityfocus.com/bid/1406). For a quick introduction to ARP and Link layer attacks such as ARP spoofing, please refer to Chapter 12, "Separating Resources."

If your system can't connect with the Internet, try pinging your default gate-way's IP address (not its host name) and then looking at your ARP table. If you don't see your gateway's MAC address, you probably have a Link layer problem. Otherwise, the problem is at a higher layer.

Tcpdump

It's no surprise that we use Tcpdump at this layer, too! Tcpdump can help debug some insidious problems. For example, consider a workstation that can't access the Internet although other workstations on the same hub have no trouble. We can ping the other workstations, but we can't ping the gateway router. If we run Tcpdump and ping the router again, we see the following:

```
# tcpdump -n host 192.168.1.130
12:17:56.782702 192.168.1.130 > 192.168.1.1: icmp: echo request
12:17:56.783309 192.168.1.1 > 192.168.1.130: icmp: echo reply
12:17:57.805290 192.168.1.130 > 192.168.1.1: icmp: echo request
12:17:57.805823 192.168.1.1 > 192.168.1.130: icmp: echo reply
```

The router (192.168.1.1) is actually replying to our pings! We try running Tcpdump again, this time with the -e switch to print the MAC addresses:

```
# tcpdump -en host 192.168.1.130
tcpdump: listening on eth0
10:27:03.650625 0:d0:09:de:fe:81 0:a0:cc:7b:9c:21 0800 98: 192.168.1.130 >
➥192.168.1.1: icmp: echo request (DF)
```

```
10:27:03.651260 0:a0:cc:7b:9c:21 0:10:5a:26:fd:41 0800 98: 192.168.1.1 >
▬192.168.1.130: icmp: echo reply (DF)
```

Note the source MAC address on the echo request that our machine sent, and the destination MAC address on the reply that the router sent. They don't match. We check the router configuration and find an old static ARP entry in its cache. Deleting the entry fixes the problem.

Revising the Example Firewall Problem with Link Layer Techniques

If you read the previous Tcpdump example, then you're probably close to solving the example firewall problem we have highlighted throughout this chapter. We have successfully accessed the web server from a workstation that is connected just outside the firewall, so the firewall rules are most likely correct. However, we still cannot access the web server from the Internet. A border router separates us from the Internet. Also recall that the firewall was replaced with a new machine just before the problems started. We execute tcpdump -en to look at the MAC addresses, and discover that the router is sending HTTP traffic to the wrong MAC address. We check the router configuration, discover a static ARP entry for the old firewall machine, and change the entry to fix the problem.

Summary

We can't overstress the importance of fostering good troubleshooting habits by developing and practicing your own methodology, as we described at the beginning of the chapter. Follow the logical steps in the process of troubleshooting closely; collect symptoms, review recent changes, form a new hypothesis, test the hypothesis, analyze the results, and repeat if necessary. Also, don't forget to apply the rules of thumb when following these steps.

With those skills in place, however, your success will depend on knowing which tools to apply for a given problem. That's why we focused so heavily, in the remainder of the chapter, on describing some of our favorite tools and providing examples of their use. The combination of solid troubleshooting skills and the right tools for the job result in success at finding the right answers for any security scenario.

References

1 University of Washington Department of Computer Science and Engineering. "Determining Your Ethernet Address." `http://www.cs.washington.edu/lab/sw/wireless/yourmac.html`. January 2002.

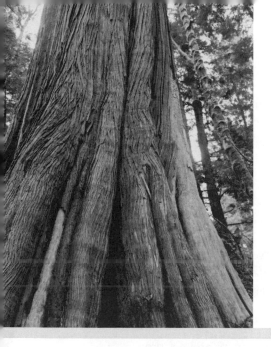

20

Assessment Techniques

THROUGHOUT THIS BOOK, WE HAVE DISCUSSED various methods of incorporating security into the network. You have learned how to apply recommended security concepts to perimeter components, such as routers, firewalls, VPNs, and host systems. This chapter changes your focus from a defensive approach to an offensive one as we examine how to assess your environment for possible security holes.

This chapter is designed to help you plan an assessment to determine whether your security perimeter is operating according to your expectations. When performing such an audit, you can use similar attack techniques and information-gathering tools that attackers use to fingerprint and enumerate a remote target. Going through the process of assessing the effectiveness of your security infrastructure helps improve the resiliency of your security perimeter and allows you to locate weaknesses before attackers can exploit them.

We examine two complementary types of the assessment processes that have different perspectives on the audited infrastructure: internal and external. An external assessment can be performed without initial knowledge about the target; it is initiated from outside the network boundaries of the organization. The auditor's traffic must pass through border devices, such as routers and firewalls, which are supposed to restrict access to internal resources. The primary goal of the external assessment is to determine what sensitive information attackers might obtain by probing the network, and what vulnerabilities they might be able to exploit. An internal assessment requires the administrator to test the configuration of each perimeter component to verify that it is implemented in a way that meets its requirements, and it assumes that the auditor is intimately familiar with the perimeter's design and the company's security policy.

External Assessment

To prepare you for performing an external security assessment, we present you with the roadmap of exploring the network to eventually locate exploitable vulnerabilities. Attackers often follow the same techniques when attempting to penetrate your defenses, which is why an external assessment is a critical step in fortifying the network. An external assessment consists of the following core phases:

1. Planning. Determine how you will conduct the assessment and get proper approvals to perform it.

2. Initial reconnaissance. Obtain basic technical and non-technical information on the organization and known public hosts, such as mail, web, and DNS servers.

3. System enumeration. Determine which additional hosts and network devices on the targeted network can be accessed from the outside.

4. Service enumeration. Gather detailed technical information about each discovered system, such as its operating system and remotely accessible services.

5. Vulnerability enumeration. Probe discovered systems and remote services for vulnerabilities that might provide the attacker with elevated access to the network.

As you go through the assessment process, you obtain information about probed systems, which you can use to construct a matrix that documents your discoveries. This system matrix is typically a logical layout of uncovered systems, operating systems, services, and potential vulnerabilities. Each step of your assessment is based on information in the matrix, and each step contributes additional information until you obtain sufficient information.

For instance, Table 20.1 documents the presence of an SMTP and FTP server for `xyz.com`. (We use xyz.com as an example to represent the audited organization.) It reflects hostnames and IP addresses of discovered systems, service ports that are accessible from the Internet, likely OS types, and information regarding the version of available services or applications.

Table 20.1 **A System Matrix to Document Information that Is Gathered During an Assessment**

System	IP Address	Available Services	OS Version
smtp.xyz.com	xxx.xxx.xxx.10	25	SunOS 2.6
ftp.xyz.com	xxx.xxx.xxx.15	21	Possible UNIX

Tip

Creating a system matrix using spreadsheet software, such as Excel, provides easy access when searching for various services or versions when attempting to locate possible vulnerabilities. Users of UNIX systems might be interested in trying Nlog (http://www.digitaloffense.net/nlog/), a program that can create a database file from Nmap scan logs and can be integrated with a web server to provide a searchable system matrix.

Planning

Have you heard the old saying, "If you fail to plan, you plan to fail?" This saying rings true when you perform a security assessment. You must choose the appropriate time to execute the assessment, evaluate possible risks, determine costs, and obtain management's approval. That sounds like a lot of preparation to determine the strength of your defenses, but remember: Hindsight is 20-20.

The proper time to conduct an assessment is when the risk to the network at attached systems is lowest, which is typically during non-business hours. Keep in mind that performing a vulnerability assessment carries with it the inherent risk of disrupting service through crashing target systems or generating excessive network traffic. Therefore, administrators should be available during your assessment to deal with any issues that might arise.

Tip

When deciding on a time to perform the assessment, be sure to account for differences in time zones across the organization.

Finally, written management approval must be obtained before the assessment commences. Written approval has saved the careers of many people when critical systems went down as a result of simple scanning. In general, communication is one of the most important aspects of planning the assessment. You need to verify that all parties involved in supporting the targeted systems, as well as management, have been informed of your activities. Keep communication and risk awareness in your thoughts as you plan and perform the assessment.

When preparing for an assessment, it is handy to have a list of commonly used TCP and UDP ports as a reference. One such relatively extensive list is available at `http://www.neohapsis.com/neolabs/neo-ports/neo-ports.html`. During the planning stage, you also want to make sure you install and configure assessment tools that you need to use, such as those mentioned throughout this chapter. It is advantageous to have Windows and UNIX systems available to utilize the plethora of OS-dependent utilities.

Tip

If you do not have extra computers lying around to run multiple operating systems, check out VMware (`http://www.vmware.com/`). VMware software enables you to run an OS within another OS. For example, if you use Windows 2000 Professional, you could use VMware Workstation on it, which would enable you to run Red Hat Linux at the same time on the same machine. Note that you might have to increase your system's RAM or disk space for proper performance.

After establishing a time frame, considering risks involved, and, most importantly, receiving written permission, you can continue the assessment by gathering publicly available information about the organization and incorporating it into the system matrix.

Initial Reconnaissance

The heart of the initial reconnaissance stage is to gather publicly available information about the organization without actually probing targeted systems directly. This often includes general business information, as well as the organization's IP address range and the names and IP addresses of its public services, such as DNS, web, and mail. We also want to gather non-technical information that might be used in a social engineering attack.

To begin the reconnaissance, surf the organization's web page to learn what type of organization you are assessing. Chances are, this is what an attacker would do, and you might be surprised to see how much you can learn about your organization based on publicly available information. You can also use your favorite search engines or download tools, such as Copernic (`http://www.copernic.com/`), to gather additional background information. Sites often unknowingly publish private information to the Internet, such as usernames or corporate contact information, that could be very helpful for social engineering. Next, you gather information about the organization's IP addressing schema and critical services by querying Whois and DNS services.

You can use Whois databases at sites such as `http://www.internic.net/whois.html` or `http://www.arin.net/` to identify the IP range that is associated with an organization and to determine geographical location and contact information that attackers might use to perform a social engineering attack.

Tip

For an informative description of social engineering techniques, take a look at the "Social Engineering Fundamentals" article by Sarah Granger at `http://www.securityfocus.com/infocus/1527`.

It is also useful to use the `nslookup` command to determine DNS-related information, such as the Start of Authority (SOA) and Mail Exchange (MX). Some DNS servers might also allow you to obtain a listing of all registered names and addresses via a zone transfer, and might tell you the version of DNS software that is running.

Various web sites and utilities are available to make many aspects of the initial reconnaissance phase almost effortless. One such site is `http://www.all-nettools.com/tools1.htm`, which provides web-based access to tools, such as `whois` and `nslookup`. You can also use utilities, such as NetScanTools, which run on your workstation and incorporate miscellaneous investigative tools into a single interface.

NetScanTools Pro (`http://www.nwpsw.com/`) is the Swiss-army knife of surveying tools; it combines several commands and utilities into one graphical user interface (GUI). Professional or trialware versions of NetScanTools are available. To perform a DNS query using NetScanTools Pro, you can do the following:

1. Select the Name Server Lookup tab and execute an *NSLOOKUP* query for the company's web server. This provides you with the server's IP address.

2. List the `xyz.com` domain computers that are registered in the authoritative name server. This displays the SOA name servers that are responsible for responding to requests about the target's domain.

3. Change the DNS Server selection to point to `SOA.xyz.com` by selecting the Adv Qry Setup button. This allows you to direct your requests to the name server that has the authoritative permission to answer them.

4. Execute a zone transfer for the domain by selecting the Dig w/AFXR button. This lists all the devices that are registered in DNS if the server allows zone transfers. (A well-configured DNS server would not permit this.)

Locating additional targets that might be registered in DNS can provide valuable information for your developing system's matrix. To external hosts, your DNS servers should provide information only about systems that require external access, such as FTP, SMTP, or web servers. Your investigation of the DNS information is performed in an attempt to locate devices, such as firewalls, printers, or workstations, that should have their identity concealed.

Figure 20.1 shows the GUI interface of NetScanTools Pro performing a simple nslookup query for xyz.com. This can also be performed using the nslookup command; however, it is often easier to point and click than to issue multiple commands via the command line. Listing 20.1 shows how the same investigative steps would look when using nslookup from the command line. The bold text indicates commands, and the rest indicates displayed output.

Listing 20.1 **Using nslookup to Query DNS**

```
C:\>nslookup
> set type=any
> xyz.com

Non-authoritative answer:
xyz.com nameserver = www.xyz.com
xyz.com nameserver = NS.JEDWARDS.NET
xyz.com nameserver = NS1.RDROP.com
xyz.com nameserver = NS2.RDROP.com
xyz.com internet address = 199.26.172.28

xyz.com nameserver = www.xyz.com
xyz.com nameserver = NS.JEDWARDS.NET
xyz.com nameserver = NS1.RDROP.com
xyz.com nameserver = NS2.RDROP.com
www.xyz.com      internet address = 199.26.172.28
NS.JEDWARDS.NET internet address = 4.61.211.86
NS1.RDROP.com    internet address = 199.26.172.34
NS2.RDROP.com    internet address = 209.162.200.178
> server 4.61.211.86
> ls xyz.com
```

You have now completed the initial reconnaissance phase of the assessment. At this point, you should have some general knowledge about the organization, its IP address range, and addresses of at least a few publicly accessible servers, such as DNS, web, and mail. Given that these systems are available in some capacity directly from the Internet, they are the most likely systems to be attacked; therefore, you should pay special attention to them. After the initial reconnaissance phase is done, you need to continue by gathering more in-depth information about the targeted network.

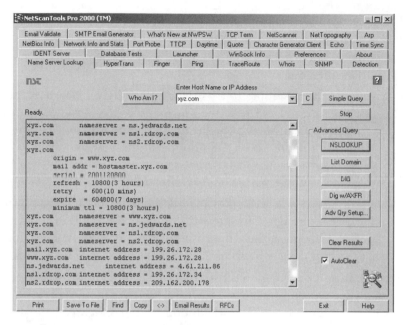

Figure 20.1   NetScanTools can be used to obtain detailed DNS information about the organization.

System Enumeration

In the system enumeration phase of the assessment, you use information that is gathered during the initial reconnaissance phase to learn more about the targeted network. It is quite likely that in the previous phase, we have not discovered all hosts that are accessible from the Internet, which is why network scanning is frequently a core aspect of performing system enumeration. At the same time, the defense perimeter might be configured to block certain scans, which is why information that is discovered in the initial reconnaissance phase helps to target further inquiries. Unlike in the previous stage, during system enumeration, you directly probe the targeted network to gather information. This prepares you for subsequent phases, in which you probe discovered systems to determine their operating system versions, open ports, and potential vulnerabilities.

System enumeration combines discovery and analysis techniques to locate systems that can be used as access points into the network. In this section, we go over several tools that can assist you in this process.

Traceroute

You can begin the enumeration process by performing a traceroute. The following are some ways to use `traceroute` (or `tracert` under Windows) to learn about the targeted network:

- If you are tracing a route to a particular IP address, `traceroute` attempts to perform a reverse DNS resolution to find the fully qualified domain name for that IP address. Many DNS names are descriptive and can provide valuable information about the purpose of the host, as well as its location, because many organizations use geographic information in their host-names. For example, what do you think `londonfw.example.com` could be?

- A traceroute to a targeted host reports the networks and systems that the traffic passes through. This information might be useful in determining which paths connect the targeted network to the Internet, and, potentially, what internal devices route packets to publicly accessible systems.

- Sometimes a traceroute returns unexpected IP addresses. For example, you might see an address such as 10.3.1.70, which is most likely an internal network address being "leaked" through a misconfigured pr malfunctioning device that performs Network Address Translation (NAT).

Network Scanners

One way to attempt to enumerate devices on the targeted network is to perform an ICMP scan, which simply issues ICMP echo request messages in hopes of receiving ICMP echo replies. SuperScan, available from `http://www.foundstone.com/knowledge/free_tools.html`, is a free Windows utility that, in addition to supporting other techniques, can perform ICMP scans. Some of the many ICMP scanners for UNIX systems are fping (`http://www.fping.com/`) and pinger (`http://packetstorm.widexs.nl/groups/rhino9/`).

Figure 20.2 illustrates hosts and devices that are discovered when performing an ICMP scan using SuperScan. Keep in mind that results of an ICMP scan are not always exhaustive because routers and firewalls might block ICMP traffic, effectively hiding internal systems from ICMP scans. This is why we employ several network scanning techniques: to determine the presence of network devices and hosts that might be invisible to a particular scanner.

Figure 20.2   SuperScan can perform ICMP scans to detect systems that are available on the targeted network.

Tip

When performing the assessment, a good rule of thumb is to start small by scanning one subnet at a time. Performing scans in smaller increments allows for the assessment of a large network to become a more manageable task. Additionally, controlling the rate and breadth of network scans aids in the prevention of network saturation and possible failure.

Even if ICMP traffic is blocked at the border of the audited network, you locate remotely accessible hosts by performing scans using TCP or UDP packets. In this case, you would use a network scanner, such as SuperScan or Nmap, to probe all IP addresses in the targeted address range on commonly open ports. Figure 20.3 shows the results of a network scan that SuperScan performed. Instead of issuing ICMP packets, we configured the program to locate all hosts that answer to connections on TCP ports 25 (SMTP), 80 (HTTP), and 21 (FTP). In this case, only two hosts were located, both apparently running web server software.

At this point of the external assessment, you have gone through several stages of learning about the targeted network. You started off with planning, performed initial reconnaissance, and enumerated systems that were accessible from the Internet. You are now ready to focus on configuration details of individual hosts that you have uncovered so far.

Figure 20.3 SuperScan can locate remotely accessible systems by attempting to connect to commonly used ports.

Service Enumeration

Now that you have mapped the targeted network, you are ready to probe individual systems in an attempt to determine which operating system they are running and locate ports that can be accessed remotely. This prepares you for the next phase, in which you probe discovered systems and services for exploitable vulnerabilities.

Port scanners can probe individual systems and network ranges to locate open ports that are associated with commonly used services, potential vulnerabilities, or specific exploits. For example, an attacker can run Nmap to find devices that have TCP port 8787 open, which might represent a listening Back Orifice 2000 trojan.

Nmap

Nmap (`http://www.nmap.org/`) is one of the most popular and powerful tools for identifying open ports in a system. Nmap can perform different types of scans that help you determine which traffic is allowed to pass through your access control devices. You can use Nmap to perform scans with TCP, UDP, and ICMP packets in an effort to acquire system information. Each Nmap option attempts to connect with the target system in a different way. Nmap is one of the most favored network scanners because of its flexible scanning options and its availability on multiple OS platforms.

The following is an example of a SYN scan directed at a remotely accessible server. Listing 20.2 shows the nmapNT (Nmap for Windows NT) command performing a SYN scan, as specified by the -sS parameter. The -O option specifies that Nmap should attempt to guess what type of OS the target system is running.

Listing 20.2 **Using Nmap to Port-Scan and Fingerprint a Remote Host**

```
C:\>nmapNT -sS -O target

Starting nmapNT V. 2.53 SP1 by ryan@eEye.com
eEye Digital Security ( http://www.eEye.com )
based on nmap by fyodor@insecure.org  ( www.insecure.org/nmap/ )

Interesting ports on (xxx.xxx.xxx.xxx):
(The 1508 ports scanned but not shown below are in state: filtered)
Port       State       Service
21/tcp     open        ftp
23/tcp     open        telnet
79/tcp     open        finger

Remote OS guesses: Linux 2.1.122 - 2.2.14, Linux kernel 2.2.13

Nmap run completed -- 1 IP address (1 host up) scanned in 272 seconds
```

> **Tip**
>
> Using Nmap to perform only a SYN scan does not exhaustively assess accessibility of remote systems and services; additional scans, such as FIN, XMAS, and UDP, should be executed as well.

In this example, Nmap not only determined which ports were open on the host, but also was able to guess its operating system, which might help later when assessing the system for vulnerabilities. Knowing open ports on the remote host enables you to determine versions of the services that are listening on those ports. Often, all you have to do is connect to the ports using a tool as commonplace as `telnet`.

Telnet and Banner Retrieval

Knowing which versions of applications are in use on the targeted system can help you locate vulnerabilities that might be exploitable over the network. After you know which TCP ports are open on the targeted hosts, you can try connecting to those ports that look particularly interesting. Some of the services that often announce their version when you simply connect to them via `telnet` are Telnet (TCP port 23) and SSH (TCP port 22). For example, you can often obtain the version of the SSH server running on the target by connecting to its TCP port 22 as follows:

```
C:>telnet target 22
SSH-1.99-OpenSSH_2.9
```

Some services, such as SMTP (TCP port 25) and HTTP (TCP port 80) require you to issue a request after you connect with Telnet before revealing their version. For example, you can determine the version of the remote web server by connecting to its port 80 using `telnet`, typing HEAD / HTTP/1.0, and pressing Enter twice:

```
C:\>telnet target 80
HEAD / HTTP/1.0

HTTP/1.1 200 OK
Date: Sat, 02 Mar 2002 00:09:55 GMT
Server: Apache/1.3.19 (Unix) Resin/1.2.2 PHP/4.1.2 mod_ssl/2.8.1 OpenSSL/0.9.6
Last-Modified: Thu, 08 Mar 2001 00:08:32 GMT
ETag: "9cf48-244-3aa6cd80"
Accept-Ranges: bytes
Content-Length: 580
Connection: close
Content-Type: text/html
```

As you can see, this web server seems to be running Apache version 1.3.19 on a UNIX platform, with several modules that might contain vulnerabilities. Port and vulnerability scanners might be able to automatically obtain versions of certain applications. For example, Figure 20.4 shows that SuperScan, which we introduced earlier in the chapter, was able to determine versions of SSH and web servers on the targeted system.

Some port scanners are better at probing specific operating systems or applications than others. LANGuard, for example, is a powerful scanner for probing systems regardless of their OS, but we think it is particularly effective for obtaining detailed information about Windows hosts.

LANGuard

LANGuard Network Scanner (`http://www.gfisoftware.com/languard/lanscan.htm`) provides robust functionality for scanning networks and individual hosts. This tool performs especially well when assessing Windows-based systems that respond on TCP ports 135 and 139. Among other techniques, LANGuard can utilize Windows NULL session connections to execute information-gathering and enumerating processes. LANGuard also comes in handy when assessing any device that accepts Simple Network Management

Protocol (SNMP) connections. If you are able to guess the target's SNMP community string, which is just like a password, you might be able to access extensive amounts of information regarding this device.

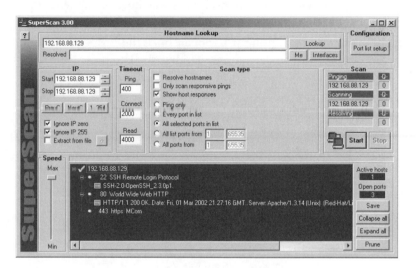

Figure 20.4   Scanners such as SuperScan can determine versions
of some remotely accessible services on the targeted system.

In Figure 20.5, LANGuard discovers enough information to plan an attack against this Windows NT 4.0 domain controller called Tweety. Let's break it down and see what information LANGuard enumerated.

- It gives you the computer name (Tweety) and the operating system (Windows NT 4.0). This helps you focus on exploits that are specific to Windows NT 4.0.

- You can see the computer's NetBIOS names and domain name, which is helpful during a brute force password attack. You also have several NetBIOS services available on this system.

- Look at those shares! There are 10 entry points, from administrative shares (C$, IPC$) to possible personal directories.

- You see 570 usernames configured on the backup DC. This is great information; combined with the domain name, you have several accounts (\\WIN2K\Administrator) to penetrate this target.

- Take special notice of the password age and last logon time for Administrative user accounts. You might find the same password used for extended amounts of time, from which you can infer that no account policies are configured. By viewing the last logon date, you might be able to locate long durations because administrative accounts have logged on, especially service accounts. Any attacker would love to see this information because it suggests that no one is watching the system.

- What can you deduce from knowing the system's uptime? This information shows you how long it has been since the host's last reboot and can sometimes help you determine whether the latest service pack is applied.

- LANGuard performs a quality effort in retrieving various service banners, such as FTP, HTTP, POP, SMTP, and so on.

Figure 20.5 In this example, LANGuard enumerates sensitive information from an NT domain controller.

Going through with the assessment, you have been gradually learning about the environment of the audited network. As we suggested at the beginning of this chapter, you should use this information to populate the system matrix that reflects what you know about targeted systems. Table 20.2 presents an example of one such matrix, which you might have obtained by going through planning, system enumeration, and port enumeration.

Table 20.2 **A System Matrix Helps Keep Track of Detailed Information that Is Discovered During the Assessment**

System	IP Address	Available Services	OS	Version
br2-dc1.abtltd.com	x.x.x.1	25	Cisco 3600	IOS 12.0(5)
smtp.xyz.com	x.x.x.10	22,25,53,110	SunOS 2.6	ESMTP-Sendmail 8.11.1
ftp.xyz.com	x.x.x.15	21,22,5631	Possible UNIX	WU-FTP 2.6.0(1)
www.xyz.com	x.x.x.28	80,443	Linux	Apache 1.3.22 OpenSSL 0.9.6a
ns1.xyz.com	x.x.x.53	25,53	SunOS 5.8	BIND 8.2.3

Network and port scanners bring you closer to the target by locating and analyzing open service ports. Scanners that are able to obtain detailed information about remotely accessible applications and determine whether they are vulnerable to known exploits are called *vulnerability scanners*. Vulnerability scanners are used to locate exploitable weaknesses in applications and operating systems, as we discuss in the following section.

Vulnerability Discovery

Vulnerability scanners often possess network and port-scanning capabilities of scanners that we have discussed so far, but can also probe audited systems for vulnerabilities. Unlike port scanners, which typically operate at the Transport layer and lower, vulnerability scanners have the ability to locate vulnerabilities at the Application layer. By using both port and vulnerability scanners, you can achieve a comprehensive awareness of the state of your network's defenses.

In the assessment process, we have been showing you how to use specialized reconnaissance tools to attempt to strip away layers of perimeter protection one by one. This is an effective way to understand weaknesses of your network. You could conduct many of the steps we have shown so far with vulnerability scanners that we discuss in this section; however, then you would not have the benefit of knowing the effect of less invasive or more stealthy attacks on your network. Let's continue the assessment process by enumerating vulnerabilities on hosts and devices that you discovered during earlier phases of the assessment. We begin by looking at Nessus, a free vulnerability scanner, which we will then compare to several commercially available alternatives.

Nessus

Nessus (`http://www.nessus.org/`), a high-quality, free vulnerability scanner, offers the ability to scan for accessible service ports, and it can perform security checks to determine whether known exploits can be applied to discovered systems. Nessus comes with hundreds of different plug-ins to assess many types of devices.

While you are performing the vulnerability discovery phase of the assessment, you might decide to audit your systems in stages, according to the function they perform. For example, consider first focusing on your high-profile devices, like your firewalls. You would then configure Nessus to test for only commonly exploited firewall vulnerabilities. You might then focus special attention on your web servers because of their high visibility and accessibility. Whatever the case, you simply have to select the Nessus plug-in family you require and specify which systems to scan. Nessus plug-ins are grouped into categories, such as backdoors, small services, Microsoft Windows, and CGI abuses.

After performing a vulnerability scan, Nessus compiles a summary report, illustrated in Figure 20.6, which helps to focus your attention on security weaknesses that require your immediate attention. In this example, Nessus was able to enumerate various user accounts while assessing a Windows file server.

Figure 20.6 A Nessus assessment report summarizes findings of the vulnerability scan—in this case of a Windows system.

Tip

Visit `http://www.vulnerabilities.org/` to obtain a quick assessment report of your personal workstation without downloading Nmap or Nessus.

ISS Internet Scanner is another popular vulnerability assessment tool, which rivals the thoroughness of Nessus and has the advantages and the disadvantages of being a commercial product.

ISS Internet Scanner

ISS Internet Scanner (`http://www.iss.net/`) can perform many of the same functions as Nessus, including port scanning, service verification, and software fingerprinting. ISS Internet Scanner is a commercial product that requires little technical know-how to be able to install it and perform various assessment scans.

ISS Internet Scanner offers tailored sessions depending on the OS, the role of the system, and the level of thoroughness you desire. For example, if your plan is to assess a UNIX system that is running Apache, you might select the UNIX web session with the desired level of thoroughness. The higher the level, the more vulnerability checks will be performed. ISS Internet Scanner also produces high-quality, flexible reports that can be tailored to executives, management, or technicians. One helpful way to organize the data is to sort it by severity.

Figure 20.7 illustrates a technician's report that is organized by severity. It clearly exhibits your greatest vulnerability risks, tagged from high to low. As you review the vulnerability report, you have a comprehensible description of the vulnerability as well as a path to remedy the problem. In this illustration, you can see that a high risk is apparent from an IISURLDecoding vulnerability, allowing an attacker to perform directory traversal to glean sensitive system information. You are also directed to Microsoft Security Bulletin MS00-086 to understand how to resolve this vulnerability.

ISS Internet Scanner provides an extensive vulnerability database of approximately 1,000 known exploits. In addition, it offers an easy-to-use update feature guaranteeing that the most current data is available. When a new vulnerability is discovered or when new malicious code becomes publicly available, ISS's X-Force team quickly updates its vulnerability database to allow customers to scan for these. Another tool with a backing of a knowledgeable security team is Retina, which we discuss in the next section.

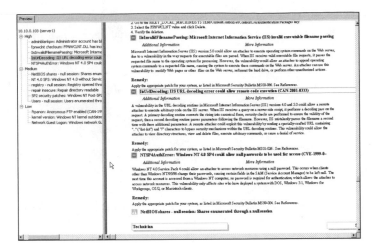

Figure 20.7 An ISS technical vulnerability report can be sorted by severity to highlight the highest risks to the scanned system.

Retina

Retina is a commercial scanner produced by eEye Security (http://www.eeye.com/) that competes with ISS Internet Scanner. Retina provides a clean Windows-based interface, illustrated in Figure 20.8. Retina offers a single interface that incorporates a vulnerability scanner, an Internet browser, a system miner module (which simulates hacking stimulus), and a tracer utility (which offers traceroute-like functionality). Retina offers a quality solution because of its user friendliness, technical robustness, ability to automatically correct some vulnerabilities, as well as detailed explanation for resolving discovered issues.

All three vulnerability scanners that we discussed offer many similar options and functionality. Let's summarize how they relate to each other:

- Nessus is a wonderful free tool whose scanning engine runs on UNIX. It is perfect for small business or personal assessments. Nessus might also be a viable solution for larger organizations if the budget does not allow for the more expensive and user-friendly scanners like ISS Internet Scanner or Retina.

- ISS Internet Scanner offers mid-size to large corporations a robust vulnerability scanning tool, complete with easy software updates and excellent reporting that can be catered for specific audiences.

- Retina is great for scanning mid-size to large corporations. Retina and ISS Internet Scanner are both intelligent and comprehensive by locating the vulnerability and offering, if not fixing, resolution for the exposed weakness. Retina, however, offers an interface that is somewhat easier to navigate and configure.

Figure 20.8   In this example, Retina discovers several exposed service ports along with a potential FTP security weakness, and outlines a recommended resolution path.

You have now completed several steps in your external assessment, starting with planning and continuing to enumerate systems, services, and vulnerabilities. By using a variety of network and vulnerability scanners, you can gain an understanding of the possible weaknesses in your security perimeter. You can learn which service ports can be accessed and exploited from the outside world, and discover configuration errors that might result in the network's defenses operating differently from what you originally expected.

You have used these network and vulnerability scanners to gather information about your organization, and your system matrix should be fully populated with an assortment of information about your external devices. The next step of the assessment is to further research what vulnerabilities are likely to affect your systems that are publicly accessible.

Vulnerability Research

Put your completed system matrix alongside the vulnerability reports generated from Nessus, ISS Internet Scanner, or Retina. This is the point where an attacker and security analyst take separate paths. The attacker continues efforts to exploit your systems, whereas the security analyst begins the process of patching and rectifying any discovered vulnerabilities.

As a security analyst, you can research vulnerabilities in efforts to determine risks that are associated with them and determine the best ways of mitigating them. An excellent source of information on vulnerabilities and their resolutions are your software vendors' web sites, along with vulnerability announcement mailing lists, such as Bugtraq. You can conduct additional research by checking security-oriented web sites, such as the following:

- `http://www.securityfocus.com/`
- `http://packetstorm.widexs.nl/`
- `http://www.cotse.com/`
- `http://www.infosyssec.com/`
- `http://searchsecurity.techtarget.com/`

You are now armed with the tools and techniques used to perform an external assessment. You can use this knowledge to find security holes in your defense perimeter and to locate vulnerable or misconfigured systems that are accessible from the Internet. In addition to examining your network from the perspective of an attacker, you can also audit the configuration of your perimeter components under more controlled conditions. Such internal assessment is critical for ensuring that all layers of your defense-in-depth infrastructure are operating properly, even if they cannot be immediately targeted from the Internet. In the next section, we discuss how to perform an internal audit on your network.

Internal Assessment

In the "Change Management" section of Chapter 17, "Maintaining a Security Perimeter," we described the need to thoroughly test hosts, devices, and applications before deploying them on a production network. Components of the security perimeter should undergo such testing as well, both in the lab environment before deployment and as part of routine internal assessments. The internal assessment incorporates many of the tools and techniques gleaned from the external assessment, but it focuses on ensuring that access restrictions that are implemented by security devices are properly implemented, even if they cannot be immediately circumvented via an external assessment. To test whether access controls are properly implemented, you need to be intimately familiar with your security policy so that you can locate deviations from it. This is different from the external assessment, which did not assume prior knowledge of the audited environment.

In this section, we concentrate on verifying controls that are implemented by a border firewall to demonstrate what's involved in testing the configuration of a perimeter component; however, the same techniques should be used to verify proper application of the security policy on any other device that restricts the way traffic moves across your network.

As a security analyst who is about to audit the security policy implemented by your firewall, you need to make sure that a plan is laid out to systematically validate mechanisms that control components of your infrastructure. The internal assessment focuses on verifying that rule sets and ACLs have the intended effect. For each rule in your firewall, whether it allows or blocks traffic, you need to verify that network traffic travels as expected.

Preparing for the Internal Assessment

Your border firewall is primarily responsible for controlling the flow of traffic between the internal network and the Internet. The firewall's internal assessment should verify that network traffic complies with the intent of the firewall rules. For example, if the firewall rulebase is configured to allow SMTP traffic from the Internet to a mail server that is located in a screened network, you will attempt to connect to the mail server from the Internet to guarantee that traffic passes through the firewall as defined in the rulebase. You must further validate that only SMTP traffic from the Internet is allowed to pass and that all other traffic is rejected by the firewall and logged accordingly. In the event that you are able to connect to the mail server from an unapproved network, you must inspect the firewall configuration to determine the cause of the deviation from your security policy.

Figure 20.9 provides an example of a common network configuration, which we will use to demonstrate how to perform an internal assessment of the firewall. To test how traffic from the Internet traverses the firewall, we have set up an assessment station outside of the organization's network. We have also configured listener systems to see what packets are able to pass through the firewall. The assessment station is equipped with network and vulnerability scanners that we discussed in the "External Assessment" section of this chapter. Listener systems are configured to monitor network traffic in promiscuous mode on internal subnets. The listening systems are configured with packet-sniffing software, such as Tcpdump (`http://www.tcpdump.org/`) on your UNIX systems and Windump (`http://netgroup-serv.polito.it/windump/`) on your Windows systems. Another commonly used sniffer is Ethereal (`http://www.ethereal.com/`), which is available free and can be used on UNIX and Windows systems.

Tip

Another powerful tool that can help you audit your security policies is Snort (`http://www.snort.org/`). Snort is an intrusion detection tool that can be configured on a "listener" station to watch the network for specific patterns and types of traffic to determine whether your defense lines are filtering against such traffic.

Figure 20.9 Assessment and listener stations are placed at key points of the network to conduct an internal assessment of the border firewall.

Your listener systems monitor packets that pass the firewall and help determine whether access controls succeeded or failed. With logging enabled on the firewall, you can view the log file to determine which packets were accepted or dropped during the audit, but these logs rarely provide as much detail as a listening station that is equipped with a sniffer. To fully audit the border firewall, you must move the assessment station from the Internet to another network segment to validate access controls for each firewall interface.

Verifying Access Controls

To verify that the firewall properly enforces access controls, you can utilize scanners, such as Nmap and LANGuard, to perform the following tests:

- Verify that the firewall service ports that should be explicitly blocked are indeed blocked and that approved traffic is allowed to pass.
- Verify controls over broadcasts and other types of discovery traffic.
- Verify that authorized firewall management stations are the only devices allowed to establish an interactive session.
- Verify that only authorized traffic can cross boundaries of internal subnets.

Your audit of the firewall's configuration begins by attempting to access systems and services that are behind the firewall.

Traffic Restrictions

During the external assessment, you used network scanners, such as Nmap, to determine what devices can be accessed from the Internet. We use the same process, depicted in Figure 20.10, to ensure that unauthorized traffic is blocked by the firewall and that approved traffic is allowed to pass. The arrows represent the inbound discovery requests from the assessment station directed toward the devices that are located in the screened network.

Figure 20.10 The assessment station issues discovery packets in an attempt to reach servers that are located behind the firewall.

To use Nmap for determining whether the firewall blocks ICMP echo request traffic, you can use the -sP parameter to perform an ICMP scan like this:

```
# nmap -sP  192.168.1.0 - 192.168.1.255
```

If your security policy prohibits inbound ICMP traffic, the firewall should block this scan as the assessment station attempts to incrementally scan the 192.168.1.0/24 network. To ensure that the firewall blocked ICMP packets, you can check firewall logs, as well as sniffer logs, on the listener system.

Next, you can attempt to verify that your firewall drops all UDP and TCP SYN packets that are not destined for approved network devices. Nmap can perform such scans using the following syntax:

- UDP: `# nmap -sU 192.168.1.0 - 192.168.1.255`

- SYN: `# nmap -sS 192.168.1.0 - 192.168.1.255`

To obtain Application layer information about accessible services, you can utilize a vulnerability scanner, such as Nessus, Retina, or IIS Security Scanner. You can use these tools to probe systems that are located during the network scan in an attempt to access approved and denied application service ports and verify that any potential vulnerabilities discovered during the external assessment have been resolved. To learn more about the types of probes that the vulnerability scanner performs, as well as to verify whether traffic was blocked, look at sniffer logs on the listening station. Figure 20.11 shows one such log, captured using Ethereal during the examination of a publicly accessible FTP server. You see the three-way handshake reflected by the leading SYN, followed by the SYN ACK, and completing the connection with the server responding with the ACK. In this case, the assessment station has been verified as connecting to the destination server through the firewall.

Figure 20.11 A sniffer that is running on the listener station can capture traffic that is directed at the servers—in this case, an FTP session initiation.

As you examine results of your network and vulnerability scans, compare them to your security policy and make sure that the firewall only accepts approved communications.

Information Leakage

By this point of the internal assessment, you have confirmed that approved systems and services can be accessed through the audited firewall. Now it is time to make sure that the firewall blocks traffic that might allow attackers to obtain sensitive information about internal systems. Certain protocols, such as those depicted in Table 20.3,[1] offer attackers valuable system information and should be blocked under most situations. Windows and UNIX hosts use these services to advertise system information and available services to others on the network. It is good practice to filter these advertisements from passing through the firewall in an inbound, as well as outbound, direction. Some of these advertisements include information about shared or exported directories, which might have read-write access. Many firewalls are configured to drop the following network packets by default, but they should verify that this is functioning as expected.

Table 20.3 Services Known to Leak Sensitive System Information Should Be Explicitly Blocked at the Firewall

Service Name	Port
Ident	TCP 113
RPC Portmapper	TCP 111
DHCP/BOOTP	UDP 67
NetBIOS Datagram	UDP 138
NetBIOS Name	UDP 137
NetBIOS Session	TCP 139
Windows RPC Portmapper	TCP 135
Windows 2000 SMB without NetBIOS	TCP 445
Windows 2000 LDAP	TCP/UDP 389 TCP/UDP 636
Windows 2000 Global Catalog LDAP	TCP 3268, TCP 3269
Windows 2000 Kerberos	UDP 88, TCP 464, TCP/UDP 750, TCP/UDP 751, UDP 752, UDP 753, TCP 754

You can use scanners, such as Nmap, to verify that these packets are not allowed to pass through the firewall in either direction unless your security policy explicitly authorizes them. You would analyze firewall and listener station logs to verify that only approved traffic can leave the internal network and that no traffic destined to the Internet is received. This part of the internal assessment helps to verify that attackers will not be able to enumerate system information using these advertising service ports from devices that are located in the screened or internal networks.

Firewall Management

The next step in the internal assessment is to validate firewall-management rules that grant administrators the ability to configure the firewall remotely. You want to verify that an attacker will not be able to connect directly to the firewall. Generally, the firewall should be configured to a finite number of administrative hosts, residing on a trusted internal management network, to establish a management session with the firewall. To verify that this is the case, attempt to connect to the firewall using its management console from the assessment station that is located on various network segments.

Adjacent Network Traffic

One of the last tests to perform during the internal assessment is to verify that the firewall does not pass unauthorized traffic between adjacent subnets. For example, if an attacker compromises a server in the screened network, she is likely to attempt to gain access to systems on the internal subnet. This phase of the audit verifies that proper access controls are defined in the firewall rulebase to prevent undesired access across boundaries of internal subnets. Figure 20.12 illustrates a failed access attempt, where the firewall denies traffic originating from the screened network and destined to the internal network. Management access to systems on the screened subnet from the internal network is still allowed, as defined by the organization's security policy.

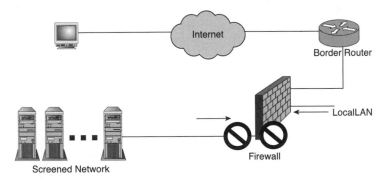

Figure 20.12 Access between adjacent internal subnets is controlled by the firewall, according to the organization's security policy.

You have analyzed the firewall rulebase and performed an audit to verify that traffic is allowed or denied according to controls that are defined in the security policy. Performing such an internal assessment is critical to locating misconfigurations or vulnerabilities of which an attacker might take advantage. As part of the assessment, you have clearly defined which traffic flows through the firewall. Your next step in the internal assessment would be to validate access controls on your border router and other devices that impose access restrictions.

Summary

In this chapter, we examined techniques for assessing the effectiveness of your security perimeter. We described two complementary approaches—one that was aimed at determining how an attacker might be able to penetrate through layers of our defense, and another that focused on ensuring that all layers of the perimeter are implemented according to the intended design.

The external assessment consisted of several discovery steps that gradually unveiled information about the audited infrastructure. The more information an attacker can gather, the more likely he can determine how to compromise a target. Table 20.4 summarizes phases of the external assessment that we discussed.

Table 20.4   The External Assessment Consists of Several Discrete Stages that We Discussed Throughout the Chapter

Step	Purpose	Utilities
PLANNING		
1. Permission! Communication!	Obtain written management and support staff buy-in.	
2. Assessment station	Obtain necessary tools and reference materials.	
INITIAL RECONNAISSANCE		
3. Background information	Gather published organizational information.	www.google.com www.altavista.com Copernic
4. Whois query	Locate contact and IP addressing information.	whois NetScanTools
5. DNS query	Obtain DNS information for internal and external domains.	nslookup dig NetScanTools

continues ▶

Table 20.4 **Continued**

Step	Purpose	Utilities
SYSTEM ENUMERATION		
6. Network topology discovery	Locate network topology information and identify potential access control devices.	traceroute NetScanTools
7. System accessibility	Determine which systems are accessible from the Internet.	pinger fping SuperScan Nmap
SYSTEM ENUMERATION		
8. Service port discovery	Determine which TCP/UDP services on accessible systems.	LANGuard SuperScan Nmap
9. Banner retrieval	Grab banner information to determine the specific OS, versions, and applications that are available.	Telnet LANGuard
VULNERABILITY DISCOVERY		
10. Vulnerability discovery	Assess network devices for known vulnerabilities in OS, services, and applications.	Nessus ISS Internet Scanner Retina
11. Vulnerability research	Understand the vulnerability scope and risk and define a path to remedy.	www.securityfocus.com packetstorm.widexs.nl www.cotse.com www.infosyssec.com

We also discussed the process of performing an internal assessment, which allows administrators to compare the implementation of the security perimeter to the organization's security policy. We showed you how to conduct an internal assessment by focusing on the organization's border firewall to ensure that the firewall's access restrictions correspond to the engineer's intentions. This process should be repeated for other components of your security perimeter that control access to network resources.

Because the security perimeter around your resources evolves together with your business needs, be sure to perform external and internal assessment on a regular basis; that way, you have a chance to validate the effectiveness of your controls before attackers exploit vulnerabilities in your defenses.

References

1 Microsoft Corporation. "Exchange 2000 Server Resource Kit, Appendix B."
`http://www.microsoft.com/technet/treeview/default.asp?url=/technet/`
`prodtechnol/exchange/reskit/ex00res/resguide/appendb.asp`. March 2002.

21

Design Under Fire

THIS CHAPTER DEALS WITH *DESIGN UNDER FIRE,* which means the practice of looking at our network security designs the same way an attacker would. Analyzing how attackers can compromise our networks helps us find the networks' weaknesses so that we can improve their security. Analysis is a natural follow-up to the testing procedures discussed in Chapter 20, "Assessment Techniques." To implement design under fire, we discuss a process called *adversarial review,* which offers one way to protect our networks, even from vulnerabilities we are unaware of.

Performing an adversarial review might seem redundant because you already included security in your design from the start. However, testing that occurs in the design stage attempts to determine whether a design functions according to its requirements. Such testing is an essential part of system design, but it tells you little about how secure the design is. It is entirely possible for a network to perform all of its functions exactly right, yet be completely insecure. An entirely different mental process is required to understand how someone else might intentionally break your design, but it is exactly the type of thought process that is necessary to eliminate subtle security problems that are introduced into our networks.

To prepare you to perform an adversarial review, we begin this chapter with a discussion of how an attacker thinks about attacking a network. Then, we ask you to watch over our shoulders while we subject the designs in this chapter to the type of attention they would receive every day if they were implemented and placed on the Internet.

The Hacker Approach to Attacking Networks

Attackers choose the path of least resistance when attacking a network. They start with efforts to discover the architecture of the network and then attempt to exploit any weaknesses that they find. Most attackers possess a limited set of attack methods (exploits), which they can use only when particular technologies and configurations (preconditions) exist on their target's network. The discovery process enables them to find out whether the network possesses any of the required prerequisites, so the first line of defense for a network is to prevent as much discovery activity as possible. You can reduce an attacker's ability to learn whether your network is vulnerable by limiting the unnecessary information that your network releases using techniques such as filtering ICMP messages, changing application headers, and employing split DNS configurations.

The attacker who gets by your anti-discovery defenses begins to map out the vulnerabilities on your network and match them up against the available exploit techniques. If the attacker finds a match, he can launch the exploit in an attempt to subvert some part of your network. An attacker who does manage to gain some access can use it to leverage more access into the network. The attacker repeats this discovery/exploit process until he runs out of techniques or achieves his attack goals. One of your goals when designing the security for your network should be to frustrate attackers long enough that they go away in search of an easier target. Failing that, slowing them down gives you a chance to detect them.

The designs that we review in this chapter are already good at frustrating attackers. It is our job to see if we can add some additional frustration into their lives by thinking about how they might subvert our networks and using this knowledge to design additional security controls.

Adversarial Review

During an adversarial review, we look for ways that an attacker might make use of the devices and the configurations of those devices that you have used to create your network. This process is especially important for those devices that you have used to implement your security infrastructure. Remember that the overall security of your network relies on the individual components that make up the network. Security settings on one device can have a dramatic effect on the security of another device. To gain a complete view of the security of the entire network, you must take a careful look at each of the devices that implement your security infrastructure and then analyze how the interaction between devices affects security. Adversarial review provides a useful method for exploring the impact of these interactions.

We are not actually attacking the network during an adversarial review. Instead, we are conducting an analytical thought process that allows us to develop scenarios that someone else might use to attack the network. By creating these scenarios and identifying measures that could be used to prevent them, we can locate flaws in the architecture of the perimeter or potentially weak links that do not follow defense-in-depth principles.

To conduct an adversarial review, you must perform the following activities.

1. Decide what you are trying to prevent. For example, the goal of your adversarial review might be to find a way to deface a web site, access an internal database, or perform a denial of service (DoS) attack.

2. Decide where to start the attack. The attack conceived during the adversarial review is frequently launched from the Internet, but it is also useful to start from an internal network segment to see how to defend against the insider threat.

3. From the viewpoint of the attacker, determine the access that remains after all of the security device configurations have been taken into account. For example, if your goal is to access a system located behind a firewall, and the firewall only allows TCP port 80 traffic through to this system, your review will have to locate a way to either attack the server using TCP port 80 or locate a vulnerability in the firewall to circumvent this restriction. To complete this step, you must review configurations and research vulnerabilities for each device that you can communicate with. If you discover vulnerabilities, you must make a judgment about how feasible an attack based upon the vulnerability is.

4. Determine the impact of taking advantages of any misconfigurations or exploiting any vulnerabilities. Any increases in access gained can then be used to attack additional systems on the network. For example, if you locate a vulnerability that would allow you to take control of an internal server, you can now consider that server under your control and proceed with the review using the system to reach other systems on your network.

5. Repeat steps 3 and 4 as necessary until you have reached the maximum amount of access to the network that you can.

6. Identify additional security controls that would have prevented any of the attacks from succeeding.

One of the most time-consuming parts of the review is step 3. To determine the amount of access that an attacker has, you must conduct a detailed analysis of each security device on your network. You will be looking for three key pieces of information:

- What access does the device have to provide to allow normal network usage? For example, a border firewall normally needs to allow TCP port 80 traffic to the public web server.

- What extraneous access is the device providing? Too frequently, the configuration of security devices is overly permissive, allowing access that is not required but that is useful to the attacker. For example, a firewall might allow TCP port 80 traffic to the entire De-Militarized Zone (DMZ), not just to the public web server. If a device on the DMZ is running a vulnerable service on port 80, an attacker can exploit it even though access to the device is unnecessary to the operation of the network.

- Does the device have any vulnerabilities that would allow you to circumvent the security controls? You can use many sources of information on the Internet to research vulnerabilities, including Carnegie Mellon's Computer Emergency Response Team (CERT) at `http://www.cert.org` and the vulnerability database maintained by SecurityFocus at `http://www.securityfocus.com/bid`. If you find a vulnerability announcement for your device, you need to carefully review the information to see whether it applies to your environment, and if it does, what you should do to mitigate the problem.

In step 4, you use the access you have discovered to "attack" your network. Thinking like the attacker, you attempt to see whether the access that remains after you have considered each device is sufficient to do significant damage.

Even if you did not find exploitable access in step 3, it is occasionally useful to act as if you had and proceed with the review anyway. New vulnerabilities are discovered in software every day. As an example, if you had been using the latest version of the wu-ftpd daemon at the end of October 2001, you would have had no way of knowing that it contained a buffer overflow condition (`http://www.securityfocus.com/bid/3581`). You would have had to wait until the end of November 2001 for the vulnerability to be made public. This vulnerability had actually been in the software since version 2.5.0, which was released in April 1999. This means that sites that installed this version or its successors (up to version 2.6.1) might have been vulnerable to this attack for two years. Simulating vulnerabilities during your review allows you to experiment with the impact that an undiscovered vulnerability would have on your network.

Step 5 is an iterative process that requires you to look at where the attacker starts to determine how far he can penetrate the network. If you were analyzing your exposure to an external attack, you would likely start the attack with your public systems. These systems normally come under attack first because they are the most exposed to the Internet. If you have (or simulate that you have) a vulnerability in one of these systems, your next step is to think what attackers could do if they were able to exploit the vulnerability successfully.

Gaining control of one of these systems would allow you to start launching more attacks using the public system as the source. If the access you have discovered during the review allows this public system to attack other computers on your network, and these other systems also had exploitable vulnerabilities, you would be able to control these other systems, moving further into your network. You continue this thought process until you run out of systems that an attacker could access or until you have circumvented the security controls that you care about. At this point, you can look to see how far you, as the attacker, got in the network and what security controls you could implement that would have stopped the attack at each step in the process. Assuming their implementation, you can re-run the analysis to see whether you can figure out any other ways to attack your network. When you have run out of ideas, you are done.

Step 6 ends the adversarial review with the identification of the additional security controls that are necessary to protect your network. Especially for reviews in which you have included simulated vulnerabilities, the review helps you identify the controls necessary to implement defense in depth. This is the real power of the adversarial review: the identification of the layers of defense needed to help protect you against the unknown.

GIAC GCFW Student Practical Designs

We will draw our examples for this chapter from practical assignments that GIAC students produced as part of the requirements for their GIAC Certified Firewall Analyst (GCFW) certification. The students were asked to create a secure network for a fictitious entity named GIAC Enterprises (GIACE), which is in the business of selling fortune cookie sayings. This is the same source we used for case study four in Chapter 16, "Sample Designs." In Chapter 16, we explored the major security features for one of the GCFW student's practicals. In this chapter, we will take a decidedly different approach when reviewing their designs.

The GCFW students have produced a wide variety of designs for us to choose from. We have chosen to discuss two of them that were awarded honors by the GCFW Advisory Board. During each review, our goal will be to determine if a reasonable scenario exists that would allow an attacker to gain access to the fortune sayings database. As a secondary goal, we will attempt to gain control of as many GIACE systems as possible. Also, both reviews will assume a starting viewpoint of an Internet attacker. A listing of completed practical assignments can be found at `http://www.giac.org/GCFW.php`.

Practical Design 1

The first design we look at is the security architecture created by Angela Orebaugh, who obtained her GCFW certification in March 2002. Angela's design is shown in Figure 21.1 and can be downloaded at `http://www.giac.org/practical/Angela_Orebaugh_GCFW.zip`. It has several interesting features, including the following elements:

- Extensive use of redundancy to produce a high-availability network
- Two levels of firewalls from two different vendors to provide defense in depth
- Ingress and egress filtering at the network border
- A screened subnet network to separate publicly accessible servers from internal systems
- A separate management network segment to monitor and administer the network
- The use of VPNs to allow suppliers and partners to gain access to the GIACE network
- IDS systems to monitor the DMZ and internal network segments

As previously mentioned, our goal is to determine if a reasonable scenario exists that would allow an attacker to gain access to the fortune sayings database. Our review will assume that the attack originates from the Internet. Because steps 1 and 2 of the adversarial review process have already been determined, our adversarial review of Angela's design will begin with step 3: determining the access that remains. By examining the security settings of each security device that stands between the Internet and the fortune database, we will determine whether an external attacker can access the fortune database. Looking at Figure 21.1, you can see that this will require us to examine the screening filtering routers at the border of the network, the external firewalls, the internal firewalls, and the database server. After we have finished discussing a device's configuration, we will perform step 4 for that device: determining the impact. After all of the devices have been discussed, we will then show how step 5—repeat as necessary—can be used to combine the discovered vulnerabilities to reach our review goal.

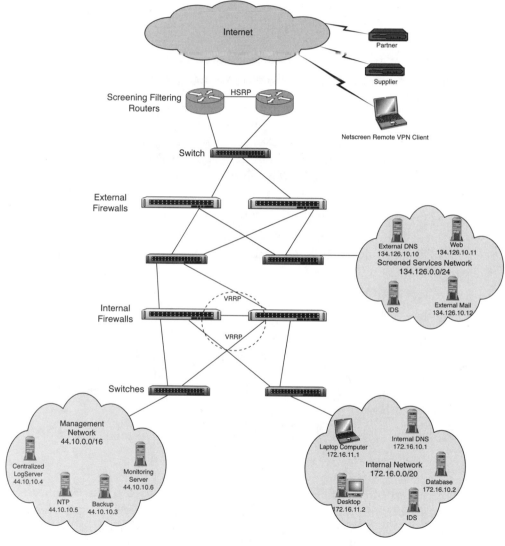

Figure 21.1 Angela Orebaugh's GIACE secure network architecture makes extensive use of redundancy.

Determining the Access that Remains: Screening Filtering Routers

Our discussion begins at the interface between the GIACE network and the Internet. At the border of the network are two Cisco 7200 series routers running IOS 12.x. They connect the GIACE network to the Internet and are configured to use Cisco's proprietary Hot Standby Routing Protocol (HSRP) to enable one of the routers to take over should the other fail. The routers also provide the first opportunity to protect the GIACE network from external attackers by implementing ingress and egress filters. Because the exact filter settings are essential to the implementation of the security architecture, we spend some time going over them.

The Ingress Filter

An ingress filter on the border router of a network can be an effective first step toward securing it. Properly implemented, an ingress filter can block potentially damaging packets before they enter the network. Here is a summarization of the ingress rules for this design, which are applied to the serial interface that is connected on the border routers to the WAN link to the Internet:

- Deny and log packets that have invalid source IP addresses.
- Deny and log incoming packets that are destined to the ports normally associated with FTP, Telnet, Secure Shell (SSH), SunRPC, Network File Service, and Windows Common Internet File Service.
- Allow HTTP and HTTPS packets that are addressed to the web server.
- Allow SMTP packets that are addressed to the mail server.
- Allow IPSec and IKE packets that are addressed to the external firewall.
- Allow "established" TCP packets (with the ACK or RST bits set) that have a destination port greater than 1024. This rule is intended to allow in TCP packets that are part of ongoing TCP conversations initiated from internal hosts.
- Deny and log any other inbound traffic.

The Egress Filter

The egress filter can prevent your site from being used to attack other sites should an attacker manage to gain control of internal systems. The egress filter prevents spoofed packets from leaving the network and is applied on the Ethernet interface that connects the border routers to the interior network:

- Permit traffic to leave if its source address is valid (that is, from 134.126.0.0/16). This is the address that is assigned to the company's internal network.
- Deny and log any other outbound traffic.

As mentioned in Chapter 2, "Packet Filtering," it is a shame that more sites do not implement egress filters. If they did, the opportunity for an attacker to launch attacks on other networks, including distributed DoS attacks, would be sharply limited.

Other Filters

In addition to the ingress and egress filters, the router also has been configured to prevent other activities that can cause security problems:

- No Source Routing
- No IP Directed Broadcasts
- No IP Unreachable Messages
- No Cisco Discovery Protocol (CDP) Messages

The first setting, No Source Routing, prevents the router from accepting packets with source routing enabled. If you allow source-routed packets, an attacker can circumvent ingress filters by spoofing packets with addresses that are allowed by the router, which allows the attacker to set up full TCP connections that appear to originate from a trusted external host. Preventing source-routed packets is a setting that should be used on all border routers.

The second setting, No IP Directed Broadcasts, prevents IP-directed broadcasts. This setting is important for preventing the network from being used in a Smurf attack. Without this setting in place, it is possible that the GIACE network could be used to launch a DoS attack on another network. To prevent this, the routers have been configured to drop packets that are destined to broadcast addresses.

The third setting, No IP Unreachable Messages, helps prevent network discovery activities by telling the router not to generate ICMP unreachable messages. A router generates ICMP unreachable messages on two occasions when it receives a packet that is destined for itself on a port that it is not listening to, and when it receives a packet that it does not know how to deliver.

Shutting off ICMP unreachable messages makes it harder for an attacker to determine what services are running on the router. It also prevents inverse network scans. If a router generates an ICMP unreachable message when it receives a packet destined for a host that does not exist on a network that the router is directly connected to, an attacker can map the network for live hosts by sending a packet to each address on the network and then watch to see which addresses result in an ICMP unreachable message. A probe that does not return an ICMP packet indicates a live host at that address.

The last setting, No Cisco Discovery Protocol (CDP) Messages, prevents the generation of CDP messages. Cisco routers use CDP to discover information about other neighboring Cisco routers. This information is also useful to attackers, so it has been disabled in this design.

Protecting the Routers

Any device that enforces the security policy of a network is a tempting target, and this definitely includes the border routers. Cisco routers have a few popular ways that attackers can attempt to gain access. These include logging in to the router using Telnet, downloading or modifying the router's configuration using SNMP, or accessing the router through its http administrative interface. The following steps were taken to prevent these types of accesses:

- Allow login access only from the monitoring server.
- Replace the Telnet protocol with SSH.
- Enable SNMP read access, but restrict it to the monitoring server.
- Enable SNMP read/write access, but restrict it to the monitoring server.
- Disable the http administrative interface.
- Disable other unnecessary services.

Now that we have described the security settings of the routers, let's see if we can figure out a way that they might be compromised.

Determining the Impact: Routers

We start step 4 of our adversarial review of the screening filtering routers by looking at the access that remains after all of the router's filter settings are considered. The major items that we note are the settings that allow outside users access to the web, mail, DNS, and VPN servers. This information will be useful to us later when we look at the security of those devices. Meanwhile, some additional items are worth noting about the routers.

The security settings of the border routers are relatively good, and little access remains after the filters and other configuration settings are considered. However, a few areas remain that we should take note of during the review:

- The ingress filter allows anonymous established packets.

- The egress filter allows any internal packet to exit the network as long as its source address is valid.
- SNMP version 1 is enabled.
- There are weak authentication logs in to the router.

To start with, the ingress filter is allowing established packets through. This allows an attacker to use ACK scanning to discover services on computers behind the routers. In this design, depending on how the external firewalls are configured, this might not be a problem. However, if a firewall was not between the routers and the GIACE network, a context-based access control (CBAC) filter could have been used to allow internal users to establish TCP connections to the Internet without requiring a generic All Allow Established Packets rule. CBAC filters can be CPU intensive, so be careful when using them that you do not affect their primary purpose of routing packets. More details about CBAC can be found in Chapter 6, "Role of a Router."

The next area to look at is the egress filter. It allows any internally generated packet to leave the network as long as its source address is valid. This is overly permissive. A number of ICMP packet types should probably be blocked at the egress filter to prevent certain types of discovery activities. For example, ICMP TTL exceeded messages should be dropped to prevent the attacker from using traceroute to discover the structure of the network. In addition, most types of ICMP destination unreachable messages should be dropped to prevent attackers from learning what hosts and services are running on the network.

Note

One type of ICMP destination unreachable message that should not be filtered is code 4 (fragmentation needed and don't fragment are set). RFC 1191 compliant systems use this destination unreachable message to set the optimum maximum transmission unit (MTU). See Chapter 6 and Chapter 15, "Tuning the Design for Performance," for more details.

In addition to filtering ICMP messages, it is worthwhile to block other types of outbound traffic that are unnecessary to the operation of the network. If an attacker were to gain control of an internal system, this would make it harder for him to use the system to attack other systems outside the network. It can also complicate the attacker's ability to download additional exploit tools. In the case of a live attacker, this is probably just an inconvenience. However, if the attacker actually sends a piece of malicious code, such as a worm or virus, egress filtering can prevent the attack from working.

Beyond these issues with the filters, certain problems might allow an attacker to gain control of the actual router. The first of these is the use of SNMP. An attacker who knows the read-only SNMP community name and has access to the SNMP service on the router can learn substantial information about the configuration of the router. An attacker who knows the read-write SNMP community name can change the configuration of the router, including the access control lists (ACLs). To prevent this from happening, the routers have been configured to accept SNMP requests only from the management console. In addition, community names have been chosen that might be hard to guess. Accepting connections that originate from the only monitoring server's address is completely effective at blocking requests from outside the network. If the attack originates from inside the network, though, the attacker might be able to successively impersonate the monitoring server, allowing him to access the SNMP service if he knows a valid SNMP community name.

Discovery of the community names might be relatively easy. First, the read-only community name was set to giacpublic. It is realistic to expect that a determined attacker might guess this community name. Second, SNMP version 1 does not encrypt its packets. An attacker who manages to take control of a system that is on the network path between the management server and the router might be able to sniff the community names (including the read-write community name) as they are transmitted to the router. This would allow the attacker to completely compromise the border routers. It is important to mention that the community name weakness has been eliminated in version 3 of the SNMP protocol. Cisco routers fully support this version of SNMP; unfortunately, many SNMP management tools have not been updated to support this enhanced version of the protocol.

The second way that an attacker might be able to gain control of the routers is by logging into them. Similar to the technique used to protect SNMP, the routers accept login only from the monitoring server, and again, similar to SNMP, an internal attack might be able to bypass this restriction. Additional security has been added by changing the login protocol from Telnet to SSH. Because SSH encrypts the network conversation, an attacker won't be able to sniff a valid password from the network when a login to the routers occurs. However, an attacker could still guess the password. No strong authentication system (such as SecurID) is being used. A simple (weak) user-name password combination is all that is needed to access the router. Brute force techniques can be used to guess this password, although the monitoring server would log this activity.

It is also possible that vulnerabilities in the SSH version 1 protocol might be used to gain access to the routers (`http://cve.mitre.org/cgi-bin/ cvename.cgi?name=CVE-2001-0144`). In particular, SSH version 1 has a vulnerability that might allow an attacker to recover a session key and allow the session to be decrypted. This could reveal the username and password of the administrator, allowing the attacker to log in to the router.

Tip

SSH supports public key authentication, but the Cisco implementation of SSH does not.

Mention of SSH vulnerabilities is not meant to imply that you should not use SSH to protect your Cisco logins. It is still a useful technique to protect the routers. To make it more effective, consider implementing stronger authentication methods than are used in this design.

Determining the Access that Remains: The External Firewalls

The next layer of defense is a pair of stateful packet filter firewalls that are being used to implement the external firewall and to terminate the VPNs that allow the business partners and the suppliers to connect to the internal network. The products that are being used are two NetScreen-100 security appliances. Like the border routers, these appliances are running a high-availability protocol to allow one to take over should the other fail.

The NetScreen-100 comes with three network interfaces: untrusted, trusted, and DMZ. In this design, the untrusted interface is connected to the border routers, the trusted interface is connected to the internal network, and the DMZ interface is connected to the screened service network. It uses four different rulebases to control which packets to allow, based on the interface at which the packet arrives. These rulebases are incoming, outgoing, to DMZ, and from DMZ. For example, packets that come from the untrusted network and are destined to the internal network are filtered based on the incoming rulebase. Packets that enter the untrusted network and are destined for the DMZ are handled by the to DMZ rulebase, and so on. The following sections present the configurations for each rulebase.

Incoming

Table 21.1 shows the rulebase that controls packets heading from the untrusted interface to the trusted interface.

Table 21.1 **Incoming Rulebase for the External Firewalls**

Source	Destination	Service	Action
Border Routers	Log Server	Syslog	Allow
Border Routers	NTP Server	NTP	Allow
Outside Any	Inside Any	Any	Deny

Outgoing

The rulebase in Table 21.2 controls the traffic that is entering from the trusted interface and destined for the untrusted interface.

Table 21.2 **Outgoing Rulebase for the External Firewalls**

Source	Destination	Service	Action
Monitoring Server	External Firewall	SSH	Allow
Inside Any	External Firewall	Any	Deny
Backup Server	Border Routers	Backup	Allow
Monitoring Server	Border Routers	Ping, SNMP, SSH	Allow
Internal Network	Outside Any	Any	Allow
Inside Any	Outside Any	Any	Deny

To DMZ

The rulebase in Table 21.3 controls the traffic that is heading for the DMZ network regardless of which interface the traffic entered from (untrusted or trusted).

Table 21.3 **Rulebase for Packets that Are Heading Toward the DMZ**

Source	Destination	Service	Action
Outside Any	Web Server	HTTP, HTTPS	Allow
Outside Any, Internal Network	External Mail Server	Mail	Allow
Internal Network	Web Server	HTTP, HTTPS	Allow
Internal Network	External Mail Server	IMAP	Allow
Monitoring Server	DMZ Any	Ping, SNMP	Allow
Backup Server	DMZ Any	Backup	Allow
Inside Any	DMZ Any	Any	Deny
Outside Any	DMZ Any	Any	Deny

From DMZ

The last rulebase, shown in Table 21.4, defines what traffic is allowed to leave the DMZ network.

Table 21.4 Rulebase for Packets that Are Leaving the DMZ

Source	Destination	Service	Action
Web Server	Database	TCP Any	Allow
External DNS	Outside Any	DNS	Allow
External Mail Server	Outside Any	Mail	Allow
DMZ Any	Log Server	Syslog	Allow
DMZ Any	NTP Server	NTP	Allow
DMZ Any	Monitoring Server	SNMP	Allow
DMZ Any	Inside Any	Any	Deny
DMZ Any	Outside Any	Any	Deny

Determining the Impact: The External Firewalls

The cumulative effect of these rulebases is to dramatically limit what type of traffic can flow between the three network zones. It is our job as adversarial reviewers to look for any access that remains after all the rules on the firewalls are put into place and for any vulnerabilities that might exist in the firewalls that an attacker could make use of. A careful review of these settings reveals the following issues:

- Network traffic to the web and mail servers is not tested for invalid requests.
- The web server is allowed unrestricted access to the database server.
- The NetScreen appliance might have a vulnerability that allows the filters to be bypassed.

As stated at the beginning of this chapter, attackers target what they can talk to. In this case, the web server and mail server must be accessible to outside users. If the web server software or the mail server software contains vulnerabilities, this design would not prevent them from being taken over, which is a major concern because services that have had the worst history for security vulnerabilities are web and mail server software. Stateful packet filtering firewalls rely primarily on the contents of the packet header to make their security decision, so they would be unable to detect an attack that uses malformed requests targeted at the web or mail server software. The use of a web proxy and a mail proxy would provide the ability to look at the application data in the packet to determine whether an invalid request is being made. Although this method is not perfect, it would provide better security than relying entirely on the packet header to make the security decision.

The next problem is the permissive setting between the web server and the database server. An attacker who managed to gain control of the web server could use it to attack any TCP service that is running on the database server. This rule should be more restrictive, permitting only the minimum TCP traffic necessary to allow the web server to make the necessary database queries. It is worth noting that the internal firewall does provide this restriction. It only allows the web server to send SQLnet1 (TCP Port 1521) traffic to the database server. You might ask why it is important to restrict the traffic between the web server and the database server at the external firewall when the internal firewall is going to accomplish the same thing. As was stated previously, whenever you can stop a particular problem with multiple defensive techniques, you increase the resiliency of the network to attack.

The last items worth talking about are potential vulnerabilities in the NetScreen devices. Some versions of the NetScreen software are vulnerable to an attack that allows packets into the DMZ that should have been filtered (`http://cve.mitre.org/cgi-bin/cvename.cgi?name=CAN-2001-0589`). Ensuring that version 2.5r6 or higher is installed on the NetScreen devices will prevent this attack.

Determining the Access that Remains: The Internal Firewalls

The internal firewalls are the last line of network filters for the GIACE network. Their purpose is to provide design redundancy for the NetScreen appliances while protecting the internal and management networks.

The internal firewalls are implemented using a pair of Nokia IP330s firewall appliances that are running Check Point FireWall-1 version 4.1. Like the NetScreen-100s, the Nokias are stateful inspection firewalls; however, unlike the NetScreen configuration, the Nokias have a single rulebase to control all filtering decisions. Table 21.5 is the configuration of this rulebase.

Table 21.5   **Rulebase for the Internal Firewalls**

No.	Source	Destination	Service	Action
1	Monitoring Server	Internal Firewall	FireWall-1, SSH, ICMP, SNMP	Allow

No.	Source	Destination	Service	Action
2	Any	Internal Firewall	Any	Drop
3	Web Server	Database	SQLnet1	Allow
4	Internal Network	Screen Service Network	http, https	Allow
5	Internal Network	NOT (Screen Service Network)	Any	Allow
6	Partner and Supplier VPN	Database	IPSec	Allow
7	Screened Service Network, Internal Network, Border Routers	Log Server	Syslog	Allow
8	Screened Service Network, Internal Network, Border Routers	NTP Server	NTP	Allow
9	Backup Server	ScreenService Network, Internal Network, Border Routers	Backup	Allow
10	Monitoring Server	Screen Service Network, Internal Network, Border Routers	SNMP, ICMP	Allow
11	Monitoring Server	Border Routers, External Firewall	SSH	Allow
12	Any	Any	Any	Deny

Determining the Impact: The Internal Firewall

This filtering layer provides additional protection for the internal network over and above that provided by the external firewalls. Separation of the management network and the internal network is a particularly good idea. As with the external firewalls, though, some access remains after the firewall's security controls are considered. Here are three issues that should be addressed:

- The internal network is granted access to the management network.
- Screened service network hosts can communicate with some internal systems.
- The SSH daemon on the firewall might contain vulnerabilities.

The first issue to address is the protection of the management network. Separating the management network from the rest of the network is a good safety precaution. As is the case in this design, management systems frequently have more access rights to the network than other systems, which make them tempting targets. An attacker who manages to gain control of the monitoring server, for example, would be able to attack most of the security devices on the network. For this reason, the management network needs to be carefully protected; yet this rulebase allows internal systems free access to the management network. Rules 4 and 5 are meant to restrict the internal networks' access to the screened services network while allowing them free access to the Internet, but the rules are more permissive than necessary. Rule 5 says that as long as the destination address is not the screen services network, then the packets—including packets that are destined for the management network—are allowed.

The next issue to talk about is the control of traffic between the screened services network and the internal network. This rulebase does a good job of limiting screened service systems access to the bare minimum required to allow the network to function; however, any time you allow communication between networks at different trust levels, you need to be extremely careful. To allow logging and time synchronization, the screen services network hosts are allowed to send syslog entries to the log server and make NTP requests from the NTP server. Both of these systems are located on the management network. If either of the daemons (Ntpd or Syslogd) contains security vulnerabilities, an attacker could gain a foothold on the management network. Because of this, special care should be taken to harden these services. See Chapter 9, "Host Hardening," for more details.

The rulebase also allows the web server to establish connections with the database server over the SQLnet1 protocol. Again, as with the NTPd and syslogd daemons, if the service, which handles the SQLNet1 requests, contains vulnerabilities, it is possible for an attacker to gain control of the database server. In addition, even if the service contains no vulnerabilities, the web server has a normal amount of access to the database service that is running on the database server. An attacker who controls the web server could cause the database server to perform malicious transactions, such as creating fake supplier invoices. These transactions would be hard to prevent if the web server is normally allowed to request them. Only careful application design that includes substantial validity checks on each transaction could help mitigate this problem.

The last issue to discuss is the reliance on the SSH protocol to administer the firewalls. The Nokia IP330s prior to release 3.4.1 have the same SSH vulnerability that we described for the Cisco routers. IP330s running older versions of software that require SSH support should be upgraded.

Repeating as Necessary, Attacking the Whole Network

So far, we have talked about the individual devices that make up the security of the network and how their configurations might open up the network to attack. Let's see what might be possible if we combine all of this information.

Our attack will start by looking for vulnerabilities in the web server, the mail server, and the DNS server. The reason for this is simple; after the routers and firewalls have done their jobs, these are the only systems that we can still establish connections to. If any of these systems contain vulnerabilities, we might be able to gain access. For example, if we assume that the web server is running Internet Information Server 5.0, it is possible that the web server is vulnerable to a buffer overflow attack[1].

A successful attack would place us in complete control of the web server.

But wait! Look back at the network diagram in Figure 21.1. Isn't there an IDS located on the screened services network that might detect the attack? The important word here is *might*. Most IDS tools are signature based. If the attack is new or the IDS has not been updated, it is possible that the IDS does not contain a signature for the attack, in which case it would not be able to produce an alert[2]. In addition, in some cases, attacks can be re-engineered to specifically avoid detection by IDS tools[3].

Assuming that we are now in control of the web server, what should we do? This depends on the review goals. If the goal was to embarrass GIACE, we now have enough privileges to deface the web site. If we are trying to steal data, we are in a good position to accomplish this as well. The web server needs to be able to query the database server to fulfill its role. We could potentially use this access to query customer account information, steal fortune sayings, or capture any other information that the web server would normally have access to on the database. We could also *trojanize* the web server, replacing the scripts that implement the web site (CGIs, JSPs, and so on) with versions that record the transactions between the users and the site.

If we want to gain control of more hosts on the GIACE network, then the other screened service network systems would be good targets. By using the web server to launch the attacks, we can circumvent the external firewalls and attack any system on the screened service network. What about attacking systems on the internal network?

We still have two layers of firewalls between the internal networks and us. The result of both layers leaves us with limited access from the screened services network. We can send Syslog packets to the log server, NTP packets to the NTP server, and SQLnet1 packets to the database server. As with the web server, we need a vulnerability in the service software if we want to continue the attack. In this case, if GIACE is running Oracle 8i on the database server, it might be possible to proceed. Some versions of Oracle 8i's listener services contain a buffer overflow vulnerability that allows an attacker to gain remote access to the server (`http://cve.mitre.org/cgi-bin/ cvename.cgi?name=CAN-2001-0499`).

Taking over the database server allows us direct access to any of the internal systems, including user workstations. In addition, it allows us to attack any of the systems on the management network. Remember: The internal firewalls do not prevent hosts on the internal network from communicating with the management network. The likely reason for this is that the administrator is using a workstation located on the internal network to log into management network systems. As was mentioned in Chapter 12, "Separating Resources," using ARP poisoning techniques makes it possible to eavesdrop on the conversations between the internal network and other networks even though the network is implemented using a switch instead of a hub. If the administrator wants to access Management Network systems by using Telnet, FTP, or any other protocols that do not encrypt authentication information, we will be able to capture the administrator's username/password combination and use it to log in. This would pretty much be game over because we would then have control of every major system on the network.

You might be asking yourself how realistic this example attack was. We had to rely on vulnerabilities on the web and database servers to accomplish the attack, and we had to assume that the IDS would not pick up the attack. This is a key point to consider when performing your review. Even when you cannot find a vulnerability for a particular service or system that you are running, it can still be useful to assume the vulnerability to discover the impact that a vulnerability could cause should one be discovered in the future. It is almost beside the point that the products we chose to use to illustrate the example actually contained exploitable vulnerabilities. It is much more important to recognize that even good security architectures can be improved.

These additional steps can be used to improve this design:

- Use proxy firewalls for high-risk services. Web and mail service software does not have a good history for security. If we want to strengthen our border defenses, we need to use firewalls that can look at the content of the message, not just its source and destination.

- Do not allow direct access from publicly accessible systems to back-end systems. Instead, implement middleware systems that enforce reasonable security checks between your public servers and your back-end databases.

- If you must use SNMP, use version 3.0 of the protocol and implement its strong authentication mechanisms. If you cannot use version 3.0, make sure to enable SNMP trap alerts—especially for authentication failures—to enable you to detect when someone is attempting to attack the SNMP service.

Practical Design 2

The second design that we will look at is the security architecture created by Sam Campbell, who obtained his GCFW certification in April 2002. Sam's design is shown in Figure 21.2 and can be downloaded at `http://www.giac.org/practical/Sam_Campbell_GCFW.zip`. This is an interesting design that has many sophisticated security features:

- The design uses multiple layers of firewalls that are not only from different vendors, but also are different firewall types (proxy versus stateful inspection).

- All internal systems use private addresses.

- The public web server is hosted on a server that is running a security-hardened version of HP UNIX.

- Standard daemons for DNS and mail have been replaced with more secure alternatives (djbdns (`http://cr.yp.to/djbdns.html`) for DNS and Qmail (`http://cr.yp.to/qmail.html`) for mail).

- A centralized authorization database is maintained using an LDAP server. This server authenticates external customers, suppliers, and partners.

- The RSA SecurID system authenticates remote users who are then allowed to establish an IPSec VPN with the internal firewall.

- The Aventail extranet product allows suppliers and partners access to the network. This is a form of reverse proxy server, which encrypts sessions and tunnels them through firewalls by making them look like HTTPS sessions.

Sam's design has five security devices that need to be examined: the border router, the external firewall, the public web server, the internal firewall, and the extranet server. Each of these devices plays a role in determining how much access we can get to the GIACE network. Just as in the previous case study, we provide a discussion of the access that remains for each of these devices and what impact this access would have to the network's security. We wrap up our discussion by showing how all the vulnerabilities can be combined to reach the review goals as well as provide recommendations to improve the security of the design.

Figure 21.2 This security architecture uses a security-hardened version of UNIX to protect the web server.

Determining the Access that Remains: The External Firewall

As in the previous review, we want to look at each security device to determine what access remains to the attacker after the device is added to the network and find any additional vulnerabilities that might exist in the device. Where appropriate, we assume vulnerabilities so that we can analyze where additional security measures might be warranted.

Because this design's border router is set up similarly to the first design we looked at, we will not spend time discussing it. Beyond the border router, there are two paths into the network: toward the external firewall or toward the public web server. We will begin our discussion by looking at the security implemented by the external firewall.

The design uses a Symantec Raptor firewall to provide access control between the Internet and the internal networks. Unlike the stateful firewalls used in the previous design, the Raptor is a proxy firewall. As was covered in Chapter 4, "Proxy Firewalls," this type of firewall acts as a go-between for network connections. This method provides some security benefits, including the ability to hide the structure of the internal network and to make security decisions based on the content as well as the header of the packet.

Proxy firewalls can hide the structure of the network because they act as a middleman for all the network connections. All incoming connections are negotiated at the firewall, which then negotiates a second connection with the system that will actually handle the transaction. This configuration makes it difficult for an attacker to discover details about the host he is attempting to attack. As an example, if an Nmap scan with operating system detection was conducted against a network protected by a Raptor firewall, the result would look like all of the public servers were Raptor firewalls.

Discovering a Network Behind a Proxy Firewall

Proxy firewalls are good at hiding the structure of the internal network, but they are not perfect. In a penetration testing assignment I recently conducted, I ran up against a Raptor firewall that allowed external users to FTP into a particular host on the internal network. Raptor's FTP proxy requires that you FTP into the firewall and then specify which host on the internal network that you want to connect to. If you specify the correct host and provide a valid username/password combination, the connection is established. A small programming error in this arrangement allowed me to map the internal network. Here's how it worked. The Raptor firewall returns an authorization error if you specify the IP address of a valid host, but it does not provide a good username/password. If you specify the address of a non-existent host, you get a `connection refused` message. Using this difference, I created a script that attempted to access IP addresses within the typical private ranges (10.0.0.x, 192.168.x.x, and so on). Any address that returned an authorization error meant that I had detected the address of a live host.

The method that proxy firewalls use to protect networks also allows for inherent Network Address Translation (NAT). Because the firewall will act as the public front for all of the protected systems, it is the only one that needs to have any public IP addresses. The protected systems can be numbered using any private addressing scheme. This does require that the firewall know which system will handle a particular incoming request. Table 21.6 shows the translation settings used to allow external requests to reach the appropriate internal system.

Table 21.6 **Translation Settings on External Firewall for the Public Services**

Destination Address	Destination Service	Redirected Address	Description
1.1.1.3	SMTP	Mail Relay	Accept incoming mail
1.1.1.3	DNS	External DNS	Accept incoming DNS requests
1.1.2.1	IPSec–ESP	Internal Firewall	Allow remote employees in
1.1.1.5	HTTPS	Extranet Server	Allow suppliers, partners in

Because these systems are the only servers that have an external IP address, they are the only systems protected by the firewall that an external attacker will be able to directly communicate with. In our review, we will want to look at the chance that an attacker could use this capability to attack these systems.

Hosts on the inside of the network that will require the ability to initiate external network connections must also have translation rules established on the firewall. Table 21.7 shows the rules for this design.

Table 21.7 **Translation Rules to Allow Outbound Network Connections**

Server	Address to Translate To	Description
Mail relay	1.1.1.3	Allow outbound mail
Web proxy	1.1.1.3	Allow outbound http requests
Internal Firewall	1.1.2.2	Needed for IPSec UDP key exchange between remote users and internal firewall

The implication of this table is that these are the only hosts (besides the public web server, border router, and external IDS) on the GIACE network that will be allowed to initiate connections to the Internet. This means that any attempts to attack the Internet from the service network need to be launched from one of these systems.

Of course, the main purpose for the firewall is to provide access control. Table 21.8 shows the access control settings used in this design.

Table 21.8 **External Firewall Rulebase**

Incoming Interface	Outgoing Interface	Source	Destination	Service	Action
Internet	Service	Any	Ext. DNS	DNS	Allow
Service	Internet	External DNS	Any	DNS	Allow
Internet	Service	Any	Mail Relay	SMTP	Allow
Service	Internet	Mail Relay	Any	SMTP	Allow
ANY	Extranet	Any	Extranet Server	HTTPS	Allow
Internet	Corporate	Any	Internal Firewall	IPSec-ESP, IPSec-IKE	Allow
Corporate	Internet	Internal Firewall	Any	IPSec-ESP, IPSec-IKE	Allow
Service	Corporate	Mail Relay	Mail Server	SMTP	Allow
Service	Internet	Web Proxy	Any	HTTP, HTTPS, FTP	Allow
Corporate	Service	Desktop LAN	Web Proxy	HTTP, HTTPS, FTP	Allow
Corporate	Service	Desktop LAN	Any	SSH	Allow, Log
Corporate	Service	Mail Server	Mail Relay	SMTP	Allow
Corporate	Internet	Any	Any	Any	Deny
Internet	Any	Any	Any	NetBIOS over IP	Deny

Note

Raptor firewalls include the incoming and outgoing interface in each access rule. The names of the interfaces are configured during installation of the firewall. In this design, the interface names are pretty self-evident, but it is worth noting that the corporate interface is the one connected to the internal firewall.

Determining the Impact: The External Firewall

This external firewall implementation doesn't give us much to complain about. Assuming that the firewall does not contain vulnerabilities that would allow us to circumvent its security rules, the only systems protected by the firewall that an external attacker could initiate a connection with are the mail relay, the external DNS server, the internal firewall, and the extranet server. For an attack to succeed, one of these servers would have to be vulnerable. However, even if one of the servers is vulnerable to some exploit, the proxy nature of this firewall might prevent the attack from succeeding. As an example, suppose that the Qmail software that is running on the mail relay server had a buffer overflow vulnerability in its handling of the SMTP HELO command. The Raptor mail proxy limits the format and length of the data that the HELO command supplies. It is unlikely that the data the attacker would need to provide to successfully attack this system would meet these length and format restrictions. This does not mean that this solution is bulletproof. Remember that we should also consider vulnerabilities in the security device. In this case, a quick search on the vulnerability database at http://www.securityfocus.com reveals two problems that could affect its security:

- Raptor 6.5 is susceptible to a DOS attack (http://www.securityfocus.com/bid/3509). The attack is possible because Raptor 6.5 does not properly handle zero length UDP packets. This attack would normally be easy to prevent by blocking UDP packets heading toward the firewall at the border router. Unfortunately, this will not work because the firewall must pass UDP packets to allow the remote employees to set up IPSec tunnels with the internal firewall. Upgrading to version 7.0 of the product eliminates this problem.

- Raptor 6.5 has a bug in its handling of http proxy requests that allows an attacker to connect to web servers behind the firewall as long as the web service is on a non-standard port (http://cve.mitre.org/cgi-bin/cvename.cgi?name=CAN-2001-0483). This vulnerability would not help an attacker browse web materials on this network because no web servers are running on non-standard ports on the GIACE network. It would enable the attacker to discover what hosts are running on the network, though. A hotfix is available to fix this problem.

Neither of these vulnerabilities would help an attacker gain unauthorized access to this network. If no other potential access paths were available for an attacker to use, we might decide to analyze the impact that adding an artificial vulnerability to the network would have. In this case, though, other areas in the network show a greater potential for problems, including the public web server.

Determining the Access that Remains: The Public Web Server

This design uses the highly unorthodox approach of locating the public web server on a host that is connected directly to the Internet with no firewalls in-between. This host is also acting, for all intents and purposes, as a proxy firewall between the Internet and the Fortune Application LAN. The designer felt comfortable doing this because this is no ordinary web server. The product that he has used is an HP Virtual Vault Server. HP Virtual Vault is an HP UNIX-based system that has been heavily modified to increase its security. The biggest change is the absence of an all-powerful root account. Instead, the power of the root user has been separated into 50 distinct privileges. These privileges can be granted or revoked as needed on a per user, process, or file basis. This provides tremendous power in limiting the impact of service vulnerabilities. Even if an attacker can successfully take over a service on a Virtual Vault, the service might not have enough privileges on the Virtual Vault to allow the attacker to do anything useful. In addition, the vault comes installed with nothing activated by default. You must manually add interface cards, the web server, and so on, which eliminates the possibility that a vulnerability in a service that is not being used could be used to compromise the vault. More information on trusted OSs like the Virtual Vault can be found at http://csrc.nist.gov/secpubs/rainbow/std001.txt.

Note

HP Virtual Vault Server has clear security advantages over standard Internet servers and is easy to recommend from a functionality standpoint. However, before you rush out to implement one, you might want to think about two possible downsides. First, these servers can be tricky to configure correctly. The added flexibility in permissions adds complexity in implementation. Second, and most important for most sites, these servers are expensive. At the time this design was created, the server with software cost around $190,000.

The version of Virtual Vault that is being used for this design comes with an integrated Netscape Enterprise web server. This web server hosts the public web site for the GIACE network and is the primary public interface between GIACE and its customers. To perform this role, the web server connects to the Fortune Application Server using its second network interface, which is connected directly to the Fortune Application LAN. This application server implements the back-end processing for the site, including storing and retrieving transaction information in the corporate database and authenticated customers by querying the corporate LDAP server.

Determining the Impact: The Public Web Server

This is an interesting way of implementing the public web server for this site, but it is also somewhat risky. The security of the most critical parts of the GIACE network depends on the strength of a single product: the Virtual Vault. If the Virtual Vault security should fail, an attacker would have access to the "crown jewels" of this network. Placing the public web server behind the external firewall, while increasing the load on the firewall, would provide some additional protection for this critical GIACE resource.

Determining the Access that Remains: The Extranet Server

The extranet server allows partners and suppliers access to the hosts on the Fortune Application LAN. The extranet server is implemented using an Aventail extranet server. The Aventail extranet server is a form of reverse proxy that allows external users, after they have authenticated, to connect to internal systems. To protect the confidentiality of these transactions, including the exchange of authentication data, the Aventail solution encrypts these conversations.

Table 21.9 shows the configuration details for the extranet server.

Table 21.9 **Rulebase for the Extranet Server**

Source	Destination	Destination Port	User	Authentication Method
Any	Application Server	5656	Any	LDAP username/password
Any	Application Server, Shares Server	5656, 80	Any	LDAP username/password and Client Certification
Any	Shares Server	NetBIOS over IP	Any	LDAP username/password and Client Certification

As you can see from this information, two classes of access are available. Suppliers are granted access to the application server by providing a valid username/password. After this is performed, the supplier is granted access to port 5656 on the application server, which is where the customer GIACE fortune application is hosted. Partners are granted additional access to the network, but they are required to also provide a client certificate in addition to a valid username/password. All authentication data, including the client certificates, is held on the corporate LDAP server.

The added access that is granted to the partners includes the ability to connect to a web service located on the application server as well as to connect to the NetBIOS ports on the shares server. This shares server is not shown on the network diagram, but it is located on the Fortune Application LAN. It is used as a place to share files between GIACE and its partners.

Determining the Impact: The Extranet Server

This solution does allow secure access from partners and suppliers, but there are still a couple of points to be made:

- The use of simple username/password authentication might allow an attacker to guess or brute force a valid password, granting him access to the fortune application. If the fortune application has any exploitable vulnerabilities, the attacker might gain a foothold on the Fortune Application LAN. The use of certificates here would eliminate this risk, but it might not be practical with numerous suppliers. Other strong authentication alternatives, such as SecurID tokens, could also be used; however, if this is not feasible, the only alternative is to make sure that the fortune application is carefully designed to prevent misuse.

- The extranet server shares an authentication server (the LDAP server) with the public web server. If the web server is allowed to request new user accounts, it is possible that an attacker could add a web user account and then use it to authenticate to the extranet server. Proper application design would eliminate this possibility, but it is still a good idea to separate the storage of customer and business partner authentication databases.

- The location of the shares server places the GIACE "crown jewels" at unnecessary risk. Authenticated partners are allowed to connect using the NetBIOS protocol to the shares server to share files with GIACE. Depending on the configuration of the shares server, though, this might be sufficient access to allow a motivated attacker to gain control of the server, which in this case would allow him to gain a foothold on the Fortune Application LAN. Although this risk is only a concern if the partner is the attacker or has had his certificate stolen, it is a risk that could easily be mitigated by relocating the shares server.

Determining the Access that Remains: The Internal Firewall

The internal firewall protects the desktop and corporate LANS while allowing remote users to establish IPSec tunnels to the GIACE network. These remote users are authenticated using SecurID tokens. The firewall is implemented using a Nokia IP440 appliance running Check Point FireWall-1 version 4.1. Table 21.10 shows its configuration.

Table 21.10 **Rulebase for the Internal Firewall**

Source	Destination	Service	Action
Desktop LAN	Corporate LAN	DNS, IMAP, LDAP, POP3, SMTP, SSH	Allow
Corporate LAN	Desktop LAN	X, SNMP, Ping	Allow
Mail Relay, Mail Server	Mail Server, Mail Relay	SMTP	Allow
Corporate LAN	External DNS	DNS	Allow
trustedusers@GIACE	Corporate LAN	Any	Client Encrypt
normalusers@GIACE	Corporate LAN	DNS, IMAP, LDAP, POP3, SMTP, SSH	Client Encrypt
normalusers@GIACE	Desktop LAN	Any	Client Encrypt
Fortune LAN	Corporate LAN	LDAP	Allow
Fortune LAN	Any	Any	Deny, Log
Desktop LAN	Web Proxy	HTTP, HTTPS	Allow
Any	NTP-Server	NTP	Allow
Any	Any	Any	Deny, Log

Determining the Impact: The Internal Firewall

This is a reasonably secure rule set, especially considering all the other security measures in effect on this network. One point of concern is worth discussing, though.

The use of SSH might allow an internal attacker access to the corporate network. The internal firewall allows the desktop LAN to communicate with the corporate LAN using several protocols, including IMAP and SSH. The use of SSH is probably to allow an administrator, while he is at his desk, to administer corporate LAN systems. At the same time, protocols that allow unencrypted authentication, such as IMAP, are also allowed between the two networks, which might create an opportunity for an internal attacker to gain administrative access to corporate servers.

This access would rely on a couple of configuration details. First, the SSH daemons on the corporate network would need to accept username/ password authentication (their default configuration). Second, an administrative user would need to have used the same password for his mail account and his user accounts on a corporate server. We'll leave it up to you to decide how realistic you think this would be.

To implement the attack, the internal attacker would first use ARP poisoning techniques to convince the local systems that the MAC address of the local interface of the firewall is actually the MAC address of the attacker's system. This method results in all of the desktop LAN traffic that is destined for other networks to be redirected to the attacker's machine. By eavesdropping on all of this traffic, the attacker can capture the IMAP authentication session when the administrator goes to retrieve his mail. Using the username/password from this session, the attacker would be able to use SSH to log into any corporate servers in which the administrator has used the same password.

Prevention of this attack is simple. Make sure that all SSH servers are configured to only accept public key authentication and make sure that the SSH private keys are well protected. Also, if you must use the non-encrypted mail access protocols (as opposed to IMAP+SSL, for example), create a different set of usernames/passwords just for mail access.

Repeating as Necessary, Attacking the Whole Network

All in all, this is a good security design that would be extremely difficult to attack from the outside. An attack is not impossible, though. Here is a potential scenario that might grant access to the "crown jewels."

As previously mentioned, an inordinate amount of trust has been placed in a single server. If the HP Virtual Vault contained sufficient vulnerability, an attacker would have free access to the Fortune Application LAN. As luck would have it, the version of Virtual Vault that was used contains two key vulnerabilities that might be useful to an attacker.

The first is a buffer overflow in the publisher module of the iPlanet web server. This is the same web server that is included with Virtual Vault (http://cve.mitre.org/cgi-bin/cvename.cgi?name=CAN-2001-0746). If the web-published module were installed on the Vault, it is possible that an attacker could use this vulnerability to execute arbitrary code at the privilege level of the web server, although this is somewhat unlikely because HP has rated the publisher module as "high risk" and does not include it as part of the standard distribution.

The second vulnerability is in Virtual Vault's mkacct command, which creates a new account on the server (http://www.securityfocus.com/bid/1843). This program contains a vulnerability that can allow a local user to add privileges to his account. Using these in combination might allow an attacker to gain control of the web server's account and then elevate his privileges to the point where he is as close to root equivalent as is possible on a Virtual Vault system.

Unfortunately for the attacker, it is unlikely that the web server would have the `mkacct` privilege, making the second half of this attack impossible. This is the strength of the Virtual Vault system. By limiting permissions to just those required for the job at hand, you drastically reduce the risk of exploitation.

All is not lost for our attacker, though. The web server must have sufficient rights to perform its normal activities. This includes the ability to retrieve customer data, retrieve fortunes, and capture other sensitive data that the web server would normally have access to. In this case, even web server access might meet the goals of the attacker. The lesson here is never to rely too heavily on one solution. Moving the web server behind the external firewall would prevent this attack from succeeding.

Summary

In this chapter, we analyzed the security of two good security designs. Each provided multiple layers of defense using different security techniques to provide defense in depth, and each would prove difficult for a real-world attacker to break into. However, as good as they were, we were able to identify areas in each that could be improved.

The process we used to accomplish this was adversarial review. Instead of concentrating on what the security architecture prevented, we concentrated on what it might allow. As is often the case, a design might allow far more than you expect. When performing your own adversarial review, keep a few things in mind:

- It is not important what a device is *supposed* to do. Think about what it *could* do.

- Pay special attention to services that are accessible to the attacker. These are where the attack must start.

- Do not assume that the attacker will always be external. It is a useful exercise to look at each of your network segments to see what an attacker could accomplish if he started his attack from it.

- Pay attention to ways that your design can reduce an attacker's ability to discover your network, but conduct your own review as if the attacker has full knowledge of your design. This might seem unfair, but it is much better to weed out all vulnerabilities, not just the vulnerabilities that you think will be easy for an attacker to discover.

It is much better for you to conduct this review than to allow the vast collection of Internet attackers to perform it for you. We hope that this chapter provided you with the incentive to look at your designs in a new light.

References

1 Eeye Advisory AD20010618. "All Versions of Microsoft Internet Information Services Remote Buffer Overflow (SYSTEM Level Access)." `http://www.eeye.com/html/Research/Advisories/AD20010618.html`. June 2001.

2 M. Handley, C. Kreibich, and V. Paxson. "Network Intrusion Detection: Evasion, Traffic Normalization, and End-to-End Protocol Semantics (HTML)." (Compressed PostScript) (PDF) Proc. USENIX Security Symposium. 2001.

3 Eeye Advisory AD20010705. "%u Encoding IDS Bypass Vulnerability." `http://www.eeye.com/html/Research/Advisories/AD20010705.html`. September 2001.

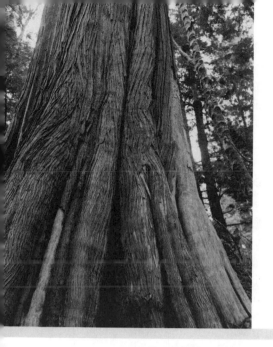

22

Importance of Defense in Depth

THROUGHOUT THE BOOK, WE HAVE TOUCHED ON defense in depth. We have made an assertion that no single defensive component is a silver bullet—that no single technology or tool adequately protects our information assets. We are at a crossroads as a community, in our desire for ease of use; the most prevalent desktop operating systems simply cannot be secured. Do you remember the discussion of rickety operating systems in the Preface of this book? If security was as simple as putting a firewall between the Internet and the system needing to be defended, that would be great, but it is not that simple. Even if the system is robust, there is more to do to achieve a reasonable level of risk. The lesson of devastating attacks, such as Nimda, is that a vulnerable system simply has to browse from a hostile web server and it can be infected. Does this depress you? We hope not. Life is full of risk, damage, and mayhem, yet we not only survive, but we prosper. To prosper, defense in depth is imperative as a design paradigm. Bad things are going to happen. We need to limit the damage to a minimum.

This chapter gives you a lot to think about and helps to tie all of the topics of the book together. In the first half of this chapter, we employ the classic castle analogy to help make our perimeter defense points crystal clear as we introduce the problem of the rigid perimeter. At the end of that discussion, we focus on static packet filters and Network Address Translation (NAT) from a defense-in-depth perspective. Then we consider softer perimeter solutions that tie up the attacker's time by absorbing the attacks, much like the crumple zone of your automobile absorbs energy in a crash.

We discuss internal defenses, which are the information technology equivalent of the watertight doors built into ships. Finally, we consider defense in depth for information.

Castles: An Example of Defense-in-Depth Architecture

Castles are often used as an information security analogy; castles typically have a perimeter control that includes one way in and out. Castles also use chokepoints. It is easy to see the defense in depth in action; to rescue the princess in the tower, you have to cross the moat and bash down the big door. Then you are in a sallyport area, a sallyport is similar to an airlock, you have external control doors, an assembly area and an interior set of doors and only one set of doors should open at a time. So even if you break down one set of doors, you have to cram into the assembly area, there may be ports where the insiders can shoot at you and you have another set of doors to go. We can employ many elements from castle architecture in our networks. The border routers and firewalls are used in the same way as moats and sallyports. The castle is not invincible, but the defense-in-depth architecture is one to carefully consider. Castles aren't still in military use today because it turns out they had a number of problems that relate to modern perimeter defense. Cannons were a big problem. Backdoors and secret passages did more than a few castles in, and the fact they were stationary and easy to find was a significant disadvantage. With our networks, we have similar problems. 802.11 wireless access points and modems, especially on autoanswer, are the backdoors and secret passages of our networks. Sites with public address space, like castles, are exposed, stationary, and easy to find and attack.

In the next section of this chapter, we use the analogy of a castle to explore some of the components of defense in depth.

Hard Walls and Harder Cannonballs

Gunpowder and cannon use were primary forces that put castles out of business. Even if you build the walls 60 meters thick—a huge investment of building resources—the attackers can hammer that wall into dust and then breach the perimeter. By using denial of service (DoS) techniques of SYN floods or UDP floods as cannonballs, attackers might not be able to turn your firewall into dust, but they might well be able to shut down your site.

If a firewall—especially an application gateway firewall—is directly connected to the Internet, it probably doesn't have the speed in terms of CPU cycles to withstand a DoS attack. As we covered in Chapter 11, "Design

Fundamentals," the border router and firewall deployed together are more robust because the router is faster and can be configured to block many DoS attacks. Thus, a couple layers of defense are more effective than a single layer.

Before the cannon was available, the perimeter breach device of choice for castles and keeps, (keeps are the inner sanctuary in a castle), was the battering ram. The actual doorway of the castle tended to be made of metal and wood and was connected into stone, each of which reacts differently to the ram's attack. Wood, for instance, is softer than iron; therefore, the metal fasteners tend to erode the wood as the doorway withstands the shock. The holes in the wood get bigger, the joints weaken, and pretty soon the defense is breached. The functional equivalent for the battering ram is the DoS attack. As we discussed in the Preface to this book, in our networks, we have the firewall applications on top of operating systems, and attackers might target either the firewall application or the underlying operating system. In fact, there have been cases, such as the flaw in Intel Pentium chips in which a single op code command series, `F0 0F C7 C8`, could halt the processor (`http://catless.ncl.ac.uk/Risks/19.45.html#subj5`).

We have already discussed using border routers to shield firewalls from attack, but border routers are also susceptible to attack. Many of them do not respond well to ping floods that are directed against them. In fact, a sufficiently large number of attacking systems directed against the primary backbones might be able to drop portions of the Internet. The solution against an attack against the Internet is outside the scope of this book, but the best answer is related to defense in depth; design the routers and network to be managed by an out-of-band network. A solution to the ping flood against your border router might be to add one more layer. This book's Preface mentions an Attack Mitigator from Top Layer, which is an example of a very fast box that can be optimized to stop DoS attacks to the point that unless they can saturate your entire data pipe, this layer can withstand the attacker's battering ram. Several companies are currently developing similar defenses against distributed DoS attacks, and additional products should be available by the time this book is printed.

Secret Passages

Although it is certainly true that a castle's perimeter can be breached, we should also take a second to think about how well those ancient perimeters worked. Thick stone walls, like firewalls, do work well to help keep the barbarians out. Because they work so well, people invested a lot of effort trying to get around perimeter defenses. A favorite movie trick to circumvent these perimeters is the secret passage. Let's take a minute to examine how easy and likely it is that you might have a tunnel through your firewall that acts as a secret passage, or a leak you are not aware of in your perimeter.

Tunnels Through the Firewall

If the firewall is perceived to be too restrictive, users find ways to get through it; one of the most common ways is to tunnel through HTTP. Dozens of tools, such as the original GNU `httptunnel`, encapsulate a communication stream in HTTP. For one example, you might want to visit `http://www.nocrew.org/software/httptunnel.html`. If you look at the data, you will see `GET`, `PUT` and `POST` commands passing through the tunnel. Most even incorporate HTML tags, making these tunnels a bit tough to spot.

If you have an intrusion detection system (IDS), such as Snort, that can perform statistical analysis, or a traffic measurement tool, such as Cisco's NetFlow, you can often detect these HTTP tunnels. If you think about it, when you surf the web, you click a URL, wait, and then the page starts to display. In terms of the traffic signature, the client initiates the connection and sends a few bytes to the server, and the server sends a considerable amount of data back to the client. Now to be sure, some web applications enable the client to `PUT` or `POST`, so there is a potential for a false positive; however, with a bit of practice, you can detect a number of these tunnels. Of course, technology is not enough. After you detect a tunnel, your organization's policy dictates your next move. Is there a policy against unauthorized connections at your site? Would your organization's policy define a tunnel as an unauthorized connection? If the answer to the preceding two questions is yes, then what actions does the policy permit or require you to take?

Effects of Filtering

You might be thinking that your users are not bright enough to tunnel through your firewall, or that they would never violate your security policy. If you think so, think again. I recently worked on an intrusion detection visualization project on a military base in Honolulu. This base hadn't put in a firewall yet, but it did have a router. The router had a single defensive ACL that had just been applied. They blocked inbound TCP port 6699 because someone in charge was concerned about the bandwidth being used by Napster. One of the network traffic analysis tools this base had was Cisco's NetFlow, so I took at look at it to get a feeling for the network's traffic for several weeks, and all of a sudden there was a lot of traffic on port 8888. When I see a port I don't understand, I like to use Google (the search engine `http://www.google.com/`) and do a query, such as "TCP port 8888". The various discussions on the port often give me one or two options, and that is a big help. In this case, there was a discussion about a tool called Chatster, a chat program related to Napster. Isn't that amazing? The base had blocked a single port, but it didn't watch its traffic and enforce its policy controls. The base had sprung a leak.

Change in the Perimeter Configuration

Even a performance problem or the perception of a performance problem can lead to the creation of a secret passage—a leak in the perimeter. People just want to get their work done, and if the perimeter is slowing them down, they find ways to get around the perimeter. A bit further on in our discussion of defense in depth in the SYN/FIN section, we review just how easy it is to penetrate static packet filters.

Even at highly secured DoD facilities or other high value assets, security officers might discover that the firewall administrator has changed the web or some other proxy application on the firewall to a simple packet filter. If it happened to you, would you be at a loss as to why the officer would have done such a thing? It does make sense. The primary task of firewall administrators is to create ACLs or rules that open up the firewall. Firewalls might ship with a default rule to deny anything that is not specifically allowed (deny all), but that does not mean that the firewall administrator is oriented to deny all. We should never forget the human element. From time to time, this administrator will almost certainly get phone calls or emails from people saying that the firewall is too slow. He knows packet filters are faster than proxy applications, so one day he decides to fix the firewall and switch it from a proxy to a packet filter.

If you are not monitoring your firewall configuration, the first time you realize something is wrong might be when you start seeing attacks from the Internet that were clearly operating-system specific. HTTP, for instance, often gives away operating system information in the protocol headers; therefore, if the attackers run a web site, they might know exactly what to target. Of course, this would only be an issue if certain web sites on the Internet were malicious. This would be a serious problem for a site that is not interested in using NAT and making all the internal machines private addresses.

An emerging best practice to help protect your site from administrative changes is to continually scan your perimeter from the outside using assessment tools. Services, such as Qualys (`http://www.qualys.com/`) and DigitalDefense (`http://www.digitaldefense.com/`), have subscription services so that you can schedule these scans via a web browser interface. They maintain a database of your configuration and provide a variety of canned reports. They also have an interface so that you can build your own reports. This way, if a new port is open or a new IP address becomes active, you can get a report to that effect. From a defense-in-depth perspective, you should seriously consider an active scanning program for any of your systems that can be reached from the Internet. Attackers will certainly scan you, so you had best probe your systems so that you see what the attackers see.

Insider Threats

It never hurts to mention that throughout history, one of the best ways to get into a castle, bank, SCIF, or perimeter defense is to pay someone off. Money is a powerful tool. If a firewall administrator would put a site at risk for free, imagine what a bit of coercion and $100,000 might be able to do. The defense-in-depth strategy here is to employ good background checks when hiring, do a bit of random monitoring, and keep an eye out for people who come in early, leave late, and work weekends. (Although all my peers work long hours, this is still a classic indicator of problems.) Sudden changes in financial status, signs of alcohol or drug use, and talk of entitlement ("They owe me.") can all be signs of an insider problem.

Hiding in the Mist

In a recent TV series called the *Mists of Avalon*, the castle dwellers did one smart thing: They used magic to call up mists to hide their castle. The location of castles is one of the big problems in the whole castle concept from the standpoint of military strategy. After the cannon was developed, it became apparent that castles were the perfect targets. They were so big that it was hard to miss them and waste the cannon ball, and you knew just where to find them because they were not mobile and they couldn't be hidden. The great news is that we can deploy the functional equivalent of the *Mists of Avalon* on our networks by using NAT. Someone can attack a perimeter in many ways, but if you have private addresses and NAT, the attacks or probes might still work to some extent, but they won't be as useful to the attacker. Suddenly, your internal systems become difficult to find, as if they are hidden in the mists. Imagine listening in on an IRC chat room discussion, and you realize the attackers are experimenting with the latest technique to slip through the perimeter. As you are watching the chat room discussion between Attacker 1 (A1) and Attacker 2 (A2), you see something resembling the following scroll across your screen:

A1: Did it work for you? I've got 10 bots banging.

A2: I got through the firewall and got a box to answer.

A1: Lamers, what OS is it? I bet I can crack it in 10 minutes or less.

A2: Passive fingerprinter indicates it must be a windoze box. It reports its IP is 192.168.1.238.

A1: NAT, better keep scanning.

A2: I don't get it. We found one.

A1: Yeah, but which 192.168.1.238 is it exactly?

There are easily 100,000 networks that start with 192.168.1, and unless you can nail up a source route or come through a tunnel, then you probably can't get to and from one of these across the Internet. If you do have public addresses for the internal machines at your site, you should seriously consider transitioning to a NAT and private address structure. It can be the single most valuable tool to prevent successful reconnaissance by those who desire to be your enemy. In the next section, we briefly discuss three classic techniques that are used every day to penetrate perimeters: setting additional flags with a SYN, fragments, and echo replies. These are merely a sampler to illustrate the point about public and private addresses. For a more complete discussion, please see *Network Intrusion Detection: An Analyst's Handbook,* by Northcutt and Novak, New Riders Publishing.

SYN/FIN

Many of the buffer overflows from 1998–2001 used a combination of flags found in byte 13 from offset zero in the TCP header and set both the SYN and FIN flags or bits. The idea behind the SYN/FIN attack is to add an additional spurious flag to the SYN to attempt to originate a connection behind a perimeter. Many packet-filtering systems, especially static packet filters mask on byte 13 of the TCP header checking for a 2, the value of the SYN flag as the only bit set. The TCP flags are URG, ACK, PSH, RST, SYN, and FIN. FIN is the low-order bit, with a value of 1 if set, the SYN is 2, RST is 4 and so on. This is what RFC 793 specifies, so it makes sense that designers of perimeter systems would inspect for a value of 2 in byte 13. SYN/RST, for instance, would not meet the logical test and would be allowed through the packet filter into the internal network, as would SYN/ACK, an ACK only, and so on. The kicker is that both UNIX and Windows systems will respond to a SYN/FIN with a SYN/ACK. SYN/FINs are used to penetrate perimeters and to establish a connection.

This attack is the most dangerous perimeter penetration we are going to discuss; fragments and echo replies are primarily for reconnaissance as opposed to system compromise attacks.

Reconnaissance with Fragments

In this section, we examine the use of incomplete fragments. When this reconnaissance technique is used on a vulnerable site, attackers get a positive answer as to the existence, or lack thereof, of a live host at every address that is checked. Fragmentation occurs when a packet is larger than the maximum transmission unit (MTU) of the next hop in its journey to its destination host.

Only the first fragment has the true header from the original datagram. The other fragments have only the IP header generated by the router that breaks up the original datagram; those fragments do not get their true protocol headers until the destination host reassembles them. This lack of protocol header makes them ideal reconnaissance tools for attackers. Many perimeter devices do not choose to make the blocking decision on anything but the first fragment. An attacker can intentionally send in fragments without the protocol information; these fragments tend to pass through the perimeter to internal systems. If the internal systems have public addresses, a number of things, all bad, could happen. If the system being probed exists, it might receive the fragment. Then when the other fragments do not arrive, the probed system might respond with an ICMP error messages saying that the reassembly time was exceeded, which tells the attacker that there is a live host at that IP address. If the system being probed does not exist, an internal router might respond with an ICMP host unreachable error message. The attacker then knows an IP address is not active. To defend against this technique, the perimeter must block both outgoing ICMP time exceeded in reassembly and also ICMP host unreachable messages.

Next, we look at one more way that attackers can penetrate perimeter defenses for reconnaissance using echo replies.

Reconnaissance with Echo Replies

ICMP has two forms: error messages that are never replied to and error messages that take the form of request-reply. ICMP Type 8, Code 0 is an echo request, although it is also known as a ping, after the ping program. If an ICMP listener receives an echo request, the listener generally responds with an ICMP Type 0, Code 0 echo reply to tell the original ICMP speaker that the datagram was received.

These request/reply types of ICMP are usually used for network management, for instance, to see if hosts or routers are up. It can also be used for reconnaissance in many cases because echo replies often pass through perimeters; to block them would break outbound ping, and people like to use ping. Therefore, attackers send in echo replies to cause internal routers to respond with `ICMP host unreachable` error messages. This is known as inverse mapping. The only active response from the probed site is for systems that do not exist.

The defense strategy is obvious here. As you learned in Chapter 3, "Stateful Firewalls," stateful firewalls maintain a table and might be able to determine whether the echo reply is not a response to a ping that is initiated from within your site. Your design should have a stateful perimeter layer. As an additional layer of protection, you learned about the importance of squelching the outbound ICMP error messages in Chapter 6, "Role of a Router." If we drop outgoing ICMP unreachable messages even if our state stable fails, we have this second layer of defense. Of course, the best defense would be to employ all of the this with a NAT.

Defense on the Inside

Even if you are able to enter a castle though a secret passage, a number of barriers still exist, including those pesky guards with swords before you can rescue the princess in the tower. This is not so with most of our sites. We do not typically use internal barriers or internal instrumentation, and that needs to change.

The Need for Compartmentalization

I worked for a Navy lab once that was a loose group of multiple Navy bases in different states. They each did different kinds of work and had fairly low interaction, but one day, some "genius" decided that the bases needed a common email system. They selected what I consider the riskiest email client on the face of the earth: Microsoft Outlook. That wasn't the half of it, though; the servicemen wanted a single domain controller for all of the users at all of the bases. Chapters 11, "Design Fundamentals," and 16, "Sample Designs," talk about single points of failure, but this was the most vulnerable design I have ever seen. If an attacker was able to compromise the single domain controller, every login for every user at every one of those bases was exposed. If you think about the way they build ships with multiple compartments, each protected by doors, you have a good analogy for building a robust internal network. We need to employ internal barriers, such as appliance firewalls, and place and monitor IDS sensors inside our systems.

If attackers get through the perimeter, we still want to employ layers of defense and instrumentation. Chapter 18, "Network Log Analysis," discusses the kind of information that is available in log files. The following sections of this chapter review some of the technologies we can employ to really get a clue as to what is going on in our networks as well as how to harden them. These technologies include personal, or host-centric firewalls; appliance firewalls and air gaps; as well as the emerging log fusion products.

Host-Centric Firewalls as Sensors

Personal, or host-centric, firewall technology is one of the great breakthroughs in the past couple of years, and it is clearly a defense-in-depth technology. Firewalls are barriers—one more layer of defense—and that additional layer is valuable in and of itself. Some do not even allow systems to answer a ping. If you have read this far in the book and do not have a host-centric firewall on your system, we might have taught you facts, but we have failed to truly educate you.

In addition to being an additional layer of defense, host-centric firewalls are equally as valuable as canaries in a coalmine. In the past century before modern sensors were developed to detect poison gas, miners took canaries into coalmines. Canaries are more sensitive to poison gas than people, so when the canaries started keeling over, it was time to get out of the mine. Because we have very little instrumentation internally in our sites, a personal firewall can be a sensor, much like a canary can alert us to a serious problem of which we might otherwise not be aware.

If all of the writers and editors of this book could be in a very large room with each of you, the readers, we could conduct a poll. If we asked all of you to raise your hands if you use a personal firewall, about 70% of your hands would go up. If you were asked who runs a personal firewall at work behind your corporate firewall, maybe 40% of you would raise your hands. If the members of that last group were asked how many had ever received an alarm on their work personal firewall, almost every hand would stay up. The implications of those alarms are startling. You can chalk those alerts to one of three things:

- False positive, or an error by the firewall detection
- Real attack generated from outside your organization
- Real attack generated from within your organization

When we instrument an internal network, the results have included finding compromised systems that were being used to attack other systems and finding employees who were involved in hacking. When choosing a personal firewall solution, you might want to make a console a priority. As an example, BlackICE has the ICEcap and also the third-party ClearICE consoles available. This is not to push one product over another, but it was one of the first personal firewall products to offer the central console. If you start seeing reports of attacks in your internal network, behind your firewall showing up on your console, you could have a serious problem. In addition, because BlackICE has the capability to log the attack as a binary file, you can examine it with Ethereal and determine for yourself if this is a false positive or a serious concern. In terms of maintaining, situational awareness, or knowing what is going on inside your network by having reports coming to a central place, is a great aid.

Internal Firewalls/Appliances

A number of tools are logwatchers and correlation engines. These are major improvements on the original swatch. Almost all of these include a relational SQL database to manage the information. Examples include Big Brother—which is free—and NetForensics, Silent Runner, and Intellitactics' NSM, which are all costly. By the time this book is printed, about a dozen of these tools will be on the market, which should help get the price down. As these tools mature, they will enable us to do the same sorts of attack detection and trend analysis—possibly even more than we can do by using a personal firewall console. If we design our networks with multiple internal compartments, possibly using firewall appliances, we have the opportunity for both protection from attacks and detection of attack attempts inside our internal network.

Two new groundbreaking free tools, Hogwash and the commercial UnityOne by TippingPoint, integrate firewall and intrusion-detection capabilities. These devices go by various names, including packet scrubber and filtering gateway. They have the advantage of using intrusion detection rule sets to help the firewall component make access or control decisions. Also, although there are some exceptions—including the Linux firewalls and Raptor—in general, firewall logs do not contain enough data to determine whether a particular record is a false positive. With intrusion-detection capabilities, more data tends to be logged for later analysis. Because these technologies are new, it might not be a good idea to put them into the outer perimeter until the product developers get the bugs worked out. However, when this technology is a bit more mature and is available in appliances, it should be useful on the inside of our networks where false positives are less likely. The tools are there to put internal barriers and instrumentation into our networks. Filtering gateways might be the next generation, but if you want defense in depth, a case can be made for the oldest and most reliable perimeter of all: the air gap.

The Case for Air Gaps

This section is not talking about the new products, called network air gaps (NAGs), which use relays or something else so that an interface can only be open for reading or writing. (NAG devices are discussed in Appendix C, "Air Gaps.") NAGs are the computer equivalent of a well-engineered sallyport; however, nothing beats a genuine, old fashioned, not-connected-to-the-net air gap. The department of defense has a rule that a classified network has to be air gapped from any unclassified network. That is a sensible rule.

You need an air gap where your critical information is. What is the information that truly differentiates you from your competition? Almost surely, your customer contact and history list is a critical piece of information.

In your quest for defense in depth, you can even have a high tech air gap if you want. We have discussed the notion of the hard crunchy perimeter and the soft chewy interior. The next section of this chapter suggests that we should think a bit about softer, absorbent perimeters. Although that might conjure up thoughts of paper towels, the plan is to discuss honeypots, rate limiting, and failover.

Absorbent Perimeters

For years, the primary advance in perimeter security was the silent drop where a probe was dropped without a response, such as an ICMP administratively prohibited message. Today, it is possible to construct perimeters that are even harder to probe from an attacker's point of view than these black hole style systems. Chapter 10, "Host Defense Components," discusses a number of host-based firewalls, including Sun Screen and Psionic PortSentry. One such host-based firewall that might be a bit ahead of its time is NFR's BackOfficer Friendly (`http://www.nfr.com/products/bof/`). This technology incorporates a kind of active defense. If the attacker is scanning for a web server, NFR's BackOfficer Friendly provides a valid HTTP response. It answers to telnet requests or even Back Orifice pings. The logic is to keep the attacker off base. Raptor firewalls have a similar capability at the perimeter. These devices, possibly in conjunction with the occasional silent drop, make reconnaissance a more challenging proposition for attackers. Other technologies that we can employ to create a perimeter that is able to absorb attacks include honeypots, rate limiting, and failover.

Honeypots

One early example of a honeypot was the deception toolkit (DTK) developed by Fred Cohen and available from his web site (`http://www.all.net/`). DTK was a state machine written in Perl that made it possible to emulate almost any service. The software came preconfigured to emulate about 20 network services, including a Telnet written in the C language. NFR's BackOfficer Friendly, which we just discussed, can also be considered a state machine. It is a honeypot as well as a personal firewall. Such technology has two major advantages for the organization that deploys it. It tends to tie up the attacker's resources as they are burning their time and effort against the honeypot, and it provides you with information about what the attackers are trying to do.

In the early days of the Global Incident Analysis Center, the web site that later became incidents.org, the site was seeing a dramatic increase in probes to port 137, NetBIOS name service. It turned out to be a worm looking for unprotected shares on Windows systems and was detected by a honeypot set by Bryce Alexander. In this case, the honeypot was the actual Windows operating system with an unprotected share. The malicious code took advantage of the share and then was captured and analyzed. This happened again with the Ramen work, a Linux worm, and was one of the most helpful tools for analyzing the sophisticated Leaves worm. In each of these cases, the honeypot was the actual operating system, not a state machine. The state machine is advantageous because it is unlikely that an attacker can break out of the state machine and use the honeypot to attack someone else. The native operating system is advantageous because it becomes a thousand times more difficult for the attackers to figure out they are dealing with a fake system.

No discussion of honeypots is complete without mentioning the Honeynet project (http://www.honeynet.org/) championed by Lance Spitzner and a number of security researchers. The Honeynet continues to add to our understanding of attacker techniques and motivation. Today, a Honeynet Alliance is available for organizations that are interested in fostering research about honeypots. The Honeynet Alliance tends to use actual operating systems for its technology; the original Honeynet was an actual network with firewalls, targets, and an IDS. Today, through the magic on VMware, it is possible to simulate an entire network using only a single computer. This solution is much cheaper and less complex, and might allow the defensive community to deploy more honeypots.

Should your organization consider a honeypot? It is an advanced technique. If you already have your perimeter functioning well, an IDS collecting data, and host-based intrusion detection on at least the critical systems, a honeypot might be a next logical step. A honeypot can be deployed on the screened subnet or DMZ as a third DNS server, an FTP server, or any other server, and it would draw fire and not be obviously out of place. A honeypot might be the only way to actually capture the full attack if the perimeter is knocking down the traffic. As defenses advance and defenders consider automated response, this technology can be used to help assess threat. Originally, the primary auto-response capabilities were to drop the connection, forge a reset to knock down the attack, and shun the attacker's IP address. Each of these has drawbacks, and a significant potential exists for self-inflicted DoS. Nevertheless, as the attacks we face become ever more sophisticated, auto response must be considered as a defense-in-depth tool.

In addition to the types of active response we have discussed in this section, another tool to consider is rate limiting.

Rate Limiting

Rate limiting, or managing the amount of bandwidth granted to a connection, was developed for quality of service (QoS) reasons. Throughout the history of networking, we have had to deal with various degrees of service and capability. Researchers have long proposed various QoS solutions, including buffering, advances in queuing theory, and protocol advances. These are primarily for performance, especially with services that do not react well to changes in throughput, such as streaming audio or video; however, QoS solutions offer fascinating possibilities for creating perimeters that absorb attacks as a defensive methodology. Like any other auto response, these techniques come with their own problems and dangers, but they are worth considering, especially to buy time to evaluate and respond to an attack. The primary advantage is to avoid tipping our hand to the attacker whose activity we have identified. Rate limiting is similar to the active response and honeypot-style defenses. Also, if we do accidentally target the wrong host with our active defense, we do less damage because we slow them down more than stopping them. Three possible ways to implement rate limiting are in the network switch that we control, in effective use of the protocol, and at the application.

Network switches are rapidly becoming more sophisticated, and quality of service is available in off-the-shelf products, such as the Entarasys switch. If the IDS detects an attack, it can simply begin to modulate the available bandwidth to the attacker. This might be a security option that managed service providers could deploy. You can't have a conversation with someone in this business for five minutes before you start hearing about a customer who made a change without informing them, setting off the security alarms and whistles. At SANS, we make every effort to employ solid configuration management; yet we have set off the alarms at Altenet, our managed care provider, at least five times in the past year. With rate limiting instead of cutting off our service, Chris Brenton and company could simply reduce the bandwidth a bit at a time. Eventually, the VPN tunnels would become so slow that the eager beaver developer who forgot to inform the security department would become aware of what had happened and fess up to making a change without notifying security. Slowing down a system admin's connection will do more to modify his behavior than yelling at him. Not all switches support rate limiting, but there are some fascinating things that we can implement with existing and emerging protocols.

If an attack were UDP based, it would be simple for the perimeter defense mechanisms to issue an ICMP source quench message. This tells the sender to slow down. You can modify the performance of a TCP connection in several ways. If the other side is Explicit Congestion Notification (ECN)-capable, we can send a congestion message and ask the sender to back off. Even if the attacker does not run ECN, we can take a page out of the LaBrea work done by Tom Liston and send an initial response with a small TCP window size and then set it to zero from time to time to keep the attacker from sending data.

These first two approaches—setting a limit using hardware, such as a switch or ICMP source quench—can easily be set in motion by an IDS as an auto response, and there have been applications of both. One simple example at the Application layer is when a user mistypes his password several times. The response can be to slow down the rate at which the system tells the user that the password is incorrect. We can also consider defense at the application, although this will not be practical until we start using better practices in coding. That said, it is worth noting that the software application might be the best place to detect and respond to certain attacks, such as illegal values and buffer overflows. It would be interesting to see sendmail and named implementations with a built-in defensive capability. Named, for instance, could trivially identify attempts to use the obsolete query class chaosnet. It could send an alert to the defensive systems, respond by delaying the answer, and then possibly transmit a BIND version number that would send attacks down the wrong path, such as 4.9.1, an ancient version of BIND. If such technology does become available, it certainly would help us implement defense in depth.

In this section of the chapter, we have considered several techniques to implement perimeters that are more flexible than the standard border router firewall type perimeter. None of these techniques should ever be used in lieu of those technologies, but they can supplement and enhance our perimeter defense. One of the critical issues in a perimeter, of course, is uptime or availability, and one of the most important technologies to help us achieve this is automated failover.

Failover

Failover is the practice of maintaining a hot standby and transferring operations to the standby if the primary fails. When considering purchase requirements for firewalls and other perimeter devices, one crucial capability is failover. Many commercial and freeware products and designs seek to balance security and degree of polling, usually through Hot Standby Routing Protocol

(HSRP), maintaining NAT tables and connection state, as well as load and performance balancing. If you plan to implement failover, buy all the firewalls at the same time and maintain strict configuration management so that they have the same patch level at all times to avoid problems.

Failover products are dynamic by nature, but it never hurts to ask the manufacturer's technical representatives if it is possible to deploy their products in a failover mode that allows both failover and static routing between the secure or intranet sides of perimeter devices. Static routing helps you avoid the risk that compromise of a single router could lead to manipulation of the organization's dynamic routing tables. If an attacker can manipulate the routes, he can cause traffic to pass through an arbitrary IP address he controls. The security mechanisms for routing tend to be a password, or MD5 hash, and they are not considered fully robust. Passwords can be sniffed, and although MD5 is a strong security mechanism, cryptographic experts have asserted that the implementation for routing was hastily done and is not perfect. Static routes are read from a table; therefore, even if a router is compromised, as long as the remaining routers do not accept ICMP redirects or router discovery messages, they and their routes will remain intact.

Maintaining a near 100% uptime is great, but it also means that a failure in our security design, process, or procedures results in our precious information leaking all the faster. Next, we will consider defense in depth with information, covering the problems and some solutions that we can employ.

Defense in Depth with Information

Defense in depth as a concept goes beyond the protocol to an architecture and orientation of protecting the information. One of the goals of this book is a holistic treatment of the perimeter. This includes not just routers, firewalls, and VPNs, but policy, system hardening, intrusion detection, and software architecture. In the final major section of our discussion of defense in depth, we want to revisit the problem of information leakage and also restate the case for encryption.

The Problem of Diffusion

One fascinating security problem is the diffusion of information. An organization might have three levels of information confidentiality: top secret, secret, and confidential. Sooner or later, a classified piece of data ends up on a system or network that is not rated for that level of information.

Today, business can be characterized by intense competition where a single misstep in information control can be disastrous. We label critical information proprietary, but laptops are lost and systems become infected with the Sircam worm and send random files out onto the Internet. AOL version 6 and 7 both occasionally decide to attach a file that has been recently sent to a mail message to someone else. You realize it is happening, and if you have a slow enough connection, you can cancel it; however, if you are on broadband and it is a small file, it's impossible to retrieve. It turns out that it is nearly impossible to prevent information diffusion, but we can develop architectures to minimize the problem. Some of the problems that we need to design and plan for to minimize diffusion include backdoors, wireless devices, remote-controlware, email, and social engineering.

In the beginning of the PC deployment, modems were controllable problems. They were slow, expensive, and external so you could find them by walking through your organization. You would think your top firewall and network administrators would know not to leave a modem on a critical system on auto answer, but administrators can be the worst culprits. After all, it is a lot easier to roll out of bed, dial up the organization, fix whatever is wrong, and go back to sleep than to drive in. Defensive measures include war dialing your own phone numbers with toneloc, a free tool or phone sweep from sandstorm if you need to use commercial software.

802.11 wireless access points bring a whole new dimension to the problem. At less than $200 each, these are going to end up all over your organization whether you prohibit them or not. They do not require much skill to set up, and they are simple to eavesdrop on with tools, such as AirSnort. The best advice is to get a wireless card with an external antenna, download a copy of NetStumbler, and walk your perimeter on a regular basis before someone else does.

The term remotecontrolware is made up, but we needed something to describe the suite of products ranging from Symantec's pcAnywhere, which can be identified by access to port 22, 5631, or 5632, to www.Gotomypc.com, which seeks to be invisible by tunneling through HTTP. Policy and security awareness training are your primary tools for managing these types of technologies.

If you don't think you have a problem with information leakage via email, try scanning just your email headers for a month. If you want to collect information to demonstrate the problem with diffusion to your management, this can be one of the most powerful ways to do it. Many times, your management will agree to allow you to copy just the subject lines because that is part of the header, the equivalent of the outside of an envelope. You will quickly learn that a lot of sensitive information is sent via email. In addition to policy and awareness training, one old trick is to create a fake acronym and add it to particularly sensitive documents. After all, no one will notice one more acronym. Then you can add this as a string to your IDS so that it alerts if the word you have created crosses your perimeter. Think of it as marker dye for tracking information diffusion.

We have made a case for understanding a bit about how diffusion of information happens in the organization. Although we have offered a number of technical solutions, the best answer is an active and powerful security awareness program. Most security awareness programs consist of a canned brief and a poster or mouse pad with a catchy slogan. We need to do better than this, and we can. The users in our organization are not stupid; they can set up a modem in autoanswer mode and deploy a wireless access point. The best security awareness program is one that treats them as peers. Get involved! Perhaps your information security officer is not the most technical person in the organization; if that is the case, help him out. With permission from your manager and security officer, set up a wireless access point and demonstrate Air Snort. In most awareness programs, you see the users nodding off, eyes fixed, brain in a wait state. When you show someone decrypting what people normally think are private communications, the lights go on. After that, the person will think twice before using that wireless in the office or at a conference without a VPN. The more your users know, the more capable they will be of making educated decisions. That said, information diffusion happens. There are just too many ways information can become exposed. This final section of the chapter and this book is a reminder of the importance of cryptography in defense in depth.

Cryptography and Defense in Depth

What is free for personal use and reasonably priced commercialware, provides defense in depth instantly, is exhaustively reviewed, yet underused? One answer would be PGP. Microsoft is often flamed for their cryptography and security practice, yet Windows 2000 shipped with Kerberos, IPSec, and encrypting file system support for certificates as part of the operating system. We have the tools that we need; we just need to implement them. Many organizations implement VPNs as a remote dial-in replacement, but we can also implement them internally. One government organization in Crystal City implemented VPNs from the desk of government officials to the printers. This kept an insider who was not trustworthy from intercepting and reading sensitive data off the network. We should think about their example. Encrypting data at rest and in transit takes a bit of work and a bit of discipline to manage the keys, but it is the most bombproof way to implement defense in depth.

Summary

On behalf of the author and reviewer team, we want to thank you for reading and applying what you have learned in this book. We learned a lot from working together as a team. Some of us are old friends, and others are new, but we are all committed to building great perimeters and defense in depth and we know you are as well. The threat against our systems and information has never been greater, yet the primary reason we lose is because we sometimes fail to apply good security design and practice. 2001 was the year of the worm with Sircam, Code Red, Nimda, and others, but almost all of the attacks exploited known vulnerabilities where the patches were available. If we take the responsibility to implement sound design and security practice, we can move forward. There is no single silver bullet, no magic product, no vendor that will do it all for us. On the other hand, tools both free and commercial are available that can be used to build an architecture that layers defense in depth. This book is not finished because it doesn't have your experiences yet. The remaining chapters of this book are yours to write, with your experiences as you apply the concepts, techniques, and designs on your networks. We look forward to seeing your chapters!

Send your mail to `nrfeedback@newriders.com`.

V

Appendixes

A

Cisco Access List Sample Configurations

THIS APPENDIX COMPRISES TWO ACCESS lists that demonstrate possible ways to securely configure a Cisco router as a standalone security device. These sections use best practices as described in Chapter 2, "Packet Filtering" and Chapter 6, "Role of a Router," listed out so that a complete configuration can be seen in its entirety. The first access list is used to demonstrate a network that has no publicly shared resources, and the second access list illustrates an example of a network with publicly accessible mail, DNS, and web servers.

Complete Access List for a Private *Only* Network

The following example access list is appropriate for a network that has outbound and return traffic only, with no public servers or screened subnets. Most likely, this network is a low-risk/low budget setup in which security is not first priority. Therefore, a single inexpensive security device is chosen. For an example of an access list that works with public servers, see the next section. Both are designed to work on a Cisco router that runs IOS version 12.0 or later.

```
no ip source-route
no service tcp-small-servers
no service udp-small-servers
no service finger
```

Next are all of the commands to be applied directly to the external serial interface, including the access–group commands that apply the inbound and outbound filters to it. The `serial 0` interface connects the router to the Internet. We also stop all services that need to be disabled at the interface configuration level.

```
interface serial 0
 ip access-group filterin in
 ip access-group filterout out
 no cdp enable

 no snmp
 no ip direct-broadcast
 no ip redirects
 no ip unreachables
```

The next section is an inbound, reflexive access list called `filterin`. `Filterin` begins with an ingress filter to prevent spoofing; it is followed by a permit list that only allows in ICMP packet-too-big statements. `Filterin` concludes with an `evaluate packets` statement, which checks the reflexive list "packets" to see if the incoming traffic matches it and will be permitted through. Any traffic that fails the `evaluate packets` check is dropped by an implied `deny all`. However, we append a `deny ip any any log-input` statement so that we can keep track of all denied traffic. If you wanted to open any other services or ports inbound, the permit statements would be added here, before the `evaluate packets` line.

```
ip access-list extended filterin
deny ip 190.190.190.0 0.0.0.255 any
deny ip 10.0.0.0 0.255.255.255 any
deny ip 127.0.0.0 0.255.255.255 any
deny ip 172.16.0.0 0.15.255.255 any
deny ip 192.168.0.0 0.0.255.255 any
deny ip 224.0.0.0 15.255.255.255 any
deny ip host 0.0.0.0 any
permit icmp any any packet-too-big
evaluate packets
deny ip any any log-input
```

`filterout` is next. It is the outbound reflexive access list that was applied to interface serial 0. It lists all the traffic types that we are allowing out of our network. Through the use of the packet's reflexive access list, the `evaluate packets` statement in the `filterin` access list will determine the return traffic that is allowed back in. You might notice that the last statement under `filterout` is an ICMP `packet-too-big` statement. This statement allows outbound information to other routers who send acceptable return traffic, but with too large of a packet size. This statement is not reflexively inspected;

therefore, it doesn't allow for return traffic. ICMP traffic has varying results when it is used in a reflexive access list, so for most applications, it is best to simply apply ICMP in individual inbound and outbound non–reflexive access lists. If your security policy specifies for any other outbound (and in turn, return) traffic that isn't already listed here, add the `permit` statements to the bottom of the list, following the pattern of the other reflexive statements. To make sure that the statement is treated reflexively, verify that it ends with the

keyword `reflect` followed by the identifying list name packets.

```
ip access-list extended filterout
permit tcp any any eq 21 reflect packets
permit tcp any any eq 22 reflect packets
permit tcp any any eq 23 reflect packets
permit tcp any any eq 25 reflect packets
permit tcp any any eq 53 reflect packets
permit tcp any any eq 80 reflect packets
permit tcp any any eq 110 reflect packets
permit tcp any any eq 119 reflect packets
permit tcp any any eq 143 reflect packets
permit tcp any any eq 443 reflect packets
permit udp any any eq 53 reflect packets
permit icmp any any packet-too-big
```

The `ethernet 0` interface is configured and has extended access list number 112 applied inbound as an egress filter, only allowing packets to pass with addresses that match the internal network's address range. This prevents programs that spoof addresses when performing malicious actions from being able to leave your network. This way, you remain a good Internet neighbor. An extended access list format was chosen because it facilitates the use of the `log-input` command. Notice that we add a `deny ip any any log-input` rule to track inappropriate traffic as it attempts to exit the network segment and use `log-input` to enable tracking of MAC addresses.

```
interface ethernet 0
 ip access-group 112 in

access-list 112 permit ip 190.190.190.0 0.0.0.255 any
access-list 112 deny ip any any log-input
```

Explanations

In the previous examples, the following information is assumed:

- We have two router interfaces: a `serial 0` interface that connects us to the Internet, and an `ethernet 0` interface that connects us to our private network.

- This list is a template with suggestions; it shouldn't be considered a full solution for any particular network.
- We want to limit the outbound traffic (and return traffic) to the services that are listed in `filterout`.
- The internal private network number is 190.190.190.0.
- We want to limit our ICMP message interactions to allow `packet-too-big` statements as the *only* type we allow out—none is allowed back in. (`Ping` and `traceroute` are disallowed internally.)
- Any use of FTP outbound requires a passive (PASV) FTP client and server support for the same.
- The listing format for the access list information is this way for easier reading.

Listing A.1 shows the complete router access list.

Listing A.1 **The Complete Router Access List for a Private-Only Network**

```
no ip source-route
no service tcp-small-servers
no service udp-small-servers
no service finger

interface serial 0
ip access-group filterin in
ip access-group filterout out
no cdp enable

no snmp
no ip direct-broadcast
no ip redirects
no ip unreachables

ip access-list extended filterin
deny ip 190.190.190.0 0.0.0.255 any
deny ip 10.0.0.0 0.255.255.255 any
deny ip 127.0.0.0 0.255.255.255 any
deny ip 172.16.0.0 0.15.255.255 any
deny ip 192.168.0.0 0.0.255.255 any
deny ip 224.0.0.0 15.255.255.255 any
deny ip host 0.0.0.0 any
permit icmp any any packet-too-big
evaluate packets
deny ip any any log-input
```

```
ip access-list extended filterout
permit tcp any any eq 21 reflect packets
permit tcp any any eq 22 reflect packets
permit tcp any any eq 23 reflect packets
permit tcp any any eq 25 reflect packets
permit tcp any any eq 53 reflect packets
permit tcp any any eq 80 reflect packets
permit tcp any any eq 110 reflect packets
permit tcp any any eq 119 reflect packets
permit tcp any any eq 143 reflect packets
permit tcp any any eq 443 reflect packets
permit udp any any eq 53 reflect packets
permit icmp any any packet-too-big

interface ethernet 0
ip access-group 112 in

access-list 112 permit ip 190.190.190.0 0.0.0.255 any
access-list 112 deny ip any any log-input
```

Complete Access List for a Screened Subnet Network that Allows Public Server Internet Access

The following is an access list that takes the preceding section's access lists and incorporates inbound access to a screened subnet containing web, mail, and DNS servers. This example would most likely be used for a lower risk, lower budget network that needs to use its router as its sole security device. By using an additional interface to serve as a "screened subnet," we allow increased protection while implementing publicly accessible services. All public access servers are assumed to be properly hardened, and because of their volatile nature, any available defense-in-depth measures should be implemented.

In this initial section, we disable unneeded global services. These commands must be configured in global configuration mode.

```
no service finger
no ip source-route
no service tcp-small-servers
no service udp-small-servers
```

Next are all the commands to be applied directly to the external serial interface, including the `access-group` commands that apply the inbound and outbound filters to it. The `serial 0` interface is the one that connects the router to the Internet. We also stop all services to be disabled at the interface configuration level.

```
interface serial 0
 ip access-group filterin in
```

```
ip access-group filterout out

no snmp
no ip direct-broadcast
no ip redirects
no ip unreachables
no cdp enable
```

Next is the `filterin` access list, which includes antispoofing commands. This list is followed by ingress lines that allow any web, SMTP, or DNS inbound traffic to the server that would handle such a request. It next allows ICMP `packet-too-big` packets, followed by an `evaluate packets` line that reflexively examines any remaining inbound traffic to see if it matches any of the currently temporarily formed reflexive access lists that `filterout created`. It is followed by a statement to log all denied inbound packets.

```
ip access-list extended filterin
deny ip 190.190.190.0 0.0.0.255 any
deny ip 10.0.0.0 0.255.255.255 any
deny ip 127.0.0.0 0.255.255.255 any
deny ip 172.16.0.0 0.15.255.255 any
deny ip 192.168.0.0 0.0.255.255 any
deny ip 224.0.0.0 15.255.255.255 any
deny ip host 0.0.0.0 any
permit tcp any host 200.200.200.2 eq 80
permit tcp any host 200.200.200.3 eq 25
permit tcp any host 200.200.200.4 eq 53
permit udp any host 200.200.200.4 eq 53
permit icmp any any packet-too-big
evaluate packets
deny ip any any log-input
```

`filterout` is next, and it starts by allowing response traffic back from the web, mail, and DNS servers. Notice the `est` (established) keyword at the end of these lists. This confirms that only replies are leaving the servers, behaving like an egress list for our screened subnet. Following that is the reflexive access lines that permit outbound traffic and create the reflexive lists that allow inbound traffic. To grant other services outbound access, you would need to add a reflexive access list here. `Filterout` is ended with an ICMP filter allowing `packet-too-big` messages to go through.

```
ip access-list extended filterout
permit tcp host 200.200.200.2 eq 80 any gt 1023 est
permit tcp host 200.200.200.3 eq 25 any gt 1023 est
permit udp host 200.200.200.4 eq 53 any gt 1023
permit tcp any any eq 21 reflect packets
permit tcp any any eq 22 reflect packets
permit tcp any any eq 23 reflect packets
permit tcp any any eq 25 reflect packets
```

```
permit tcp any any eq 53 reflect packets
permit tcp any any eq 80 reflect packets
permit tcp any any eq 110 reflect packets
permit tcp any any eq 119 reflect packets
permit tcp any any eq 143 reflect packets
permit tcp any any eq 443 reflect packets
permit udp any any eq 53 reflect packets
permit icmp any any packet-too-big
```

Progressing to interface ethernet 0, no outbound list is applied; therefore, any traffic that matches the private network's address range is passed on.

```
interface ethernet 0
 ip access-group filterin1 in
```

Filterin1 is applied inbound to the ethernet 0 interface. Filterin1 contains an egress filter, only allowing traffic that is addressed from the private network's address range to be forwarded to the serial interface. It also contains a deny statement, logging all non–standard egress traffic.

```
ip access-list extended filterin1
permit ip 190.190.190.0 0.0.0.255 any
deny ip any any log-input
```

ethernet 1 contains filterout2 and filterin2.

Filterout2 permits network traffic in from the Internet to be forwarded to the web server if it's HTTP traffic, to the mail server if it's SMTP traffic, and to the external DNS server if it's DNS traffic. Notice that these first three lines serve as a basic ingress filter. Filterout2 also permits ICMP packet-too-big messages to pass and supports logging of undesirables through its last statement.

```
interface ethernet 1
ip access-group filterout2 out
ip access-group filterin2 in

ip access-list extended filterout2
permit tcp any gt 1023 host 200.200.200.2 eq 80
permit tcp any gt 1023 host 200.200.200.3 eq 25
permit tcp any host 200.200.200.4 eq 53
permit udp any host 200.200.200.4 eq 53
permit icmp any 200.200.200.0 0.0.0.255 packet-too-big
deny ip any any log-input
```

Filterin2 allows *reply* traffic from each of the three public servers out to the serial interface. This serves as a basic egress filter. Packet-too-big messages are also forwarded. The deny any 190.190.190.0 line disables communications between the screened subnet and your private network. This is necessary because the outbound traffic on ethernet 0 is open to the screened subnet.

The next lines allow SMTP and DNS traffic from their particular servers to the Internet. Serial one's `filterout` then passes this traffic through its reflexive access lists so that it will have the same level of protection as the private network's outbound traffic. If any other outbound traffic is desired from the screened subnet, this is where additional filters are added. These additional filters are added after the deny statement that prevents everything except reply traffic from entering the private segment, but before the last statement that logs undesirables. DNS support for the private segment would most likely be handled internally (split DNS) or by an outside party. No DNS zone transfers would take place between the private and screened subnets.

```
ip access-list extended filterin2
permit tcp host 200.200.200.2 eq 80 any gt 1023 est
permit tcp host 200.200.200.3 eq 25 any gt 1023 est
permit udp host 200.200.200.4 eq 53 any gt 1023
permit icmp 200.200.200.0 0.0.0.255 any packet-too-big
deny ip any 190.190.190.0 0.0.0.255
permit tcp host 200.200.200.4 any eq 53
permit udp host 200.200.200.4 any eq 53
permit tcp host 200.200.200.3 any eq 25
deny ip any any log-input
```

Explanations

In the preceding example, the following information is assumed:

- This list is a template with suggestions; it shouldn't be considered a full solution for any particular network.
- The screened subnet's network number is 200.200.200.0.
- The internal private network number is 190.190.190.0.
- The screened subnet's web server's address is 200.200.200.2.
- The screened subnet's SMTP mail server's address is 200.200.200.3.
- The screened subnet's DNS server's address is 200.200.200.4.
- No other hosts are on the screened subnet.
- We have three router interfaces: a `serial 0` interface that connects us to the Internet, an `ethernet 0` interface that connects us to our private network, and an `ethernet 1` interface that connects us to our screened subnet.
- We want to limit the outbound traffic (and return traffic) to the services that are listed in `filterout`.

- We want to limit our ICMP message interactions to allow `packet-too-big` statements as the only type we allow out—none is allowed back in. (`Ping` and `traceroute` are disallowed internally.)
- Any use of FTP outbound requires a PASV (or passive) FTP client and server support for the same.
- The listing format for the access list information is for easier reading.

Listing A.2 shows the complete router access list.

Listing A.2   The Router Access List for a Screened Subnet Network that Allows Public Server Internet Access

```
no service finger
no ip source-route
no service tcp-small-servers
no service udp-small-servers

interface serial 0
ip access-group filterin in
ip access-group filterout out

no snmp
no ip direct-broadcast
no ip redirects
no ip unreachables
no cdp enable

ip access-list extended filterin
deny ip 190.190.190.0 0.0.0.255 any
deny ip 10.0.0.0 0.255.255.255 any
deny ip 127.0.0.0 0.255.255.255 any
deny ip 172.16.0.0 0.15.255.255 any
deny ip 192.168.0.0 0.0.255.255 any
deny ip 224.0.0.0 15.255.255.255 any
deny ip host 0.0.0.0 any
permit tcp any host 200.200.200.2 eq 80
permit tcp any host 200.200.200.3 eq 25
permit udp any host 200.200.200.4 eq 53
permit icmp any any packet-too-big
evaluate packets
deny ip any any log-input

ip access-list extended filterout
permit tcp host 200.200.200.2 eq 80 any gt 1023 est
permit tcp host 200.200.200.3 eq 25 any gt 1023 est
permit udp host 200.200.200.4 eq 53 any gt 1023
permit tcp any any eq 21 reflect packets
permit tcp any any eq 22 reflect packets
```

continues ▶

Listing A.2   **Continued**

```
permit tcp any any eq 23 reflect packets
permit tcp any any eq 25 reflect packets
permit tcp any any eq 53 reflect packets
permit tcp any any eq 80 reflect packets
permit tcp any any eq 110 reflect packets
permit tcp any any eq 119 reflect packets
permit tcp any any eq 143 reflect packets
permit tcp any any eq 443 reflect packets
permit udp any any eq 53 reflect packets
permit icmp any any packet-too-big


interface ethernet 0
ip access-group filterin1 in

ip access-list extended filterin1
permit ip 190.190.190.0 0.0.0.255 any
deny ip any any log-input

interface ethernet 1
ip access-group filterout2 out
ip access-group filterin2 in

ip access-list extended filterout2
permit tcp any gt 1023 host 200.200.200.2 eq 80
permit tcp any gt 1023 host 200.200.200.3 eq 25
permit tcp any host 200.200.200.4 eq 53
permit udp any host 200.200.200.4 eq 53
permit icmp any 200.200.200.0 0.0.0.255 packet-too-big
deny ip any any log-input

ip access-list extended filterin2
permit tcp host 200.200.200.2 eq 80 any gt 1023 est
permit tcp host 200.200.200.3 eq 25 any gt 1023 est
permit udp host 200.200.200.4 eq 53 any gt 1023
permit icmp 200.200.200.0 0.0.0.255 any packet-too-big
deny ip any 190.190.190.0 0.0.0.255
permit tcp host 200.200.200.4 any eq 53
permit udp host 200.200.200.4 any eq 53
permit tcp host 200.200.200.3 any eq 25
deny ip any any log-input
```

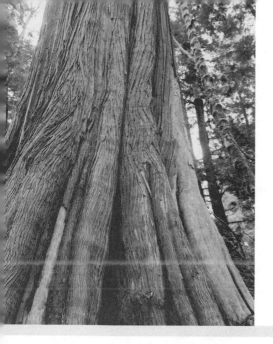

B
Crypto 101

CRYPTOGRAPHY IS THE PRACTICE AND STUDY of encryption and decryption. Cryptography is an important part of what makes a VPN work. This Appendix is a primer on how cryptography works. It defines the various terms that are used for the cryptographic processes so that you can better understand the technologies that are part of the VPN. Cryptography is an immensely complicated and varied field. The purpose of this Appendix is to briefly describe the encryption technologies that are necessary to better understand VPNs and how they work. It is meant to be a supplement for the VPN material that appears throughout the book.

> **NOTE**
>
> Quite a few specific terms are used regularly when speaking of cryptographic technologies. Throughout this Appendix, we will define these terms and briefly explain them to facilitate the understanding of the VPN. Don't worry—we only cover those terms that you actually need to know!

A discussion of cryptography rarely occurs without the mention of encryption keys. *Keys* are secret values that are used to encode and decode messages. These values can vary in length, with the length of the key corresponding directly to the security of the encoded message. Encryption keys come in symmetric and asymmetric varieties, which we will discuss in greater detail later in this appendix.

Cleartext and *plain text* are terms that define information before it is placed into an encrypted form. After the same information is encrypted, it is called *ciphertext*.

The formula or method by which information is encrypted is called the *encryption algorithm*, or *cipher* (also spelled *cypher*). An *algorithm* is a mathematical means by which cleartext is transformed into encoded ciphertext.

Encryption Algorithms

Many encryption algorithms are commonly used to protect data. Of these, most can be categorized as symmetric or asymmetric key algorithms—two very different approaches to encryption.

Shared Key—Symmetric

A *shared key,* or *symmetric key,* is an encryption method that uses the same key value for both encryption and decryption. Its use assumes that everyone has had time in advance to securely exchange a secret key that no one else knows. This key value is then used to encrypt information that is exchanged. This means of encryption can be fast because the mathematics needed to create ciphertext from a shared secret key does not have to be as complex as the type used with asymmetric algorithms. The main disadvantage to the symmetric algorithm is that it is difficult to remotely exchange keys or start a symmetric exchange with an unknown party and authenticate that person is who he says he is. How can you give a remote party your key if he doesn't already have it? You would need to have a secure channel to pass the key. Because you most likely don't have such a channel (otherwise you wouldn't need to pass the key), you are in the middle of a catch-22. With a symmetric algorithm, we have established confidentiality of data as long as the key remains secret, and we have some basic key exchange issues.

Many symmetric encryption algorithms are available for use today, including Data Encryption Standard (DES), 3DES, Rijndael, Blowfish, and International Data Encryption Algorithm (IDEA). Of these, DES and an enhanced version, 3DES, are heavily used as encryption algorithms of choice in today's VPNs. DES was an encryption standard set by the National Institute of Standards and Technology (NIST) in 1977. DES, a symmetric algorithm with a 56-bit key, seemed unbreakable with the technology of the time. However, as time has passed and processing power has multiplied, DES has been proven breakable many times. The quickest recorded crack so far was just more than 22 hours in RSA's DES challenge III (`http://www.rsasecurity.com/rsalabs/des3/index.html`).

Does this mean that DES is not a suitable algorithm to use for your VPN? Maybe. You have to weigh the value of your data against the price paid to retrieve it. No one wants his payroll posted on a billboard, but by the same token, it is unlikely that you will install a walk-in vault to protect it from interlopers. (If you would, don't use DES.) Many businesses that are exchanging standard transactions that have no real value to outside parties are effectively using DES as their VPNing algorithm. If you operate a financial institution or you have top-secret information that you are exchanging, don't use DES.

As an interim solution to the vulnerability of DES, 3DES has become a new popular standard. Most popularly used with three 56-bit keys for a total of a 168-bit key strength, 3DES provides considerably more protection. Even so, with the breaking of DES, a call went out for a new Advanced Encryption Standard (AES). The winner was Rijndael, an algorithm made by Vincent Rijmen and Joan Daemen, two highly respected Belgian cryptographers. Despite the fact that a new standard has been enacted, this might not effect you personally for some time to come. Rijndael is not yet heavily implemented, although it is considered the future of symmetric cryptography. 3DES is still a fine solution for most secure implementations today; therefore, don't feel that you have to be the first kid on your block with the new technology unless your security policy or your company's regulations requires so.

Symmetric algorithms are important to VPNs because they supply the confidentiality component that the VPN supplies. They work well to protect the heavy burden of the VPN's data flow because of their speed per strength advantage over other encryption algorithm types.

Public-Private Key—Asymmetric

Asymmetric key algorithms use a different method of encryption. Two different keys are used: a public key and a private key. The *public key* is used to encrypt the ciphertext, and the *private key* is used to decode it back to cleartext. The interesting thing about this process is the relationship between these two keys. The public key cannot be used to reverse engineer the private key. Therefore, although ciphertext can be generated by anyone with a copy of the public key, only the person who possesses the private key can decrypt it. For this reason, the mathematics behind asymmetric algorithms is considerably more complex than that used in symmetric algorithms. In turn, asymmetric algorithms are also much slower and more processor intensive.

We still haven't resolved the issue of how to start an encrypted communication session with someone whom you haven't previously been able to exchange keys with. Because the public key cannot compromise the ciphertext, it can be freely distributed. This does not guarantee, however, that the message is coming from the person it claims to be. Despite still lacking guaranteed authentication, integrity, and non-repudiation, we still have confidentiality of our data and no more key exchange issues.

One popular example of asymmetric key encryption is Pretty Good Privacy (PGP). PGP is a means to exchange information securely with persons whom you might not ever have met face to face. It uses publicly dispersible keys (in coordination with private keys), and even has specific key servers set up for the distribution of these public keys. This way, if the person with whom you are exchanging information has "posted" his public key on a key server, you can search for it by the person's email address or name. Then the communication can begin. Posting public keys to a key server is not a necessary part of the process; keys can just be emailed back and forth.

The two most commonly used asymmetric algorithms are Diffie-Hellman and RSA's public-key algorithm. Diffie-Hellman is used heavily in VPN technology, as a part of the Oakley key exchange protocol. It and Internet Security Association Key Management Protocol (ISAKMP) make up the standard negotiation and key-management option of IPSec, called Internet Key Exchange (IKE) protocol. Whitfield Diffie and Martin Hellman created Diffie-Hellman in 1976. It was the first of the public key algorithms[1].

Diffie-Hellman is most commonly used in VPNs as a means to exchange information to set up a symmetric algorithm tunnel using a protocol, such as DES or 3DES. The advantages of public-key cryptography are used to allow the creation of an outside connection without previous knowledge. This connection is used to pass the vital symmetric-key information and configuration data that cannot be securely transferred otherwise. Then the symmetric algorithm communication can begin. When using the Diffie-Hellman algorithm in conjunction with a VPN, you have to choose the group type that will be used: group 1 or group 2. The differences between the groups include the size of the prime number that is used (768 bit for group 1 and 1024 bit for group 2) and the length of the prime modulus in 32-bit words: 24 for group 1 and 32 for group 2. Group 2 provides more security but takes more processing power to implement.

Although asymmetric algorithms are too slow to be practical as a means to encrypt the main data flow transmitted via the VPN, they are an effective way to exchange key information in the negotiation and key exchange phase of VPN initialization. Because symmetric algorithms have key-exchange woes and faster encryption speeds, asymmetric and symmetric algorithms make an excellent pair. By using asymmetric algorithms to exchange keys to be used for a symmetric connection, you have removed your key exchange issues, while benefiting from the speed advantage of the symmetric algorithm.

Digital Signatures and Hash Algorithms

Digital signatures and hash functions are the missing pieces in our secure communication method. They help provide integrity of data, additional authentication, and non-repudiation. *Digital signatures* are meant to prove that a piece of information came from a certain individual or entity. This authentication is accomplished with encryption. If you receive a message that was encrypted with a key that only one other person has, then it is most likely from that person.

However, a symmetric key does not function well in this model because you have all of the same key-management issues that occur with standard symmetric key transactions. For this reason, asymmetric encryption has become a popular means to integrate digital signature capability. You can encrypt a document with your private key, and the person to whom you are sending the document can decrypt it with your public key, proving (because you are the only individual with your private key) that the message was from you. Therefore, we have non-repudiation and integrity checking because any changes in the encrypted text result in jumbled output. However, we lack true confidentiality because anyone with our public key can decrypt the message. The biggest disadvantage of this as a signing method is the sluggishness of asymmetric encryption. A signature should be able to be retrieved in a timely fashion or it loses its practicality. Also, anyone with your public key can read the document, so the document loses its confidentiality unless you then encrypt it a second time, adding even more time to the whole process. Wouldn't it be nice to have a means to ensure integrity, authentication, and non-repudiation and not have the speed disadvantage of asymmetrically encrypting an entire message?

Enter the hash algorithm. *Hash algorithms* are used to create a "fingerprint" of a piece of information or file. You can use this fingerprint, called a *hash* or *message digest*, to verify that the file has not been changed. If the file changes, so will its hash. This helps guarantee the integrity of the information without having to verify the entire file bit-by-bit. With a one-way hash, it is difficult to reverse-engineer the original source information, or like information from that can produce the same hash. People are confused about how one-way hashes can be verified. If these hashes can't be reversed, how do you know that they correctly represent the original information? The answer is deceptively simple. You take the document for which you are verifying integrity and create a second hash using the same algorithm. You then compare the hashes. If the documents are the same, the hashes will be as well. And because a one-way hash function is being used, it is unlikely that you just happened upon a document that produced the same hash.

Two of the more popular hash algorithms are Message Digest 5 (MD5) and Secure Hash Algorithm (SHA-1). SHA-1 is the more secure hash algorithm of the two, but it is slower than MD5. In practical applications, it is okay to use either, unless your security policy dictates the use of the more secure SHA-1. Both algorithms are available and commonly used in VPN setups for integrity checking of information.

Summary

Understanding the basics of cryptography is essential for designing, implementing, and maintaining VPN solutions. The use of speedy symmetric encryption algorithms keep data flows confidential, and asymmetric algorithms allow for easy key exchange. Hash algorithms ensure integrity with digital signatures, which provide authentication and ensure non-repudiation. Combine these technologies and the three goals of a secure communication channel—confidentiality, integrity, and authentication—can be successfully established.

References

1 W.Diffie and M. Hellman, "New Directions in Cryptography." IEEE Transactions on Information Theory, vIt-22, n.6. November 1976.

C

Network Air Gaps

THROUGHOUT THIS BOOK, WE HAVE LOOKED into various elements of the network security perimeter. At times, devices do not neatly fall into categories that are related to specific types of security mechanisms (firewalls, routers, intrusion detection systems, and so on). One such type of mechanism is the network air gap (NAG). Some call these devices "air gap firewalls," although vendors clearly state that NAGs are not to be confused with firewalls and actually offer complementary services to be implemented in conjunction with firewalls when the environment demands it. The objective of this Appendix is to provide a high-level overview of NAGs. We explain the core concepts of NAGs and point out resources where you can obtain additional information about their uses and related products.

A Case for Air Gaps

In designing firewall systems, one argument for using dual-homed bastion hosts is to make a well-defined separation between an internal *trusted* network and an external *untrusted* network. However, keep in mind that one network card in the host is physically connected to your protected network. An attacker can exploit this connectivity to gain further access to internal resources.

To further protect the internal network, you can place the bastion hosts in a DMZ or a screened subnet. This placement helps ensure that the bastions do *not* have a direct connection to the internal network—meaning that the internal network card on the host is not physically connected with the internal protected network. This configuration provides an additional layer of separation between the bastion host and systems on the internal network.

Perhaps the best way to protect a computer from being compromised over a network is not to connect it to the network at all. This so-called *air gap* means that a physical disconnect exists between the internal computer and the network connecting with the outside world (the Internet). This type of configuration is also useful in providing a physical disconnect between networks with different trust or risk levels. With the air gap, the internal computer is protected; however, if information is needed from the outside, the information must be carried in some manner to the protected computer.

How does an air gap facilitate security but still permit communication between networks? Take a look at a sneakernet example in Figure C.1.

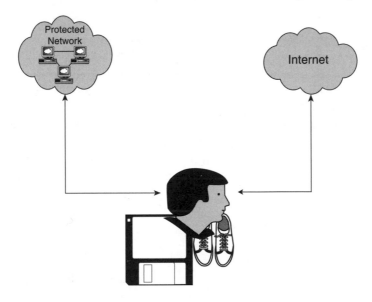

Figure C.1 A "sneakernet" or "floppy firewall" provides a low-tech air gap gateway for providing a method to transport information between physically disconnected environments (networks or computers).

The communication mechanism in the sneakernet example of Figure C.1 is a user. The data from one network is copied to some kind of storage medium, and the user physically carries the data and files from one network to another. (Note the sneakers, which aid in traction and speed.) The two networks are *never* connected. You can think of this kind of setup as a crude store-and-forward environment. You can understand such an environment if you consider how your own important information is stored, backed up, and archived.

The air-gap technique is sometimes called an *ultimate firewall*. Even so, the sneakernet approach has several limitations. Perhaps the foremost is performance. It takes time to copy the data and manually shuttle it between networks. (We're not talking about real-time speed here.)

In Figure C.1, the user who is transporting the data acts as a courier between the two networks.

Digital couriers can also be used to transport and terminate connectivity in one network and establish connectivity in another. This idea of a controlled environment to establish and drop connectivity as necessary is the basic idea behind the digital NAG solution.

Defining NAGs

NAGs are hardware devises that literally provide a physical disconnect between two networks. (One of the networks is typically more trusted than the other.) NAGs also provide the mechanics to shuttle information between the networks without forwarding TCP header information or commands. A NAG can function as the first step in a store, analyze, and forward process that allows the packet information as well as the data to come under scrutiny by whatever means the user or organization warrants before being passed to the internal network.

You can use NAGs in conjunction with other security mechanisms, such as firewalls, routers, and intrusion detection systems (IDSs) to provide an additional layer of security between the internal protected network and the outside world. Figure C.2 illustrates a digital NAG.

Vendors who provide NAG solutions want to emulate the benefits of the sneakernet:

- Physical disconnect of the networks.
- Static data in transit. (Commands cannot be executed between networks.)

NAG vendors are attempting to address the sneakernet limitations by providing the following:

- High-speed network performance. Near real-time processing is desired with large throughput.
- Support of command execution as well as file/data distribution across the gap.

Figure C.2 A NAG can be implemented as part of a De-Militarized Zone (DMZ) and provide a means to store and forward data between networks.

The diagram in Figure C.2 illustrates a NAG providing a single physical connection for data transmission. Information can travel only one way at a time. The basic function of the NAG is to connect to the external network and read data into the buffer. The connection to the external network is severed and a connection is made to the internal network. The buffered data is then read from the buffered storage and passed to the appropriate internal devices. Based on this crude description, we can easily see that such a "read–write" switch will have some kind of latency and does not take advantage of the available bandwidth.

One way to address the bandwidth issue is to employ an additional switch for data connectivity and storage for the data that is being transmitted. As the information from the external network is being written to one storage device, the internal network is reading information from the other storage device. (SpearHead's NetGAP product supports such a configuration.) Figure C.3 provides an illustration of such a configuration.

Figure C.3 illustrates two networks that are separated by a NAG. A client in the internal network makes a request from the Internet. The command sequence or data is sent to the switch device, which temporarily stores the request sequence. The connection with the internal network is broken and the TCP information is removed. A connection is made between the switch and the Internet, and the command sequence is pushed to the Internet. The same type of connectivity takes place when the response is sent back to the internal network. However, the two networks have no direct connection.

Figure C.3   NAG solutions with two storage buffers address efficiency concerns in handling data between networks.

Using Air Gaps in Conjunction with Firewalls

NAGs can be used in conjunction with firewalls. Although some functionality might cross over between these two product types, having a mix of products in your security solution provides for a better defense in depth. Each of the components addresses an aspect of security, and each has various forms of vulnerabilities to be mitigated. NAGs enforce a store-and-forward environment. Such an environment buffers the internal protected network from the outside world and allows for the data being transmitted to fall under tighter scrutiny.

The core difference between NAGs and other mechanisms for providing secure communications is the physical disconnect in the data stream. A common problem within network security has to do with misconfiguration of components and services, whether they are firewalls, filters, IDSs, unused services, or scripts. Many functions that NAG vendors advertise can be implemented through combinations of filters and proxies. However, using various filters and proxies still provides some physical connectivity and can be complicated to configure. NAGs help protect the internal network by addressing the problem of proxy servers or bastion hosts coming under attack. The disconnect that NAGs provide also allows for the analysis of transmitted data to counter application-specific attacks.

Implementing NAGs

NAGs are more than just nice ideas; products actually do exist. At the time of this writing, NAG products were continuing to evolve. NAG vendors suggest an array of implementation ideas, although many can be sufficiently addressed with proxy and filter firewalls. Three NAG vendors are Whale Communications, providing e-Gap solutions (`http://www.whalecommunications.com`); Spearhead Security Technologies, which offers NetGAP (`http://www.sphd.com`); and RVT Technologies, which has a line of STOP-IT products (`http://www.rvttech.com`).

Deciding when or whether a NAG should be implemented depends on the sensitivity of your trusted environments and the security practices, procedures, and policy you must enforce. Some organizations and even countries employ NAG-like environments to ensure that all data that is being transmitted has been authorized or appropriately "scrubbed" of illicit, damaging, or unwanted material.

> **Note**
>
> The *scrubbing* process is not necessarily part of the NAG. The NAG provides an interim storage point where the data can be examined or processed, if required.

You can deploy NAGs for one-way communication that will only transfer data in one direction, thus preventing data from "leaking out" of a trusted environment. An implementation of this type allows data transfer from an unclassified network into a highly confidential network but does not allow transmission in the other direction. Implementing networks at various trust levels is possible if information cannot be passed from a higher trust environment to a lower trust environment. NAGs provide mechanisms to ensure this relationship.

Summary

In this Appendix, we provided you with a high-level overview of NAG devices. As we discussed, NAGs, when used in conjunction with more traditional defense components, can help improve the resiliency of your security perimeter. They attempt to achieve physical separation between segmented networks. To allow communications to take place, NAGs automate data transfer across the gap under highly controlled conditions. This automation does not allow you to achieve true separation between the two networks, but it does assist in protecting against some network-level attacks, allows you to set up uni-directional communication channels, and offers an opportunity for "scrubbing" shuttled traffic of unwanted materials. If you are interested in learning more about NAG technologies and related products, please explore the NAG vendor web sites that are mentioned in this Appendix.

Index

I

M

Q-R

T

VOICES THAT MATTER

VISIT OUR WEB SITE

WWW.NEWRIDERS.COM

On our web site, you'll find information about our other books, authors, tables of contents, and book errata. You will also find information about book registration and how to purchase our books, both domestically and internationally.

EMAIL US

Contact us at: **nrfeedback@newriders.com**

- If you have comments or questions about this book
- To report errors that you have found in this book
- If you have a book proposal to submit or are interested in writing for New Riders
- If you are an expert in a computer topic or technology and are interested in being a technical editor who reviews manuscripts for technical accuracy

Contact us at: **nreducation@newriders.com**

- If you are an instructor from an educational institution who wants to preview New Riders books for classroom use. Email should include your name, title, school, department, address, phone number, office days/hours, text in use, and enrollment, along with your request for desk/examination copies and/or additional information.

Contact us at: **nrmedia@newriders.com**

- If you are a member of the media who is interested in reviewing copies of New Riders books. Send your name, mailing address, and email address, along with the name of the publication or web site you work for.

BULK PURCHASES/CORPORATE SALES

The publisher offers discounts on this book when ordered in quantity for bulk purchases and special sales. For sales within the U.S., please contact: Corporate and Government Sales (800) 382-3419 or **corpsales@pearsontechgroup.com**. Outside of the U.S., please contact: International Sales (317) 581-3793 or **international@pearsontechgroup.com**.

WRITE TO US

New Riders Publishing
201 W. 103rd St.
Indianapolis, IN 46290-1097

CALL/FAX US

Toll-free (800) 571-5840
If outside U.S. (317) 581-3500
Ask for New Riders
FAX: (317) 581-4663

Solutions from experts you know and trust.

www.informit.com

- OPERATING SYSTEMS
- WEB DEVELOPMENT
- PROGRAMMING
- NETWORKING
- CERTIFICATION
- AND MORE...

Expert Access.
Free Content.

New Riders has partnered with **InformIT.com** to bring technical information to your desktop. Drawing on New Riders authors and reviewers to provide additional information on topics you're interested in, **InformIT.com** has free, in-depth information you won't find anywhere else.

- **Master the skills you need, when you need them**

- **Call on resources from some of the best minds in the industry**

- **Get answers when you need them, using InformIT's comprehensive library or live experts online**

- **Go above and beyond what you find in New Riders books, extending your knowledge**

As an **InformIT** partner, **New Riders** has shared the wisdom and knowledge of our authors with you online. Visit **InformIT.com** to see what you're missing.

www.informit.com ■ www.newriders.com

New Riders

Colophon

The image on this book's cover is of an old growth cedar on Vancouver Island, British Columbia. The cedar was photographed by Spike Mafford. The tree in the image is likely hundreds of years old. Many animals, including salamanders, woodpeckers, squirrels, foxes, and snails make their homes in either fallen or standing old growth trees. Old growth cedar trees are known to decompose in such a way that when they fall, their branches grow into new trees.

This book was written and edited in Microsoft Word, and laid out in QuarkXPress. The fonts used for the body text are Bembo and MCPdigital. It was printed on 50# Husky Offset Smooth paper at Phoenix Color in Hagerstown, MD. Prepress consisted of PostScript computer-to-plate technology (filmless process). The cover was printed at Moore Langen Printing in Terre Haute, Indiana, on Carolina, coated on one side.